Economic Complexity and Evolution

More information about this series at http://www.springer.com/series/11583

Andreas Pyka • Uwe Cantner
Editors

Foundations of Economic Change

A Schumpeterian View on Behaviour, Interaction and Aggregate Outcomes

Springer

Editors
Andreas Pyka
University of Hohenheim
Stuttgart, Germany

Uwe Cantner
Department of Economics
Friedrich Schiller University Jena
Jena, Germany

ISSN 2199-3173 ISSN 2199-3181 (electronic)
Economic Complexity and Evolution
ISBN 978-3-319-62008-4 ISBN 978-3-319-62009-1 (eBook)
DOI 10.1007/978-3-319-62009-1

Library of Congress Control Number: 2017957725

Printed on acid-free paper

This Springer imprint is published by Springer Nature
The registered company is Springer International Publishing AG
The registered company address is: Gewerbestrasse 11, 6330 Cham, Switzerland

Contents

Introduction: Foundations of Economic Change—Behavior, Interaction and Aggregate Outcomes

Uwe Cantner and Andreas Pyka

The theme of the 15th International Joseph A. Schumpeter Conference, held from July 27 to 30, 2014 in Jena (Germany), was "Foundations of Economic Change—Behavior, Interaction and Aggregate Outcomes". This topic was intended first to cover core dimensions of innovation driven evolutionary economic development and to be broad enough to attract a wide range of papers from evolutionary economics, economics of innovation, science and technology studies, complexity economics, behavioral economics, institutional economics, regional economics, and others more. Secondly, the topic was chosen in order to represent the research achievements, agendas and programs that have been developed in Jena since 1991: institutionally to mention here are the Max Planck Institute of Economics with its focus on evolutionary and behavioral economics as well as entrepreneurship, completed by and cooperating with research projects on economics of innovation, behavioral economics and entrepreneurship at the Department of Economics and Business Administration at the Friedrich Schiller University, as well as the University's research major "Social and Economic Change" with research projects in psychology, sociology, law, regional sciences, ethics, and political sciences; major research training groups located in Jena that trained and advised young scholars from all over the world have been pushing these research topics: the DFG graduate school (GRK 1411) "The Economics of Innovative Change", the International Max Planck Research School on "Adapting Behavior in a

U. Cantner (✉)
Department of Economics, Friedrich Schiller University Jena, Jena, Germany

Department of Marketing and Management, University of Southern Denmark, Odense, Denmark
e-mail: uwe.cantner@uni-jena.de

A. Pyka
University of Hohenheim, Stuttgart, Germany
e-mail: a.pyka@uni-hohenheim.de

A. Pyka, U. Cantner (eds.), *Foundations of Economic Change*, Economic Complexity and Evolution, DOI 10.1007/978-3-319-62009-1_1

Fundamentally Uncertain World", and the Jena Graduate School "Human Behavior in Social and Economic Change". Third, and finally, the choice of behavior, interaction and aggregate outcomes followed a specific rationale: that of representing the multilevel focus of analysis and the 'division of labor' of Neo-Schumpeterian and Evolutionary economists that over the years committed themselves to uncover the dynamic nature of economic phenomena from the individual and single technology (in production and consumption) up to changes in whole systems. In this sense, the title of the conference was at the same time a tribute to (and a suggestion to proceed on) the inquiry of the Economy from a systemic and systematic viewpoint.

In July 2014, 369 scholars from all over the world, one third of which were young researchers, attended the Jena conference, discussed up-to-date problems and questions under the general topic's umbrella and presented 313 appropriate papers. The conference program was developed along seven plenary sessions, a final outlook session, as well as "semi-plenary" sessions and 89 parallel sessions. Each plenary session featured two eminent speakers—of which, usually one 'senior' and one 'junior' scholar, a decision taken with the declared aim to foster the intergenerational dialogue within the community—who discussed topics revolving around the main "building block" of the event, that is *Behavior, Interaction*, and *Aggregate Outcomes*, developed along the following themes: *Behavioral Foundations, Complexity Economics and Innovation, Industrial Dynamics, Schumpeter meets Keynes?: ABM and the "Macro"*, *Smart Specialization and Innovation Policies*, *Entrepreneurship in Context*, as well as *Productivity and Innovation*. A final outlook session on The Future of Capitalism completed this sequence. It was a pleasure to listen to the inspiring talks of W. Brian Arthur, David B. Audretsch, Giulio Bottazzi, Guido Bünstorf, Wesley Cohen, Herbert Dawid, Giovanni Dosi, Magda Fontana, Dominique Foray, Koen Frenken, Daniella Laureiro, Mariana Mazzucato, Stan Metcalfe, Pierre Mohnen, Richard R. Nelson, Carlotta Perez, Mario Pianta, and Ulrich Witt. The semi-plenary sessions were dedicated to topics considered of high interest and potential and of wider interest: Core Issues in Agent-Based Modelling (ABM), Evolutionary Economics: Welfare, Entrepreneurship: Behavior and Traits, Core Issues in Innovation, From Micro to Macro, Demand and Evolution of Preferences, Europe in a Globalized World, Schumpeter and Keynes, Core Issues in Industrial Dynamics.

This conference proceeding represents the breadth of the discussion during the Jena conference and addresses behavioral dimensions of economic change, the mechanisms of actor interaction driving change, and the aggregate outcomes of these interactions. The collection here is the result of a review process and selection of a larger number of papers submitted after the conference.

1 Part I: Foundations of Economic Change

The first part comprises three chapters and deals with the core topic of the Jena conference. This section is opened by Uwe Cantner's Presidential Address entitled *Foundations of Economic Change,* which has to be considered the intellectual skeleton of this volume. Understanding the process of change, either incremental or disruptive and competence-destroying, is the core of the Schumpeterian research program. The Presidential Address includes a broad theoretical analysis supplemented by empirical accounts of endogenous processes of change and development which places heterogeneous actors and their interaction central. For this purpose, Uwe Cantner also borrows important insights from behavioral and complexity economics, however keeping a critical eye open on the mainstream side of economic theory, so to be able to present Neo-Schumpeterian economics as a valid alternative for a comprehensive study of economic phenomena. The result is at the same time a consistent review of contributions at the different level of analysis, conflating the 'division of labor' mentioned above, and a roadmap for the research to come. In his chapter *Behavior and Cognition of Economic Actors in Evolutionary Economics* Richard Nelson develops further considerations concerning routinized and creative behavior of economic agents. He highlights the importance of the evolving framework of cultural context in which explorative and exploitative human agents are embedded in, and which is responsible for adaptive responses. Needless to say that this kind of behavior does not resemble any optimization but is coping with the complexity of the real world. Kurt Dopfer, Jason Potts and Andreas Pyka address the issue of an endogenously evolving environment in which economic agents are embedded in and which in turn is shaped by the actions and interactions of economic agents. In their paper *Upward and Downward Complementarity: The Meso Core of Evolutionary Growth Theory* the authors show that a major source for the qualitative changes economic systems undergo over time, comes from cross-fertilization of so far not connected knowledge, which is behind upward complementarities. Upward complementarities are responsible for the long-run innovative changes causing qualitative change and structural development so central in evolutionary economics.

2 Part II: Aggregate Outcomes

One of the conclusions of the first part is that we have to expect rather heterogeneous aggregate outcomes in different economic systems, caused by differences in the capabilities of economic agents interacting in market and non-market environments. The five chapters of the second part of this volume are dedicated to the aggregate outcomes of economic systems and shed light on their plurality. Heterogeneity is a fundamental property not only of firms, but of wider economic systems too. Martin Shrolec's chapter entitled *Global Dynamics, Capabilities and the Crisis* exactly addresses these issues from an empirical point of view in his analysis of the consequences of the 2007 financial crisis which is far from being uniquely processed in Europe, Asia and Africa. In *Convergence or Divergence: A Nonparametric Analysis on China's Regional Disparity* Xiang Deng, Jing Song and Jianping Li address divergent economic developments on the regional level in China. Instead of long run convergence suggested by mainstream economic growth theories the authors detect an increasing divergence since 1978 and analyze the reasons for this observation. Gunnar Eliasson uses his chapter, *Micro to Macro Evolutionary Modeling – On the economics of self organization of dynamic markets by ignorant actors*, to demonstrate that a computable general equilibrium is only a special case in his experimentally organized economy when all experimental features of agents are ignored. All other cases generate a wide variety of results which depend on the empirical information of the model. Maureen McKelvey also addresses the context dependence as an important explanation for varying innovation performance of firms in her contribution *Firms Navigating Through Innovation Spaces: A Conceptualization*. Innovation activities of firms are embedded in different geographical contexts which are responsible for access, generation and co-evolution of ideas in R&D cooperations. The specific mix of available resources, technologies, creative people stimulate business innovation and leads to rather heterogeneous products, process and services. Hans-Jürgen Engelbrecht makes *A Proposal for a 'National Innovation System Plus Subjective Well-Being' Approach and an Evolutionary Systemic Normative Theory of Innovation* which addresses the open flank of evolutionary economics: because of taking serious strong uncertainty, the benchmark corresponding to the optimum optimorum of a social planner's solution in a mainstream model is not available in evolutionary economics. Engelbrecht analyses possibilities to apply normative theories related to happiness approaches to explore possibilities of closing this fundamental gap.

3 Part III: Behavior

Aggregate outcomes result from economic behavior which is the central topic of the six chapters in this part of the book. The replicator dynamics approach already used by Uwe Cantner in his Presidential Address also is central in the chapter *Confounded, Augmented and Constrained Replicator Dynamics: Complex Selection Processes and Their Measurement* by Jacob Rubæk Holm, Esben Sloth Andersen and J. Stanley Metcalfe. An extension of replicator dynamics to overcome the restrictions stemming from the concentration of a single characteristic evolving in a single environment is introduced. So-called confounded selection becomes visible by considering the co-variance matrix of heterogeneous characteristics, which opens opportunities for new empirical analysis building on replicators. Michael Joffe addresses the most central form of economic behavior in Schumpeterian economics: Entrepreneurship. His chapter *The Roots of Growth: Entrepreneurship, Innovation and the Capitalist Firm* shows that although entrepreneurship can be observed in all societies, only the combination with capitalistic institutions generates growth characteristic for the industrialized countries for the last 200 years. A similar important role of co-evolving institutions are highlighted in Jorge Niosi's chapter *The Journey of Innovation—From Incremental to Radical Innovation and High-Tech Innovation Cascades: The Case of Biotechnology*. Guido Bünstorf, in his chapter *Schumpeterian Incumbents and Industry Evolution*, sheds light on an observation most often not so in the foreground, namely the creative role of established companies. Incumbents provide fertile grounds for innovative spin-offs by both allowing the foundation of new companies and also by acquiring entrepreneurial companies to support the diffusion of new technologies. Also when it comes to industry-university relationships incumbents often offer better prerequisites to digest and integrate new basic knowledge. In a similar vein, in *Incremental by Design? On the Role of Incumbents in Technology Niches An Evolutionary Network Analysis,* Daniel Hain and Roman Jurowetzki analyze the role of incumbents in technological niches, while Erik Stam and Zori Kambourova, in *Entrepreneurs' Overoptimism during the early Life Course of the Firm,* address the critical role of over-optimism of entrepreneurs for firm growth in early periods of the life-cycle.

4 Part IV: Interaction

The last part of this conference proceedings with its six chapters focuses on interaction between different economic agents. Obviously, in evolutionary economics learning and knowledge exchange play an utmost important role. Traditionally, external knowledge flows are considered as involuntary externalities and are summarized under the heading of technological spillovers. As this volume in particular emphasizes that heterogeneity matters, also external knowledge sources are to be considered in more detail as there a vast differences between e.g. innovation networks and industrial espionage. Muhammad Ali, Uwe Cantner and Ipsita Roy in their contribution *Knowledge Spillovers Through FDI and Trade: Moderating Role of Quality-Adjusted Human Capital* shed new light on the particularities of foreign direct investments and thereby help to disentangle the confusion around technological spillovers. In their empirical analysis they employ a quality-based indicator of human capital to investigate the varying effects of FDI in 20 European economies between 1995 and 2010. Dario Guarascio, Mario Pianta and Francesco Bogliacino also investigate European industries and find characteristic patterns which distinguish between Northern economies and Mediterranean economies. Their contribution *Export, R&D and New Products. A Model and a Test on European Industries* focuses on three relationships explaining the varying innovative performance in the two groups of countries, namely the capacity of firms to transfer R&D into new products, the meaning of innovation to gain export market shares and the relationship between successful exports and innovation. In the Northern economies a positive feedback emerges which is missing in the other countries club. Thomas Brenner and Johann Peter Murmann apply simulation analysis to explain the different settings of the German and the U.S. synthetic dye industries dominating the evolution of this industry in the second half of the nineteenth century. Their numerical experiments in their chapter *Using Simulation Experiments to Test Historical Explanations: The Development of the German Dye Industry 1857–1913* show the important role of University-Industry-links responsible for the global dominance of German companies in this field. The complexity of economic interactions is the major motif of agent based modelling approaches. In *From the Marshallian search for Equilibrium to Schumpeterian Dynamics. A Simulation Model* Cristiano Antonelli and Gianluigi Ferraris apply this methodology to develop the Schumpeterian and Marshallian microfoundations of economic interaction. In the following chapter *Understanding the complex nature of innovation network evolution* Muhamed Kudic and Jutta Günther analyze structural properties of innovation networks which constitute the platform of interactions in innovation processes. The final chapter *Why Does Sports Equipment Sometimes Become Too Sophisticated and Expensive?: A Case Study of the Overshooting Hypothesis in Board Sports* by Stuart Thomas and Jason Potts highlights positive feedbacks between the innovation activities of suppliers and sensitivity towards fashion phenomena on the demand side which eventually lead to a market collapse.

To conclude, all contributions in this proceedings volume of the Jena conference of the International Joseph Alois Schumpeter Society in 2014 emphasize the role of heterogeneity of economic actors concerning e.g. their knowledge-base, the meaning of different modes of interaction between various actors within economic systems as well as the important mutual feedback relations between the economic agents and their environment responsible for varying contexts in which innovation-driven dynamics take place. Without doubt, the explicit emphasis on the overwhelming heterogeneity to be observed in different realms of economic systems is responsible for the extra explanatory power of modern evolutionary economics. Finally, and besides the stress on the idea that 'heterogeneity matters', all chapters have to be praised as they ennoble the general guideline traced by the Conference title 'Foundations of Economic Change'. The contributions extend, enrich and deepen our understanding of processes of evolution and change at all the levels of analysis, and certainly push forward the frontier of knowledge, to the benefit of the Neo-Schumpeterian and Evolutionary Economics community of scholars. In this sense, this conference proceeding is a taste of a more general academic success and should be considered as an additional evidence of the increasing relevance of Evolutionary Economics; for all these reasons, we are convinced that this volume will become a source of insight, motivation, and inspiration for a wave of novel research in the spirit of Schumpeter.

Part I
Foundations of Economic Change

Foundations of Economic Change: An Extended Schumpeterian Approach

Uwe Cantner

Abstract This paper employs the Schumpeterian approach to the development of economies in order to identify the core building blocks of a theory of endogenous economic change. Borders and insights are widened by combining concepts and findings from behavioral economics, from evolutionary economics, and from complexity economics. Actor heterogeneity, on the one hand, and mechanisms of actors' interaction, on the other, are suggested to be fundamental elements of that theory. Theoretical analyses and empirical accounts are presented, achievements are discussed, and further avenues of research are suggested.

1 A Changing World and Innovations in the Thick of It

That the social and economic world is developing continuously and thereby changes its structures—sometimes smoothly and sometimes rather abruptly—is nothing new to social scientists. The social sphere in general and the economic sphere in particular are in continuous flux. Economic and technology historians (e.g. Mokyr 1992) inform us that, at least since the industrial revolution about 250 years ago, such changes are not rare and have even become routine in our days. New ideas, often but not only of a technological nature, and respective innovations following from them are considered the main drivers of structural change, affecting the composition of an economic and social system (Saviotti 1996). Locally and globally, on the individual level as well as on the level of populations and even higher levels of aggregation, such changes are observable. They appear at various speeds and velocities, they are not always foreseeable, they are often the result of intended actions but in some cases they are due to unintended side effects.

The analysis of such change is a challenging task as we attempt to understand short and long term (even historical) pattern and causes, with the sources of

U. Cantner (✉)
Department of Economics and Business Administration, Friedrich Schiller University Jena, Carl-Zeiss-Strasse 3, 07743 Jena, Germany

Centre for Integrative Innovation Management, Department of Marketing & Management, University of Southern Denmark, Odense, Denmark
e-mail: uwe.cantner@uni-jena.de

A. Pyka, U. Cantner (eds.), *Foundations of Economic Change*, Economic Complexity and Evolution, DOI 10.1007/978-3-319-62009-1_2

emerging newness, the nature of those actors who create, implement, propagate, compete with, use and refuse the new, and the mechanisms that connect these activities into a stream of changes at its core. To address these dimensions in an integrative way, a conceptual framework is needed. Here the economics literature offers two alternatives to comprehend the described rich dynamics: The first suggests a rather complicated machine at work that runs on the basis of a certain plan combined with some randomness (just as exogenous shocks) which determines the economic outcomes—the dynamics being the result of a rather carefully drafted plan. A second concept renders the economy as a complex ecology that does not act and respond in always predictable ways—the dynamics observed is the result of activities devoted to experimentation in a not-well-understood environment, often facing strong uncertainty and being confronted with unintended outcomes.

It is the latter concept that underlies the foundations of economic change to be developed in this address. We draw on Schumpeter and his ideas presented in the *Theory of Economic Development* (1934/2008) and in *Capitalism, Socialism and Democracy* (1942). The former identifies the entrepreneur as a rather special and rare actor who initiates innovative change. The latter highlights the notion that newness and innovation as well as the related entrepreneurial activities are major *dei ex machina* of change, be that in markets or in the economy as a whole:

> The opening up of new markets, foreign or domestic, and the organizational development from the craft shop to such concerns as U.S. Steel illustrate the same process of industrial mutation—if I may use that biological term—that incessantly revolutionizes the economic structure from within, incessantly destroying the old one, incessantly creating a new one. This process of Creative Destruction is the essential fact about capitalism (Schumpeter 1942/1950, 83).

Hence, structural change is here seen as induced by innovations that (attempt to) drive out of the market existing technologies, processes and products. At the very core of such newness driven structural development is the *homo agens* (as opposed to *homo oeconomicus*) as a *micro* unit that induces (as inventor and innovator of new ideas) and/or propagates change (as imitator and adopter of newness).

On this basis, we go beyond Schumpeter by indicating that insights from (i) behavioral economics, (ii) evolutionary economics and (iii) complexity economics are helpful in understanding better the intricate dynamics of innovation driven change. The first offers findings to the behavioral nature of the agents of change who act in a world not perfectly comprehensible to them; this allows going beyond Schumpeter's rather parsimonious description of the entrepreneur in sociological terms. The second and third address the mechanisms of interaction between individuals (and group of individuals) that lead to creative destruction in Schumpeter's sense and beyond when long term dynamics are concerned. Competition as well as cooperation, market exchange as well as non-market transactions and relations comprise important modes of interaction among these actors of change providing for structures in markets and industries.

To develop these basic elements of a theory of economic change, we proceed as follows. Section 2 looks at the individual level of actors and provides arguments for actor heterogeneity being analytically and empirically relevant for the analysis of innovative change. The mechanisms of interaction in a population of heterogeneous agents are introduced in Sect. 3 and an account of their empirical validity is offered in Sect. 4. The final section summarizes and, on basis of the core elements of economic change addressed, suggests an extended, even more general approach to analyzing economic change.

2 Actors of Change: A Heterogeneous Landscape

2.1 Homo agens*: Some Principle Remarks*

With human beings at the core of any theory of social change in general and of economic change in particular, the conceptualization of economic actors occupies a central position. The concept of a *homo agens* or actor of change is required. As Schumpeter informed us, these actors can be individuals (Schumpeter 1912 [1934/2008]) or teams/groups of individuals under the umbrella of a firm or firms (Schumpeter 1942/1950). More recently, even larger entities where different actors work together such as in cooperative R&D projects and networks and also value-chains have been frequently suggested.

How should we conceptually deal with these actors of change? It appears that in a theory of economic change with endogenous forces and determinants of transformation an economic actor modelled along the ideal of *homo oeconomicus* as a decision maker[1] whose decisions are based on a fully rational calculus in a sense of an optimum optimorum is less suitable. Schumpeter (1912 [1934/2008]) justified such a conceptual idea for all those economic activities that are ongoing and for which economic actors have enough time to arrive at the optimal solution; in decision situations of that type, the concept of *homo oeconomicus* may serve well as an abstraction and workhorse. However, whenever, instead of known problems new ones have to be solved, this abstraction and the underlying assumptions appear to be farfetched or, as Schumpeter puts it:

> The assumption that conduct is prompt and rational is in all cases a fiction. But it proves to be sufficiently near to reality, if things have time to hammer logic into men. Where this has happened, and within the limits in which it has happened, one may rest content with this fiction and build theories upon it. [. . .] Outside of these limits our fiction loses its closeness to reality. To cling to it there also, as the traditional theory does, is to hide an essential thing and to ignore a fact which, in contrast with other deviations of our assumptions from reality, is theoretically important and the source of the explanation of phenomena which would not exist without it (Schumpeter 1934/2008, 80).

[1] This conceptualization is the core backup of the mainstream approach and whether one looks into research on the individual and the firm, on market interaction and industries performance, or on the macro level of economies, explicitly or implicitly the *homo oeconomicus* concept is applied. In this sense it is a major binding element, it is the backbone of the approach and it is consistency-preserving.

Hence, when we think of innovation driven change, an alternative concept of economic man that comes closer to a behavior towards the creation of newness than the concept of *homo oeconomicus* is required. For that we again draw attention to Schumpeter (1912 [1934/2008]) who was among the first to address an agent of change, the *entrepreneur,* inclined to provoke change, which he contrasts to the *static host,* an agent engaged in the same types of known and manageable tasks. The bottom line is that the introduction of the 'entrepreneur' has been the first step in acknowledging actor heterogeneity, which nowadays is rendered as being based on several types, with different preferences, competences and ambitions. It is this diversity or heterogeneity of actors that, through interaction, is a fundamental source of newness and change.

As is well known, Schumpeter did not stick solely to the notion of the *entrepreneur* as the driver of innovation and economic development. In *Capitalism, Socialism and Democracy* (Schumpeter 1942/1950) he considered an additional category, the established *firm,* and its importance for innovation driven development. This twist in argumentation led to a surge of empirical research on the so-called Neo-Schumpeter hypotheses (e.g. Cohen and Levin 1989; Cohen 2010), which attempt to clarify the question whether the small or the big firm—respectively, a competitive market or a monopoly—shows higher incentives to innovation.

In line with these two categories of a *homo agens,* two strands of research have been pursued over the past decades: entrepreneurship research enhanced by insights from psychology, on the one hand, and research on the innovative firm which draws on insights from behavioral economics and its manifestation in the theory of the firm, on the other. In the following, we briefly address these directions.

2.2 *Schumpeter's Entrepreneur as* homo agens: *Insights from Entrepreneurship Research*

2.2.1 The Concept of Schumpeter's Entrepreneur

Schumpeter identified *his* agent of change as someone beyond the norm, someone with a special character. His entrepreneur is a quite peculiar actor willing to break through traditional structures and challenge established ways of doing things. The Schumpeterian entrepreneur is individualistic, self-directed, has an inner drive to innovate, and, as stated by Leskinen (2011), seeks autonomy and "independence from other people" in order to be "in control of one's own destiny" (p. 5). Schumpeter (1912 [1934/2008]) further argued that the fascination of entrepreneurship is especially strong for people "who have no other chance of achieving social distinction" (p. 93).

This suggests that, first, the Schumpeterian entrepreneur is a different social "animal"; neither average nor representative, but rather an outlier in the skewed distribution of propensities to innovate and change. Second, an approach going beyond the boundaries of economics and drawing on insights from psychology and sociology may be required to get an understanding of that "animal". Hence, agents' personality traits [as represented by the Big Five (McCrae and Costa 1997)], their respective self-identity (e.g. Obschonka et al. 2015), their motivations and attitudes (Göthner et al. 2012), their social attitudes and norm perceptions (Cantner et al. 2017), their competences and, related to that, their respective perceived behavioral control (Göthner et al. 2012) are dimensions that are at the core of understanding individual behavior, problem solving and decision making.

Along these lines an impressive body of literature in entrepreneurship research has been built, which is primarily focused on deep psychological factors that "construct" an entrepreneurial personality; high levels of openness and extraversion combined with low levels of agreeableness and neuroticism characterize individuals who tend to entrepreneurship (e.g. Schmitt-Rodermund 2004). However, lacking predictive power of these deep factors, the discussion has been directed towards context factors-especially the social context, on the one hand, and so-called characteristic adaptations (McAdams 1995) comprising an individuals' desires, beliefs, concerns, and coping mechanisms, on the other. In this context, recently a literature has developed going beyond deep entrepreneurial traits, one focused on entrepreneurial intentions, a step just before action is started. Intentions, as conceptualized by the *Theory of Planned Behavior* (Ajzen 1991), depend, next to attitudes (which are closely related to deep personality traits[2]), on social norms and on belief in one's own abilities.

With the help of these insights from psychology, in the following we attempt to develop Schumpeter's characterization of the entrepreneur as a special and deviant type of actor towards an account of actor heterogeneity with respect to innovation.

2.2.2 Entrepreneurship Heterogeneity with Respect to Innovation

The phenomenon of the entrepreneur as Schumpeterian deviant, to be distinguished from a follower and the resulting heterogeneous entrepreneurial landscape, can be analyzed in various ways. Two of them are briefly presented here, the first focusing on factors influencing the intention to found a new firm (hence more "input"-oriented) and the second focusing on the innovative output generated by entrepreneurs' newly founded firms.

Starting with entrepreneurial intentions, in their seminal study applying the Theory of Planned Behavior, Krueger et al. (2000) argued that the prototypical entrepreneur is an "iconoclastic individualist" with a strong "tendency toward inner-directedness" (p. 424). More recently, Krueger (2007) further highlighted the salience of entrepreneurial self-identity (as opposed to a salient social identity, see Tajfel and Turner 1979) for the entrepreneurial type. Hence, an entrepreneur is someone fighting *against all odds* to create a successful enterprise.

[2]Here, attitudes can be considered characteristic adaptations of the Big Five traits.

Table 1 Schumpeterian deviants and followers [adapted from Cantner et al. (2017)]

Peer group identification		Low		High		
Peer group support		Low	High	Low	High	Totals
High entrepreneurial intentions	No.	44	34	24	53	155
	%	11.0	8.5	6.0	13.3	38.8
Realization	%	1.1			2.5	

Drawing on that literature, Cantner et al. (2017)—using scientist data from the Thuringian Founder Study—analyzed via observed entrepreneurial intentions whether potential entrepreneurs are rather of the Schumpeterian type or follow the norm or the crowd. Using the Theory of Planned Behavior by Ajzen (1991), next to individual level variables, attitudes and behavioral control contextual dimensions such as social norms and group identification (from social identity theory; Tajfel and Turner 1979) play a role. Entrepreneurial intentions (Bird 1988) are cognitive representations of a person's readiness to engage in entrepreneurship—that is, to found a new firm on the basis of a new idea/business model—measured by three levels, high medium, and low intentions. The degree of an individual's social embeddedness is proxied by the dimension *group identification* which represents the relation to a subject's peers; identifiers (with a high level of *group identification)* are distinguished from non-identifiers (with a low level of *group-identification*). This leads to two subsamples with 213 non-identifiers and 187 identifiers. As to social norms, explanatory power is found in the variable *injunctive norm,* which informs whether the peer group of a potential entrepreneur would encourage or support the founding of a new firm based on a new idea; higher and lower levels of perceived social expectations towards engaging in entrepreneurship are distinguished.

A potential entrepreneur of the Schumpeterian type is identified by the combination of high intentions to found a new firm, a low degree of group identification and a non-supportive social norm. The follower type goes with high intentions, high degree of group identification and a supportive social norm. Table 1 delivers information on these types out of a sample of 400 scientists. First, 38.8% of all subjects show a high entrepreneurial intention. Out of these, 11% fulfill the criteria of a Schumpeterian deviant and 13.3% are considered followers. There is a third group between these extremes with a total share of 14.5%.

Extending the analysis from intentions to actually founding a firm (realization) a couple of years later finds, with respect to the total sample, only 1.1% Schumpeterian deviants and 2.5% followers.

Looking at the entrepreneurial landscape additionally from the angle of innovation output, a rather obvious pattern emerges. Data from the Thuringian Founder Study are used to classifying newly founded firms (entrepreneurial start-ups) by the degree of newness of their innovation (along the CIS-nomenclature).

From Table 2 it becomes immediately clear that entrepreneurs with ideas and innovations more of the follower-type are in the majority: the latter comprise at least the categories "locally" and "not new" and add up to 61.1%. Neglecting the

Table 2 Innovators and imitators by innovations' degree of newness (Thuringian founder study)

Innovations' degree of newness	Number of entrepreneurs start-ups	%
For the world	74	**20.1**
For Europe	24	6.5
For Germany	36	9.8
Locally	58	15.8
Not new	163	44.3
Don't know	13	3.5

"don't know" category, the remaining 36.4% differ in their degree of newness where the highest degree belongs to "for the world" and amounts to 20.1%. Hence, just as the number of Schumpeter entrepreneurs is lower than that of following entrepreneurs, when it comes to the newness of innovations, those who can be considered as imitators dominate those being more radical.

The Schumpeterian concept of actor heterogeneity, as formulated by Schumpeter in terms of a entrepreneur versus static host dichotomy, has been developed further and been found in more detailed characterizations and classifications. Its relevance for understanding a core driving force of economic development and dynamics, and of innovation, leading in the end to growth and economic welfare is high on the agenda of the entrepreneurship research program. On the one hand, with actor differences in opportunity recognition marshalling resources in the nascent phase, problem solving behavior should be a concern; analyses of entrepreneurial decision making and effectuation, creativity and discovery using experimental approaches (e.g. Crosetto 2010) are considered a viable route. On the other hand, and based on the aforementioned, the crucial roles different entrepreneurial styles and types may play in varying contexts and situations (e.g. situations of radical, disruptive, or directional change) still need to be investigated.

2.3 *Established Firms as* homo agens*: Change as a Normal Affair*

2.3.1 The Concept of the Established Firms as Agent of Change

Discussing entrepreneurship and its intricate sources and dynamics addresses one dimension of innovation driven structural change; another concerns the observation that (established) firms drive economic development, as discussed in Schumpeter (1942/1950). Whereas the Schumpeterian entrepreneur enters the stage with new combinations rather surprisingly and suddenly, the established firm's new ideas are generated in a systematic way and hence are something more predictable.

To understand the observed heterogeneity of established firms, it seems obvious to draw again on psychological traits and characteristic adaptations as well as individual social interaction—since established firms are an assemble of several and often a large number of economic actors. However, a fundamental, still not solved problem is how to aggregate the relevant characteristics of all members of a firm—or at least of its governing board. There are certainly approaches around attempting to explain the interaction and performance of teams (e.g. Bunderson 2005), how the competences of team members interact in innovation (e.g. Drach-Zahavy and Somech 2001), and how mental models converge during the process of working together (e.g. Cannon-Bowers et al. 1993; Sander et al. 2015).

However, in the development of the modern theory of the firm, this route has not been taken. Neglecting aggregation issues, the starting point has been a psychological one, namely, the concept of bounded rationality. This concept has been derived from a focus on decision making when the conditions of the *homo oeconomicus* approach are not given, and then transferred to the level of a firm.

In Simon (1955), the boundedly rational actor was characterized by bounded substantial and bounded procedural rationality. The former refers to a situation where a decision maker has not all the information at hand required for an optimal solution; the latter addresses the issue that a decision maker is not aware or does not know the algorithm by which an optimal solution can be derived. These two dimensions quite nicely fit into an innovation context: when a decision maker starts a new project, neither the outcome nor the procedure by which that outcome can be achieved or accomplished is (perfectly) known *ex ante*. Dosi and Egidi (1991) complement these dimensions by a concept of uncertainty in the sense of substantive and procedural uncertainty. The former refers in an analogous way to uncertainty about the availability of information and the latter with respect to the appropriate solution algorithms. In such contexts, framing and status quo orientation (as important sources of *path-dependency*), heuristics (as rules-of-thumb or *routines*) and loss aversion (as prominently formulated by prospect theory) shape choices and behavior (e.g. Tversky and Kahneman 1981; Kahneman et al. 1982; Kahneman and Tversky 1992; Thaler and Sunstein 2008); and they explain not only deviations from *homo oeconomicus* behavior but also non-uniformity and hence heterogeneity of actors' choices.

A further development of these ideas is found in Cyert and March (1963), who suggest a theory of the firm addressing inner firm structures. They suggest an understanding of the firm in terms of two concepts most relevant for the economics of innovation, namely, bounded rationality and imperfect environmental matching.[3] As to the former, Cyert and March stick to the notion of Simon in understanding bounded rationality as "limitations of information and calculation", implying that one attempts to satisfy targets (aspiration levels) instead of optimizing the best imaginable solution. In this sense, in behavioral theory, a firm is considered as being a set of (unchangeable) *standard operating procedures,* a concept taken up later by Nelson and Winter in their concept *of routines.* As to the imperfect environmental matching dimension, Cyert and March suggest that human agency is not entirely determined by an exogenously given structure

[3]There is a third dimension Cyert and March considered important, namely, unresolved conflicts.

(e.g. market structure); the dimension opens up a place for history, an issue to be taken up under individual-context interplay below. The important insight of Cyert and March concerning innovation and learning is the idea of innovations being induced by organizational slack, which provide funds for innovative activities.[4]

A few years before, Penrose (1959) suggested a resource based view of the firm (RBV), a theory of the innovating multiproduct firm facing uncertainty and pursuing objectives under bounded rationality. The latter is represented by specific human and non-human resources that embody knowledge of various types and that allow a firm to grow. By internal learning, an excess of those resources is generated, which by itself serves as an additional inducement mechanism for expansion. Excess resources provide services at (near) zero marginal costs, enabling managers to invest into innovation and growth. Fundamental are productive opportunities that arise from a difference between perceived internal and external firm environments.

How do actors decide, behave and act under those conditions? Drawing on the standard operating procedures in Cyert and March (1963), Nelson and Winter (1982) suggest the concept of a routine, defined as a *"pattern of behaviour that is followed repeatedly, but is subject to change if conditions change"* (Winter 1964, 263–264). A routine is a collective phenomenon and finds its individualistic counterpart in skills and habits. Routines in this approach refer to how tasks are accomplished, how problems are solved, and how knowledge is learned; more often they are not tangibly identifiable or necessarily codified. Routines show various characteristics: some are static and some dynamic (e.g. search and research routines); they are not easily changed and difficult to imitate since they contain quite a degree of tacitness. It is this latter dimension that relates the concept of *routines* to the concept of *resources* in the resource-based view of the firm (RBV) as envisaged by Penrose (1959) and further developed by, e.g., Wernerfelt (1984), Barney (1991) and Barney et al. (2001). Hence, human resources and firm competences in the RBV relate in this sense to skills and routines; here firms are considered as being composed of tangible and intangible assets, which are tied to the firm and are difficult to imitate. However, the RBV lacks the dynamic dimension already envisaged in routines. Further developments of the RBV to a dynamic capabilities approach of the firm, as suggested by Teece (1986), just render this nexus. This theory of the firm seeks to explain how firms achieve and sustain competitive advantage despite an ever-changing environment. Most important in this concept are what Nelson and Winter define as high-level routines, namely, those that determine the firm's ability to perceive new opportunities and those that allow the firm to alter lower-level routines to achieve these opportunities. Of utmost importance for innovative activities of firms are capabilities and routines that govern learning and allow building up competencies and skills; the difficulties in imitation them lend the firm a sustainable competitive advantage. Other firms have

[4]There is another source of innovation discussed, "problemistic search", referring to search induced by problems arising from intra-firm conflicts.

to incur non-negligible costs to build up respective absorptive capacities, a notion introduced by Cohen and Levinthal (1989, 1990), in order to copy or to imitate knowledge and competences represented by these capabilities, if they are able at all.

This focus on competences and capabilities as well as on skills and routines is at the core of a behavioral approach towards inventive and innovative actors—either being performed by an individual or by a firm—and by this towards innovation driven structural change. Boundedly rational, and facing uncertainty in the strong sense, these actors are not only driven by pure economic incentives but also, if not more so, by their competencies and their knowledge acquired via learning and experimenting. How do learning and knowledge accumulation work?

To start with information and knowledge are different when compared with commodities and goods. They show an immaterial character, on the one hand, and, on the other, they are, with a few exceptions, not of the type of a purely private good. Hence, both may be considered as pure public goods meeting the criteria of non-rivalry and of non-excludability.[5]

However, classifying information and knowledge in that way, to be transmitted between actors, requires encoding them into signals so that all potential users have the perfect ability to understand the signals' content (Denzau and North 1994). These two conditions satisfied, any consideration of the way by which the use of new information and new knowledge by others, hence imitation, could be prevented leads to the discussion of intellectual property rights. The public good nature of information and knowledge put forward can easily be questioned via three revisions.

A first kind of revision aims at distinguishing between information and knowledge (e.g. Foray 2004; Boisot and Canals 2004). The former is the representation of some knowledge by signals (words, letters, optical impressions, etc.) that can be transmitted between actors. Knowledge, by contrast, is related to the ability to take up the signals (encoding), to understand their content and to relate it to pre-existing knowledge. For a transfer or exchange of knowledge to be successfully accomplished, its codification, its transfer, its de-codification, as well as its basic understanding in the sense of connecting it to the existing knowledge stock is required.

On the basis of this distinction, a second revision refers to giving up the assumption of the perfect ability of actors to understand the content of transmitted signals. Doing so, knowledge is not to be taken as a pure public good anymore, which, by its very definition, is entirely available to everyone at every place and at any time. As per Nelson (1991), knowledge attached to innovation activities is to be considered a latent public good, implying that it enfolds its public good character whenever certain circumstances are met. Among those circumstances, most prominent is the ability of the information recipient to understand the signals, to interpret

[5]Knowledge is a peculiar kind of commodity the pricing of which is difficult to accomplish—pricing is done by describing to others the commodity's value, but once you do it in the case of information and knowledge, the potential buyers already have what they wanted and show no willingness to pay for it.

them, and to use them. Cohen and Levinthal (1990) coin the concept of absorptive capacities, which comprises characteristics (human capital, smartness, etc.) of actors to do so. Transmitting knowledge in that case from one actor to another, a certain cognitive proximity between them has to be given—if the cognitive or technological distance between them becomes too large, the communication of knowledge becomes ineffective. Recognizing this interdependence in the process of knowledge exchange, Lane and Lubatkin (1998) suggest the concept of relative absorptive capacity.

The third revision addresses the observation that some encoding of knowledge into signals is not always possible. Drawing back to Polanyi (1967), some part of knowledge has a tacit character. This implies that actors possess knowledge that they use in an appropriate way but they are incapable of explaining to others how it works in detail. They are not able to encode it into signals that may then be transferred to the recipient. Consequently, such knowledge cannot be transmitted from one actor to another (Cowan et al. 2000), at least not that easily and by the usual kinds of signals. In that case, knowledge shows the character of a private good—it is embodied within a certain actor who can be hired from the labor market. This knowledge is not available for those in the previous occupation and can entirely be used by those in the new one. Hence, the two criteria for a private good, rivalry and excludability, are met. However, beside this market based transfer channel, it seems to be the case that by sheer observation, even tacit knowledge can be copied. This requires a considerably close interaction between the sender and the recipient in the sense of having face-to-face contact and being at the same place.

With the departure from both the *homo oeconomicus* principle and the notion of knowledge being a pure public good, the door opens for actor heterogeneity,[6] in terms of different abilities, competencies, and incentives, to be successful in activities related to innovation, imitation and also adoption.[7] In this approach, the so-called knowledge-based approach, knowledge and competences of actors play a decisive role in how they design their respective change related activities—and economic incentives become of a subordinated nature.

An interesting additional dimension concerns specific characteristics of the technology to be further developed and of the process of change determining such development. The further exploitable opportunities and appropriability conditions a certain technology offers, the specific nature of knowledge required to master and to develop this technology as well as the degree of cumulativeness of

[6]For a broader discussion, see Cantner and Hanusch (2005).

[7]This concept of heterogeneity, of course, is an extraction out of all possible sources and instances of heterogeneity, but it enables us to focus on that kind of heterogeneity we consider analytically relevant in the economic theory of technical change. More generally, it refers to the degree of difference within a population of observations, let that be households, firms, sectors or even regions or countries that differ with respect to some dimension of interest: their efforts, behaviors and/or success due to—among other things—the artefacts they consume or produce, the modes of production they employ, the direction and intensity of innovative activities they pursue, or the organizational setting they choose.

(technological) change provide contexts that, together with an actor' knowledge and competencies, shape change-provoking behavior. These contextual conditions are summarized in the 'OACK' approach (with O for opportunities, A for appropriability conditions, C for cumulative change, and K for knowledge).

OACK serves as a basis for investigating industrial dynamics and industrial evolution by looking at innovative activities and market structures as complex and mutually dependent phenomena. OACK claims that the ways agents bring about new ideas and economize are considerably different (or heterogeneous); the degree of those differences depends on the four OACK features of technology. It further claims that these various ways compete among one another in markets where the degree of competition depends on the degree of heterogeneity of innovative activities and successes. The heterogeneity across firms in innovation implies both the presence of idiosyncratic capabilities (absorptive, technological, etc.) and that firms not only do different things but, and most importantly, when they do the same thing, they know how to do it in different ways. This focus on the underlying capabilities for innovation activities draws on the behavioral foundations discussed above and their embeddedness in the technological environment prevailing in a market or an industry.[8]

2.3.2 Firm Heterogeneity with Respect to Innovation, Imitation and Adoption

The empirical account of the heterogeneity among firms in terms of innovation, imitation and adoption is broad and rather comprehensive. Structural regularities as well as pattern of dynamics and change have spawned a literature on so-called *industrial dynamics* and *industrial evolution* (Marsili and Verspagen 2002; Malerba 2006; Cantner and Guerzoni 2009), which have come into vogue since the 1980s by the very fact of traditional IO approaches not being able to find robust and convincing evidence for the so-called *Neo-Schumpeter Hypotheses* (on firm size and market-concentration dependent degree of innovation activities). Research in that field succeeded in collecting a range of stylized facts and deriving certain classifications for specific structural patterns of innovation and structural dynamics.

For the description of industry structures and their dynamics, certain stylized facts (Dosi et al. 1995; Dosi 2007) have been extracted from a broad set of industry specific studies. A first addresses persistent (in terms of rank persistency) performance gaps between firms (e.g. Dosi et al. 1997; Marsili 2001; Cantner and Krüger 2004) due to learning-by-doing effects with respect to differential knowledge accumulation and innovation. A second set of stylized facts addresses regularities in non-normal distributions with respect to firm size and firm growth rates which

[8]This characterization of the behavioral side and its interaction with technological context conditions fit nicely into the general pattern of the innovation process in modern manufacturing, as suggested by Dosi (1988) (see Cantner and Guerzoni 2009).

can be explained by firm related idiosyncratic factors such as specific abilities and competencies to diversify (Bottazzi and Secchi 2006) and/or to pursue innovative activities—as proposed by the resource-based view of the firm and its further developments indicating the "guided" stochastic nature of innovation and related learning effects. Whereas the first two sets of facts address time persistent structures, a third set highlights technology (e.g. Malerba and Orsenigo 1997) and market entry and exit dynamics (e.g. Geroski 1995) as well as related market turbulences (e.g. Davies and Geroski 1997). Responsibility for such dynamics may rest with entrepreneurial activities, on the one hand, and technological regimes in which small firms are better equipped to be successful in innovation, on the other. The further stylized fact of an industry life cycle pattern (e.g. Klepper 2002a, b; Cantner et al. 2009), which accounts for the structural features of an industry from early states into maturity, can be seen as a combination of a phase of turbulent development in earlier stages followed by a phase of a more structured and selective market dynamics leading to a mature stage. Meanwhile, these bare bones of a model of selective competition have experienced various refinements in terms of, e.g., niche development (e.g. Klepper and Thompson 2006) and demand side influences (e.g. Fontana and Guerzoni 2008; Klepper and Malerba 2010).

Also in an inter-industry context, industry classifications drawing on firm heterogeneity allow for differences in the degree and breadth of knowledge accumulation, the type of innovation, reliance on innovation pursued elsewhere, and usage of means of appropriation. In line with the distinction of different types of innovative actors by Schumpeter, important milestones are the industry classifications suggested by Pavitt (1984) and by Malerba and Orsenigo (1995, 1996) as well as the latter's application to the theory of industry life cycles. Whereas Pavitt draws on institutional and economic determinants to classify innovation activities or actors and Malerba and Orsenigo relate their classification to the *Neo-Schumpeter-Hypotheses,* namely, the question whether small or large (patenting) firms are the major drivers of innovation. By these classifications, characteristic context conditions are suggested which form the pattern of innovation driven structural change.

To complement this literature and following the same line of analysis offered in the description of innovative/imitative entrepreneurship, in the following we provide a few statistics taken from the German section of the Community Innovation Survey. These indicate the innovation related heterogeneity of firms in German industries and services. The distinction between *research intensive* and *other industries,* as well as between *knowledge intensive* and *other services,* innovator rates and again the degree of innovativeness are addressed for selected time spans. In Fig. 1, innovator rates—that is, the share of innovative firms out of the total—in these subcategories are depicted from 1992 to 2014.

As one might expect, firms in *research intensive industries* show the highest innovator rate throughout the period considered, with a peak of about 81% in 1996 and then declining to about 66% in 2014. *Other industries* and knowledge intensive services show a rather similar innovator rate, which was higher than 50% before 2002 and declined to about 37% in 2014. Ranked last are *other services,* which started with 45% in 2000 and then experienced a decline to about 28% in 2014.

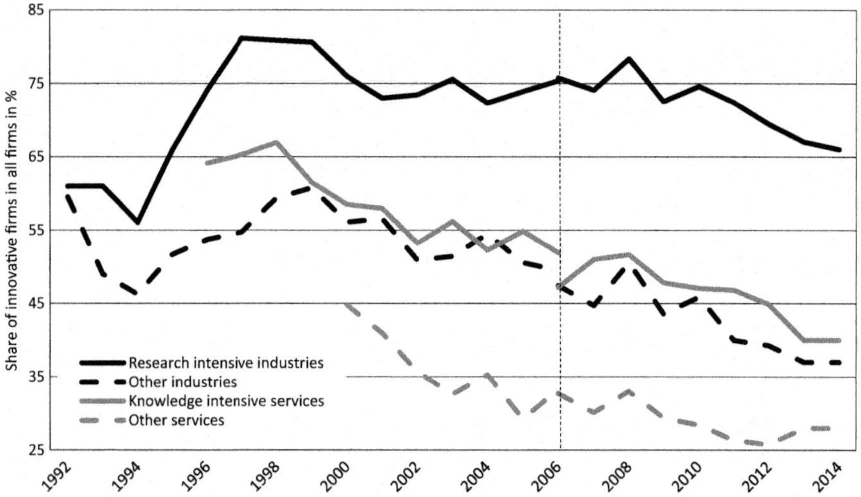

Fig. 1 Innovator rates [German CIS data; adapted from ZEW (various years)]. Note: The *scattered line* at year 2006 indicates a break in the data due to a revision of the industry classification

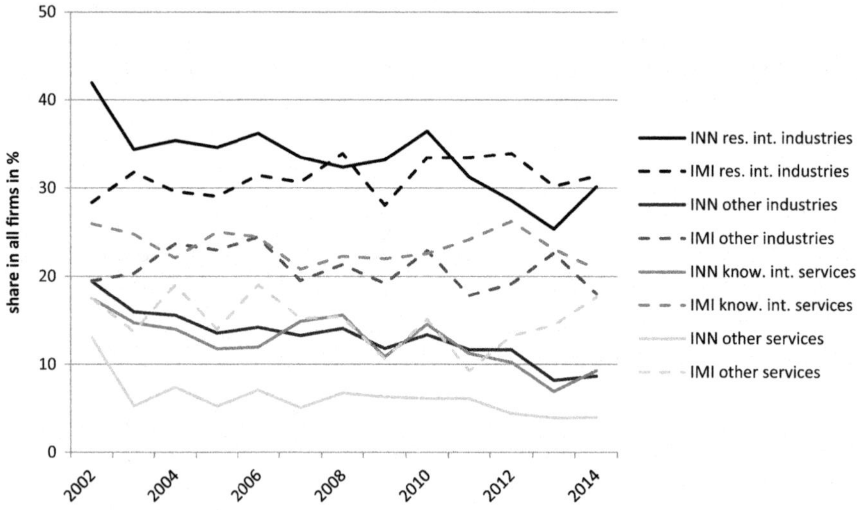

Fig. 2 Share of product innovators and product imitators [German CIS data; adapted from ZEW (various years)]

Hence, the overall picture here shows that not all firms are innovators—thus there is heterogeneity in this respect—and that the innovators' rate is declining over time.

In Fig. 2, the newness of product innovations is depicted for industries and services from 2002 to 2014 by looking at the share of innovators and imitators in all firms. The bold lines indicate product innovators, whereas the scattered lines indicate product imitators. Except for *research intensive industries,* in the other three aggregates the share of product imitators is larger than the share of product innovators throughout the considered time span. In the *research intensive industries,* the share of imitators overtakes the share of innovators in 2011. Overall, these figures complement the pattern of innovators/non-innovators by the degree of innovativeness: among those firms that admit to having introduced new products into the market—with a sub-period of exception for the *research intensive industries*—there are more imitators than innovators. In line with the development in Fig. 1, the share of product innovators for each of the four aggregates is declining, whereas imitators' shares stay relatively constant, *cum grosso modo.*

Although the foundations of a theory of the dynamic firm are partly influenced by insights from behavioral science, allowing us to move from the representative firm (based on the *homo oeconomicus* principle) to the concept of firm heterogeneity, to rely on dynamic resources and related learning effects appears only to be half the way to an explanation of businesses' choices and change. The concern here is that, in this approach, a firm is treated as an entity not to be disaggregated further, although a firm's "decisions" and behavior are the outcomes of interactions between firm employees. This does not mean that all employee and stakeholders are necessarily to be taken into account; the usual hierarchical structure of firms allowing for incomplete, pluralistic decision making enables researchers to concentrate on management teams (in R&D, in top management, etc.). The combination of research from management and from social psychology on team performance could help us to find a proper behavioral foundation of established firms. Interestingly, this would even allow specific insights into the differences between entrepreneurs (Schumpeter I) and established firms (Schumpeter II), which as yet are mainly reduced to the dimension of firm size.

2.4 Beyond Firm Boundaries and Openness

2.4.1 Concept of Cooperation in Innovation[9]

Differential accumulation of knowledge, as discussed above, does not take place in isolation but works within the context of interaction and exchange with other firms. It is actor heterogeneity that opens up collective exploration and exploitation of the knowledge space, a topic discussed early on by Allen (1983) and von Hippel (1987). For that to take place, actors have to access the knowledge of others, external knowledge, under some agreement. To accomplish that, an actor has several options. Among the options are (1) buying the required technological knowledge in appropriate markets (e.g. Arora et al. 2001) via external R&D expenditures, paying licensing fees or buying patents, (2) integrating other actors'

[9]For a more extensive discussion, see Cantner and Graf (2011).

technological knowledge into the own firm via mergers and acquisitions (e.g. Ahuja and Katila 2001) and via the market for human capital, and (3) cooperating in research and thereby formally and informally exchanging knowledge. These three cases of accessing external knowledge are related to the concept of organizational proximity introduced by Boschma (2005). In the case of market transactions, this proximity is considerably low, the relationships between contracting partners are highly flexible and governed by market prices with a unidirectional knowledge transfer from the seller to the buyer. Contrariwise, in the case of mergers and acquisitions as well as in the case of hiring human capital, here the hierarchical structure of a firm provides for close proximity, flexibility in the relation between the partners is considerably low and ruled by contract with again a unidirectional knowledge transfer. An intermediate level of proximity applies to any network type of cooperative relationship. This organizational format allows for flexibility and the switching rather easily from one cooperation partner to another. The transfer of knowledge is bidirectional and based on knowledge exchange. Here the reciprocity of exchanging knowledge is essential but neither necessarily uno actu (as in markets) nor contractually agreed upon (as in hierarchies).

Looking more closely on those cooperative relationships, one may ask for the conditions that have to be satisfied for actors to become engaged in knowledge exchange. In principle, there have to be a common (economic) interest to do so, a certain level of mutual understanding, and a certain degree of controllability and reciprocity in a continuous relation.

Looking at the common interests of actors engaging in knowledge exchange, the expected economic benefits are of utmost importance. However, intermediate targets in terms of technological solutions to be achieved commonly, or reciprocal access to specific knowledge are important as well. In the end, the motives have to be complementary so that all participating actors benefit. In this sense, on purely economic grounds research cooperation allow the participating actors to reduce the risk involved and share R&D costs as well as combine complementary assets in order to enhance the propensity of a successful development project. In addition, it is the internalization of knowledge spillovers (Griliches 1992), the possibility to exchange knowledge and the resulting interactive learning which may lead to higher inventive and innovative success of the participating actors. From the point of view of economic competition, vertical relations along the value chain are rather unproblematic as firms here do not compete in the same markets. On equal terms, the exchange of knowledge between firms from different sectors as discussed in Jacobs (1969) is not likely to harm the partners respective market positions. More problematic in this sense are horizontal relationships (with spillovers of a rather Marshallian type) between the cooperating partners. To the extent they compete on the same markets, incentive problems may arise and their cooperative venture requires a more formalized and thus controllable design.

The success of cooperative activity in invention and innovation is dependent among others factors on a mutual understanding of the partners, combined with enough creative differences in their knowledge stocks (creative potential). Boschma (2005) suggested the concept of cognitive proximity as being relevant for exchanging knowledge characterized as a latent public good and geographical proximity for knowledge of the tacit type. Of crucial importance for successful interaction is the cognitive or technological proximity between the interacting agents. The generic potential in cooperative invention and innovation rests on the actors involved being different in their knowledge and competences. However, some overlap in these knowledge bases and thus some degree of proximity in the cognitive or technological dimension is required for a common understanding. This overlap just indicates the (relative) absorptive capacities in the sense that the larger the overlap, the higher the absorptive capacities, but also the less the generic potential of the relationship. Hence, a rather general feature of proximity concepts shows up here, an inverted-U shaped relationship, suggesting an intermediate level of proximity at which knowledge exchange is highest, whereas any deviation from that level (either to lower or an increased proximity) leads to a decreased level[10] of cooperative invention and innovation. With respect to the transmittance of tacit knowledge, cognitive proximity alone is not sufficient. The face-to-face interaction of the exchanging actors requires spatial or geographical proximity, which often is just social proximity.

Contrary to knowledge transfer in markets or in hierarchies, which can in principle be contracted, in network relationships, which are often informal, trust between the cooperating actors is a controlling device and is based on the principle of reciprocity-not in the sense of *uno actu* but over time. This trust is reinforced by social proximity built up by repeated interactions as well as by institutional proximity referring to common habits and attitudes (Balland et al. 2015).

2.4.2 On Heterogeneity and Cooperation in Innovation

Having briefly outlined the conceptual basis of openness and cooperation, a brief look into some empirics (using the same German CIS data as before) is meant to provide a quantitative account of the importance of openness for startups and for established firms.

Next to founding intentions and radicalness of innovation, a characterization of entrepreneurs by their inclination to cooperate can be taken as an indicator of openness as this indicates a certain ambition to exchange knowledge and experience with appropriate partners. Table 3 depicts for each degree of newness of product innovations the share of entrepreneurs that cooperate for two sub-periods, before the first business year and alternatively in the first 3 years of business. The numbers in Table 3 indicate that cooperation in innovation is quite important for new firms. The share of innovators tends to increase with the degree of newness in both sub-periods. Comparing them, it becomes evident that, in each newness class,

[10]Given the total knowledge stock remains the same, the cooperation potential gets step by step exploited, which means that, in dynamics terms, the inverted U curve of proximity shifts to the left (less and less to gain from interaction).

Table 3 Innovation cooperation and innovations' degree of newness (Thuringian Founder Study)

	% Innovation cooperation	
Innovations' degree of newness	Before year 1	Year 1–3
For the world	52.8	71.6
For Europe	42.1	47.6
For Germany	18.8	38.5
Locally	33.3	54.5
Not new	27.5	30.9
Don't know	50.0	33.3

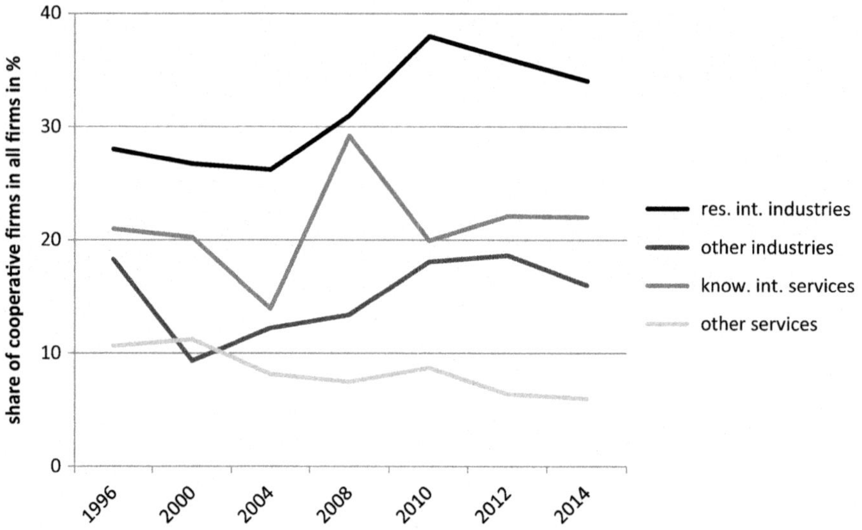

Fig. 3 Share of firms with innovation cooperation (of any type) [German CIS data; adapted from ZEW (various years)]

this share increases—except for "don't know"; hence the number of unconnected (Schumpeter) entrepreneurs ("lonely wolves") declines, in some classes considerably (e.g. "for the world" or "for Germany").

Turning to established firms, their inclination to cooperate in innovation is considered in Fig. 3, which delivers the share of firms cooperative in innovation for the four industry aggregates and for the period from 1996 to 2014. It becomes evident that cooperation in innovation is not a rare event. The research intensive industries rank here highest, with more than 30% since 2008, followed by the knowledge intensive services, with about 20%. Over time, except for other services, the inclination to cooperate has been (slightly) increasing. Other industries and other services showed roughly the same level in 2000 and then diverged considerably; for the last years from 2012 to 2014 a slight drop in cooperation activities can be observed.

3 Interaction and Structural Change on a Heterogeneous Landscape

On the basis of entrepreneurial and firm heterogeneity with respect to innovation, imitation and cooperation, the next building block of the theory of economic change addresses the mechanisms of interaction. In doing so, the analytical frame is spanned by approaches from economic evolution and economic complexity. In both, the heterogeneity of actors is a fundamental principle and is to be considered the source and the result of structural change. Selectionist approaches, synergetic approaches and developmental approaches (Cantner 2015) rely on it and account for the system's nature or structure, on the one hand, and how, on the other hand—based on this—its (structural) dynamic is affected or driven by it. However, in each approach, the way heterogeneity affects evolutionary development is quite specific: In the selectionist approach it is heterogeneity which is reduced by competition and generated by innovation. In the synergetic approach it is heterogeneity which brings about specific structural, self-organizing features with respect to learning, cooperation etc. In the developmental approach, finally, heterogeneity is a matter of the stages of development (to be) passed.

In the following, we focus on some basic dynamic mechanisms. A first, taken from evolutionary economics, takes heterogeneity as given or randomly generated and attempts to understand selective competition among heterogeneous agents. A second refers to endogenous innovation and requires that we take into account feedback mechanisms—the analytical framework is taken from complexity economics and allows for path-dependent dynamic patterns. The third mechanism concerns cooperation and mutual learning, another type of feedback effect between actors.

3.1 Competition and Structural Dynamics

The relationship between innovativeness and competition is at the core of evolutionary approaches and Neo-Schumpeterian approaches to economic change. A formal description of the fundamental underlying mechanism is given by the so-called replicator dynamics. This principle goes back to Fisher (1930) and allows the formal representation of the Darwinian principle of survival of the fittest working on the population of broadly considered heterogeneous entities. Applied to economics, the dynamic competition among heterogeneous agents in markets can be dealt with in this way.

The approach of replicator dynamics is appealing as theory and provides for a simple description of market dynamics. The quite "romantic" Schumpeterian story, that more innovative or technologically fitter firms tend to dominate a market over time whereas technologically relative less fit and non-innovative firms get dominated and outcompeted, seems to be a nice case to be handled by this formal representation. When it comes to empirics and attempts to validate the ideas of market dynamics and evolution, the results are less encouraging. The evidence is rather meager, and presumably due to that, attempts to test the pure replicator dynamics are rare—the reported results are not really in favor of the replicator mechanism.

In a number of theoretical models, replicator dynamics is used to explain the dynamic development of certain sectors or whole economies. In general, the high complexity of these models does not allow for analytical solutions and therefore it is necessary to run simulation experiments.[11] This holds especially when innovative activities are modeled as search and experimental behavior[12] and stochastic effects are taken into account. In view of this complexity, the following discussion intends to present the basic mechanisms of replicator dynamics via a quite simple deterministic model of an evolving market consisting of a population of heterogeneous firms and a given demand structure.

Replicator dynamics is formally given as follows: consider N constant magnitudes or replicators i, $i \in N$, the relative frequency of which (share within total population N) s_i changes during time. This change is dependent on the fitness f_i with respect to the average weighted fitness $\bar{f}$ of the whole population. Fitness in general is dependent on a vector $\mathbf{s}$ that contains the relative frequency of all replicators.[13] The respective market share dynamics s_i is given by the following differential equation, where is β a parameter governing the speed of the selection dynamics:

$$\dot{s}_i = \beta \cdot s_i \cdot \left(f_i - \bar{f}(\mathbf{s})\right), \quad \bar{f}(\mathbf{s}) = \sum\nolimits_N s_j \cdot f_j(\mathbf{s}) \tag{1}$$

For the analysis of market evolution, this dynamics is interpreted as follows: replicators i are considered as different firms within a market that have a respective market share of s_i. Fitness f_i can be measured looking at the level of unit costs, productivity or some other measures.[14] Replicator dynamics states, for a constant fitness function, f_i that a firm i will enhance (reduce) its market share whenever its fitness is above (below) the average weighted fitness within the market. Then, by competitive selection, those firms with comparatively low fitness are driven out of the market. In the end, the firm with the highest fitness gains a monopoly position.[15]

[11]See, for example, Silverberg et al. (1988), Kwasnicki and Kwasnicka (1992), Kwasnicki (1996) and Saviotti and Mani (1995).

[12]See, for example, Nelson and Winter (1982), Silverberg and Lehnert (1994, 1996), Silverberg and Verspagen (1994), Kwasnicki and Kwasnicka (1992), Metcalfe (1994, 1998), Mazzucato (1998) and Winter et al. (2000, 2003).

[13]This broad formulation already contains the possibility of frequency-dependent fitness.

[14]See, for example, Metcalfe (1994), Metcalfe and Calderini (1998), Mazzucato and Semmler (1999) and Cantner (2002).

[15]It can be shown that average fitness increases with the variance of unit costs: $\frac{\partial \bar{f}}{\partial t} = var(f_i) \geq 0$.

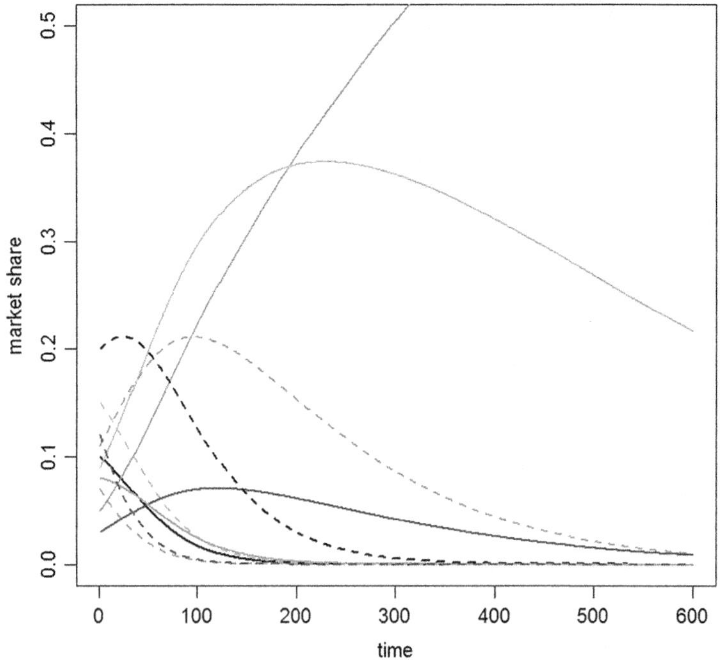

Fig. 4 Selection dynamics of firms with respective constant fitness

Figure 4 shows this development in a market consisting of ten firms that start in period 0 with different market shares and different fitness values. After a while, the firm with the highest fitness value is going to dominate the market, whereas the other firms experience a decline of market share until they exit; the lower a firm's fitness, the earlier it is forced to exit.

3.2 *The Role of Innovation Dynamics in Structural Dynamics*

At this point, it has to be critically stated that, in formulation (1), single firms have no impact on the selection dynamics; hence, the routine of producing with fitness f_i will not be changed. However, at least for real actors with a selection disadvantage $\left(f_i < \overline{f(\mathbf{s})}\right)$ a reaction is to be expected.

Assume the only kind of (re)action to be expected is that firms attempt to innovate. How can this be introduced into this formal model? Different feedback effects from the economic to the technological—innovative sphere are conceivable. Quite generally, feedbacks can be taken into account by a dependence of fitness f_i on economic success e_i and within the context of innovative activities by the way of *dynamic scale effects*. These imply that the *change of fitness*[16] depends on the success e of a firm. In principle, the following formulation holds:

$$\dot{s}_i = \beta \cdot s_i \cdot \left(f_i(e_i) - \bar{f}(\mathbf{s}) \right), \quad \bar{f}(\mathbf{s}) = \sum\nolimits_N s_j \cdot f_j(e_j) \tag{2}$$

$$\dot{f}_i = g(e_i) \tag{3}$$

Translating this into a market model, it can be asked how the economic success of a firm might be represented there. In quite a simple formulation it could be assumed that the market share s_i accounts for economic success. This market share then represents economic as well as technological aspects relevant to further innovative success. With respect to the former, (relative) firm size is related to the ability of appropriating profits and of financing R&D projects. With respect to technological abilities and know-how, a large market share and, thus, a large firm size implies that know-how can be accumulated quite easily, and a broad range of technological possibilities and directions can be covered. This case implies a model formulated *with positive dynamic scale effects* and oriented along the principle of *success breeds success*. Accordingly, this formulation fits into the regime of *Schumpeter II*, where relatively large firms are innovatively more successful (see Malerba and Orsenigo 1995, 1997).

However, it could also be argued that small firms are more flexible and therefore more innovative. This flexibility economically refers to the effect that small firms do not have large R&D laboratories that can only be directed with high product costs; in a technological context, large R&D laboratories apply very standardized routines in order to be innovative and these routines are not easily changeable. This problem should not be too difficult for small firms to solve. Therefore, an interpretation along the regime of *Schumpeter I* seems appropriate here; the respective model exhibits *negative dynamic scale effects* in innovation (see Malerba and Orsenigo 1995, 1997).

Both alternatives are discussed in Mazzucato and Semmler (1999) as well as in Cantner (2002, 2009). For the competition among firms, and for the innovations that improve the production process and therefore imply higher fitness, the following model holds:

$$\dot{s}_i = \beta \cdot s_i \cdot \left(f_i - \bar{f} \right), \quad \bar{f} = \sum\nolimits_N s_i \cdot f_i \tag{4}$$

$$\dot{f}_i = \gamma \cdot g(s_i), \quad \lim_{t \to \infty} f_i = f_{max} \tag{5}$$

The function $g(s_i)$ represents the relationship between technological improvement f: and market success: as stated, we can distinguish constant ($\partial g / \partial s_i = 0$), positive ($\partial g / \partial s_i > 0$) and negative ($\partial g / \partial s_i < 0$) dynamic scale effects which affect the rate of technological improvement. We assume that there is an upper level of

[16]When the level of fitness is affected, static economies of scale are at work (Metcalfe 1994, 1998).

technological fitness (f_{max}) which cannot be exceeded, representing the maximum technological opportunities that can be exploited. γ is a parameter that represents the intensity of the economic feedback. Imitation, spillover effects and social learning which may additionally affect innovative success, are excluded for the time being.

The case of an exogenously given rate of technological improvement is discussed first. Figure 5 contains this case of constant ($\partial g/\partial s_i = 0$) dynamic returns to scale; here all firms improve their technological performance by the combination of a constant proportional rate and a rate depending on the respective degree of exploitation of a technological potential f_{max}. To keep in mind, competitive selection s_i and technological change f_i are not directly related to each other.

The evolution of the market in Fig. 5 shows two main features: First, some firms will have to exit relatively early; those firms are not able to exploit the technological potential f_{max} fast enough and they are outcompeted, leading to a final exit. Second, other firms show a market share development that eventually reaches a stable positive level; these firms were able to exploit the potentials and therefore stay in the market, subsequently showing different market shares but at the same performance level.

Analyzing the case of *Schumpeter II*, the process of *success breeds success* is modeled with $\partial g/\partial s_i > 0$. Competitive selection s_i and scale dependent innovative success f_i go hand-in-hand and lead to increasing economic and technological

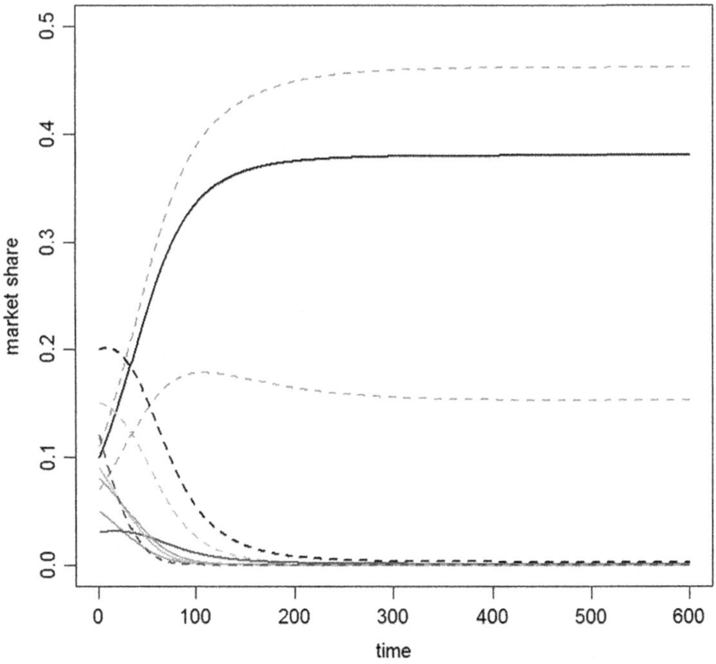

Fig. 5 Development of market shares with constant dynamic returns to scale and exploitable opportunities

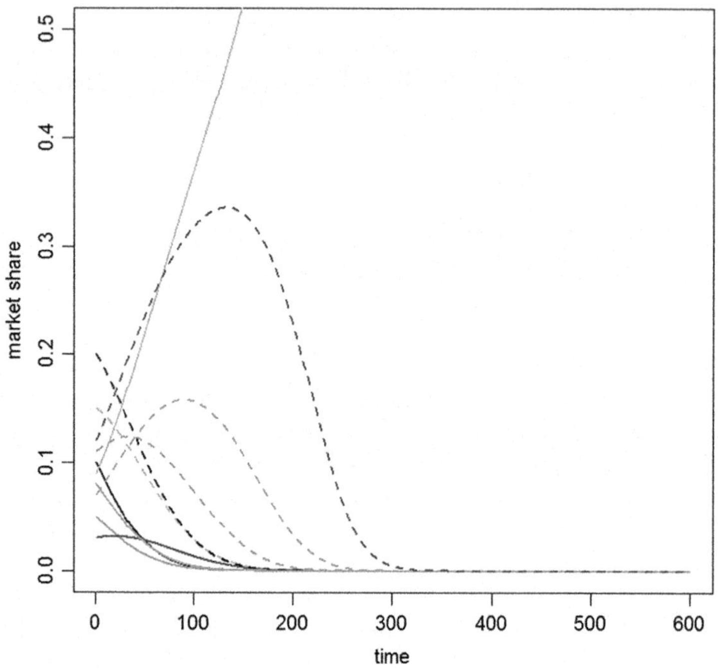

Fig. 6 Development of market shares with increasing dynamic returns to scale and exploitable opportunities

dominance of the technology leaders and, consequently, to monopolization (see Mazzucato and Semmler 1999; Cantner 2002, 2009).

Figure 6 shows this for ten firms. Here, after some time, all except one firm finally have to exit the market. Some of the exiting firms enjoy for some periods an even increasing market share. But after a while, via a success-breeds-success dynamics, the technology leader becomes dominant by outcompeting one competitor after another.

As a third case, the constellation of Schumpeter I, characterized by decreasing returns to scale in innovative activities, $\partial g/\partial s_i < 0$, is considered. Consequently, driven by selection dynamics, firms with the relatively low market share will have a relatively higher innovation performance dynamics, which provides for increasing market shares; this, however, works against further innovative performance. Thus, competitive selection s_i and innovation dynamics f_i are counteracting forces. The emergence of characteristic patterns of evolution depends on the parameters β and γ. For a large range of values, the one or the other force dominates and a smooth development to coexistence[17] or monopoly[18] is observed. However, for appropriate

[17]The rate of exploiting technological opportunities γ is high compared to the rate of competitive selection β.

[18]Here, compared to innovation dynamics γ the selection dynamics β is relatively high.

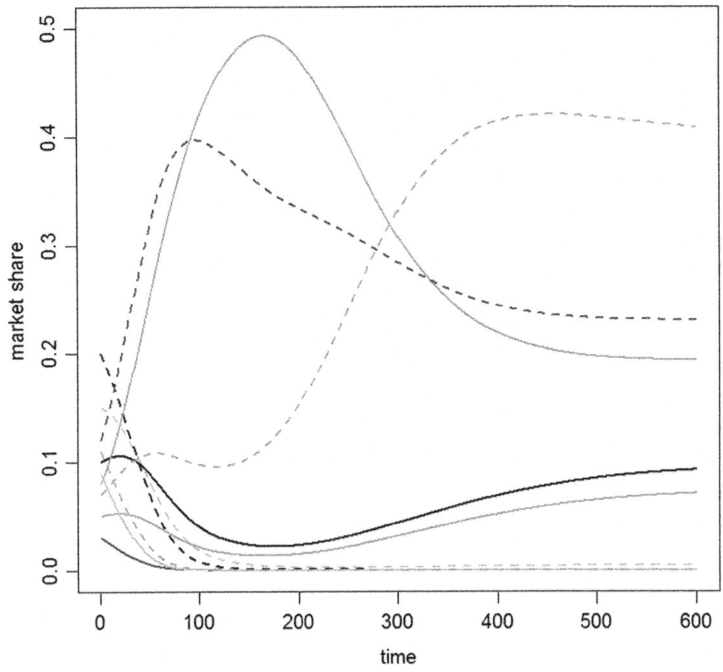

Fig. 7 Development of market shares with decreasing dynamic returns to scale and exploitable opportunities

values of parameters β and γ, it can be shown that both forces are in a continuously changing balance and the market share development is characterized by turbulence. Figure 7 shows and exemplifies this case again for ten firms.

Most of the firms are able to hold a market share that is far larger than 0. They all exploit the given opportunities completely and, in the end, show exactly the same technological performance. The observed differences in market share after exploitation are affected by the starting market share as well as by the path of competition and exploitation taken. It cannot be ruled out that the one or other firm is forced to exit. A very low technological performance in the beginning is responsible for such a final result.

3.3 *Cooperation and Networking: Interaction with Market Selection*

Based conceptually on spillovers, types of knowledge and knowledge acquisition as elements of open innovation, research on cooperation in innovation has been developed in two major branches. The first looks at institutional arrangements in term of systems of innovation such as national systems of innovation, regional systems, sectoral systems, technological systems, etc. (for an overview see Carlsson 2007).

A second line of research focuses on the core of those systems, namely, the network of actors, and analyzes network properties as well as network dynamics and their influence on the performance of the individual actor as well as the network in total.[19] The dynamics of innovation networks show some specific features quite related to the (latent) public good feature of information and knowledge. A fundamental point is addressed by comparing the situation of the cooperating partners before and after knowledge exchange. Consider two actors, I and II, who possess several knowledge categories, A to E, and differ only in their competences in B and C, with I being more competent in B and II being more competent in C. In this situation, the interests of both to exchange knowledge, the required mutual understanding, as well as the reciprocal benefits are assumed to be given. Consequently, knowledge exchange takes place and—assuming no changes in knowledge categories A, D, and E—may lead to a situation in which I and II show the same, identical expertise in each of the knowledge categories A–E. As soon as this is reached, any further exchange of information and knowledge does not lead to any additional insights for both partners. Consequently, the common interest to exchange information and knowledge has been dried out. Hence, what we observe and have to take into account in analyzing the development and evolution of networks is that the very reasons for undertaking these exchanges, the differences in competencies and knowledge between actors, vanish and thusalso their interest in further collaboration (Cowan et al. 2006; Cantner et al. 2016a).

For this dynamic, two underlying principles can be identified. The first dimension is *preferential attachment* (Barabasi and Albert 1999). It describes the dynamics as a process in which the formation of a link from actor I to actor II is dependent on the existing number of links of actor II. The number of links of an actor may serve as an indication of the precious knowledge stock this actor holds or of the cooperative success this actor already has accumulated. Hence, network position and innovation performance constitute a virtuous cycle, implying that the rate of acquisition of information and knowledge from the outside is closely linked to the internally generated expertise, and vice versa.

Preferential attachment can also be interpreted along the lines of trustworthiness. Trust within a collaboration might be given right from the beginning (*ex-ante* trust) but it may also be developed over time by repeated collaborative projects (*ex-post* trust). Network dynamics governed by preferential attachment lead to a sustained core-periphery structure with a few large (in terms of economic, innovative or collaborative success) actors in the core and smaller ones in the periphery (Orsenigo et al. 1998; Cantner and Raake 2014). Clearly, a skewed distribution of the number of ties per actor develops. Hence, preferential attachment leads to increased clustering of actors.

[19]For an overview see Cantner and Graf (2011).

Another driving force for the establishment of cooperative linkages between actors is *homophily* (Skvoretz 1991). Here, the choice of a cooperation partner is biased towards those actors that are similar. This similarity may be due to close geographical proximity as in the case of clusters or local innovation systems. It may also be based on social proximity in the sense that friends compared to others are preferred cooperation partners. Looking at innovation, however, it is doubtful whether *homophily* in terms of cognitive proximity really counts. In order to draw on a creative potential, the cooperating actors have to show a considerable difference between their knowledge stocks combined with some overlap indicating the degree of mutual understanding (Nooteboom 2009).

Based on these mechanisms the relationships between exchanging knowledge, technological overlap and further or continued collaboration follow three different dynamics. First, by the very nature of frequently exchanging knowledge there is a tendency of the technological proximity between two actors I and II to narrow. This tendency might be counteracted by a second dynamic related to the potential of any one partner I and/or II to be able to create new knowledge by collaborating with other partners. Hence it is the breadth of ego network (as measured by the number of different cooperation partners) of each of the partners which governs this potential. Third, by continuously exchanging knowledge with the same partner, a higher degree of mutual trust is built up, furthering collaboration in the future. Empirical evidence on these relationships is as yet not well developed except that by collaboration and exchanging knowhow the degree of overlap between two partners increases (Mowery et al. 1998).

Drawing on the model on market competition introduced above, now the feature of no imitation and no spillovers is given up in order to integrate into the model knowledge flows—without discussing the reason for such to happen. For that purpose, a technological gap is defined for each firm, given by the difference of the best technological performance in the market, $max(f_j)$, and a respective firm's practiced performance. For the leader in technological performance, this gap is exactly zero, while for all other firms it is positive. Out of this gap spillovers z_i can be used; this is governed by function h in (8).[20] Spillovers contribute to technological improvements in (7) with $\partial g/\partial z_i > 0$.

$$\dot{s_i} = \beta \cdot s_i \cdot \left(f_i - \bar{f}(\mathbf{s})\right), \quad \bar{f}(\mathbf{s}) = \sum_N s_i \cdot f_i \tag{6}$$

$$\dot{f_i} = \gamma \cdot g(s_i, z_i) \tag{7}$$

$$z_i = h\left(\max\left(f_j\right) - f_i\right) \tag{8}$$

[20]The h function can be made explicit via a linear and alternatively a bell-shaped formulation as in Verspagen (1992).

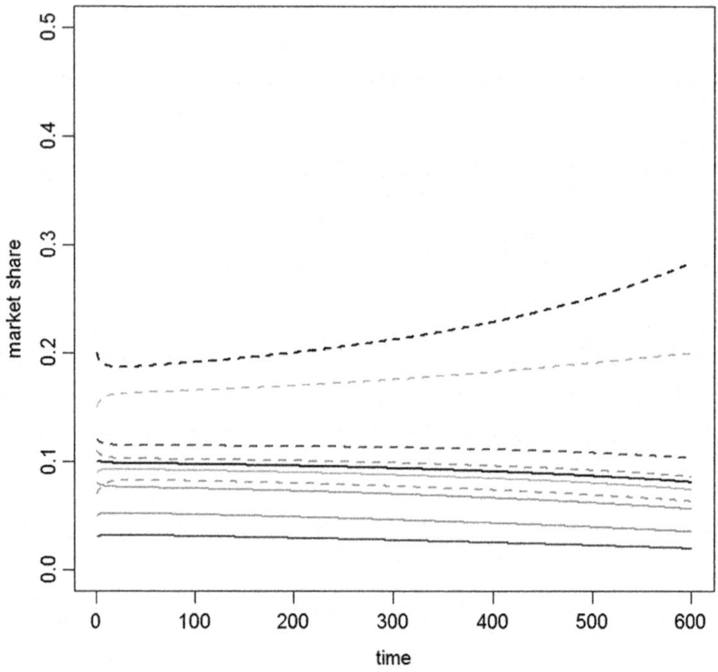

Fig. 8 Development of market shares with imitation and exploitable opportunities

The effects of spillovers are shown in Fig. 8. Obviously, market share development is rather smooth; no clearly directed tendency towards dominance or monopoly is found but rather long periods of coexistence with no market exit.

This effect is dependent on the strength of the spillover effect governed by the functions *h* and *g*. The higher the (potential) spillovers (*h* function) and the more they can be absorbed (*g* function), the less are the differences between the technological levels among firms and consequently the lower is the selection effect. Market evolution is relatively smooth and structural change less strong.

Given this theoretical analysis of evolutionary and complex mechanisms of interaction in populations consisting of heterogeneous actor as conceptualized in Sect. 2, the empirical validity of these mechanisms is our next concern.

4 Structural Change *in* Heterogeneous Actor Populations

Our "test" addresses an idealistic (if not "romantic") interpretation of the suggested mechanisms of interaction: Innovation and related market competition should lead to an increase in the heterogeneity of actors within a population, in terms of competences, technology and also in economic terms (firm size, profitability, market share); hence, competitive dynamics and resulting structural changes should be pronounced and fast. Contrariwise, imitation and cooperation should be drivers towards a more homogeneous population not affected by intense structural dynamics due to a low degree of competitive selection.

The account of empirical phenomena suitable to explanation by such a concert of underlying mechanisms is rich. Testing the aforementioned relationships as yet has been partly successful when looking at the one or other of these mechanisms; convincing evidence on the interplay between the different mechanisms is still missing. In the following, a few of these dimensions and results will be addressed.

4.1 Empirics on Selective Competition

In view of the central theoretical position of replicator dynamics in evolutionary economics, it is quite astonishing that empirical attempts trying to answer the question of whether market selection is operating as proposed by evolutionary theory are rare. In principle we can distinguish direct and indirect empirical approaches. The former do not directly test a version of (1) above but look at the implicit relationship between variables representing relative economic success, on the one hand, and fitness related variables, on the other. The latter, contrariwise, consider the replicator formulation (1) rather closely and address respective empirical tests. There are approaches just between these two types; in indirect approaches, the working of replicator dynamics, although formally taken into account, is rather a side result.

A first type of an indirect empirical analysis of replicator dynamics to work is interested in differential growth rates of firms—where differential growth rates imply a market share dynamics as suggested in the selection equation in (1). For example, using a database of Italian manufacturing firms, Bottazzi et al. (2008) investigate how profitability and productivity are related to firm growth. Their results show that the overall selection process is only weakly operating in the expected way. In fact, they do not find a significant relationship between profitability (or productivity) and firm growth (see also Dosi 2007). In a related study on French manufacturing firms, Coad (2007) raises doubts about the validity of the principle of "growth of the fitter". He finds only a minor influence of profits on growth and concludes that evolutionary models should abandon the assumption of a direct relationship. Coad (2010) indeed shows that subsequent firm growth is initiated by employment growth rather than by growth of profits or sales.

Relatedly, empirical studies on the industry life cycle and of the market exit phenomena in general look at the relationship between a firm's technological and/or innovative performance, on the one hand, and the survival or exit hazard, on the other. An example is Cantner et al. (2011) who investigate survival curves of 333 German automobile firms from 1886 to 1940. They distinguish automobile producing firms by their innovativeness and their accumulated experience. Crossing these two dimensions, four types of automobile firms can be distinguished: (1) early innovators, (2) late innovators, (3) early non-innovators and (4) late non-innovators. Here "early" implies that, on the scale of the ILC, these actors are older and already have accumulated experience, whereas "late" means relatively young firms with a low level of accumulated knowledge. The analysis shows that innovative firms clearly dominate non-innovative ones, as measured by the survival probability. In terms of accumulated knowledge and experience, given the characteristic innovative/non-innovative, older and more experienced firms ("early") show a higher survival rate than younger and less experienced firms ("late"). This indicates that some degree of dynamic increasing returns scale plays a role. This relationship only can be broken by late entrants when they are innovative. These results can be interpreted with respect to market selection dynamics; however, it is not the market share dynamics itself but the related exit dynamics that is addressed.

A second type of indirect empirical study investigates the formal mechanism of replicator dynamics more closely by linking it to the dynamics of the average fitness variable in a market such as the aggregate productivity development (Cantner and Krüger 2008; Krüger 2014). The decomposition of aggregate productivity change allows us to identify their driving forces, which are firm-specific productivity changes, market share changes as well as changes due to the entry and exit of firms. The analysis basically rests on the presumption that the competition of firms, market entry and exit and the related innovation activities necessarily determine the aggregate performance of an industry and its development over time. Dosi et al. (2015) analyze the manufacturing industries of selected countries in the same way.

Interpreting productivity as an indicator of technological sophistication of a firm and productivity change as a result of innovative activities, a special decomposition formula for aggregate productivity change of a group of firms has been proposed in Foster et al. (2001),[21] which is an extension of the formula of Baily et al. (1992) that also accounts for the contributions of entering and exiting firms. One term in this decomposition formula is of interest in the discussion about market selection, the so-called between-effect. It accounts for the change of the market share of a firm i between period $t - k$ and period t, Δs_{it}, and multiplies it with the deviation of the respective firm's productivity (a_{it-k}) from the share weighted average productivity $\left(\bar{a}_{t-k}^{s}\right)$ in the population of firms in the starting period $t-k$, $\left(a_{it-k} - \bar{a}_{t-k}^{s}\right)$. Summing up these products over all firms in the industry leads to the between-effect, $\Sigma_{i \in C} \Delta s_{it} \cdot \left(a_{it-k} - \bar{a}_{t-k}^{s}\right)$.

Particularly appealing is that the between component resembles a discrete-time version of the replicator dynamics mechanism $\Delta s_{it} = \beta \cdot s_{it} \cdot \left(a_{it-k} - \bar{a}_{t-k}^{s}\right), \beta > 0$. If above-average productivity levels in period $t - k$ tend to be associated with positive share growth from $t - k$ to t and below-average productivity levels tend to be associated with negative share growth on average, then the between component will be positive. This pattern is exactly the outcome if the replicator dynamics mechanism is a valid description of competition within a market.

This productivity decomposition is applied to a sample of German manufacturing firms with observations for the years 1981–1998 (or a part of that time span, in

[21]For an overview on possible decompositions, see Melitz and Polanec (2015).

the case of entering and exiting firms). Overall, 874 firms are in this sample at some time. These firms can be assigned to 11 industries at roughly two-digit (SIC) level of aggregation (construction, food and beverages, textiles and apparel, paper and printing, chemicals and petroleum, rubber and plastics, metal products, machinery and equipment, electronics, transportation equipment, instruments).

In Table 4, for the between component, we generally find positive effects, indicating a development pattern consistent with the replicator dynamics mechanism but which are rather low compared to productivity changes from within the firm. Three groups of industries can be distinguished. In a first, *wrong selection dynamics,* which only contains Food the within term is slightly negative indicating that selection via the replicator mechanism is not found here. By contrast, in the group *low selection dynamics,* with four industries listed (Textiles, Chemicals, Electronics, Transportation), selection via replicator mechanisms shows up positively and with an annual percentage rate of higher than 0.1%. The third group, *weak selection dynamics,* with six industries (Construction, Paper, Plastics, Metal Products, Machinery, and Instruments), ranks just in between the former two groups and shows, with an annual change of less than 0.08%, only slight selection working. Dividing the sample period into two parts, one before the German reunification (1981–1989) and the other after (1990–1998), reveals that the effects tend to become somewhat stronger in the later period. In general, however, in this study as well as in others, the rather low values of the between component indicate that the selection effect is not very strong and further analyses are required.

Direct approaches attempt to explicitly test (Eq. 1). Although this appears to be trivial, in practice such an analysis is not easily accomplished (Andersen 2004), since the data requirements are tremendous. A case in point of a direct empirical test is a study by Metcalfe and Calderini (1998), who compute the selection parameter β, measuring the speed of selection, for a dataset of the Italian steel industry. However Metcalfe and Calderini cannot convincingly show that a competition process according to replicator dynamics is at work; the value of the selection parameter tracked over time jumps up and down, indicating dimensions neglected in the analysis.

In view of this weak evidence for competition dynamics via the replicator formulation, a first set of explanations ranges from the choice of not appropriate

Table 4 Annual average between-effect for selected industries between 1981 and 1998

Wrong selection dynamics		Weak selection dynamics		Low selection dynamics	
Food	−0.0344	Construction	0.0298	Electronics	0.2898
		Paper	0.0649	Transportation	0.3450
		Plastics	0.0099	Textiles	0.1571
		Metal products	0.0621	Chemicals	0.2525
		Machinery	0.0790		
		Instruments	0.0428		

Reported are annual average percentage growth rates of the aggregate productivity levels due to the competitive selection effect, divided by the initial share-weighted average productivity level and multiplied by 100/(1998–1981)

variables for firm performance (fitness) to not clearly demarcated units and populations under analysis (firms vs. products, industries vs. markets/sub-markets): an industry is not a market but a collection of markets, the firms are multi-product, and the fitness variable is entirely supply-side determined, unit costs of production. Cantner et al. (2012) suggest defining specific markets and thereby shifting the analysis from the firm to the product level. They do so by looking at the market for compact cars in Germany from 2001 to 2005. Moreover, they suggest using a more appropriate fitness variable, a quality-price ratio e_{it} of product i in period t. The core variable to explain market share changes is $s_{it} \cdot (e_{it} - \bar{e}_t)$ and the estimated coefficient can be interpreted as the speed parameter in the replicator formulation. The principle result of the study is that car models with a quality-price ratio higher than the average systematically tend to gain market shares, exactly as replicator dynamics suggests—there, however, is a time dimension since this relationship shows up more strongly in the medium run. This result shows that addressing demarcated markets and using appropriate fitness indictors may be a proper way to overcome some empirical problems affecting simple analyses of industries within which firms compete.

Next to this issue of designing proper empirical settings, other explanations refer to neglected fitness relevant components [such as sunk costs, see (Hölzl 2015)] or to the exclusion of factors relevant for market share changes such as a firm's integration into a value chain (Cantner et al. 2016b).

A further line of analysis, as yet not fully exploited, needs to shed further light on the influence of knowledge spillovers and, in general, and a firm's integration into networks and clusters, in particular, on market share dynamics, survival and other performance measures. The interaction the two basic mechanisms, competition and cooperation, as already addressed via a simple setting in Sect. 3, would further enrich our understanding of competition dynamics in markets and industries. Such analyses need to integrate concepts and findings from the analysis of cooperation and networking be that of a formal or an informal type—dimensions briefly addressed in the following section.

4.2 Empirics on Cooperation and Networking

The empirics on cooperation and networking have delivered a broad account of insights and findings. In the context of networking and of the broader concept of open innovation, the ways actors interact, share and transfer information and knowledge, and how that translates into performance are intensely analyzed. With respect to the discussion here two dimensions are relevant.

The first relates to interaction structures by asking who cooperates and exchanges knowledge with whom, who receives spillovers and who sends them, and who employs an open innovation strategy and interacts with others and who does not. In this respect, analyses of network formation and development are able to explain how observed network structures came about. Network dynamics governed by preferential attachment lead to a sustained core-periphery structure with a few large (in terms of economic, innovative or collaborative success) actors in the core and smaller ones in the periphery (Orsenigo et al. 1998). In line with this, empirical evidence shows (Ahuja 2000; Stuart 2000; Cantner et al. 2016a) that firms with more patents are more likely to form further alliances than firms lacking patents—they become more attractive. Another self-reinforcing dimension is addressed by Powell et al. (1996) who find for the global biotechnology industry that firms that develop experience in managing collaborative R&D relationships garner faster access to centrally positioned organizations. Through accumulating experience in collaboration, firms are able to widen their cooperative network, increase their diversity of partners, and become more visible in the industry (Powell et al. 2005). By a feedback loop, a more central position leads to growth in size with a positive influence on the financial situation of the firm accompanied by the ability to coordinate more alliances (Powell et al. 1999). With respect to entry-exit dynamics, Cantner and Graf (2006) find that actors entering the system tie themselves rather closely to the core of the network made up by actors with a relatively high number of ties and collaboration partners. Compared to that, actors exiting the system are connected mainly to actors in the periphery of the network.

The other determinant of network dynamics is homophily, which implies tie repetition over time and contributes to some stability in the network structure. Looking at the empirical evidence, there is some indication that an intermediate level of homophily drives the formation of ties in the future. For cooperation in innovation, Mowery et al. (1998) as well as Cantner and Meder (2007) find that the technological overlap (measured on the basis of the IPC classes of their respective patents accumulated until t) between two actors in period t are positively related to the likelihood that they form a cooperation in period $t + 1$. Equivalently, Cantner and Graf (2006) find for cooperation in the case of the Jena network of innovators that the potential to cooperate in period t as identified by some commonality in knowledge and expertise (again measured by IPC classes overlap) determines the likelihood that these actors cooperate in $t - 1$.

A second line of research addresses the question of how firms design cooperation strategies in general and open innovation strategies (Chesbrough 2003) in particular. In this respect, a literature emerged that reconsidered the boundaries of the firm and analyzed which knowledge sourcing strategies reach beyond the traditional borders given by physical resources and human capital. External R&D and outsourcing, cooperation and networking, being open for inflows and outflows of information and knowledge are dimensions considered here that are regularly subsumed under the umbrella of open innovation strategies. On this basis, a small but interesting literature emerged on the complementarity of these different knowledge sourcing strategies (Cassiman and Veugelers 2006; Schmiedeberg 2008; Knudsen et al. 2016; Cantner and Savin 2014) and how they affect the performance of firms.

Although the dynamics of these network structures are increasingly better understood, their influence on the competition of firms, on market share dynamics and the pattern of market entry and exit still wait for closer inspection. An equivalent argument holds for the phenomenon of open innovation; its relation to firm competition, market share dynamics and exit pattern is still not sufficiently addressed.

5 Conclusions and Challenges

This paper is devoted to basic building blocks of a theory of innovation-driven economic change. The approach taken is Schumpeterian in the sense that agents of change are put into the focus of analysis. Following this, the discussion started with a conceptualization of actors and actor heterogeneity in terms of differential behavior in arenas of interaction which often are markets (with all difficulties of demarcation) but also networks. Actor heterogeneity considered takes into account traits, behavior, given and acquired endowments, and revealed actions related to generating and adopting new ideas as a well as of economizing on them via innovation, imitation and adoption. Conceptualized that way, agents of change resemble institutional arrangements of firms, being a newly founded entrepreneurial or an established innovative one with different perceptions of and behavioral attitudes towards innovation-driven change in a broad sense. Some empirically based classifications in line with these characterizations rounded up this part.

Given such arenas of heterogeneous actor populations, in a next step core interaction modes have been considered, competition, on the one hand, and cooperation, on the other. To understand their respective basic mechanisms, models from evolutionary and complexity economics are used. Innovation, competition, and connectedness via spillovers (implying imitation or cooperation) and their interaction were shown to deliver certain structural and dynamical pattern characterizing arenas (markets or networks). The final step took account of the empirical validity of these mechanisms and the resulting structural and dynamic pattern. The "test" had a mixed outcome with some results in favor and some against the theoretically expected pattern.

Without doubt, the dynamics discussed and analyzed so far offers room for improvement as already addressed in each of the sections above. However, looking ahead, extensions towards an all-encompassing approach should include structural change on higher levels of aggregation.

Given the empirical account discussed and the partial validity of the interaction mechanisms *in* heterogeneous populations, one may ask whether the basic mechanisms do also work *between* populations of heterogeneous actors. Here one can think of aggregates such as regions, cities, industries, or countries and country blocs. Each of these units can be considered a specific population of heterogeneous actors bound together by certain "ties" and showing a specific kind of fitness or capability. *Social capabilities,* as made prominent by Abramovitz (1986), comprise a country's or economy's abilities to absorb new technology, attract capital and participate in global markets; differences between countries in such capabilities allow for an explanation of their differential success in international competition understood in terms of catching up, forging ahead or falling behind.

The basic question addressing such aggregate fitness or capabilities is on the ties and mechanisms at work. Cultural, institutional and social factors (and proximities) are just as relevant as the mechanisms of collective learning, knowledge accumulation, and building up human capital. Actor groups or sub-populations such as technological and epistemic communities are cases in point as well as clusters, urban, local, regional and sectoral innovation systems; any further aggregation could be considered as being based on the same principles of tying actors together. As a consequence, higher order structures of heterogeneity can be observed to build up sub-populations. These structures are characterized by inter-industry, inter-regional or international differences in the ability to innovate and to pursue technological change, in the ability to absorb and to use external knowledge and in the ability to generate economic welfare.

Hence, taken that way, competition and cooperation, innovation and imitation are suggested to take place in and between heterogeneous populations and on several levels of aggregation; in a certain sense they are nested, ranging from the individual actor up to the unit of country blocks.

The phenomena to be analyzed via such a type of framework extend from market and industrial dynamics to the meso level, covering competition and cooperation between clusters, networks and regions as well as between technologies and (to a lesser extent) even industries; and also the macro level of countries with differential growth performance accessible via this framework. Dynamic pattern such as convergence/divergence and life cycles, structural regularities such as persistence and bimodal "actor" distributions, and the role of the different interaction modes here can be addressed. Rather challenging is the analysis of the relationship between the different levels of sub-populations, the well-known micro–meso–macro loops, which might be relevant in explaining phenomena such as the emergence and pervasiveness of general purpose technologies.

To dig deeper into these dimensions and to work on respective research questions will certainly lead to a considerably better understanding of economic change in general and of innovation driven change in particular. Challenges are ahead and obstacles will come up frequently. One of them is crucial and not surmountable; there is a straightforward epistemological reservation affecting all research dealing with issues related to the future. For economics no one less than Kenneth Arrow formulated that reservation when discussing research in innovation and technological change:

> Almost by definition, it is hopeless to develop a model which will genuinely predict innovations: an innovation is something new, and if you know what will be in the future, you know it now. [...] However, I do not conclude from this that dynamic models which incorporate technical change are useless. What they give you is not any predictions of specific innovations, but an idea of the statistical properties of technological progress. We may have some useful idea of the average rate of technological change, of the degree of fluctuations and the kinds of surprise that we may find in the future. We cannot, of course, predict a surprise; that is a contradiction in terms. But we can predict the kind of surprises that might occur (Arrow 1991, 473).

Hence, although not able to predict specific innovations, our knowledge and methods to extract out of observations at least the statistical properties of the new have been considerably developed and we have been able to extend the boundaries of what we can get to know. With Marshall McLuhin (1911–1980) "we drive into the future using only our rearview mirror" and our methods may us allow here and there a good guess what the future will be all about.

Acknowledgments This paper was the basis for the presidential address of the International Joseph A. Schumpeter Society held during the 15th Schumpeter Conference in Jena, July 30, 2014. The author thanks the audience for helpful questions and comments. Further thanks go to my collaborators at the Chair of Economics at the Friedrich Schiller University Jena, Holger Graf, Maximilian Göthner, Simone Vannuccini, Sebastian Döll, Johannes Herrmann, Susanne Hinzmann, Martin Kalthaus, Peggy Kelterborn, Stefanie Picard, Ivan Savin, Stefan Töpfer, and Tina Wolf, as well as all the doctoral students and colleagues in the DFG Graduate School GRK 1411 "The Economics of Innovative Change" and the International Max Planck Research School on Uncertainty. Special thanks go to Simone Vannuccini who devoted a lot of effort and time in critically commenting on the manuscript. Last not least, thank you to Chuck McCann for the English editing. Last not least, I am grateful for the financial support via the DFG GRK 1411 "The Economics of Innovative Change". The usual caveats apply.

Compliance with Ethical Standards There are no potential conflicts of interest involved.

References

Abramovitz M (1986) Catching up, forging ahead and falling behind. J Econ Hist 46(2):385–406

Ahuja G (2000) The duality of collaboration: inducements and opportunities in the formation of interfirm linkages. Strateg Manag J 21(3):317–343

Ahuja G, Katila R (2001) Technological acquisitions and the innovation performance of acquiring firms: a longitudinal study. Strateg Manag J 22(3):197–220

Ajzen I (1991) The theory of planned behaviour. Organ Behav Hum Decis Process 50(2):179–211

Allen RC (1983) Collective invention. J Econ Behav Organ 4:1–24

Andersen ES (2004) Population thinking, price's equation and the analysis of economic evolution. Evol Inst Econ Rev 1(1):127–148

Arora A, Fosfuri A, Gambardella A (2001) Markets for technology and their implications for corporate strategy. Ind Corp Chang 10(2):419–451

Arrow KJ (1991) The dynamics of technological change. In: OECD (ed) Technology and productivity: the challenge for economic policy. OECD, Paris, pp 473–476

Baily MN, Hulten C, Campbell D (1992) Productivity dynamics in manufacturing plants. In: Brookings papers on economic activity: microeconomics. Brookings Institution Press, Washington, DC, pp 187–267

Balland P-A, Boschma R, Frenken K (2015) Proximity and innovation: from statics to dynamics. Reg Stud 49(6):907–920

Barabasi A, Albert R (1999) Emergence of scaling in random networks. Science 286(5439): 509–512

Barney J (1991) Firm resources and sustained competitive advantage. J Manag 17(1):99–120

Barney JB, Wright M, Ketchen DJ Jr (2001) The resource-based view of the firm: ten years after 1991. J Manag 27(6):625–641

Bird BJ (1988) Implementing entrepreneurial ideas: the case for intention. Acad Manag Rev 13(3): 442–453

Boisot M, Canals A (2004) Data, information and knowledge: have we got it right? J Evol Econ 14(1):43–67

Boschma R (2005) Proximity and innovation: a critical assessment. Reg Stud 39:61–74
Bottazzi G, Secchi A (2006) Gibrat's law and diversification. Ind Corp Chang 15(5):847–875
Bottazzi G, Secchi A, Tamagni F (2008) Productivity, profitability and financial performance. Ind Corp Chang 17(4):711–751
Bunderson JS (2005) Team member functional background and involvement in management teams: direct effects and the moderating role of power centralization. Acad Manag J 46(4): 458–474
Cannon-Bowers JA, Salas E, Converse S (1993) Shared mental models in expert team decision making. In: Castellan NJ Jr (ed) Individual and group decision making. Lawrence Erlbaum Associates, Hillsdale, NJ, pp 221–246
Cantner U (2002) Heterogenität, Technologischer Fortschritt und Spillover-Effekte. In: Lehmann-Waffenschmidt M (ed) Studien zur Evolutorischen Ökonomik V. Duncker&Humblodt, Berlin, pp 15–40
Cantner U (2009) Competition in innovation. In: Cantner U, Greiner A, Kuhn T, Pyka A (eds) Futurity and economics. Edward Elgar, Cheltenham, pp 13–33
Cantner U (2015) Evolutionary economics of innovation – behavior, interaction, and outcomes. In: Ramser HJ, Stadler M (eds) Entwicklung und Perspektiven der Wirtschaftswissenschaft. Mohr Siebeck, Tübingen, pp 333–354
Cantner U, Graf H (2006) The network of innovators in Jena: an application of social network analysis. Res Policy 35(4):463–480
Cantner U, Graf H (2011) Innovation networks: formation, performance and dynamics. In: Antonelli C (ed) Handbook on the system dynamics of technological change. Edward Elgar, Cheltenham, pp 366–394
Cantner U, Guerzoni M (2009) Innovations driving industrial dynamics – between incentives and knowledge. Econ Polit J Anal Inst Econ XXVI(3):473–501
Cantner U, Hanusch H (2005) Empirical issues in evolutionary economics – heterogeneity and evolutionary change – concepts and measurement. In: Dopfer K (ed) Economics, evolution and the state – the governance of complexity. Edward Elgar, Cheltenham, pp 13–42
Cantner U, Krüger JJ (2004) Geroski's stylized facts and mobility in large German manufacturing firms. Int J Ind Organ 24:267–283
Cantner U, Krüger J (2008) Micro-heterogeneity and aggregate productivity development in the German manufacturing sector – results from a decomposition exercise. J Evol Econ 18(2): 119–134
Cantner U, Meder A (2007) Technological proximity and the choice of cooperation partner. J Econ Interac Coord 2:45–65
Cantner U, Raake B (2014) International research networks in pharmaceuticals: structure and dynamics. Res Policy 43(2):333–348
Cantner U, Savin I (2014) Do firms benefit from complementarity effect in R&D and what drives their R&D strategy choices? Jena Economic Research Papers #2014-023
Cantner U, Krüger J, von Rhein K (2009) Knowledge and creative destruction over the industry life cycle – the case of the German automobile industry. Economica 76(301):132–148
Cantner U, Krüger J, von Rhein K (2011) Knowledge compensation in the German automobile industry. Appl Econ 43(22):2941–2951
Cantner U, Krüger J, Söllner R (2012) Product quality, product price and share dynamics in the German compact car market. Ind Corp Chang 21(5):1085–1115
Cantner U, Hinzmann S, Wolf T (2016a) The coevolution of innovative ties, proximity and competences – towards a dynamic approach of innovation cooperation. In: Glückler J (ed) Topographies and topologies of knowledge. Springer, Heidelberg (forthcoming)
Cantner U, Savin I, Vannuccini S (2016b) Replicator dynamics in value chains: explaining some puzzles of market selection. Jena Economic Research Papers #2016-003, Friedrich-Schiller-University and Max Planck Institute of Economics, Jena
Cantner U, Göthner M, Silbereisen RK (2017) Schumpeter's Entrepreneur – a rare case. J Evol Econ 27:187–214

Carlsson B (2007) Innovation systems: a survey of the literature from a Schumpeterian perspective. In: Hanusch H, Pyka A (eds) Elgar companion to Neo-Schumpeterian economics. Edward Elgar, Cheltenham, pp 857–871
Cassiman B, Veugelers R (2006) In search of complementarity in innovation strategy: internal R&D and external knowledge acquisition. Manag Sci 52(1):68–82
Chesbrough HW (2003) Open innovation – the new imperative for creating and profiting from technology. Harvard Business School Press, Boston
Coad A (2007) Testing the principle of growth of the fitter: the relationship between profits and firm growth. Struct Chang Econ Dyn 18(3):370–386
Coad A (2010) Exploring the processes of firm growth: evidence from a vector auto-regression. Ind Corp Chang 19(6):1677–1703
Cohen WM (2010) Fifty years of empirical studies of innovative activity and performance. In: Handbook of the economics of innovation, vol 1. Elsevier, Amsterdam, pp 129–213
Cohen WM, Levin RC (1989) Empirical studies of innovation and market structure. In: Schmalensee R, Willig RD (eds) Handbook of industrial organization. North Holland, Amsterdam, pp 1059–5107
Cohen WM, Levinthal D (1989) Innovation and learning: the two faces of R&D. Econ J 99(397): 569–596
Cohen WM, Levinthal D (1990) Absorptive capacity: a new perspective on learning and innovation. Adm Sci Q 35(1):128–152
Cowan R, David PA, Foray D (2000) The explicit economics of knowledge: codification and tacitness. Ind Corp Chang 9(2):211–253
Cowan R, Jonard N, Zimmermann J-B (2006) Evolving networks of inventors. J Evol Econ 16(1–2):155–174
Crosetto P (2010) To patent or not to patent: a pilot experiment on incentives to copyright in a sequential innovation setting. In: Ågerfalk PJ, Boldyreff C, González-Barahona J, Madey G, Noll J (eds) IFIP advances in information and communication technology, open source software. New horizons, vol 319. Springer, Berlin, pp 53–72
Cyert R, March J (1963) A behavioral theory of the firm. Prentice-Hall, Englewood Cliffs, NJ
Davies SW, Geroski P (1997) Changes in concentration, turbulence, and the dynamics of market shares. Rev Econ Stat 79(3):383–391
Denzau AT, North DC (1994) Shared mental models: ideologies and institutions. Kyklos 47(1): 3–31
Dosi G (1988) Sources, procedures, and microeconomic effects of innovation. J Econ Lit 26(3): 1120–1171
Dosi G (2007) Statistical regularities in the evolution of industries. A guide trough some evidence and challenges for the theory. In: Malerba F, Brusoni S (eds) Perspectives on innovation. Cambridge University Press, Cambridge, pp 153–186
Dosi G, Egidi M (1991) Substantive and procedural uncertainty: an exploration of economic behaviour in changing environments. J Evol Econ 1(2):145–168
Dosi G, Marsili O, Orsenigo L, Salvatore R (1995) Learning, market selection and the evolution of industrial structures. Small Bus Econ 7(6):411–436
Dosi G, Malerba F, Marsili O, Orsenigo L (1997) Industrial structures and dynamics: evidence, interpretations and puzzles. Ind Corp Chang 6(1):3–24
Dosi G, Moschella D, Pugliese E, Tamagni F (2015) Productivity, market selection and corporate growth: comparative evidence across US and Europe. Small Bus Econ 45(3):643–672
Drach-Zahavy A, Somech A (2001) Understanding team innovation: the role of team processes and structures. Group Dyn Theory Res Pract 5(2):111–123
Fisher RA (1930) The genetical theory of natural selection. Clarendon, Oxford
Fontana R, Guerzoni M (2008) Incentives and uncertainty: an empirical analysis of the impact of demand on innovation. Camb J Econ 32(6):927–946
Foray D (2004) The economics of knowledge. MIT Press, Cambridge, MA

Foster L, Haltiwanger J, Krizan CJ (2001) Aggregate productivity growth: lessons from microeconomic evidence. In: Hulten CR, Dean ER, Harper MJ (eds) New developments in productivity analysis. University of Chicago Press, Chicago, pp 303–372
Geroski PA (1995) What do we know about entry? Int J Ind Organ 13(4):421–440
Göthner M, Obschonka M, Silbereisen RK, Cantner U (2012) Scientists' transition to academic entrepreneur-ship: economic and psychological determinants. J Econ Psychol 33(3): 628–641
Griliches Z (1992) The search for R&D spillovers. Scand J Econ 94:29–47
Hölzl W (2015) Mobility barriers and the speed of market selection. J Evol Econ 25(2):323–344
Jacobs J (1969) The economy of cities. Random House, New York
Kahneman D, Tversky A (1992) Advances in prospect theory: cumulative representation of uncertainty. J Risk Uncertain 5(4):297–323
Kahneman D, Tversky A, Slovic P (eds) (1982) Judgment under uncertainty: heuristics & biases. Cambridge University Press, Cambridge
Klepper S (2002a) Firm survival and the evolution of oligopoly. Rand J Econ 33(1):37–61
Klepper S (2002b) The capabilities of new firms and the evolution of the US automobile industry. Ind Corp Chang 11(4):645–666
Klepper S, Malerba F (2010) Demand, innovation and industrial dynamics: an introduction. Ind Corp Chang 19(5):1515–1520
Klepper S, Thompson P (2006) Submarkets and the evolution of market structure. Rand J Econ 37(4):861–886
Knudsen M, Tranekjer T, Cantner U (2016) Open innovation in an international perspective: how to organize for (radical) product innovation. In: Viardot E, Brems A (eds) Revolution in innovation management – international trends in research and practice. Palgrave McMillan (forthcoming)
Krueger NF (2007) What lies beneath? The experiential essence of entrepreneurial thinking. Enterp Theory Pract 31(1):123–138
Krueger NF, Reilly MD, Carsrud AL (2000) Competing models of entrepreneurial intentions. J Bus Ventur 15(5):411–432
Krüger JJ (2014) Intra-sectoral structural change and aggregate productivity development – a robust stochastic non-parametric frontier function approach. Empir Econ 46(4):1545–1572
Kwasnicki W (1996) Knowledge, innovation and economy: an evolutionary exploration. Edward Elgar, Aldershot
Kwasnicki W, Kwasnicka H (1992) Market, innovation, competition: an evolutionary model of industrial dynamics. J Econ Behav Organ 19(3):343–368
Lane L, Lubatkin M (1998) Relative absorptive capacity and interorganizational learning. Strateg Manag J 19(5):461–477
Leskinen R (2011) Success in the female entrepreneurial networking process. Ann Innov Entrep 2(1):6002
Malerba F (2006) Innovation and the evolution of industries. J Evol Econ 16(1):3–23
Malerba F, Orsenigo L (1995) Schumpeterian patterns of innovation. Camb J Econ 19:47–65
Malerba F, Orsenigo L (1996) The dynamics and evolution of industries. Ind Corp Chang 5(1): 51–87
Malerba F, Orsenigo L (1997) Technological regimes and sectoral patterns of innovative activities. Ind Corp Chang 6(1):83–118
Marsili O (2001) The anatomy and evolution of industries: technological change and industrial dynamics. Edward Elgar, Cheltenham
Marsili O, Verspagen B (2002) Technology and the dynamics of industrial structures: an empirical mapping of Dutch manufacturing. Ind Corp Chang 11(4):791
Mazzucato M (1998) A computational model of economies of scale and market share instability. Struct Chang Econ Dyn 9:55–83
Mazzucato M, Semmler W (1999) Market share instability and financial dynamics during the industry life cycle: the U.S. automobile industry. J Evol Econ 9(1):67–96
McAdams DP (1995) What do we know when we know a person? J Pers 63(3):365–396

McCrae RR, Costa PT (1997) Personality trait structure as a human universal. Am Psychol 52(5): 509–516
Melitz MJ, Polanec S (2015) Dynamic Olley-Pakes, productivity decomposition with entry and exit. Rand J Econ 46(2):362–375
Metcalfe JS (1994) Competition, Fisher's principle and increasing returns in the selection process. J Evol Econ 4(4):321–346
Metcalfe JS (1998) Evolutionary economics and creative destruction. Routledge, London
Metcalfe JS, Calderini M (1998) Chance, necessity and competitive dynamics in the Italian steel industry. In: Cantner U, Hanusch H, Klepper S (eds) Economic evolution, learning, and complexity. Physica-Verlag, Heidelberg, pp 139–158
Mokyr J (1992) The lever of riches. Oxford University Press, Oxford
Mowery DC, Oxley JE, Silverman BS (1998) Technology overlap and interfirm cooperation: implications for the resource-based view of the firm. Res Policy 27(5):507–523
Nelson RR (1991) Why do firms differ, and how does it matter? Strateg Manag J 12:61–74
Nelson R, Winter S (1982) An evolutionary theory of economic change. Harvard University Press, Cambridge
Nooteboom B (2009) A cognitive theory of the firm – learning, governance and dynamic capabilities. Edward Elgar, Cheltenham
Obschonka M, Silbereisen RK, Cantner U, Göthner M (2015) Entrepreneurial self-identity: predictors and effects within the theory of planned behavior framework. J Bus Psychol 30(4): 773–794
Orsenigo L, Pammolli F, Riccaboni M, Bonaccorsi A, Turchetti G (1998) The evolution of knowledge and the dynamics of an industry network. J Manag Gov 1(2):147–175
Pavitt K (1984) Sectoral patterns of technical change: towards a taxonomy and a theory. Res Policy 13(6):343–373
Penrose ET (1959) The theory of the growth of the firm. Wiley, New York
Polanyi M (1967) The tacit dimension. Anchor Books, New York
Powell WW, Koput KW, Smith-Doerr L (1996) Interorganizational collaboration and the locus of innovation: networks of learning in biotechnology. Adm Sci Q 41(1):116–145
Powell WW, Koput KW, Smith-Doerr L, Owen-Smith J (1999) Network position and firm performance. In: Andrews S, Knoke D (eds) Research in the sociology of organizations, vol 16. JAI Press, Greenwich, pp 129–159
Powell WW, White DR, Koput KW, Owen-Smith J (2005) Network dynamics and field evolution: the growth of interorganizational collaboration in the life sciences. Am J Sociol 110(4): 1132–1205
Sander PC, van Doorn RR, van der Pal J, Zijlstra FR (2015) Team adaptation to an unforeseen system failure: limits of the potential aids of shared knowledge and standardized communication. Eur J Work Organ Psy 24(5):796–811
Saviotti PP (1996) Technological evolution, variety and the economy. Edward Elgar, Aldershot
Saviotti PP, Mani GS (1995) Competition, variety and technological evolution: a replicator dynamics model. J Evol Econ 5(4):369–392
Schmiedeberg C (2008) Complementarities of innovation activities: an empirical analysis of the German manufacturing sector. Res Policy 37:1492–1503
Schmitt-Rodermund E (2004) Pathways to successful entrepreneurship: parenting, personality, entrepreneurial competence, and interests. J Vocat Behav 65(3):498–518
Schumpeter JA (1934/2008) The theory of economic development, 14th edn. Transaction, Brunswick
Schumpeter JA (1942/1950) Capitalism, socialism and democracy. Harper Brothers, New York
Silverberg G, Lehnert D (1994) Growth fluctuations in an evolutionary model of creative destruction. In: Silverberg G, Soete L (eds) The economics of growth and technical change. Edward Elgar, Aldershot, pp 74–108
Silverberg G, Lehnert D (1996) Evolutionary chaos: growth fluctuations in a Schumpeterian model of creative destruction. In: Barnett WA, Kirman A, Salmon M (eds) Nonlinear dynamics in economics. Cambridge University Press, Cambridge, pp 45–74

Silverberg G, Verspagen B (1994) Learning, innovation and economic growth: a long-run model of industrial dynamics. Ind Corp Chang 3(1):199–223
Silverberg G, Dosi G, Orsenigo L (1988) Innovation, diversity and diffusion: a self-organisation model. Econ J 98(393):1032–1054
Simon HA (1955) A behavioural model of rational choice. Q J Econ 69(1955):99–118
Skvoretz J (1991) Theoretical and methodological models of networks and relations. Soc Networks 13(3):275–300
Stuart TE (2000) Interorganizational alliances and the performance of firms: a study of growth and innovation rates in a high-technology industry. Strateg Manag J 21(8):791–811
Tajfel H, Turner JC (1979) An integrative theory of intergroup conflict. In: Austin WG, Worchel S (eds) The social psychology of intergroup relations. Brooks-Cole, Monterey, pp 33–47
Teece DJ (1986) Profiting from technological innovation: implications for integration, collaboration, licensing and public policy. Res Policy 15(6):285–305
Thaler R, Sunstein C (2008) Nudge: improving decisions about health, wealth, and happiness. Yale University Press, New Haven
Tversky A, Kahneman D (1981) The Framing of decisions and the psychology of choice. Science 211(4481):453–458
Verspagen B (1992) Uneven growth between interdependent economies. An evolutionary view on technology gaps, trade and growth. Avebury, Aldershot
von Hippel E (1987) Cooperation between rivals: informal know-how trading. Res Policy 16: 291–302
Wernerfelt B (1984) A resource-based view of the firm. Strateg Manag J 5:171–180
Winter SG (1964) Economic 'natural selection' and the theory of the firm. Yale Econ Essays 4: 225–272
Winter SG, Kaniovski YM, Dosi G (2000) Modeling industrial dynamics with innovative entrants. Struct Chang Econ Dyn 11(3):255–293
Winter SG, Kaniovski YM, Dosi G (2003) A baseline model of industry evolution. J Evol Econ 13(4):355–383
ZEW, Innovationsverhalten der deutschen Wirtschaft, Indikatorenbericht zur Innovationserhebung, various years, Mannheim

Behavior and Cognition of Economic Actors in Evolutionary Economics

Richard R. Nelson

Abstract An evolutionary perspective on the nature of economic activity requires a theory of human behavior and cognition that highlights human creativity and innovativeness, while at the same time recognizing that in many arenas of economic life change is slow and more routine aspects of behavior obtain. It is proposed that Herbert Simon's conception of human behavior as largely "bounded rational" is capable of suiting both aspects. However, to be able to encompass the enormous advances humans have achieved over the years in their ability to meet a variety of wants, a theory of behavior and cognition suitable for evolutionary economics needs to recognize the evolving cultural context of economic behavior and cognition.

1 Introduction

While we Schumpeterians may differ in some of the details of our theoretical orientation, we all share a view of what is going on in the economy, and the context in which economic actors are operating, that is very different than that laid out in today's standard economics texts which have been so much influenced by neoclassical theory. Those texts picture action going on in an economy that is in equilibrium, or at least is operating in a way that is stable and familiar to the participants, with the actors knowing the best course of action for them to take, and taking it. Economic actors are not seen as, in many situations, venturing out on new paths because they think that, if their venture is successful, they will be handsomely rewarded, or just because they like trying new things, or because they are forced to do so because what they had been doing no longer is viable. Yet a Schumpeterian or evolutionary (I often will use the terms interchangeably) perspective would highlight the importance of these latter contexts, and we Schumpeterians need a theory of economic behavior and cognition that deals with them.

An earlier version of this essay was presented at the 2014 meeting in Jena of the International Schumpeter Society.

R.R. Nelson (✉)
Columbia University, New York, NY, USA
e-mail: rrn2@columbia.edu

A. Pyka, U. Cantner (eds.), *Foundations of Economic Change*, Economic Complexity and Evolution, DOI 10.1007/978-3-319-62009-1_3

2 Framing the Question

What kind of a theory about the behavior and cognition of economic actors is needed if one sees what is going on in the economy through Schumpeterian or evolutionary glasses?

Any theory of economic behavior faces the problem that it must deal with a range of different kinds of economic actors, doing a variety of different things. It must deal with the behavior of households making consumption decisions, and business firms deciding what and how much to produce. In some cases economic analysis addresses the behaviors of school systems and individual teachers, and in others hospitals and doctors. If the analysis is concerned with public sector activity it must deal with government agencies, and perhaps with how regulations are set, and maybe voting behavior. As I highlighted above, Schumpeterian economics needs to encompass what goes on in the processes involved in invention and innovation, and perhaps deal with scientific research.

This need to deal with enormous variety is there whether the general theoretical perspective is neoclassical or Schumpeterian. But if it is the latter the theory also must recognize different kinds of contexts. Some of these may be relatively tranquil and familiar to the actors. But, of particular importance to Schumpeterians, others involve actors attempting something they have not done before, and often dealing with contexts with which they have little or no experience.

In the light of this diversity, one can ask whether any single theory can cover the full range of things. Neoclassical theory attempts to do so, by admitting a variety of different specifications of what is in the actor's utility function, and in the kinds of actions that are specified as in the choice set, but then assuming that actors maximize, whatever that context. Much of the criticism of neoclassical theory involves consideration of cases where this kind of a behavioral theory seems impossible to square with actual observed behavior. The rise over the last decades of "behavioral economics" largely reflects increased recognition of these kinds of cases.[1]

The lessons here are highly relevant in thinking about what kind of a broad theory of behavior and cognition would fit a Schumpeterian-evolutionary perspective. My position is that it is futile to try to build a tightly structured unified general theory of economic behavior that would cover all cases. Indeed I will argue that recognition of a variety of different modes of behavior is an important part of the understanding we want of what is going on and why. However, I also think it useful to have a broad umbrella theory that covers and, in a sense, explains this diversity.

[1]For a fine broad review of behavioral economics see Diamond and Vartianen (2007).

3 What Can We Draw from Psychology?

To some extent the agenda I am identifying overlaps some of the themes being developed by behavioral economics. And there certainly are some important insights and premises highlighted by behavioral economics that ought to be encompassed by a theory of behavior and cognition that suits how Schumpeterian and evolutionary economists see economic activity.

One is the proposition that the way an actor sees, frames, a decision problem very much affects what that actor chooses to do, and that what might be regarded as the same real problem can get framed very differently depending on how it is presented or comes to attention, or the past experience of the actor involved. A second is that it is a mistake to presume that economic actors always behave consistently; indeed the evidence is clear that actors have trouble reasoning coherently about choice problems where basic background facts are uncertain, and in particular tend to be inconsistent both in thought and in action in dealing with the probabilities involved in the problem. A third general proposition, that has been particularly highlighted recently by Daniel Kahneman (2011), is that much of human action taking actually is guided by very little explicit thinking, and that conscious deliberation about what to do is the exception not the rule. This proposition has been standard for a long time in various sub-fields of psychology, and I propose it is particularly important to take aboard in a theory of behavior and cognition that fits with evolutionary economics.

But while there is overlap of interest, the orientation of behavioral economics is not to the central issues of human behavior and cognition relevant to Schumpeterian economics. The agenda for Schumpeterian and evolutionary economics is motivated by the belief that neither the innovation going on in modern economies nor the associated shifting and previously inexperienced ground for much of decision making more broadly are treated adequately by neoclassical rational behavior theory. Our objective is to develop a theory of cognition and behavior that can illuminate what goes on in these kinds of contexts as well as more tranquil ones. The agenda of behavioral economics is motivated by the argument that observation and experiment have revealed many contexts in which what individuals do and don't do is clearly inconsistent with the canons of neoclassical rational decision theory, but the contexts studied are not in general ones that particularly interest Schumpeterian economists.

Behavioral economists seem divided on whether they see the long run goal of the discipline as finding the areas of behavior where rational behavior theory falls down worst, and providing a better theory for those areas, or whether they see the objective as the achievement of a new general theory of behavior of economic actors to replace neoclassical theory. Particularly the behavioral economists in the latter camp believe that the theory of behavior in economics ideally ought to be based on the understandings in psychology. A problem with this perspective is that modern psychology is a fragmented field, which includes a number of quite different broad perspectives on human behavior, and within each empirical research is largely oriented to particular phenomena and questions that are germane in particular contexts but not others.

Of the various branches of psychology, for our interests here cognitive science is the most important, and important lessons can be drawn from the fact that it itself is a divided field.[2]

At its inception the presently broad field of cognitive science was strongly oriented by the basic conception of artificial intelligence: the proposition that the workings of the digital computer could provide a plausible model for the workings of the human mind. The focus was on aspects of human behavior that seemed to involve sophisticated thinking about what to do, including drawing on relevant information taken into and stored in the mind relevant to a mental characterization or model of what to do, and "computational" processes assumed to be analogous to the computation that computers did. The particular cases studied by proponents of this view of human intelligence tended to be relatively complex explicitly posed analytic problems, like playing a game of chess or proving a mathematical theorem.

Relatively early in the game, a point of view began to be articulated that much of human problem solving and thinking was not like that at all, but rather involved the recognition of patterns, and tended to proceed through parallel processing of different pieces of information taken into the brain through the senses, and fitted together so as to make sense of some event or phenomena, with logical thinking playing at most a minor role. Recognizing particular faces is one prominent example. Language learning, both oral and written, a more complex one. While there clearly was dispute regarding the nature of human intelligence between those that stressed logical information processing and those that stressed pattern recognition, it was clear to many within the developing cognitive science community that many human tasks required and involved elements of both.

As cognitive science developed as a field, a number of participants called attention to the fact that much of human action seemed simply to be more or less automatic responses to particular circumstances which, to be effective, may have required some prior trial and error learning, and memory of what happened, but once learned its activation did not seem to require either subtle recognition of complex patterns or much logical processing. I note that this kind of action taking, and the nature of the learning associated with its development, was a central subject of research in psychology prior to emergence of cognitive science. And, as noted, this aspect of human behavior has been highlighted more recently by Kahneman.

More generally, as research and reflection by cognitive scientists has progressed over the years, there has been growing recognition within the discipline that humans come to the actions they take through a variety of different cognitive processes. Merlin Donald (1991) has used the term "the hybrid mind" to highlight this diversity.

[2]For a compact review of the field and how it connects to economic analysis see Nelson and Nelson (2002). For a more recent and extensive review written for psychologists see Glenberg et al. (2013).

4 Economic Behavior as Mostly "Boundedly Rational"

I propose that, rather than a comprehensive theory that purports to be relevant to all cases if tailored appropriately, the kind of theoretical perspective on the cognition and behavior of economic actors that may be achievable and useful involves a typology of different modes of cognition and action generation that tend to invoked by different contexts, and a way of assessing at least some aspects of the outcomes that are likely to be generated. But at the same time, I believe it is useful to have a broad umbrella perspective that helps one understand the variety. In my view, the proposition developed by Herbert Simon[3] and his colleagues then at Carnegie Institute of Technology that much of human and organizational behavior can be understood as "boundedly rational" can provide that general point of view.[4]

The perspective on economic behavior as mostly "boundedly rational" has the particular attractiveness for economists of being consonant with the traditional economic theory of behavior, going back to the days of Adam Smith, that sees economic actors doing what they do with purposes in mind and in many contexts at least a rough understanding of the consequences of following various courses of action. I believe that, treated with care, and recognizing human fallibility, this broad theoretical perspective has shown considerable explanatory and predictive power. The problem with the full blown rational behavior theory of neoclassical economics is that it does not recognize these caveats.

On the other hand, recognition that rationality is bounded highlights that there are limits to the power of the human mind and the knowledge actors can master and work with, and that the contexts for human action generally are too complicated or subtle for actors to understand and take into account adequately the wide range of factors bearing on what they should be doing. The formulation is quite open to significant differences across contexts in the strength of human understanding. And empirical studies guided by this broad framework have recognized a variety of particular modes of decision making and action taking in different contexts, and among different kinds of actors.

However, I would propose that, to address phenomena of particular interest to Schumpeterian economists, and to get clearly into view that bounded rationality is a concept that encompasses a variety of different kinds of behavior, several distinctions and factors need to be highlighted more than they have been in the literature to date.

---

[3]Perhaps the best general reference is Simon (1957).

[4]Giovanni Dosi has urged me to state clearly that the conception of bounded rationality I am endorsing here must not be interpreted as implying that there is something that could be interpreted as fully rational behavior that bounded rationality is not quite up to achieving. Under the perspective I develop here truly fully rational behavior is simply impossible, often even to define, much less achieve, except under tightly defined and controlled contexts that are quite unlike the contexts actually faced by economic actors.

First, it is important to distinguish between choice contexts which the economic actor considers familiar and responds to more or less automatically by taking actions that have sufficed before in this kind of context, and contexts that induce the actor to engage in serious contemplation of alternatives. And where action taking is preceded by conscious deliberation, it is important to distinguish between contexts where the actors attention is focused on courses of action the actor has followed before perhaps in another context or has other reason to believe are well within it's range of competence, and those that involve trying to do something new. Schumpeterian and evolutionary economists of course have a special interest in the latter—that is what innovation is all about—but innovation only can be understood in juxtaposition to more routine behavior, and more generally action taking that involves doing the familiar.

Second, particularly for the kinds of phenomena which particularly interest Schumpeterian economists, it is important to recognize that actors differ in the capabilities that they bring to various choice contexts. They differ in their knowledge and experience, and in the skills they possess. For these reasons they may differ significantly in what they do in contexts that, to an outside observer, may look basically the same. And some will do better than others will.

Again, I note that this aspect of behavior—differences in capabilities—has received little attention from psychologists, or from behavioral economists. Yet differences in capabilities obviously are of central interest to Schumpeterian and evolutionary economists.

A third important limitation of most of the writings on economic behavior that, in my view, needs to be remedied is failure to relate the perceptions of individual actors about the contexts they face, the courses of action that they understand are available, and their judgments about which of these actions are appropriate and likely to be effective, to the beliefs and understandings and know-how of the broader community of which the actor is a part. This can and has been raised as a criticism of modern psychology in general. And it is hardly recognized in behavioral economics.

In basically ignoring the social and cultural context within which individual and organizational actors operate, contemporary mainline economic analysis in effect blinds itself to important influences on the phenomena in which it is most interested.[5] The purchases of consumption goods and services by households clearly is strongly influenced by consumption patterns and notions about appropriate life style held by the social community of which the household is a member. The practices of individual businesses, and the broad strategies they have adopted to guide their decision making, obviously are influenced by the perceptions and norms shared by the management community and what is taught by its gurus.[6]

[5]The argument that a theory of economic behavior and cognition needs to recognize the cultural basis of human action and thought of course was a central premise of the American Institutional Economists who were an important part of the academic economic community from the beginnings of the twentieth century until after World War II. For a survey of their perspective, see Mazzoleni and Nelson (2013).

[6]For a very interesting discussion see J. C. Spender's Industry Recipes (1989).

I want to argue that it is especially important that Schumpeterian economists recognize clearly the social and cultural context of action taking. We are centrally interested in how modern capitalist economies have become so productive, and the sources and mechanisms of future progress. When one observes powerful and complex methods being used by individuals and organizations to achieve their ends, it is almost a sure thing that the heart of the knowledge base of what they are doing is shared by their professional peers, and is acquired by individuals only as they are part of this broader community.

And, where one sees action being very effective, almost always that common knowledge that enables it has been achieved through a lengthy cultural learning process. Thus characterization of the actions taken today needs to be understood as a frame in an evolutionary moving picture.

I note that these observations would not have surprised Thorstein Veblen who, over a century ago (Veblen 1898) asked "Why is Economics Not an Evolutionary Science?". The school of institutional economics, that largely grew up inspired by Veblen's views, in its early days was very much oriented to the continuing processes of evolutionary change going on in modern economies, and highlighted the cultural and sociological context of this evolution. Unfortunately this intertwining of evolutionary and institutional analysis has not carried over to the "new" institutional economics. But there is some reason to be hopeful.[7]

To return to the general theme, under the perspective on economic behavior and cognition I am proposing, economic actors are assumed to be boundedly rational. When in contexts that call for them to do something, they proceed with some notions about the outcomes they would like to see happen, a perception of at least some actions they might take that seem plausible, and some thoughts on which of these might be most appropriate. But the contexts they face differ widely, and they go about generating the actions they actually take in different ways in different kinds of contexts.

In some contexts, actors are likely to respond to the requirement to do something by following patterns of behavior that they have successfully used before. In others, for some reason this is impossible, or the context is different from what the actor has faced before, or while the context may be familiar there are strong incentives to scan and reflect on the options before acting. Simon himself made this distinction in a number of his analyses, and I note that this also is a distinction made by Kahneman.[8] Sidney Winter has reminded me that John Dewey (1992) presented a similar view of behavior, with perhaps more emphasis on the role played by emotion and anxiety in some contexts. More generally, not surprisingly the point

[7]For a history of what happened see the introduction by Hodgson and Stoelhorst (2014), to the special issue of the Journal of Institutional Economics concerned with the future of institutional and evolutionary economics.

[8]These two different modes of action taking were built into most of the models developed in Nelson and Winter (1982).

of view on how to understand economic behavior that I am espousing here is similar in many respects to arguments Winter has made (Winter 2013, 2014).

I note that Kahneman puts less weight than I do here on the argument that routine or habitual behavior is often an effective way of acting. Also, he seems to presume to a greater extent than I do that active deliberation is likely to come up with an effective course of action. My argument is that, where one does see effective problem solving, the reason almost always is that deliberation can draw on a strong fund of knowledge that has been accumulated culturally generally over a long period of time.[9]

5 Routines

Under most circumstances the range of actions that need to be taken often over a short period of time by an individual person, household, firm, research laboratory, economic actor more generally, is far too great for that actor to be able to think carefully before taking action, except in a minority of cases. And where the environment for action has been relatively tranquil actors generally have had time to learn what works and what doesn't. Most of the actions one observes in such contexts should be understood as actors following routines that have in the past yielded satisfactory outcomes, and are triggered relatively automatically by circumstances under which action along these lines seems appropriate.

I suggest that individual or household shopping for the kinds of items bought relatively regularly largely involves following routines. In my recent paper with Davide Consoli (Nelson and Consoli 2010) we propose that much of household behavior can be understood in terms of the routines they use. And of course a quite extensive empirical and theoretical literature exists arguing that firm behavior largely involves the following of established routines.[10] In our earlier work Sidney Winter and I used the term "routine" to characterize these aspects of firm behavior. Here I am using it to denote the relatively automatic behavior patterns of any economic actor.

The fact that little conscious thought is involved in the invoking and execution of a routine does not imply that routines are crude ways of doing things. The routines a store has for reordering stock and for setting prices may be quite elaborate, even though once in place they are carried out routinely. The operation of highly sophisticated technologies largely involves the use of routines. Many of the routines used by economic actors are very powerful and highly effective in meeting their objectives.

[9]There is good reason to believe that Dewey would agree with me on this.

[10]For a fine review of the literature on organizational routines, see Becker (2004).

Also, routines need not be ridged. Indeed viable routines generally have a reasonable amount of flexibility built into them to enable them to adjust to the kind of variable circumstances that are to be expected in the broad context where they are operative. Household shopping routines need to be sensitive to what is and is not available at the store, and to some degree to prices. Firm pricing routines need to take costs into account. But my argument is that in established shopping routines these adjustments generally are made relatively routinely. There may be some conscious consideration of alternatives, but so long as the context remains in the normal range, wide search and intensive deliberation is highly unlikely. Similarly, the pricing routines of firms almost always are sensitive to costs, with much of that sensitivity, if not necessarily all, built into a formula used relatively routinely.

Elsewhere (Nelson 2013) I have used the term "adaptively responsive" to denote the sensitivity of routines to broadly experienced and thus anticipated variation in the details of the context that invokes their use. My proposal is that most routines that are used for a significant time are adaptively responsive.

Economists of a neoclassical persuasion would be inclined to argue that routines persistently employed by an economic actor must be, in some sense, optimal. If one's view of human behavior is that it is "boundedly rational", then in general one would deny that choice sets are objectively defined, and if this is so it is not clear what optimal means. Relatively effective given the actors goals, and adaptively responsive to not surprising changes in the details of the context do not imply optimality. However, that an actor continues to use a particular routine indicates that the results are "satisfactory" in the sense that doing things in a significantly different way is not being actively considered.[11] On the other hand, of course, some of the actions that are carried out routinely by some actors are clearly clumsy, and likely even counterproductive given the objectives they aim to reach. An important challenge for evolutionary economics is to illuminate the conditions under which routines are effective, and those where they often are not.

From one point of view, to explain or predict what an economic actor does in a domain of activity marked by the use of routines it is sufficient to identify and analyze the routines that are in use. And this is exactly what is done in studies like those reported in the classic book by Cyert and March (1963), A Behavioral Theory of the Firm.

But for the theory of behavior to have any depth, it is important to understand why the routines in use are what they are. I have argued that the neoclassical mode of answering that question—to propose that they are optimal—is not convincing if one holds to a theory of bounded rationality, and wants an explanation, not simply a purported characterization, of observed behavior. Under evolutionary theory such an explanation needs to be posed in terms of learning and selection processes. More on this shortly.

[11]This is Herbert Simon's concept of "satisficing".

6 Deliberating, Problem Solving, Choosing

The proposition that much of the economic behavior one observes at any time should be understood as economic actors following routines is not meant to play down the role of deliberation, problem solving, and often creativity in the generation of economic activity. These more active cognitive processes are brought into play when economic actors face contexts with which they are not familiar, or where no established routine seems suitable, or more generally where the actor for whatever reason wants to do something new. And of course in many cases they are involved in the genesis of prevailing routines in the first place.

This perspective is, of course, very Schumpeterian. Chapter 1 of his Theory of Economic Development (Schumpeter 1934) is all about routine activity in an economic steady state. In the actual economic world as we know it no context is as constant as the context for economic action Schumpeter depicts in Chap. 1, or is laid out in general equilibrium theory. However, my argument is that at any time a good portion of economic activity does proceed in contexts that are regular enough so that behavior that follows an established routine can suffice to meet the actor's objectives, at least if the routine used has a certain amount of built in flexibility.

In Chap. 2 Schumpeter describes a very different kind of economic behavior: innovation. Innovation is creative by desire or necessity, uncertain as to success, often failing, sometimes winning big. But involving thinking and problem solving in an essential way.

In recent years cognitive scientists have significantly improved our understanding of how the cognitive capabilities and practices of human beings differ from those of other higher animals; the most interesting comparisons have been with other primates.[12] There would appear to be two basic capabilities that humans have that other primates do not. One is built in biologically. The other, while based on this, is essentially cultural.

Other animals share with humans the ability to solve problems by doing different things until they find something that works, and then carrying over what has been learned to subsequent experiences with situations like that. But humans have the ability, that even other primates have to a far lesser degree, to in effect reflect on a context or a way of doing something (perhaps something they have observed others doing) even when that context is not present or that action not being actually implemented, in effect anticipating future situations and actions.[13] Thus the kind of deliberation we are considering here would seem to be a capability that is largely unique to humans.

And humans are unique in having the capacity for cumulative collective learning. While the cutting edge of progress generally has been discovery or trying out of a new method by an individual, major advance over time has depended on the

[12]Donald (1991) provides a splendid discussion of these and related matters.

[13]There is some evidence that certain other animals have this capability, but to a very limited degree.

spread across the community of what has been learned, and the further building on that by others.[14] The development of shared language has been essential for this to happen to any major extent. There is no question that the ability of humans to reflect and gather and process relevant knowledge prior to action is an important capability in its own right. However, I would argue that, in the absence of strong cultural know-how that has been developed over time through collective learning on which that capability can draw, what human reflection can achieve on its own is modest.

In my view Schumpeter draws too sharp a line between innovating, and the imitative responses by followers to the innovations of others. The latter also requires ability to conceptualize a way of doing something that is new for the particular actor, and often involves considerable uncertainty.

However, what is a new situation or new activity for a particular actor will tend to be conceived very differently if that actor knows about and can draw on the experience of other actors, than if the actor is all alone, as it were. Much of what actors do that is new to them is invoked by their knowledge of the experience of others. The abandonment by an actor of an old routine and the adoption of a new one may be induced simply by knowledge that others are doing something different and doing well, as contrasted with any compelling evidence that the old routine is not yielding satisfactory results. While direct imitation often is not easy, and the efforts of one economic actor to do what another is doing may achieve something somewhat or widely different, at any time a shared body of know-how provides the basis for the range of activities used in a field, and is the reason why one generally observes a certain amount of similarity in what the various actors are doing.

7 Innovation and the Advance of Know-How

While I believe the lines are blurred not sharp, the term "innovation" as contrasted with "imitation" connotes an endeavor by an actor to do something new not only to that actor, but to the community of actors doing roughly similar things. Empirical research shows clearly that innovators, like imitators, almost always draw heavily on know-how, and more general knowledge, possessed by their peer community. And a large share of innovation is based on and aims to improve artifacts and processes that are in use, often use by the innovator. But innovators are reaching beyond what has been done before. And if they are successful, what they have achieved sooner or later becomes part of the knowledge base shared by that community. That is, know-how in an area of economic activity advances over time through an evolutionary process driven largely by the innovation going on.

The principal difference between the orientation of evolutionary and Schumpeterian economists, and that of today's more orthodox orientation to the

[14] Other species have the capability of spreading the effective behaviors learned by one individuals to others in the community, but not of building further and cumulatively from that.

study of economics, is our focus on innovation. Our argument is that what makes economic activity today so effective in meeting a wide variety of human wants is that the means we have available to achieve our ends have become so powerful as the result of cumulative innovation. It is not because economic decision makers are so effective. Human economic decision making remains, as it always has been, often mechanical, sometimes creative, but in these cases often mistake ridden.

While there has been considerable research over the years by scholars of management on what makes firms successful, there is little evidence that firm managers today are more effective than firm managers were a half century or a century ago. The failure rates of new firms, and of new ventures by established firms, remains high. Business management remains an art, in which luck is an important factor determining success.

The situation is similar regarding household purchases and other decisions regarding how they spend their money. It is not for naught that we have in place a number of regulatory agencies justified explicitly by the proposition that households often have limited understanding of what they are buying. Wesley Clair Mitchell's "The Backward Art of Spending Money", published in 1912, rings as true today as it was then.

Or consider highly trained engineers working in a field of advanced technology trying to design an artifact that will have important capabilities that presently available artifacts do not. Their design efforts may be highly sophisticated, guided by strong scientific knowledge. However, like firm managers and household shoppers, their rationality is bounded in the sense that, if they try to do something significantly different from prevailing practice, they are highly likely to make at least some mistakes. To achieve the capabilities they are aiming for will then require that they or someone else somehow finds a way that works, to a considerable extent through trial and error problem solving.

However, boundedly rational human actors, can achieve remarkably good outcomes, if the know-how they have to work with, the means they know how to use, are good enough.

For these reasons, where one observes effective human action going on the principal reason is not so much that someone or some organization earlier had effectively thought through the background problem and surmised, or calculated, a good way of doing things in that context, but rather that there has been a lot of collective learning going on generally over a considerable period of time that, cumulatively, has led to the development of ways of doing things that work reasonably, or even extraordinarily, well. Thus a key part of the theory of behavior and cognition that we need is a theory of how collective learning occurs.

Efforts at innovation clearly are the key driving force. However, a key premise of evolutionary economics, amply supported by empirical evidence, is that the efforts of economic actors to venture beyond established practice almost always are associated with uncertain outcomes. While in areas where knowledge is reasonably strong, innovative efforts are far from blind, nonetheless all areas of innovative activity are marked by failures as well as successes, and even the most knowledgeable experts sometimes turn out to be wrong. A fundamental consequence is that, while economic progress certainly depends on the creative efforts of individual inventors and innovators, it depends at least as much on the existence of a number potential innovators holding somewhat different perceptions of the most promising routes to advance, with competition in ex-post practice being a large part of the selection process determining the winners. And continuing progress depends on the essence of what has been achieved in one round of innovative effort becoming part of the collective knowledge base for the next round.

As I suggested earlier, the emphasis I am putting here on the need to recognize that the knowledge and orientation of individual economic actors regarding appropriate and effective ways of doing things, including their efforts at innovation, as largely determined by the culture they share with their peers is very much in the spirit of the old American institutional economics tradition, as is a focus on the mechanisms involved in economic progress. This overlap of perspectives and interests calls for reaching out to the institutional economics tradition that is reemerging.[15]

8 The Need for a More Eclectic and Flexible Conception of "Rational" Behavior

Earlier I noted that, since the times of Adam Smith, economists observing the behavior of economic actors in the contexts in which they had a central interest have assessed these behaviors as largely reasonably rational, given the actors' apparent objectives, and the range of options they faced. This point of view, and the kinds of behavior and contexts on which economists have focused, has given economic theorizing about behavior a very different orientation than that taken by psychologists, who mostly have focused on contexts and on kinds and aspects of behavior outside of the range where economic analysis has been concentrated.

I also have stressed that, even within the relatively constrained range that economists are interested in, there is great variety of both contexts and behaviors. For economists of a Schumpeterian and evolutionary orientation, there is special interest in behaviors associated with efforts to do something new, and contexts that economic actors have not experienced before. But as I will argue shortly, it is important not only to have a perspective on behavior and cognition that treats innovation and its consequences adequately, but does so with a broader framework that also treats behavior in more stable contexts. Within that framework there needs to be room for both creativity and habit, for both insightful understanding of the situation, and biased or simply ignorant views of what is going on.

[15]See Mazzoleni and Nelson (2013), for a discussion of that tradition of economic research. The December 2014 special issue of the Journal of Institutional Economics reviews the state of both evolutionary and institutional economics and considers their connections. See in particular the opening essay by Hodgson and Stoelhorst.

I believe that the kind of perspective on economic behavior and cognition that I have sketched here, based on the presumption that economic behavior is "boundedly rational", but emphasizing the bounded as well as the rational, and being careful to recognize important differences associated with different kinds of contexts and conditions, has the promise of doing this. It provides a much better and richer characterization of economic behavior that is for the most part purposeful and functional than the theory of full blown optimization that neoclassical theory is stuck with. It is applicable across a much wider spectrum of conditions, and it avoids some of the obvious problems. And for those that care about such matters, it provides an explanation for much of economic behavior that one actually can believe.

As Schumpeterian economists long have understood, neoclassical theory cannot deal with efforts at innovation, as we know about these empirically. A theory of innovative behavior certainly should recognize that inventors and innovators are pursuing goals, and that their efforts generally reflect their best understanding of how to achieve their goals. However, the full blown rationality assumption of neoclassical theory does not at all help the analyst to understand why different inventors generally try different kinds of solutions to the challenges they face, and that a large share of these efforts fail. A theory that inventive efforts are "boundedly" rational is quite consistent with these facts and, further, leads the analyst of innovation in a particular arena of economic activity to consider the weaknesses as well as the strengths of the current knowledge base.

Some advocates of neoclassical economics will admit the difficulties that theoretical structure has in dealing with innovation, but argue that for analysis of many other economic phenomena neoclassical economics does just fine. In particular, it provides a way of analyzing how markets work, and the determinants of prices, and of how prices influence supply and demand, that fits many of the important facts. I propose that our response should be that a theory that the behavior of economic actors is boundedly rational can generate all of the understandings of neoclassical market theory that are worth preserving, and does so with a view of how individual economic actors think and behave that is much more consistent with what is known about that. The key, I propose, is the argument that in the relevant contexts boundedly rational behavior generally is "adaptively responsive" to changes in conditions.

Earlier I argued that, in contexts that were repetitive and broadly similar from case to case, much of observed behavior involved the following of routines. I also proposed that routines that had been honed by considerable experience tended to have flexibility built into them so that what was done could be adaptive to not unexpected differences in the contexts they face. There is no case to be made that these adaptive responses are optimal. But my argument here is that they are highly likely to be in the right direction.

I would make a similar argument regarding behavior in contexts that are sufficiently different from the norm to trigger conscious thinking about what to do. Again, no case to be made that the actions taken would be optimal. However, a good case can be made that they would be adaptively responsive to the particular features of the context that induced reflection on alternatives in the first place.

This is specially likely to be so if the alternatives being considered are reasonably well established ways of doing things. But the evidence suggests that, despite the uncertainties and variation in viewpoints involved, the kinds of innovations that an economy gets also is adaptively responsive to changes in the context. What is tried and what succeeds are strongly sensitive to the kinds of returns that might be expected from a successful innovation.

In a recent article (Nelson 2013) I have argued that a theory that the behavior of economic actors is adaptively responsive in the above sense is sufficient to generate virtually all of the empirically relevant "theorems" about how markets works that one finds in neoclassical textbooks, for example responses of demand and supply to changing prices.[16] (Of course the theorem to the effect that market solutions are "optimal" has no counterpart in evolutionary theory). And it does so with assumptions that much better fit the facts that we know about individual and organizational behavior.

9 The Range of Topics Schumpeterian: Evolutionary Economic Theory Must Cover

I conclude by proposing that, if a Schumpeterian and evolutionary perspective on what is going on in a modern capitalist economy is to take hold broadly in academic economics, it is not sufficient that it provide an illuminating analysis of innovation as the driver of economic change and the nature of competition and of creative destruction that goes on in arenas of economic activity where innovation is prominent. It must a provide a general way of understanding economic behavior and activity, and how this is shaped by and shapes the way that markets work, that covers contexts and questions where innovation is not the central force at work, as well as those where innovation is the heart of what is going on.

Schumpeter's great work focused on the former of these arenas. He never developed a general "price theory" of the sort that Marshall did. And a large share of the questions asked by economists are of the sort that price theory, and the tools that Marshall developed, addresses. I believe that Schumpeter's position, at least in his Theory of Economic Development, was that economists could work with two sets of theories: Schumpeter's regarding innovation and innovation driven economic change, and the developing neoclassical price theory for the topics and questions it seemed to fit. I believe many present day Schumpeterians take a similar position.

[16]Formal proofs of important aspects of this argument can be found in Chap. 7, "Firm and Industry Response to Changed Market Conditions" in Nelson and Winter (1982).

But with the wisdom of hindsight, one can see that it is very difficult for a Schumpeterian theory of innovation and a neoclassical price theory to co-exist broadly in the economics discipline. The central reason, I believe, is that to hold a Schumpeterian theory of dynamics and a neoclassical theory when change is not disruptive is schizophrenic.[17] Particularly as neoclassical theory tightened up and its theory of behavior increasingly stressed full rationality, the awkwardness of holding both theories became more and more evident. Economists are not about ready to give up the tools of price theory. And the development of a neoclassical theory of economic growth provided main line economists with a way of understanding economic behavior and activity under relatively tranquil conditions, and how technological change driven economic growth occurred, that were intellectually compatible.

Neo Schumpeterians and evolutionary economists are rightly pleased with the major advances in understanding of innovation and it sources and effects that have been won over the last 30 years by research guided by our perspective. But we have been frustrated by how little of that literature has been picked up by our main stream colleagues, even when they are writing about technological advance.

The argument I am making is that, if we are to have a chance of becoming a significant influence within academic economics, we Schumpeterians must articulate a theory that addresses both economic questions associated with innovation and innovation driven change, and economic questions of the sort that price theory deals with, with a consistency of viewpoint between the two. I propose that the kind of perspective on the behavior and cognition of economic actors that I have sketched above can enable us to do this.

References

Becker M (2004) Organizational routines: a review of the literature. Ind Corp Chang 13 (4):643–678

Cyert R, March J (1963) A behavioral theory of the firm. Prentice Hall, Englewood Cliffs

Dewey J (1992) Human nature and conduct. Henry Holt, Mineola

Diamond P, Vartianen H (eds) (2007) Behavioral economics and its applications. Princeton University Press, Princeton

Donald M (1991) Origins of the modern mind. Harvard University Press, Cambridge

Glenberg A, Witt J, Metcalfe J (2013) From the revolution to embodiment: 25 years of cognitive psychology. Perspect Psychol Sci 8:575–585

Hodgson G, Stoelhorst J (2014) Introduction to the special issue on the future of institutional and evolutionary economics. J Inst Econ 10:513–540

Kahneman D (2011) Thinking fast and slow. Macmillan, New York

Mazzoleni R, Nelson R (2013) An interpretive history of challenges to neoclassical microeconomics and how they have fared. Ind Corp Chang 22:1409–1451

Mitchell WC (1912) The backward art of spending money. Am Econ Rev 2:269–281

[17]For a more elaborate discussion see Nelson (2012).

Nelson R (2012) Why Schumpeter has had so little influence on today's main line economics and why this may be changing. J Evol Econ 22:901–916
Nelson R (2013) Demand, supply, and their interaction on markets as seen from the perspective of evolutionary economic theory. J Evol Econ 23:17–38
Nelson R, Consoli D (2010) An evolutionary theory of household behavior. J Evol Econ 20:665–687
Nelson R, Nelson K (2002) On the nature and evolution of human know-how. Res Policy 31:719–733
Nelson R, Winter S (1982) An evolutionary theory of economic change. Harvard University Press, Cambridge
Schumpeter J (1934) The theory of economic development. Harvard University Press, Cambridge
Simon H (1957) Models of man. Wiley, New York
Spender JC (1989) Industry recipes: the nature and sources of managerial judgment. Oxford University Press, Oxford, pp 373–397
Veblen T (1898) Why is economics not an evolutionary science? Q J Econ 12:373–397
Winter S (2013) Habit, deliberation, and action: strengthening the microfoundations of routines and capabilities. Acad Manag Perspect 27:120–137
Winter S (2014) The future of evolutionary economics: can we break out of the beachhead? J Inst Econ 10:613–644

Upward and Downward Complementarity: The Meso Core of Evolutionary Growth Theory

Kurt Dopfer, Jason Potts, and Andreas Pyka

Abstract We propose that the concept of complementarity can take two distinct meanings in evolutionary economics: one referring to Adam Smith's notion of increasing specialization and the division of labour, which we denote 'downward complementarity' (wholes into new parts); and a second type that refers to the discovery of emergent complementarity between extant or new components and products, which we call 'upward complementarity' (parts into new wholes). We outline this new conception and explore some of its analytic and theoretic implications.

1 Complementarity in Generic and Operant Analysis

Progress in science often takes the form of either: (a) realizing that things thought to be different are actually similar; or (b) realizing that things thought to be similar are actually different. Neoclassical economics is often at its best in the first mode seeking topological equivalence of the structure of different decision problems: for example when Theodore Schultz and Gary Becker showed that what appeared to be qualitatively different phenomena—investment in plant and factories and educating children—could both be studied as investment in capital. But evolutionary economists have long been at their best when operating in the second mode of elaborating differences. The basic Schumpeterian approach to economic dynamics distinguishes between growth that comes from without—or exogenous growth, as accumulated factors of production or new technologies—and growth that comes from within the economic system—endogenous growth through entrepreneurship and innovation. In evolutionary economics structure matters because there is no

K. Dopfer
University of St. Gallen, St. Gallen, Switzerland

J. Potts (✉)
RMIT University, Melbourne, Australia
e-mail: jason.potts@rmit.edu.au

A. Pyka
Hohenheim University, Stuttgart, Germany

A. Pyka, U. Cantner (eds.), *Foundations of Economic Change*, Economic Complexity and Evolution, DOI 10.1007/978-3-319-62009-1_4

representative actor. Neoclassical economics, in the work of Robert Lucas and Paul Romer in the late 1980s, took this distinction and (reverting to the first mode) sought to make it conceptually similar again in their capital investment theory of technological change in so-called endogenous growth theory which portrays economic growth without development because of freeze-framed structures. But along the Schumpeterian line of advance, the purpose of the new distinction between things once thought similar was to elaborate new mechanisms and processes—such as the role of the entrepreneur, or the process of creative destruction, or the changing composition of the industrial setting of an economy, or long-term technological waves (Nelson 2005; Foster et al. 2006; Perez 2009; Saviotti and Pyka 2013; Aghion et al. 2013).

It is instructive to consider why complementarity plays a special role in evolutionary economics. Whereas neoclassical economics can be said, to a first approximation at least, to be a general theory of substitution (all goods are substitutes), *evolutionary economics is to a first approximation a general theory of complementarity* (economic evolution is a process of generic change in economic connections). Potts (2000) explained how neoclassical economics is built on field-theoretic foundations in which 'everything is connected to everything else' and therefore the only way that dynamics can be expressed is through re-allocation on the basis of known knowledge. The reason that neoclassical economics is built around a generalized analysis of price coordination in markets is that this approach best expresses a framework of generalized substitution at the level of ongoing market operations. But this does not describe economic evolution, which Potts (2000) defines over a 'non-integral space' in which the elementary dynamic is change in the knowledge connections within the system. Economic evolution is thus not a general theory of substitution—i.e., a reorganization of who has what—but a general theory of complementarity—a reconfiguration of what is connected to what. This is the sense in which evolutionary economics is at base a theory of entrepreneurs and firms, which are the agents of such change (Nelson and Winter 1982; Nelson and Dosi 1994; Hanusch and Pyka 2007), or of knowledge as generic rules, which are the objects of such change (Dopfer and Potts 2008; Dias et al. 2014). Thus where neoclassical economics generalizes the notion that agents make substitutions in markets, evolutionary economics generalizes the notion that entrepreneurs create complementarity in firms (micro), sectors (meso) and the economy as a whole (macro). Obviously there are agents, firms and markets in both neoclassical and evolutionary economics, but in the same way that sub-stitution (at the margin) is fundamental analytic focus in neoclassical economics, the dynamics of complementarity are the fundamental focus in evolutionary economics. It follows that any basic classification of types of complementarity will ramify through evolutionary economics, yet may be rather incidental to neoclassical economics.

The purpose of this paper is to elaborate the core of a theory of long run economic growth by noting that the often singular conception of *complementarity*—which is used in supply-side analysis[1] as a way to recursively construct the division of labour and technology: the division of labour is a modular decomposition of a technology in an organization; a technology is an organization of complementary inputs—can actually be separated into two distinct meanings. We will call them '*downward complementarity*' and '*upward complementarity*' (Dopfer 2015). Downward complementarity is essentially Smithian and Marshallian—proceeding by division, differentiation and reorganization; but upward complementarity is essentially Schumpeterian, and can also be read in the work of Herbert Simon (1985)—proceeding by new combination or *cross-fertilization* among seemingly different inputs.

These two types of complementarity follow from a clear distinction between generic and operant levels of economic analysis (Dopfer et al. 2004; Dopfer 2005; Dopfer and Potts 2008)—between knowledge (the generic level of analysis, over *knowledge space*) and the operations that knowledge enables (the operant level of analysis, over *operant space*)—which is to say between economic operations on the one hand, such as production and consumption, and the knowledge upon which economic operations are performed. This distinction matters for evolutionary economic analysis because it is the generic knowledge level that evolves, and which, as we point out here, expresses two different meanings of complementarity. The generic knowledge space is the locus of evolution as continual change of structure of complementary knowledge. The operant space is the layer of ongoing operations that in the main embrace production, consumption and market transactions. Economic statics and economic dynamics deal with the layer of individual operations posited as a cumulated pay-off matrix and equilibrium in commodity space. Complexity-based evolutionary—i.e., *generic*—economics deals with the static and dynamic of operations *in relation to structure and evolution of knowledge*. At the generic layer the field of analysis is not operant but instead *generic static and generic dynamic.*

2 Meso: The Analytical Unit of Evolutionary Structure and Change

We can now advance two points: first, the phenomenon of complementarity governing economic operations resides in the generic knowledge layer; and, second, that both the static aspects of knowledge structure and the dynamic aspects of knowledge evolution represent major fields of theoretical investigation. The

[1]Complementarity is also defined on the demand side as the dual of substitution, specifically as a way of classifying goods in a preference ordering: two goods are substitutes or complements depending on whether cross-price elasticity is negative or positive. Neoclassical economics is an operational analysis of price coordination that expresses a framework of generalized substitution—viz. agents reallocate by making substitutions in markets.

question then is how to define an analytical unit of knowledge that captures both its structure and its evolutionary dynamic as they govern economic operations.

We suggest the concept of meso. The integrated core element is a knowledge 'bit'—a *generic rule* (Dopfer et al. 2004; Dopfer 2012; Dopfer and Potts 2008)—that is actualized by a population along a trajectory detailing the generation, adoption and retention of the rule. As a single (generic) rule meso is a *structure component*, for instance, a particular technology (a structured composite of technical rules) is a component part of a larger technological structure. As a rule trajectory, meso is a *process component*. The rule originates in a micro unit such as a firm and is adopted by other firms and retained—as a meso rule—for recurrent operations.

Many micro units make up a meso unit—they share a meso rule and are members of a meso population—and the meso unit is a component part of a structure and evolutionary process of macro. Meso is the core element of the resultant micro–meso–macro architecture. Downward and upward complementarity driving economic evolution as a process of continual restructuring of knowledge originates in and develops from *meso*.

3 Classical Economics Revisited

Adam Smith drew a comprehensive picture of the emerging modern market economy. Though he did not address expressly the distinction between the two kinds of complementarity or employ this exact language he did variously acknowledge the significance of both. Yet his theory of the dynamics of production clearly emphasized 'downward complementarity' as epitomized in his famous example of pin factory: the many specialized operations are the downwardly complementary parts, of which further subdivisions may be possible.

Adam Smith's specialization and the division of labour (as limited by the extent of the market) are the starting point for all exchange-based theories of long-run economic growth (classical, neoclassical and evolutionary alike). Downward complementarity emerges from a process of ongoing modularization that breaks or decomposes an extant whole into parts—which firms, consumers and markets then put back together again. This is a source of economizing gains, due to specialization at the level of the parts, resulting in greater efficiency at the level of the whole. This concept is developed and expressed for instance in Alfred Marshall's evolutionary conception of the firm (Raffaelli 2003); in Young (1928) conception of 'increasing returns'; and in Baumol et al. (1988) concept of 'economies of scope' when the costs of production of two or more goods produced together by the same firm are lower than the costs of producing them separately by specialized firms. This increasing variety at the modular level also drives increasing economic complexity at the level of substitute inputs and the economic space of adjacent technological possibilities (Hidalgo and Hausmann 2009).

Downward complementarity is an expression of technological organization and operational scale in firms, as coordinated in markets. It is the primary account of the wealth of nations as an economic process that takes place in firms and markets. At the core of this is a particular conception of complementarity in which a whole—say one of Smith's pins—is seen as a particular suite of complementary parts that can be modularized into an assembly of sub-systems—the drawing of wire, straightening, cutting, making and fixing the head, whitening, and so on, each step of which can be a target of specialization and scale. Smith's point was that by having different people specialize in these (complementary) stages, or parts, greater productive efficiency was gained in the manufacture of the whole (Leijonhufvud 2007). Ricardo and Marshall noted that this could extend to entire firms or even countries in the parts within a conception of a whole that is then reassembled within a firm, an industry, or by global trade. Downward complementarity, in this example, is a story about pins and the economic efficiency and productivity potential that lies latent in their structure of complementarity—the parts that compose a pin and the limits to which these can be decomposed.

Furthermore, the idea that downward complementarity might be the only sort of complementarity is a hazardous thing to believe. Because if you do, then it is also easy to believe that economic planning might extend to planning economic growth by seeking to rationalize all the economies of specialization, scale and scope that lie latent in the downward complementarities of any particular meso conception of an economy, i.e., within a given set of demanded outputs: this many guns, that much butter, this much wine, that much cloth, and so forth in the optimization of an economy conceived as an assembly line. The problem is that the downward-complementarity view misses half of the evolutionary dynamics of complementarity, and which lies in a completely different direction. From the meso perspective of pin factories, we bring into focus structure looking 'up' to see a web of upward complementarity with other meso wholes—perhaps garment makers, iron foundries, transport services, and so on—for which the pin factory meso is a part of a larger (macro) whole. These are both complementarities, but they are very different in their evolutionary expression. Yet both are essential in explaining long-run economic growth and development.

Upward complementarity calls for the task to assemble entities into a whole previously considered to be unrelated. The mode of analysis is mereology: the study of the logic of relationships between entities as parts of a whole (Antonelli 2011; Dopfer 2011; Dias et al. 2014). As an evolutionary process, upward complementarity is the creation of new wholes from extant or new parts, which is in the first instance a creative act of entrepreneurial vision. The idea of a re-combining agent is partly captured in models of recombination that form the conceptual underpinnings of endogenous growth theory (Romer 1990; Weitzman 1998) but these models retain a reductive sense of part and whole, such that recombination is reduced to a mere probability issue as if rules are combined and recombined through some mysterious agency.

4 Unified Evolutionary Growth Theory

Modern growth theory is built on factorial aggregates describing growth as input–output function on the basis of exogenous shocks and simultaneously restored equilibria. It deals with downward complementarity, yet suffers from the inherent methodological difficulty of dealing with non-linearity which complementarity usually implies (Arthur 2014). While the issue of non-linearity may be partly resolved by "linearizing" non-linear functions (Tinbergen 1991), the aggregate view applied in modern growth theory proves essentially inadequate when it comes to dealing with upward complementarity. The process of recombining entities into a new whole is entirely different from that of comparing various degrees of differentiation and specialization of extant knowledge, such as the subsequent downward-scaling of a given technological or institutional rule. Not only are static and dynamic 'totally different kinds of analysis', as Schumpeter famously remarked (Schumpeter 1908), but also is the dynamic based on upward and on downward complementarity of an entirely different nature.

A unified evolutionary growth theory must embrace and integrate both dimensions of complementarity if it is to give a complete account of economic growth. This builds on the well-established distinction between the exploitative and explorative orientation of research and development on a firm level introduced in management theory (March 1991). This distinction re-appears at the macro-level of growth theory which depends in the short run on the profitability of mature industries and in the long run from the creativity of emerging industries. A comparative view highlighting the essential features of the two kinds of complementarity and of their implications shall suffice here as a first step in erecting the theoretical edifice.

First, the conventional measure of economic performance—*efficiency*—may be reconsidered. Efficiency means to do an existing task better, say to improve the input–output ratio or capital coefficient. The measure of downward complementarity is typically efficiency. Performing the task of assembling individual entities into a new whole requires not only efficient behavior but also one that relates to the task of combining these entities, independent of whether or not that task is performed efficiently. The idea of efficiency cannot meaningfully be applied because of its inherent mereological feature. The criterion defining here the economic task is structural adaptability and the fitting of parts. The key performance measure therefore is *effectiveness* rather than efficiency (Dopfer 2005). The dynamic of upward complementarity builds primarily on the task of combining entities into a functioning new whole and calls for behavior that is effective.

Second, the distinction into downward and upward complementarity suggests two kinds of entrepreneurship. Entrepreneurship in the mode of the former is perhaps the most common form of entrepreneurial action, in that the agent is alert to opportunities that can be seen in firms or in markets to exploit inefficiencies (Kirzner 1999). It is a kind of 'activation trigger' (Zahra and George 2002) alert to the creative prospect of an opportunity (Kirzner 1999) arbitraging (hidden) inefficiencies. For upward complementarity we absolutely need to invoke some visionary agent—the entrepreneur in general, but it may also be a user, producer or consumer (von Hippel 1986)—because they are creating novelty (Witt 2009) by assembly of existing parts into new wholes. Entrepreneurship in the mode of upward complementarity is closer to Schumpeter's original heroic and visionary conception, but we represent it here more analytically as the assembly of parts into new wholes.

This suggests a new classification system of entrepreneurship that is consistent with but differs from the equilibrating versus dis-equilibrating axis, a.k.a. the Austrian model of alertness to an opportunity (Kirzner 1999; Shane 2000) versus the Schumpeterian model of a novelty generating, dis-equilibrating agent (Baumol 1990, 2015; Metcalfe 2004, 2014). It also differs from the 'fourth factor of production' approach associated with the Marshallian model of the firm (Casson 1982), as well as the Knightean model of entrepreneurship as a special type of decision-making, namely judgment under uncertainty (Shackle 1972; Foss and Klein 2012). The taxonomy of upward and downward complementarity makes sense of the complexity of the entrepreneurial function having all of these aspects simultaneously but each representing different aspects of meso structure and meso process. The exclusivity of each singular entrepreneurial ability must be considered as artificial. To be entrepreneurial requires that the right abilities are called for at the right stage of the entrepreneurial process. Furthermore, while entrepreneurship associated with upward complementarity is expected to have a positive effect along the lines of the new meso trajectory, it will also have a disruptive or destructive effect at the meso–macro level as existing meso structures are re-coordinated (Dopfer and Potts 2008). A better understanding of the types of complementarity leads us toward a more unified approach to evolutionary economics in general and entrepreneurship in particular.

Third, the concept of complementarity duality sheds new light on the nature of networks in general and of *innovation networks* in particular. A dynamic modern economy is characterized by a strong interrelatedness between heterogeneous agents and heterogeneous knowledge. So-called combined technologies are the rule rather than the exception (e.g., Teece 1986). In many cases firms are unable of keeping pace with the development of all relevant technologies and therefore, they seek access to external knowledge sources. As a consequence, innovation networks have gained increasing significance as a mean of generating and coordinating industrial research and development (R&D) when exploiting upward and downward complementarity (Pyka 2015).

The evolution of innovation networks can be described by the development of network density that measures the number of realized cooperative links for joint knowledge development in relation to the maximum number of relationships in a fully connected network. Agents focus on their core competences and combine them with core competences of other agents leading to an increase in the number of network linkages and/or the number of agents connected in the network. The network density increases or decreases accordingly. Rationale and motivation for engaging in network relationships will depend on the kind of complementarity agents decide to engage in.

The exploration of and engagement in upward complementarity are informed by the integration of new competences and actors in the network. Consequently, the integration of new actors leads to the emergence of network structure. Economic evolution becomes change stated in terms of increasing upward complementarities monitored by network relationships. Network density is generally decreasing in the stage of exploring upward complementarities. In contrast, following the downward course an increase in the number of network interrelationships will increase divisibility, number of production steps and scale size within a network, which with respect to size remains constant. Therefore, the network density is increasing in the case of the exploitation of downward complementarities. In both kinds of complementarity *quantitative* change stated as change in relative frequency of network relationships co-relates with *qualitative* change stated as change of structure.

Let us illustrate the theoretic distinction by way of an example. Innovation networks were first studied in the 1980s as a new form of organization of industrial R&D observed in pharmaceuticals (Pyka and Saviotti 2005). Large diversified pharmaceutical companies tried to get access to the new biotechnologies via cooperation with small dedicated biotechnology start-up firms. Acquiring competences in molecular biology and unlocking new extensive technological opportunities by exploring the possibilities of cross-fertilization between inherent and innovative knowledge has led to a particular focus on upward complementarities. The aim was to reinvigorate the innovative dynamics of an industry that relied on an expiring business model based on so-called block-busters medical compounds. Each of these was expected to provide financing for R&D for another round of block-busters self-sustaining the R&D process and profits over time. However, skyrocketing costs and various other factors related to R&D challenged this old business model. A completely new way of doing things was called forth and the advent of an industrial application of biotechnology offered promising opportunities.

Traditional industrial economics considers innovation networks as a merely temporary phenomenon. For instance, in the present case innovation networks would disappear as soon as the pharmaceutical companies have built up the new biotech competences. In this picture some of the small biotech companies may become the pharmaceutical firms of the future replacing the incumbents with their outdated competences. To cooperate with existing large firms aimed at generating new knowledge by way of discovering upward complementarities was out of imagination. The advent of molecular biology and its industrial application was considered as being simply a competence destroying technological change, not a *tool of sustained co-operation on the basis of increasing upward complementarities*. From the viewpoint of the traditional doctrine the early innovators were bound to become big, or to be swallowed, or to be wiped out. They were bound to be a temporary phenomenon. Nothing like that happened, and still in the second decade of the twenty-first century large pharmaceutical and small dedicated biotech firms sprightly co-exist and cooperate. A view of the development of the underlying network densities, which first decrease and then increase again, reveals the switch from the exploration of upward complementarities to the exploitation of downward complementarities.

Fourth, the approach also suggests two kinds of industrial dynamics. The filling out of an industry through ongoing specialization, which may extend outward through industrial districts and clusters through to global patterns of specialization and trade (Kling 2011), can be characterized as downward complementarity. This leads first to the establishment of a dominant design, which then is exploited by an increasingly more efficient industry, which simultaneously matures. But the creation of a new industry or sector of the economy is the process of upward complementarity in seeing complementarity between parts that can be assembled into a new whole. With the exploration of the technological opportunity space opened by the discovery of the upward complementarity new seeds for economic development are spread out which eventually lead to new and pronounced economic growth. Upward complementarities are the factorial re-combinations between technologies, products or services to create new technologies, products and services that result in new industries and sectors (Aldrich and Fiol 1994; Cantner and Graf 2006; Antonelli 2011; Tether and Stigliani 2012; Saviotti and Pyka 2013; Kerr et al. 2014). The result is a cumulative circular causation that is propelled by the dynamic of upward complementarities between the entrepreneurial discovery of novelty and the ongoing process of the division of labour (Sarasvathy 2001; Metcalfe 2001, 2014). Long run economic growth and development is propelled by the co-evolutionary link between upward and downward complementarities: With downward complementarity, the resources required to explore potential upward complementarities are set free for entrepreneurial discovery (Arthur 2014; Hidalgo and Hausmann 2009). Upward complementarity refreshes the opportunities for further development, which are exploited over time by the operationalization of the process of specialization. The rise of the so-called ‘sharing economy’ of internet-based platforms is an example of this. Long-run evolutionary economic development is thus an interactive process of both downward and upward complementarity.

Fifth, it follows from these two conceptions of entrepreneurship and two conceptions of industry dynamics that the distinction between downward and upward complementarity will also express in two kinds of industry and innovation policy as built around the different mechanisms and institutions that support these different forms of complementarity and division of labour. Downward complementarity seeks to develop clusters associated with coordination efficiencies, scale economies, incentives to invest in R&D and spillovers. Most contemporary innovation policy is built on the logic of downward complementarity addressing market failures and system failures in innovation investment. However, evolutionary economic policy can additionally be built on the logic of upward complementarity, but here it becomes a creativity-based and experimental discovery-based approach that seeks to build connections and to develop feedback loops between existing and new technologies (Hausmann and Rodrik 2003; Potts 2011; Bakhshi et al. 2011; Foster 2013; Teubal 2013; Safarzyńska et al. 2012; Blind and Pyka 2014; Yoguel and Pereira 2014; Nelson 2016). Instead of the incentive reducing interpretation of technological spillovers, upward complementarity focuses on the idea-creation effects of technological spillovers and collaborative knowledge sharing.

5 Upward Complementarity Is the Engine of Economic Evolution

Upward complementarity is in the long-run the prime engine of evolutionary economic growth and development. But the concept has arisen piecemeal and fragmented in such a way that it has been difficult to see all of various aspects as different views on the same underlying reality. The entrepreneurial aspect, the recombination aspect, the aspects that express the formation of new goods, markets, firms and industries are all different parts of a single story that can be captured with the concept of upward (as distinct from downward) complementarity.

Upward complementarity also got lost to some extent with the increasing emphasis on the short run. Upward complementarity occurs in a time-consuming process, which could be assumed away by focusing on short-term optimal decisions. As a conjecture about the long-run pattern of economic development, we can expect that the relative importance of upward complementarity, as a species of division of labour, will increase as the number of new consumer products increases, or as factor inputs (as structured wholes) are substituted increasingly by new ones. This is especially the case in the digital and software economy that allows greater modularity and prospects for recombination (Beinhocker 2011). But the broader implication is that a conception of upward complementarity is central to an evolutionary account of macroeconomic development, and indeed is likely to become more so with the increasing complexity of economic systems. It would seem to us, therefore, that concept and language of upward and downward complementarity serves as a useful addition to the analytic lexicon of evolutionary economics.

References

Aghion P, Akcigit U, Howitt P (2013) What do we learn from Schumpeterian growth theory? Mimeo, New York

Aldrich H, Fiol M (1994) Fools rush in? The institutional context of industry creation. Acad Manag Rev 19(4):645–670

Antonelli C (2011) The complexity of technological change: knowledge interaction and path dependence. In: Antonelli C (ed) Handbook on the economic complexity of technological change. Edward Elgar, Cheltenham

Arthur B (2014) Complexity economics. Oxford University Press, Oxford

Bakhshi H, Freeman A, Potts J (2011) State of uncertainty: innovation policy through experimentation. NESTA, London

Baumol W (1990) Entrepreneurship: productive, unproductive, and destructive. J Polit Econ 98 (5):893–921
Baumol W (2015) Joseph Schumpeter: the long run, and the short. J Evol Econ 25(1):37–44
Baumol W, Panzar J, Willig R (1988) Contestable markets and the theory of industry structure. Harcourt Brace, New York
Beinhocker E (2011) Evolution as computation: integrating self-organization with generalized Darwinism. J Inst Econ 7(3):393–423
Blind G, Pyka A (2014) The rule approach in evolutionary economics: a methodological template for empirical research. J Evol Econ 24(5):1085–1105
Cantner U, Graf H (2006) The network of innovators in Jena: an application of social network analysis. Res Policy 35(4):463–480
Casson M (1982) The entrepreneur: an economic theory. Oxford University Press, Oxford
Dias M, Pedrozo E, da Silva T (2014) The innovation process as a complex structure with multilevel rules. J Evol Econ 24(4):1067–1084
Dopfer K (2005) Evolutionary economics: a theoretical framework. In: Dopfer K (ed) The evolutionary foundations of economics. Cambridge University Press, Cambridge
Dopfer K (2011) Mesoeconomics: a unified approach to systems complexity and evolution. In: Antonelli C (ed) Handbook on the economic complexity of technological change. Edward Elgar, Cheltenham
Dopfer K (2012) The origins of meso economics: Schumpeter's legacy and beyond. J Evol Econ 22(1):133–160
Dopfer K (2015) Evolutionary economics. In: Faccarello G, Kurz H (eds) Handbook of the history of economic analysis, Schools of thought in economics, vol II. Edward Elgar, Cheltenham
Dopfer K, Potts J (2008) General theory of economic evolution. Routledge, London
Dopfer K, Foster J, Potts J (2004) Micro, meso macro. J Evol Econ 14:263–279
Foss N, Klein P (2012) Organizing entrepreneurial judgment. Cambridge University Press, Cambridge
Foster J (2013) Energy, knowledge and economic growth. J Evol Econ 24(2):209–238
Foster J, Metalfe JS, Ramlogan R (2006) Adaptive economic growth. Camb J Econ 30(1):7–32
Hanusch H, Pyka A (2007) Principles of Neo-Schumpeterian economics. Camb J Econ 31:275–289
Hausmann R, Rodrik D (2003) Economic development as self-discovery. J Dev Econ 72 (2):603–633
Hidalgo C, Hausmann R (2009) The building blocks of economic complexity. Proc Natl Acad Sci 106(26):10570–10575
Kerr W, Nanda R, Rhodes-Kropf M (2014) Entrepreneurship as experimentation. J Econ Perspect 28(3):25–48
Kirzner I (1999) Creativity and/or alertness: a reconsideration of the Schumpeterian entrepreneur. Rev Austrian Econ 11:5–17
Kling A (2011) Patterns of sustainable specialization and trade: a Smith-Ricardo theory of macroeconomics. Capital Soc 6(2):1–18
Leijonhufvud A (2007) The individual, the market and the division of labor in society. Capital Soc 2(2):1–19
March J (1991) Exploration and exploitation in organizational learning. Organ Sci 2(1):71–87
Metcalfe JS (2001) Evolutionary approaches to population thinking and the problem of growth and development. In: Dopfer K (ed) Evolutionary economics: program and scope. Kluwer, Dordrecht, pp 141–164
Metcalfe JS (2004) The entrepreneur and the style of modern economics. J Evol Econ 14:157–175
Metcalfe JS (2014) Capitalism and evolution. J Evol Econ 24(1):11–34
Nelson RR (2005) Technology, institutions, and economic growth. Harvard University Press, Cambridge, MA
Nelson RR (2016) Behavior and cognition of economic actors in evolutionary economics. J Evol Econ 26:737–751

Nelson RR, Dosi G (1994) An introduction to evolutionary theories in economics. J Evol Econ 4 (3):153–172
Nelson RR, Winter S (1982) An evolutionary theory of economic change. Harvard University Press, Cambridge
Perez C (2009) Technological revolutions and techno-economic paradigms. Camb J Econ 34 (1):185–202
Potts J (2000) The new evolutionary microeconomics. Edward Elgar, Cheltenham
Potts J (2011) Creative industries and economic evolution. Edward Elgar, Cheltenham
Pyka A (2015) Avoiding evolutionary inefficiencies in innovation networks. Prometheus 32:265–279
Pyka A, Saviotti PP (2005) The evolution of R&D networking in the biotechnology-based industries. Int J Entrep Innov Manag 5:49–68
Raffaelli T (2003) Marshall's evolutionary economics. Routledge, London
Romer P (1990) Endogenous technical change. J Polit Econ 98:71–102
Safarzyńska K, Frenken K, van den Bergh JCJM (2012) Evolutionary theorizing and modeling of sustainability transitions. Res Policy 41(6):1011–1024
Sarasvathy S (2001) Causation and effectuation: toward a theoretical shift from economic inevitability to entrepreneurial contingency. Acad Manag Rev 26(2):243–263
Saviotti PP, Pyka A (2013) The co-evolution of innovation, growth and demand. Econ Innov New Technol 22(5):461–482
Schumpeter JA (1908) Wesen und Hauptinhalt der theoretischen Nationalökonomie. Duncker & Humblot, Leibzig
Shackle GLS (1972) Epistemics and economics. Cambridge University Press, Cambridge
Shane S (2000) A general theory of entrepreneurship. Edward Elgar, Cheltenham
Simon H (1985) What do we know about the creative process? In: Kuhn R (ed) Frontiers in creative and innovative management. Ballinger, Cambridge, MA
Teece D (1986) Profiting from technological innovation: implications for integration, collaboration, licensing, and public policy. Res Policy 15:285–305
Tether B, Stigliani I (2012) Toward a theory of industry emergence: entrepreneurial actions to imagine, create, nurture and legitimate a new industry. Paper presented at DRUID
Teubal M (2013) Israel's ICT-oriented, high tech, entrepreneurial cluster of the 1990s: a systems/ evolutionary and strategic innovation policy perspective. KDI, Global Industry and Economy Forum, Seoul
Tinbergen J (1991) The functioning of economic research. J Econ Issues 25(1):33–38
von Hippel E (1986) Lead users: a source of novel product concepts. Manag Sci 32(7):791–805
Weitzman M (1998) Recombinant growth. Q J Econ 113(2):331–360
Witt U (2009) Propositions about novelty. J Econ Behav Organ 70(1–2):311–320
Yoguel G, Pereira M (2014) Industrial and technological policy: contributions from evolutionary perspectives to policy design in developing countries. Munich University, MPRA
Young A (1928) Increasing returns and economic progress. Econ J 38:527–542
Zahra S, George G (2002) Absorptive capacity: a review, reconceptualization, and extension. Acad Manag Rev 27:185–203

Part II
Aggregate Outcomes

Global Dynamics, Capabilities and the Crisis

Jan Fagerberg and Martin Srholec

Abstract The financial crisis started in 2007–2008, initially in the US, but its consequences have been felt throughout the global economy. However, its effects were far from uniform. While parts of Asia and Africa continued to grow fast, Europe experienced a large set back. This paper emphasizes three important factors: differences across countries in technological development; differences in capacities to exploit the opportunities offered by technology; and differences in the ability to compete in international market. A formal model, based on this approach, is developed and applied to data for 100 countries in the period 1997–2012. Empirical indicators reflecting the various factors are developed, a dataset constructed and econometric estimates of the model performed. The results are used to explore the factors behind the slowdown in economic growth, with a particular emphasis on the continuing stagnation in Europe. A major factor turns out to be the increased financialization of the economy. The negative effect of the growth of finance prior to the crisis is especially pronounced for the countries that suffered most during the crisis.

1 Introduction

The financial crisis started in 2007–2008, initially in the US, but its consequences have been felt throughout the global economy. However, although most countries in the world were affected in one way or another, the effects were far from uniform. While several industrializing countries in Asia and Africa continued to grow relatively fast, in Europe the financial crisis marked the transition to a period of

J. Fagerberg
Center for Technology, Innovation and Culture (TIK), University of Oslo, Oslo, Norway

IKE, Department of Business and Management, Aalborg University, Aalborg, Denmark

CIRCLE, Lund University, Lund, Sweden

M. Srholec (✉)
CIRCLE, Lund University, Lund, Sweden

CERGE-EI, Economics Institute, Czech Academy of Sciences, Prague, Czech Republic
e-mail: martin.srholec@circle.lu.se

A. Pyka, U. Cantner (eds.), *Foundations of Economic Change*, Economic Complexity and Evolution, DOI 10.1007/978-3-319-62009-1_5

stagnation and—in parts of the continent—outright decline. This paper is concerned with the explanation of such differences in performance. What are the most relevant factors? Do they work in the same way during the downturn as before the crisis struck? If not, what are the implications?

In addressing these questions, we analyze global growth from a perspective that emphasizes three, interacting factors. The first has to do with technological development, the levels of which differ enormously around the globe. As emphasized by a series of economists and economic historians (Veblen 1915; Cornwall 1976; Abramovitz 1986; Maddison 1991), countries that lag technologically have a potential for high growth through exploitation of more advanced technology already in use elsewhere. But having a large potential for growth is not sufficient; it also needs to be taken advantage of in practice, and for this a country's capacity for doing so has proven to be essential (Gerschenkron 1962). Such national capacities, which have invariably been called "social capability" (Abramovitz 1986), "national technological capability" (Lall 1992) or "social filter" (Rodríguez-Pose 1999), also vary. Thus, the gap in national capacities is the second factor taken into account here. Third, in a global world, a country's growth is also influenced by how what it produces is assessed by customers all over the world, i.e., competiveness (Fagerberg 1988). Failing to meet the required standards, trade and current account deficits may occur, and this may—at least in the longer run—hamper growth (Thirlwall 1979; Kaldor 1981).

Section 2 lays out the facts about global growth from the early 1990s onwards for a sample of 100 countries at different levels of development. A formal model, based on the above approach, is outlined in Sect. 3. Then, in Sect. 4, empirical indicators reflecting the three factors are developed, and a panel dataset constructed, the final period of which covers the financial crisis. The estimation of the model is carried out with particular attention to the possibility of changes in the way variables work across time, such as a different impact during the crisis. The estimated model is then used to explore the factors behind the slowdown in economic growth since the outbreak of the financial crisis. The final section sums up the lessons with respect to the impact on global dynamics and considers the implications for the future research agenda in this area.

2 The Stylized Facts: The Global Economy Before and After the Crisis

Although economists and historians of different leanings, from Veblen (1915) via Gerschenkron (1962) to Solow (1956), often have been very positive in their assessments of the prospects for convergence in productivity and income in the global economy, in practice it has not always worked out that way. In fact, some periods have seen a lot of convergence, such as the decades following the end of the Second World War, while, in other periods, it has been more or less absent. For

Table 1 Annual GDP growth, four periods, 1992–2012

	N	1992–1997	1997–2002	2002–2007	2007–2012
Northern EU and EFTA	14	2.9	3.2	3.1	−0.1
Southern EU	6	2.7	3.3	2.6	−1.1
Eastern EU	11	2.3	3.7	6.1	−0.1
Other developed	9	4.8	3.2	3.9	2.1
Other former socialist	10	−4.2	4.4	7.5	2.6
Latin America	14	3.9	1.5	5.3	3.0
Eastern Asia	6	7.0	3.4	6.8	5.3
Southern Asia	4	5.0	4.3	6.7	5.6
Middle East and North Africa	8	4.0	3.7	5.8	3.3
Sub-Saharan Africa	18	3.7	4.1	5.5	5.0
World	100	3.0	3.4	5.2	2.5
Testing for β-convergence: Log of GDP per capita	100	−0.33 (0.21)	−0.39 (0.15)**	−0.66 (0.16)***	−1.39 (0.15)***

See Table 2 for source and definition of GDP growth. N is the number of countries. Countries included in the groups are listed in Appendix Table 7. Robust standard errors are in parentheses. *, **, *** denote significance at the 10, 5 and 1% levels

example there was a virtual standstill in the 1980s and 1990s, leading Easterly (2001) to characterize these years as "lost decades" for development.

Nevertheless, important changes were taking place in the global economy around that time, which eventually would lead to higher growth, particularly in the developing part of the world, and more convergence. Technological change, particularly in ICTs, spurred the emergence of new business models facilitating coordination of activities on a global scale, as did advancements in transport technology. Moreover, the gradual integration of previously Socialist economies in Asia and Europe into the capitalist world economy added many new workers and even more consumers. The combination of these two trends resulted in rapidly increasing trade and higher economic growth in large parts of the world.

Table 1 reports growth of GDP for ten country groups in four consecutive time periods from 1992 onwards. As the table shows, global growth was particularly strong during the years preceding the outbreak of the financial crisis, with most low income countries growing substantially faster than the developed part of the world. However, since that time, growth has been sluggish. On average, the rate of GDP growth was more than halved between 2002–2007 and 2007–2012. The slowdown has been far from uniform, though. While many countries in Asia and Africa were only marginally affected and continued to catch up with the developed world at a rapid rate, Europe experienced a large set back. As a result, global convergence was particularly strong after the crisis struck.

The diversity in performance is also evident from Fig. 1, which plots growth before the crisis (2002–2007) on the horizontal axis against growth in the years that followed (2007–2012, vertical axis). This leads to a division of the countries into four quadrants, depending on their growth performance. The countries in the upper

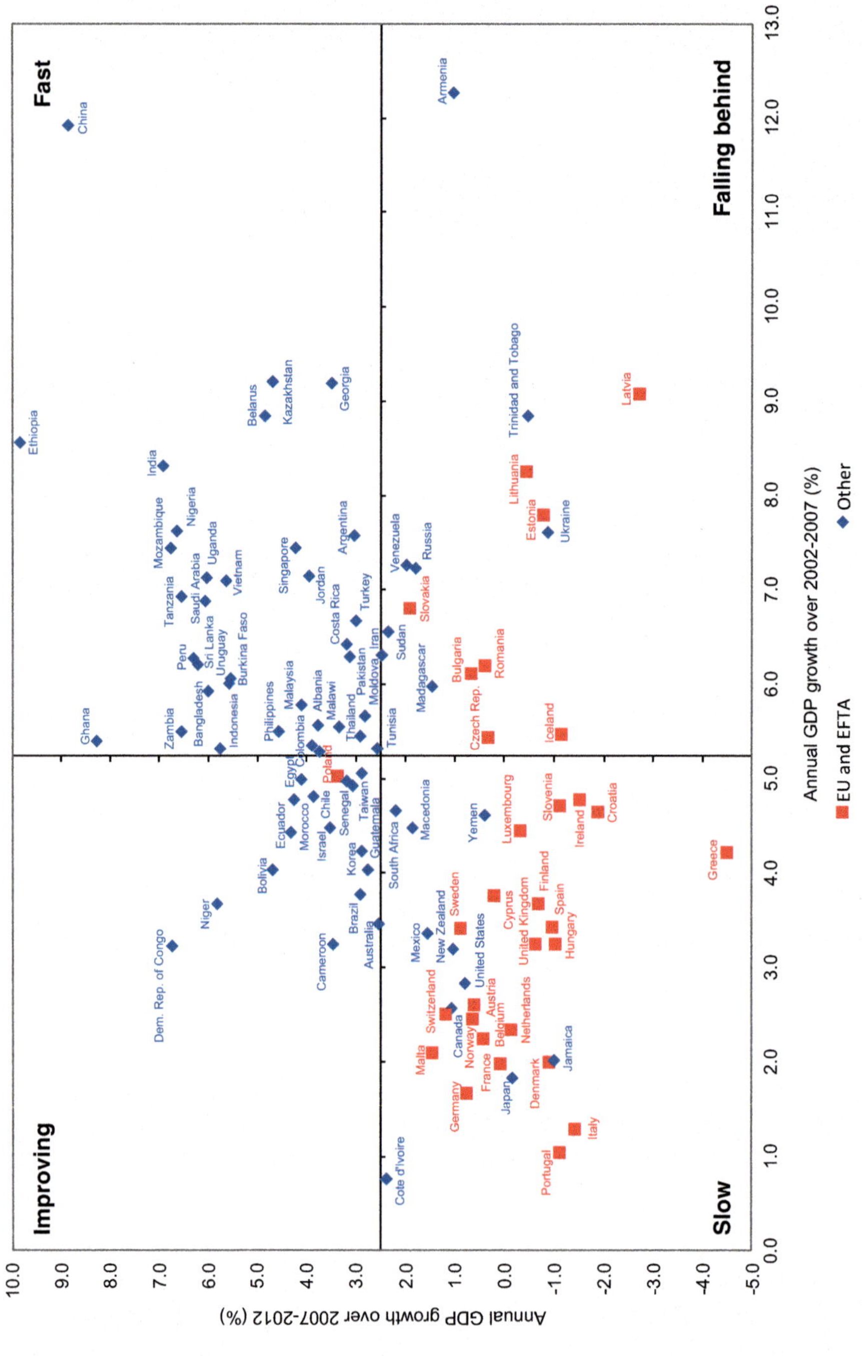

Fig. 1 Growth before and after the financial crisis

right quadrant ("Fast") are those that performed above average in both periods. Asian and African countries dominate in this category. Among the Asian countries, China is arguably in a class of its own, but India and Vietnam also experienced fast growth in both periods. On the African continent, Ethiopia, Nigeria, Mozambique, Tanzania and Uganda may be mentioned as examples of fast-growing economies. Those in the upper left quadrant ("Improving") consist of countries that, at least in relative terms, improved their growth performance after the crisis struck. Several countries in Africa and South America belong to this category. In contrast, the countries in the bottom left quadrant grew at a below average rate in both periods ("Slow"). Most European countries and other developed economies are to be found here. Finally, in the bottom right quadrant ("Falling behind") we find the countries that were most severely affected by the crisis, i.e., previously fast growing countries that now perform below average. A number of previously socialist countries in Eastern Europe and elsewhere are included here.

Hence, the impression of a "global" economic crisis is to some extent misleading. Clearly, Europe has slid into stagnation and the change is especially evident for the countries of Eastern Europe, which grew fast and caught up rapidly prior to the crisis. However, although most countries were affected to some extent, many developing countries continued to grow and catch up with the developed part of the world at a rapid rate.

3 Analyzing Global Growth: A Formal Model

To analyze the diversity in growth performances highlighted above, we use a framework that allows for the interaction of three important factors, namely differences across countries in technological development, in capacities to exploit the opportunities offered by technology and, finally, in the ability to compete in international market and the repercussions that this may have on a country's growth. The model builds on previous work by Fagerberg (1988) and Fagerberg et al. (2007).[1]

Consider a two-economy model, in which one country interacts with the "rest of the world". Let exports be X, imports be M and W be world (foreign) demand, all measured in terms of volume. In addition, we take into account the country's level of technological development (T) and its (social) capacity to exploit technology commercially (C), and we also allow for the possible impact of differences in price competitiveness (P), i.e., relative prices on tradeables in common currency.

[1]However, while this earlier work assumed strictly balanced trade, the model presented below allows for deviations from this rule.

The exports of a country can be expressed as:

$$X = f(T, C, P, W), \tag{1}$$

where T, C, P is technology, capacity and price competitiveness in country i, relative to the world: $T = \frac{T_i}{T_{world}}, C = \frac{C_i}{C_{world}} P = \frac{P_i}{P_{world}}$

Since imports in this model are the "world's" exports, we can model imports in the same way, noting that the competitiveness variables in this case are the inverse of those in Eq. (1) and that domestic demand (Y) replaces world demand:

$$M = g\left(\frac{1}{T}, \frac{1}{C}, \frac{1}{P}, Y\right) \tag{2}$$

If we take world demand and technology, capacity and price competitiveness as given, Eqs. (1)–(2) give us two relationships between three endogenous variables (Y, X and M). To solve the model for, say, GDP growth we need an additional constraint linking growth to trade. It is common to assume in the literature that there exist economic mechanisms[2] that prevent a country from continuing on paths that would not be sustainable in the long run, such as accumulating ever-increasing debt or claims on a grand scale vis-à-vis the rest of the world. A simple way to take this into account, suggested by Thirlwall (1979), would be to assume strictly balanced trade. However, in the real world, deviations from this requirement do occur and such deviations arguably have economic effects that should be taken into account. For the sake of realism, we will therefore allow the balance (B), defined as the ratio between the value of exports and that of imports, to vary:

$$B = \frac{XP}{M} \tag{3}$$

Our expectation is that, in the longer run, dY/dB $>$ 0, which means that an increase in the deficit will have a negative effect on growth (and vice versa).

Technology does not only depend on national sources *(N)* but also on diffusion (D) from abroad:

$$T = h(N, D). \tag{4}$$

It will be assumed, as is common in many models, that the contribution from diffusion of technology from abroad follows a logistic curve (Metcalfe 1988). This implies that the contribution is an increasing function of the distance between the level of technology appropriated in the country and that of the country on the technological frontier. Hence, for the frontier country, this contribution will be zero by definition.

[2]This may occur through adjustments of the fiscal and monetary policy stance, but it may also be the result of the working of markets, such as the capital, labor and currency markets.

Let the total amount of technology, adjusted for differences in country size (e.g., per capita), in the frontier country and the country under consideration, be T_* and T_i respectively and let d be the rate of growth of knowledge diffused to the region from the outside world (D):

$$d = \gamma - \gamma T^{gap}, where\, T^{gap} = \frac{T_i}{T_*} \tag{5}$$

By totally differentiating (1)–(5), substituting and rearranging, we arrive at the following solution for growth of GDP, using small case letters for growth rates (e.g., $y = \mathrm{d}Y/Y$ etc.)[3]:

$$\begin{aligned} y = \gamma\, \varepsilon_{TD} \frac{\varepsilon_{XT} + \varepsilon_{MT}}{\varepsilon_{MY}} - \gamma \quad \varepsilon_{TD} \frac{\varepsilon_{XT} + \varepsilon_{MT}}{\varepsilon_{MY}} T^{gap} + \varepsilon_{TN} \frac{\varepsilon_{XT} + \varepsilon_{MT}}{\varepsilon_{MY}} n \\ + \frac{\varepsilon_{XC} + \varepsilon_{MC}}{\varepsilon_{MY}} c + \frac{\varepsilon_{XP} + \varepsilon_{MP} + 1}{\varepsilon_{MY}} p - \frac{1}{\varepsilon_{MY}} b + \frac{\varepsilon_{XW}}{\varepsilon_{MY}} w \end{aligned} \tag{6}$$

where $\varepsilon_{YT} = \frac{\partial Y}{\partial T}\frac{T}{Y}$ refers to the partial elasticity of GDP with respect to technology (similar for other variables).

Hence, following this approach the growth of a country depends on five factors: (1) the potential for exploiting technology developed elsewhere, which depends on the country's level of technological development relative to the world frontier, this potential being largest for less-developed countries; (2) domestic efforts to increase the technological capability of the country; (3) change in the (social) capacity to exploit knowledge; (4) change in relative prices in common currency[4]; (5) change in the trade balance (as reflected by the exports to imports ratio); and (6) growth of world demand.

In the following, we are going to exploit this framework to assess the impact of each of these explanatory factors on economic growth. We will do this in the form of a regression of indicators reflecting the right hand side variables in (6), which will be treated as exogenous, on the dependent variable. Reverse causation, from economic growth to the various factors assumed to explain it, cannot be excluded a priori, but is considered less likely.[5] However, to reduce the possibility of simultaneity bias as much as possible, a one period lag between the explanatory factors and economic growth is introduced. The exception to this rule is growth of world

[3]See Appendix 4 for details on how Eq. (6) was derived.

[4]As can be seen from Eq. (6), the expected sign of the effects of changing relative prices on growth depends on whether or not the so-called Marshall-Lerner condition is satisfied.

[5]We hold it as unlikely that changes in a country's technological capability and social capacity can be seen as mere reflections of its rate of economic growth. A stronger case may exist for an effect of economic growth on price growth, since the price-level by definition is a relation between the value and quantity of what is produced. However, the largest share of value added consists of wages, which often are determined through negotiations of various sorts, and subject to influence by institutions, politics etc., which we in the present context have chosen to consider as exogenous.

demand, which is assumed to have an instantaneous relationship with economic growth.[6]

4 Explaining the Diversity

To study global growth, a dataset with broad country coverage, relevant and reliable information, and long time series is desirable. In practice, broad country coverage may easily come into conflict with the latter. For example, some types of data, such as R&D statistics, are often not available on an annual basis. Furthermore, time-series going back much longer than the mid-1990s may be problematic for the former socialist countries. Hence, the dataset used here contains 100 countries between 1997 and 2012. Since annual data were not always available, a panel of three periods was constructed: 1997–2002; 2002–2007; and 2007–2012. In a few cases, there were missing data points that had to be estimated.[7]

Table 2 gives the definitions and sources. As an approximation to the growth rates of the theoretical model, log differences were used, whenever appropriate.[8] While some of the variables are reasonably straightforward to measure, other variables—especially the growth of technology and (social) capacity—require careful consideration. For the level of technological development we use, as is common in the literature,[9] a broad productivity measure, i.e., GDP per capita. Regarding the growth of domestic technological capability, we use a broad set of indicators reflecting aspects such as the quality of science and engineering, invention, R&D expenditure and capabilities in ICT.

Factor analysis was used to summarize the growth of the technology indicators taken into account here into a synthetic measure, which we for convenience label "Technology". The results of the analysis are reported in Table 3. One eigenvalue higher than unity (1.51), explaining 37.7% of the total variance, was retained. As the table shows, the four indicators taken into account are closely correlated, lending support to the procedure.

In the case of the growth of (social) capacities, we include the three aspects particularly emphasized by Abramovitz (1986, 1994a, b), namely, the supply of

[6]In principle, this increases the possibility for reverse causation. Arguably, most countries are too small to have a significant influence on world demand. Nevertheless, there may be a few countries among the one hundred taken into account here for which this assumption can be questioned, and we will test for the sensitivity of the estimates to this.

[7]Missing observations were estimated using the impute procedure in Stata 11.2, for more information see Stata (2005, pp. 217–221). The procedure, which is regression-based, uses information from other variables in the data set to fill in missing values. This applies to the following cases (% of estimated observations in brackets): R&D expenditures (11%); gross tertiary enrolment (1%); quality of bureaucracy (9%), freedom from corruption (1%) and external debt (10%).

[8]If necessary unity was added to avoid logs of zero.

[9]See Fagerberg (1994) for an overview and discussion.

Table 2 Variables, data and sources

Label	Name	Description	Source
Y	GDP	GDP (USD converted to 2013 price level with updated 2005 EKS PPPs)	Conference Board (2014)
T^{gap}	Gap	$\ln(T_i/T_{us})$; T is GDP per capita (USD converted to 2013 price level with updated 2005 EKS PPPs), the frontier is represented by the United States	Conference Board (2014)
N	Technology	Scientific and engineering articles (per mil. people)	National Science Board (2012, 2014)
N	Technology	USPTO utility patents granted (per mil. people)	USPTO (2014)
N	Technology	R&D expenditures (% of GDP)	UNESCO (2014), OECD (2014), Castellacci and Natera (2011) and national sources
N	Technology	Internet users (per 100 people)	World Bank (2014)
C	Education	Gross tertiary enrolment ratio (%)	UNESCO (2014) and World Bank (2014)
C	Governance	Quality of bureaucracy (index)	Kaufmann et al. (2014) based on Economist Intelligence Unit
C	Governance	Freedom from corruption (index)	Heritage Foundation (2014), based on the Corruption Perceptions Index by Transparency International
C	Governance	Judicial independence (index)	Kaufmann et al. (2014), based on Global Insight Business Condition and Risk Indicators
C	Finance	Domestic credit to private sector (% of GDP)	World Bank (2014)
P	Price	Real effective exchange rate	Darvas (2012)
B	Trade balance	Export–import ratio of goods and services (in current USD)	World Bank (2014)
W	Demand	Demand index (for details see Footnote 5)	UNCTAD (2014)

Variable symbols (the first column) refer to the theoretical model, while variable names in second column refer to the empirical model below

skills (education), access to finance and the quality of governance. The latter is measured by three different indicators (based on surveys and expert assessments) reflecting the quality of bureaucracy, freedom from corruption and the working of the legal system, respectively. In these data, countries are ranked on a fixed-point scale, which makes calculation of growth rates problematic. Hence, for these three indexes, changes from one period to the next were used instead. As previously, factor analysis was used to synthesize the evidence into one, common variable, "Governance" (Table 4). One eigenvalue higher than unity (1.23), explaining 41.2% of the total variance, was retained. As in the previous case, the selected indicators turned out to be closely correlated.

Table 3 Technology: results of the factor analysis

	Factor loadings
Scientific and engineering articles (per mil. people)	0.63
USPTO patent grants (per mil. people)	0.71
R&D expenditures (% of GDP)	0.68
Internet users (per 100 people)	0.39
Number of observations	200

The extraction method is principal-component factors based on pooled data of growth rates in 100 countries in 1997–2002 and 2002–2007, hence 200 observations in total. Due to the choice of a one period lag in the estimated model, and in order to avoid unnecessary estimation of missing values for the most recent year, only data for the two first periods is used here

Table 4 Governance: results of the factor analysis

	Factor loadings
Quality of bureaucracy	0.68
Freedom from corruption	0.64
Judicial independence	0.61
Number of observations	200

The extraction method is principal-component factors based on pooled data of changes in the quality of governance for 100 countries in 1997–2002 and 2002–2007, hence 200 observations in total. Due to the choice of a one period lag in the estimated model, and in order to avoid unnecessary estimation of missing values for the most recent year, only data for the two first periods are used here

Growth of world demand is computed by weighting the growth of global demand by product (g_j) with the initial composition (specialization) of each country's exports (s_{ij})[10]:

$$w_i = \sum_{j=1}^{m} \left(g_j \times s_{ij}\right), s_{ij} = \frac{X_{ij}^{t-1}}{\sum_{j=1}^{m} X_{ij}^{t-1}} \text{ and } g_j = \ln\left(\sum_{i=1}^{n} X_{ij}^{t}\right) - \ln\left(\sum_{i=1}^{n} X_{ij}^{t-1}\right), \quad (7)$$

where X_{ij} denotes country's $i(i = 1 \ldots n)$ exports of a product group j ($j = 1 \ldots m$) and t is time. A high score indicates favorable demand conditions for a country's exports.

The empirical model to be estimated, which corresponds to the theoretical model derived above, is:

[10] Both merchandise trade and trade in services are included. While merchandise trade is used at 3-digit level of SITC, rev. 3, with 255 product categories, the available data on trade in services only allow us to distinguish three service categories (transport, travel and other services).

$$\Delta \text{GDP} = a_0 + a_1 \text{Gap} + a_2 \Delta \text{technology} + a_3 \Delta \text{education} + a_4 \Delta \text{governance} + a_5 \Delta \text{finance} + a_6 \Delta \text{price} + a_7 \Delta \text{trade balance} + a_8 \Delta \text{world demand} + a_i X_i + e_i \quad (8)$$

where X_i is a set of control variables and e_i is the error term.

As noted above, these core variables, except the "Gap", were used in the estimates in log-differences or changes (denoted by "Δ"). With the exception of growth of world demand, the independent variables were lagged one period to reduce simultaneity bias in the estimates. This restricts the number of periods included in the estimations to two, which implies that panel data estimation techniques are not suitable. However, to reduce the possible omitted variable bias as much as possible, a set of control variables, reflecting differences in economic structure, geography, nature and culture (see Appendix Table 8 for their definitions and sources),[11] were added to the model.

Table 5 reports the estimates.[12] The results are broadly consistent with the theoretical model. As expected, differences across the globe in levels of technological development, given by the gap variable, present poorer countries with promising opportunities, the realization of which requires continuous upgrading of technological and social capabilities. The important role played by world demand for growth is confirmed. As expected, deviations from balanced trade tend to be followed by a correction. Price competitiveness is, consistent with earlier studies (Fagerberg 1988; Fagerberg et al. 2007), found to be of minor importance. The results are robust to the inclusion of control variables (Table 5, column 2) and to the exclusion of the two largest economies in the world, the USA and China (for which the usual small-country assumption is questionable). The estimates of the crisis (2007–2012) dummy are insignificant in all cases. Finally, the model was re-estimated by a regression method robust to outliers, using the procedure suggested by Li (1985). The results are very similar to those reported in the paper.[13]

However, in contrast to previous research (Fagerberg and Srholec 2008), an increase in a country's financial capacity (as reflected in private credit) was not found to have a significant positive effect on growth. A similar finding has been reported by Arcand et al. (2015) in a cross-country study of finance and economic growth over the period 1990–2010. A possible explanation for this finding is that, while access to finance may be essential for growth and development, "too much

[11] Several other potentially relevant control variables were tested for possible inclusion in the model. However, as the estimated coefficients did not come out anywhere close to being significant at conventional levels, they were not retained in the model. This includes the size of government (general government final consumption expenditure as % of GDP), income inequality as measured by the Gini index, access to ocean or navigable rivers, Köppen–Geiger ecozones, Holdridge life zones and the composition of religious adherence.

[12] Beta values are reported, i.e. the variables enter the analysis with mean of zero and standard deviation of one, thus the estimated coefficients refer to the impact of change by one standard deviation.

[13] Results from these additional tests are available from the authors on request.

Table 5 Explaining GDP growth (pooled OLS for periods 2002–2007 and 2007–2012)

	(1)		(2)		(3)		(4)		(5)		(6)	
	Basic model		With control variables		With interaction between the growth and level of finance		With interaction between the growth of trade balance and level of external debt		With interaction between the growth of finance and the crisis dummy		Full model	
Gap	−0.44	(7.89)***	−0.53	(5.94)***	−0.48	(5.16)***	−0.52	(6.10)***	−0.58	(6.56)***	−0.52	(6.16)***
Δ technology	0.15	(2.95)***	0.10	(1.99)**	0.11	(2.17)**	0.10	(1.95)*	0.12	(2.35)**	0.13	(2.53)**
Δ education	0.12	(2.54)**	0.12	(2.48)**	0.11	(2.28)**	0.11	(2.30)**	0.11	(2.53)**	0.10	(2.12)**
Δ governance	0.15	(2.77)***	0.14	(2.99)***	0.13	(2.81)***	0.13	(2.78)***	0.14	(2.91)***	0.12	(2.54)**
Δ finance	−0.07	(1.32)	−0.08	(1.51)	0.10	(1.30)	−0.07	(1.38)	0.08	(1.47)	0.29	(2.71)***
Δ price	−0.03	(0.64)	−0.04	(0.76)	−0.03	(0.53)	−0.02	(0.42)	−0.02	(0.45)	0.01	(0.11)
Δ trade balance	0.16	(2.90)***	0.15	(3.22)***	0.14	(3.01)***	−0.38	(1.63)	0.13	(2.60)***	0.41	(1.54)
Δ demand	0.41	(7.38)***	0.49	(3.48)***	0.48	(3.57)***	0.48	(3.50)***	0.43	(3.24)***	0.41	(3.23)***
Natural disasters			−0.09	(2.23)**	−0.10	(2.39)**	−0.09	(2.23)**	−0.08	(1.91)*	−0.09	(2.09)**
Malaria			−0.19	(2.54)**	−0.17	(2.26)**	−0.19	(2.50)**	−0.22	(2.85)***	−0.19	(2.54)**
Oil and gas			−0.23	(3.54)***	−0.24	(3.64)***	−0.25	(3.72)***	−0.21	(3.34)***	−0.23	(3.61)***
External debt			−0.14	(2.22)**	−0.14	(2.32)**	−0.15	(2.47)**	−0.12	(1.93)*	−0.13	(2.29)**
Industry			0.13	(1.92)*	0.12	(1.73)*	0.15	(2.18)**	0.15	(2.30)**	0.16	(2.37)**
Cultural diversity			0.14	(2.76)***	0.13	(2.55)**	0.14	(2.82)***	0.15	(2.93)***	0.14	(2.78)***
Crisis (2007–2012) dummy			0.06	(0.45)	0.05	(0.35)	0.04	(0.32)	0.09	(0.66)	0.09	(0.70)
Δ finance × finance					−0.21	(2.67)***					−0.22	(2.46)**
Δ trade balance × external debt							0.54	(2.36)**			0.53	(2.02)**
Δ finance × crisis (2007–2012) dummy									−0.26	(3.70)***	−0.28	(4.08)***

F-test	28.61***		22.19***		24.15***		21.79***		23.79***		19.95***	
R^2	0.56		0.64		0.65		0.65		0.66		0.69	
Number of countries	100		100		100		100		100		100	
Number of observations	200		200		200		200		200		200	

See Table 2 and Appendix Table 8 for sources and definitions. Beta values are reported. Absolute values of robust t-statistics are in parentheses. *,**,*** denote significance at the 10, 5 and 1% levels finance" may actually be a bad thing, because it may lead to increased volatility and crowding out of resources from other sectors of the economy. If so, the contribution from an increase in financial capability to economic growth should be expected to depend on the level of financial capability. We test for this by introducing an interaction variable between the growth of financial capability and its level. The interaction variable is found to have a significant, negative impact on economic growth (Table 5, column 3), which is consistent with the thesis of diminishing returns to further increases in the size of the financial sector for countries in which this sector is already fairly well developed.[14]

Moreover, an interaction variable between the growth of the external balance and the level of country's foreign debt was added to test for the possibility that the strength of the correction following a change in the external balance depends on the country's degree of indebtedness. The argument is that countries with a high debt may be under much stronger pressure to restore the external balance through adjustments in the macro-economic policy stance than countries with little or no debt, and hence more freedom to pursue the policies they want. The result confirms (Table 5, column 4) that the correction is indeed much stronger in countries with high debt.

Taking the basic model as the point of departure, we also tested for the possibility that there are differences over time in the way the various variables work. This was done for one variable at a time, by allowing the estimated coefficient to vary between the pre-crisis and crisis period (see Appendix Table 9 for the results). Only one highly significant difference was found, for finance, the impact of which changed from positive (though not significant) to strongly negative (and significantly so) after the crisis struck (Table 5, column 5).[15]

The model with the highest explanatory power is reported in the final column in (Table 5, column 6). This model includes the interaction terms for the growth and level of finance and for the growth of trade balance and the level of external debt, and allows the impact of finance to differ between the two periods. The results suggest that there has been a change in the relationship between finance and economic growth. Before the crisis, increases in financial capability had a positive impact on growth for the majority of countries in our sample. This effect was particularly pronounced in developing countries with poorly developed financial capabilities. However, with the crisis, this positive impact completely disappears.

Table 6 provides a prediction of the slowdown in GDP growth based on the estimated model (Table 5, column 6). For most of the country groups, particularly

[14]Arcand et al. (2015) suggest that the effect of financial development (F), measured in different ways, on economic growth should be modelled as $F = a_1 S + a_2 S^2$, where S is an indicator of the size of the financial sector. However, according to the model developed in this paper, it is the growth of financial capability, not its initial level, that should be expected to affect subsequent economic growth, and this leads to a different specification. Note that, by totally differentiating F we get $dF = a_1 dS + 2 a_2 S dS$, i.e., the two terms included in the model here.

[15]We also tested for a possible change in the impact of the interaction terms [(Δ finance × finance) and (Δ trade balance × external debt)] during the crisis; however, this hypothesis was not supported.

Table 6 Explaining the slowdown in annual GDP growth after 2007 (difference between the 2007–2012 and 2002–2007 periods)

	N	Actual slowdown	Predicted slowdown	Estimated contributions								
				Gap	Technology	Education	Finance	Governance	Price	Trade balance and debt	Demand	Other
Northern EU and EFTA	14	−3.1	−3.7	0.0	−0.6	−0.1	−0.7	−0.2	0.0	−0.4	−2.2	0.7
Southern EU	6	−3.7	−2.8	0.0	0.0	0.0	−0.6	−0.2	0.0	−0.5	−2.0	0.5
Eastern EU	11	−6.2	−4.0	−0.3	−0.2	−0.2	−1.5	0.1	0.0	−0.3	−2.3	0.6
Other developed	9	−1.8	−2.6	−0.1	−0.5	0.0	−0.1	0.0	0.0	0.0	−2.0	0.1
Other former socialist	10	−4.9	−5.0	−0.3	−0.1	−0.1	−2.1	0.1	0.0	−0.4	−2.5	0.3
Latin America	14	−2.3	−2.1	−0.1	0.0	0.0	−0.2	0.1	0.0	−0.2	−2.2	0.5
Eastern Asia	6	−1.6	−1.7	−0.2	0.0	−0.2	−0.3	0.2	0.0	0.0	−1.9	0.6
Southern Asia	4	−1.1	−1.3	−0.2	0.2	0.3	−0.5	0.0	0.0	−0.1	−1.6	0.7
Middle East and North Africa	8	−2.5	−2.4	−0.1	0.1	0.0	−0.5	0.0	0.0	−0.2	−2.3	0.5
Sub-Saharan Africa	18	−0.4	−1.2	−0.1	0.2	0.1	−0.6	0.2	0.0	0.4	−2.0	0.6

Based on Table 5, last column. N is the number of countries. See Appendix Table 7 for definition of the country groups. Column "other" reports the contribution from the control-variables and the crisis (2007–2012) dummy. Sums of contributions may not add up because of rounding

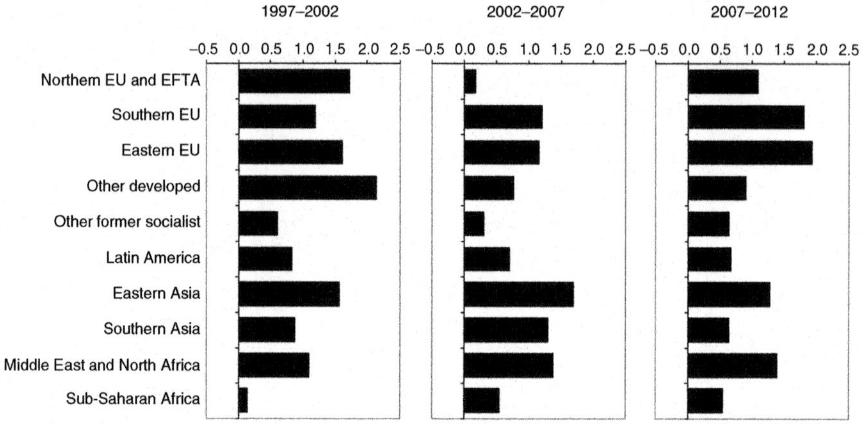

Fig. 2 Growth of technology, 1997–2012

for the developing part of the world, the drop in world demand goes a long way in explaining the difference, which is to be expected, given the high degree of interdependencies that exist globally. However, there are also other factors at play. First, while before the crisis rich countries managed to compensate for the increasing competitiveness of the developing world by advancing their technological lead (Fagerberg et al. 2007), this is no longer the case, leading to slower growth in the developed part of the world. Second, high debt and deteriorating trade balances have slowed down growth, particularly among the other former socialist countries. Finally, a major factor turns out to be the increased financialization of the economy prior to the crisis. The negative effect of the growth of finance is especially pronounced for the countries that suffered most during the crisis years, i.e., the Eastern Europe, for which around one third of the predicted slowdown can be explained in this way.

Slower growth in technological capabilities in the rich part of the world was pointed to as one of the factors behind the slowdown of their economic growth. To analyze this issue in more depth, Fig. 2 depicts the growth of technological capability from the end of the 1990s onwards. There was a notable change taking place early in the new millennium when the global economy grew particularly fast. Before that (left panel), the developed countries had actually managed to increase their technological lead vis-à-vis the developing part of the world. During the high growth period that preceded the crisis (mid panel), growth in technological capability in the richest countries slowed down considerably, while several other country groups, Eastern Asia in particular, expanded their technological capabilities at a faster rate than before. The relatively high growth in technological capability in Eastern and Southern Europe during this period is also noteworthy. This pattern essentially continues in the most recent period, after the financial crisis struck (right panel). If sustained this may indicate that the world is undergoing a transition to a new growth regime in which growth of technology will no longer be based just on advances in a few, highly developed economies but will draw on much larger and geographically less concentrated base.

Figure 3 delves deeper into the other major factors emphasized above by plotting the contribution of the increased financialization against the combined contributions from growth in external balance and external debt. The countries in the lower left quadrant are those that are most negatively affected, while those in the upper right quadrant have benefitted. It is interesting to observe that those that have benefitted from these developments are low-income countries in Asia, Africa and Latin America, while those that were most negatively affected are predominantly European. In fact, almost the entire EU belongs to this category, while a number other developed countries do not. This clearly begs further questions about the nature of EU integration and policies prior to the crisis.[16]

5 Conclusions

This paper has analyzed the growth of the global economy with particular emphasis on the period after the financial crisis. It was shown that, although most countries were affected to some extent, the impact has been far from uniform. To explore this diversity, the paper has made use of a perspective that takes into account three interrelated phenomena: differences in levels of technological development and trends; differences in (social) capacities for exploiting (technological and economic) opportunities; and differences in "competitiveness". The empirical analysis, based on data for 100 countries from all over the globe, suggests that such differences go a long way in explaining the variations in growth performance. On a general level the policy implications of the analysis for countries in the process of development are clear. Catching up, technologically and economically, is possible, but requires continuous improvements of technological and social capabilities. Arguably, without such complimentary investments in capability-building, catching up is likely to run into problems.

However, technological and social capabilities, and their distribution in space, are not carved in stone but evolve, and this presents countries with new challenges and opportunities. One finding that deserves to be highlighted concerns the role of technological capability in global growth. Gone are the days when it could be assumed, as Raymond Vernon famously did in his "product cycle model" (Vernon 1966), that technological capability is something that only exists in the US (and possibly a few other highly developed economies), from which the results diffuse to the rest of the world in an orderly fashion. Rather what is emerging is a global system in which technological capabilities, including advanced ones, are widely dispersed. As the analysis shows, this transformation is ongoing, and at a high

[16]See Fagerberg and Verspagen (2015) for a more in-depth discussion of this issue.

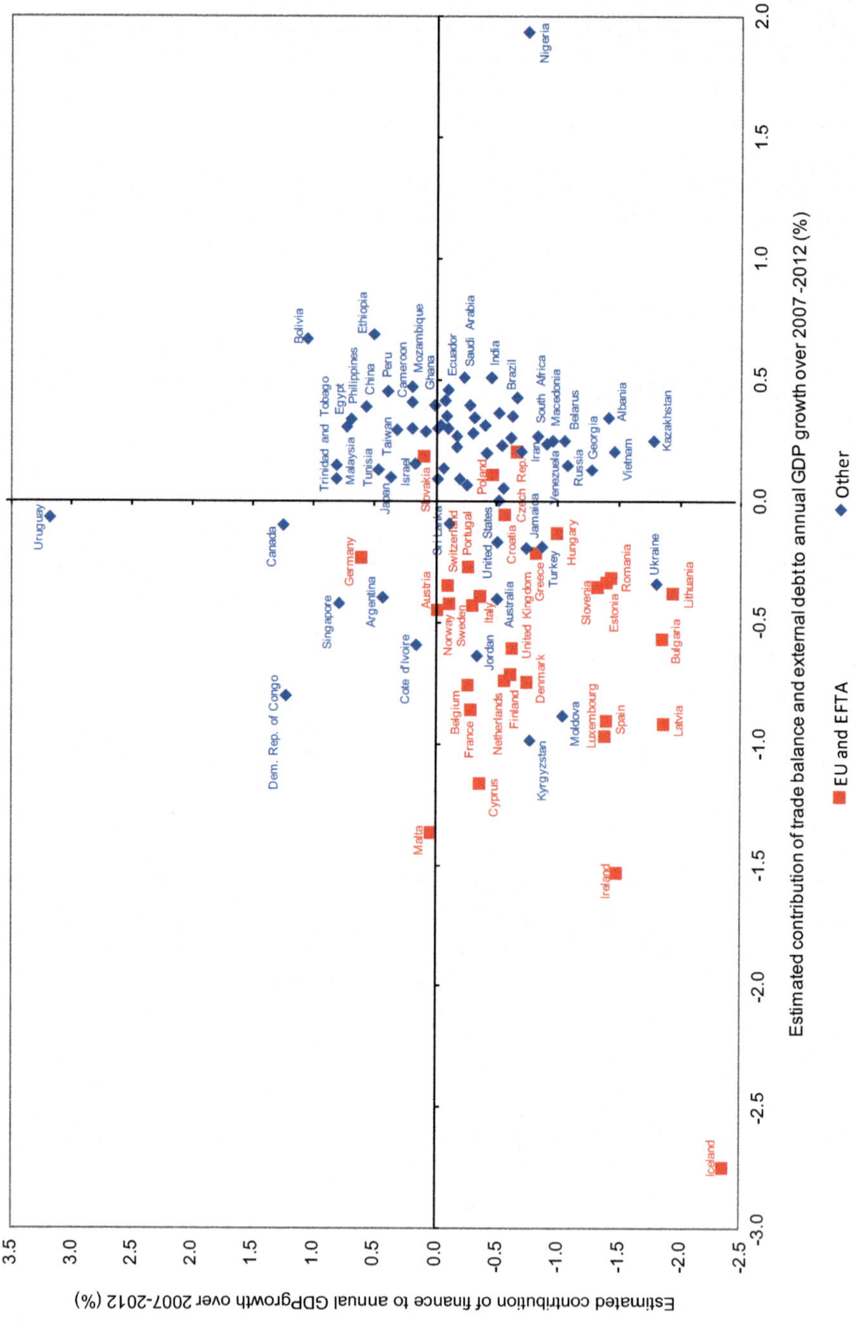

Fig. 3 The impact of finance, trade balance and external debt and on the slowdown

speed. Thus, we would expect developing countries with rapidly increasing technological capabilities to continue increasing their role in the global economy.

As for social capability, earlier work (Gerschenkron 1962; Abramovitz 1986, 1994a, b) placed strong emphasis on developing financial institutions and markets. The results provide a more chilling picture. Recent research has provided evidence suggesting that expanding finance beyond a certain threshold might have a negative effect on economic growth (Cecchetti and Kharroubi 2012; Law and Singh 2014; Arcand et al. 2015), and this is also confirmed by the present study. However, our results also indicate that the virtuous relationship between the expansion of finance and growth, however limited, completely broke down during the crisis. Thus, from being a capability supporting economic growth, further growth of the financial sector has turned into a liability, dragging down the rest of the economy. Whether this is a change for the longer run, or a more specific feature characterizing the recent past, remains to be seen. Nevertheless, these findings clearly beg further work, theoretically as well as applied, on the role of finance in growth and development.

As pointed out earlier, the economic downturn following the outbreak of the financial crisis was very uneven across the globe. While many fast growing countries in Asia and Africa were only marginally affected, if at all, Europe moved into recession. The analysis conducted here points to two factors behind the particularly large slowdown in Europe. First, prior to the crisis, many European countries were characterized by a rapid build-up of their financial sectors, making them vulnerable when the crisis truck; this was particularly evident for the previously socialist countries. A second factor leading to the slowdown, highlighted by this paper, concerns the increasing trade deficits in these countries and, hence, also levels of foreign debt, a pattern that also extended to the comparatively more developed Southern Europe, which proved unsustainable and contributed to the depression that followed. As a consequence, the catching up of Eastern Europe relative to its more advanced neighbors, and of Europe as a whole vis-à-vis the USA, came to an almost immediate halt, from which Europe has still not recovered. Arguably, the question of how Europe can escape the present deadlock, and instead start to profit from the increases in technological and social capabilities that are documented in this paper, deserves a high place on the agenda.

Acknowledgments Financial support from the VINNOVA Core Funding of Centers for Innovation Systems (project 2010–01370 on 'Transformation and Growth in Innovation Systems: Innovation Policy for Global Competitiveness of SMEs and R&I Milieus'), Czech Science Foundation (project P402/10/2310 on 'Innovation, productivity and policy: What can we learn from micro data?') and Czech Academy of Sciences (institutional support RVO 67985998 and agenda 'Strategie AV21') are gratefully acknowledged. Earlier versions of the paper were presented at the 15th ISS Conference, 27–30 July, 2014, Jena, Germany, the 2013 Eu-SPRI Forum Conference on Management of Innovation Policies, 10–12 April 2013, Madrid, Spain and the Joint UNU–MERIT/School of Governance Seminar, 6 June 2013, Maastricht, Netherlands.

Appendix 1

Table 7 Regional groups of countries

Regional group	Country
Northern EU and EFTA	Austria, Belgium, Denmark, Finland, France, Germany, Iceland, Ireland, Luxembourg, Netherlands, Norway, Sweden, Switzerland, United Kingdom
Southern EU	Cyprus, Greece, Italy, Malta, Portugal, Spain
Eastern EU	Bulgaria, Croatia, Czech Rep., Estonia, Hungary, Latvia, Lithuania, Poland, Romania, Slovakia, Slovenia
Other developed	Australia, Canada, Israel, Japan, Korea, New Zealand, Singapore, Taiwan, United States
Other former socialist	Albania, Armenia, Belarus, Georgia, Kazakhstan, Kyrgyzstan, Macedonia, Moldova, Russia, Ukraine
Latin America	Argentina, Bolivia, Brazil, Chile, Colombia, Costa Rica, Ecuador, Guatemala, Jamaica, Mexico, Peru, Trinidad and Tobago, Uruguay, Venezuela
Eastern Asia	China, Indonesia, Malaysia, Philippines, Thailand, Vietnam
Southern Asia	Bangladesh, India, Pakistan, Sri Lanka
Middle East and North Africa	Egypt, Iran, Jordan, Morocco, Saudi Arabia, Tunisia, Turkey, Yemen
Sub-Saharan Africa	Burkina Faso, Cameroon, Democratic Rep. of Congo, Cote d'Ivoire, Ethiopia, Ghana, Kenya, Madagascar, Malawi, Mozambique, Niger, Nigeria, Senegal, South Africa, Sudan, Tanzania, Uganda, Zambia

Appendix 2

Table 8 Control variables

Name	Description	Source
Natural disasters	Log of the number of people killed in natural disasters over the period (per million people)	Université catholique de Louvain (2014)
Oil and gas	Log of the initial level of oil and gas exports, SITC, rev. 3 categories 333, 334, 335, 342, 343 and 344, (% of exports of goods and services);	UNCTAD (2014)
Malaria	Malaria fatal risk (estimate of % population at risk of contracting falciparum malaria in 1994)	Sachs (2003)
External debt	Log of the total debt owed to nonresidents repayable in foreign currency, goods, or services (% of GDP)	World Bank (2014, 2015)
Industry	Industry value added (% of GDP)	World Bank (2014)
Cultural diversity	Cultural fractionalization based on the structural distance between languages (index)	Fearon (2003)

Appendix 3

Table 9 Testing for differences in variable impact between the pre-crisis period of 2002–2007 and the crisis period of 2007–2012 (pooled OLS)

	Coefficient	t–statistics
Gap	−0.46	(4.70)***
2007–2012 (dummy)	−0.12	(0.73)
Gap × 2007–2012 (dummy)	−0.17	(1.75)*
Δ technology	0.15	(2.15)**
2007–2012 (dummy)	0.05	(0.37)
Δ technology × 2007–2012 (dummy)	−0.07	(1.08)
Δ education	0.12	(1.86)*
2007–2012 (dummy)	0.05	(0.34)
Δ education	−0.01	(0.07)
Δ governance	0.16	(2.30)**
2007–2012 (dummy)	0.04	(0.31)
Δ governance × 2007–2012 (dummy)	−0.03	(0.39)
Δ finance	0.08	(1.47)
2007–2012 (dummy)	0.09	(0.66)
Δ finance × 2007–2012 (dummy)	−0.26	(3.70)***
Δ price	−0.01	(0.07)
2007–2012 (dummy)	0.05	(0.36)
Δ price × 2007–2012 (dummy)	−0.05	(0.85)
Δ trade balance	0.18	(2.81)***
2007–2012 (dummy)	0.04	(0.30)
Δ trade balance × 2007–2012 (dummy)	−0.04	(0.65)
Δ demand	0.44	(2.88)***
2007–2012 (dummy)	−0.07	(0.29)
Δ demand × 2007–2012 (dummy)	0.08	(0.56)

Other variables are the same as in Table 5, column 2. Beta values are reported. Absolute values of robust t-statistics are in parentheses. *, **, *** denote significance at the 10, 5 and 1% levels

Appendix 4: Derivation of the Model

From (3):

$$x - m = b - p \tag{9}$$

From (1)–(2):

$$x = \varepsilon_{XT}t + \varepsilon_{XC}c + \varepsilon_{XP}p + \varepsilon_{XW}w \tag{10}$$

$$m = -\varepsilon_{MT}t - \varepsilon_{MC}c - \varepsilon_{MP}p + \varepsilon_{MY}y \tag{11}$$

By subtracting (11) from (10):

$$x - m = (\varepsilon_{XT} + \varepsilon_{MT})t + (\varepsilon_{XC} + \varepsilon_{MC})c + (\varepsilon_{XP} + \varepsilon_{MP})p + \varepsilon_{XW}w - \varepsilon_{MY}y \quad (12)$$

From (9) and (12) follows, by eliminating $x - m$:

$$b - p = (\varepsilon_{XT} + \varepsilon_{MT})t + (\varepsilon_{XC} + \varepsilon_{MC})c + (\varepsilon_{XP} + \varepsilon_{MP})p + \varepsilon_{XW}w - \varepsilon_{MY}y$$

By solving for y:

$$y = \frac{\varepsilon_{XT} + \varepsilon_{MT}}{\varepsilon_{MY}}t + \frac{\varepsilon_{XC} + \varepsilon_{MC}}{\varepsilon_{MY}}c + \frac{\varepsilon_{XP} + \varepsilon_{MP} + 1}{\varepsilon_{MY}}p - \frac{1}{\varepsilon_{MY}}b + \frac{\varepsilon_{XW}}{\varepsilon_{MY}}w \quad (13)$$

From (4)–(5)

$$t = \varepsilon_{TN}n + \varepsilon_{TD}d$$
$$t = \gamma\varepsilon_{TD} - \gamma\varepsilon_{TD}T^{gap} + \varepsilon_{TN}n \quad (14)$$

By substituting (14) into (13):

$$y = \gamma\varepsilon_{TD}\frac{\varepsilon_{XT} + \varepsilon_{MT}}{\varepsilon_{MY}} - \gamma\varepsilon_{TD}\frac{\varepsilon_{XT} + \varepsilon_{MT}}{\varepsilon_{MY}}T^{gap} + \varepsilon_{TN}\frac{\varepsilon_{XT} + \varepsilon_{MT}}{\varepsilon_{MY}}n + \frac{\varepsilon_{XC} + \varepsilon_{MC}}{\varepsilon_{MY}}c + \frac{\varepsilon_{XP} + \varepsilon_{MP} + 1}{\varepsilon_{MY}}p - \frac{1}{\varepsilon_{MY}}b + \frac{\varepsilon_{XW}}{\varepsilon_{MY}}w$$

References

Abramovitz M (1986) Catching up, forging ahead, and falling behind. J Econ Hist 46(386):406

Abramovitz M (1994a) The origins of the postwar catch-up and convergence boom. In: Fagerberg J, Verspagen B, von Tunzelmann N (eds) The dynamics of technology, trade and growth. Edward Elgar, Aldershot, pp 21–52

Abramovitz M (1994b) Catch-up and convergence in the postwar growth boom and after. In: Baumol WJ, Nelson RR, Wolf EN (eds) Convergence of productivity – cross-national studies and historical evidence. Oxford University Press, Oxford, pp 86–125

Arcand J, Berkes E, Panizza U (2015) Too much finance? J Econ Growth 20:105–148

Castellacci F, Natera JM (2011) A new panel dataset for cross-country analyses of national systems, growth and development (CANA). Innov Dev 1:205–226

Cecchetti SG, Kharroubi E (2012) Reassessing the impact of finance on growth, BIS Working Papers No. 381, Bank for International Settlements, July 2012

Conference Board (2014) Total economy database, January 2014. http://www.conference-board.org/data/economydatabase/

Cornwall J (1976) Diffusion, convergence and Kaldor's Law. Econ J 86:307–314

Darvas Z (2012) Real effective exchange rates for 178 countries: a new database. Working Paper 2012/06, Bruegel, 15 Mar 2012 (Update, 26 June 2014). http://www.bruegel.org/datasets/real-effective-exchange-rates-for-178-countries-a-new-database/

Easterly W (2001) The lost decades: explaining developing countries' stagnation in spite of policy reform 1980–1998. J Econ Growth 6:135–157
Fagerberg J (1988) International competitiveness. Econ J 98:355–374
Fagerberg J (1994) Technology and international differences in growth rates. J Econ Lit XXXII (3):1147–1175
Fagerberg J, Srholec M (2008) National innovation systems, capabilities and economic development. Res Policy 37:1417–1435
Fagerberg J, Verspagen B (2015) One Europe or several? Causes and consequences of the European stagnation. In: Fagerberg J, Laestadius S, Martin BR (eds) The triple challenge for Europe economic development, climate change and governance. Oxford University Press, Oxford, pp 33–59
Fagerberg J, Srholec M, Knell M (2007) The competitiveness of nations: why some countries prosper while others fall behind. World Dev 35:1595–1620
Fearon JD (2003) Ethnic and cultural diversity by country. J Econ Growth 8:195–222
Gerschenkron A (1962) Economic backwardness in historical perspective. The Belknap Press, Cambridge
Heritage Foundation (2014) 2014 Index of economic freedom, all index data. The Heritage Foundation. http://www.heritage.org/index/explore?view=by-region-country-year. Accessed 13 June 2014
Kaldor N (1981) The role of increasing returns, technical progress and cumulative causation in the theory of international trade and economic growth. Econ Appl (ISMEA) 34:593–617
Kaufmann D, Kraay A, Mastruzzi M (2014) Worldwide governance indicators, on-line. World Bank. http://info.worldbank.org/governance/wgi/index.aspx#doc-sources. Accessed 13 June 2014
Lall S (1992) Technological capabilities and industrialization. World Dev 20:165–186
Law SH, Singh N (2014) Does too much finance harm economic growth? J Bank Financ 41:36–44
Li G (1985) Robust regression. In: Hoaglin DC, Mosteller F, Tukey JW (eds) Exploring data tables, trends, and shapes. Wiley, New York, pp 281–340
Maddison A (1991) Dynamic forces in capitalist development: a long-run comparative view. Oxford University Press, New York
Metcalfe JS (1988) The diffusion of innovation: an interpretive survey. In: Dosi G (ed) Technological change and economic theory. Francis Pinter, London
National Science Board (2012) Science and engineering indicators 2012. National Science Foundation, Arlington
National Science Board (2014) Science and engineering indicators 2014. National Science Foundation, Arlington
OECD (2014) OECD.Stat. OECD, Paris. Accessed 8 Aug 2014
Rodríguez-Pose A (1999) Innovation prone and innovation averse societies: economic performance in Europe. Growth Chang 30(1):75–105
Sachs JD (2003) Institutions don't rule: direct effects of geography on per capita income. NBER Working Paper No. 9490. http://www.nber.org/papers/w9490
Solow RM (1956) A contribution to the theory of economic growth. Q J Econ 70(1):65–94
Stata (2005) Stata data management, reference manual, release 9. Stata Press, College Station
Thirlwall AP (1979) The balance of payments constraints as an explanation of international growth rate differences. Banca Nazionale del Lav Q Rev 32:45–53
UNCTAD (2014) UNCTAD handbook of statistics 2012. UNCTADstat on-line. UNCTAD, Geneva. Accessed 16 Oct 2014
UNESCO (2014) Science, technology and innovation; Data Centre. UNESCO Institute for Statistics, Geneva. Accessed 8 Aug 2014
Université catholique de Louvain (2014) EM-DAT: The OFDA/CRED International Disaster Database. Brussels. www.emdat.be. Accessed 8 Aug 2014

USPTO (2014) Extended year set – patents by country, state, and year utility patents (December 2013). U.S. Patent and Trademark Office. http://www.uspto.gov/web/offices/ac/ido/oeip/taf/cst_utlh.htm. Accessed 8 Aug 2014

Veblen T (1915) Imperial Germany and the industrial revolution. Macmillan, New York

Vernon R (1966) International investment and international trade in the product cycle. Q J Econ 80:190–207

World Bank (2014) World development indicators 2013. World Bank, last updated 18 Dec 2013. Accessed 8 Aug 2014

World Bank (2015) Quarterly external debt statistics. World Bank. Accessed 6 Aug 2015

Convergence or Divergence: A Nonparametric Analysis on China's Regional Disparity

Xiang Deng, Jianping Li, and Jing Song

Abstract By applying key notions of evolutionary economics, this study develops an analytical framework to explain the differentiated evolutionary paths of convergence and divergence in the economic growth across China's provinces since 1978. We adopt the nonparametric approach in the study, including both univariate and multivariate kernel density estimation. We find evidence that the convergence in economic growth across provinces does not take shape. Instead, a divergence exists in the economic growth of China. Furthermore, the evolutionary dynamics revealed by our kernel estimation suggests that the disparity of the economic growth rate continuously increases since 1978, not only among different provinces, but also among different areas within a single province.

1 Introduction

Whether economic growth will converge or diverge has been perplexing economists and policymakers for a long time. The research on convergence and divergence can be traced back to the neoclassical models of growth. For instance, Barro and Sala-i-Martin identify the β-convergence distribution and σ-convergence ($\lim_{t\to\infty}\sigma_t^2 = \sigma^2$) by employing the neoclassical growth model (Barro and Sala-i-Martin 1992). Taking one step forward, Young et al. (2008) provide evidence that β-convergence serves as a sufficient condition for σ-convergence.

X. Deng
School of Economics, Sichuan University, Wangjiang Lu 29, 610064 Chengdu, People's Republic of China
e-mail: dengxiang@scu.edu.cn

J. Li
School of Economics and Management, Southwest Petroleum University, No.8 Xindu Avenue, Xindu District, Chengdu 610500, People's Republic of China
e-mail: lee.jp@hotmail.com

J. Song (✉)
School of Economics and Management, Southwest Jiaotong University, Chengdu 610031, People's Republic of China
e-mail: jsong@swjtu.edu.cn

A. Pyka, U. Cantner (eds.), *Foundations of Economic Change*, Economic Complexity and Evolution, DOI 10.1007/978-3-319-62009-1_6

However, neoclassical economists have not reached a consensus on this issue so far. Findings on the convergence estimation have been mixed and largely inconclusive. On one hand, Barro and Sala-i-Martin (1992) provide evidence on convergence by studying the American economy from 1963 to1986. Researchers who employ OLS and 3SLS to analyze the USA or OEDC countries also reach the conclusion of convergence or conditional convergence (e.g., de La Fuente 2003; Higgins et al. 2006; Young et al. 2008). On the other hand, researchers adopting other methods drew different conclusions, which generally support club convergence (e.g., Corrado et al. 2005; Pittau and Zelli 2006; Krause 2015) or divergence (e.g., Acemoglu 2009; Caggiano and Leonida 2009). These researchers use various econometric inferences, including regression, density estimation, or ACF (autocorrelation function), and different datasets consisting of world-wide countries, OECD countries, or EU countries.

Similarly, findings of most China-based studies are mixed as well. Some researchers provide evidence on convergence (e.g., Shi and Zhao 2011; Zhang 2004) or conditional convergence (e.g., Cai and Wang 2002; Wu 2006; Xu and Li 2004; Zou and Zhou 2007). In these studies, researchers employ regression, SGMM or DEA approach, respectively, to analyze Chinese province-level data. In contrast, Cai and Du (2000) find that while China's economic growth is featured by club convergence, there is no significant absolute convergence based on the data from 1978 to 1998. The similar results are obtained by Xu and Shu (2005) with 1D kernel density estimation. Additionally, some other researchers draw the conclusion of divergence (Fan 2006; Ou et al. 2006; Wang and Fan 2004) or inter-provincial divergence in China through DEA estimation (Yan and Wang 2004; Zhang and Gui 2008).

In short, all these substantive differences in the empirical findings imply that it is merited to revisit the issue of convergence using other theoretical perspectives. Interestingly, the evolutionary theory provides such an alternative theoretical lens that has the potential to reconcile the controversies and contradictions. The evolutionary theory places a key emphasis on the dynamics during the evolutionary process. Put differently, it stresses that economic processes be path-dependent to the extent that future action is largely constrained by historical development (Bathelt and Glückler 2003). More specifically, the evolutionary school of economic thinking is strongly related to such key evolutionary notions as selection, path-dependency, chance and increasing returns (Boschma and Lambooy 1999), which can be well utilized to investigate the spatial clustering of the industry and regional disparities. By integrating these evolutionary thoughts into the current study, we take an econometric approach to delineate the evolutionary dynamics in the regional economic development in China, with a particular focus on the issue of convergence/divergence.

2 An Evolutionary Perspective on China's Regional Disparity

Since China implemented the economic reform and opening-up policy, its economy has been growing fast for nearly 40 years. GDP grows 14 times since 1978, making China the second largest economy in this world. However, there exists a great disparity in the regional economic development across different provinces in China, especially between the inland provinces and the coastal ones.

Mechanisms of selection and chance play a critical role in the success of the eastern provinces in China. One major factor driving China's economic growth is institutional changes. Almost all the experimentations of marketization policies began in the coastal area. As a consequence, the implementation of reform and opening-up policies encouraging trials and discoveries makes the economic growth in the eastern area remarkably faster than that in the western area which was then dominated by the planning economy. The reform from the 1980s through 1990s in the twentieth century endowed the eastern area with the unprecedented chance to outperform the middle and western area. Even though the firm cannot make globally rational decision in the market competition due to information imperfection, the inherent bias in the entrepreneur's calculation, and the ever-changing market environment, the market does select the winner that can approximate global rationality. During this selection process, it is the pioneering marketization in the eastern area that makes more winners selected from this area than from other areas. As the economic reform unfolds, such disparities among regions gradually widen, which results in an increasingly evident phenomenon of divergence.

Additionally, the presence of increasing returns is to some extent held responsible for the growth disparities between the eastern and other areas in China. The concept of increasing returns is often associated with other concepts such as the lock-in effect (Grabher 1993) and knowledge spillover (Caniëls and Verspagen 2001). The apparent policy advantage of the eastern area attracts a great number of firms to agglomerate, which is further reinforced by the rapid growth in this area. Consequently, numerous firms agglomerate in the eastern area and even start to create their own regional milieu to support their goals (Bathelt and Glückler 2003). At the same time, the rate and character of technological advance is greatly influenced by certain institutional structures supporting R&D and/or other innovation activities. This policy-technology interaction makes the eastern area take a lead in economic growth. With the widening gap in economic growth between the eastern and other areas, a divergence inevitably appears.

It takes different ways for path dependency to play a role at different stages of the evolutionary process of China's economic growth. Path dependency means that the technological and organizational change is a cumulative process, constraining firms in the possibilities of what they can do, by what they have done in the past (Laursen 2000). At first, the policy of economic reform and opening-up was piloted in China's coastal areas and then implemented nationally. At this specific stage of the evolutionary process, the growth of the eastern area greatly benefited from taking a lead in shaping new growth paths and calculation routines for firms to coping with challenges and opportunities in the new market environment. Therefore, this early stage of the economic growth is featured by increasing divergence across different areas. Later on, with the diffusion of both policies and technologies, the negative effect of path-dependency gradually occurred as a result of adhering to the outdated calculation routine by firms which neglected the changes in the market and institutional environment. In other words, the outdated path dependency made many pioneering firms in the eastern area at a disadvantageous position in the competition. In contrast, the less-developed provinces in the middle and western area made good use of the late-comer advantage to create path dependency more appropriate to the new institutional environment and the new pattern of economic growth. At this later stage of the evolutionary process, path dependency enables the less-developed areas to accelerate to catch up with the eastern area, and may eventually allow economic convergence to emerge.

This study contributes to the literature in the following three aspects. First, we adopt multivariate kernel density estimation to well capture the evolutionary dynamics in the process of economic growth. Many of the extant studies depend on the 1D kernel density estimation, instead of a multivariate one, to conduct cross-sectional tests. Consequently, these studies cannot analyze the evolution process of the GDP per capita, and are likely to lead to arbitrary results. Given the complicated situation of the economic development and institutional environment in contemporary China, it is critically important to detect whether convergence, club convergence, or divergence exists across provinces. Therefore, departure from most of the existing studies, we employ both 1D and 2D kernel density estimation to analyze the evolution dynamics of the China's province-level GDP per capita at different time points.

Second, the combined use of critical bandwidth (CB) and Silverman test allows us to determine whether the density distribution estimated via the kernel density estimation is unimodal or multimodal, and to analyze the development of club convergence and de-clubbing based on the CB value. As such, we provide an objective and statistical method to distinguish different patterns.

Third, the neoclassical AK model is only utilized to describe the characteristics of increasing returns. Although the evolutionary perspective casts doubt on the assumption of rationality, it is still necessary to figure out to which parameters and variables the growth pathway is related before we can conduct empirical analysis. Therefore, we build our theoretical model by combining neoclassical models with the evolutionary analysis of increasing return and institutional factors, aiming to explain the stable long-term evolution and lay a mathematical foundation for our empirical analysis.

3 The Emergence and Explanation of Divergence Among Regional Economies in China

To address the evolution process, a model of explicit distribution dynamics has been advocated by several authors (e.g., Quah 1996, 2002). Distribution dynamics can be evaluated according to two aspects: shape dynamics and intra-distribution mobility. Although this approach is controversial as it is too sensitive to the sample size and the selection of time intervals (Kremer et al. 2001), it is still more powerful in analyzing complicated economic convergence and the evolution of GDP compared with the regression estimation which was used by Laursen (2000) to analyze the patterns of export and technological specialization.

In this study, we introduce the preferential policy granted by the central government as a parameter into our model, and take into account of the difference in technological level between regions. The application of AK model is in accordance with the investment-driven growth pattern in China, as it is emphasized in this model that capital input promotes growth. Additionally, the conclusion derived from the AK model fits well with the data on China's economic growth.

As for the representative household, we employ the CES type of utility function to depict the 'agent's consumption and saving behavior'.

$$
\begin{aligned}
&MaxU(c_t)\\
&U(c_t) = \int_0^{\infty} e^{-(\rho-n)t}\frac{{c_t}^{1-\theta}-1}{1-\theta}dt\\
&s.t.\dot{a}_t = (r_t - n)a_t + w_t - c_t
\end{aligned}
$$

Where a_t, w_t, and c_t represent household asset, received wage and consumption, respectively. Drawing on the present-value Hamilton equation, we can derive the first-order condition for maximizing household consumption:

$$\frac{\dot{c}_t}{c_t} = \frac{r_t - \rho}{\theta}$$

We further get the consumption at period t:

$$c_t = c_0 \exp\left(\frac{r_t - \rho}{\theta}t\right)$$

As for the representative firm, we adopt parameter τ to describe how the government preferential policy distorts market system, as it is a critically import factor in the regional economic growth in China. When τ is equal to zero ($\tau \in [0,1)$, no policy intervention is exerted on the market. The higher the value of τ, the stronger the government intervention (distortion) in the capital market. It is noted that a considerable number of regional growth policies in China tend to provide preferential land and taxation policies, so as to attract business and investment.

$$y_t = Ak_t$$
$$s.t.C_t = (1 - \tau)rk_t$$

Where C_t is firm cost. The government preferential policy leads to the increase in the rate of return on capital, which enables the regional capital to generate a higher net return on capital investment $r_t = r - \delta = \frac{A}{1-\tau} - \delta$, where δ is a depreciation rate. The firm's increment of capital stock and GDP per capita are given by:

$$\dot{k}_t = \left(\frac{A}{1-\tau} - \delta - n\right)k_t - c_t$$

$$\dot{y}_t = A\dot{k}_t = \left(\frac{A}{1-\tau} - \delta - n\right)y_t - Ac_0 \exp\left(\frac{A/(1-\tau) - \delta - \rho}{\theta}t\right)$$

Solving the differential equation $\dot{k}_t$ at period t, the growth rate of per capita GDP is equal to that of per capita capital stock:

$$\frac{\dot{y}_t}{y_t} = \frac{\dot{k}_t}{k_t} = \frac{A/(1-\tau) - \delta - \rho}{\theta} \tag{1}$$

Although we cannot identify the exact difference between the rate of time preference (ρ) and the inter-temporal substitution rate of consumption among different areas (θ), the difference in policies (τ) and the difference in technologies (A) among areas can be directly observed. The government preferential policy distorts the market mechanism, leading to the high return and high growth of capital in the coastal area, where the first mover advantage and advanced technological level (A) ensure a relatively high rate of productivity acceleration. At the same time, the coastal area obtains sufficient and cheap labor, which in turn leads to rapid growth, an obvious consequence for this region.

However, we note that even if similar areas enact the same incentive policy, it is not necessary that these areas result in the same development path, due to the inherent uncertainty within the economic system. Second, since the regional technological level A, ρ, θ and τ are not deterministic variables, we need to view the domestic per capita GDP as a stochastic process. From Eq. (1), we can derive the following result:

$$y_t = y_0 \exp(W_t),$$

where $W_t = W(t; A, \tau, \theta, \delta, \rho)$, represents a random variable with unknown probability distribution. Furthermore, the stochastic process y_t satisfies the Markov assumption with probability distribution function F_t, and F_{t+s} is expressed as the F_t's mapping based on F_t's own space:

$$\forall y_t, y_{t+s} \in R : F_{Y,t+s}(y_{t+s}) = \int_{-\infty}^{+\infty} M_s(y_{t+s}|y_t) dF_{Y,t}(y_t) \tag{2}$$
$$M_s : R \times R \to [0,1]$$

where M_s is probability transition function that describes the probability that the stochastic distribution y_t at period t transiting to y_{t+s} over a time interval of S. And M_s is connected with W_t. To make Eq. (2) hold, the expression of y_t should contain only first order lag terms and no higher lag terms.

Taking Eq. (2) to the limit as $t \to \infty$ provides the ergodic (long-run) density implied by the transition function. It can be found as the solution to:

$$F_{Y,\infty}(y_\infty) = \int_{-\infty}^{+\infty} M_s(y_\infty) dF_{Y,\infty}(y_\infty)$$

In order to understand the dynamics of regional economic growth, we can use the data on y_t and y_{t+s}, and employ kernel density estimation to estimate their probability density.

4 The Kernel Density Estimation

In this section, we will focus on describing the probability distribution of y_t and the dynamics of distribution function.

Considering the stochastic process y_t in Eq. (1) and expressing the stochastic distribution function of y_t at period t as $F_{y,t+s}$, we have the following estimation function for $F_{y,t}$:

$$\hat{F}_{Y,t}(y_t) = \frac{1}{n} \sum_{i=1}^{n} S(y_t - y_{i,t})$$
$$S(u) = \begin{cases} 1, u \geq 0 \\ 0, u < 0 \end{cases},$$

where $i = 1, 2, 3 \ldots n \in \mathrm{I}$ represents the sample identity, namely, the identity label for provinces, and $S(u)$ is the indicative function. We then obtain the following estimation of a probability density function of y_t:

$$\hat{f}_{y,t}(y_t) = \frac{\hat{F}_{Y,t}(y_t + h) - \hat{F}_{Y,t}(y_t - h)}{2h} = \frac{1}{nh} \frac{1}{2} \sum_{i=1}^{n} [S(y_t + h - y_{i,t}) - S(y_t - h - y_{i,t})]$$

Here, the expression within the summation symbol denotes the number of sample points within the interval of $[y_t - h, y_t + h]$. We thus can set an appropriate weight function K, assigning weights to the sample point i defined by the Euclidean distance $|y_t - y_{i,t}| \leq h$. As such we can obtain the estimation of a density function. That is, the kernel density estimate in this study is expressed as follows:

$$\hat{f}_{y,t}(y_t) = \frac{1}{nh}\sum_{i=1}^{n} K\left(\frac{y_t - y_{i,t}}{h}\right)$$

Equation (2) is expanded from one dimension to multiple dimensions and used for empirical analysis. Since the probability density function can be estimated as Lebesgue measure on R^d, the kernel density estimation equation of the point range $\{y_i\}$ can be redefined as:

$$\hat{f}(y) = \frac{1}{nh^d}\sum_{i=1}^{n} K\left(\frac{y - y_i}{h}\right),$$

where h is bandwidth, the size of which influences how well the density curve fits the sample. Generally speaking, the smaller the value of h, the better the density curve fits. K, the kernel function, is in nature a kind of weight function. We use Gauss kernel in the following estimation: $K(u) = (2\pi)^{-\frac{1}{2}} e^{-u^2/2}$. Researchers may also choose Epanechikov kernel or other kernel functions (Quah 1996). However, in practice, when considering the goodness of fit, it is generally accepted that the selection of bandwidth is far more important than the selection of kernel function (Weißbach and Gefeller 2004). The selection of bandwidth usually follows the standard of minimizing the asymptotic integrated mean square error (AIMSE). For instance, one can adopt direct insertion method or cross validation method defined by the minimum residual sum of squares.

In this study, we adopt the rule-of-thumb method to select the bandwidth:

$$h = \left(\frac{8\pi^{1/2}\int_R K^2(x)dx}{3n\left(\int_R xK(x)dx\right)^2}\right)^{1/5} \hat{\sigma}$$

In calculation, this method is corresponding to a 'rule-of-thumb' algorithm proposed by Silverman (1981) and Scott (1992). To minimize AIMSE, we simplify the bandwidth selection function under the assumption that the data follow a normal distribution.

5 Empirical Analysis of Regional Economic Divergence and Its Pattern in China

5.1 Methodology and Data Sources in Estimating Divergence

The basic methods for estimating convergence/divergence include cross-sectional, time series and panel data method. Cross-sectional method is questioned as it is vulnerable to the ad hoc selection, and it does not allow time series method to deal with multiple cross-sectional samples. Relatively speaking, the panel data model allows researchers to make sufficient use of the cross-sectional and time information in the data, and employ cointegration and/or ADF test. However, it is noteworthy that the selection of exogenous variables is somewhat arbitrary, which may make the results of empirical analysis depart from the conclusion derived from the theoretical model.

The multivariate non-parametric kernel density estimation is suitable for analyzing the phenomenon of convergence, particularly club convergence, or multimodal convergence. This method overcomes the drawbacks of parametric models and does not need to preset the model structure and parameters.

All the data on provinces, autonomous regions and municipalities are obtained from China Statistical Yearbook and China Compendium of Statistics from 1978 to 2013. In the convergence estimation, we use data on all the 31 provinces, municipalities and autonomous regions in China's mainland.

5.2 The Distribution of Inter-Provincial Per Capita Real GDP Based on the Univariate Kernel Density Model

Figure 1 presents the results of the univariate kernel density estimation based on the data on real GDP per capital in 1978, 1990, 2000, 2010 and 2013. Here, all data have been standardized.

As Fig. 1 shows, after China embarked on economic reform, its GDP per capita, based on the price of year 1978, continuously increases, and the inter-provincial disparity, measured by the difference in GDP per capita, widens at the same time. In the 1980s, the curves of GDP per capita across provinces are rather concentrated, whereas they gradually separate from each other since 1990s. At the early stage of reform and opening-up, the average GDP per capita is very low (461 RMB *yuan* in 1978 and 524.8 RMB *yuan* in 1980), and the regional GDP per capita is concentrated around the mean level. In recent years, however, the aggregate level of GDP per capita increases from 1083.2 *yuan* in 1990 to 2940.8 *yuan* in 2000, and further to 10771.89 RMB *yuan* in 2013. Moreover, the disparity in GDP per capita GDP across regions increases.

Based on the mean of the probability density curve, it is found that the curve kurtosis shifts to the right continuously, and the variance in the provincial-level data increases. The gap between the curves becomes increasingly apparent since 1990s.

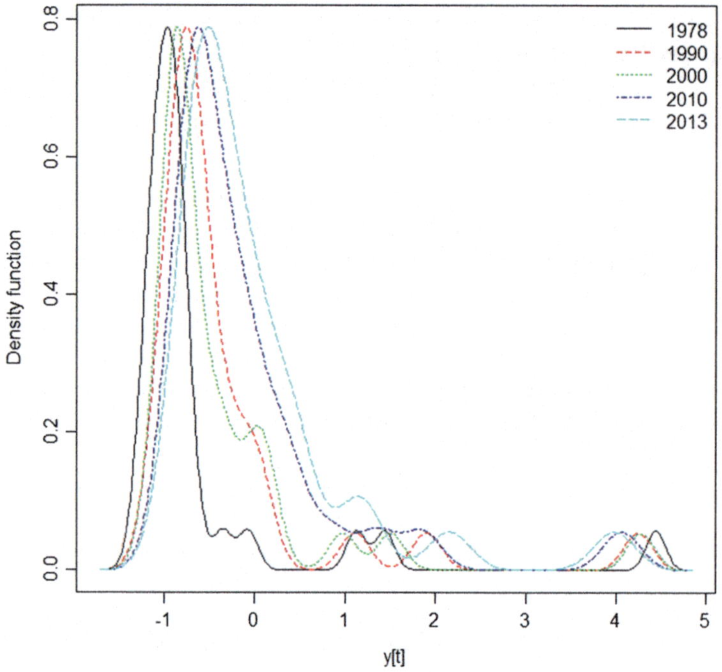

Fig. 1 Distribution curve of inter-provincial GDP per capita (Year 1978, 1990, 2000, 2010 and 2013)

We cannot infer whether there is absolute convergence or club convergence (i.e., bimodal distribution or multimodal distribution). However, we can conclude that since the implementation of reform and opening-up policies, China's economic growth is characterized by growing GDP per capita, and a process of divergence of economic growth across provinces.

5.3 The Multivariate Estimation and Dynamics of Inter-Provincial Convergence in China

The multivariate kernel density estimation provides the straightforward description of the dynamics of inter-provincial convergence in China. This is conducive to gaining a better understanding of whether there is twin-peak or multi-peak in the inter-provincial economic growth. Aziz and Duenwald (2001) estimate growth dynamics based on China's provincial-level data. However, they make comparisons based on the provincial data of 2 years, which makes their sample points largely limited.

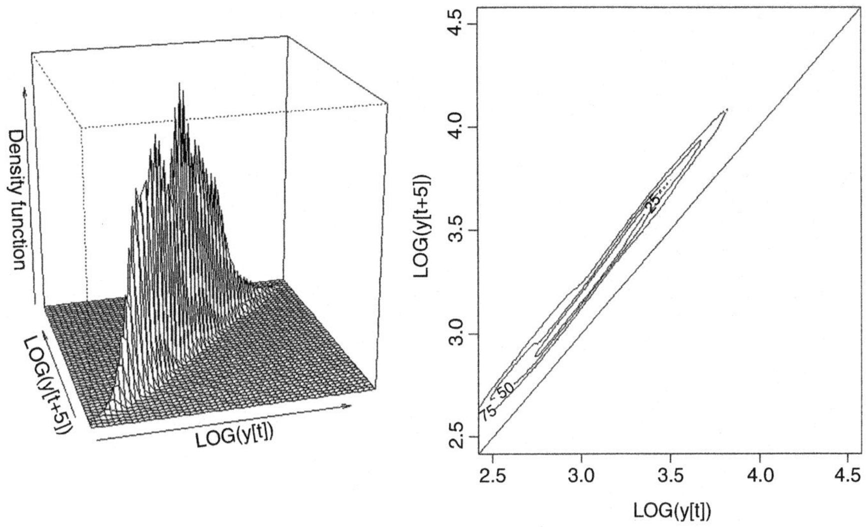

Fig. 2 The inter-provincial dynamics of the real GDP per capita (Year 1978–2013), s = 5

In our estimation, we set the transition period to cover 5 years and 10 years, respectively. This is because there are abundant data on the inter-provincial per capita GDP, and the growth rate of post-reform China is faster than that of the 117 countries in Quah's study. Therefore, if time interval is set to be too long, one may run the risk of overlooking some features of the transition in the dynamic process. We use Gauss kernel in the estimation, and the bandwidth is determined by using the rule-of-thumb method. The variable is expressed as 2 two-dimensional matrices: lny_t and lny_{t+5}, lny_t and lny_{t+10} denoting the logarithm value of per capita GDP at period t, period t+5 and period t+10, respectively. $N = 962$ represents the size of sample points (including all the provincial-level data points on per capita GDP from 1978 to 2013). The estimation results are presented in Fig. 2.

As is shown in Figs. 2 and 3, there is no club convergence in the changing process of provincial GDP per capita, and the dynamic process of the disparity in provincial GDP per capita is still characterized by a unimodal distribution. Instead, the disparity across provinces further widens. The ridge projection of the probability density curve in the right panel of Fig. 2 is just a little higher than 45° $\left(1 = \frac{d(\text{lny}_{t+s})}{d(lny_t)} = \frac{\dot{y}_{t+s}}{y_{t+s}} / \frac{\dot{y}_t}{y_t}\right)$, which suggests that both low- and high-income areas experience economic growth at a relatively high rate, and it shows no sign of decelerating by so far. This means that for both the regions with low GDP and those with high GDP, the probability for them to maintain this acceleration is higher than that to cut their economic growth rate. As a result, the disparity across regions will keep widening, which is in consistent with the result of univariate density estimation. There is a unimodal structure on the projection chart of the growth

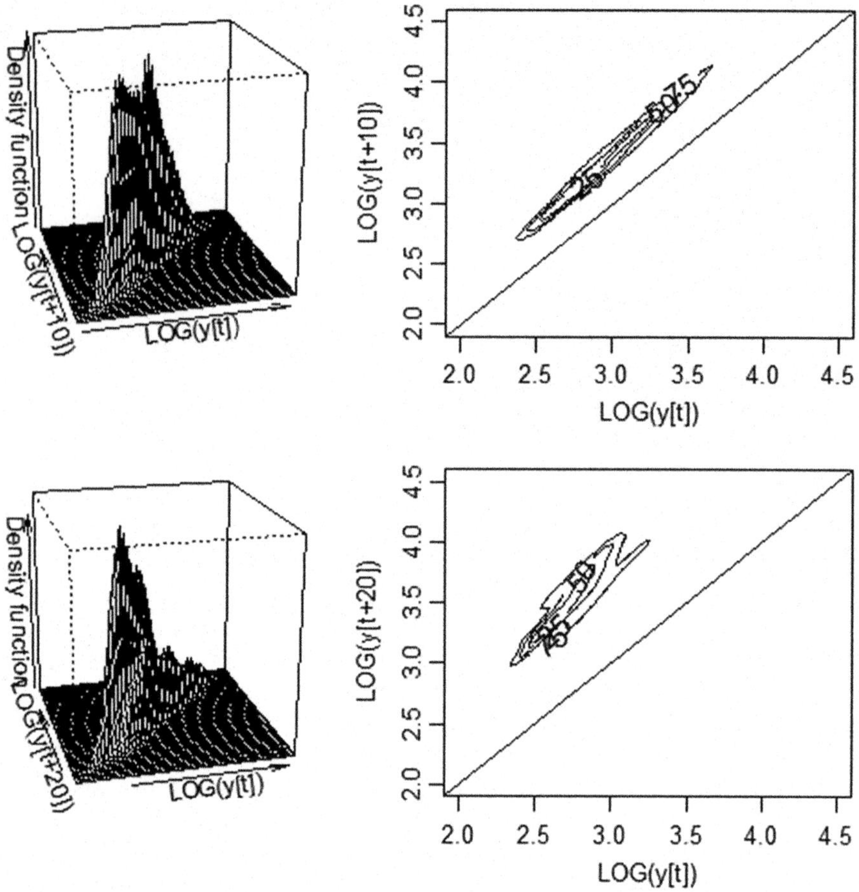

Fig. 3 The inter-provincial dynamics of the real GDP per capita (Year 1978–2013), s = 10 and 20

dynamics of GDP per capita, and this suggests that there is not yet a convergence in the process of growth in provincial GDP per capita in China.

To further test this conclusion, we also conduct bivariate kernel density estimation with longer time spans (10-year and 20-year term, respectively), which yields the same conclusion that there is no multimodal distribution, hence no club convergence. Although there is a tendency of deviation along the periphery of the probability density chart of the 20-year term, there is only one center.

5.4 Detecting the Club Convergence

Given that the foregoing analysis rejects the hypothesis of convergence, it still remains unanswered whether there exists divergence in a general sense or club convergence.

It allows us to determine whether the probability density curve is unimodal or multimodal by using the critical bandwidth (CB) in the kernel density estimation. The CB is expressed as follows:

$$\mathrm{CB} = \inf\left\{\mathrm{h};\hat{f}(\mathrm{y},\mathrm{h})\mathrm{has\ at\ most\ m\ modes}\right\}$$

For instance, when the probability density curve is a mixture distribution composed of m different probability density curves, we can calculate the smallest bandwidth fitting the m modes of the estimated kernel density, namely the critical bandwidth. Additionally in a kernel density estimation of f(x) with a Gaussian kernel, the number of modes is a right-continuous decreasing function of the bandwidth (Silverman 1981). Hence, it is possible for us to use the CB value to find whether there is club convergence or a de-club phenomenon.

Specifically, f(x) is the density of standardized income per capita with at most two modes, and it is observed at two time points, $t = 1, 2$. The critical bandwidths for unimodality at $t = 1$ and $t = 2$ can be calculated as CB_1 and CB_2, respectively. In such a case, there is club convergence if and only if $CB_2 > CB_1$, or de-clubbing if and only if $CB_2 < CB_1$.

Furthermore, Silverman proposes a method to test multimodality which depends on the value of Silverman test with the help of a bootstrap procedure. This method can be used to track the changes in the modes of the probability density curve estimated via the kernel density estimation, and determine whether club convergence or de-clubbing trend occurs.

Figure 4 presents the kernel density estimates of the standardized real GDP per capita from 1978 to 2013, where the variance increases over time. Moreover, a peak can be easily observed, and there are some bumps in the tail area, on which we next run the Sliverman multimodality test and calculate the CB value.

We calculate the critical bandwidth of the kernel density estimation of the province-level GDP per capita in China from 1978 to 2013. By drawing a bootstrap sample of the China's provinces including 5000 data points with replacement, we calculate the corresponding Silverman test statistic, where the null hypothesis is that there exists at most one mode. As is shown in Fig. 5, the CB value rises transitorily between 1991 and 1998 from 0.9188 to 1.0476, which results in a short-time multimodality of the distribution of the GDP per capita. This helps explain why some researchers argue that there is club convergence across provinces in China (e.g., Xu and Shu 2005). In contrast, the CB value declines in other time periods, suggesting a de-club status for the provincial real GDP per capita in China. The results of the Silverman test also show that a statistically significant multimodality occurs for the China's economic growth between 1997 and 2004

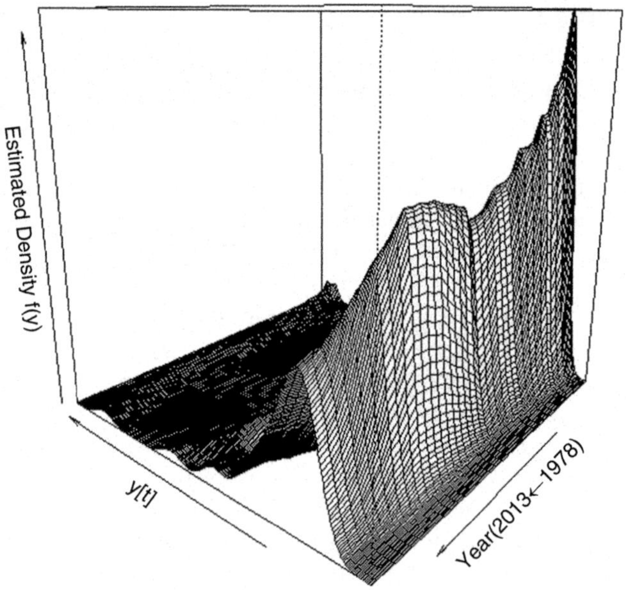

Fig. 4 Distribution curve of inter-provincial GDP per capita over time (Year 1978–2013)

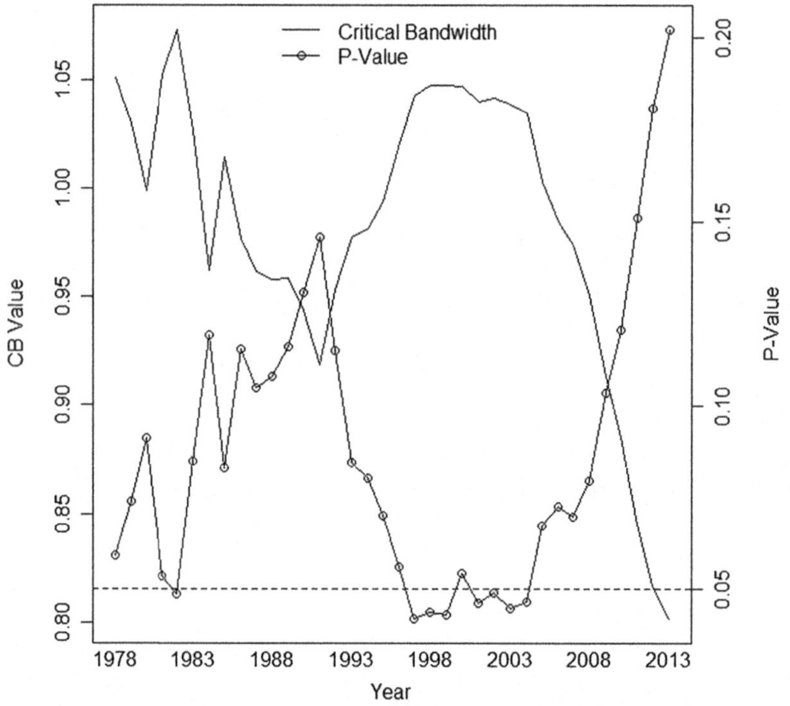

Fig. 5 Critical bandwidth and Silverman modality test (Year 1978–2013)

(i.e., the p-value of the Silverman multimodality test $< 5\%$). After this time period, this trend inverses, which does not provide support for the club convergence any more.

6 Conclusion

Based on the analytical results, we find that there is no convergence of the provincial economic growth in China, regardless of using univariate or multivariate kernel density estimation.

It is shown by the divergence estimation that the regional economic growth in post-reform China is featured by a considerable level of disparity. Although the overall economy grows rapidly and continuously, the economy of the eastern coastal regions (high-income regions) grows much faster than that of the western regions (low-income regions). Moreover, the differences in growth rate across regions tend to increase. Therefore, there exists no convergence of economic growth across provinces, instead there is a divergence in China.

Acknowledgements The authors would like to thank the anonymous reviewers for their constructive and helpful comments on an earlier draft of this paper. The authors are grateful for the financial support from the National Natural Science Foundation of China, No. 71473169, No. 716731947 and No. 71473168 for Xiang Deng, No. 71402151 for Jing Song, and the Humanities and Social Sciences of Ministry of Education in China (No. 13XJA790002) for Jianping Li.

References

Acemoglu D (2009) Introduction to modern economic growth. MIT Press, Cambridge, MA

Aziz J, Duenwald C (2001) China's provincial growth dynamics. International Monetary Fund, Washington, DC

Barro RJ, Sala-i-Martin X (1992) Convergence. J Polit Econ 100(2):223–251

Bathelt H, Glückler J (2003) Toward a relational economic geography. J Econ Geogr 3(2): 117–144

Boschma RA, Lambooy JG (1999) Evolutionary economics and economic geography. J Evol Econ 9(4):411–429

Caggiano G, Leonida L (2009) International output convergence: evidence from an autocorrelation function approach. J Appl Econ 24(1):139–162

Cai F, Du Y (2000) Convergence and divergence of regional economic growth in China. Econ Res J (in Chinese) 10:30–37

Cai F, Wang D (2002) Comparative advantages: differences, changes and their impact on regional disparity. Soc Sci China (in Chinese) 5:41–54

Caniëls MC, Verspagen B (2001) Barriers to knowledge spillovers and regional convergence in an evolutionary model. J Evol Econ 11(3):307–329

Corrado L, Martin R, Weeks M (2005) Identifying and interpreting regional convergence clusters across Europe. Econ J 115(502):C133–C160

de La Fuente A (2003) Convergence equations and income dynamics: the sources of OECD convergence, 1970–1995. Economica 70:655–671

Fan J (2006) Industrial agglomeration and difference of regional labor productivity: Chinese evidence with international comparison. Econ Res J (in Chinese) 11:72–81
Grabher G (1993) The weakness of strong ties: the lock-in of regional development in the Ruhr area. In: Grabher G (ed) The embedded firm: on the socio-economics of industrial networks. Routledge, London, pp 255–277
Higgins MJ, Levy D, Young AT (2006) Growth and convergence across the United States: evidence from county-level data. Rev Econ Stat 88(4):671–681
Krause M (2015) The millennium peak in club convergence—a new look at distributional changes in the wealth of nations. J Appl Econ 32:621–642. https://doi.org/10.1002/jae.2542
Kremer M, Onatski A, Stock J (2001) Searching for prosperity. Carn-Roch Conf Ser Public Policy 55(1):275–303
Laursen K (2000) Do export and technological specialisation patterns co-evolve in terms of convergence or divergence? Evidence from 19 OECD countries, 1971–1991. J Evol Econ 10(4): 415–436
Ou X, Shen Z, Wang R (2006) Spatial structure evolution of regional economic growth and its inequality in China since 1978. Sci Geogr Sin (in Chinese) 26(6):641–648
Pittau MG, Zelli R (2006) Empirical evidence of income dynamics across EU regions. J Appl Econ 21(5):605–628
Quah DT (1996) Convergence empirics across economies with (some) capital mobility. J Econ Growth 1(1):95–124
Quah DT (2002) Spatial agglomeration dynamics. Am Econ Rev 92(2):247–252
Scott DW (1992) Multivariate density estimation: theory, practice and visualization. Wiley, New York
Shi X, Zhao S (2011) The regional economic convergence and its mechanism in China: 1978–2009. J Quant Tech Econ (in Chinese) 1:51–62
Silverman BW (1981) Using kernel density estimates to investigate multimodality. J R Stat Soc Ser B Methodol 43(1):97–99
Wang X, Fan W (2004) Analysis on the regional disparity in China and the influential factors. Econ Res J (in Chinese) 1:33–44
Weißbach R, Gefeller O (2004) A rule-of-thumb for the variable bandwidth selection in kernel hazard rate estimation. Technical Report//Universität Dortmund, SFB 475 Komplexitätsreduktion in Multivariaten Datenstrukturen
Wu Y (2006) A spatial econometric analysis of China's provincial economic growth convergence. J Quant Tech Econ (in Chinese) 12:101–108
Xu X, Li X (2004) Convergence in Chinese cities. Econ Res J (in Chinese) 5:40–48
Xu X, Shu Y (2005) Physical capital, human capital, and regional twin-peak convergence in China. J World Econ (in Chinese) 28(1):47–57
Yan P, Wang B (2004) Technical efficiency, technical progress & productivity growth: an empirical analysis based on DEA. Econ Res J (in Chinese) 12:55–65
Young AT, Higgins MJ, Levy D (2008) Sigma convergence versus beta convergence: evidence from US county-level data. J Money Credit Bank 40(5):1083–1093
Zhang H (2004) The application of the augmented Solow model diversities and convergence among Chinese provinces. China Econ Q (in Chinese) 3(3):605–618
Zhang X, Gui B (2008) The analysis of total factor productivity in China: a review and application of Malmquist index approach. J Quant Tech Econ (in Chinese) 6:111–122
Zou W, Zhou H (2007) The estimation and analysis on the China's inter-provincial growth disparities (1978–2002): an empirical study based on the counterfactual income approach. Manage World (in Chinese) 7:37–46

Micro to Macro Evolutionary Modeling: On the Economics of Self Organization of Dynamic Markets by Ignorant Actors

Gunnar Eliasson

Abstract The Micro to Macro model MOSES, for Model of the Swedish Economic System, is presented as a synthesis of Austrian/Schumpeterian and Swedish/Stockholm school economics. That connection unfortunately failed to be achieved at the time, as Swedish economists abandoned their ambition to take their Ex ante Ex post analysis down to the micro level for neoclassical static equilibrium economics, and therefore also failed to establish a Swedish platform for evolutionary economics. I argue that evolutionary models have to be micro based to make sense as driven by entrepreneurial competition and selection among autonomous market agents, be economy wide as an economic system, and should feature *endogenous evolutions of firm populations*, a complex dynamic that makes the model unsolvable for a market clearing equilibrium. The initial state dependency of such highly non linear selection models furthermore makes them unavoidably empirical. Since empirical models are always related to a case economy, the Moses model has been drawn up within the general theoretical framework of what I call an *Experimentally Organized Economy* (EOE), and applied to the Swedish economy. The estimation/calibration problems associated with such models are addressed, and the empirical credibility of the *surprise economics* that they generate discussed.

Entrepreneurial entry drives competition and growth of the Micro to Macro model economy through a Schumpeterian type Creative Destruction process, that however also endogenously both raises the rate of exit, changes the population of actors, and lowers (because of the consequent structural change) the reliability of market price signaling as predictors of future prices. Simulation experiments suggest that *an optimal growth maximizing rate of firm turnover exits*.

Revised version of paper presented at the 15th International Joseph A. Schumpeter Conference in Jena, Germany, July 27–30, 2014. Discussions with Uwe Cantner, Bo Carlsson, Keith Drake, Rolf Henriksson and Brian Loasby have been very helpful in getting the story of econmic doctrines right.

G. Eliasson (✉)
Royal Institute of Technology (KTH), Stockholm, Sweden
e-mail: Gunnar.elias@telia.com

A. Pyka, U. Cantner (eds.), *Foundations of Economic Change*, Economic Complexity and Evolution, DOI 10.1007/978-3-319-62009-1_7

When MOSES is deprived of its micro based evolutionary features and firms are aggregated to sectors a traditional computable general equilibrium (CGE) sector model is shown to emerge as a special case. The static equilibrium properties of that model, however, are incompatible with the operating domain of the dynamic MOSES model, and *a neoclassical capital market equilibrium comes out as an undesirable state to aim policies for*. I conclude by demonstrating that the Wicksellian Cumulative Process can be nicely fitted into the Micro to Macro model.

1 Problem Formulation Against the Background of Economic Doctrines

The Micro to Macro modeling project was empirical from the start. The ambition was to design an economy wide dynamic model economy populated by "live" actors, all being always, but differently ignorant about circumstances that might fundamentally change their ways of life, or even threaten their existence, and on a foundation of observable and relevant "facts". This model design still turned out to have a recognizable place in the familiar history of economic doctrines. So I begin from there.

Economic actors make up ex ante plans, or set up business experiments, that more or less fail to be realized ex post, as conceived. Thus economic mistakes are an unavoidable determining element in the evolution of an economy as a complex economic system of behaving agents that interact and compete in markets. Endogenous entrepreneurial competition forces the "creation of novelty", to use a term from the evolutionary economics literature, or new innovative "ideas"[1] to be commercialized, and an irreversible selection on the population of actors, favoring viable actors, and forcing others to exit. This endogenous evolution of a complex population of heterogeneous actors makes the economy highly non transparent from any observation point, gross ignorance of circumstances (that may be critical for survival) a pervasive characteristic, and unpredictability and the making of (non random) economic decision mistakes a normal occurrence at individual as well as central policy levels. *This all occurs at the intersection of Austrian/Schumpeterian and Stockholm School economics*. A model of an economic system that fails to embody those characteristics, such is my argument, will fail to convey a credible understanding of the behavior of a real economy. The analyst relying on the wrong model might however be unaware of its empirical shortcomings, which raises the problem of empirical credibility.

A key, and controversial element in modeling economic evolution concerns the endogeneity of innovation and entrepreneurial competition. Innovation means

[1]Just for information, in neoclassical growth literature you find R&D based "innovation" or "Ideas production functions" [see i.e. Jones and Williams (1998)] that, as I will argue below, come very close to the idea of an "innovation system", the latter often claimed to be evolutionary.

venturing into the unknown, and therefore by definition defies explicit explanation and modeling of ex post outcomes. This, referring to Witt (2002) has cast doubt on the proposition that Schumpeter was an evolutionary economist. It all, however, depends on what one means by evolutionary economics, and the Micro to Macro model Moses turns out to be an ideal instrument to discuss that question.[2] The trick is to endogenize the conditions that are necessary for *the creation of novelty in the form of creating and selecting improved technology in terms of the characterization of what market agents* (firms) do in the model. As a consequence modeling the evolution of an economic system as moved by entrepreneurial competition, to make sense, has to begin at the micro "behavioral" level, and be explicit about how that selection of agents occurs in the markets of the model.

The characteristics of economic behavior so emphasized were the characteristics of two, of the three competing schools of economics that were developed during the late part of the nineteenth and the early twentieth centuries; the *Austrian*, the *Swedish* (Stockholm) and the *French*, with their respective founding fathers; Menger/Schumpeter, Wicksell and Walras. The winner at the time, the Walrasian, or neoclassical model, soon eclipsed the other two. The Walrasian model, however, lacked the critical characteristics of a dynamic evolutionary economy, and is currently, more than a century later, subject to competitive pressure from Austrian/Schumpeterian related economists for its failure to recognize ignorance, its incompatibility with a meaningfully defined entrepreneur, and its lack of relevant dynamic content.

While Schumpeter verbally gave his exogenous innovator/entrepreneur a role in economic development, the concept of Ex ante and Ex post of the Stockholm school economists, and their emphasis of expectations and plans that constantly fail to be realized, defined not only an opening for modeling the role of meaningfully defined entrepreneurship in a macro economy, but also for modeling the endogenous economic evolution of a complex economic system through "Darwinian" selection (Winter 1964), and an economic system set in unavoidable perpetual evolution by competition. The Stockholm School economists, however, missed that opportunity by refusing to take their analysis down to the micro level, arguing that it would not add to our understanding of economics. The Austrian economists never really attempted the formidable task of explicitly modeling all interacting economic agents within a coherent dynamic market systems framework. In fact, Carl Menger was against mathematical modeling of the economy, which I am not, and was frustrated to learn that his best students (Eugene von Böhm–Bawerk and Friedrich von Wieser) had fallen into the trap of easy Walrasian modeling, which I will not.

The followers of Walrasian economics soon eclipsed the two alternative schools by their ingenious design of transparency, easy teachability and convenient

[2]To understand that, however, requires some technical understanding of the Moses model economy. The literature reference list therefore becomes quite long to make it possible for the interested reader to access the details of the model he needs. Some technicalities that clarify the evolutionary nature of the model furthermore have been moved to the Supplement.

mathematical representation. Austrian and Swedish school economics therefore failed to connect. Since Swedish school economics had an element of Keynesian economics, or even predated Keynes in several respects (Schumpeter 1954: 1173f), the world got the general (static) equilibrium (GE) model, on the one hand, which that still fails to recognize a meaningfully defined entrepreneur and (non random) economic mistakes, and, on the other, the Keynesian policy model that confers more theoretical leverage to politicians interfering ambitiously with the economy, than the understanding they (and their economic advisers) have, and that rational voters should trust that they have. As a consequence both the Austrians and the Swedes of the original descent shut up for half a century.

This "Grand System of Economic", writes George Shackle (1967: 4f) on the general equilibrium model, was complete in essentials" before the end of the nineteenth century, and "in its arresting beauty and completeness this theory seemed to need no corroborative evidence from observation". Alfred Marshall was the academic authority on the Walrasian model at the time, and was highly critical of its empirical shortcomings. During the early post WWII years Walrasian minded static equilibrium economists nevertheless managed to disconnect a promising merge of the Austrian/Schumpeterian and Stockholm Schools, and for decades more or less block the development of evolutionary economics.

On the neo Walrasian, or general equilibrium (GE) model, Hansen and Heckman (1996) write that it is "practically devoid of economic content, close to trivially true, and therefore hard to reject empirically". It is "vacuous" Clower et al. (1998) adds. How could such an empirically empty model gain such dominance in economic teaching and research?

Hansen and Heckman (1996: 101) continue to deplore the lack of attention paid in literature to the transition from Micro to Macro. A redirection of micro empirical research towards providing inputs into well defined GE models would move the economics discussion towards the intellectually (more) important task of clarifying how micro estimates can be used to illuminate well-posed macro economic questions. The GE model, despite its empirical emptiness, might then be used as a synthesizing device to aggregate from Micro to Macro, Hansen and Heckman (1996) add, or as I prefer to express it; as a neutral economic measurement instrument that imposes a minimum of prior content on the data. "A widely accepted empirical counterpart to the general equilibrium theory" however still "remains to be developed", they continue, or a model that can be rejected by data, if wrong.

I will present such a desirable counterpart to the general equilibrium model, which however still remains to be widely accepted; the Swedish Micro (firm) to Macro model MOSES, that celebrated its 40th anniversary in 2014. I will demonstrate its original conception as what was later called an evolutionary model, and demonstrate how those properties derive from the merge of Austrian Schumpeterian and Swedish Stockholm, school economics.

After this background of the history of economic doctrines, the theory of an *Experimentally Organized Economy (EOE)*, and its model approximation, the *Micro to Macro model MOSES,* will be presented in the next Sect. 2 as evolutionary, and distinctly different from the standard neoclassical model, and its empirical application the Computable General Equilibrium (CGE) model in that economic development occurs through explicitly modeled market intermediated selection among autonomously behaving agents. I then continue in Sect. 3 to present the Micro to Macro model, the mathematical code of which will be seen to feature such non linear complexity as to pose a number of difficult but interesting estimation/calibration problems to be addressed in Sect. 4. While the a priori specifications of the model are empirically reasonable and well researched, they give rise to unusual economic systems behavior that is absent in the received economic models. Such *surprise economics* raises a credibility problem that is addressed in Sect. 5. Finally, and quite in keeping with the doctrinary origin of this whole modeling venture, I derive a stylized version of the Wicksellian cumulative process, the ultimate variant of Stockholm School economics, from the Micro to Macro model in Sect. 6. (For practical reasons most of the technical and philosophical discussion of what distinguishes the evolutionary Micro to macro model from received and familiar equilibrium theory has been moved to the Supplement).

2 Life in an Experimentally Organized Economy (EOE)

The system of general postulates and building blocks of an Experimentally Organized Economy (EOE), to be verbally presented here, serves as a theoretical frame for its approximation, the quantified Micro to Macro model empirically set up for the Swedish economy. The theoretical design of an EOE has been used to interprete and generalize from the simulation experiments to other economies.

For reasons to be briefly explained below, but being already presented in Eliasson (1991a, 1992, 2005b, 2009) the Micro to Macro model should therefore be seen as a narrowed down model version of a more general theory of an *Experimentally Organized Economy (EOE),* that frames the empirically implemented model. Four postulates govern life in an EOE;

1. The *Särimner proposition*, that defines the business opportunities space[3] of the theoretical Micro to Macro economy. This proposition establishes universal and everlasting ignorance as the normal state of affairs among market agents, and economic mistakes as a normal and determining element in economic evolution
2. *Schumpeterian Creative Destruction*, or economic growth through competitive selection
3. *Competence bloc theory* that governs the dynamic or Schumpeterian evolutionary efficiency of that selection
4. *Endogenous entrepreneurial entry* that moves competition and keeps the creative destruction machinery perpetually activated.

[3]Or the state space of the corresponding mathematical model.

The ambition of the Micro to Macro modeling project has been to be up to those general guiding theoretical principles.

2.1 The Business Opportunities Space and the Särimner Proposition

The state of information in, and the size and complexity of the space of opportunities which economic agents explore are the fundamental postulates of economics (Eliasson 2005a, 2009). Fundamental ignorance among agents of an economy was one foundation of Austrian/Menger economics. Since agents explore the opportunities space, and learn about its content, it becomes necessary to have something to say of what *prevents* agents from learning all about the interior of that opportunities space such that the model economy cannot reach the state of full information, taken for a fact in traditional Walrasian economics. That prevention is provided by the Särimner[4] postulate, which simply states that we are getting increasingly ignorant about all that can be learnt about, or the economic opportunities space, because *the rate of expansion of that space, driven by its exploration and learning, is faster than the rate of learning of its content*. Let us for the time being leave that proposition of the relative rates of learning and expansion as an empirical proposition that can be tested, and proceed on the assumption that so is the case, and that the Särimner proposition will keep all actors in the economy in perpetual ignorance, and constant unrest and anxiety to be overrun by competition, forcing them to counteract by innovation, or be competed out of business. The point made is that entrepreneurial competition in a viable EOE forces innovative performance on the agents in the market. There is no need to assume anything about entrepreneurial spirit or innate entrepreneurial capabilities on the part of agents. If they don't do anything, or don't know how to do it, they perish. This dynamic keeps the economic system diverse and viable, and from collapsing into a state of full information. As a consequence systematic wedges between ex ante plans and ex post outcomes are created that not only provide a bridge between Austrian and Stockholm School economics, but also introduce the economic mistakes of Menger and von Hayek, and mistake prone selection as the normal vehicle for economic progress. This is also the basic economics behind the growth promoting Schumpeterian Creative Destruction of the Micro to Macro model as stylized in Table 1, which makes up a credible story of endogenous growth through competition driven selection.

[4]From the pig in the Viking sagas that was eaten for supper, but came back again the next morning to be eaten again, and so on. The difference in the theory of the EOE is that the opportunities space grows from being explored through learning. The Särimner proposition was first presented as one of three information paradoxes in Eliasson (1987a: 29, 1990b: 46ff).

Table 1 The four mechanisms of Schumpeterian creative destruction and economic growth—going from micro to macro

1.	Innovative entry *enforces* (through competition)
2.	Reorganization
3.	Rationalization or
4.	Exit (shut down and business death)

Source: Eliasson (1996a: 45)

2.2 Schumpeterian Creative Destruction: A Graphic Salter Curve Presentation

The population of firms in a market can be ranked according to a number of criteria and statistically presented in Salter curve graphics. Figure 1a ranks the entire manufacturing firm population of the Micro to Macro model to be presented below by labor productivity and wage costs 1983 and 1997. Figure 1b shows the corresponding distribution (for 1983 only) of rates of return over the interest rate ($R - i = \varepsilon$),[5] all data coming from the MOSES Data Base (Albrecht et al. 1992).

---

[5]A large number of persons have been involved in the Moses project from its initiation by IBM Sweden in 1974, without whom the project would have been stranded along the way. That Axel Iveroth, then President of the Federation of Swedish Industries, not only allowed the project to be located at my Department of Economic Policy, but acively encouraged it, was of course critical. Ola Virin at my department was instrumental in setting up the Planning Survey to firms, which not only served the model with firm data, but also became increasingly useful in the business forecasting activities of the Federation. The computer programming skills of Mats Heiman and Gösta Olavi at IBM Sweden have to be specially mentioned. Thomas Lindberg, Lars Arosenius, Ingemar Hedenklint and Ulf Berg, also at IBM Sweden were not only extremely helpful in setting the project up, but also actively interested in its progress. Their constant interested attention definitely contributed to the model being up and running on time. Ragnar Bentzel of Uppsala University, once my thesis adviser, was constantly acvailable for discussing the project during its early formative years.

Jim Albrecht, then at Columbia University, joined the project when it had moved with me to the IUI, as did later Ken Hanson from USC. Bot were instrumental in broadeing the model specification, and keeping it running, as it constantly hit the capacity ceiling of even large mainframe computers. Thanks also go to Fredrik Bergholm, Tomas Lindberg, Jörgen Nilson and many others at IUI without whom we would never have got the large database work in order. Bo Carlsson's early economy wide, dynamic cost benefit calculation on the Moses model of the Swedish industrial support program during the 1970s and 1980s, and his studies on how technical changes at the micro levels worked themselves through the model economy generating structural change, in many respects pioneered new analytical methods, but also helped promote the model in the policy community.

With Erol Taymaź arrival at the IUI from CWRU in Cleveland in the late 1980s modelling took a great leap forward, and thanks to the continued cooperation with Erol, now at Middle East Technical University (METU) in Ankara, and with Gerard Ballot at Paris II, Pantheon, the Moses model is still progressing according to some tacitly udnerstood general design. Without the strict

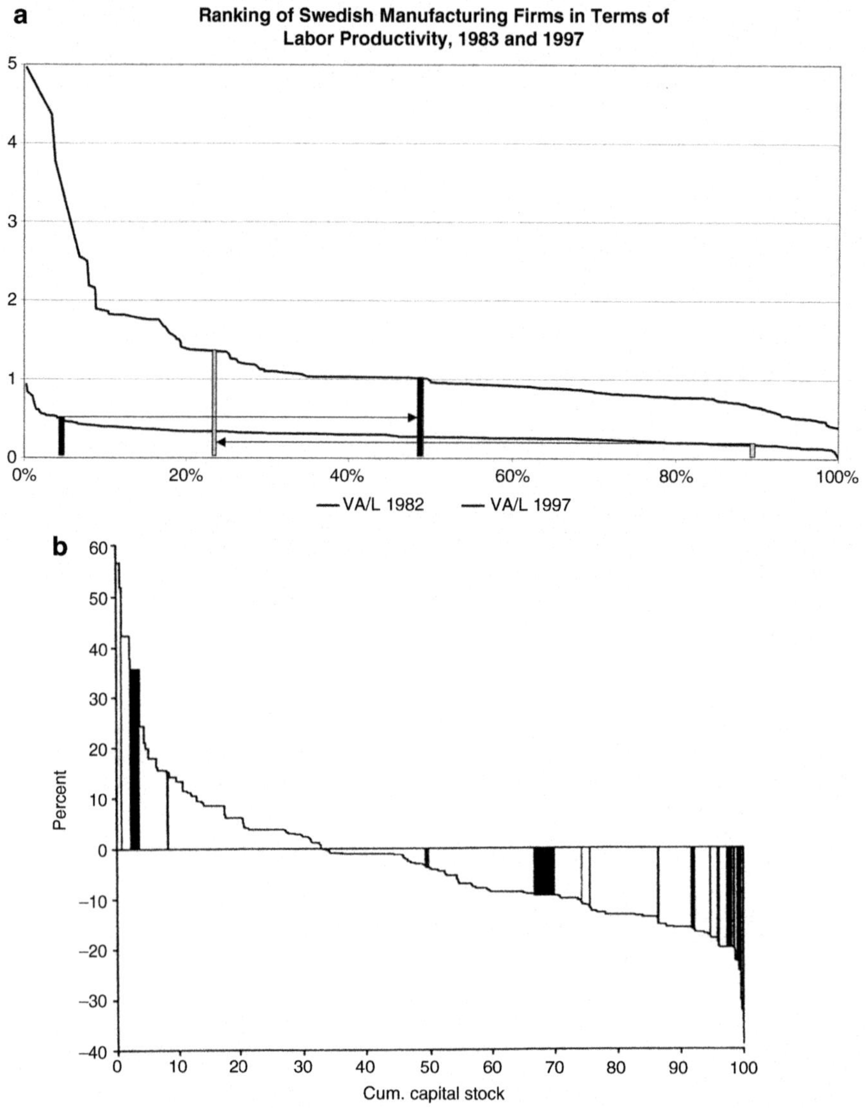

Fig. 1 (**a**) Labor productivity Salter distributions 1982 och 1997. *Source*: Moses Data Base (1992). (**b**) Salter rate of return over interest rate (= ε) distributions. *Source*: Taymaz (1992a: 158)

---

protocol of econometric method voiced by Anders Klevmarken from the beginning of the Moses project, we most certainly would not have taken Moses calibration as seriously as we now have.

Thanks also go to an anonymous referee who wondered whether Moses really was evolutionary, and if so urged me to clarify how exactly the evolutionary nature of Moses distinguishes it from the received neoclassical, or the Keyenes-Leotief sector models. That should have been achieved with the Supplement in Sect. 8.

To the left in Fig. 1a we have the most productive firms with the largest profit margins (difference between productivity and wage cost curves), provided they are not particularly capital intensive, in which case they will be ranked lower in Fig. 1b. Far down to the right on both curves are the low productivity and loss making firms. The columns show two Swedish firms, the width measuring their size as a share of total value added in Swedish manufacturing, one firm (solid column) having lost in ranking between 1983 and 1997, while the other has improved its ranking.

If a firm is generally ranked below another firm it is challenged by that firm to improve its performance through innovation, or be competed down to the right along the Salter curve. For the same reason the superior firm is challenged both by superior firms to its left, and by the inferior firms to its right, the latter trying to leap frog their positions through innovation to avoid the competition, and so on over the entire range of businesses.

And this is not enough. In the wings potential entrepreneurs lurk, waiting for opportunities to enter the market. The general characteristics of those firms is that on average they are inferior to the incumbents, but their performance spread is very wide, and being entrepreneurs they are optimistic about their opportunities to succeed (Why would they otherwise try?), so whenever possible they enter the market, challenging a whole range of incumbents.

As higher productivity firms survive, and improve their productivity performance, and lower productivity firms shrink or exit (in Table 1) the Salter productivity distributions shift outwards, and the macro economy grows.

Technology is, however, not sufficient to explain economic growth, but necessary to frame the growth potential of the economic system as embodied in the Särimner proposition. *New technology has to be commercialized to result in economic growth, and the commercialization process is far more resource demanding than innovative technology development itself, not least because of all the business selection mistakes made along the way.* Given the opportunities space and the competition forcing business actors to explore it, there is a need to explain the dynamic efficiency of that exploration, of identifying the winning opportunities and to carry them on to industrial scale production and distribution that together make up the *commercialization process*. Competence bloc theory does that job in an EOE (Eliasson and Eliasson 1996, 2009). A competence bloc lists (in Table 2) the minimum number of actors needed to create, identify, capture and carry winning projects on to industrial scale production and distribution.

2.3 Competence Bloc Theory Determines Dynamic Efficiency of Project Selection

The competent customer (Item 1 in Table 2) occupies the top position in the selection hierarchy. *In the long run no better products will be developed and*

Table 2 Actors in the competence bloc

1.	Competent and active *customers*
	Technology supply
2.	*Innovators* who integrate technologies in new ways
	Commercializtion of technology
3.	*Entrepreneurs* who identify profitable innovations
4.	*Competent venture capitalists* who recognize and finance the entrepreneurs
5.	*Exit and private equity markets* that facilitate ownership change
6.	*Industrialists* who take successful innovations to industrial scale production

Source: Eliasson and Eliasson (1996)

manufactured than there are customers who understand the products, and are willing to pay. All other downstream actors in the competence bloc have to pay attention to these demands of the customers.

We have the *innovators* (Item 2) that are governed by visions of technologically feasible innovations with also an eye to the demands of the customer. The innovators create the technology supplies in the markets for innovation. From there on selection in the commercialization process begins with the *entrepreneurs* (Item 3) who select what they ex ante consider profitable innovations. Entrepreneurs, however, rarely have sufficient financial resources of their own to carry their selected projects on, and therefore have to fall back on industrially competent *venture capitalists* (Item 4). Access to industrially competent venture capitalists is critical for the efficiency of project selection. Industrially competent venture capitalists are a rare species. When incompetent they charge too much for participating in projects, or dare not participate in winning projects they don't understand (Eliasson 2003b, 2005b: Chap. IV).

When the entrepreneur and the venture capitalist have developed the project further, tested its economic viability and made it ready for the market it might be turned over to the *private equity market* populated by industrially less competent, but financially more resourceful actors (Item 5). The project should now have been cleared ("branded") as a winner that financial market actors can fairly "safely" invest in (Eliasson and Eliasson 2005: 224f).

Finally, if a winner has been discovered, an entirely new competence clicks in, when the *industrialist* (Item 6) takes the project on to industrial scale production and distribution.

The *actors of the competence bloc are functionally defined*. In practice the functions, however, often mix within one empirically defined actor. The innovator may also be an entrepreneur, the entrepreneur may also be the venture capitalist, and quite often a large firm internalizes almost an entire competence bloc.

Normally the range of technologically defined innovation supplies is far wider than the competence range of *experienced based commercializers*. Since there will therefore always be more technical business opportunities than there are competent actors to identify, capture and commercialize them, a *positive failure rate can be demonstrated to always exist* (Eliasson 2005b: 40ff). Hence more or less mistaken choices abound in a progressing economy, which makes the commercialization phase in the competence bloc the by far most resource using one because of mistaken selections.

Commercialization can occur within large firms that internalize entire competence blocs, or over markets. In that sense competence bloc theory provides a dynamic version of Coase's theory of the firm (Eliasson and Eliasson 2005). Internalization by definition narrows the range of competencies and threatens the firm by bad selection efficiency. [IBM, for instance, internalized almost an entire competence bloc in the 1980s, and entered a crisis that almost wrecked the company during the last years of the decade (Eliasson 1996a: 183ff)]. External commercialization is more costly, but offers a broader range of evaluation competence. Provided the external diversified commercializing markets are in place, the risk of losing winners is minimized.

Vertical completeness is necessary to prevent (winning) projects from getting stuck along the commercialization sequence. A broad range of diverse competences, furthermore, is needed at each functional category of the selection range (*horizontal diversity*) to make sure that maximum competence is applied to each selection, and that each project is understood by the resource providers. *A vertically complete and horizontally differentiated competence bloc therefore defines an attractor and a spillover source characterized by intense entrepreneurial competition that drives creative destruction* (in Table 1), and makes sure that only winners survive and can access local resources. The potential winner entrepreneur can now continue to look for resources (financing) being confident that a resource provider will soon understand his project and support it at reasonable terms. If a winner, the probability that s/he will obtain the needed resources is maximized. Since belief in one's idea is the characteristic of entrepreneurial spirit, the more lively entrepreneurial supply, the faster growth, but also the larger the exit rate of mistaken business ventures, and the faster the turnover of firms (entries and exits in Table 1). Endogenous growth now occurs.

While the competence bloc facilitates the establishment and development of winning projects into successful businesses, differentiated markets for specialized subcontractors form a platform for selection of promising growth candidates. But such markets in turn have a history of evolution to begin with, that has the same explanation of experimental innovative entry. *To study the evolution of a complete economic system the initial state of the economy therefore has to be empirically precisely established.*

2.4 Allocative Efficiency in the EOE

Allocative efficiency in the evolutionary EOE economy will have to be something entirely different from the market clearing definition of the static GE model. We are now talking Schumpeterian efficiency in terms of a viable selection of winning projects or firms, or (Eliasson and Eliasson 2005) minimizing the economic loss to society (in the form of lost output) from keeping losing projects too long in production (Error Type I), and from losing winners (Error Type II), or minimizing the economic losses from Errors Type I & II. Error Type I can then be interpreted as being mostly made up of static inefficiencies, while Error Type II, or the costs to society of losing winners, is not even definable in the GE model. The first point to be made of the above efficiency definition is that by pushing policies to eliminate losers of type I too hard, the risk of rejecting winners is raised. Dynamic Schumpeterian evolutionary selection efficiency therefore means that some, perhaps even *significant slack, or static inefficiency* (Error Type I) *has to be allowed for to minimize the loss of the far more valuable winners.* It is however perfectly possible to simulate an approximate Min (Error type I&II) combination through repeated simulation experiments on the Micro to Macro model. The simulations in Eliasson (1991a), attempting to police the economy on to a zero Error Type I static equilibrium (reported on in Sect. 5) illustrates how that can be done.

In practical policy reality, however, the advice of the Micro to Macro model will rather be that achieving maximum Schumpeterian selection or allocative efficiency is not a responsibility that central policy makers will be capable of shouldering. It is instead a matter of maximizing the exposure of innovations to the wealth of knowledge existing in markets through entrepreneurial competition to promote a viable selection of projects/firms, partly through entries and exits. This is illustrated by the firm turnover experiments reported on in Sect. 5, but also through forcing positive change on incumbents (Item 2 in Table 1).

The population of actors (firms) was endogenized from the beginning with endogenized exit (Eliasson 1976b), but became fully endogenized when Taymaz (1991a: 63f, 199) made firm entry dependent on the expected industry profitability. This endogenous evolution of the populations of agents (by quarter) from an initial state reflects the intensity of entrepreneurial competition, and of course also defines the utter and unpredictable complexity that I associate with an evolutionary model (See further Supplement).

2.5 Restless Competition Moves the Model Economy

The totality of an endogenously evolving experimentally organized economy can now be visualized by combining the analogue of a Salter curve in Fig. 1 with the Creative destruction process in Table 1, exactly as the dynamics of this economic system is also expressed in mathematical language in the Micro to Macro model to follow.

Extreme diversity across micro agents and over time characterizes a healthy progressing economy, and this diversity exercises a fundamental influence on the progress of the entire economy. To model this economy it has to be characterized (measured) by its initial state, a diversity that in a healthy economy is then replicated without losing its complexity. In fact, and as a corollary to the Särimner proposition, diversity will rather increase. Two conclusions can now be drawn:

1. At each point in time large numbers of incumbent and potential firms challenge each other along the Salter curves. If not protected by natural or legal monopolies there is **no rest anywhere**. Each actor has to constantly attempt to overcome its competitors to the left through innovative performance in order not to be overtaken. And each actor is threatened by actors to its right that attempt to avoid the competition through innovation.
2. Since not everybody can be superior, firms edge upwards the Salter curves, or are competed down along them. New firms enter (Item 1 in Table 1), *subjecting the whole population of firms to competition* and force change in the form of reorganization and rationalization (Items 2 and 3), or if hopelessly inferior to begin with, force them to exit (Item 4) together with incumbents that have failed in the competition. As a consequence the Salter curves shift outwards from period to period. Macro economic growth occurs.

Together this becomes a highly nonlinear economic system, the dynamics of which is governed by competing incompatible choices and selections. This economic system has no external equilibrium solution. If pushed too hard for a "market clearing solution" the model economy is likely to collapse (Eliasson 1991a); an "infinite regress" occurs. Complexity therefore rules in the EOE, and economic mistakes at all levels abound, including at the policy levels. Ambitious policies based on advice from empirically faulty economic theorizing is however potentially far more harmful to the economy (because of the large resources moved around at that level), than the many individual business mistakes that cancel against the business successes, many of which would not have been realized if not accompanied by the mistakes. Since this characterization is inherently empirically reasonable, it also becomes important to keep it as a characteristic of the Micro to Macro model approximation of an Experimentally Organized Economy.

3 The Swedish Micro to Macro Model MOSES

The Micro to Macro modeling project MOSES was initiated by IBM Sweden in 1974 with the accompanying message that a generally felt sentiment in the Swedish business community was that of a lack of understanding among politicians and academics alike of the role of business actors and entrepreneurship in economic development. After my field study of business economic planning practices (published as Eliasson 1976a) I was inclined to agree. I was in fact very enthusiastic about the proposition, and found no problem to get acceptance for my personal demand that the macroeconomic system should be based on the explicit behavior of micro agents in dynamic markets, even though there was no such model to be found in the global academic community. It was also understood that the model should preferably be economy wide, dynamic, empirical, and relate to some known economy, an ambition that my doctorate work at IUI made me willing to accept, even though that ambition made the Micro to Macro modeling project much larger than I originally understood. In the process of setting up the project in 1974 and 1975 Kenneth Arrow was very helpful in getting me in contact with economists in general positive to my ambitions, among them Richard Day, Harvey Leibenstein, Herbert Simon and Sidney Winter.

My doctorate thesis (1967, 1968) on the econometrics of investment plan realizations in Swedish manufacturing had set me on the Swedish School track early, and my field study (1976a) on business economic planning practices, made it clear that Micro based Macro economics was the only way to achieve serious progress in economic theory, an orientation that however ran against the ideas of most Stockholm School economists. The experience from my field study went directly into the specification of the agent decision models, and experimenting with the model told me that pursuing market self regulation of the economic system was the theoretically right way to proceed. The non linear complexity of a complete selection based economic systems model, and the consequent non existence of a traditionally defined exogenous equilibrium, was something that simply had to be faced. Progress in computer science also soon made reliance on the traditional mathematical tools less important.

The project was first located at the Economic Policy Department at the Federation of Swedish Industries, that I headed at the time. In the business community it was rather considered an obvious fact that such a modeling project should have a micro foundation to be capable of saying anything meaningful on how the dynamics of an economy functioned from the market level and up to long term macro economic growth. The academic home of the project first became the University of Uppsala, before the project followed me in 1977 to the Industrial Institute of Economic and social Research (IUI) in Stockholm. Without the generous programming and computer support of IBM the project would however have been a hopeless proposition, and without the Planning Survey to Swedish manufacturing firms, initiated for the project at the Federation of Swedish Industries, it would not have been a feasible empirical proposition.[6]

To achieve an *economy wide understanding* of economic dynamics the micro based manufacturing industry was placed in the midst of an existing, but for our purpose modified eleven sector Keynesian–Leontief CGE type model of the Swedish economy developed at the Industrial Institute for Economic and Social Research (IUI).[7] The Micro to Macro model structure was however such that any part of the CGE sector model could be converted into micro and be populated by individual firms, if the micro data were available. Thus Johansson (2001) carved out the Swedish Computer & Communications (C&C) industry from the service

[6]The solid columns in Fig. 1b are firms that exited the firm population when the MOSES model was simulated from the base year 1982 to create a synthetic data base for 1990 available externally for public use (Taymaz 1992a).

[7]That model was eventually published in Ysander (1986).

production sector and combined it with existing C&C firms in the four manufacturing markets for his Micro to Macro analysis of growth in that industry.

The Swedish Micro to Macro model therefore became a business division and firm-based economy wide Macro model, initialized on a consistent Micro to Macro database, and calibrated ("estimated") against Swedish national accounts data. Work on the model began in late 1974, and MOSES, for Model of the Swedish Economic System soon became the acronym for the model. While the original design of its dynamic core still remains intact, its *modular design* with well defined interfaces has allowed a number of realistic later improvements of its specification. And this presentation of the model will focus on how it looked in the late 1990s when the population of firms had become fully endogenized with both endogenous entry and exit, and an early version of endogenous innovations and the Särimner proposition "installed".

From the start the ambition of the project was to understand the micro entrepreneurial dynamics of a market economy that was growing endogenously through competitive selection. This dynamic core was designed on the model of a Schumpeterian Creative Destruction as stylized in Table 1 (Eliasson 1977, 1978a, 1985, 1996b). One important concern was to explicitly account for the economy wide consequences of both the behavior of business agents in markets and the presence of a large non market and inflexible public sector in a "mixed economy". So economy wide long run (dynamic) competitive selection became key concerns. *For this it was necessary both to begin at the micro market level and "aggregate up", and to move far beyond partial analysis.* Besides that, the preoccupation of the economics profession at the time with large scale macro modeling had created an obvious need to take economy wide economic systems analysis down to its micro economic foundations. Since aggregation by definition reduces the information content of a data base, and notably the diversity of its structure, Micro to Macro analysis can be seen as a method to exploit the information content of available data better (Klevmarken 1983). As a consequence we decided to begin at a micro level where autonomous business decision makers could be defined empirically, their behavior studied, and their internal statistical information system accessed for information. My own field study of business economic planning (Eliasson 1976a) was of course extremely useful here, not only for information access, but also for not getting locked up by the priors of neoclassical micro economic theory. Aggregation above all eliminates the heterogeneity that figures so importantly in the market allocation of resources in an economy. To exclude that information from the analysis on a priori grounds the possibility to understand the role of agent behavior in a market economy is eliminated and almost as scientifically unsound as to believe that macro economic growth can be explained solely in macro economic terms.[8] *Economic growth can be described by Keynesian macro aggregates, but to understand it analysis has to be taken down to the micro level* where decisions are taken (Eliasson 2003a).

[8]Even if Keynes, and notably some of his followers, entertained that idea.

By going micro we therefore expected to open up a vista of new analytical opportunities. The Micro based Macro model was also found to be ideally suited (1) for the study of evolutionary historic processes in which economic, technical and institutional circumstances interact in markets, and (2) to answer questions of the type: What happens to the economic system if it is subjected to particular micro events, or the enactment of particular policies, when it is important to capture the economy-wide and dynamic (over time) consequences. Dynamic cost benefit analysis of policy programs was one example. Economic forecasting was, however, one application that we gave up from the beginning, and for reasons I will return to below.

Empirical application and quantification were an early concern, and a criterion for that was that the entities of the model be observable and measurable. So the firm or business agent was defined as a hierarchical decision system with its own statistical information system[9] that could be accessed through the Planning Survey of the Federation of Swedish Industries. The rationale for that definition of a micro agent is that the firm as a financial decision system is a fairly stable entity that reorganizes itself in response to external market events through mergers, acqusitions and divestments (Eliasson and Eliasson 2005) but can be observed statistically as an evolving entity. In principle we disliked to play around with unmeasurable concepts.

The empirical foundation of the MOSES model was further reinforced by placing the model in a macro national accounting framework. This also allows me now to use the familiar CGE model as a pedagogical reference to present the Micro to Macro model as the desirable counterpart to the GE model that Hansen and Heckman (1996) asked for. The engineering firms populating four markets are however the engine that endogenously moves the entire Moses economy. So my presentation will begin by putting empirical economic life into the accounting or measurement frame of the GE or Keynesian–Leontief (K–L) model shown in Fig. 2.[10] Beginning with this bird's view of the Micro to Macro model also serves the two purposes of demonstrating that the GE model (1) is a special case of the Micro to Macro model when stripped of "economic life", or "evolutionary dynamics". (2), by being almost devoid of economic content, to quote Hansen and Heckman (1996), the CGE model also becomes a useful accounting framework for economic analysis.

After having presented this bird's view I go through the most important model modules briefly, one at the time, and then tie up the presentation in terms of the model's dynamic systems features. Since the model has been published in many bits and pieces over the years, this document also serves the purpose of presenting "a whole". Since the space allowed for often important detail is limited, the reader will have to excuse the many references for technical detail to myself and my collaborators.

[9]Parallel work on a matching household decision system data base was began early (Eliasson and Klevmarken 1981), but has so far only resulted in a unique data base (The HUS project), and a number of econometric studies not directly related to the Micro Macro modeling project.

[10]To make the point of the 40 year anniversary I will throughout the text use the diagrams from the first MOSES model as they were published in Eliasson (1976b,1977,1978a).

3.1 A Bird's View

When seen from above in Fig. 2 the Micro to Macro model appears as a familiar eleven sector Leontief supply, Keynesian demand (K–L) feed back model, and when stripped of further economic content, such as Keynesian private demand feed back, an eleven sector CGE model. A consistent production, financial and labor supply eleven sector Micro to Macro accounting framework has been put together for the initial year of each simulation experiment (Albrecht et al. 1992). Since the Micro to Macro model is (partly) populated by "live" observable and behaving firms facing each other in product, labor and financial markets, the Swedish input output table has had to be redefined on the OECD end use classification to be compatible with the internal firm data used by, and collected from the firms (Ahlström 1978, 1989). As can be seen from Fig. 2 manufacturing industry in this CGE accounting framework has been divided up into four markets; Durable investment goods (DUR), Intermediate goods (IMED), Non durable consumption goods (NDUR) and Basic industry goods and raw materials (RAW). (For practical reasons the exogenous variables will be presented together after the dynamic properties of the model have been discussed, and before Sect. 4 on calibration).

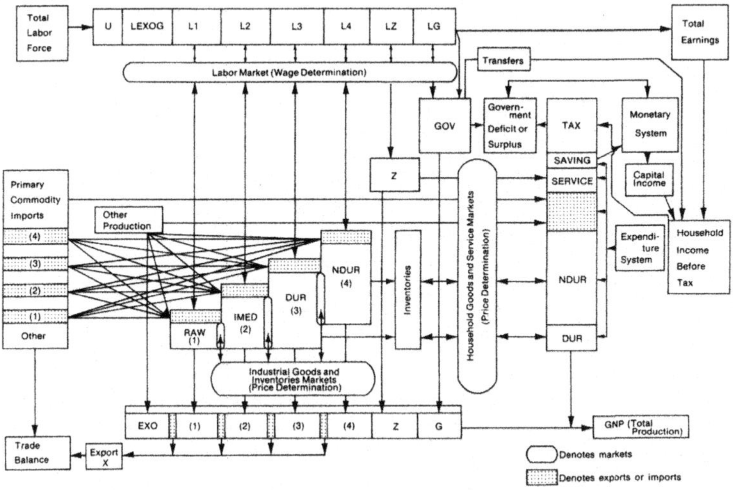

Micro to Macro delivery, income determination and financial flows structure of MOSES. Sectors (Markets) populated by micro agents: 1. RAW = Raw material production; 2. IMED = Intermediate goods production; 3. DUR = Durable household and investment goods production; 4. NDUR = consumer, nondurable goods production.

Source: Eliasson (1980)

Fig. 2 A bird's view of the Micro to Macro model

3.2 The Micro Decision Units

The macro aggregates of each of the four micro defined industries have been carved out in product, labor and financial dimensions, and have been replaced by real firms from a special survey conducted annually by the Federation of Swedish Industries. The firm data have been collected from the firms' own internal statistical information systems, and individual firm decisions are modeled on the basis of what firms know from their own statistical information systems as short term (budgeting) and long term investment planning models, all as observed in more than one hundred interviews with US, European and Japanese firms (in Eliasson 1976a), and in Fig. 3.

Real firm data are added up in all dimensions for each industry the initial year and the remaining residual firm in each market has been chopped up into several small synthetic firms where total size distributions of firms in each industry to the extent possible have been preserved the initial year. Statistical ex post Micro to Macro accounting consistency in all three market dimensions (product, labor and finance) could thus be achieved for the initial year, and is maintained ex post throughout quarterly simulations. New initial conditions after the starting quarter are endogenously redetermined through the simulations each quarter.[11] Ex ante expectations of individual firms rarely add up consistently, and ex ante ex post differences are the major element of dynamics of the model; one heritage of the Swedish/Stockholm School.

3.3 Production System of a Firm

The production frontier $Q = QTOP\ (1 - e^{-\gamma L})$ of each firm is shown in Fig. 4. Q is production (value added in constant prices), L is labor input and γ defines the curvature of the frontier (Eliasson 1977, 1991a[12]). New technology enters through

[11]In a growth simulation some initial circumstances, such as plan realization differences, may cumulate over time, as may also measurement errors in the initial state. Plan realization differences represent market "disequilibria" that reflect the dynamic evolution of the model, but not the measurement errors. Good quality initial state measurement therefore is critical for the empirical characteristics of simulations.

[12]In this verbal presentation of the model I have kept the mathematics at a minimum. Eliasson (1976b) includes a complete early mathematical specification of the model. In addition there are *five* technical *MOSES books* (Eliasson 1985; Bergholm 1989; Albrecht et al. 1989, 1992; Taymaz 1991a, b) that together give a complete state of the art mathematical presentation of the MOSES model through the mid 1990s, including the major updating during the early 1990s, introducing endogenous entry. Learning, human capital accumulation, innovation and endogenous technical change using genetic algorithms was entered by Ballot and Taymaz (1997, 1998). The *five MOSES books* are unfortunately either out of print or difficult to find. All MOSES related publications published from 1976 through 1994 can however be accessed on line, either from the home page of IUI/IFN WWW.IFN.se/eng (under English publications), or from the journals where they were published. For technical detail I will, however, in the first hand make page references to

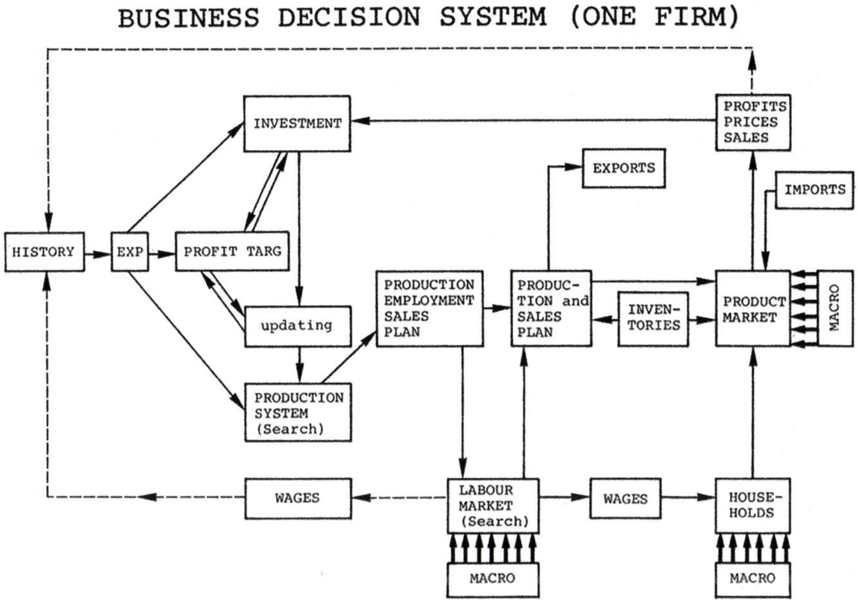

Fig. 3 Financial planning (budgeting) system

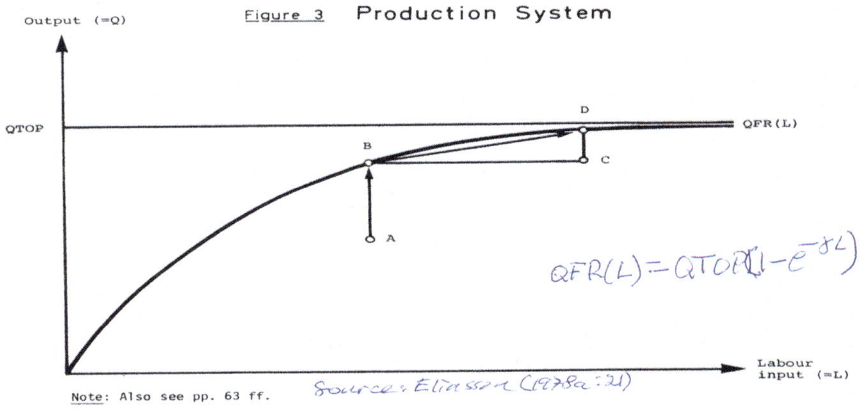

Fig. 4 MOSES production system

publications that are fairly easy to access. They are Eliasson (1977, 1980, 1984, 1991a, 1992) and Ballot and Taymaz (1997, 1998). Also see Ballot et al (2014) for a survey of related Agent Based or Micro to Macro models.

the upgrading of γ.[13] This gives QFR the desired convexity properties and defines the marginal productivity of labor to be γ QTOP in origin. A is the firm's operating position. Both A and QFR are estimated for the initial year on data collected annually in the special Planning Survey of the Federation of Swedish Industries, and then reestimated each quarter on firm investments endogenously generated throughout the simulation. The planning survey questionnaire was originally designed on what I had learned about internal statistical information systems of firms (in the field study Eliasson 1976a), and on the format of the MOSES Micro to Macro model. Firms were always found to be operating far below the estimated frontier, signifying constantly unused production capacity. Competition, however, ensures that firms are constantly striving to move closer to the frontier through reorganizing themselves and rationalizing (Items 2 and 3 in Table 1), thus pushing the frontier further upwards through investment and the introduction of new technology.

3.4 *Expectations*

For the Stockholm School economists the distinction between ex ante and ex post (see Myrdal 1927 in particular), and the role of expectations in shaping the economy were basic. Ex ante plan incompatibilities forced plan realizations to be modified. These "realization functions" are central in the MOSES model which features individual firms drawing up their ex ante expectations of prices, sales and wages on the basis of past experiences to convert history into future projections. To this an extra "caution correction" was added that depended on the magnitude of previous expectational errors, and the volatility of the price, sales or wage histories. Conventional smoothing algorithms are used. There is also an option to incorporate extraneous information on what other firms know and are doing (Eliasson 1977, 1991a: 161f), and expectations can be modified to include exogenous considerations, and "learning from" or imitating competitor firms.[14]

3.5 *Ex Ante Profit Hill Climbing in an Endogenously Changing Competitive Business Environment*

Individual firms set up their own profit targets based on the principle that past rates of return be restored, maintained or preferably improved. This *Maintain or Improve*

[13]Since the production frontier shifts outward by investment, $Q = QTOP\,(1 - e^{-\gamma L})$ can be derived from a generalized CES-type production function with capital stock explicit.

[14]On one occasion managers from several Volvo divisions participated in a calibration game where they set their own expectations, profit targets and parameters.

Profits (MIP) targeting principle was almost universally observed in the more than hundred interviews reported on in Eliasson (1976a: 159, 236ff). Given expected prices (P) and wages (W) a minimum labor productivity (Q/L) line can be computed and entered in Fig. 4.[15] Management can also modify its profit target by observing the performance of other firms, or to accommodate changes in the interest rate. The latter is important in that when firms happen to be challenged by superior firms, they may be forced to opt for a high risk, innovation expansion strategy that will succeed if the innovation experiment succeeds, and fail if the opposite occurs. Alternatively firms can also opt for contraction, or even exit if a positive outcome does not generate satisfactory expected profits. On the other hand high rate of return firms tend to be bolder and opt for high risk expansion strategies, and they may be sufficiently profitable to survive even if the strategy fails (Ballot and Taymaz 1998: 312). Within the area above the upward sloping line, and below the feasible production frontier the firm finds itself in an ex ante satisfactory profit situation. When the operating point is below, it strives to move itself inside the satisfactory range by raising productivity, either by lowering planned production and laying off labor, or by investing and scaling up. The labor market production search process was quite elaborate from the beginning in that we attempted to represent Swedish labor market rules as closely as possible (see below).

The unique Swedish Stockholm School feature of the MOSES model is that the ex ante profit hills that firms are attempting to climb change endogenously because of all the climbing going on. As a consequence firms constantly commit production planning and investment mistakes in that the expected upwards profit climb may turn out a decrease in ex post profits. These ex ante plan and ex post realization differences then feed back into next period's decision making.

3.6 Competition, Business Turnover and Endogenous Populations of Firms

Investment in incumbent firms and new firm entry puts competitive pressure on the entire firm population in both product and labor markets (Item 1 in Table 1). Firms may suddenly find themselves outside the satisfactory operating range in Fig. 4 and are forced to rationalize and/or reorganize themselves (Items 2 and 3), or, if unsuccessful, exit (Item 4). From the outset innovation was present in the model through exogenous Schumpeterian entry, together with endogenous exit (Eliasson 1978a: 52ff). As a matter of curiosity, and an instance of "surprise economics" (Sect. 5) it should be mentioned that the early academic seminar "trials" of MOSES specifications revealed a more or less compact disinterest among participants in having innovation and entrepreneurship economics represented in the model. The advice

[15]Demonstrated graphically and mathematically in Eliasson (1991a: 160 f). Also see Eliasson (1977).

was to turn off the entry module, which we did for some time, soon to discover that the loss of diversity in MOSES structures (with no entry, but exit) soon pushed the entire model economy into unstable systems domains, that again disappeared when the entry mechanism was turned on (Eliasson 1984, 1988, 1991b; Hanson 1989).

Endogenous innovative entry [as introduced in Taymaz (1991a: 59ff), Ballot and Taymaz (1998) and Eliasson and Taymaz (2000: 274)] represents the most forceful competition that (under the Särimner proposition) keeps all incumbent firms constantly restless and on tip toe to improve their positions, and the economy constantly and endogenously evolving/growing.

3.7 Labor Market Matching

When the Micro to Macro modeling project was initiated 40 years ago mobility and flexibility in the Swedish labor market had been increasingly restricted by regulations, that were later gradually softened, as their destructive allocation effects on the economy were understood. In the original labor market search module (Eliasson 1978a: 73ff), however, the productivity of the worker was determined by the equipment in the firm that s/he operated, a specification that was empirically acceptable at the time, but is no longer, as job performance is increasingly determined by the "entrepreneurial qualities" of the worker (Eliasson 2006). Originally both wages and productivities therefore increased as high productivity firms recruited labor from less productive firms, and from the pool of unemployed. The labor market could then be presented as a dynamic market for workers´ services that could be modified as desired to correspond to the various imperfections that characterized normal labor markets. This meant that the labor market of the Micro to Macro model was more of a market for labor than in reality. The modular design of the model has however made it possible to introduce different regulations as they have been introduced in reality.

In the original labor market search module firms made up their production plans and gradually offered new jobs at their expected wages. Labor supply was forthcoming from other firms if wage offers were significantly (the coefficient can be varied, but has been set on the basis on studies of *reservation wages* made) above the wages of their current employment, and from the unemployed if the wage offered was significantly above unemployment insurance benefits. Firms, however, gradually modified their wage offers upwards when they couldn't recruit the labor they needed, and wages drifted upward. In the opposite situation, when the firm was planning to reduce production and laying off labor, laid off workers were allocated to the pool of unemployed.

The original specification of the labor market search module included the only stochastic element of the model in that firms were ranked in descending order according to their wage offers. The market was then stochastically informed about the wages offered in that order each quarter.

Labor market matching could be modified in many ways to incorporate the new regulations enacted during the 1970s and 1980s. One of the first simulation experiments (Eliasson 1977) was on the new regulation (The "Åman law") that required firms to give 6 months' notice before labor could be laid off. The experiments showed this regulation to slow macro economic growth and demand for labor, thus counteracting its original purpose. Furthermore, if decision making in firms was characterized by tough (rather than soft) profitability targeting, the device both prompted firms to look for more productive plans through lowering output, or expanding output through investment, and/or to restore profitability by lowering wages. The long run effects on their rates of return were marginal, and most of the incidence of the Åhman regulatory device fell on wages.

During the early 1990s Ballot and Taymaz (1996, 1997, 1998, 1999, 2000, 2001) introduced workers' training, learning and human capital accumulation that not only raised firms' capacity to innovate and choose the right technologies, but also to learn from each other, and thus raised the performance of the company. Those improvements have moved the labor market specification closer to what it really is; a market for competence (Eliasson 1990a, 1994, 2006).

3.8 Investment, Innovative Technology and the Särimner Effect

Investments in each firm is governed by its expected profitability and brings in new technology that both shifts the production frontier outwards, and changes its shape at a rate determined by best practice technologies available in global markets. To begin with the best practice technologies were externally given through a survey to Swedish manufacturing firms conducted by the Industrial Institute of Economic and Social Research (IUI) in cooperation with the Swedish Academy of Engineering Sciences (IVA), and reported on in Carlsson et al. (1979) and Carlsson (1981). Until the mid 1990s exogenous best practice technologies were brought into the individual firms through their endogenous investments, and improved labor and capital productivities shifted and reshaped the QFR frontier (Eliasson 1991a: 165ff). Technology change was endogenized by Ballot and Taymaz (1997, 1998) who introduced investments in R&D and in both general and specific workers´ training to raise human capital. This way the technological *receiver competence* and the ability of firms to capture and exploit globally available technologies was raised, as was their endogenous capacity to innovate in radically new technologies. Because of the quasi rents generated by successful radical innovations it became profitable for firms to invest in general training despite the increased risk of losing now better trained labor to poaching firms. The increase in general human capital had both raised the innovative capacity of the firm, and its capacity to pay higher wages (Ballot and Taymaz 1997: 205/3).

With Ballot and Taymaz (1997, 1998) investments in R&D and employee training were added to investments in physical assets and financial assets. Total investments so defined were made dependent on the profitability of the firm, the interest rate it had to pay on borrowed funds and its size, very much as physical investments had been previously determined. Together the difference between the expected rate of return on total assets and the borrowing rate, individual to the firm, now determined total funds available for investments. The share of total investments allocated on R&D was in turn made dependent on its stock of general human capital and the firm's propensity to pursue radical innovations. Investments in training or human capital were in turn made dependent on the existing stock of human capital, the inverse of unused capacity to manufacture, and the size of the firm measured by sales revenue.

Through R&D investments and investments in (general) training the best practice technologies brought into the firm through physical investments could now be endogenized. Using genetic algorithms the technological level of a firm was determined in relation to the "global technology" level of best practice technologies within the technological paradigm the firm was operating. The closer to that globally best practice level the more of the R&D investments the firm would direct towards investing in the creation of radical innovations. The probability of successful outcomes of that strategy now depended on the firm's stock of general knowledge, or receiver competence (Ballot and Taymaz 1998: 307, 313f), investments in which are also endogenous and determined as R&D. The firm's probability of successfully creating radically new innovations also depended on its capacity to pick up spillovers from other firms (Ballot and Taymaz 1997: 205/11), which in turn depended positively on the same general human capital or receiver competence. By hiring from firms with a higher per employee level of human capital the hiring firm could increase its own level of human capital, but then it also had to be capable of paying the higher wages that this firm was paying. Together all this meant that *the best practice technology of a technological paradigm* (a global technology) *was endogenously pushed upwards*. Since the opportunities space is composed of all best practice technological paradigms *the opportunities space is* also *endogenously pushed upwards*, possibly faster than it is being searched, thus preventing the Micro to Macro model economy from collapsing into a CGE model.

3.9 Private Consumption Demand and the Tax System

For decades Sweden has taxed its citizens more than any other country. To obtain a "Sweden like" Micro to Macro model economy the progressive Swedish personal income tax system had to be reasonably well represented, and this also required that Keynesian private demand feed back be properly represented. The latter was done in macro (all "representative" households were assumed to be equal), using a marginal tax rate function developed by Jakobsson and Norman (1974) to calculate disposable income (after taxes and transfers) from the endogenously determined wages, and fed through a Stone type household expenditure system. An estimated linear version of such a system was brought into the MOSES model from Klevmarken and Dahlman (1971), modified somewhat to add a non linear consumption component that maintained stable consumption ratios to real income in the long run ("habit formation"), and complemented with an extra *savings/insurance balance* that maintained a long run stable relationship between household financial wealth and disposable income. The latter corresponded to a Modigliani–Brumberg type life cycle permanent income savings behavior in which savings could be said to *represent a demand for future consumption*. In addition, households could swap between saving and buying durable consumption goods (such as cars) over the business cycle depending on the interest rate. In the end, final ex post quarterly saving was residually determined (Eliasson 1978a: 76ff, 1985: 218ff). We also found it quite interesting to experiment with the adjustment dynamics and the changes in resource allocations associated with a change in the Swedish tax system (Eliasson 1980) from an emphasis on payroll taxes to value added taxes, and to study the macro economic consequences of varying various tax parameters.[16] [It is interesting to note that the progressiveness of the Swedish income tax rates affected the calculated cost benefits of the industrial support program of defunct shipyards in Carlsson (1983a, b), a study that we revisited in a companion paper to this in Carlsson et al. (2014).]

3.10 Financial Markets

From the beginning the standard MOSES specification featured firms depositing their cash surpluses, and borrowing in "the bank" at individual interest rates that depended on their endogenous debt equity ratios. Over the years the financial system has been improved upon to introduce parts of the competence bloc (venture capital. Ballot et al. 2006), a stock market and a financial derivatives market (Taymaz 1999; Eliasson and Taymaz 2001). On this Broström (2003) demonstrated that the Capital Asset Pricing Model (CAPM) was utterly unreliable when the economy operated away from what could be called a capital market equilibrium (i.e. when there was a wide spread in the ε in Fig. 1B) which is the normal situation both in reality and in MOSES simulations, and has to be so for sustained economic systems stability.

[16] A fairly detailed presentation of the tax system of the model as it still looks is presented in Eliasson (1980) together with the simulation results.

3.11 Moses Goes Global Through Spillovers and Trade in General Purpose Technologies

Recently Ballot and Taymaz (2012) have cloned the Moses model into ten national models that are linked by spillovers and learning across national boundaries. They combine the already installed mechanism of endogenous radical innovation creation with a more or less generic technology spillover feature, and thus are able to link the economies through the global diffusion of technologies. Interesting new and realistic (observed) economic developments, referred to as stylized facts, are simulated. Ballot and Taymaz therefore take exception to the Solow (1956) and Swan (1956) type models that feature convergence among national economies by assumption. Quite the opposite, they argue, divergence is what you see around you, and should be a possibility embodied in both theoretical and empirical models. Poor countries do not generally catch up to the wealthy industrial economies, and clusters of close and equally wealthy and structurally similar neighboring economies that they call "clubs", may rather race ahead of the rest of the world.

Since Ballot and Taymaz (1998) the Moses model has been equipped with a spillover/learning feature among firms with similar technologies, a feature that is now enhanced with a geographical proximity feature. Since some technologies are more generic and spillover intensive than others interesting evolutionary growth patterns arise that are not stochastic, as they are in all other similar models, and seem to match the stylized facts reported in empirical literature better.

3.12 Non Linearity, Path Dependency and Economic Turbulence Demands Precise Economic Measurement and Credible Estimation by the Analyst

The Moses model economy is highly non linear. It evolves endogenously through competition driven firm turnover and selection carried by the Schumpeterian type creative destruction process stylized in Table 1, and the entire spectrum of Micro Macro market transactions is fed back for a new decision round each quarter. It is therefore initial state and path dependent and features endogenous populations of firms. *Such models are empirical since their initial state has to be measured before a simulation experiment can be run, and with that a case economy has been characterized, that should preferably feature characteristics that belong to a real economy*. Model simulations also exhibit unpredictable phases of turbulence or chaos, and not least the surprise economic systems behavior and the Wicksellian Cumulative process that I address in Sects. 5 and 6 respectively, surprises that are not properties of the received economic models, but may still be quite realistic features that should not be assumed away from the analysis.

Since chaos economics by definition means that there is no way to derive the underlying model that generates the chaos from observed data during the phase of turbulence, once the economy has entered such a phase, initiated perhaps by a sometimes small disturbance or policy action decades earlier ("the butterfly effect") policy makers will have practically no informed way to correct a socially undesirable economic systems behavior once it has begun. Since turbulence is equally impossible to predict, since it may have originated in a small disturbance a decade or so before it shows up, the policy maker will be stuck in a Catch 22 situation, being likely to do worse in the long run, when trying to do better in the short run.[17] Since the origin of economic turbulence cannot credibly be established, and since worse chaos may be created in the long run by actions to contain it, there is a policy morale to pay attention to. *To minimize socially undesirable economic systems behavior "caution", not "ambition" should be the general rule of policy.*

3.13 Exogenous Variables and Economic Systems Behavior

The evolutionary features of the micro to macro model give it uniquely different dynamical systems properties compared to the standard macro models of economics. Exogenous variables, however, keep this surprise behavior within bounds. Some of them are currently being endogenized to make the model more general, but still serve the same purpose.

The five important sets of exogenous variables are:

1. The initial state variables that we measure directly through a survey
2. The labor force
3. The global environment assumed to be in a steady state foreign prices and interest rate equilibrium
4. The global pool of best practice technology
5. Policy

Global conditions 3 and 4 have to be consistently specified over future time for that equilibrium to obtain. Thus, (until Ballot and Taymaz 1997), best practice technology, expressed as total factor productivity in the global pool of technology for the four micro markets that firms tap into through their investment decisions, was determined such that the rate of return of marginal investments in those best practice technologies equaled the global interest rate ex post (Eliasson 1983: 313, 1991a). Locally, firm by firm expectational errors, different individual (endogenous) prices and interest rates, linked to the global price environment through export/import and trade credit transactions, and firms´ own wage setting practices violated that equilibrium rate of return constraint ex post. The exogenous steady state global rate of return restriction on new best practice investment vintages was endogenized and significantly modified with Ballot and Taymaz (1997, 1998). As

[17] In one very early analysis of chaotic economic behavior (Ysander 1981) tax wedges that distorted the price system was the initiating factor.

described above this allowed firms to improve on globally available technology (productivity) through more or less radical R&D investments, and learning from one another, and in such a way that the global opportunities space was positively affected. Work is currently under way to further endogenize the business opportunities space along the lines of the Särimner Proposition. The Ballot and Taymaz (2012) paper can furthermore be seen as a step in the direction of endogenizing the global technology pool by allowing sophisticated MOSES firms to contribute improved technologies to that pool.

In general policy making is treated as an exogenous input in the Moses model and a general experience from work on the model that will be discussed below is that the Moses model economy, due to its complexity and non linear market intermediated selection processes is extremely difficult to control through exogenous policy, in the fashion taken for granted in Keynesian policy models (Eliasson 1983). Misunderstanding the evolutionary dynamics of the model economy may drastically raise the risk of policy failure from interfering with its self regulating market mechanisms.

As long as the exchange rate of the Moses economy is fixed the global economy exercises a restraint on excessive surprise economics of the Moses model. A possible pedagogical value of static equilibrium economics is perhaps illustrated by the final discussion in Sect. 6 of the Wicksellian Cumulative process where the exchange rate constraint is lifted.)

4 Estimation, Calibration and Empirical Credibility

Throughout the large part of the 1980s simulation experiments on MOSES were first run on mainframes, and then on a Prime minicomputer. In the beginning even 5 year experiments by quarter, involving less than 100 firms required overnight use of IBMs largest computer system in Europe, which would have been prohibitively costly on an academic budget. Limited computer capacity thus prevented us both from ascertaining that simulations behaved well over the long term, and from carrying out Monte Carlo experiments to check the initial state sensitivity of model trajectories. Since the late 1980s PC technology has taken care of these practical problems, and an advanced PC can now accommodate a population of firms in the thousands, 100 year simulations by quarter and very elaborate parameter calibration using Monte Carlo experiments (Taymaz 1991a, 1992b, 1993). From the beginning "surprise" behavior of the MOSES model economy (Sect. 5) arose skepticism in the academic reference group, and we had to make up our minds on the empirical credibility of what the model told us (Eliasson 1978b, 1983, 1984; Klevmarken 1978).

Early on, efforts were made to investigate the existence of an external "equilibrium" steady state within the Moses model, which was argued from the academic audiences to be desirable. More precisely, could the model equations be solved for such a steady state? We understood intuitively, before sufficient computer capacity became available, that we would not "find" such a steady state, and that we did not want it. Neither should evolutionary models be solvable for equilibrium steady states (see Supplement). In fact, we found early that forcing the model too close to a capital market equilibrium where all firms operated at roughly the same rates of return, and barely above the interest rate (all $\{\varepsilon\}$ in Fig. 1b being close to zero) positioned the entire model economy in a collapse-prone mode. Without entry, model structures fast lost diversity and became highly sensitive to even small external disturbances, and again collapse-prone (Eliasson 1983, 1984, 1991a).

Using an eleven sector Leontief supply and Keynesian demand feed back model (Fig. 2) to frame the micro market based growth engine of the MOSES model (as explained above) *first allowed* economy wide consequences of a micro occurrence to be quantified, even though the transmission of those consequences beyond the manufacturing industry then became linear and conventional. *Second*, this however posed no principal problem. MOSES is composed of empirically defined modules, including firms, linked together by markets. If considered empirically important all sectors can be micro based. It is all a matter of cumbersome and costly data collection, costs that are however in reality almost negligible compared to the social costs caused by mistaken policy action. *Third*, and not least important, there is an instructional advantage to consider. The links to the CGE model and conventional economics that all trained economists are familiar with are now exactly defined. If you aggregate the four micro-defined manufacturing sectors of the Micro to Macro model, and remove the Keynesian private demand feed back you obtain a complete eleven-sector Computable General Equilibrium (CGE) model with an exogenous equilibrium. This eleven sector model is in turn placed in a global economy assumed to be in static equilibrium.[18] If you keep the Keynesian feed back element you obtain the eleven sector model that already existed at the IUI and was brought in to frame the micro defined part of the Micro to Macro model.

To achieve the required Micro to Macro stock-flow consistency the initial year, the I/O table furthermore had to be redefined according to the OECD end use classification to correspond to the internal market-oriented classifications of the statistical systems used in the firms loaded into MOSES the initial year. The firm data was collected in the Planning Survey of the Federation of Swedish Industries (Albrecht 1978a, b, 1979, 1992; Ahlström 1978, 1989).

All CGE models have a calibration problem, and the calibration methods used have been subjected to the harsh criticism of Hansen and Heckman (1996), a critique that affects this model as well, but not to the full extent. We argue that we have carried out credible empirical calculations, so a few paragraphs on the empirical method are in place. The main thing is to be precise about where exactly we depart from a correct estimation protocol. *First*, you have to argue the case for the particular model specification you use (which is the real "art of economics").

[18] There are exogenous global prices for each sector/market determined such that that capital and labor best practice technologies when introduced in firms earn a return on the margin equal to the exogenous global interest rate (Eliasson 1983: 313).

That specification then enters your estimation procedure as a priori assumption and conditions all parameter estimates. (Moses is *no universal model*, but it is sufficiently general to embody most of the general characteristics of an evolutionary theory that we attribute to an Experimentally Organized Economy (EOE), and to enclose a CGE, or more generally a Keynesian–Leontief (K–L) model as a special case. So before an empirical application one has to argue the advantages of a Moses choice, or the reasons for not using one of the special cases. There is also the possibility of studying the sensitivity of simulated outcomes to Moses parameters, and features that distinguish the full scale Moses model from its special cases.) *Second*, we should resist modifying the model specifications to facilitate proper estimation. Then specification and estimation errors won't mix unmanageably. Even though rarely practiced, it is a great analytical benefit if both errors can be made explicit in the estimation or calibration procedure. Estimating the wrong model perfectly is no merit. Estimating the right model less than perfectly is a problem that can be dealt with. This refers exactly to the accompanying paper on the Swedish industrial subsidy program 1975–1984 (Carlsson et al. 2014). The empirical problem of estimating the social costs incurred in that program relates solely[19] to the "estimation" or "calibration" of parameters to obtain an "empirically credible "Micro to Macro, or agent-based model representation of the Swedish economy. Table 3 describes the calibration procedure.

There are four principal calibration, verification, estimation and testing problems to address. *First*, the exogenous assumptions have to be presented (Items 1 in Table 3). *Second*, the hierarchical structures of both the economy wide model and the firm decision system have to be specified (Items 2 and 3). Together that makes up the a priori specifications of the model that have to be credibly argued *before* parameter calibration/estimation begins. The business decision module of the firm models involves specifying

- The internal firm-to-firm interfaces, and firm-to-market interfaces, and
- Market processes, *how ex ante plans are confronted and realized in dynamic market confrontations*. (This is one place where the influence of the Swedish/ Stockholm School heritage is reflected.)

That micro specification is part of the overall specification of the total economic system that has been carefully researched prior to the design of the Micro to Macro model (as documented in Eliasson 1976a).

Third (Item 4), initial conditions have to be consistently *defined and measured.*

Fourth (Item 5), the critical time reaction parameters of firms that also determine Stockholm School feed backs in the model economy[20] have to be "estimated",

[19]And of course also to the choice of the MOSES model which, given the above, is the empirically superior choice to other kinds of conventional CGE, L&K, or partial models.

[20]Modigliani and Cohen (1961) coined the term *realization function* for that Stockholm School phenomenon, however, without quoting a Stockholm School economist.

Table 3 What has to be measured, estimated, calibrated or assumed?

Exogenous assumptions/forecasts
1a. **World economy** assumed to be on a consistent capital market equilibrium steady state growth path (Exogenous Prices, interest rate) 1b. **Pool of best practice technologies** that firms tap endogenously into through investments [Survey based to begin with Carlsson et al. (1979) and Carlsson (1980, 1981)] Endogenized (the Särimneer proposition. Endogenized through learning and human capital accumulation in Ballot and Taymaz 1997, 1998, 2012) 1c. **External domestic macro environment** (Exogenous 11-sector K&L model)
Internal structures of Micro to Macro model
2. **Hierarchical structures of national micro based model** – Organization of market processes – Modified end use National Accounts and I/O classification (Ahlström 1978, 1989; Nordström 1992) 3. **Hierarchical structure of business decision system** – Internal firm to market decision processes, ex ante profit hill climbing (Eliasson 1976a, and other interviews) – Firm to firm and firm to market interfaces, competition 4. **Initial state measurement** – Individual firm structures [Special statistical survey to firms (Planning Survey of Federation of Swedish Industries, Albrecht 1978a, b, 1992)] – Residual firms to ensure internal micro to macro consistency (Eliasson 1978a; Taymaz 1992a)
Calibration & verification
5. **Calibrating micro to macro time reaction parameters** that move the dynamics of transition over time – Calibration against historical macro time series and micro distributions (Eliasson and Olavi 1978; Taymaz 1991b, 1993) – Monte Carlo experiments to determine long run model behavior (Taymaz 1992b) 6. **Calibration possibility**; Arrange a business game and make real firms enter their own parameters (Volvo)

preferably by a method that makes it possible to determine their stochastic properties.

The first three steps pose no particular problems, except that choice of specification will determine the difficulties of estimation. The exogenous assumptions define what we don't know well, even though the expansion of the opportunities space, or the Särimner proposition, still remains to be endogenized in a sophisticated way. Model specifications under 2 and 3 represent the important "art of setting the priors right", which is a matter of economic knowledge and good common sense. High quality data base work is necessary to minimize measurement errors, because of the sensitivity of the Micro to Macro model to initial state conditions (Item 4). After these three steps estimation of the critical time reaction parameters of individual firms (ten in total, but six of them identical for all firms, at the time of the subsidy study, Carlsson 1983a, b), follows.

At the time of the industrial subsidy study, calibration of the time reaction parameters was done manually as described in Eliasson and Olavi (1978), but in principle executed as in the pioneering calibration program for Micro to Macro models developed by Taymaz (1991b, 1993). Calibration against macro time series data, however, is not sufficient to identify the micro parameters of the model. Individual firms may have different parameters, and there may be several parameter combinations that fit the same time series data equally well. At the time of the subsidy study it was impossible to determine the stochastic properties of the calibrated parameters. Today we also calibrate the parameters against micro distributions of firm characteristics, although that does not solve the identification problem.

We use partial estimates of parameters, which is allowed if there are only negligible *cross-market and over-time interdependencies between micro agents*. Since such interdependencies *define the core dynamics of the Micro to Macro model economy* we deliberately commit a principal estimation error here.

All these shortcomings on the estimation side become part of the "empirical credibility" of the Micro to Macro model. For anyone familiar with the "estimation" of large-scale economy-wide models of the Keynesian type in the 1960s and 1970s, and the CGE models that became fashionable in the 1980s, this problem is known to be universal. Limited computer capacity at the time also prevented us from checking sensitivity to initial conditions with Monte Carlo experiments the way we now do routinely (Taymaz 1992a, b).

The final solution to the problem of estimating and identifying the parameters of complex selection-based dynamic models of the Swedish Micro to Macro type (Item 6 in Table 3) is to do what we once began, but so far have not completed, namely to *organize the entire Micro to Macro model as an interactive evolutionary game* and to invite a sample of managers of the real firms to set their own parameters. This would also make it possible to determine, using small sample methods, the stochastic properties of the parameters. Volvo budgeting and planning management participated in such an interactive experiment in the 1970s, and plans were to expand that activity (Eliasson 1985: 151ff; Taymaz 1991a) that so far, unfortunately, have not been realized.

So even though its principal specification is generic, the Swedish Micro to Macro model becomes empirical whenever implemented numerically, and the empirical credibility of the model, like all models, not only rests on its a priori specifications, the quality of data collection and measurement, and the estimation protocol, but also on how the model is used. It is ideal, if you take the trouble to do a careful calibration/estimation job to quantify the long run economy wide consequences of particular micro events, such as the industrial support program in Carlsson et al. (2014), analyses for which CGE models and K–L models should be avoided. It is of course superior to macro models in general for quantitative analyses of resource allocation problems, and in particular when production structures can be expected to change endogenously over time. In addition, as a general intellectual tool to understand the evolutionary dynamics of a complex market based economic system through simulation experiments MOSES type models is the only available instruments for increased understanding. The best example of this is for the study of "mixed economy" problems and the consequences for the entire economy of an inflexible non market sector, or for investigating the limits of policy control of a complex economic system (see conclusions Sect. 7).

For a highly complex micro based non linear economy wide model with chaotic properties that cumulates errors of measurement and estimation, forecasting, if at all interesting, is of course ruled out, unless one wants to invoke the Friedman (1953) proposition that anything goes as long as the model predicts well, whatever that means. But with such a low ambition, why would you take all the trouble of building and loading a complete Micro to Macro model with data?

Still the Swedish Micro to Macro model, as all other large scale economic systems models, will always have to be a compromise application between a theoretical and an empirical exercise, and the credibility of the model analysis will have to be conditioned by the complementary judgment that has been entered through a priori specification, the quality of the data and errors of estimation; that is on the care, sound judgment and competence of the analyst.

Let us therefore conclude with some apt illustrations that I call *surprise economics,* because they are stories that cannot be told out of received economic theorizing.

5 Surprise Economics

Familiar models of the received type taught at universities across the Western academic world also have familiar answers embodied in their a priori specifications. Depending on their parameter settings the magnitudes of model pronouncements will differ, but for the trained analyst there will be no surprises coming out of his analysis. One "advantage" with the transparent linear CGE or K–L models therefore is that you don't really need much analysis to predict what principal answers the model will give to your queries. Not so with the highly complex non linear selection based, initial state dependent and economy wide Micro to Macro model. It aggregates data both across dynamic markets with endogenous price determination, and over time, and keeps throwing surprise answers at you, or answers that are not embodied in the priors of traditional CGE or K–L models. Part of the reason is the complexity of the model, which is also a natural feature of reality, as current (2015) zero interest zero inflation economics among industrial economies illustrates. So given the estimation problems discussed above let us consider what empirical credibility should be given to some surprise empirical statements the MOSES model has thrown at us over the years on a couple of controversial economic policy issues.

First, in an early policy experiment Eliasson and Lindberg (1981) demonstrated that the costs to society incurred by failed investments, even large ones, are negligible as long as production is shut down as soon as the investment mistake has been identified, and labor reallocated on more promising projects. This reallocation should therefore not be prevented by policy. The large social costs in the form of lost output were incurred when manufacturing was continued in what turned out to be an inferior production facility. [As demonstrated on the MOSES model in Carlsson et al. (2014) a massive drag on the Swedish economy was incurred for more than a decade during the 1970s and 1980s by locking up (skilled) labor in the worst performing large companies through subsidies, to achieve a minor temporary employment benefit.]

Second, a CGE model economy achieves maximum efficiency and utility (welfare) when costs of production are minimized and profits maximized, but eliminated by competition, such that all markets are cleared and rates of return of producers are all equal to the interest rate. In such a capital market equilibrium all excess profits in Fig. 1b are equal to zero (all $\varepsilon = 0$). Such a situation can be approximated on the Micro to Macro model by artificially raising market competition through repeat simulations. The surprise answer is that such an equilibrium does not exist as an operating domain of the Micro to Macro model (Eliasson 1991a), and that the MOSES economic system gets increasingly destabilized as it is being pushed closer to a market clearing situation by competition, eventually to collapse. It was therefore concluded that the state of static capital market equilibrium is entirely undesirable to be pursued by policy. Should you therefore avoid such models, and on what grounds, or what should you do when the journal referees demand that the equilibrium properties of your model be mathematically clarified? Magda Fontana (2010) has an interesting story to tell about the equilibrium syndrome of the Santa Fee Institute which claims to be a pioneer in economic complexity theory. The point she makes is that the closer to challenging the equilibrium the computer simulation analyses of increasingly non linear and complex economic models became, the more reluctant several early sponsors of the Santa Fee institute to embrace its idea became.

Third, Walras introduced the auctioneer, or central planner to make sure that the equilibrium be achieved. Given strict convexities of the production and consumption sets, and continuous derivatives it could be mathematically demonstrated to exist through "repeated (transactions cost less) interactions" between producers and the central planner. The MOSES model needs no central auctioneer to coordinate the economy. It is done by costly self regulation among agents in markets. Coordination, however, does not mean that markets are cleared to allow the economy to go to sleep in equilibrium. To the contrary, Antonov and Trofimov (1993) demonstrated on the MOSES model that centrally imposed coordination to raise static efficiency reduced long term growth by preventing firms from discovering even better opportunities within the opportunities space.

Self regulation over markets draws resources (positive transactions costs), not least due to ignorance, in the form of failed business decisions and systematic differences between ex ante plans and ex post realizations. An illusion of a socially costly organization of the economy is therefore created compared to central planning to clear all markets for a general equilibrium under a regime with (assumed) zero transactions costs (Pelikan 1988). *Transactions costs* in the MOSES model by their very nature have to *include business mistakes* (Eliasson and Eliasson 2005) which are indeterminate, as are then also the evolutionary trajectories the model economy follows. Coordination is thus achieved through competition among all actors of the economy, or by the invisible hand Adam Smith[21] introduced in academia almost 250 years ago. When deprived of its evolutionary specifications markets disappear and a CGE model emerges. A central Walrasian auctioneer is suddenly needed to costlessly coordinate the economy. Technically that can be done if the mathematical model equations can be solved for such an external equilibrium. The above mentioned (Antonov and Trofimov 1993) simulation experiments not only suggest that the CGE model is based on empirically faulty specifications, but also should not be used for empirical quantification, and above all that carrying out policies based on the CGE model are unadvisable.

Four, the entrepreneur of Joseph Schumpeter was for long considered an unnecessary element of economic analysis, and therefore also forgotten in conventional economic analysis, and in economics teaching (Johansson 2004; Rosen 1997: 149), and Baumol (1968) declared that the phenomenon as such, except as a stochastic phenomenon, was incompatible with static general equilibrium, and most probably would continue to be. Not only did any notion of a role for an entrepreneur in economic theory disturb the "beauty" of the GE model, to quote Shackle (1967). It also caused insurmountable mathematical problems to be made compatible with that model.

Not until the realities of the post oil crises global economy had made themselves felt, it was understood that new production structures had to be developed. The question raised at the time was whether Central Government should do the entrepreneurial job as a new type of "Central Innovation Auctioneer". This idea became popular in some industrial economics circles and appeared at the policy level as government sponsored R&D programs and national innovation systems proposals (Freeman 1987; Lundvall 1992 or Nelson 1992, 1993). The alternative to fall back on entrepreneurial incentives and private businesses for recovery, with no intermediate central policy hands involved, took longer to reach the minds of policy makers, but gradually made inroads on the policy agenda.[22] One reason for launching the Micro to Macro modeling project 40 years ago in fact was to explore the rationale for the then common ambition to take typical business decisions up to central policy levels which lacked the competence to pursue (national) innovation systems ambitions. Today, in the wake of a decades long European stagnation after the oil crises of the 1970s, and the miraculous and unexpected entrepreneurial surge in the US economy out of the IT paradox (Solow 1987) during the Internet age from

[21]When Gerard Debreu was awarded the Price in Economics in Memory of Alfred Nobel in 1983 the reason given was that he had helped clarify the role of the invisible hand in GE theory. The invisible hand of Adam Smith, however, had very little to do with static equilibrium.

[22]Cf. Cantner and Pyka (2001) for the change in the German policy mind. Also compare the rapid recovery of the Swedish economy in the "do nothing" policy reference case in Carlsson et al. (2014) when crisis firms were allowed to exit rapidly and workers were reallocated over the efficient model labor markets. The study recognized that the labor market and entrepreneurial incentives in the model were more "efficient" than in reality. It was however also observed, that when the Swedish policy regime was changed in the direction of MOSES model specifications from the mid 1990s, actual Swedish manufacturing growth dramatically shot up to recapture by 2010 more or less the growth the Swedish economy had lost compared to Europe during the subsidy years of the 1970s and the 1980s.

the mid 1990s, this is no longer found surprising. It is furthermore being increasingly understood that central policy makers had little to do with the return of growth.

Five, in their Moses based "Tsunami economics" paper Eliasson et al. (2004), show that the *gestation period* needed for the generic new Computing & Communications (C&C) technologies[23] to be commercialized and to show in resumed macro economic growth *may be very long*. Agents in the market (and in Moses) first have to learn and to build the necessary *receiver competence*, and the information accumulated during this learning process and reflected in market transactions did not give off the statistical signals needed for outside econometric analysts to predict the sudden "tsunami" that heralded the emergence of a "New Economy". Due to the complexity of initial conditions, of the learning and incentives guiding entrepreneurial entry in the model, and of the commercialization process in general there is no guarantee that even a very large input of new technology will at all boost economic growth. No New Economy wave in fact occurred in several simulation experiments because of lacking incentives and commercialization competence. So it is fairly safe to conclude that there was no guarantee that the learning and entrepreneurial new business formation required for a successful outcome would at all take place.

Let us therefore finally (and *sixth*) see what happens when we change the time reaction parameters of the endogenous entrepreneurial entry functions in the Micro to Macro model such that the rate of entry is steadily raised. Increased entrepreneurial entry now raises competition in the Micro to Macro model, and forces positive change on incumbent firms through the Schumpeterian Creative Destruction process of Table 1, and increased exit. As can be seen in Figs. 5a, b faster structural change through faster firm turnover lowers the predictability of market prices that in turn raises the business failure rate, and eventually turns the positive macroeconomic effects of entry into reverse. An *optimal growth maximizing rate of firm turnover appears to exists.*

6 Wicksell's Cumulative Process

I began by presenting the Micro to Macro model MOSES as a model approximation of an Experimentally Organized Economy (EOE), which is in turn a synthesis of a number of salient features of Austrian Schumpeterian and Wicksellian/Stockholm School theorizing of the early twentieth century, features that pry our analysis loose from the general equilibrium modeling tradition. The two schools however failed to connect at the time, and then were more or less forgotten for decades (Eliasson

[23]The "fifth generation of computing" and the entry into the Internet era began around the mid 1990s with the commercialization of new integrated computing and communications (C&C) technologies.

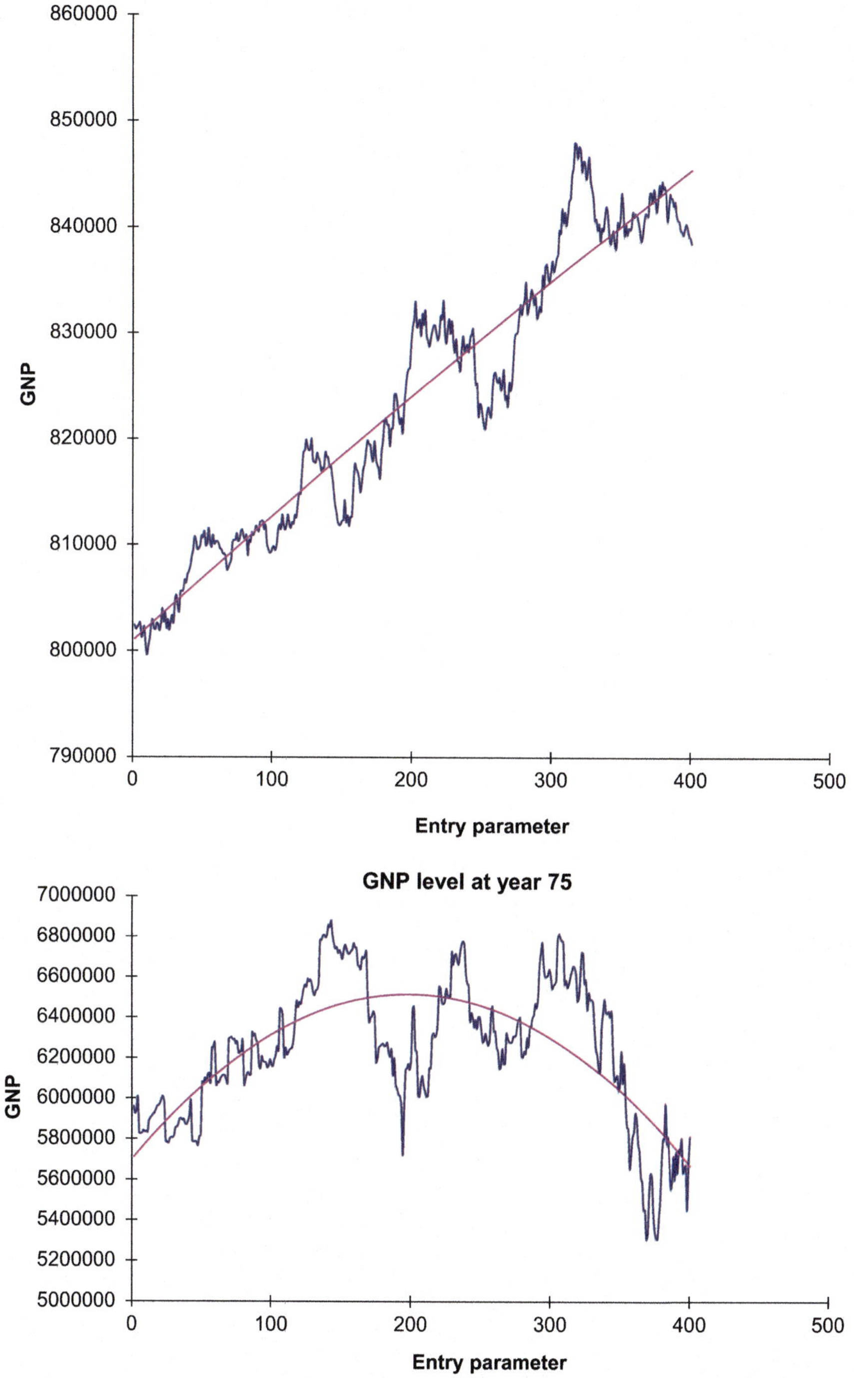

Fig. 5 (**a**) GNP levels at year 15 for different entry rate specifications. (**b**) GNP levels at year 75 for different entry rate specifications

2015). What could therefore be more fitting than to conclude this essay with a stylized MOSES based version of the ultimate dynamics of the Swedish Stockholm School, Wicksell's (1898, 1906) *cumulative process*, which can be theoretically represented within the MOSES economic system.

During his visit to Austria in 1898 Knut Wicksell came in contact with Eugene von Böhm–Bawerk's work in capital theory. Wicksell's use of the concept of marginal capital productivity has made some place him in the neoclassical camp. On the other hand, when Wicksell contrasted the notion of marginal productivity, or the natural rate of return to capital with the money rate of interest, as determined outside the real production system, he quietly did away with the notions of both money as a "veil", Say's Law, and the equilibrium "requirement" that total factor compensations exhaust total production value. When Wicksell finally indicated the possibility of a cumulative inflation process fueled by a "maintained discrepancy" between the money and the real interest rates ($R - i = \varepsilon > 0$. Figure 1b), and a potentially unlimited capacity of the banks to create substitute money (credits), he was no longer in the neoclassical camp (Wicksell 1898: 102ff).

The difference between the natural or real, and the monetary interest rates can be interpreted both as a capital market disequilibrium, and as entrepreneurial rents (the ε Salter curves in Fig. 1b). It was therefore appropriate to ask (above) what would happen if these rents are competed away, to what extent the difference between the natural and the monetary rates could be artificially maintained by policy, and if the quantity theory of money makes sense if the velocity of money, and/or money itself can theoretically escalate out of all proportions. The latter would at least refute the strict version of the quantity theory.[24] Wicksell might have meant that the latter was a phenomenon of the short run, and in the long run the quantitative theory of money should operate as a limit to the cumulative process. At least this is Patinkin's (1952) reading of Wicksell. And Patinkin may in that sense be right when he argues that Wicksell's primary interest does not lie "in describing an *unstable* economy continuously moving away from equilibrium, but in giving a detailed account of how a *stable* economy achieves equilibrium after an initial disturbance". It is however still unclear how that restriction of the quantity theory of money can be imposed on the economy in practice, if credit can be expanded out of all bounds in the short run, and the price system collapses. On this Wicksell (1898: Chap. 7) introduces the interest rate as a regulator of prices.

I have argued above on the basis of MOSES simulations that a capital market with zero rents ($\{\varepsilon\} = 0$) in equilibrium should not at all be a desirable state to aim policies for. Vigorous competition that reigns in the differences but does not eliminate (structural) diversity is desirable. When entrepreneurs react to those rents by investing and/or entering the market (a Kirznerian proposition), they both contribute diversity, force incumbents to improve performance, or exit, and perform a socially desirable endogenous market coordination and balancing act.

[24]Wicksell (1898: 62, 70). Rolf Henriksson has pointed out that Wicksell here in effect presented the quantity theory equation of Irving Fisher.

It is, however, difficult to find documented evidence that Wicksell really attempted to build his "model" such that it should be solvable for an exogenous steady state, which is what Patinkin (1952) suggested. And the Stockholm School economists were rather picking up on the idea of an economy constantly out of equilibrium with ex ante plans and ex post realizations constantly and significantly out of touch, an economy that could never be perfectly coordinated, and that might grow as a consequence of that disequilibrium. [In fact (see Supplement) in my version of an evolutionary economy the notion of out of equilibrium economics does not make sense, since an external equilibrium neither can be defined nor exits]. I have found no argument of Wicksell to the effect that Ex ante plan/Ex post realization differences should be random, something modern Neo Walrasian economists have proposed to accommodate the entrepreneur. The interesting question still is how the difference between the natural and the monetary interest is maintained, and how self coordination takes place in such a "disequilibrium" economic system. An even more interesting question is how the real economy will react to the rate of return and the rate of interest differences. Wicksell in fact unknowingly placed himself in the midst of the currently (2015) hot discussion of the dangers that arise when the financial system is decoupled from the real production system through layers of layers of financial derivatives. The vagueness of Wicksell's own writing therefore leaves room for some relatively free, but interesting interpretations.

Critical for sorting out Wicksell's own position is what he thought about the relationships between the natural interest, or the marginal return to capital, and the monetary interest determined in the monetary system. In his 1898 treatise he took some steps towards bridging the divide between the real and the monetary system, at least in the short run. The Swedish economists also expressed different views on whether Wicksell's notion of a cumulative process was a singular monetary phenomenon, or also embodied an embryo of a growth theory. Ohlin (1937) and Dahmen (1980) suggest the latter, but Landgren (1957, 1960) thinks not. Whatever, Wicksell's own writing can accommodate both interpretations, and includes openings that can be extended into a merge of the real and the monetary system in the form of a simple growth model that can also be derived from MOSES. I say so even though one can find quotes of Wicksell to the opposite. The distinguishing notion is to what extent observed average $\{\varepsilon\} \neq 0$ should be interpreted as investment and growth stimulating entrepreneurial rents, or an inflationary or deflationary monetary disequilibrium (Eliasson 1987a: 95f,b).

Thus, for instance, Gustaf Åkerman (1921, 1923), a brother of Johan Åkerman, in his doctoral dissertation extended Böhm–Bawerk's (1889) theory of capital deepening from circulating capital to fixed capital (Brems 1988) in an attempt to integrate the real and monetary dimensions. On this Wicksell (1923) commented that normally the real economy was held constant when monetary analyses were conducted, and vice versa. Apparently, however, Wicksell thought that this integration could be achieved, but that the "gymnasium mathematics" of Åkerman was not sufficient for that achievement. Many have tried later without succeeding, and the reason is that integrating the real and the monetary dimensions of an economy wide model in a meaningful way takes you out of the confines of the standard calculus of neoclassical equilibrium theory into non linear models that cannot be solved analytically for an external equilibrium.

Today we are not restricted by the traditional mathematical tools. Simulation modeling is a more advanced mathematical tool that makes the integration possible and does not trick the analyst into imposing the restrictions necessary to achieve an analytically tractable equilibrium model along the lines suggested by Patinkin (1952). So we don't have to impose the ceteris paribus clause, holding the rate of return and the rate of growth constant when studying inflation caused by a discrepancy between the monetary and the real rates of interest, and vice versa.

The Micro to Macro model features ignorant firms and entrepreneurs that entertain rate of return expectations on their planned investments that change the allocation of resources and therefore affect economic growth.

A run away cumulative inflation in MOSES is automatically checked by exogenous foreign prices, and rising unemployment, if wages are allowed to run away. Total credits in the system would automatically be checked. But in a closed economy with irresponsible banks, or in the global economy those restrictions may not be there. And if government in an open economy tries to hold back rising unemployment by allowing the currency to be devalued, the self regulation is disconnected.

If devaluation and inflation lower the real monetary interest compared to the real rate of return on new investment, investment and growth may increase and hold back inflation, and also check the cumulative inflation process. Where the balance between real growth and monetary growth ends up is an entirely empirical question. So the "Wicksellian" (1898) cumulative process analysis is quite applicable to the current (2015) situation in the global economy (i e the US, EU and Japan) primed with idling money, ready to be activated.

The Wicksellian proposition could also be reformulated in a different way. Suppose it is desirable to achieve such a balance between the monetary and the market interest rates, and return the economy to some kind of steady state, non inflationary growth. There is a handful of proposed such models (Keynesian and neoclassical) that can be solved for steady states where the real and monetary interest rates are equal and (also) equal to the rate of growth in the economy. Already Cassel (1903) discussed such models, and von Neuman (1945) demonstrated the existence of a neoclassical steady state where the expansion of an economy *under the restriction of no structural change* equaled the interest rate, and no profits above the interest rate could be earned (cf. Smale 1967 on structural stability). The capital market is then in static equilibrium with all entrepreneurial rents competed away. But we have already demonstrated what happens if we attempt to push the MOSES model economy onto such a steady state.

Part of the Wicksellian problem was addressed in Eliasson (1987a: 95f, b). MOSES has a fully integrated monetary and real production system (Eliasson 1985: Chap. IV). Money creation is endogenous, through depositing in, and lending "by the bank". Government can control credit expansion through depository demands on the bank. There is also a financial derivatives module that can boost endogenous credit expansion and further decouple the monetary system from the production system (Taymaz 1999; Eliasson and Taymaz 2001). The exogenous global interest rate and a vector of exogenous global prices for each micro defined market, however, keep MOSES firms from losing control of their wages. That restraint is taken off if policy makers in MOSES allow the currency to depreciate.

Firms pay individually determined loan rates that depend positively on their endogenous debt equity ratios. Local bank lending and depositing rates are determined by supply and demand in financial markets, and link up to the exogenous global interest rate through foreign trade credit transactions as an alternative to direct bank lending. Complete accounting stock flow consistency is created in the initial data base and maintained through the quarterly simulations.

Firms invest (INV) and upgrade their capital equipment and productivities endogenously in response to their expected rates of return ("rents" = ε) over the loan rate:

$$\mathrm{INV} = \mathrm{F}[\mathrm{EXP}(\varepsilon)] \tag{1}$$

$$\varepsilon = \mathrm{R} - \mathrm{i} \tag{2}$$

R is the nominal ("natural") rate of return on capital of the firm, and i is the nominal loan rate of the individual firm (See Fig. 1b). Then:

$$\mathrm{EXP}(\varepsilon) = [\mathrm{EXP}(\mathrm{p}) \cdot \mathrm{EXP}(\mathrm{Q}) - \mathrm{L} \cdot \mathrm{EXP}(\mathrm{w})]/\mathrm{K} - (\mathrm{i} + \rho) \tag{3}$$

where p is the product price of gross product Q. L is labor input, w the wage, and ρ is the rate of depreciation on capital K. EXP is an operator for expectations.

The interest paid by firm j is:

$$\mathrm{i_j} = \mathrm{F}(\phi), \partial\mathrm{F}/\partial\phi \geq 0 \qquad \phi = \mathrm{BW/SH} \tag{4}$$

where BW stands for debt, and SH for shares or equity on the books (Eliasson 1985: Chap. IV on money in Moses).

Given this a cumulative process experiment on MOSES can be set up:

(A). Endogenize politicians by making the exhange rate against foreign currencies = F(RU), $\partial F/\partial \leq 0$, where RU is the employment rate.
(B). Increase market speeds such that all $\{\varepsilon\} \rightarrow 0$.

If unemployment concerns make policy makers give up on currency discipline, inflation in the model economy may escalate out of all proportions. Speeding up markets flattens the {ε} distributions in Fig. 1b and force them close to 0. Self regulation in markets is reduced or decoupled altogether. Cumulative inflation could then occur. It is however theoretically unclear whether the real economy collapses before inflation goes through the roof.

If the initial state of the model economy is such that all {ε} are significantly >0 a balancing act will occur between real economic growth through investment in (1), and inflation through the policy equation (A). Market pricing and predictability are disturbed by inflation and growth reduced. In the "Wicksellian case" with no positive investment and growth response the increased unemployment might start up a cumulative inflation process. Investment and growth stimulus through (1), on the other hand, should raise growth and reduce unemployment and soften a devaluation prone inflationary policy. My point is that in a complete model scenario with integrated monetary and real systems the investment growth response to large positive expected $\{\varepsilon\}$ may be sufficiently large to prevent cumulative inflation from occurring. The latter may be the case Wicksell really considered, but that the Swedish economists failed to agree on.

7 Conclusions on the Economic Modeling of Complexity

This has been my illustrated story of the evolution of the MOSES Micro to Macro model as a merger of Austrian/Schumpeterian and Stockholm School economics. As will be further detailed in the Supplement, a new and highly complex theoretical economic world emerges that can be clearly distinguished from the market clearing general equilibrium tradition, that exhibits all the qualities that we want to associate with evolutionary economics. A helpful instructional result is that an eleven sector computable general equilibrium (CGE) model emerges as a special case when the Micro to Macro model is deprived of its evolutionary features and aggregated to the industry sector level.

The complexity and unpredictability of the evolutionary Moses model economy not only raises uncertainty in the life of explicitly modeled micro agents, who constantly fail to realize their Ex ante plans, but should also alert policy makers, comfortably lodged in the security of fail safe Keynesian or GE thinking, to the high risks of significant policy failure when interfering with the self regulating market mechanisms of the Moses economy. Even seemingly minor policy measures may accidentally cumulate into major events. Policy failure thus is a far more serious problem than the many instances of uncoordinated individual business failures because of the large resources systematically moved around at that level. *The smooth development or macro growth of an evolutionary economic model requires a minimum of unpredictable disorder at the micro market level in the form of business successes and failures.*

The Micro to Macro model, instead of offering guidance for fine tuning economic systems evolution with corrective policies, presents itself as a potentially useful instrument for dynamic cost benefit analyses, especially when further advance has been made on developing credible calibration/estimation methods of the parameters of very complex non linear Micro to Macro selection models. Research investment here should be socially very profitable because of the small resources needed compared to the potentially large social costs of policy makers messing unwittingly with the economy. For the time being the great insight from evolutionary economic modeling is that big Government now appears on the scene as only one of many market agents liable to make serious mistakes. The new morale therefore is for policy makers to be cautious, rather than ambitious.

Supplement

The Evolutionary Nature of the Swedish Micro to Macro Model

I have argued that the theory of an *Experimentally Organized Economy (EOE)*, and its model approximation, the *Micro to Macro model MOSES,* are evolutionary and distinctly different from the standard neoclassical equilibrium model, as well as its empirical application, the Computable General Equilibrium (CGE) model, or for that matter Keynesian & Leontief type sector models. The existence, or non-existence of a traditional exogenous equilibrium is what distinguishes these two theoretical worlds from one another. I have added that that same distinction should also be made the distinguishing feature of evolutionary economics, and that this will cast doubt on the evolutionary nature of the popular (national) innovation systems models. To say that they may not be evolutionary, however, is also close to saying that Schumpeter's (1911) theory, and even more so that his dismal foreboding of 1942, are not evolutionary (Witt 2002).

To motivate such heretic suggestions let me begin with some quotations from literature, and to begin with a sympathizing neoclassical economist from Chicago. Even though "neoclassical economics would be enriched by a more fully articulated view of competition as a selection device, ...and as a generator of economic change", writes Rosen (1997: 150), disequilibrium analysis is probably not compatible with "the neoclassical scheme". In neoclassical equilibrium, Rosen continues, "there is nothing for entrepreneurs to do", a view voiced already by Baumol (1968). Austrian economics, on the other hand, with entrepreneurial competition as "the main instrument of change" within the economy, therefore "offers a valuable perspective of the economy as an evolutionary process".

Like Rosen, I am perfectly aware that enormous academic effort has been devoted to introducing non equilibrium dynamics into the neoclassical model, without, however, violating its central dictum of the existence of an external equilibrium, and that it may be unfair to those who have tried, to compare with a highly stylized model that they have tried unsuccessfully to abandon. But the preoccupation with static equilibrium with those who still insist not only makes it appropriate, but correct to use the market clearing neoclassical model as a reference bench mark for clarifying the differences to the evolutionary alternative I am going for. Unfortunately this means ripping open the mathematical foundation of market clearing general equilibrium economics. My auxiliary reason, however, is that we now have a well defined mathematical alternative, the Micro to Macro model

Moses that can speak for itself, so we don't have to be overly critical of orthodox economics to make our points.

While Schumpeter has been a standard reference for evolutionary economics, Witt (1993, 2002: 9) takes a polite exception to that view. He requires as a minimum that evolutionary theory be capable of self transformation of the economic system through the "endogenous creation of novelty", or innovation and entrepreneurship. Not much of evolutionary modeling I have seen is however up to that requirement.

In Schumpeter (1911), and even more so in 1942, the innovator, or "creator of novelty" is exogenous and not explained, while the entrepreneur is the endogenous "doer" who turns the exogenous innovations into the kick starter of economic development (Hanusch and Pyka 2007a, b), or perhaps the discoverer of new profit opportunities, which is Kirzner's (1997) perhaps alternative idea of entrepreneurship. But this is not enough to make the creator of novelty endogenous according to Witt, and also Dopfer (2012). By substituting administrative routinization of R&D management for the innovator/entrepreneur, Schumpeter (1942) removed himself even more from the notion of entrepreneurial competition sketched in his 1911 treatise. He has instead inspired the invention of both the central administrative national innovation systems artifacts as policy instruments for the 1990s to help failing markets to allocate R&D spending better, and the "ideas production functions" of New Growth Macro theory, sometimes referred to as "Schumpeterian", very succinctly formulated in Jones and Williams (1998).

The Informational Assumptions About the Unknown

A central premise of evolutionary economics therefore has to be the assumptions made about how unknown to the actors the content of the economic or business opportunities space is. The assumptions made about the state of information in the economy are central for economics (Eliasson 1987a, 1992, 2009). For Carl Menger (1871), and also restated by Rosen (1997: 141), "there is an enormous amount of ignorance in the (economic) system" and "out of the totality of what is known in the economy at large, any single person knows essentially nothing".

Here I venture to add (Eliasson 2005a, 2009) that there is a lot more to learn about in the business opportunities space that none in the economy yet knows about, but may learn about by exploring that unknown totality. By exploring that unknown terrain adventurous innovators and entrepreneurs use their knowledge and experience, significant and critical parts of which they cannot articulate (being *tacit*), to discover new avenues of progress, and not only come up with new ideas. They also, in doing so, expand the opportunities space and prevent it from being fully searched and all opportunities exhausted (The Särimner proposition). In doing so they however also frequently fail to come up with a god design of their business experiment, and *the resources lost through mistaken entrepreneurial ventures become a transactions cost that should be balanced against the gains from the same exploration of the opportunities space* (Eliasson and Eliasson 2005). The economy thus has a capacity to generate new ideas through entrepreneurial ingenuity and discovery.[25] The circumstances favoring, or disfavoring such innovative exploration can be observed and modeled, and the outcome expressed in terms of the productive performance of the innovator/entrepreneur, without characterizing the type of novelty created.

The rate of business failure accelerates if exploration (read entrepreneurial competition) is speeded up (Eliasson 1991a, 2009). Entrepreneurial competition can, however, only occur in markets populated by autonomously behaving business agents. It draws transactions costs in the form of business failure. It has gradually been endogenized in the Moses model in ways to be explained below. The totality of such an endogenous entrepreneurial exploration and selection process must satisfy Witt's general definition of an evolutionary economy. A model of such an evolutionary economy of course soon becomes too complex to be compacted into an equation system that can be solved for a market clearing equilibrium. Coordination of the model economy thus has to be achieved by other means than assuming that a central political chieftain, or Walrasian auctioneer, be around to do the job free of charge (zero transactions cost assumption). We therefore have to think in terms of the emergence of (Lesourne and Orléan 1998) stable systems of coordination as the result of a "collective learning process", and evolutionary self-organizing among agents in markets guided for instance by the constantly changing price and quantity signals from market transactions. Rosen (1997) concludes by paying his respects to the great Austrian economists´ legacy of paying attention to the systems aspects of economic theory,[26] and how "open competition and survival of the fittest work to aggregate highly decentralized knowledge and information into" ...a "mostly smoothly operating, but rudderless social organization". The Moses model features such self regulating market processes in the form of algorithms that mimic the solution of the model for an external equilibrium that does not exist because of the non linear complexity of the millions of selection processes that make up the Moses model (see Moses code in Eliasson 1976b: 193ff, 1978a: 175ff). Obviously such a convergence process (it normally converges in the short run!) won't be perfectly stable, because it also changes the structures of the economy that

[25] In neoclassical growth theory R&D is the resource that goes into that creative activity, but since failed business experiments, that neoclassical theory fails to recognize, appear as unpredictable transactions costs in the Micro to Macro model, the model economy also fails to come to rest in static equilibrium.

[26] As a matter of curiosity, Blaug (1962) failed to give Schumpeter a chapter of his own, because (Op cit, p. 416) he "failed in any way to provide either a systematic theory or classification of innovations or an analysis of the manner in which innovating "entrepreneurs"—the source of all dynamic change in the Schumpeterian system—appear on the historical scene. And so economists continued by and large to abstract from technical progress." The Austrian chapter is about Böhm-Bawerk's theory of interest and roundabout production, where also Wicksell appears (in his critique of Böhm-Bawerk) as a neoclassical economist. Wicksell, however, appears again in the chapter on neoclassical monetary theory, where his cumulative process, created by a discrepancy between the market rate of interest and the expected yield on investment, is mentioned as a curiosity. Menger appears as one of the three creators of marginalism. Von Hayek gets footnote attention. But Ex ante investment plan Ex post differences with reference to Wicksell, Myrdal and

in turn affects the predictive information content of price signals negatively, and therefore subjects the analyst to frequent surprise experiences.

Hence, the policy maker, or his economic adviser, will be as prone to significant misunderstanding and policy failure, as are all other market agents to business failure. Due to gross ignorance on the part of the central policy auctioneer of the Moses model he therefore cannot solve the neo classical coordination problem analytically. And the macro consequences of failed policy action are potentially far more serious than individual business mistakes that are balanced by business successes, because of the large resources the policy maker can move around. *Evolutionary economics*, as I see it in terms of the Moses model, *makes the central policy maker into only one of the many other failure prone market agents* (Eliasson 1991a).

So the distinguishing features between the neoclassical model and evolutionary economics are (1) the existence, or *non existence, of an external equilibrium* for which the model can be solved,[27] (2) the necessity of modeling coordination through *competition driven self coordination in markets* among autonomous micro agents, and (3) to model the endogenous creation of eternal entrepreneurial competition. So it remains to explain how perpetual entrepreneurial competition through endogenous novelty creation can be maintained indefinitely in the Moses economy.

Agents Forced by Competition to Venture into the Unknown

The business actor can always act on more knowledge than s/he can articulate. Such *tacit knowledge* guides the firm when exploring the unknown segments of the opportunities space, or when being forced to act prematurely to avoid being overtaken by competitors acting similarly (Eliasson 1992, 2005a: 435f, 439f). During that exploration agents upgrade their human capital (Ballot and Taymaz 1998) and spill parts of that same human capital to other actors to imitate or improve upon.

As a consequence of entrepreneurial competition the Micro Macro model economy features the evolution of *endogenous populations of firms*, most importantly through firm entry, and forced exit. Such endogenous structural change first of all affects the reliability of market price signals negatively as predictors of future prices, and raises market uncertainty. Competition furthermore forces firms to innovate in order not to be overrun by innovative competitors, and all constantly risk failure because they have to act long before they have satisfactorily understood

Lindahl are commented upon in the context of Keynes' investment and savings schedules. Knowledge capital and information economics are hardly mentioned. So most of what my paper has been about had no place in the economic doctrines half a century ago.

[27] As a consequence evolutionary models should not be referred to as disequilibrium analysis, since the standard neoclassical equilibrium cannot be defined in terms of such models.

their business situations, and because competitors may turn out more successful. The rationality of this behavior is that rational *actors in an EOE understand that they are grossly ignorant of circumstances that may eventually threaten their survival*. They are "boundedly rational" to use Herbert Simon's term.[28] This state of constant *market anxiety* leaves little margin for rest, and prevails for ever, if not reduced by regulation or monopoly formation. An important *part of explicit evolutionary modeling therefore is to characterize what information/knowledge firms base their expectations and plans on, or how ignorant they are when they make their decisions.*

Firms innovate by exploring the business opportunities space within which all economic action takes place, by imitating, learning and recombining technologies. But those innovations are also added to the opportunities space for other firms to imitate, learn and recombine again. The opportunities space thus increases from being explored by agents that are forced by competition to explore its interior. This Särimner proposition prevents the evolutionary Micro to Macro model from collapsing into its special case, the full information state of a general equilibrium model. In the case of the Micro to Macro model this state obtains when all evolutionary characteristics have been removed and agents have been aggregated to sector levels, namely a Keynesian–Leontief, or a CGE sector model. As explained in the main text a stylized version of the Särimner proposition (Eliasson 1987a: 29, 1991a, 1992, 2009) has been in the Micro to Macro model since Ballot and Taymaz (1997, 1998), and the two are currently working on an improved specification. As a consequence the Moses model will feature a Micro to Macro market based model economy that evolves within, but constantly trails the endogenously evolving business opportunities space.

Endogenous Market Self Coordination Without a Central Policy Auctioneer

The unpredictable endogenous evolution of the Moses model economy is moved by millions of entrepreneurial decisions and guided by prices and quantities determined in markets, all being based on a wide variety of individual and endogenously evolving circumstances. The evolution of the Moses economy may take very different directions depending on these circumstances, and the reliability of prices as predictors of future prices is critical for how markets coordinate that evolution. Things may therefore temporarily, sometimes permanently, go all wrong, and the economy collapses, but normally the model economy follows a cyclical well behaved growth path well underneath the upper bounds of the opportunities space, and extreme systems movements are endogenously corrected through

[28]But they are also grossly ignorant, not only marginally uninformed, which is as far as neoclassical asymmetric information theorist can go without coming up with problems.

micro based demand and supply decisions in markets.[29] Since the economy is bounded from above, excessive movements in one direction tend to be reversed by corrective supply and demand decisions in markets (the Le Chatelier principle). Well behaved macro behavior, however, is normally matched by a corresponding disorder at the micro level, and vice versa. The social and political capacity of a nation to cope with such micro market disorder and unpredictability can be said to also define its capacity to become, and to continue to be a wealthy and growing economy (Eliasson 1983, 1984, 1992).

Statistical learning theory has taught us that the requirements for reliable price signaling are strict (Lindh et al. 1993). Economic transactions only emit reliable and interpretable price signals if the (model) economy features a (sufficiently) stable endogenous quantity structure (the fundamentals) to be revealed by the price signals (Eliasson 2005a: 451).[30] If structures change because of firms´ production and investment decisions the reliability of price signals are negatively affected with a feed back on quantities/structures, and so on. It is no coincidence that both von Neuman (1945) and Smale (1967) formulated very elegant equilibrium growth models under the assumption of no structural change. That mathematical elegance disappears when structures, as in Moses, change endogenously in response to firms´ price expectations and investment decisions. You then also learn that growth cannot occur without a concomitant endogenous structural change, and that perfect coordination onto an equilibrium trajectory is impossible.

Moses as an Evolutionary Design

I will therefore clarify the evolutionary origin of the Micro to Macro model by directly relating it to its two inspirational sources (the Austrian/Schumpeter and the Swedish Stockholm School tradition), and to recognize the empirical tradition of the Carnegie Mellon School of Herbert Simon and followers. When explicitly modeling Micro to Macro, the information and knowledge agents base their individual expectations and plans on, and how they do it, have to be specified.

To begin with the evolutionary nature of the Micro Macro model, as conceived already in 1974, was the consequence of the assumptions made, not originating in an ambition to do evolutionary modeling. The necessity to take macro economics down to its micro economic foundations was singularly overwhelming after my field study (1976a). That field study also suggested that I should stay away from the

[29]Recovery may however take a long time. Cf. Eliasson (1983: 315ff, 1984) where the Moses economy collapses after being tripped by a small micro event, that created a ripple of downstream economic systems reactions, cascade effects of exactly the same kind as those modeled by Acemoglu et al. (2012) who challenged Lucas (1977), and several other besserwissers, who had claimed that such microeconomic shocks would average out and leave only small ripples at the systems macro level. That was clearly wrong as we had already understood.

[30]In static equilibrium mathematical duality prevails, and prices map exactly into quantities and vice versa.

limitations of neoclassical doctrine, as evidenced in Fisher (1972), and later in Weintraub (1979). To explain the dynamics of an economic system populated by autonomously deciding and behaving agents in product, labor and financial markets, we had to know what these agents actually knew, and according to what rules they were preparing and making their decisions (Eliasson 1976a, 2005a). Quite in line with the Stockholm School ideas, firms made up ex ante plans, and responded to their realizations ex post when confronted with the plans of other agents in markets, all staged on an evolving quarterly format.

The empirical ambition made it necessary to model observable Micro agents that made decisions according to information and rules that could also be observed., An advantage of that approach was that the *Moses firm model then could be related directly to the internal statistical information systems of firms that could be directly accessed through a statistical survey*, the Planning Survey of the Federation of Swedish Industries (see below).

To meaningfully theorize and model competition driven selection among agents in markets unavoidably takes you into non linear mathematics and initial state and path dependent empirical models. To study the evolution of such models you have to specify (measure) the initial state of the economy and be empirical (see below).

The next step was to model how firms′ behavioral rules observed appeared in their supply decisions and competition strategies in markets, and how they contributed to a converging price and quantity determining market process from period to period (Eliasson 1976b: 68ff, 185ff; Albrecht et al. 1989: 155ff, 314ff). If I may borrow some terms from evolutionary game theory (Weibull 1995, also see Ballot and Taymaz 1998: 312), without therefore implying that the evolutionary process moves from one price quantity equilibrium to another, the variety necessary for evolutionary economic systems stability is achieved by investment and R&D based innovative improvements in firm performance ("mutations"), while innovative firm competition, inter alia through new firm entry enforces the selection among agents ("replicator dynamics"[31]) that raises the performance of the entire economic system. One experience from early model work (see further below) is that seemingly insignificant events may have a major impact on the long run development of the entire economic systems model.

Since the ex ante plans made up and executed by agents are both highly varied, inconsistent, and, as a consequence, rarely well tuned to the emerging business environment,[32] plan realization differences are large (but not stochastic), *economic mistakes frequent* and normal, and the model highly non linear and too complex to be solvable for an external equilibrium that does not exist even as an approximation. In fact, when speeding up market arbitrage in the model through

[31]In the first model version selection among firms is enforced through competition in markets, forcing upgrading of performance or exit through the Schumpeterian type creative destruction process (in Table 1 in the main text). In later versions various functions of the competence bloc theory of the main text that governs selection and commercialization of technologies within firms, or in markets have been introduced (e.g. Ballot et al. 2006).

[32]An environment largely made up of all competing agents, and therefore also endogenous.

exogenous policy interference, forcing it closer to an approximate external market clearing equilibrium,[33] the economic system eventually collapsed (Eliasson 1984, 1991a). This non existence of an external equilibrium, and a preserved micro heterogeneity (through innovation) should therefore be considered both a prerequisite for preserved economic systems stability, and a typical characteristic of an evolutionary model (at least as I define it), and one consequence of the Wicksellian ex ante and ex post based theorizing of the Swedish Stockholm School economists. These ideas were also an early source of inspiration of mine both in my doctorate thesis (1967, 1969), my field survey of business economic planning (1976a), and when designing the Micro to Macro model (1976b, 1977), ideas that were unfortunately abandoned by later Swedish economists in favor of the then popular general equilibrium model (Eliasson 2015).

So both on empirical and theoretical grounds I make the Stockholm School notion of ex ante agent plans and ex post realizations when confronted in markets, a distinguishing feature of evolutionary economics. There boundedly rational ("ignorant") agents act on intuition, and their successes and failures in markets feed back to influence next period decisions, and so on ad infinitum. With millions of such decision being made each quarter it should be no surprise that the ensuing quite delicate dynamic balancing act may go wrong now and then. To the contrary it is surprising how rarely it happens both in MOSES simulation and in reality. The advantage with the MOSES model is that you can then trace the reason for the occurrence. That notion of feed back economic systems stability, however, does not come out clearly in the many characterizations of evolutionary economics in literature, not all of which have an explicit micro market foundation. I will therefore present my version, and to the extent possible relate that version to some chosen evolutionary economics papers.)

What Does a Selection of Literary Sources Have to Say On This?

While selection is practically always referred to in economic literature called evolutionary, the roles of the market and autonomously behaving agents, and the firms intermediating that selection is conspicuously absent. Here Schumpeter (1942) may be partly to blame in that he envisioned the possibility of an invincible firm that eliminated other firms in the market (including the market) through

[33]Technically the market arbitrage mimics the solving of the highly non linear Moses model for such an equilibrium. Since such an equilibrium point or trajectory does not exist the solution process starts to diverge dramatically when the model economy comes too close to an approximate capital market clearing equilibrium. Prices and quantities are registered along the way per period. If forced to the extreme this solution or competition process eventually forces the economic system to collapse when diversity has been dangerously reduced, rates of return have become fairly equal across the firm population and close to the interest rate, and in addition, the number of firms has been reduced through exit such that market processes can no longer be meaningfully supported (Eliasson 1984).

superior routine R&D management, an idea that recurs in the policy model both of a (national) innovation system, that is often called evolutionary, and in neoclassical new growth theory models, such as Jones and Williams (1998), ideas that to my mind contradict the concept of evolutionary economics.

Selection moved by market competition among satisfying firms is an important element in Winter's (1964, 1971) early evolutionary modeling. The role of the market in economic selection has however faded considerably in Nelson and Winter (1982),[34] who relies more on Schumpeter (1942) than Schumpeter (1911), show a preference for premarket or non market selection, and in the end come up with typical neoclassical arguments of under or overinvestment in R&D and arguments against leaving the allocation of industrial R&D entirely in the hand of "profit-seeking firms and competitive markets" (Op cit, p. 390ff). These are arguments for central policy interference to correct market failure, arguments that soon thereafter show up in the national innovation systems literature aimed at replacing prostrate centralist Keynesian demand policy with centralist policies of the "picking winners" type. I mention this since the Nelson and Winter (1982) volume is generally referred to as a herald of evolutionary modeling. Evolutionary modeling, as I see it, should not only underline the equally, and far more serious high risk of policy failure when Governments doped by Keynesian or neoclassical policy advice ambitiously interfere with the self regulatory market mechanisms of a complex economic system they do not understand. The latter is a possibility not mentioned in the Nelson & Winter volume, that is far more socially costly than individual business failure. "Overspending on certain types of R&D as well as underspending on others" (op cit, p. 390), furthermore, is a natural feature of experimental (evolutionary) market selection by ignorant actors, and something one can only pass judgment on Ex post, and that the market still understands best Ex ante. So there remains the reasonable neoclassical argument of underinvestment in public goods type infrastructures with large positive externalities. But that conclusion is classical neoclassical.

Unfortunately Nelson and Winter (1982) has become an intermediate step in the transfer of the Darwinian market selection of Winter (1964) to the policy oriented innovation systems of Freeman (1987), Lundvall (1992) and Nelson (1992), which appear as central administrative business systems to correct the failure of markets to allocate R&D spending "efficiently" and in sufficient volume. Typical neoclassical arguments are offered in support of such policies, and the role of entrepreneurial competition is downplayed, if at all mentioned.

I therefore see a need to repeat the entrepreneurial competition argument that Rosen (1997) makes the distinguishing feature, and therefore minimum requirement of evolutionary economics, and that such competition requires a micro based market representation to make sense. Hence evolutionary models will have to be agent or firm (micro) based, and feature *endogenously evolving populations of agents (firms) through new business creations, their life and final death (exit)*, or

[34]That is so even though Winter (1964, 1971) appear as Chap. 6 in condensed form.

for simplicity the role of endogenous new firm creation, growth and exit in economy wide systems behavior. Moses then becomes an excellent illustration of such a model since it featured endogenous exit and populations of agents from the beginning (Eliasson 1976b), and definitely since Taymaz (1991a:59ff), when also firm entry was endogenized, as well as explicit market intermediation and selection among those firms.[35]

This places emphasis on the nature and the role of the entrepreneur in economic evolution and whether Schumpeter's exogenous innovator/entrepreneur qualifies Schumpeter (1911) as evolutionary theory. Witt's argument, and also that of Dopfer (2012), is that Schumpeter fails to explain the creation of new economic ideas, and only how the entrepreneur carries out those ideas, or to use my term, *commercializes the innovations*. My inclination is to take exception to that position. New ideas are unique by definition, and their nature cannot be explained Ex ante by theory, only observed Ex post.

Bo Carlsson (1995) and Carlsson and Stankiewicz (1991) presented their technological innovation system as an alternative to the Freeman, Lundvall and Nelson innovation system. Theirs is a design to show how innovation supply is stimulated, created and selected without carrying on to a policy model aimed at controlling the outcomes. Even though they mention the presence of an entrepreneur as a facilitator, the ambition is to improve the selection of technically defined innovations, for instance how they appear in Table 2. In that sense they answer up to Witt's (2002) creation of novelty in designing the complex of institutional circumstances explaining novelty without detailing the nature of that novelty. Theirs can also be seen as a more sophisticated institutionally specified micro version of the R&D based macro innovation ideas production functions you find in neoclassical growth theory (e.g. in Jones and Williams 1998).

Neo-Schumpeterian Complexity Economics

Since the above characteristics all appear in the Micro to Macro model I will finally try to frame my characterization of this model as evolutionary in the terminology of Hanusch & Pyka's (2007a, b) identification of the five intellectual sources of Neo-Schumpeterian economics; (1) the Schumpeterian (1911) exogenous entrepreneur, (2) the path dependencies and irreversibilities of evolutionary economics (Dopfer 2005), (3) the interactions and feedbacks of complexity economics (Kirman 1989; Frenken 2006; Fontana 2010; Allen 2014), (4) the endogenous innovation and competition process that both drives and regulates the entire economic system, including the learning that expands the opportunities space of the economy (Eliasson 1992, 2009), and finally (5) the notion of an evolutionary economy as a dynamic economic system that in my version cannot be controlled, only influenced,

[35]Introducing endogenous entry in an economy wide model is very difficult. Dosi et al. (2013) have used the Dasgupta and Stiglitz (1981) modeling trick of making entry equal to exit.

by policy, and not rarely for the worse. All five dimensions figure explicitly in MOSES. Hanusch & Pyka's general concept is Neo Schumpeterian economics, so the MOSES model becomes both Neo Schumpeterian and evolutionary and the complexity dimension should be obvious from what has already been said.

Irreversible feed back dynamics of historic selection is one economically relevant property of the micro based Experimentally Organized Economy the origin of which can be traced to the merger of Wicksellian, Schumpeterian and Smithian economics (Eliasson 1992) that you don't find in the received CGE model. I demonstrated in the main text that the static standard CGE model, falls out as a special case of MOSES when all the dynamics of firm behavior, market processes and competition have been removed. Similarly, a stylized version of the Wicksellian Cumulative Process has been shown in Sect. 6 to be embodied in the Micro to Macro model.

A non linear selection—based and initial state—and path dependent model by definition has to be micro based, and features endogenous populations of firms (structures) and complicated irreversible trajectories. As a rule it cannot be solved for an external equilibrium trajectory, the non existence of such an external equilibrium therefore also becomes a distinguishing feature of the evolutionary model.

The other side of the same property is that the evolution of the economy follows different paths depending on initial conditions and the composition of price and quantity feed backs in the economy (path dependency). This makes the number of possible outcomes extremely large, the totality immensely complex and the future utterly unpredictable. This complexity is cumulated as the economy progresses through history and new initial conditions are constantly redetermined by the model from period to period. This is again a typical characteristic of non linear economic systems, and notably micro based economic systems, moved by selection in firm populations characterized by endogenously sustained variety. Since initial conditions cannot be determined with infinite exactitude, neither can the evolutionary orbit (or future trajectory) of the model population of firms (Puu 1989: 5). We therefore experience phases of "chaos" when seemingly small events may cumulate historically into major macro economic events. Future evolutionary outcomes hence become unpredictable and optimization therefore not a rational mode of behavior, something Herbert Simon understood decades ago. Since this is a property of both evolutionary and complexity economics, these two intellectual sources of neo Schumpeterian economics emphasized by Hanusch and Pyka (2007a, b) come together nicely.

Selection furthermore can only occur among diverse, non representative firms, and that diversity has to be sustained over time for economic systems stability. Consequently, the key notion in evolutionary economics, both in its verbal form of an EOE, and its mathematical model approximation MOSES, becomes embodied in the Särimner proposition. As an assumption it theoretically prevents the evolutionary model from collapsing into the full information state of a static general equilibrium model. Empirically, however, looking at the economic world around us, the evidence is overwhelmingly in favor of that same proposition, and that it describes a state of the world economic that must have been true since the Stone age.

Furthermore, and already indicated in Hanusch and Pyka (2007a, b: 276), the evolutionary model therefore also has to feature uncertainty as distinct from calculable risks (Eliasson 1985: 315ff), and now and then exhibit "potential surprises" (Shackle 1949).

The third (or rather first) intellectual source of Neo Schumpeterian economics of Hanusch and Pyka (2007a, b) is the exogenous Schumpeterian innovator/entrepreneur who disrupts the "regular circular flow" of Schumpeterian economics, and "kicks off economic development".

One problem is to verbalize the evolutionary concept, which I do in terms of the theory of an Experimentally Organized Economy (EOE). The difficult problem, however, is to mathematically formalize the full evolutionary model, including the endogenous entrepreneurs that keep the economy on the move through endogenous innovation driven competition of Schumpeterian Creative Destruction, or the dynamic forces that both create and preserve diversity of the evolving firm population over historic time. During this economic systems evolution both the cyclical balancing of macroeconomic stability and microeconomic "disorder", and the possibility of systems reversals (the Le Chatelier principle) present the "policy maker" of the MOSES model economy with difficult, but interesting tasks, that s/he cannot study, and practice on the received economic policy model. I have referred to *surprise economics* in the main text as one property of the MOSES model we have learned about from the beginning of modelling work (Eliasson 1983: 272, 1984), as well as the initial state and path dependency typical of non linear models that makes evolutionary selection driven models unavoidably empirical, and model specification, database quality and parameter estimation/calibration a critical part of economic analysis.

Path dependency arises in initial state dependent models with periodic feed back and updating of the initial state, as in MOSES. With no feed back path and initial state dependency are the same thing. I think this would be Paul David's (who came up with the term) characterization, but I am not sure. It relates to so called non ergodic models with a memory, that loosely speaking end up differently depending upon where they start and which path they take. This property has been referred to in the criticism levied against the "ahistorical" nature of neoclassical economics. David (2002: 15) argues the case for path dependent and non ergodic models to make economics the "historic social science that economics should become". For the record, MOSES is both path dependent and probably non ergodic and historical in that sense, and in addition features the interesting historical systems property that seemingly minor occurrencies with time may cumulate into major historical events.

It has long been known that exogenous disturbances can generate long waves of economic development (growth cycles) in non linear models, but then a constant exogenous input is needed to generate sustained economic growth. To become truly evolutionary that same entrepreneurial input has to be endogenized.

The Endogenous Entrepreneur in the EOE, in MOSES and in Literature

MOSES achieves that endogenization in a straighforward way, but it can be verbalized in a much more sophisticated and easy to understand fashion for the theory of the Experimentally Organized Economy (EOE). I therefore begin with the latter. Three assumptions are needed to endogenize the Schumpeterian (1911) innovator/entrepreneur: (1) *innovative competition* by endogenous entrepreneurs forces all agents to innovate, (2) *learning* when the entrepreneurs are forced (by competition) to explore the (business) opportunities space to come up with innovative ideas, (3) such that *the opportunities space expands from being explored*, when agents learn from each other (the spillover property of a competence bloc). That expansion is likely to be faster (an empirical question) than its content is being searched and exhausted (The Särimner proposition). The first information paradox of economics therefore is that we are becoming increasingly ignorant of all that we can know about.[36] Under those assumptions each individual agent in the market will be constantly challenged by a sufficient number of incumbent and new actors to be forced to successfully innovate to avoid being competed out of business (exit), and that this situation of constant unrest and market anxiety prevails for ever, if not prevented by regulation and monopoly formation. Then new firms will be induced to enter markets where they see Ex ante profit opportunities (This is the specification we have of endogenous entry in MOSES since Taymaz 1991a:59ff). Together a sufficient number of incumbent and new agents will then constantly challenge each agent in the market and force it to act innovatively not to be competed out of business, which it is if it fails on the innovation side, and agents constantly do. In this way endogenous entrepreneurial competition keeps the Schumpeterian creative destruction process (in Table 1) going, and endogenous macro economic growth is achieved that constantly lags the faster expanding opportunities space. The latter (3) finally signifies the necessary requirement to prevent the model from collapsing into a static general equilibrium model.

This is a verbal rendering of how the evolutionary growth process takes place both in an EOE and in MOSES. I am not sure this satisfies Witt's (2002) criterion for endogenous creation of novelty or innovation. The theory of an EOE and Moses offer no endogenous explanation of the outcome of the innovation process, except that it creates improved technology in firms in terms of the specification of technology improvement in the firm model, and that innovations that do not succeed are

[36]See Eliasson (1990b: 34f, 46f, 1992, 1996a: 27f).The second information paradox states that because of the increased share of difficult to measure qualities in economic inputs and outputs we are increasingly losing statistical control of what is going on in the economy. The third information paradox combines the first two and states that due to the immense complexity of the economic system gross ignorance prevails at all levels. In order to act and make necessary decisions all actors have to fall back on simplistic personal interpretation models, or ask information consultants with similar personal interpretation models for advice. I believe this last notion of a "misinformation society" is very Mengerian/Austrian in spirit.

eventually forced to exit (selection). *The conditions under which the market competition game forces innovation (novelty) to be created are* however *explicitly modeled.* This will have to satisfy Witt's requirement, since it is by definition not possible to model the creation of something previously entirely unknown.

Menger, despite being one of the fathers of what later became mathematical economics and the static GE model, was not enthusiastic of quantification and mathematization of economic theory. Similarly Dopfer et al. (2004) emphasize the intellectually limiting nature of neoclassical economic analysis, or what they call *algebraicism.* Even though Dopfer et al. (2004) are right, this still does not make it necessary to take exception to algebraicism, only to empirically incorrect specifications, such as those of the static general equilibrium (GE) model. Quantification does not necessarily limit intellectual reasoning, and being empirical should not be a bad word in economics. And we have put great effort into using measurable concepts and empirically correct specifications in the Micro to Macro model MOSES. Most evolutionary models I have seen are however "theoretical" in the sense that they quantify a stylized evolutionary process of a synthetic economy, or (more commonly) a subsystem of an economy. That may limit or distort the empirical understanding of the evolutionary nature of a real economy.

Quite often you also want to quantify the economy—wide consequences of some micro phenomena that stretch over historic time, for instance the macroeconomic consequences of the large Swedish industrial subsidy program in the 1970s in Carlsson (1983a, b), calculations revisited in Carlsson et al. (2014): What did it cost Swedish society in terms of lost output to temporarily save a few jobs on the defunct Swedish shipyards? One may also want to know the "invisible" civilian productivity benefits of large military procurement projects to balance the measured, and very "visible" costs incurred (Eliasson 2017). The standard model used for such cost benefit analyses is the static CGE model, which is unsuitable for such analyses. It is normally sector-based which makes quantification of the initial micro event awkward. It is static, and lacks feed backs while the consequences of the micro, say policy, event progresses through a real non linear selection based economy. The CGE model is however often economy wide, which is good, and a property needed for such analyses.

Post-script on Evolutionary Economics

From the beginning the Micro Modeling project was set up to be empirical and possible to relate quantitatively to a real economy. (This may have been the wrong strategy academically because academics familiar with non linear selection based economic modeling, read evolutionary theory, regarded Moses as a specific country model. Scientifically it has however been the right strategy to pursue. It has forced us close to the limits of quantitative modeling and made us realize that a relevant Micro to Macro theory of an economy, despite the difficulties of the three information paradoxes, has to be empirical to make sense.) Hence great effort was spent on measuring the initial state of the Swedish economy through a firm survey of the entire manufacturing sector. Since dynamics is the essence of an evolutionary model we did our best to estimate or calibrate the model parameters (Eliasson and Olavi 1978; Klevmarken (1978) and above all Taymaz 1991b, 1993). The economy wide dimension was obtained by placing four firm based markets of manufacturing industry in the midst of an eleven sector Keynesian–Leontief model enclosed in the markets of a complete financial system. The macro Keynesian–Leontief sector model part is, however, primarily used to scale simulations up to the national accounts level of the particular economy chosen, to make calibration of parameters against official statistical data, and quantification of the economy wide consequences of particular occurrencies possible. The static nature of that economy wide frame also makes it ideal as a national accounting measurement frame for the entire model economy, within which the evolutionary Micro Macro model growth engine Moses is an integral part.

References

Acemoglu D, Carvalho VM, Ozdaglar A, Tahbaz-Salehi A (2012) The network origins of aggregate fluctuations. Econometrica 80(5):1977–2016

Ahlström L (1978) The market oriented inter-industry stock and flow data aggregation scheme used in the Swedish model. In: Eliasson G (ed) A micro-to-macro model of the Swedish economy. Papers on the Swedish model from the symposium on micro simulation methods in Stockholm, September 19–22. IUI and Almqvist & Wiksell International, Stockholm

Ahlström L (1989) A micro-to-macro data base. Supplement to Bergholm, Fredrik. In: MOSES handbook, Research report no. 35. IUI, Stockholm

Åkerman G (1921) Inflation, Penningmängd och Ränta. Ekonomisk Tidskrift, Årgång 23, Häfte 9:143–162

Åkerman G (1923) Realkapital und Kapitalzins. Dissertation, Lund University, Lund

Albrecht JW (1978a) Expectations, cyclical fluctuations and growth – experiments on the Swedish model. In: Eliasson G (ed) A micro-to-macro model of the Swedish economy. Conference reports 1978:1. IUI, Stockholm

Albrecht JW (1978b) Production frontiers of individual firms in Swedish manufacturing 1975 and 1976. In Carlsson B, Eliasson G, Nadiri I (eds) The importance of technology and the permanence of structure in industrial growth. IUI Conference Reports 1978:2, Stockholm

Albrecht JW (1979) A look at capacity utilization in Swedish industry 1975–1976. In: Industrikonjunkturen (Spring). Federation of Swedish Industries, Stockholm

Albrecht J (1992) Chap. III: Documentation of the planning survey data: cross-sector and panel. In: Albrecht JW, Braunerhjelm P, Eliasson G, Nilsson J, Nordström T, Taymaz E (eds) MOSES database. Research report no. 40. IUI, Stockholm

Albrecht JW et al (1989) MOSES code, Research report no. 36. IUI, Stockholm

Albrecht JW, Braunerhjelm P, Eliasson G, Nilsson J, Nordström T, Taymaz E (1992) MOSES database. Research report no. 40. IUI, Stockholm

Allen PM (2014) Evolution: complexity, uncertainty and innovation. J Evol Econ 24(2):265–289

Antonov M, Trofimov G (1993) Learning through short-run macroeconomic forecasts in a micro-to-macro model. J Econ Behav Organ 21(2):181–203

Arthur B (1999) Complexity and the economy. Science 284(2):107–109

Ballot G (1994) Continuing education and Schumpeterian competition: elements for a theoretical framework. In: Asplund R (ed) Human capital creation in an economic perspective. Physica Verlag, Berlin, pp 160–171

Ballot G, Taymaz E (1996) Firm sponsored training, technical progress and aggregate performances in a micro–macro model. In: Harding A (ed) Microsimulation and public policy. North-Holland, Amsterdam
Ballot G, Taymaz E (1997) The dynamics of firms in a micro-to-macro model with training, learning and innovation. J Evol Econ 7:435–457
Ballot G, Taymaz E (1998) Human capital, technological lock-in and evolutionary dynamics. In: Eliasson G, Green C (eds) The micro foundation of economic growth. University of Michigan Press, Ann Arbor, pp 301–330
Ballot G, Taymaz E (1999) Technological change, learning and macro-economic coordination: an evolutionary model. J Artif Soc Soc Simul 2(2)
Ballot G, Taymaz E (2000) Competition, training, heterogeneity, persistence, and aggregate growth in a multi-agent evolutionary model. In: Ballot G, Weisbuch G (eds) Applications of simulation to social sciences. Hermes Science, Oxford, pp 335–352
Ballot G, Taymaz E (2001) Training policies and economic growth in an evolutionary world. Struct Chang Econ Dyn 12(3):311–329
Ballot G, Taymaz E (2012) Love thy neighbor—a firm based multi-country model with international technology spillovers and growth regimes. Revised and extended version of paper presented to the DIME workshop, Universite Antilles Guyanes, 2–4 Dec 2009
Ballot G, Eliasson G, Taymaz E (2006) The role of commercialization competence in endogenous economic growth. Paper presented to the international J.A. Schumpeter Society 11th ISS Conference, Nice-Sophia Antipolis, 21–24 June 2006
Ballot G, Mandel A, Vignes A (2014) Agent-based modeling and economic theory: where do we stand? J Econ Interac Coord 10(2):199–220
Baumol WJ (1968) Entrepreneurship in economic theory. Am Econ Rev Pap Proc LVIII:64–71
Bergholm F (1989) MOSES handbook. Research report no. 35. IUI, Stockholm (Earlier IUI working paper no. 118)
Blaug M (1962) Economic theory in retrospect. Richard D. Irwing, Homewood, IL
Brems H (1988) Capital quickening and the rate of interest. Faculty working paper no 1470, July. BEBR, University of Illinois, Urbana-Champaign
Broström A (2003) The reliability of the CAPM in different macro economic environments. Master thesis, Linköping Institute of Technology and Royal Institute of Technology, Stockholm, Linköping: LiTH IPE Exarb 2003.672
Cantner U, Pyka A (2001) Classifying technology policy from an evolutionary perspective. Res Policy 30:759–775
Carlsson B (1980) The content of productivity growth in Swedish manufacturing. In: IUI 40 years 1939-1979-the firms in the market economy. IUI, Stockholm
Carlsson B (1981) The content of productivity in Swedish manufacturing. Res Policy 10(43): 336–354
Carlsson B (1983a) Industrial subsidies in Sweden: macro-economic effects and an international comparison. J Ind Econ XXXII(1):9–14
Carlsson B (1983b) Industrial subsidies in Sweden: simulations on a micro-to-macro model. In: Microeconometrics, IUI yearbook 1982–1983. IUI, Stockholm
Carlsson B (ed) (1995) Technological systems and economic performance: the case of factory automation. Kluwer Academic, Boston
Carlsson B (2007) Innovation systems: a survey of the literature from a Schumpeterian perspective. In: Hanusch H, Pyka A (eds) Long term economic development: demand finance, organization, policy and innovation in a Schumpeterian perspective. Springer, Heidelberg, pp 191–222
Carlsson B, Stankiewicz R (1991) On the nature, function and composition of technological systems. J Evol Econ 1(2):93–118
Carlsson B, Dahmén E, Grufman A, Josefsson M, Örtengren J (1979) Teknik och industristruktur – 70-talets ekonomiska kris i historisk belysning. IUI and IVA, Stockholm

Carlsson B, Eliasson G, Sjöö K (2014) The Swedish industrial support program of the 1970s revisited – a study in micro to macro analytical method. Paper presented to the 15th International Joseph A. Schumpeter Conference, Jena, July 2014

Cassel G (1903) The nature and necessity of interest. Macmillan, London

Clower RW (1998) A theory of economic growth. In: Eliasson G, Green C (eds) The microfoundations of economic growth. University of Michigan Press, Ann Arbor

Dahmén E (1980) Hur studera industriell Utveckling. In: Dahmén E, Eliasson G (eds) Industriell utveckling i Sverige. Teori och verklighet under ett sekel (Industrial development in Sweden. Theory and practice during a century). IUI, Stockholm

Dasgupta P, Stiglitz J (1981) Industrial structure and the nature of innovative activity. Econ J 90:266–293

David PA (2002) Path dependence, its critics and the quest for "historical economics". In: Cowen T, Crampton E (eds) Market failure or success—the new debate. Edward Elgar, Cheltenham

Day R, Chen P (eds) (1993) Nonlinear dynamics and evolutionary economics. Oxford University Press, New York

Dopfer K (2004) The economic agent as a rule maker and rule user—Homo Sapiens Oeconomicus. J Evol Econ 14(2):177–197

Dopfer K (2005) The evolutionary foundations of economics. Cambridge University Press, Cambridge

Dopfer K (2012) The origin of meso economics. J Evol Econ 22:1323–1160

Dopfer K, Foster J, Potts J (2004) Micro–meso–macro. J Evol Econ 14(3):263–280

Dosi G, Fagioli G, Napoletano M, Roventini A (2013) Income distribution, credit and fiscal policies in an agent-based Keynesian model. J Econ Dyn Control 37:1598–1625

Eliasson G (1967) Kreditmarknaden och Industrins Investeringar – En ekonometrisk studie av företagens kortsiktiga investeringsbeteende. Almquist & Wicksell/Industriens Utredningsinstitut (IUI), Uppsala/Stockholm

Eliasson G (1969) The credit market, investment planning and monetary policy – an econometric study of manufacturing industries. IUI, Stockholm

Eliasson G (1976a) Business economic planning – theory, practice and comparison. Wiley, London

Eliasson G (1976b) A micro-to-macro model of the Swedish economy. Preliminary documentation (with the assistance of Gösta Olavi and Mats Heiman). Economic research report B15. Federation of Swedish Industries, Stockholm

Eliasson G (1977) Competition and market processes in a simulation model of the Swedish economy. Am Econ Rev 67(1):277–281

Eliasson G (1978a) Micro-to-macro model of the Swedish economy. Conference reports, 1978:1. IUI, Stockholm

Eliasson G (1978b) How does inflation affect growth? – Experiments on the Swedish micro to macro model. In: Eliasson G (ed) Micro-to-macro model of the Swedish economy, Conference reports, 1978:1. IUI, Stockholm

Eliasson G (1980) Experiments with fiscal policy parameters on a micro-to-macro model of the Swedish economy. In: Haveman RH, Hollenbeck K (eds) Microeconomic simulation models for public policy analysis, vol 1 & 2. Academic Press, New York

Eliasson G (1983) On the optimal rate of structural adjustment. In: Eliasson G, Sharefkin M, Ysander B-C (eds) Policy making in a disorderly world economy, Conference reports, 1983:1. IUI, Stockholm

Eliasson G (1984) Micro heterogeneity of firms and stability of growth. J Behav Econ Org 5 (3–4):249–298 (also in Day RH, Eliasson G (eds) (1986) The dynamics of market economies. IUI and North Holland, Stockholm and Amsterdam

Eliasson G (1985) The firm and financial markets in the Swedish micro-to-macro model – theory, model and verification. IUI, Stockholm

Eliasson G (1987a) Technological competition and trade in the experimentally organized economy. Research report no. 32. IUI, Stockholm
Eliasson G (1988) Schumpeterian innovation, market structure and the stability of industrial development. In: Hanusch H (ed) Evolutionary economics – applications of Schumpeter's ideas. Cambridge University Press, Cambridge, pp 151–199. Also IUI WP Nr 164 (1986)
Eliasson G (1990a) The firm as a competent team. J Econ Behav Organ 13(3):275–298
Eliasson G (1990b) Chap I: The knowledge-based information economy. In: The knowledge based information economy. IUI, Stockholm
Eliasson G (1991a) Modeling the experimentally organized economy – complex dynamics in an empirical micro–macro model of endogenous economic growth. J Econ Behav Organ 16(1–2): 153–182
Eliasson G (1991b) Deregulation, innovative entry and structural diversity as a source of stable and rapid economic growth. J Evol Econ 1:49–63
Eliasson G (1992) Business competence, organizational learning and economic growth – establishing the Smith-Schumpeter-Wicksell (SSW) connection. In: Scherer FM, Perlman M (eds) Entrepreneurship, technological innovation, and economic growth: studies in the Schumpeterian tradition. University of Michigan Press, Ann Arbor, pp 251–277
Eliasson G (1994) Educational efficiency and the markets for competence. Eur J Vocat Train 2:5–11
Eliasson G (1996a) Firm objectives, controls and organization – the use of information and the transfer of knowledge within the firm. Kluwer Academic, Boston
Eliasson G (1996b) Endogenous economic growth through selection. In: Harding A (ed) Microsimulation and public policy. North Holland, Amsterdam
Eliasson G (2003a) Global economic integration and regional attractors of competence. Ind Innov 10(1):75–102
Eliasson G (2003b) The venture capitalist as a competent outsider. In: Alho K, Lassila J, Ylä-Anttila P (eds) Economic research and decision making. ETLA-Taloustieto Oy, Helsinki
Eliasson G (2005a) The nature of economic change and management in a new knowledge based information economy. Inf Econ Policy 17:428–456
Eliasson G (ed) (2005b) The birth, the life and the death of firms—the role of entrepreneurship, creative destruction and conservative institutions in a growing and experimentally organized economy. The Ratio Institute, Stockholm
Eliasson G (2006) From employment to entrepreneurship. J Ind Relat 48(5):633–656
Eliasson G (2009) Knowledge directed economic selection and growth. Prometheus 27 (4):371–387
Eliasson G (2015) The incomplete Schumpeter Stockholm school connection. J Evol Econ 25: 45–56
Eliasson G (2017) Visible costs and invisible benefits-military procurement as innovation policy. Springer, New York
Eliasson G, Eliasson Å (1996) The biotechnological competence Bloc. Revue d'Economie Industrielle, 78-40^{0}. Trimestre: 7–26
Eliasson G, Eliasson Å (2005) The theory of the firm and the markets for strategic acquisitions. In: Cantner U, Dinopoulos E, Lanzilotti R (eds) Entrepreneurship. The new economy and public policy. Springer, Berlin, pp 91–115
Eliasson G, Eliasson Å (2009) Competence and learning in the experimentally organized economy. In: Bjuggren P, Mueller D (eds) The modern firm, corporate governance, and investment. Edward Elgar, Cheltenham
Eliasson G, Klevmarken A (1981) Household market and non-market activities – Research program and proposal. IUI research report no. 12:1981
Eliasson G, Lindberg T (1981) Allocation and growth effects of corporate income taxes. In: Eliasson G, Södersten J (eds) Business taxation, finance and firm behavior, Conference reports 1981:1. IUI, Stockholm, pp 381–435

Eliasson G, Olavi G (1978) Stepwise parameter estimation on a micro simulation model. In: Eliasson G (ed) A micro-to-macro model of the Swedish economy, IUI conference reports, 1978:1. IUI, Stockholm

Eliasson G, Taymaz E (2000) Institutions, entrepreneurship, economic flexibility and growth – experiments on an evolutionary model. In: Cantner U, Hanush H, Klepper S (eds) Economic evolution, learning and complexity – econometric, experimental and simulation approaches. Physica Verlag, Heidelberg, pp 265–286

Eliasson G, Taymaz E (2001) Modeling financial derivatives in a firm based evolutionary macro model (MOSES) – The integration of computing, communications and financial services. Mimeo, KTH, Stockholm

Eliasson G, Johansson D, Taymaz E (2004) Simulating the new economy. Struct Chang Econ Dyn 15(3):289–314

Eliasson G, Johansson D, Taymaz E (2005) Chap. VI: Firm turnover and the rate of macroeconomic growth. In: Eliasson G (ed) The birth, the life and the death of firms-the role of entrepreneurship, creative destruction and conservative institutions in a growing and experimentally organized economy. The Ratio Institute, Stockholm, pp 305–356

Fisher FM (1972) On price adjustment without an auctioneer. Rev Econ Stud 39:1–15

Fontana M (2010) The Santa Fe perspective on economics: emerging patterns in the science of complexity. Hist Econ Ideas (HEI) XVIII(2):167–196

Freeman C (1987) Technology policy and econonmic performance. Pinter, London

Frenken K (2006) Technological innovation and complexity theory. Econ Innov New Technol 15(2):137–155

Friedman M (1953) The methodology of positive economics. In: Friedman M (ed) Essays in positive economics. The University of Chicago Press, Chicago, IL

Hanson KA (1989) Firm entry. In: Albrecht JW et al (eds) MOSES code. Industriens Utredningsinstitut (IUI), Stockholm

Hansen LP, Heckman JJ (1996) The empirical foundations of calibration. J Econ Perspect 10 (1 (Winter)):87–104

Hanusch H, Pyka A (eds) (2007a) Elgar companion to neo-Schumpeterian economics. Edward Elgar, Cheltenham, pp 1055–1076

Hanusch H, Pyka A (2007b) Principles of neo-Schumpeterian economics. Camb J Econ 31: 275–289

Jakobsson U, Normann G (1974) Inkomstbeskattningen i den ekonomiska politiken. IUI, Stockholm

Johansson D (2001) The dynamics of firm and industry growth – the Swedish computing and communications industry. Doctorate thesis, Department of the Organization and Management. KTH, Stockholm

Johansson D (2004) Economics without entrepreneurship and institutions: a vocabulary analysis of graduate textbooks. Econ J Watch 3(1):515–538

Jones CI, Williams JC (1998) Measuring the social returns to R&D. Q J Econ 113(4):1119–1135

Kirman A (1989) The intrinsic limits of modern economic theory: the emperor has no clothes. Econ J 99(395):126–139

Kirzner IM (1997) Entreprenurial discovery and the competitive market process: an Austrian approach. J Econ Lit 35(1):60–85

Klevmarken A (1978) On estimation and other problems of statistical inference in the micro simulation approach. In: Eliasson G (ed) A micro-to-macro model of the Swedish economy. IUI conference reports, 1978:1. IUI, Stockholm

Klevmarken A (1983) There is a need for applied microeconometrics – survey research about the household. In: Microeconometrics, IUI yearbook 1982–1983. Industriens Utredningsinstitut (IUI), Stockholm

Klevmarken A, Dahlman CJ (1971) Den Privata Konsumtionen 1931–1975. IUI/Almqvist &Wiksell, Stockholm/Uppsala

Landgren K-G (1957) Economics in modern Sweden. Library of Congress, Washington

Landgren KG (1960) Den "nya ekonomin" i Sverige. J.M. Keyenes, E.Wigforss, B.Ohlin och utvecklingen 1927–39. Almqvist & Wiksell, Uppsala
Lesourne J, Orléan A (1998) Introduction. In: Lesourne J, Orléan A (eds) Advances in self-organization and evolutionary economics. Economica, London
Lindh T (1993) Lessons from learning about rational expectations. In: Day RH, Eliasson G, Wihlborg C (eds) The markets for innovation, ownership and control. IUI/North-Holland, Stockholm/Amsterdam
Lucas RF (1977) "Understanding business cycles", paper presented for the Kiel conference on *Growth Without Inflation*, 22–23 June 1976
Lundvall B-Å (1992) National systems of innovation. Pintner, London
Menger C (1871) Grundsätze der Volkswirtschaftslehre. Wilhelm Braumüller, Vienna
Modigliani F, Cohen KJ (1961) The role of anticipations and plans in economic behavior and their use in economic analysis and forecasting. Studies in business expectations and planning, no 4, Urbana, IL
Myrdal G (1927) Prisbildningsproblemet och föränderligheten, Uppsala och Stockholm
Nelson R (1992) National innovation systems: a retrospective on a study. Ind Corp Chang 1(2): 347–374
Nelson R (ed) (1993) National systems of innovation: a comparative study. Oxford University Press, Oxford
Nelson RR, Winter SG (1982) An evolutionary theory of economic change. Harvard University Press, Cambridge, MA
Ohlin B (1936) "Introduction" to Knut Wicksell. Interest and prises. English translation of Wicksell K (1898) Geldzins und Guterpreise, Jena
Ohlin B (1937) Some notes on the Stockholm theory of saving and investment. I–II. Econ J *47*:53–69; 221–240
Patinkin D (1952) Wicksell's "cumulative process". Econ J 62(248):835–847
Pelikan P (1988) Can the imperfect innovation systems of capitalism be outperformed? In: Dosi G et al (eds) Technical change and economic theory. Pintner, London
Puu T (1989) Nonlinear economic dynamics. Springer, Berlin
Rosen S (1997) Austrian and neoclassical economics: any gains from trade? J Econ Perspect 11(4): 139–152
Shackle GLS (1949) Expectations in economics. Gibson Press, Westport
Shackle GLS (1967) The years of high theory: invention and tradition in economic thought 1926–1939. Cambridge University Press, Cambridge
Schumpeter JA (1911) Theorie der Wirtschaftlichen Entwicklung. Page references to the English 1934 translation
Schumpeter JA (1942) Capitalism, socialism and democracy. Routledge, London
Schumpeter JA (1954) History of economic analysis. Oxford University Press, New York
Smale S (1967) Differential systems and structural stability. Bull Am Math Soc 73
Solow RM (1956) A contribution to the theory of economic growth. Q J Econ 70(1):65–94
Solow RM (1987) We'd better watch out. New York Times Book Review, 12 July, p 36
Swan TW (1956) Economic growth and capital accumulation. Econ Rec 32:334–361
Taymaz E (1991a) MOSES on PC: manual, initialization, and calibration. IUI research report no 39. IUI, Stockholm
Taymaz E (1991b) Chapter III: Calibration. In: Taymaz E (ed) MOSES on PC: manual, initialization, and calibration. IUI research report no 39. IUI, Stockholm
Taymaz E (1992a) Chapter II: A description of the initial 1982 and the synthetic 1990 databases. In: Albrecht JW et al (eds) MOSES database. IUI, Stockholm
Taymaz E (1992b) Chapter VI: Initial state dependency – sensitivity analyses on MOSES. In: Albrecht JW et al (eds) MOSES database. IUI, Stockholm
Taymaz E (1993) A calibration algorithm for micro-simulation models. Paper prepared for the special intensive course in "microanalytic simulation" at ERMES, Universite de Paris II, Paris, 2 Feb 1993. Also published and available on line as IUI working paper No 374

Taymaz E (1999) Modeling the stock and derivatives market in MOSES. KTH, TRITA – IEO-R 1999–09. Stockholm
Tomas N (1992) MOSES macro accounting system-updating procedures, in Albrecht et al (1992), *MOSES database*, Research report no 40. IUI, Stockholm
von Böhm-Bawerk E (1889) Positive Theories des Kapitales. Wagner'sche Universitäts – Buchhandlung, Insbruck (trans: Smart W (1891) Positive theory of capital. Macmillan, London)
von Neuman J (1945) A model of general economic equilibrium. Rev Econ Stud 13:1–9
Weibull JW (1995) Evolutionary game theory. The MIT Press, Cambridge, MA
Weintraub ER (1979) Microfoundations – The compatibility of microeconomics and macroeconomics. Cambridge University Press, Cambridge
Wicksell K (1898) Geldzins und Guterpreise, Jena. Page references to the 1936 English edition; Interest and prices, Augustus M. Kelley, Bookseller, New York
Wicksell K (1906) Föreläsningar i Nationalekonomi: Del II Om pengar och krediter. C F Fritzes Hofbokhandel, Stockholm
Wicksell K (1923) Realkapital och kapitalränta. Ekononmisk Tidskrift, Häfte 5–6:145–180
Winter SG (1964) Economic 'natural selection' and the theory of the firm. Yale Econ Essays 4(1—Spring):225–272
Winter SG (1971) Satisficing, selection, and the innovating remnant. Q J Econ LXXXV (May):237–261
Witt U (1993) Emergence and dissemination of innovations: some principles of evolutionary economics. In: Day R, Chen P (eds) Nonlinear dynamics and evolutionary economics. Oxford University Press, New York
Witt U (2002) How evolutionary is Schumpeter's theory of economic development. Ind Innov 9(1–2):7–22
Ysander BC (1981) Taxes and market stability. In: Eliasson G, Södersten J (eds) Business taxation, finance and firm behavior, IUI conference volumes, 1981:1, Stockholm
Ysander B-C (1986) Structural change as an equilibrium or a disequilibrium process. In: Ysander B-C (ed) Two models of an open economy. IUI, Stockholm

Firms Navigating Through Innovation Spaces: A Conceptualization of How Firms Search and Perceive Technological, Market and Productive Opportunities Globally

Maureen McKelvey

Abstract The main contribution of this paper is a theory-based conceptual framework of innovation spaces, and how firms must navigate through them to innovate. The concept of innovation systems—at the regional, sectoral and national levels—have been highly influential. Previous literature developing the concept of innovation systems has stressed the importance of institutions, networks and knowledge bases at the regional, sectoral and national levels. This paper primarily draws upon an evolutionary and Schumpeterian economics perspective, in the following three senses. The conceptualization of 'innnovation spaces' focuses upon how and why firm search for innovations is influenced the opportunities within certain geographical contexts. This means that the firm create opportunities and can span different context, but they are influence by the context in term of the access, flow and co-evolution of ideas, resources, technology, people and knowledge, which help stimulate business innovation in terms of products, process and services. The paper concludes with an agenda for future research and especially the need to focus on globalization as a process of intensifying linkages across the globe.

1 Introduction

An area of important contribution—but also a key conceptual problem—for evolutionary approaches to social science is how and why to link micro-level data with macrolevel theorizing. van den Bergh and Gowdy (2003) outline the promises and problems of developing the micro-foundations of macroeconomics, from an evolutionary perspective. They address a range of approaches, from multi-agent models including complexity and hierarchy to group selection as well as the need to recognize heterogeneity of firms in analyzing macro processes. More specifically in this line of reasoning, Dosi et al. (2008:601) stress that four basic notions are:

M. McKelvey (✉)
Department of Economy and Society, Institute for Innovation and Entrepreneurship,
School of Business, Economics and Law, University of Gothenburg, Gothenburg, Sweden
e-mail: maureen.mckelvey@handels.gu.se

A. Pyka, U. Cantner (eds.), *Foundations of Economic Change*, Economic Complexity and Evolution, DOI 10.1007/978-3-319-62009-1_8

(1) innovation is a key driver of economic growth; (2) the heterogeneity of firms; (3) markets are selection devices that affect decentralized decisions like entry and exit; and (4) the above three Schumpeterian micro-foundations are complementary with a Kuznetsian perspective on industrial dynamics. Within management literature inspired by evolutionary economics and organizational learning, a key concept has been 'firm search', often related to the creation of economic opportunities (Laursen 2012). This paper focuses upon how to help explain how and why firms differential abilities to 'navigate' through three dimensions of innovation spaces influence their ability to recognize opportunities, and therefore, in longer run, be able to compete and generate aggregate economic growth. This paper is an initial step in developing this understanding. This paper therefore uses elements of existing theoretical and empirical understanding in a new combination, in order to propose a new synthetic conceptualisation of the innovation process in firms as the navigation of a complex space involving different types of opportunities.

Empirically, these topics are increasingly important to both firms and economies, due to the globalization of all types of business activities—from research and development through production, service and customers. Archibugi and Iammarino (2002:99) define globalization as 'a high (and increasing) degree of interdependency and interrelatedness among different and geographically dispersed actors.' Similarly, the authors provide empirical evidence of globalization, and why this shift matters for invention and innovation. Taking this proposition of globalization seriously also means that firms increasingly have to search and develop opportunities globally. Globalization thus also requires a more complex theoretical understanding of how such interdependencies and interrelatedness affect firms, and the observation that firms struggle with search and opportunities on a global scale prompted this line of research to better conceptualize the processes.

A key concept used in this paper is opportunities. Opportunities are most often discussed in recent years within entrepreneurship literature, although also inherent in Schumpeter's (1934, 1942) conceptualization of the dynamics of the economy. Within entrepreneurship literature, there has been a debate about whether opportunities are created or discovered (Alvarez and Barney 2007; Alvarez et al. 2013). In the creation theory within entrepreneurship literature, the nature of opportunities means that the actions of the entrepreneurs create opportunities, as compared to the situation where opportunities exist and are simply uncovered. *Ex ante*, the persons who become entrepreneurs may not be significant different from those who do not become entrepreneurs—but the process of having been and becoming entrepreneurs probably does change them, *ex post*. Given that firms develop innovations in relation to the creation of opportunities, their knowledge about the future is limited yet as they act, they also create new knowledge (Holmèn and McKelvey 2013). Accordingly, some work has stressed that the firms' innovative search occurs in an environment of co-evolution with market, technologies and institutions, as widely acknowledge in the innovation system literature (Nelson 1993; Lundvall et al. 2002) and related literature (McKelvey 1996, 2004; McKelvey and Holmèn 2006).

This paper therefore starts from the viewpoint that opportunities are created over time, which is also in line with an evolutionary epistemology (Buenstorf 2007;

McKelvey et al. 2015). In order to conceptualize whether, how and why firms do, or do not, move through complex space, it is necessary to start from two insights from evolutionary economics: (a) that firms search for opportunities under conditions of selection and (b) that the ability to identify and exploit that knowledge is related to firm internal capabilities (see review in Salter and McKelvey 2016). The implication is that firm search is necessary because this ability to innovate—and to create opportunities—is not randomly spread over the population of firms in an industry, but is concentrated in firms with certain capabilities and routines. Moreover, in the existing literature addressing evolutionary economics, there are different approaches, methodologies and theories, which this paper makes no claim to address all of them.

This paper only focuses on three core questions of an evolutionary approach to the development of knowledge and innovations in the economy—namely from where do different types of opportunities emerge? Why do we assume that firm search is necessary for innovation? And how does the innovation system help define the industrial, regional and national context, within which firms search? The answers to these questions are used to develop a conceptualization, which includes the microfoundations of firm search with the macro processes involving technology, markets and institutions.

2 From Where Do Different Types of Opportunities Emerge?

The first question is, From where do different types of opportunities arise? This question is explicitly addressed within evolutionary economics, in that capitalism is restless (Nelson 1996; Metcalfe 2002). Evolutionary economics focus upon dynamics and emergent systems as well as the peculiar role of knowledge and the appropriation of value of innovation. Industrial dynamics is driven through innovation in large companies and through entrepreneurship through new companies (Schumpeter 1934, 1942). Recent literature has both examined to what extent that Schumpeter was evolutionary and dynamic in his theorizing, as well as strived to define principles for evolutionary economics (Andersen 2011; Witt 2010; McKelvey and Holmèn 2006; Foster and Metcalfe 2001). Metcalfe (2002, 2008) argues that the restless nature of capitalism has to do with knowledge as the pre-eminent source of variation, but that there is a difference between knowledge and information which helps explain why heterogeneity of firms also matters. Here as well, markets are the primary arenas of selection for micro-processes.

From this literature, a key insight for this paper is thus that the creation of opportunities is a process of knowledge accumulation (Metcalfe 2002; McKelvey et al. 2015), and therefore one must understand firm search in relation to the innovation spaces within which they navigate. Moreover, opportunities are generated endogenously through the dynamics of the economic system and not through exogenous shocks. In other words, the phenomena of innovation and entrepreneurship exist because the actors create different types of opportunities, which involve engaging in decisions and actions under conditions of uncertainty and risk-taking.

Existing literature defines innovative opportunities as "the possibility to realize a potential economic value inherent in a new combination of resources and market needs, emerging from changes in the scientific or technological knowledge base, customer preferences, or the interrelationships between economic actors" (Holmén et al. 2007, p. 37). As such, an innovative opportunity consists of the following three components: (a) an economic value for someone; (b) mobilization of resources; and (c) the ability of the actor pursuing the opportunity to appropriate some of the economic value.

Three types of opportunities can be identified in the literature, and the issue is from where each type of opportunity emerges—which leads to the follow-on question for this paper, namely where should the firm be searching?

The first type that firms monitor is technological opportunities, which arise from scientific and technological knowledge (Scherer 1965; Nelson and Winter 1982; Breschi et al. 2000; Oltra and Flor 2003; Palmberg 2004). Note that there appears to be a relatively uneven distribution of 'technical opportunities' at different times and in different technologies and industries (Nelson and Winter 1982; Dosi 1982). Breschi et al. (2000) further develop the 'technological regime' proposed by Nelson and Winter (1982). They argue that *'Technological opportunities* reflect the likelihood of innovating for any given amount of money invested in search' (ibid). Differences between industry help explain where the generation of these types of opportunities occur. Breschi et al. (2000: 390–391) state that 'observed sectoral patterns of innovative activities are related to the nature of the relevant technological regime….defined by the specific combination of technological opportunities, appropriability of innovations, cumulativeness of technical advances and the properties of the knowledge base underlying firms' innovative activities. This research implies that sectoral differences impact the ability to find new opportunities and to appropriate the value to the firm.

Technological knowledge is also related to how technology develops more generally in society, usually though a combination of public and private investment into new knowledge (McKelvey 2014; Archibugi and Filippetti 2015). Technological opportunities are thus created through the development of related areas of knowledge, including a range of relevant scientific and technological knowledge bases, techniques, and instrumentation.[1] Technologies can be seen as general bodies of human knowledge, which are often created and further developed within specific application areas, such as within firms, industries or other societal contexts of use; one must distinguish the stock of 'useful human knowledge as well as the

[1]The rate and distribution of change across technological areas can be measured empirically in many different ways, including studies of technical aspects, such as performance of new materials, as well as studies of more interrelated economic-technological aspects, such as the ratio of price to performance, or second-order effects on demand.

continuous addition of new knowledge' (Moykr 2002).[2] Literature within the history of science and technology and in economic history suggests that such knowledge development is an on-going process, usually driven forward by specific individuals and acting within specific societal institutions (Rosenberg 1982, 1994). Some technologies develop quickly and general purpose technology, whereas other technologies develop slowly.

Technological knowledge is useful because it helps to solving problems, and so there are evolutionary dynamics in the underlying system of innovation whereby solving one technological problem often opens up new technical opportunities and new technical problems of relevance for developing complex engineering products. Solving one technical problem often focuses the attention of decision-makers on the need to improve related complementary technologies, which are known as 'focusing devices' for bottlenecks and as 'reverse salients' in a large technical system (Rosenberg 1982; Hughes 1983). These technical problems often require search activities in a variety of technological areas, and these search activities and problem-solving activities involve technological and market learning by diverse actors. Relatedly, Stankiewicz (2002) calls the opening up of new areas of 'cognitive space' and 'design space' as the exploration of new search space, to develop new technological opportunities. This helps explain why the science and university system are potent drivers of economic change. However, the science and business system need to have interdependencies and be interconnected because there are feedback loops between practical application of knowledge within an industry and the broader scientific and technological knowledge (Kline and Rosenberg 1986).[3] Biotechnology is one example, where scientific progress has stimulated extensive economic development, regeneration of existing firms, and knowledge intensive entrepreneurship (Audretsch and Feldman 1996; Senker 1999; McKelvey 1996; Faulkner and Senker 1995).

The second type of opportunity that firms must monitor is market opportunities. Entrepreneurship literature originally focused upon market imperfections and arbitrage profits, and therefore had a particular focus on how the entrepreneur could use that knowledge to engage in purposeful action (see discussion in Holmén et al. 2007). Shane (2000) demonstrated how the individual entrepreneurs' prior knowledge affected cognition and the interpretation of opportunities. This is one type of the market opportunities of interest here, whereby information asymmetries may exist due to the differences in individual cognition, thereby opening up market opportunities.

More broadly, in the economics of innovation literature, however, a debate was originally formulated about the driving forces for the development of new

[2] Moykr (2002) also proposes a conceptualization of two types of useful knowledge, namely 'propositional' (what) and 'prescriptive' (how). He argues that much of technology is about 'prescriptive' knowledge but is based upon much 'propositional' knowledge.

[3] The use of techniques and instrumentation as well as the use of machines and capital equipment in factories were initially studied, as places where users impacted technical development.

knowledge, which is useful in the economy. A dichotomy was proposed between 'technology' and 'market' in a dynamic sense, as one classical distinction is between 'technology push' and 'market pull' (Mowery and Rosenberg 1991). Technology push means that the investments into research and technology lead to the development of new ideas that can be tested and introduced to the market. The technology 'pushes' out new ideas. The notion of market pull means that the inventor or innovating firm comes up with an idea, because they are responding to the perceived wants and preferences of customers. In other words, the market 'pulls' out creativity and new ideas. In more recent years, the discussion focuses not on markets in general but on the role that lead users often significantly impact the direction of technology development in an early phase (von Hippel 1988; Franke and von Hippel 2003). As the technology matures and diffuses, new types of user groups may express quite different needs than the early ones, thereby influencing both the technology per se as well as the range of potential future uses.

Innovations require both, and because business innovations must ultimately be sold, recent innovation literature stresses that customers, and relevant knowledge about customers and societal links, needs to be integrated into business innovation theory (Dodgson et al. 2014). New business models is one tool to integrate ideas, technology, markets and so forth into what the firm offers to different types of customers and how the firm appropriates value.

The third type of opportunity that firms must monitor is the productive opportunity. This relates to how the firm should organize its resources internally. Penrose (1959) argued that the firm has the possibility to combine its internal resources in many new ways. The 'productive opportunity' limits the number of combinations, especially as perceived by managers in the firm. A key issue involves the managers' capacity to envision alternative modes of using the resources at hand (Penrose 1959:31–42, 111). In more recent literature, one can argue that the notion of productive opportunities relates to internal firm issues, and what is known as capabilities. By capabilities, we mean the knowledge, experience and skills that firms have which are appropriate for carrying out specific activities (Richardson 1972). Capability building is seen as a major source of sustained competitive advantages for the firm. Combinative capability can be defined as the ability to integrate and synthesize internal resources and external learning and deploy them in a competitive environment (Kogut and Zander 1992). Recent literature includes many contributions about capabilities, dynamic capabilities and capabilities as specifically related to innovation (Helfat and Lieberman 2002; Bingham et al. 2007; Teece 2007; Hine et al. 2014). Helfat and Lieberman (2002:725) distinguish between resources 'as stocks of available factors that are owned or controlled by the firm, and capabilities as the firm's capacity to deploy resources for a desired end result'. The literature on dynamics capabilities stresses that the firm must adapt to demands in the external environment, and reconfigure resources (Teece et al. 1997). Firms with high levels of motivation and the capacity to learn should be more open to gaining experience from different situations; this makes them more likely to seize pre-emptive opportunities than more defensive firms which employ static resource-exploitation strategies (Teece et al. 1997). Hine et al. (2014:17) distinguish between different types of capabilities, across the dimensions of predominate resources, routine patterning, learning focus and strategic intent. The three levels of capabilities are 'higher-order dynamic learning capabilities' which involve creative ability; 'lower-order dynamic functional capabilities' which involve dynamic ability; and 'first-order ordinary capabilities' which involve static ability. The latter category involves general resources, rigid routine patterning, exploitative focus of learning tasks and subsistent strategic intent. Search processes involve higher-order and lower-order ones.

In summary, this section has addressed evolutionary literature that helps to answer the question, From where do different types of opportunities emerge? These theories help to conceptualize how and why firms are searching for new opportunities, and especially in relation to technological, market, and productive opportunities. Given the evolutionary epistemology, this paper also follows the conceptualization that the firm involved in innovation processes must also be engaged in, and help to create, these three types of opportunities. An active firm—with high levels of motivation and the capacity to learn—is more likely to search and be able to create opportunities across all these three dimensions. Moreover, the literature specifies that firms can be analyzed as engaging in specific, identifiable processes, specifically to identify economic value; mobilize resources; and appropriate at least some of the economic value.

In terms of the conceptualization of firms navigating innovation spaces, a first constituent element is:

> Firm help to seize and create opportunities in their innovation space, over time. The innovation space can be thought of—and analyzed—through three axes. The first axis is of creation of technological opportunities through scientific and technological knowledge. The second axis is the creation of market opportunities related to new market and customer knowledge. The third axis is the creation of productive opportunities, dependent upon using business knowledge of how to operate innovation in the firm locally and globally and leading to a reconfiguration of capabilities.

3 Why Do We Assume That Firm Search Is Necessary for Innovations?

The second question to address, is what does the literature say about, Why do we assume that firm search is necessary for innovation? Search is core to evolutionary thinking, because, a key notion is that firms are heterogeneous in a way that matters to economic change. Selection takes place at the population level, and therefore differences at the unit level matter for determining which organization disappears, or else continues to exist. If the firm does not search—or does not find opportunities—they are likely to disappear, due to market selection.

In relation to firms search for technical innovations, McKelvey (1996) specifies three key points in a conceptualization based upon evolutionary economic theories. Firstly, there is an assumption of intentionality, and that humans generate novelty and diversity, which are intended to satisfy environment conditions. Secondly, because of intentionality in relation to perceived environmental conditions, firms explore certain 'search spaces which can be presented as a three-dimensional space, full of hills, valleys and plains'. Because the search for innovation does not occur randomly in time and space, this means that certain parts of search space are more explored than other. Thirdly, there is an expectation of diversity at the micro level of firms, which will in turn impact future performance of firms and also of their ability to search for, and learn about, innovations. The reason is that the firm needs to access ideas and information in order to take advantage of different types of opportunities and to innovate in different geographic contexts and cognitive frameworks. A key insight is also that due to heterogeneity, firms will have explored different parts of the innovation space.

Hence, search is not just a question of identifying 'the right information' which exists out there. Focusing on search means that the firm's internal combinations of routines, resources, capabilities, and learning must be taken into consideration, and will also change over time, in response to internal and external conditions (Nelson 1996; Penrose 1959; Teece et al. 1997; Teece 2007). Theories in innovation management explicates how the internal capabilities of the firm is linked to opportunities arising in the environment, thereby stressing the role of relationships and networks for the firm to search, identify and seize relevant business opportunities (Brusoni et al. 2001; Dodgson et al. 2014). The proposition here is thus that firms will have different capabilities to search for information related to opportunities, as well as different abilities to process and use that information to create new opportunities. Moreover, because the focus here is on search activities related to invention and innovation, this means that the firm is searching under conditions of uncertainty and also in an increasingly globalized context.

From an evolutionary perspective, the argument has been put forth that firms have difficulties in developing innovation relevant to new situations, whether these arise from changes in the industry or in the country. Nelson and Winter (2002:29) call it the competence puzzle:

> "How can the same organizations be so impressively competent from one perspective and yet so strikingly" bounded "in their rationality? . . . In the evolutionary view, the key to the puzzle lies in the contrasting demands of different types of situations. High competence is often achievable where skills and routines can be learned and perfected through practice. For individuals and organizations (not to speak of animals), learning guided by clear short-term feedback can be remarkably powerful, even in addressing complex challenges. But that sort of learning does little to enable sophisticated foresight, logically structured deliberation and/or the improvisation of novel action patterns and situations that demand these are rarely handled well."

This quote suggests that firm have difficulties dealing with the future—and explicitly states that decisions that must rely upon foresight, logically structured deliberation and novel action patterns. This suggests that search is difficult.

Still, a key aspect of understanding innovation spaces is the role of firms, and explicitly that firms must search for new innovative opportunities, and search for solutions to their technical and market problems (Holmén et al. 2007; Laursen 2012). So, one answer as to why firms must search is related to the types of knowledge involved in invention and innovation as well as the particular role of learning. Existing literature outlines that there is an imperative for firms to learn, develop routines, and access new types of inputs as sources of competitive advantage (Nelson and Winter 1982; Fleming and Sorenson 2001; Rosenkopf and Nerkar 2001; Katila and Ahuja 2002). Another way to understand what firms do is that they need to find new knowledge, which helps them solve different types of problems. According to the problem-solving perspective as developed within the knowledge-based theory of the firm, the key task of the manager is to 'not how to organize to exploit already developed knowledge or capability, but rather how to organize to efficiently generate knowledge and capability' (Nickerson and Zenger 2004:617). Firms are recognized as the actors, which play the key role in the development of incremental changes in existing technologies and products along a trajectory (Pavitt 1991; Dosi 1982).

Uncertainty is, by definition, a characteristic of the firm search activities, because novelty is involved in invention and innovation. Business innovation in a broad sense can be defined as 'novelty of economic value'.[4] Because innovations require novelty, this implies that the processes leading to innovation will occur under conditions of limited knowledge about the future. Therefore, the decision-making context is uncertain, in the meaning proposed by Knight (1921) of not being able to predict or assess the probability of potential outcomes. Firms face uncertainty rather than risk in that uncertainty cannot be measured nor calculated. In contrast, risk refers to situations where the odds can be predicted, even if we do not predict the outcomes.

But what does it mean that innovation processes involve uncertainty and risk taking? This paper proposes that: (1) innovation by definition includes an element of novelty for the future, and the novel idea may or may not work; (2) decision-makers are unable to access or process all relevant information; (3) often the future is uncertain in the sense of unknown-able rather than risky in the sense of calculate possible alternatives and (4) multiple possible paths of scientific and technological alternatives can exist to solve any identifiable user needs.

From the firm's perspective, they are investing in search activities about innovations of which they cannot predict future outcomes. In order to innovate, the firm must make complex decisions under conditions of uncertainty about future technologies and future market preferences. In the Campbell (1960) sense, blind-variation helps explain that the development of knowledge cannot necessarily be predicted, but once new knowledge is developed, there is a change in the later direction of search for new knowledge. In relation to innovations and technical development, these blind-search paths whereby later search is affected should lead to path dependency. In that sense, failures are an inherent part of testing and

[4]Note that the concept of business innovation as economic phenomena includes a notion of 'economic value'. Thereby innovation must be linked to a conceptualization of customer and markets, and not just remain at the stage of an idea. That is why the innovation literature generally distinguishes invention—such as an idea or technical item—from innovation—such as a new product introduced to the market.

selection among a variety of alternatives to solve any one problem (Basalla 1988; Vincenti 1990; Dosi 1982, 1988). The literature on radical versus incremental innovations suggests that the degree of uncertainty and the degree of risk may, however, be different in different industries and types of innovations.

In summary, this part of the literature motivates the focus here upon firm search, under conditions of uncertainty about the future as well as making decisions involving risk. An evolutionary perspective of creation of opportunities suggests that the firms (actors) must be understood as heterogeneous actors, with diverse sets of knowledge and capabilities. That is a given, if selection is to occur over time on the population level. Moreover, firms have difficulties in searching for areas further away from their existing resources and capabilities and focus on knowledge that is useful for problem-solving.

In terms of the conceptualization of firms navigating innovation spaces, a second constituent element is:

> Firms must navigate through an innovation space, in an evolutionary process, as they search and develop different types of business innovations. By definition, an innovation entails the unknown, as the concept focuses upon novelty of economic value.

4 How Does the Innovation System Help Define the Industrial, Regional and National Context, Within Which Firms Search?

This section addresses the question, How does the innovation system help define the industrial, regional and national context, within which firms search?

Previous literature developing the concept of innovation systems has stressed the importance of institutions, networks and knowledge bases at the regional, sectoral and national levels, known as innovation systems (Malerba 2002, 2009; Edquist 2006; Lundvall et al. 2002; Cooke et al. 1997; Nelson 1993; Edquist and McKelvey 2000). This provides an understanding of the context for innovation processes. Perhaps because economic geographers develop notions of space and proximity, it makes sense to help define the context from their discussions first (Boschma and Frenken 2006; Boschma and Martin 2010; Boschma 2012). In Boschma and Martin (2010:6–7), an ambitious range of scholarship for an evolutionary economic geography approach is staked out:

> The processes by which the economic landscape—the spatial organisation of economic production, circulation, exchange, distribution and consumption—is transformed over time....spatialities of economic novelty (innovations, new firms, new industries, new networks), with how the spatial structure of the economy emerge from the micro-behaviours of economic agents (individuals, firms, organisations); with how, in the absence of central coordination or direction, the economic landscape exhibits self-organisation, and with how the processes of both path creation and path dependence interact to shape geography of economic development and transformation, and why and how such processes may themselves be place dependent.

The current paper shares an intellectual heritage and interest in these types of questions; although the purpose here is much more narrow than their agenda. Still this quote identifies many of the core issues about self-organization, path dependency and microfoundations that are also found in evolutionary economics.

That leaves us with the task of exploring how theoretical insights can be applied to understand the micro-behavior of firms, as agents navigating through complex spatial and industrial dimensions, and in ways this will impact their future development of innovations.

This brings us back to how microfoundations are linked to macro processes. In this conceptualization, it is useful to define an innovation space, because there is a relationship between the development of firm capabilities and the innovation system. The innovation system provides many elements, such as access to networks, institutions, as well as technology and science. Firms do not search randomly, nor does it only occur inside the firm. Innovation processes rely upon search outside the firm, and innovation is distributed in the sense that actors are distributed across countries, industries and different types of firms and organizations (Metcalfe 2008).

Thus, the proposal here is to draw upon these insights from innovation systems, to express that firm search activities must span industries as well as regions/countries. This is visualized in Fig. 1 below.

The firm is conceptualized as spanning the industry and the region/country level, in the sense that they must search this external environment in order to find relevant new knowledge and create opportunities. The visualization in Fig. 1 suggests that there are interdependencies, or co-evolution, between the firm and contexts in which the firm is active, as explained below.

At the industry level, the innovation space takes it specific form (expression) through a combination of industrial conditions, global patterns, and local dependencies. The industrial sector, or sectoral system of innovation is likely the basis of

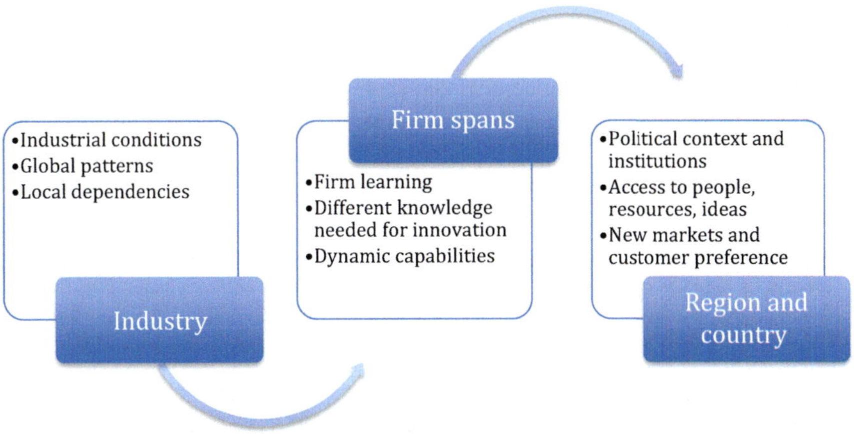

Fig. 1 Interactions as the firm spans between industry and region/country

firm search and learning, rather than the nation (Malerba 2002). The industry life cycle literature claims that rapidly changing technologies lead to the development of new industries (see Abernathy and Utterback 1975; Utterback 1994; Klepper 1996). In the early phase, many competing firms exist, and they compete on alternative product designs; in the later phase, a dominant design emerges; competition is based on economies of scale; and the firms tend to become larger in order to reap scale economies while managing such processes. Hence, the stage in the industry life cycle will also affect the ability and direction of the firm's search for innovations.

At the region and country level, the innovation space takes it specific form (expression) through a combination of political context, agglomeration effects such as access to people, resources and ideas, and the development of new markets and customer preferences, the national innovation system, including societal structures and institutions. Some literature links this national level of technological and market learning to institutions and social structure, which are simultaneously embedded in the firm, sector and/or region (Fransman 2001; Harvey et al. 2003). Much of economic geography suggests that regions and nations are key geographical spaces, and scales include the regional and national. Therefore, even though this literature is vast and different arguments about the importance of local, regional, national, international levels have been put forward: the concepts of geographical scales or level of analysis are useful here.[5] This line of research provides the insight that (1) geographical contexts can differ in important ways at different scales; and (2) firm networks can help link different innovation spaces to each other through the operations of the firm.

In summary, the firm is said to be searching in space, which links different actors, and the definition of that space consists of innovation systems, where the context may be industrial regional and national, or all three at the same time. From the perspective of the firm, they need to use their networks and organizational structure in order to explore the different opportunities possible in different geographical scales. What is key to the conceptualization here is that firms are the actors, which are spanning between the industry and the regional/national institutional setting. The proposition is: the notion of distributed innovation processes implies that geographic space, context and scale may matter, but that the international knowledge flows as well as firm actions mean that innovation is not restricted to specific places or contexts.

In terms of the conceptualization of firms navigating innovation spaces, a third constituent element is:

> An innovation space constitutes a geographical context, which affects innovation through a process of interaction of firms spanning industry as well as the regional/national institutional setting. Because innovation space can be analyzed as this interplay, the innovation

[5]Economic geography and human geography have extensive work on related concepts, including a recent special issue of *Regional Studies* (Boschma 2012; Healy and Morgan 2012; Shearmur 2011).

space is not bounded by geography per se. Geography matters in that certain regions and countries tend to have a concentration of potential opportunities. However, firms can span across several spaces through networks and through activities in multiple countries and thereby the firm can configure its capabilities to link innovation spaces through the operations and capabilities of the firm.

5 Conclusions: A Conceptualization and Future Research Agenda

The contribution of this paper is intentionally at a high level of abstraction in conceptualization, given the early stage of this line of research, although a few comments related to research design are included below. This paper has focused on three core questions of an evolutionary approach to the development of knowledge and innovations in the economy—namely from where do different types of opportunities emerge? Why do we assume that firm search is necessary for innovation? And how does the innovation system help define the industrial, regional and national context, within which firms search? The answers to these questions have been used to develop a conceptualization, which includes the microfoundations of firm search with the macro processes involving technology, markets and institutions.

The proposed concept of 'innovation spaces' developed in previous sections—and synthesized below—can thus be understood as a systematic manner in which to organise the various models of the nature and function of what firms do as they search through the space of opportunities, under conditions of uncertainty, seeking to discovery new source of value.

5.1 *Conceptualization*

Putting together the three constituent elements, the conceptualization of firms navigating innovation spaces, as proposed in this paper is:

> Firm help to seize and create opportunities in their innovation space, over time. The innovation space can be thought of—and analyzed—through three axes. The first axis is of creation of technological opportunities through scientific and technological knowledge. The second axis is the creation of market opportunities related to new market and customer knowledge. The third axis is the creation of productive opportunities, dependent upon using business knowledge of how to operate innovation in the firm locally and globally and leading to a reconfiguration of capabilities.
>
> Firms must navigate through an innovation space, in an evolutionary process, as they search and develop different types of business innovations. By definition, an innovation entails the unknown, as the concept focuses upon novelty of economic value.

An innovation space constitutes a geographical context, which affects innovation through a process of interaction of firms spanning industry as well as the regional/national institutional setting. Because innovation space can be analyzed as this interplay, the innovation space is not bounded by geography per se. Geography matters in that certain regions and countries tend to concentrate opportunities. However, firms can span across several spaces through networks and through activities in multiple countries and thereby the firm can configure its capabilities to link innovation spaces through the operations and capabilities of the firm.

The perspective taken here is that of the economist, using tools from an evolutionary analysis of knowledge for invention and innovation, in order to understand why and how the microfoundations matter. The focus is put upon the firm searching and creating opportunities, of which three types have been identified. The three types of opportunities that are created are proposed to entail technological, market, and productive opportunities. Given the focus on invention and innovation, the business managers are making decisions in a dynamic context with Knightian uncertainty. The metaphor of firms navigating innovation spaces suggests the importance of directionality, spatial, and context.

5.2 Future Research Agenda

Researchers interested in the future research agenda should tackle key theoretical issues, including develop testable hypotheses as well as tackle empirical issues related to research design and especially, how to use data to capture what firms are doing and why it differs.

In order to help structure a future research agenda, Table 1 provides a synthesis of the conceptualization, as divided into the three constituent parts. The left hand column summarizes the main points, when answering the three questions relevant to evolutionary approaches. The middle column states the main theoretical challenges, which should be further developed, including proposing hypothesis. The right column identifies some of the empirical challenges, which are naturally aligned with the theoretical challenges as well.

In terms of empirical strategy for the research design, the following provides some initial comments about how to tackle the issues. A key scientific challenge is that given the theoretical propositions about the heterogeneity of firms in terms of both capabilities and search, this implies that the research design must take into consideration how the firm interprets its environment, and cannot just assume 'objective data' will be processed the same way by all firms.

For the first constituent element in developing a research design to study opportunities, the existing innovation and management literature provides multiple tools that have already been operationalized and validated. In order to study technological opportunities, there are a range of refined indicators of publications and patents as being indicators, respectively, of science and technology as well as many measures of 'impact' through citations, referencing, authorship/ownership and so forth. In order to study market opportunities, the data often used includes both quantitative numbers of the size of markets, usually on the vector of increase,

Table 1 Conceptualization of firms navigating innovation spaces: constituent elements, theoretical and empirical challenges

	Theoretical challenges	Empirical challenges
Part I: Opportunities are created in process These represent different types of innovative opportunities	Explain the creation of opportunities Delineate the three types of opportunities—technological, market and productive	Propose how the search for certain types of innovations involve different degrees of uncertainty vs risk Describe firm search and problem-solving in the context of uncertainty and knowledge accumulation
Part II: Firms navigate and search for innovation, under conditions of uncertainty	Discuss uncertainty vs risk Define innovations Describe firm search and problem-solving	Propose how heterogeneous firms can span the context of sectoral, regional and national innovation systems in ways which affect the direction and rate of innovations introduced Explain in detail how the firm can use networks and organizational/operational capabilities to access multiple innovation spaces
Part III: Firms span the industrial, regional and national institutional context	Define context of sectoral, regional and national innovation systems Discuss how the firm can use networks and organizational/operational capabilities to access multiple innovation spaces	Explore how the firm engages in the creation of opportunities while spanning the industry and regional/national context Delineate whether the three types of opportunities—technological, market and productive—are visible to firm managers

as well as more qualitative input on the role of users within innovation processes. In order to study productive opportunities, quantitative tools that relate to internal management control as well as to more qualitative concepts like dynamic capabilities are needed, in a longer time frame. Interesting questions about opportunity creation, for example, is whether, how and why entrepreneurial firms transit from being focused upon technological opportunities primarily, to also take into consideration market and productive opportunities?

For the second constituent element of firms navigating, the research design should take into consideration that innovation spaces are multi-dimensional. Moreover, the word 'navigating' indicates the active and heterogeneous nature of firms. Firms may not always be moving and navigating—but search suggests the firms are engaged in exploring new areas and thereby must develop maps and navigate their ways towards new goals. Thus, a detailed empirical strategy combined with an historical methodology could be a useful approach. Search could be made more specific, relative to existing literature, such as existing taxonomies of different kinds of innovations as related to a specification of the degree of uncertainty and/or risk-taking. For example, firm search activities can be mapped in terms of high/low uncertainty and in terms of whether the search pertains to technological, market or productive opportunities. Finally, especially in industries in crises, such as the pharmaceutical industry in recent years, firms at time congregate around the same innovation spaces and use the same search strategies, while at other times, much diversity can be observed. One interesting question is then, How firm who change their strategy to more globalized networks also change their global networks? This could also be done comparative, between firms initially having similar technological knowledge (as signaled by patents and publications for example).

For the third constituent element, developing a research design should draw extensively on concepts and variables found in economic geography and innovation systems. This literature can be used to operationalize and validate the importance of variables such as institutions, networks, flows, etc. For example, literature could further develop the analysis of firms in emerging markets, which try to catch up with developing countries, as a dynamic process of co-evolution, between firms and countries (Malerba and Nelson 2012; Bell and Pavitt 1993). Finally, given that co-evolution over time is expected to occur, then theoretical as well as empirically grounded propositions can be developed. These propositions may help explain different trajectories of development, when firms search in different geographical contexts.

In terms of theoretically interesting issues, there are many to tackle. This paper started by focusing upon the challenges of research based upon microfoundations, and the four basic notions, as outlined by Dosi et al. (2008:601) are: (1) innovation is a key driver of economic growth; (2) the heterogeneity of firms; (3) markets are selection devices that affect decentralized decisions like entry and exit; and (4) the above three Schumpeterian micro-foundations are complementary with a Kuznetsian perspective on industrial dynamics. Each of these notions could be further developed, specifically in relation to innovation spaces and firm search. For example, because search and innovation processes generally occur before, as well as concurrently with, market processes, this means that market selection is not the only selection mechanism. Thus, from an evolutionary and Schumpeterian economics perspective, future research should return to fundamental theoretical issues, such as which mechanisms and processes tend to generate novelty, retain capabilities and attributes, and select amongst alternatives.

Finally, an important topic for future research is to develop the conceptualization, in order to more deeply understand the globalization of invention and innovation. Indeed, this paper was inspired by earlier empirical work to try to understand the rise of Asia—both as economies and as companies located in those countries (McKelvey and Bagchi-Sen 2015). The resulting book examined ongoing process of global interdependencies and interrelatedness, by looking within Asia as well as Asian firms moving to Western countries and at Western firms moving into Asia. In other words, the book provides some empirical evidence and some conceptualization of what Asia means to global invention and innovation. The book argues that four myths are debunked: (a) There is a lot of talk about Asia, but it is only talk. Government policy and national institutions are not supportive of technological development and innovation (b) Firms from Asia tend not to be entrepreneurial (c) Large firms from Asia tend not to be innovative. They focus on low cost, and not on investing in resources to compete through technology and innovation (d) Western firms can easily move to outsource customer development, technological development and research and development to Asia. Hence, much more work should be done on issues of globalization in general and of Asia in particular, because Asia is quickly becoming a key innovation space where technological, market and productive opportunities are being created. The complexities of globalization of invention and innovation involving firms and countries is an area where theoretical developments are needed, and aligned with empirical studies.

Acknowledgements Acknowledgements to the financiers, specifically the Sten A Olsson Foundation for Research and Culture; Getinge; Volvo AB; and SKF. I would also like to acknowledge my co-author Sharmistha Bagchi-Sen, especially our co-edited book on related topics.

References

Abernathy W, Utterback J (1975) A dynamic model of process and product innovation. Omega 7:379–394
Alvarez SA, Barney JB (2007) Discovery and creation: alternative theories of entrepreneurial action. Strateg Entrep J 1:11–26
Alvarez SA, Barney JB, Anderson P (2013) Forming and exploiting opportunities: the implications of discovery and creation processes for entrepreneurial and organizational research. Organ Sci 24:301–317
Andersen ES (2011) Joseph A Schumpeter: a theory of social and economic evolution. Palgrave Macmillan, New York
Archibugi D, Filippetti A (2015) The handbook of global science, technology and innovation. Wiley, Oxford
Archibugi D, Iammarino S (2002) The globalization of technological innovation: definition and evidence. Rev Int Polit Econ 9(1):98–122
Audretsch D, Feldman M (1996) R&D spillovers and the geography of innovation and Production. Am Econ Rev 86:630–640
Basalla G (1988) The evolution of technology. Cambridge University Press, Cambridge
Bell M, Pavitt K (1993) Technological accumulation and industrial growth: contrasts between developed and developing countries. Ind Corp Chang 2(2):157–210
Bingham C, Eisenhardt K, Furr N (2007) What makes a process a capability? Heuristics, strategy, and effective capture of opportunities. Strateg Entrep J 1(1–2):24–47
Boschma R (2012) Proximity and innovation: a critical assessment. Reg Stud 34(3):213–229
Boschma R, Frenken K (2006) Why is economic geography not an evolutionary science? Towards an evolutionary economics geography. J Econ Geogr 6(3):273–302
Boschma R, Martin R (2010) The handbook of evolutionary economic geography. Edward Elgar, Cheltenham
Breschi S, Malerba F, Orsenigo L (2000) Technological regimes and schumpeterian patterns of innovation. Econ J 110:388–410
Brusoni S, Prencipe A, Pavitt K (2001) Knowledge specialisation, organizational coupling, and the boundaries of the firm: why firms know more than they make. Adm Sci Q 46(4):597–621
Buenstorf G (2007) Creation and pursuit of entrepreneurial opportunities: an evolutionary economics perspective. Small Bus Econ 28:323–337
Campbell DT (1960) Blind variation and selective retentions in creative thought as in other knowledge processes. Psychol Rev 67:380–400
Cooke P, Gomez UM, Etxebaria G (1997) Regional innovation systems institutional and organizational dimensions. Res Policy 26(4–5):475–491

Dodgson M, Gann D, Phelps N (2014) The handbook of innovation management. Oxford University Press, Oxford
Dosi G (1982) Technological paradigms and technological trajectories. Res Policy 11(3):147–162
Dosi G (1988) Sources, procedures and microeconomic effects of innovation. J Econ Lit XXVI (3):1120–1171
Dosi G, Gaffard J-L, Nesta L (2008) Schumpeterian themes on industrial evolution, structural change and their microfoundations: an introduction. Ind Corp Chang 17(4):601–609
Edquist C (2006) Systems of innovation. Perspectives and challenges. In: Fagerberg J, Mowery DC, Nelson RR (eds) The oxford handbook of innovation. Oxford University Press, Oxford
Edquist C, McKelvey M (eds) (2000) Systems of innovation. A reference collection. Edward Elgar, Cheltenham
Faulkner W, Senker J (1995) Knowledge frontiers: public sector research and industrial innovation in biotechnology, engineering ceramics and parallel computing. Clarendon, Oxford
Fleming L, Sorenson O (2001) Technology as a complex adaptive system: evidence from patent data. Res Policy 30(7):1019–1039
Foster J, Metcalfe JS (2001) Frontiers of evolutionary economics: competition, self-organization and innovation policy. Edward Elgar, Cheltenham
Franke N, von Hippel E (2003) Satisfying heterogeneous user needs via innovation toolkits: the case of apache security software. Res Policy 32:1199–1215
Fransman M (2001) Designing dolly: interactions between economics, technology and science and the evolution of hybrid institutions. Res Policy 30(2):263–273
Harvey M, Quilley S, Beynon H (2003) Exploring the tomato: transformations of nature, society and economy. Edward Elgar, Cheltenham
Healy A, Morgan K (2012) Spaces of innovation: learning, proximity and the ecological turn. Reg Stud 46(8):1041–1053
Helfat C, Lieberman M (2002) The birth of capabilities: marke entry and the importance of pre-history. Ind Corp Chang 11(4):725–760
Hine D, Parker R, Pregelj L, Verreynne M-L (2014) Deconstructing and reconstructing the capabilities hierarchy. Ind Corp Chang 23(5):1299–1325. https://doi.org/10.1093/icc/dtt046
Holmèn M, McKelvey M (2013) Restless capitalism and the economizing entrepreneur. Econ Innov New Technol 22(7):684–701
Holmén M, Magnusson M, McKelvey M (2007) What are innovative opportunities? Ind Innov 14:27–45
Hughes T (1983) The networks of power: electrification in western society, 1880–1930. John Hopkins Press, Baltimore
Katila R, Ahuja G (2002) Something old, something new: a longitudinal study of search behavior and new product introduction. Acad Manag J 45(8):1183–1194
Klepper S (1996) Entry, exit, growth, and innovation over the product life cycle. Am Econ Rev 83 (3):562–583
Kline S, Rosenberg N (1986) An overview of innovation. In: Lanau R, Rosenberg N (eds) The positive sum strategy: harnessing technology for economic growth. National Academy Press, Washington, DC
Knight F (1921) Risk, uncertainty and profit. Houghton Mifflin, Boston
Kogut B, Zander U (1992) Knowledge of the firm, combinative capabilities and the replication of technology. Organization Science. Vol 3, Issue 3, August, pp 383–397
Laursen K (2012) Keep searching and you'll find: what do we know about variety creation through firms' search activities for innovation? Ind Corp Chang 21(5):1181–1220
Lundvall BÅ, Johnson B, Andersen ES, Dalum B (2002) National systems of production, innovation and competence building. Res Policy 31(2):213–231
Malerba F (2002) Sectoral systems of innovation. Res Policy 31:247–264
Malerba F (2009) Sectoral systems of innovation: concepts, issues and analyses of six major sectors. Cambridge University Press, Cambridge

Malerba F, Nelson RR (2012) Economic development as a learning process: variation across sectoral systems. Edward Elgar, Cheltenham
McKelvey M (1996) Evolutionary innovations: the business of biotechnology. Oxford University Press, Oxford
McKelvey M (2004) How and why dynamic selection regimes affect the firm's innovative activities. Innov Manag Policy Pract 1(6):3–24
McKelvey M (2014) Science, technology and business innovation. In: Dodgson M, Gann D, Phelps N (eds) The handbook of innovation management. Oxford University Press, Oxford
McKelvey M, Bagchi-Sen S (2015) Innovation spaces in asia: entrepreneurs, multinational enterprises, and policy. Cheltenham: Edward Elgar Publishers
McKelvey M, Holmèn M (2006) Flexibility and stability in the innovating economy. Oxford University Press, Oxford
McKelvey M, Zaring O, Ljungberg D (2015) Creating innovative opportunities through collaborative research: an evolutionary framework and empirical illustration from engineering. Technovation 39–40:26–36. https://doi.org/10.1016/j.technovation.2014.05.008i
Metcalfe S (2002) Knowledge of growth and growth of knowledge. J Evol Econ 12(1):3–13
Metcalfe S (2008) Restless capitalism – the evolutionary nature of capitalism. Princeton University Press, Princeton
Mowery D, Rosenberg N (1991) Technology and the pursuit of economic growth. Cambridge University Press, Cambridge
Moykr J (2002) The gifts of athena: historical origins of the knowledge society. Oxford University Press, Oxford
Nelson RR (1993) National systems of innovation: a comparative analysis. Oxford University Press, Oxford
Nelson RR (1996) The sources of economic growth. Harvard University Press, Cambridge
Nelson R, Winter S (1982) An evolutionary theory of economic change. Belknap Press of Harvard University Press, Cambridge
Nelson RR, Winter S (2002) Evolutionary Theorizing in Economics. Journal of Economic Perspectives. Vol 16, No 2, Spring, pp 23–46
Nickerson JA, Zenger TR (2004) A knowledge-based theory of the firm-the problem-solving perspective. Organ Sci 15(6):617–632
Oltra MJ, Flor M (2003) The impact of technological opportunities and innovative capabilities on firms' output innovation. Creat Innov Manag 12(3):137–144
Palmberg C (2004) The sources of innovation looking beyond technological opportunities. Econ Innov New Technol 13(2):183–197
Pavitt K (1991) What makes basic research economically useful? Res Policy 20:109–119
Penrose ET (1959) The theory of the growth of the firm. Wiley, New York
Richardson GB (1972) The organisation of industry. The Economic Journal. Vol 82, No 327 September, pp 883–896
Rosenberg N (1982) Inside the black box: technology and economics. Cambridge University Press, Cambridge
Rosenberg N (1994) Exploring the black box: technology, economics and history. Cambridge University Press, Cambridge
Rosenkopf L, Nerkar A (2001) Beyond local research: boundary-spanning, exploration, and impact in the optical disk industry. Strateg Manag J 22(4):287–306
Salter A, McKelvey M (2016) Evolutionary analysis of innovation and entreprenuership: Sidney G Winter, recipient of the 2015 global award for entrepreneurship research. Small Bus Econ. https://doi.org/10.1007/s11187- 016-9702-4
Scherer FM (1965) Firm size, market structure, opportunity, and the output of patented inventions. Am Econ Rev 55:1097–1125
Schumpeter J (1934) The theory of economic development. Harvard University Press, Cambridge
Schumpeter JA (1942) Capitalism, socialism and democracy. Harper & Brothers. Reprint by George Allen & Unwin (Publishers Ltd)

Senker J (ed) (1999) Biotechnology and competitive advantage: Europe's firms and the US challenge. Edward Elgar, Cheltenham

Shane S (2000) Prior knowledge and the discovery of entrepreneurial opportunities. Organ Sci 11 (4):448–469

Shearmur R (2011) Innovation, regions and proximity: from neo-regonalism to spatial analysis. Reg Stud 45(9):1225–1243

Stankiewicz R (2002) The cognitive dynamics of biotechnology and the evolution of its technological systems. In: Carlsson B (ed) Technological systems in the Bio industries. Kluwer Academic Publishers, Boston, pp 35–52

Teece D (2007) Explicating dynamic capabilities: the nature of (sustainable) entreprise performance. Strateg Manag J 28(13):1319–1350

Teece DJ, Pisano G, Shuen A (1997) Dynamic capabilities and strategic management. Strateg Manag J 18(7):509–533

Utterback J (1994) Mastering the dynamics of innovation. Harvard Business School Press, Boston

Van den Bergh J, Gowdy J (2003) The microfoundations of macroeconomics: an evolutionary perspective. Camb J Econ 27:65–84

Vincenti WG (1990) What engineers know and how they know it. The Johns Hopkins University Press, Baltimore

Von Hippel E (1988) The sources of innovation. Oxford University Press, Oxford

Witt U (2010) How evolutionary is Schumpeter's theory of economic development. Ind Innov 9 (2):7–22

A Proposal for a 'National Innovation System Plus Subjective Well-Being' Approach and an Evolutionary Systemic Normative Theory of Innovation

Hans-Jürgen Engelbrecht

Abstract It is argued that development of a 'National Innovation System plus Subjective Well-being' (NIS+SWB) approach would be a natural extension of current research into innovation systems, 'happiness' research and attempts to develop a normative theory of innovation that tries to avoid what can be called the long-run fallacy of normative innovation economics, i.e. the axiomatic assumption that innovation and economic growth are always desirable. After reviewing the literature on national innovation systems and recent contributions, from diverse literatures, relevant to the development of a normative theory of innovation, some of the implications of a NIS+SWB approach are explored. In particular, it is argued that the approach requires an evolutionary systemic normative theory, because of the systemic and co-evolving nature of both the NIS and SWB. This has to be clearly distinguished from individualistic (micro-level) welfare theory, although both are best seen as complementary. Confusing societal and micro-level analysis is an example of the ecological fallacy. Further, the choice of SWB measure is highlighted. It is suggested that life satisfaction is the currently preferred SWB measure for a NIS+SWB approach. However, more research into a merger of SWB research and Sen's capability approach seems called for. Last but not least, some general implications of a NIS+SWB approach for innovation policy are discussed.

1 Introduction

The development of a normative theory of innovation has become an active area of research in recent years. Fagerberg et al. (2013, p. 1), addressing the evolution and future challenges of innovation studies, argue that "..., to recognize that innovation is desirable because of its assumed beneficial effects is not sufficient in itself." As highlighted by, among others, Soete (2013), although there is a widespread

H.-J. Engelbrecht (✉)
School of Economics and Finance, Massey Business School, Massey University, Palmerston North, New Zealand
e-mail: H.Engelbrecht@massey.ac.nz

A. Pyka, U. Cantner (eds.), *Foundations of Economic Change*, Economic Complexity and Evolution, DOI 10.1007/978-3-319-62009-1_9

tendency in the literature to assume that innovation is always good, it does not necessarily benefit society at large. It might benefit the few instead of the many, or it might lead to unsustainable consumption growth and environmental degradation. Assessing the distribution of rewards of innovation is perhaps the most important issue currently facing innovation researchers (Nelson 2013).

How can this issue be addressed? Considering recent developments in evolutionary economics, the move to go 'beyond GDP' in assessing welfare (Stiglitz et al. 2009; European Commission 2014) and the maturing of 'happiness' or subjective well-being (SWB) research, use of a 'SWB lens' as an additional tool for assessing the impacts of innovation seems a promising, and so far mostly unexplored, way forward. Engelbrecht (2014) proposes a general model of the innovation-SWB nexus and advocates measurement of a wide variety of SWB impacts of not only outcomes, but in particular of *processes*, as an additional indicator in the assessment of innovation and in innovation policy-making.[1] The innovation-SWB nexus is a complex adaptive system, consisting of a number of elements and linkages between them, allowing for complex reverse causality and feedback effects, thereby highlighting many impacts usually neglected in innovation research. Broader societal factors are regarded as framework conditions that impact on the elements and links between them.

A number of other recent developments also indicate that it is timely to explore the relationships between innovation and SWB. Empirical work linking the two is beginning to appear outside of the psychological literature (e.g., Dolan and Metcalfe 2012). Also, the 2013 Global Entrepreneurship Monitor Report (Amorós and Bosma 2014) for the first time links entrepreneurship indicators and SWB measures. Amorós and Bosma (2014, p. 11) find that "... in all regions, entrepreneurs exhibit relatively higher rates of subjective well-being in comparison to individuals who are not involved in the process of starting a business or owning-managing a business." In several economies, 10–30% of the labour force could be considered early-stage entrepreneurs or business owners. If it is correct that they have high levels of SWB, this could raise *aggregate* SWB (ibid., p. 62).

More generally, there is increasing 'hard' evidence on the objective benefits of SWB for a broad range of behavioural traits and life outcomes. For example, De Neve et al. (2013) find that SWB predicts future health, mortality, productivity, and income, after controlling for other possible determinants. SWB seems to be associated with greater cooperation, motivation and creativity, and these are important for success in the workplace and life in general. A moderate degree of SWB seems to be optimal for achieving these effects.

Noting similarities between some aspects of the general model of the innovation-SWB nexus and the National Innovation Systems (NISs) approach, Engelbrecht (2014) suggests that an exploration of the relationship between the model and the literature on NISs might be a promising area of further research. This paper begins to explore more closely the rationale for a NIS+SWB approach and tries to draw out

[1] On the importance of procedural utility for human well-being, see Frey et al. (2004).

some of the general implications for the development of a normative theory of innovation.

The chapter is organised as follows. Section 2 reviews the NIS approach. It discusses some of its basic features, perceived strength and weaknesses, and some normative and policy aspects. Section 3 discusses some recent contributions, from a number of disciplines, relevant to the development of a normative theory of innovation. Section 4 explores how such a normative theory might be integrated with the analysis of NISs to form the NIS+SWB approach. Section 5 provides some concluding comments.

2 The National Innovation Systems Approach

2.1 *Basic Features, Perceived Strengths, Weaknesses and Challenges*

The NISs approach builds on the insight that in modern economies, innovation is ubiquitous and the outcome of many interactions and interactive learning among individuals and organisations that are shaped by the (mostly national) institutional framework. It adopts a systems perspective where elements are linked in many different ways, that include many feedback effects, creating distinctive national innovation system 'patterns' (Johnson and Lundvall 2013). There are many, often similar, definitions of NISs focussing on the complex, interactive, dynamic and systemic character of innovation and the important role of learning processes and government policies.[2] Although they appear to be fairly comprehensive, it is less clear what the elements and linkages contained within the NIS are or should be (Edquist 2005). From the start, this created diversity within the approach.

Edquist (2005, pp. 184–186) summarises the strengths and weaknesses of the innovation systems approach as follows. Its strengths are that it (a) places innovation and learning processes at the centre of focus, (b) adopts a holistic and interdisciplinary perspective, (c) employs historical and evolutionary analysis, which makes the notion of optimality irrelevant, (d) emphasises interdependence and non-linearity, (e) can encompass both product and process innovations, as well as subcategories of these types of innovation, and (f) emphasises the role of institutions. Its chief weaknesses are its conceptual diffuseness, i.e. key terms like institutions are defined differently by different authors, its unclear boundaries, and the lack of formal theory. Moreover, given the system features of the approach, even if we knew all of the determinants of innovation, policy can only influence the development of NISs to a limited extent (ibid., p. 191).

[2]The contributions by Freeman (1987), Lundvall (1992a) and Nelson (1993) are commonly credited with having started the by now very large modern literature on NISs. For surveys of the NISs literature, see Balzat and Hanusch (2004), Edquist (2005), Carlsson (2007), Soete et al. (2010), Johnson and Lundvall (2013), Teixeira (2014).

In a new chapter added to the re-print of his classic 1992 book, Lundvall (2010) argues that the wide diffusion of the NIS concept, both in academic and policy-making circles, has distorted its original meaning. A narrow focus on R&D and science too often seems to dominate, incorrectly suggesting that experienced-based learning and tacit knowledge have become less important over time. Lundvall (2010) remains convinced that a broader view is needed if we want to understand innovation and its impacts.

Johnson and Lundvall (2013) see five main challenges for future NISs research. *First*, it needs to further improve our understanding of learning, capability building and innovation, in particular how they interact and how to better combine learning processes based mostly on codified knowledge and mostly on tacit knowledge. *Secondly*, future research needs to provide a better understanding of how work organisation (i.e. the 'learning organisation') affects innovation. This is a central topic for NISs research because work organisation differs greatly between countries. *Thirdly*, future research needs to focus on welfare and inequality in society. Building on Sen's capability approach, Johnson and Lundvall (ibid., p. 1344) emphasise that "learning capability is the most dynamic of the human capabilities, and it is conditioned by national institutions ... an uneven access to learning and competence improvement is a central dimension to inequality". *Fourthly*, the interrelationships between the NIS and regional and urban innovation systems warrant further analysis. *Fifthly*, there is a bias in NISs research that regards innovation as progress. Future NISs research needs to be better able to analyse system failure, i.e. cases where user-producer relationships and the institutional framework lead to unsatisfactory paths of innovation. We suggest that adoption of a NIS+SWB approach would go some way towards meeting these challenges.

2.2 The Normative Dimension of National Innovation Systems: From Long-Run Fallacy to...?

Advocates of the NISs approach have long struggled with its normative dimension. For example, Lundvall (1992b, pp. 6–8) acknowledges that there seems to be a broad social acceptance of international competitiveness and economic growth being the main goals. However, he already argued that we must go beyond this. In particular, the trade-off between growth and environmental sustainability needs to be taken into account.

Despite these comments, other NISs researchers, and innovation and growth researchers in general (i.e. be they neo-classical or not), have subscribed to a mostly uncritical 'innovation and economic growth are good' view. This view can be called the long-run fallacy of normative innovation economics.[3] It is usually

[3]There are exceptions. Witt (1996), e.g., recognises the trade-off between long-term (economic) gain and short-term pain for some members of society and suggests a contractarian approach to navigate the trade-off.

regarded as self-evident, i.e. axiomatic, in light of the rise in general living standards in developed countries over the last two centuries, or what Witt (1996) calls 'Schumpeterian progress'. McCloskey (2013, p. 1710) puts this view harshly by arguing "the historical facts speak loudly enough. Clearly, *some* people are hurt by economic change, every time." However, the "Win-Win-Win-Win-Wins far outnumber the lone Lose" (ibid.). She then seems to argue that anyone objecting to this must be a Neo-Luddite!

The long-run fallacy comes close to assuming that the ends justify the means, even if the means greatly impact negatively on some people in the present and the beneficiaries are members of future generations.[4] Suffice to say, even while subscribing to such a view, many researchers have pointed out that performance measurement is a major challenge for the NISs approach (Carlsson et al. 2002; Fagerberg 2013; Lundvall 2013; Nelson 2013; Soete 2013).

In a recent survey of the NISs literature based on a quantitative description using bibliometric analysis, Teixeira (2014) argues that the NISs approach has not yet converged on an integrated analytical framework. This reflects persistent methodological weaknesses, in particular the lack of formal and diversified quantitative methodologies for assessing the performance of NISs.[5] This echoes earlier assessments of the NISs approach (e.g., Balzat and Hanusch 2007). We would argue there are good reasons for this state of affairs, a major one being the lack of an appropriate normative theory of innovation.

Teixeira (2014) agrees with Dodgson et al. (2011) that the current weaknesses of the NISs approach are likely to result in ill-defined policy design and evaluations. In particular, Dogson et al. (ibid.) argue that despite acknowledging the importance of national differences for innovation, innovation policy prescriptions still tend to be uniform and related to addressing market failure that are applicable in all nations at all times. Using the case of Australia as an example, they argue that notions of system failure, instead of just market failure, can improve future policy-making.

These views about policy are similar to those expressed earlier by, e.g., Nelson and Winter (1982), Metcalfe (1995, 2007), Nelson (2009), Malerba (2009). They are based on well recognised basic properties of evolutionary economics that eschew neo-classical economic notions of equilibrium and optimisation, and policies based on them that aim to correct 'market failure' (i.e. deviations from a theoretical optimum) to bring an economy closer to Pareto-optimality. Innovation, by definition, involves extensive externalities and (massive) spillovers. Market

---

[4]Hanusch and Pyka (2007, p. 277) argue that the future developmental potential of socio-economic systems is the normative principle of Neo-Schumpeterian Economics. Their Neo-Schumpeterian corridor, i.e. a goldilocks development path between bubbles and stagnation, is defined in innovation and economic terms. Although an improvement over the usual long-run fallacy, on its own it seems of limited use when trying to develop a normative theory of innovation.

[5]To give but two examples of quantitative studies, see Guan and Chen (2012) and Castellacci and Natera (2013). In both cases normative aspects are limited to the 'innovation is good' view and methodological features common in neo-classical economic analysis (i.e. efficiency, optimality and maximisation) are adopted.

failure is a misnomer as such 'failures' are an essential feature of innovation (Metcalfe, 2007).[6]

By necessity, i.e. given the characteristics of innovation, NISs are complex evolving systems characterised by path dependence and positive as well as negative feedback effects. As pointed out by Antonelli (2009), individual and systemic path dependence can be identified and articulated. Moreover, the

> ... architectures of the system into which firms are localized exert a key role in shaping the dynamics both at the aggregate and the individual level. The structure of interactions, the networks of cooperation and communication, the flows of technological externalities, the structure of the markets for products and processes and the forms of competition that prevail in each of them, the geographical distribution of firms, their density in regional and technological spaces, the forms of organization within and among firms, the institutional context are the meso-economic carriers of history and, as such, embody the memory of the system. They change through time, albeit at a slow rate, as a result of the dynamics of agents and of the aggregate ... *[and]* act as a filter between the dynamics at the individual and the aggregate level.
>
> (Antonelli 2009, p. 639)

This supports the view that analysis at *both* the micro level and system level is not only legitimate but necessary in the context of NISs, and that they should not be confused. Below it will be argued that this applies even more so to the analysis of SWB in a NIS context.

3 Contributions to the Development of a Normative Theory of Innovation

This section briefly discusses some recent contributions, from researchers based in a variety of disciplines, that either try to develop their own normative theory of innovation and/or provide insights that are useful in the context of trying to develop a normative theory for a NIS+SWB approach.

3.1 Some Recent Contributions by Evolutionary Economists: Schubert and Binder

In a series of papers, Schubert (2012a, b, 2013, 2014) argues for an evolutionary theory of well-being that incorporates aspects of SWB and procedural utility, but in

[6]Some neo-classical economists have also recognised the pervasiveness of massive direct and indirect externalities associated with innovation. The prime example is Baumol (2002). He emphasizes the trade-off between innovation and beneficial spillovers, and struggles with Pareto-optimality: Zero spillovers cannot be Pareto-optimal, but there is no one level of positive spillovers that is clearly optimal, or, interpreted differently, they are all optimal (ibid., p. 122).

some ways goes beyond them. Schubert (2012a) proposes a well-being measure based on 'effective preference learning'. This is based on an individualistic viewpoint, i.e. based at the micro level, as Schubert regards system-level views as being at odds with basic tenets of evolutionary thinking. He (ibid., p. 609) sees a resemblance between his notion of well-being and parts of Sen's (1985, 1999, 2009) capability approach. However, he regards his approach as more subjectivist than Sen's.

In another contribution, Schubert (2012b) again strongly argues against the use of aggregate measures of SWB as a proxy for an empirical social welfare function, i.e. as something to be maximised (the hedonic maximisation approach). Instead, he prefers the constitutional approach to SWB politics that focuses on procedural sources of SWB arising from the design of the institutional framework of society, but argues it needs to be extended because the pursuit of 'happiness' transcends procedural utility. More precisely, it should include anticipation of hedonically valuable outcomes (and path-dependency, i.e. the time profile, in general), as well as preference learning.

Schubert and Cordes (2013) introduce a formal model that allows for learning biases that can result in desirable and undesirable paths of preference learning. Their focus is on consumption preferences, and specifically on the negative impacts of status consumption and status races.[7] Schubert (2013) tries to further strengthen his case for effective preference learning, and against the use of SWB, by taking guidance from Schumpeter's writings.

Last but not least, Schubert's (2014) criticism of Generalized Darwinism as a basis for an evolutionary theory of policy-making again focuses on the individualistic versus systemic approach to an evolutionary welfare economics. He criticises Hodgson and Knudsen (2006) as deficient because their approach runs the risk "to ... stress, in a one-sided way, the supra-individual ("systemic") level of welfare to the detriment of the level of individual well-being" (Schubert 2014, p. 500).

To summarise, Schubert makes some valuable points about the dangers of adopting system-level analysis that ignores impacts on the quality of life of individuals and about hedonic maximisation. They need to be taken seriously in the context of a NIS+SWB approach. However, his emphasis on preference learning and on an individualistic approach seems overdone and limiting. We suggest an evolutionary normative theory needs to come to terms with the complex issue of *both* individual and collective (i.e. systemic) 'welfare'. Moreover, Schubert does not make clear how preference learning can be empirically measured. Last but not least, he seems to equate SWB, life satisfaction (LSF), happiness, hedonic well-being and hedonic utility. This is inappropriate as they capture different

[7]Some aspects of their model are confusing. For example, they associate experienced utility (i.e. the hedonic approach) to mean happiness maximisation (Schubert and Cordes 2013, p. 139), and they limit procedural utility to (consumption) preference learning. This seems a major limitation of their theory, a fact they themselves acknowledge when suggesting that what one might call 'procedural utility in the wider sense' (e.g. that derived from work and political participation) could be targeted by policy.

psychological aspects and have different correlates. Engelbrecht (2014) argues for LSF as the appropriate SWB measure in the context of the innovation-SWB nexus. Further evidence supporting this view is presented below in Sects. 3.4 and 4.2.

In contrast to Schubert, Binder (2013) argues that research has progressed to a stage where SWB measures can be used to assess the welfare effects of innovative change. Theories of SWB enable "a nuanced and comprehensive assessment of the effects that innovativeness has on a society" (ibid., p. 561). Binder acknowledges many of the diverse dimensions of the innovation-SWB nexus. For example, he emphasises that impacts at the micro and macro level, as well as production and consumption impacts, have to be taken into account.[8] However, his views on policy are rather hands-off and similar to Schubert's constitutional approach. Policy is to focus on creating the institutional frameworks that allow individuals to pursue SWB.

In a further contribution, Binder (2014) sketches a promising way forward in the development of a well-being theory of innovation, i.e. he suggests using features of Sen's capability framework to enrich the SWB perspective. He is not the first to link SWB with aspects of Sen's capability approach. However, reviewing the relevant literature, he argues that most of the earlier attempts have focussed on incorporating and subsuming SWB into Sen's approach, e.g. by making SWB a valuable functioning.[9] Instead, Binder argues that welfare assessments should be based on the assessment of 'SWB capabilities', i.e. on the substantive opportunity of individuals to achieve SWB. This arguably overcomes some major weaknesses of both the capability and the SWB approaches (i.e. the problem of hedonic adaptation; the lack of an agency perspective of SWB; how to select a list of valuable functionings in the capability approach). Binder does not implement his proposal empirically, and a dynamic perspective of this approach remains to be developed. Furthermore, he continues to advocate an institutional approach to policy and, like Schubert, uses the terms SWB and happiness inter-changeably.

---

[8]Binder (2013) suggests two evaluation rules to impose some structure on the analysis of SWB impacts of innovation. The 'life domain evaluation principle' restricts analysis to life domains that impact on SWB regardless of context and culture. He mentions health, the social domain and the work domain (ibid., 572). When compared to the model in Engelbrecht (2014), this principle seems like a rather restrictive rule for selecting system elements. Secondly, the 'welfare dynamics principle' aims to impose structure on the analysis over time by taking into account the time dimension of domain-specific hedonic adaptation patterns.

[9]Sen (1999, p. 75) explains the key concepts of his capability approach as follows: "The concept of "functionings,"...reflects the various things a person may value doing or being...A person's "capability" refers to the alternative combinations of functionings that are feasible for her to achieve. Capability is thus a kind of freedom: the substantive freedom to achieve alternative functioning combinations...". 'Alternative functioning combinations' can be interpreted as different lifestyles and capabilities reflect a person's freedom to choose between lifestyles (Clark 2006).

3.2 *The Search for a Normative Dimension of Social Innovation and Social Entrepreneurship*

Social innovation and social entrepreneurship researchers are also exploring normative perspectives, and some contributions emphasise Sen's capability approach and/or SWB research, but so far this literature seems separate from that of evolutionary economics.

Pol and Ville (2009) suggest a definition of 'desirable social innovation' that includes the notions of quality and quantity of life as integral parts. Quality of life is defined in objective, not subjective, terms, i.e. what they call 'macro-quality of life' that is characterised by "the set of valuable options that a group of people has the opportunity to select" (ibid., p. 882). Pol and Ville include things like material well-being, education opportunities, health, job security, family life, environment, political stability and freedoms. Ziegler (2010) suggests using the capability approach as a normative framework for the assessment of social innovation and social entrepreneurship. He defines social innovation as the carrying out of new combinations of capabilities, and social entrepreneurship as creating such new combinations.

Both Pol and Ville (2009) and Ziegler (2010) explicitly dismiss notions of SWB. In contrast, Wobbe (2012, p. 321) suggests that a 'happiness indicator' might be a relatively simple indicator for monitoring the effects of social innovations, but he does not take this suggestion any further. Mulgan (2012a, b) emphasises the potential importance of *both* SWB and capabilities for assessing the outcomes of social innovation. He argues they "could provide both the theoretical and practical glue to hold social innovation practice together, and provide some common measures of success" (Mulgan 2012a, p. 61).

Furthermore, it should be noted that in the chapter of the World Happiness Report 2013 that focuses on policy implications of SWB research (i.e. O'Donnell 2013), many of the examples from around the world where SWB analysis has influenced policy decisions have led to actions that can be described as social innovation and social entrepreneurship. They include, e.g., government policy and social mobilisation in Brazil to clean up polluted water-ways, improve waste management and train fencers drawn from favelas, and policies in Singapore to improve prison service outcomes for prisoners and society. A strong case can be made for increased collaboration between SWB researchers and social innovation and social entrepreneurship researchers.

3.3 *Political Scientists Analysing Subjective Well-Being Across Many Countries*

Another strand of research relevant to the development of a normative theory of innovation that is not usually cited by evolutionary economists is associated with Ronald Inglehart, a political scientist, and his co-researchers. They adopt an evolutionary perspective that links changes in values, agency and freedom to SWB. Using comparable data for large samples of countries collected by the World Values Surveys and the European Values Study, they progressively develop and empirically test evolutionary theories of human development, emancipation, cultural and institutional change (Inglehart and Welzel 2005; Inglehart et al. 2008; Welzel and Inglehart 2010; Welzel 2013).

Some findings from this literature relevant in the current context are: (1) LSF and happiness, i.e. two alternative SWB measures, can move in different directions for significant periods of time, with LSF being more sensitive to economic conditions. In short, the choice of SWB measure matters. (2) Average levels of SWB for entire societies do change; they do not stay fixed. (3) Factors like free choice (Inglehart et al. 2008), agency (Welzel and Inglehart 2010), action resources and freedoms (Welzel 2013) that are closely related to Sen's capability approach are found to be important for SWB, i.e. they have positive impacts on it. (4) There is reciprocal causality between historical, cultural and institutional factors, and SWB. This needs to be taken into account, especially when considering applying the NIS+SWB approach over long time periods. (5) Analysis is usually conducted at both the individual (micro) and societal (country-average) level. Results can and often do differ. It indicates that analysis should be conducted at both levels in order to avoid wrongly assuming that findings at one level also apply at the other. The findings strengthen the case for pursuing the same approach in the context of NIS+SWB. Wrongly assuming that societal level results apply at the individual level is known as the 'ecological fallacy' (O'Dowd 2003).

3.4 Psychologists Analysing Gallop World Poll Data

In a number of recent papers, a group of researchers associated with Ed Diener, a psychologist, re-assess some of the main issues raised in SWB research and explore some new ones using Gallup World Poll data available from 2005 onwards, which are arguably the best SWB data for cross-country comparisons currently available (Diener et al. 2010a, 2013; Tay and Diener 2011). Compared to Inglehart and Welzel's contributions, their approach is more empirical and less aimed at developing an over-arching theoretical framework. Never-the-less, some of their findings are highly relevant. For example, they provide further evidence for the view, advocated in Engelbrecht (2014) in the context of the innovation-SWB nexus, that LSF (or life evaluation[10]) is the more appropriate of the SWB measures for a NIS+SWB approach, despite sometimes appearing contradictory on the issue.

All three studies use three SWB measures, i.e. a life evaluation measure, and positive and negative feelings. Diener et al. (2010a, 2013) re-examine the

[10] In this paper, we regard LSF and life evaluation as synonymous. They arguably assess the same aspects of SWB. This is discussed further in Sect. 4.2.

relationships between SWB measures and income. They re-confirm that life evaluation is closer related to income than are the feelings measures, and that this is somewhat stronger in wealthy countries. Diener et al. (2013) also find this applies to the relationship between life evaluation and changes in income. The implication is that income and LSF are closer inter-twined than often assumed. Interestingly, relative income considerations were found to be based on a mostly global standard of income, not on within-country differences.

The workplace is an important element of the innovation-SWB nexus (Engelbrecht 2014). However, Diener et al. (2010a) relate 'flow' experiences in the workplace, as well as novelty and learning, to positive feelings. This seems highly questionable. Flow occurs when a person's skills are fully engaged in overcoming a challenge that is just manageable (Csikszentmihalyi 1997, p. 30). On theoretical grounds, many positive psychologists argue that flow is more associated with LSF and not with positive emotions like happiness. Csikszentmihalyi (ibid., p. 32) explicitly states that it is "flow, rather than happiness, that makes for excellence in life. When we are in flow, we are not happy, because to experience happiness we must focus on our inner states, and that would take away attention from the task at hand".[11] Seligman (2011, p. 11) argues that "if you ask people who are in flow what they are thinking and feeling, they usually say, "nothing"."

Tay and Diener (2011) address somewhat different questions by focussing on the relationships between the three SWB measures and the fulfilment of needs.[12] They find that basic needs are the strongest predictor of life evaluations. This weakens, but persists, when income is taken into account. Low needs fulfilment is associated with low life evaluation and vice versa. Importantly, they find a difference between life evaluation and feelings measures when it comes to societal need fulfilment:

> ... a person with a certain level of need fulfilment will have a higher life evaluation if living in a society with high need fulfilment than a person with identical personal need fulfilment living in a society in which needs are not as frequently fulfilled. By contrast, positive and negative feelings appear to be tied to individual-level conditions rather than country-level conditions.
>
> (Tay and Diener 2011, p. 360)

The authors conclude there are universal need predictors of well-being, i.e. needs and the three measures of SWB are closely related, but they display different patterns. Focussing on life evaluation, lack of needs is found to lead to low

---

[11]This is easily illustrated by some examples: "If a rock climber takes time out to fell happy while negotiating a difficult move, he might fall to the bottom of the mountain. The surgeon can't afford to feel happy during a demanding operation, or a musician while playing a challenging score" (Csikszentimihalyi 1997, p. 32). In fact, one might even feel 'unhappy' doing some of these activities, e.g. mountain climbing. In most of his writings, Csikszentimihalyi seems to associate flow with leading the good life, i.e. something closely associated with LSF.

[12]The Gallup World Poll includes questions about the following six needs: Basic needs for food and shelter; safety and security; social support and love; feeling respected and pride in activities; mastery; self-direction and autonomy (Tay and Diener 2011, p. 355).

life evaluations, but needs fulfilment is not sufficient for high life evaluation, i.e. additional factors are relevant. Arguably, Tay and Diener's findings provide further support for the use of LSF as the SWB indicator at the system level. Somewhat surprisingly, Sen is not referenced in Tay and Diener (2011). Further research, both theoretical and empirical using Gallop World Poll data, on how Sen's capability approach relates to needs fulfilment and SWB, seems to be called for.

3.5 Sen, Subjective Well-Being, and the Further Development of the Capability Approach

Some of the literature reviewed so far suggests that an evolutionary theory of SWB with a focus on LSF that also takes Sen's capability approach into account might be a useful basis for a normative theory of innovation. Hall (2013) directly addresses similarities and differences between the SWB literature and the capability approach and expresses surprise that they are not closer aligned. However, the suggestion that they should be might seem strange to some readers, especially when considering some of Sen's statements. For example, Schubert (2012a) reports Sen's conclusion that purely subjectivist accounts of welfare should be abandoned in favour of the more objective account of capability (i.e. in order to avoid the 'happy peasant' syndrome). Never-the-less, a closer look at some of Sen's writings and those of some other researchers that have explored the SWB-capability links reveals that the two literatures are less antagonistic than sometimes thought.

Turning first to Sen's writings (Sen 1999, 2008, 2009), he mostly uses the terms pleasure and happiness when referring to modern SWB research. This usage suggests a somewhat biased portrayal of SWB research not uncommon in economics (e.g. compared to psychology). This said, it is also clear that Sen (2009, p. 274) is quite conciliatory towards SWB research, regarding it as extremely important. However, the "... central issue is not the significance of happiness, but the alleged insignificance of everything else, on which many advocates of the happiness perspective seem to insist" (ibid., p. 273). This is a dismissal of the 'happiness maximisation' approach to policy. Importantly, Sen (2008, p. 27) says that although happiness is not all that matters, it can often provide useful evidence on whether we achieve our objectives. Happiness thus has evidential merit.

While it is correct that agency and freedom are different from LSF, they are often positively correlated (see, e.g., Welzel 2013, p. 43), a fact acknowledged by Sen (2009, p. 287). This raises the question, 'how important are differences between SWB (and in particular LSF) and capabilities empirically'? Some findings indicate that although discussions about conceptual differences will continue (partly due to stake-holder interests and scientific silos), differences might be less pronounced when it comes to measurement and policy advice.

Veenhoven (2010) asks what capabilities are required to lead a satisfying life and how happiness contributes to capabilities, and finds that "Capability is typically conducive to happiness, while happiness enhances capability" (ibid., p. 350).[13] Moreover, capabilities improve happiness not only to the extent that they are functional in mastering the problems of life, but also by aiding in the process of functioning (although Veenhoven doesn't explicitly refer to 'flow' experiences, that seems to be what he has in mind). The main causal effect by which happiness affects capabilities is by fostering activity, which in turn fosters the maintenance and development of skills.

In short, the differences between the two approaches are likely to be overstated. With reciprocal causality, there might be little conflict between policies that prioritise either LSF or capabilities! This should not be surprising. Hall (2013) argues that both approaches were developed, at least in part, to tackle the same problem, i.e. 'to go beyond GDP' when measuring human achievement. The two approaches are not antagonistic. Rather, they provide complementary pictures of, and offer improvements to, human lives, and they can benefit from each other.

However, Sen does not say much about analysis at different levels of aggregation, presumable reflecting the micro-level character of his theory. The Human Development Report 2013 (UNDP 2013) suggests that the capability approach should become less individualistic, and this is elaborated in more detail in the background paper by Stewart (2013):

> Individuals cannot flourish alone: indeed, they cannot function alone. The human development approach, however, has been essentially individualistic, assuming that development is the expansion of individual's capabilities or freedoms. Yet there are aspects of societies that affect individuals but cannot be assessed at the individual level... (UNDP 2013, p. 36, Box 1.7)

> The capability approach, developed by Sen (1999) and Nussbaum (2000), provides the theoretical underpinning of much discussion of human development ... the primacy of individualism in the capability approach is at odds with the flourishing of social beings. (Stewart 2013, pp. 1–2)

Acknowledging this, the Report (UNDP 2013) focuses on the nature of social institutions and social competencies that are favourable to human flourishing, raising many questions about the relationships (and mutual causation) between individuals and social institutions.[14] Social institutions are defined as "all institutions in which people act collectively (that is, involve more than one person), other than profit-making market institutions and the state" (ibid., Box 1.7, p. 36). They include, among others, formal non-governmental organisations, informal associations (like neighbourhood associations, social clubs), cooperatives and producer associations, sports clubs, savings associations, as well as norms and rules of behaviour. They interact with the state and markets, but have been much less

---

[13]Note that Veenhoven uses 'happiness' to denote LSF, i.e. the enduring satisfaction with one's 'life-as-a-whole'.

[14]Stewart (2013, p, 2) argues that Sen (2009, pp. 244–247) has begun to hint at the more fundamental role of society in determining individual capabilities. Sen seems to argue he always has done so, if indirectly.

researched (Stewart 2013, p. 2). Social competencies are defined as "what such institutions can be and do—i.e. they are in a sense the capabilities of institutions, . . ." (ibid., p. 2). Although only a partial step towards a more *societal or systemic view* of capabilities (such a view would potentially include *all* institutions), it suggests that such a view is not impossible and should not be dismissed.

4 Towards a NIS+SWB Approach

We now begin to explore how a normative theory of innovation might be integrated with the analysis of NISs. After commenting on some general aspects of evolutionary methodology as espoused by Foster and Potts (2009), and on an earlier attempt of interpreting NISs from an evolutionary perspective, there is a more detailed discussion of the choice of SWB measure, the issue of aggregation and level of analysis and, last but not least, of general implications of an evolutionary systemic normative theory of innovation for NISs policy.

4.1 Neo-Schumpeterian Evolutionary Methodology

Foster and Potts (2009) have suggested building an integrated mixed-method methodology for evolutionary economics based on a micro-meso-macro perspective. They see the economy as driven by a variety of rules (cognitive, behavioural, socio-cultural, organisational, technical, institutional). Microeconomic analysis refers to individual carriers of rules and their local operations, a meso unit refers to a rule and its population of carries, and macroeconomic analysis studies coordination and change in the meso structure of an economy (ibid., p. 57/58). Foster and Potts (2009, pp. 58, 60) argue that ". . .economic evolution involves the origination, adoption and retention of a novel meso rule in the micro and macro structure of the economy. . ." and that "The goal is to identify the different kinds of generic rules that enable value-generating connections between the components of identifiable systems."

Foster and Potts equate value with economic value, i.e. with output or utility from consumption, which suggests that their implicit normative perspective is of the 'innovation is always good' variety. Never-the-less, features of their evolutionary view of the economy might lend themselves to analogies in terms of the innovation-SWB nexus and the development of a NIS+SWB approach. There are obvious parallels between economic structures as an incomplete network of connections (ibid., p. 58) and the innovation-SWB nexus with its many links between elements (Engelbrecht 2014). Moreover, institutional features not only greatly affect the evolution of the economic system and the NIS, but also of SWB.

In a footnote, Foster and Potts (2009, Note 6, p. 60) state that the institutional context, which they explicitly label the meso, has often been neglected by neo-classical economists and also by neo-Schumpeterian evolutionary economists.[15] It is therefore not surprising that there exists little research addressing the issue of how to interpret NISs from an evolutionary perspective. Kastelle et al. (2012) are an exception. Echoing Foster and Potts' sentiment they argue that much of the NISs literature is biased towards a macro perspective of institutional engineering that regards the NIS as static and exogenous. Instead, they propose to endogenise NISs by adopting a micro-meso-macro framework. This enables them to view such systems as macro rules within a micro-meso-macro rule system. Change in the NIS can then be "defined by the entry of a new meso unit, which thus requires micro adoption and retention" (ibid., p. 7). More precisely (ibid.):

> The study of innovation systems from the evolutionary perspective thus proposes a micro meso macro framework in which: micro refers to the adoption of new innovation system rules; meso refers to the resultant set and respective populations of innovation system rules; and macro, refers to the emergent complex structure of meso rules that compose the (macro) innovation system. This framework enables us to conceptualize innovation systems (as a macro construct) composed of interacting meso populations that are themselves composed of micro adoptions of these rules.

Viewing economic and innovation systems as co-evolving in this way leads Kastelle et al. (2012) to develop three propositions. First, different innovation systems (e.g. NIS, regional, sectoral) interact at the level of the actors (i.e. through micro evolution). Actors are simultaneously embedded in different types of innovation systems and "all of these systems are able to contribute meso rules that might influence the process of innovation" (ibid., p. 11). This highlights the diversity subsumed under the NIS and enables us to better understand how different innovation systems interact. Secondly, by according an important role to actors at the micro level, mutual causation and co-evolution is emphasised. Innovation systems (i.e. their institutional set-ups) affect actors, but actors can also change innovation systems by spreading new meso rules. Thirdly, innovation systems are best analysed using population dynamic methodologies. This implies that such systems are heterogeneous.

Conceptualising the NIS as being driven by different meso rules raises interesting questions, such as 'what combination of meso rules is most effective' and 'which rules do not interact well and why' (ibid., p. 17). However, Kastelle et al. (2012) seem to judge 'effective' and 'well' in terms of economic outcomes, which we argue is not an appropriate basis for a normative assessment.

The task of developing an evolutionary systemic normative theory of innovation requires not only that the institutions forming the NIS are endogenised using an evolutionary methodology, but that the evolution of the normative criterion is also included (and the latter needs to be broad enough to include procedural utility in the wider sense). NISs (and other innovation systems) and their actors co-evolve, and so does SWB. At this point one may speculate how to proceed to

[15] Also see Nelson (2002) on this point. In hindsight this seems odd, given the importance of the meso for evolutionary methodology.

develop a NIS+SWB approach. While NIS and SWB are interconnected, a starting point may be to separately analyse the NIS and SWB meso rules, and then explore their interactions. We currently have little knowledge about the feasibility and usefulness of a micro-meso-macro analysis of SWB, let along how this might interact with micro-meso-macro analysis of the NIS.

4.2 Choice of SWB Measure

The choice of SWB measure to be used in the context of a NIS+SWB approach is an important issue. The term happiness is often used to denote all kinds of SWB. This is misleading and conceptually confusing. The practice should be stopped. This plea is addressed, in particular, to economists, but also to the popular media for whom happiness is more attention-grabbing and often intuitively appealing (OECD 2013). The OECD (ibid., p. 184), therefore, recommends against using only the term happiness, especially for releases of SWB data by national statistics agencies. They also note another source of confusion, i.e. the practice of some authors to use the term wellbeing as shorthand for SWB.

The OECD (2013) guidelines on measuring SWB provide much needed clarification that is also of help in the current context. They identify three broad subcategories of SWB, i.e. *life evaluation*, *affect* and (so far less researched) *eudaimonia* or psychological flourishing. Life evaluation is recommended as the core measure that should be measured by all member states. There are two main candidate questions to assess life evaluation. They are the Self-Anchoring Striving Scale (Cantril Ladder of Life scale, e.g. as adopted by the Gallup World Poll) and a version of the commonly used LSF question (e.g. as used in the World Values Surveys). As noted earlier, we treat LSF and life evaluation as equivalent SWB measures. Both the Cantril Ladder of Life scale question and the LSF question account for longer-term considerations instead of short-term emotions. Diener et al. (2010b) argue that both reflect primarily a judgement, and Helliwell et al. (2010) find that both show similar correlations with key underlying structural variables, although LSF values tend to be higher than Cantril Ladder values.

For both conceptual and pragmatic reasons, LSF seems to be the most appropriate systemic measure in the context of a NIS+SWB approach. It is the most commonly available, and most recommended, SWB measure. If possible, it should be reported not only at the aggregate level, but supplemented with life domain specific and group specific data. This will be especially important when trying to identify and assess policy interventions. OECD (2013, Chap. 4) discusses in some detail how SWB data should be presented and reported. In any empirical application, besides reporting mean values (the preferred measure of central tendency), due consideration needs to be given to alternative ways of reporting levels, the distribution of values, aggregation across life domains, reporting changes over time and between groups etc.

An issue that requires further clarification, especially in the context of a NIS+SWB approach where procedural utility is important, is how LSF and eudaimonia are related. OECD (2013, p. 32/33) notes that psychological flourishing has fairly low correlations with the other SWB measures. It remains to be seen whether this will be confirmed in future studies using larger data sets. OECD (ibid.) further notes that eudaimonia has more to do with capabilities than the other SWB measures, and therefore has a more instrumental focus, but that its conceptual structure is less fleshed out. Eudaimonia might prove to be an important link between SWB and Sen's capability approach.

4.3 Societal (System-Level) Versus Individualistic (Micro-level) Analysis

Not only does use of an inappropriate SWB measure lead to misunderstandings, so does confounding different levels of analysis. Foster (2011) notes that much of the evolutionary restlessness observed at the micro-economic level is averaged out at more aggregate levels of analysis. This also applies in the case of SWB measures. Much confusion and mutual miscomprehension in academic discussions probably arises when different researchers argue about the advantages and disadvantages of linking innovation and SWB while implicitly assuming different levels of analysis or ignoring systemic aspects. Confusing system-level phenomena with micro-level processes is an example of the ecological fallacy. We briefly discuss some evidence highlighting the importance of distinguishing between the two.

Veenhoven (2010) points out that the relationships between capabilities and SWB can be addressed at both levels. At the micro level, analysis focuses on the relationships between capabilities and SWB of persons. At the societal or system level, the focus is on the level of capabilities in society and average SWB. Relationships can differ between the two levels. For example, schooling does not seem to make pupils happier, but it does so indirectly at the societal level because modern societies require high levels of education. Therefore, it seems to make sense to distinguish between 'individual capabilities' and the 'level of capabilities in nations' (ibid.).

Similarly, Tov and Au (2013) observe that societal-level and person-level correlates of SWB often differ. There is usually not a direct and perfect relation between factors at the different levels of analysis. To illustrate this, consider an increase in GDP. It is unlikely to improve a person's well-being if he or she remains unemployed. Suicide rates are another example. They may not affect well-being if they apply to a small segment of society rather than one's close friends and family (ibid., p. 456). Importantly,

> The point is that we must not make assumptions about the individual motives and desires of *all* people in a country based on societal SWB alone ... interpreting aggregated data requires a shift in perspective toward broad, societal conditions and norms.
>
> (Tov and Au 2013, p. 457)

Consider, e.g., the case of divorce rates. They are positively correlated with average SWB, despite married people having higher SWB than un-married people (ibid.). In general, assessing impacts at the individual and system levels might highlight important trade-offs that need to be considered by policy-makers. Binder (2013, p. 570/1) provides another example: International competitiveness of countries, a system-level indicator, might only be achieved by reducing SWB of individuals.

Recent research on the complex relationships between SWB and entrepreneurship using Global Entrepreneurship Monitor (GEM) data indicates the feasibility and usefulness of societal-level analysis of this important aspect of a NIS+SWB approach. Naudé et al. (2014) empirically explore whether the presence and nature of entrepreneurship impacts on national 'happiness', and whether nations with 'happy' citizens are better for entrepreneurs to start new businesses.[16] They find some support for both hypotheses, and also that the nature of entrepreneurship (i.e. whether it is 'early stage', opportunity driven or necessity driven) matters greatly. An extended analysis is reported in the Global Entrepreneurship Monitor 2013 Global Report (Amorós and Bosma 2014). It uses both overall LSF and work domain-specific LSF. Amorós and Bosma (2014) provide many interesting, if preliminary, empirical insights and indicate that a larger, dedicated report on the issue is forthcoming. In principle, GEM data can be used for analysis at both the micro and societal levels. They seem to be a prime candidate for use in an empirical application of a NIS+SWB approach.

4.4 An Evolutionary Systemic Normative Theory of Innovation and NIS Policy

There seems to be agreement among prominent NISs researchers and evolutionary economists that public policy has to be based on systems thinking (Nelson 2009; Malerba 2009). Malerba (2009) argues that policies should generate a satisfactory performance in terms of technological change and rate of innovation. 'Optimal intervention' and 'best' policies cannot be identified in a changing and uncertain world where direct, let alone indirect, consequences of policies are difficult to predict and often surprising. However, public policy is necessary to address evolutionary and systems failures, such as learning failures, competence lock-ins, and trade-offs regarding exploration and exploitation, variety generation and selection, appropriability and the distribution of competences (ibid.).

This similarly applies to SWB. A normative theory associated with a NIS+SWB approach should focus on identifying evolutionary and systemic LSF failures and weaknesses that then might be addressed by policy in order to keep systemic LSF at

[16]They measure 'happiness' by LSF, i.e. like many researchers, they are not specific enough in their use of SWB terms.

a satisfactory level. More positively, it can be described as supporting externalities and spillover effects that might raise, but not maximise, systemic LSF.[17] This is emphasised by, e.g., De Neve et al. (2013). They suggest that this enables people to flourish across all life domains, ranging from health to traffic safety and, one may add, innovation. Such an approach is different from the two main perspectives on the 'politics of happiness', i.e. SWB maximisation and the constitutional approach. It is a third approach that is evolutionary and experimental, relying explicitly on trial and error. For example, if we can identify major negative LSF impacts in a particular life domain, they could be targeted by policy. By aiming to counteract major known negative LSF impacts, policy might also help to reduce anti-innovation views.

A key example of an element of the innovation-SWB nexus that is of great importance to both NISs and SWB researchers is the workplace. Hall (2013, p. 146), among others, reports that there is a strong correlation between job satisfaction and overall life evaluation across countries. Procedural utility derived from work matters greatly. NISs researchers seem to agree. As noted earlier, Johnson and Lundvall (2013, p. 1344) regard a better understanding of how work organisation affects innovation as one of the major challenges facing NISs research. They agree that well-being in the work domain and innovation performance are correlated. In fact, there is a large literature, across many disciplines, on the contribution of the work domain to procedural utility and SWB. To give but a few recent examples, contributors include economists (Helliwell and Huang 2011; Phelps 2013), management researchers (Dewe and Cooper 2012; Erdogan et al. 2012), sociologists (Gershuny and Fisher 2014), organisational and industrial psychologists (Warr 2013). In short, analysis of workplace impacts, and the design of policies to address any shortcomings in the work domain, should have a prominent place in a NIS-SWB approach.

In general, we should take advantage of increasing knowledge about the source and impacts of SWB and develop an evolutionary systemic normative theory of innovation that takes into account as many of the impacts suggested by the general model of the innovation-SWB nexus as possible. LSF at the system level is probably best viewed as a 'SWB thermometer' or broad warning indicator that might highlight shortcomings of the NIS in terms of measured LSF. To what extent a particular level of systemic LSF should be tolerated or acted upon is ultimately a separate political issue that will also be informed by analysis of LSF at the micro-level, and other policy considerations. Hopefully, my making the impacts and trade-offs involved visible, systemic policies remain connected to their impacts on individuals.

[17]This also implies that a NIS+SWB approach should not be described as utilitarian. Utilitarianism requires maximisation; it is one of its defining features (Eggleston 2012).

5 Concluding Comments

Development of a NIS+SWB approach seems a natural extension of current research into NISs, SWB and attempts to develop a normative theory of innovation. Adding the analysis of SWB to that of the NIS probably strengthens the 'N' in NIS, because SWB is, in important ways, influenced and shaped by national factors (formal and informal institutions, e.g. laws, regulations, social conventions). This should reduce doubts (see, e.g. Balzat and Hanusch 2004) about the continuing significance of the national perspective. However, given the systemic and co-evolving nature of the NIS and SWB, there are potentially so many direct and indirect links between them that we cannot possible hope to capture them all. Using the model of the innovation-SWB nexus adapted to a specific country as a guide and focusing devise, it should be possible to make progress in determining the more important links and impacts.

Moreover, development of a NIS+SWB approach has to overcome some special challenges associated with the long-run fallacy of normative innovation economics and with the danger of committing the ecological fallacy. The former is addressed using SWB, or more precisely, a particular form of SWB (i.e. LSF), as a normative indicator. By measuring LSF across 'life-as-a-whole', as well as for specific life domains (e.g. the work place) in order to assess the impacts of processes as well as of outcomes, it is made clear that innovation should raise human well-being not just in the multi-generational long-run, but also for the people more immediately affected.

The ecological fallacy highlights the importance of clearly distinguishing between analyses at the systemic or societal level from that at the micro level. A NIS+SWB approach, being a systems approach, requires a systemic normative dimension. The NIS and SWB co-evolve as a complex adaptive system, and 'SWB maximisation' is simply impossible. That is why we advocate development of an evolutionary systemic normative theory of innovation that aims at an 'acceptable' level of (systemic) LSF. This does not preclude individualistic or micro level analysis. In fact, it will be desirable to undertake both. In this way, a NIS+SWB approach should be able to overcome Schubert's (2014) criticism of Generalized Darwinism, i.e. as being completely detached from the realm of individuals' concerns.

The case for the development of a NIS+SWB approach put forward in this paper is, by necessity, exploratory and tentative, focussing on broad general issues. Never-the-less, it is an important step that puts innovation firmly in the context of the search for well-being indicators that go 'beyond GDP'. It remains to be refined and many potential extensions and implications need to be explored.

One area of further research is the relationship between Sen's capability approach and SWB research. Both NISs researchers (e.g. Lundvall 2010) and evolutionary economist trying to develop a normative theory of innovation seem to be converging on the view that Sen's approach should be an important element of any normative assessment of innovation. How should 'SWB capabilities', to use

Binder's (2014) term, be measured empirically? The answer to this question might also affect to what extent 'objective' well-being indicators are separately included in the analysis. The use of LSF data is advocated as a pragmatic first step when trying to implement a NIS+SWB approach, but it might not be the last word on how to measure SWB.

Research is also required on the possible implications of extending a NIS+SWB approach to other innovation systems, e.g. regional and technological systems, as well as to global systems of innovation. Last but not least, most of the NISs literature focuses on innovation in highly developed countries (Teixeira 2014). It has been recognised that it needs to be extended to developing countries. This will pose additional challenges for a NIS+SWB approach as such countries are much more diverse, e.g. with respect to institutions. To some readers, the long-run fallacy might seem more justifiable in the context of poor countries. We would argue that such a view is incorrect.

References

Amorós JE, Bosma N (2014) Global entrepreneurship monitor 2013 global report: fifteen years of assessing entrepreneurship across the globe. Global Entrepreneurship Research Association. www.gemconsortium.org. Accessed 20 May 2014

Antonelli C (2009) The economics of innovation: from the classical legacies to the economics of complexity. Econ Innov New Technol 18(7):611–646

Balzat M, Hanusch H (2004) Recent trends in the research on national innovation systems. J Evol Econ 14:197–210

Balzat M, Hanusch H (2007) Fundamentals of the concept of national innovation systems. In: Hanusch H, Pyka A (eds) Elgar companion to neo-Schumpeterian economics. Edward Elgar, Cheltenham, pp 926–939

Baumol W (2002) The free-market innovation machine: analysing the growth miracle of capitalism. Princeton University Press, Princeton

Binder M (2013) Innovativeness and subjective well-being. Soc Indic Res 111:561–578

Binder M (2014) Subjective well-being capabilities: bridging the gap between the capability approach and subjective well-being research. J Happiness Stud 15:1197–1217

Carlsson B (2007) Innovation systems: a survey of the literature from a Schumpeterian perspective. In: Hanusch H, Pyka A (eds) Elgar companion to neo-Schumpeterian economics. Edward Elgar, Cheltenham, pp 857–871

Carlsson B, Jacobsson S, Holmén M, Rickne A (2002) Innovation systems: analytical and methodological issues. Res Policy 31:233–245

Castellacci F, Natera JM (2013) The dynamics of national innovation systems: a panel cointegration analysis of the coevolution between innovative capacity and absorptive capacity. Res Policy 42:579–594

Clark D (2006) Capability approach. In: Clark D (ed) The Elgar companion to development studies. Edward Elgar, Cheltenham, pp 32–45

Csikszentmihalyi M (1997) Finding flow. Basic Books, New York

De Neve JE, Diener E, Tay L, Xuereb C (2013) The objective benefits of subjective well-being. In: Helliwell J, Layard R, Sachs J (eds) World happiness report 2013. United Nations Sustainable Development Solutions Network, New York, pp 54–79

Dewe P, Cooper C (2012) Well-being and work: towards a balanced agenda. Palgrave Macmillan, Basingstoke

Diener E, Kahneman D, Tov W, Arora R (2010a) Income's association with judgements of life versus feelings. In: Diener E, Helliwell J, Kahneman D (eds) International differences in well-being. Oxford University Press, Oxford, pp 3–15
Diener E, Ng W, Harter J, Arora R (2010b) Wealth and happiness across the world: material prosperity predicts life evaluation, whereas psychological prosperity predicts positive feeling. J Pers Soc Psychol 99(1):52–61
Diener E, Tay L, Oishi S (2013) Rising income and the subjective well-being of nations. J Pers Soc Psychol 104(2):267–276
Dodgson M, Hughes A, Foster J, Metcalfe S (2011) Systems thinking, market failure, and the development of innovation policy: the case of Australia. Res Policy 40:1145–1156
Dolan P, Metcalfe R (2012) The relationship between innovation and subjective well-being. Res Policy 41:1489–1498
Edquist C (2005) Systems of innovation: perspectives and challenges. In: Fagerberg J, Mowery D, Nelson R (eds) The Oxford handbook of innovation. Oxford University Press, Oxford, pp 181–208
Eggleston B (2012) Utilitarianism. In: Chadwick R (ed) Encyclopedia of applied ethics, 2nd edn. Academic Press/Elsevier, London, pp 452–458
Engelbrecht HJ (2014) A general model of the innovation – subjective well-being nexus. J Evol Econ 24(2):377–397
Erdogan B, Bauer T, Truxillo D, Mansfield L (2012) Whistle while you work: a review of the life satisfaction literature. J Manag 38(4):1038–1083
European Commission (2014) Beyond GDP: measuring progress, true wealth, and the well-being of nations. http://ec.europa.eu/environment/beyond_gdp/index_en.html. Accessed 22 May 2014
Fagerberg J (2013) Innovation – a new guide. The working papers on innovation studies, No. 20131119. Centre for Technology, Innovation and Culture, University of Oslo, Oslo. http://www.sv.uio.no/tik/InnoWP/tik_working_paper_20131119.pdf. Accessed 20 May 2014
Fagerberg J, Martin B, Andersen E (2013) Innovation studies: towards a new agenda. In: Fagerberg J, Martin BR, Andersen ES (eds) Innovation studies: evolution and future challenges. Oxford University Press, Oxford, pp 1–17
Foster J (2011) Evolutionary macroeconomics: a research agenda. J Evol Econ 21:5–28
Foster J, Potts J (2009) A micro-meso-macro perspective on the methodology of evolutionary economics: integrating history, simulation and econometrics. In: Cantner U, Gaffard J-L, Nesta L (eds) Schumpeterian perspectives on innovation, competition and growth. Springer, Dordrecht, pp 55–70
Freeman C (1987) Technology policy and economic performance: lessons from Japan. Pinter, London
Frey B, Benz M, Stutzer A (2004) Introducing procedural utility: not only what, but also how matters. J Inst Theor Econ 160:377–401
Gershuny J, Fisher K (2014) Post-industrious society: why work time will not disappear for our grandchildren. Sociology Working Paper 2014-03. Centre for Time Use Research, Department of Sociology, University of Oxford. http://www.sociology.ox.ac.uk/materials/papers/wp20143.pdf. Accessed 20 May 2014
Guan J, Chen K (2012) Modeling the relative efficiency of national innovation systems. Res Policy 41:102–115
Hall J (2013) From capabilities to contentment: testing the links between human development and life satisfaction. In: Helliwell J, Layard R, Sachs J (eds) World happiness report 2013. United Nations Sustainable Development Solutions Network, New York, pp 138–153
Hanusch H, Pyka A (2007) Principles of neo-Schumpeterian economics. Camb J Econ 31:275–289
Helliwell J, Barrington-Leigh C, Harris A, Huang H (2010) International evidence on the social context of well-being. In: Diener E, Helliwell J, Kahneman D (eds) International differences in well-being. Oxford University Press, Oxford, pp 291–327
Helliwell J, Huang H (2011) Well-being and trust in the workplace. J Happiness Stud 12:747–767

Hodgson G, Knudsen T (2006) Why we need a generalized Darwinism, and why generalized Darwinism is not enough. J Econ Behav Organ 61:1–19
Inglehart R, Foa R, Peterson C, Welzel C (2008) Development, freedom, and rising happiness: a global perspective (1981–2007). Perspect Psychol Sci 3(4):264–285
Inglehart R, Welzel C (2005) Modernization, cultural change, and democracy: the human development sequence. Cambridge University Press, Cambridge
Johnson B, Lundvall BÅ (2013) National Innovation Systems (NIS). In: Carayannis EG (ed) Encyclopedia of creativity, invention, innovation, and entrepreneurship. Springer, New York, pp 1341–1347
Kastelle T, Potts J, Dodgson M (2012) The evolution of innovation systems. Paper presented at the 14th International Schumpeter Society Conference, Brisbane, Australia, 2nd–5th July
Lundvall BÅ (ed) (1992a) National systems of innovation: towards a theory of innovation and interactive learning. Pinter, London
Lundvall BÅ (1992b) Introduction. In: Lundvall BÅ (ed) National systems of innovation: towards a theory of innovation and interactive learning. Pinter, London, pp 1–19
Lundvall BÅ (2010) Post script: innovation systems research – where it came from and where it might go. In: Lundvall BÅ (ed) National systems of innovation: toward a theory of innovation and interactive learning. Anthem Press, London, pp 317–349
Lundvall BÅ (2013) Innovation studies: a personal interpretation of 'the state of the art'. In: Fagerberg J, Martin BR, Andersen ES (eds) Innovation studies: evolution and future challenges. Oxford University Press, Oxford, pp 21–70
Malerba F (2009) Increase learning, break knowledge lock-ins and foster dynamic complementarities: evolutionary and system perspectives on technology policy in industrial dynamics. In: Foray D (ed) The new economics of technology policy. Edward Elgar, Cheltenham, pp 33–45
McCloskey D (2013) Tunzelmann, Schumpeter, and the hockey stick. Res Policy 42:1706–1715
Metcalfe S (1995) Technology systems and technology policy in an evolutionary framework. Camb J Econ 19(1):25–46
Metcalfe S (2007) Policy for innovation. In: Hanusch H, Pyka A (eds) Elgar companion to neo-Schumpeterian economics. Edward Elgar, Cheltenham, pp 943–966
Mulgan G (2012a) The theoretical foundations of social innovation. In: Nicholls A, Murdoch A (eds) Social innovation: blurring boundaries to reconfigure markets. Palgrave Macmillan, Basingstoke, pp 33–65
Mulgan G (2012b) Social innovation theories: can theory catch up with practice? In: Franz HW, Hochgerner J, Howaldt J (eds) Challenge social innovation: potentials for business, social entrepreneurship, welfare and civil society. Springer, Berlin, pp 19–42
Naudé W, Amorós JE, Cristi O (2014) "Surfeiting, the appetite may sicken": entrepreneurship and happiness. Small Bus Econ 42:523–540
Nelson R (ed) (1993) National innovation systems: a comparative analysis. Oxford University Press, New York
Nelson R (2002) Bringing institutions into evolutionary growth theory. J Evol Econ 12:17–28
Nelson R (2009) Building effective 'innovation systems' versus dealing with 'market failures' as ways of thinking about technology policy. In: Foray D (ed) The new economics of technology policy. Edward Elgar, Cheltenham, pp 7–16
Nelson R (2013) Reflections on the study of innovation and on those who study it. In: Fagerberg J, Martin BR, Andersen ES (eds) Innovation studies: evolution and future challenges. Oxford University Press, Oxford, pp 187–193
Nelson R, Winter S (1982) An evolutionary theory of economic change. The Belknap Press of Harvard University Press, Cambridge
Nussbaum M (2000) Women and human development: a study in human capabilities. Cambridge University Press, Cambridge

O'Donnell G (2013) Using well-being as a guide to policy. In: Helliwell J, Layard R, Sachs J (eds) World happiness report 2013. United Nations Sustainable Development Solutions Network, New York, pp 98–111
O'Dowd L (2003) Ecological fallacy. In: Miller R, Brewer J (eds) The A-Z of social research: a dictionary of key social science research concepts. SAGE, London
OECD (2013) OECD guidelines on measuring subjective well-being. OECD, Paris
Phelps E (2013) Mass flourishing: how grassroots innovation created jobs, challenge, and change. Princeton University Press, Princeton
Pol E, Ville S (2009) Social innovation: buzz word or enduring term? J Socio-Econ 38:878–885
Schubert C (2012a) Is novelty always a good thing? Towards an evolutionary welfare economics. J Evol Econ 22:585–619
Schubert C (2012b) Pursuing happiness. Kyklos 65(2):245–261
Schubert C (2013) How to evaluate creative destruction: reconstructing Schumpeter's approach. Camb J Econ 37:227–250
Schubert C (2014) "Generalized Darwinism" and the quest for an evolutionary theory of policy making. J Evol Econ 24(3):479–513
Schubert C, Cordes C (2013) Role models that make you unhappy: light paternalism, social learning, and welfare. J Inst Econ 9:131–159
Seligman M (2011) Flourish. Free Press, New York
Sen A (1985) Commodities and capabilities. North-Holland, Amsterdam
Sen A (1999) Development as freedom. Anchor Books/Random House Inc., New York
Sen A (2008) The economics of happiness and capability. In: Bruni L, Comim F, Pugno M (eds) Capabilities and happiness. Oxford University Press, Oxford, pp 16–27
Sen A (2009) The idea of justice. The Belknap Press of Harvard University Press, Cambridge
Soete L (2013) Is innovation always good? In: Fagerberg J, Martin BR, Andersen ES (eds) Innovation studies: evolution and future challenges. Oxford University Press, Oxford, pp 134–146
Soete L, Verspagen B, Ter Weel B (2010) Systems of innovation. In: Hall BH, Rosenberg N (eds) Handbook of the economics of innovation, vol 2. North-Holland/Elsevier, Amsterdam, pp 1159–1180
Stewart F (2013) Capabilities and human development: beyond the individual – the critical role of social institutions and social competencies. Occasional Paper 2013/13. United Nations Development Programme Human Development Report Office, New York
Stiglitz J, Sen A, Fitoussi JP (2009) Report by the commission on the measurement of economic performance and social progress. www.stiglitz-sen-fitoussi.fr. Accessed 22 May 2014
Tay L, Diener E (2011) Needs and subjective well-being around the world. J Pers Soc Psychol 101 (2):354–365
Teixeira A (2014) Evolution, roots and influence of the literature on national systems of innovation: a bibliometric account. Camb J Econ 38:181–214
Tov W, Au E (2013) Comparing well-being across nations: conceptual and empirical issues. In: David S, Boniwell I, Conley Ayers A (eds) The Oxford handbook of happiness. Oxford University Press, Oxford, pp 448–464
United Nations Development Programme (UNDP) (2013) Human development report 2013 – the rise of the south: human progress in a diverse world. United Nations Development Programme, New York
Veenhoven R (2010) Capability and happiness: conceptual difference and reality links. J Socio-Econ 39:344–350
Warr P (2013) Jobs and job-holders: two sources of happiness and unhappiness. In: David S, Boniwell I, Ayers AC (eds) The Oxford handbook of happiness. Oxford University Press, Oxford, pp 733–750
Welzel C (2013) Freedom rising: human empowerment and the quest for emancipation. Cambridge University Press, New York

Welzel C, Inglehart R (2010) Agency, values, and well-being: a human development model. Soc Indic Res 97:43–63
Witt U (1996) Innovations, externalities and the problem of economic progress. Public Choice 89:113–130
Wobbe W (2012) Measuring social innovation and monitoring progress of EU policies. In: Franz HW, Hochgerner J, Howaldt J (eds) Challenge social innovation: potentials for business, social entrepreneurship, welfare and civil society. Springer, Berlin, pp 309–324
Ziegler R (2010) Innovations in doing and being: capability innovations at the intersection of Schumpeterian political economy and human development. J Soc Entrep 1:255–272

Part III
Behaviour

Confounded, Augmented and Constrained Replicator Dynamics

Complex Selection Processes and Their Measurement

Jacob Rubæk Holm, Esben Sloth Andersen, and J. Stanley Metcalfe

Abstract The quantitative methodology derived from replicator dynamics for empirical studies of economic evolution is becoming increasingly well developed in theory but is rarely applied in practice. One reason is the relatively naïve nature of current methods, which focus on the evolution of a single characteristic in a single environment. This assumption constrains the analysis of real selection processes in which firms operate in several markets and their products have several characteristics that interact to determine fitness. This entails that measurement of economic selection becomes confounded: characteristics that are associated with firm growth are not becoming more frequent in the population. The reason for confounded selection is that characteristics interact to augment or constrain the rate and direction of evolution and one-dimensional, single trait replicator dynamics cannot cope with confounded selection. The contribution of this paper is to develop an approach that serves to explicitly analyse confounded selection. The primary elements of the method are the selection gradients of the characteristics and the covariance matrix of the characteristics. Based on these, the method motivates a taxonomy of selection based on the interaction of characteristics. Applying the method to a population of firms will shed light on potentially confounded selection. It will reveal the indirect effects of characteristics on selection and the augmentation and constraints created thereby.

1 Introduction

Although economic evolution is in principle an easily understandable process, in practice it is surprisingly difficult to analyse. For practical reasons, it therefore remains necessary to develop a formal theory of economic evolution, one that

J.R. Holm (✉) • E.S. Andersen
Department of Business and Management, Aalborg University, Fibigerstræde 11, 9220 Aalborg Ø, Denmark
e-mail: jrh@business.aau.dk

J.S. Metcalfe
Manchester Institute of Innovation Research, University of Manchester, Manchester, UK

A. Pyka, U. Cantner (eds.), *Foundations of Economic Change*, Economic Complexity and Evolution, DOI 10.1007/978-3-319-62009-1_10

addresses the key Schumpeterian questions, that is empirically robust at the relevant levels of analysis, and that might illuminate the problems faced by decision makers whether in firms or in government. Moreover, this formal theory should reconcile many different pieces and make connections with existing branches of economic theory and the pioneering insights of Schumpeter.

Within the context of how wealth is created from knowledge, the question of how innovations impact the economic system is crucial. This is not a matter of innovation alone, but of providing an explanation of how the system adapts to the possibilities immanent in any innovation and how it draws them out such that adaptation and innovation react to one another. The system must be understood as if every solution to an economic problem only serves to open up further problems somewhere in the system. The problems are dynamic, they relate to process, and it is process that we have to elucidate.

To be precise, we wish to explain the rate at which innovations are absorbed into the economic structure, displacing established methods in the process. We are addressing creative destruction in matters small and the large, and this involves structural change in the economy and differential growth in the use of innovations and their rivals. Differential growth is the essence of economic evolution, the analogue to fitness in formal biological theory.

Standard evolutionary theory gives the following formal answer for economic systems that select with respect to only one dimension:

1. Technical characteristics of innovations are converted into economic characteristics through the prevailing price system, to define effective variation in the unit costs and qualities of products and services. Formal evolutionary theory analyses the varying characteristics individually.
2. Differential effective variation is the source of economic profit in Schumpeter's sense.
3. Differential profit is the basis of the differential growth of rival methods, and hence two activities that have equal profitability are selected for at the same rate. Growth and profitability are positively correlated, and this correlation is grounded in an economic explanation of processes in single markets. This is one of the oldest ideas in dynamic economic analysis.

This standard theory is very restricted. Selection is limited to one dimension (typically the unit cost characteristic), and selection is analysed in the context of only one market process, that in the product market. The theory is of great pedagogic value, but it is far too narrow to explore the questions raised in part 1 of the above answer. One problem is that the theory emphasises differential growth of methods, which generally translates into differential growth of firms, while firm turnover is neglected (Baldwin and Rafiquzzaman 1995; Baldwin and Gu 2006b). Another problem is that differential growth may be caused by structural transformations that are unrelated to differential profit (Holm 2014). However, the main problem is that each particular process of evolution normally involves multiple technical and economic characteristics and multiple markets (such as markets for products, labour and capital).

Progress towards the analysis of these more complex forms of economic evolution thus requires two additional steps:

4. The articulation of multiple dimensions of effective economic variation.
5. The extension of the market process to cover simultaneous selection in multiple markets, adding labour and capital markets to the list.

When considering multiple characteristics, the correlation between the different characteristics is crucial for evolutionary change. Firms compete not only for customers but also for employees and access to capital. Thus labour and capital markets substantially condition the rate and direction of evolution across populations of firms. The different markets do not always select upon the same characteristics. Furthermore, some of the multiple characteristics of a firm might be strongly correlated. For instance, an innovation that changes a characteristic of positive relevance in the product market might be strongly correlated with other characteristics that are valued negatively in the labour market or capital market. Formal theory based on replicator dynamics thus not only needs to account for different markets but also for the confoundedness created by correlated characteristics.

With inspiration from Rice (2004), we show that it is possible and practically feasible to quantify economic selection in empirical studies even when simultaneous selection on multiple characteristics of firms is confounding the relationship between covarying characteristics and fitness. The confounding effects of investment behaviour and financial performance may be disentangled with this methodology. However, it also has other uses such as the study of simultaneous selection in factor and output markets. Even in a straightforward model of competition in which firms compete by undercutting one another's prices, the simple assumption that labour markets are less than perfect and that growing firms hence must offer a relatively high wage rate to attract employees, and thus have higher unit costs, entails that the relationship between profitability and growth becomes confounded (Metcalfe 1997; Baldwin and Gu 2006a; Metcalfe and Ramlogan 2006). Once profits are imperfectly correlated with investment decisions, we must go beyond traditional versions of replicator dynamics. This is necessary because it is not assured that the most competitive firm in terms of unit costs is also the fittest firm, in the evolutionary sense of having the fastest rate of growth among its population of rivals. The contribution of the paper is to extend the usefulness of replicator dynamics in both modelling and empirical studies in a way that makes replicator dynamics able to describe economic selection when selection depends on multiple and interacting factors.

This paper proceeds as follows. In Sect. 2, we highlight the proliferating use of replicator dynamics for both modelling and empirical analysis, and emphasise the limitations of current theory for analysing selection in markets. In Sect. 3, we present a framework and a methodology for addressing the confoundedness produced by multivariate selection. In Sect. 4 we apply the methodology to simulated data.

Section 5 summarises and concludes. The paper is followed by an appendix with a guide for applying the proposed method with empirical data.

2 Applications of Replicator Dynamics

The replicator dynamics based methodology for empirical studies of economic evolution is becoming increasingly well developed theoretically. However, empirical and simulation application remain highly limited as replicator dynamics still only address a single variable at a time and hence only allows for analysis of a single characteristic in a single environment. This limits the analysis of real selection processes in which firms operate in several markets and their products have several characteristics that interact to determine fitness. Characteristics interact to augment or constrain selection, and one-dimensional, single trait replicator dynamics cannot cope with such confounded selection.

Replicator dynamics represent a basic tool in evolutionary game theory and are also widely applied in modelling in evolutionary economics (Hodgson and Huang 2012; Safarzynska and van den Bergh 2010; Windrum 2007; Metcalfe 1998). Replicator dynamics are also linked to empirical studies, as the “selection”, “reallocation” or “inter-agent” term of productivity decomposition studies is often a version of replicator dynamics (Hölzl 2015; Holm 2014; Metcalfe 2008; Andersen 2004). Simple replicator dynamics can be applied to numerous areas, but attempts at extending either replicator dynamics or the derived decomposition equations for empirical application have nevertheless proliferated (Andersen and Holm 2014; van Veelen 2011; Safarzynska and van den Bergh 2011). Ultimately, replicator dynamics are a formalisation of the evolution of frequencies of strategies in a population. Replicator dynamics describe how the change in the frequency of one strategy depends on the frequencies of other strategies by specifying that the change in the frequency of a strategy depends on the fitness of that strategy relative to the average fitness in the population. Replicator dynamics can be formalised in a number of ways, but they share the common features of being deterministic, monotonic and, often, non-linear transformations of fitness to growth. The formalisation in Eq. (1) is chosen here because it relates directly to the model employed in Sect. 4 of the current paper.

$$s_i' = s_i \frac{W_i}{\overline{W}} = s_i w_i \tag{1}$$

s_i is the population share of strategy i, and s_i' is the population share at a later point in time. W_i is the absolute fitness of strategy i, $\overline{W} = \sum_i s_i W_i$ is the average fitness and w_i is the relative fitness. Fitness is determined in a non-linear manner based on the characteristics of the strategy, the vector z_i. In the simple case in which z_i only contains one characteristic and higher values of the characteristic monotonically translate into greater fitness, there will be positive covariance between a strategy's characteristic z_i and the change in the frequency of the strategy, $\Delta s_i = s_i' - s_i$. This principle is applied in empirical decompositions in the tradition of Foster et al. (1998) and related approaches, where the contribution from economic selection to the change in the average characteristic in a population is quantified by Eq. (2).

$$\text{Selection effect} = \sum_i (\Delta s_i)(z_i - \bar{z}) = Cov(w_i, z_i) \tag{2}$$

The close relationship between the replicator dynamics of Eq. (1) and the selection effect of Eq. (2) is discussed in detail in Cantner (2014). Equation (2) is an example of what may be called positive directional selection, as the average characteristic in the population is driven continuously towards higher values by selection. Andersen and Holm (2014) derive alternative specifications for other types of selection. In the current paper we generalise the selection effect in Eq. (2) so that it can be applied in empirically more relevant cases where fitness can depend on more than one characteristic.

In empirical application, a strategy (i) is normally a firm and its frequency, s_i, is the population share of the firm measured using a relevant size variable. In an empirical study of firm growth, it would not be reasonable to assume that growth depends only on one characteristic. Other characteristics, which are potentially correlated with z_i, will also affect growth and hence whether the average, $\bar{z}$, will tend to grow in the population. Studying the relationship between correlated characteristics and the evolution of $\bar{z}$ leads us to a taxonomy of confounded selection, which is closely linked to our methodology for empirically accounting for such confounding effects of additional variables on the selection effect of Eq. (2). In order to explore and demonstrate the method and taxonomy in a controlled setting allowing for pure cases we rely on simple simulated data.

The primary elements of the method are the selection gradients of the characteristics and the covariance matrix of the characteristics. Based on these, the method motivates the taxonomy of selection based on the interaction of characteristics. This is done in a formal way but thinking in terms of confounded, augmented and constrained selection can help a variety of statistical approaches that dig deeper into the muddles of economic evolution.

3 Analytical Framework for Multivariate Selection

Metcalfe (1994) moved from R. A. Fisher's specific theorem of genetics-based natural selection to the general "Fisher Principle" to make the work of the great statistician and evolutionary biologist relevant for evolutionary economics. The Fisher Principle states that "in the context of a population of diverse behaviours across which selection is taking place in a constant environment, the rate of change of mean behaviour is a function of the degree of variety in behaviour across the population". Under such circumstances, the gradually evolving mean behaviour becomes increasingly informed about and adapted to the environment of the population. Evolutionary economists have formalised and applied this principle in the study of simple selection and evolution in simple environments in a variety of ways, which are generalised by replicator dynamics. However, the conditions of Fisher's Principle are seldom fulfilled. First, the stability or lawful patterning of the environment of an economic population obviously cannot always be taken for granted. Second, selection can work on a number of more or less conflicting behavioural characteristics. For example, a fluctuating environment may repeatedly shift the characteristics on which selection focusses. Furthermore, the input markets and the output markets can emphasise conflicting population characteristics. Third, the importance of multiple and shifting characteristics means that it is often not obvious which characteristics of behaviour have to be recreated when old variance has been used up by the selection process.

The development of Fisher's Principle towards an extended and more operational toolbox for theoretical and applied evolutionary economics involves a large research agenda. The turbulent environment and its shifting focus on different behavioural characteristics have, to some extent, been addressed by innovation studies. Furthermore, industrial dynamics examined the systematic change in selective focus across behavioural characteristics during the industry life cycle. However, we nevertheless lack general principles and statistical methods for coping with the selection and evolution of multiple and potentially conflicting characteristics of behaviour. The lack of analytical tools seems to have slowed the move from the well-understood univariate analysis to the general analysis of multivariate selection and evolution. In turn, the lack of multivariate analysis has decreased the analytical clarity and power of evolutionary economic studies attempting to extend Fisher's Principle in other directions.

The move from univariate to multivariate selection has already been made within evolutionary biology. The statistical procedures for theorising and data analysis can be traced back to Fisher (1930), but a very helpful advance was made by the Chicago School, a group of Chicago biologists working within quantitative genetics in the late 1970s and early 1980s (Lande and Arnold 1983; Connor and Hartl 2004). The Chicago approach to phenotypical selection and evolution is based on the statistical analysis of the fundamental requirements for any evolutionary process: the variance of the characteristics of the population, the covariance between characteristics and the reproduction of members, and the intertemporal inertia of the characteristics. By focusing on these requirements for phenotypical evolution rather than on the direct study of genetic evolution, this approach has been very successful for studying "natural selection in the wild" (Endler 1986; Brodie et al. 1995; Kingsolver et al. 2001; Kingsolver and Pfennig 2007). This use has been eased by reformulations and developments by, e.g., Rice (2004) of the Chicago school approach in relation to the very general analytical framework of Fisher and George Price. With some caution and modification, the approach can also be used for the analysis of economic selection and evolution.

As we have already developed the basic analytical framework elsewhere (Andersen 2004), in the following we move quickly from Price's Equation to the Chicago novelties with respect to evolutionary economics.

3.1 Univariate Selection as a Starting Point

Price (1970, 1995) worked at a deeper level than the Chicago School. He thought in terms of a population that is studied at two subsequent points of time, t and t'. He assumed that any member of the t'-population can be connected to a member of the t-population. This made it possible for him to define absolute fitness for each t-member as the number by which to multiply its size at t to determine its representation in the t'-population. Then, Price defined evolution as the change in the population mean of a characteristic between the two points in time. He also defined selection as the part of evolution that can be explained by the covariance between the characteristic values of the members of the t-population and their fitness. The residual of the evolutionary change in the mean characteristic is explained fully by mean intra member change evaluated in the t'-population. Thus Price's Equation–or Price's Identity–can be written as

$$\text{Total evolutionary change} = \text{Selection effect} + \text{Intra member effect} \tag{3}$$

Equation (3) suggests basic analyses that apply two subsequent population censuses. As we emphasise selection, we call them the pre-selection census and the post-selection census. When necessary, we distinguish by adding a prime to variables that relate to the post-selection census. The two censuses provide the basis for calculating statistics on fitness and characteristics and the relationships between them. This procedure can be presented in three basic steps (Andersen and Holm 2014):

A-1. In each of the two censuses, we measure the population share of each member. Then, we calculate the relative fitness of each member as the ratio of its population shares after and before selection relative to the fitness of the population as a whole. Thus the population has mean relative fitness $\overline{w} = 1$.

A-2. The censuses provide information on a focal characteristic, z_1, of the members of a population. In each census, we measure the characteristic value of z_1 for each member, and we calculate the member-level change in z_1 between the two censuses. We then calculate the weighted means of z_1 in each of the two censuses, $\overline{z}_1$ and $\overline{z}'_1$, and the change in the mean between censuses, $\Delta\overline{z}_1$. We also calculate the weighted mean of the member-level change in the characteristic, $E(w\Delta z_1)$. However, in the present paper, we focus on selection and assume that $\Delta z_1 = 0$ for all members such that $E(w\Delta z_1) = 0$.

A-3. We use the member-level information to calculate the covariance between fitness and the characteristic z_1, $Cov(w, z_1)$, which corresponds to replicator dynamics, cf. Eq. (2). This covariance is equal to the product of the regression of fitness on the characteristic and the variance of the characteristic, $\beta_{w,z_1}^{Total} Var(z_1)$. (The superscript "Total" is used to distinguish $beta_{w,z_1}^{Total}$ from later β_s which are all partial regressions coefficients).

Much can be learned by following this procedure. For example, we can turn to simple applications of Price's Equation as Eq. (4) for analysing the relative importance of the selection effect and the intra member effect with respect to individual characteristics

$$\Delta\bar{z}_1 = Cov(w, z_1) + E(w\Delta z_1) = \beta_{w,z_1}^{Total} Var(z_1) + E(w\Delta z_1) \tag{4}$$

The practical implementation of Price's Equation as Eq. (4) serves to study the process of directional univariate selection. However, the Chicago school has promoted an analytical distinction between different types of selection. Although we have already addressed this contribution (Andersen and Holm 2014), it is worth repeating that it is important to add other types of selection to the directional selection implied by Fisher's Theorem and Fisher's Principle. While most thinking on selection within evolutionary economics has been dominated by the–positive or negative–directional selection that results in a change in the mean of a characteristic, it is possible to define other types of selection that can occur with a constant mean of the population.

3.2 Multivariate Selection

The developers and users of the Chicago approach share an interest in the directional selection of Fisher and Price. However, they normally focus on more concrete problems connected with artificial selection and natural selection in the wild. In the context of artificial selection, the emphasis is on the selection differential, i.e., the difference between the mean value of the parents chosen for breeding and the mean value of all potential parents in the population. In other words, the selection differential is the change in $\bar{z}_1$ that can be ascribed solely to selective reproduction and thus can be modelled with replicator dynamics. In terms of Eq. (4), the selection differential is $Cov(w, z_1)$. However, this selection differential is the combined result of direct selection on the studied characteristic and the indirect effects on that characteristic of (artificial) selection working on other characteristics. In these connections, the problems of addressing selection on multiple characteristics are obvious. For example, when breeders are performing artificial selection, they recognise that by selecting on a single characteristic, they are often co-selecting unwanted characteristics. The Chicago approach addresses this and similar problems by thinking of total evolutionary change as a vector that consists of the changes in a number of different characteristics (e.g., Lande and Arnold 1983).

To confront such issues, the Chicago school has provided two new tools. The first tool is the vector of selection gradients, i.e., the direct effects of selection on the different characteristics. While a selection differential includes both the direct and the indirect selection on a characteristic, a selection gradient is the partial regression of relative fitness on a characteristic. Thus the selection gradient ignores indirect selection due to other analysed characteristics and measures only the direct selection of the characteristic in question. The selection gradient in Eq. (4) is β_{w,z_1}^{Total}. As Eq. (4) is Price's Equations for a single characteristic, there are no indirect effects and the distinction between the selection gradient and selection differential is trivial in Eq. (4). The second tool for coping with multiple characteristics is the matrix of phenotypic covariances between characteristics. This matrix reflects the fact that different characteristics may be interdependent. For example, we have the case in which members of the t-population that have high values of one characteristic also tend to have high (or low) values of coupled characteristics. This means that when selection acts directly on one characteristic, it also influences the population mean of more or less closely coupled characteristics. The elements of the phenotypic covariance matrix can be zero, positive, or negative.

By combining the two new tools, we can understand the strange ways in which the process of selection on coupled characteristics might operate. For instance, a change in the mean of the focal first characteristic is potentially influenced by all the studied characteristics. The selection effect in Eq. (3) now consists of one direct effect and multiple indirect effects. The direct effect is derived by multiplying the first element of the covariance matrix by the first element of the vector of selection gradients. Thus, we are multiplying a covariance by a partial regression coefficient. However, as we are here concerned with the covariance of the first characteristic with itself, we are actually multiplying the variance of the first characteristic by the efficiency of direct selection on that characteristic. The indirect effects might involve important covariances (and thus correlations). For example, the first indirect effect on the change in the mean of the first characteristic is obtained by multiplying the covariance between characteristics z_1 and z_2 by the selection gradient of characteristic z_2.

Surprising observations can result from this multiplication because the covariance might be negative and the selection gradients of characteristics z_1 and z_2 might have opposite signs. Thus this indirect selection of characteristic, z_1, might remove or invert a positive direct selection on characteristic z_1. However, although the effects of such couplings of characteristics have been analysed intensively by evolutionary biology, discussion persists concerning the frequency of this phenomenon in nature (Agrawal and Stinchcombe 2009).

The Chicago approach to multivariate selection can be clarified by extending the above procedure for studying univariate selection. We still have two censuses and calculate statistics on fitness and characteristics as well as the relationships between them. Furthermore, we continue to exploit the convenience of operating in the short run. In contrast to long-term analysis, this approach allows to concentrate on selection to a greater degree and thus minimise the importance of some of the huge differences between economics and biology. We also believe that the simple short-term framework helps to think clearly about concepts and measurements of selection. Finally, in numerous countries, immensely rich data on each firm and each citizen have become available for relatively short-term social science analysis.

To apply the Chicago approach, we must redefine the three steps in the procedure.

B-1. We extend the censuses beyond the focal characteristic to cover a set of new characteristics labelled from 2 to n. We do so by repeating steps (A-1) and (A-2) for each additional characteristic. One of the results is that we are provided with a vector of changes of mean characteristics

$$\Delta\bar{\mathbf{z}} = \begin{bmatrix} \Delta\bar{z}_1 \\ \vdots \\ \Delta\bar{z}_n \end{bmatrix}$$

The aim is to explain this vector with particular emphasis on $\Delta\bar{z}_1$. We have much of the information needed for this analysis, but steps (B-2) and (B-3) provide us with crucial tools.

B-2. For the pre-selection census, we check whether the characteristics are correlated by extending step (A-3) and calculating the "phenotypic" covariance matrix

$$\mathbf{P} = \begin{bmatrix} P_{11} & \cdots & P_{1n} \\ \vdots & \ddots & \vdots \\ P_{n1} & \cdots & P_{nn} \end{bmatrix} = \begin{bmatrix} Cov(z_1, z_1) & \cdots & Cov(z_1, z_n) \\ \vdots & \ddots & \vdots \\ Cov(z_n, z_1) & \cdots & Cov(z_n, z_n) \end{bmatrix}$$

where the diagonal represents variance, because, e.g., $Cov(z_1, z_1) = Var(z_1)$. The phenotypic covariance matrix is computed from a census rather than a sample, and hence it is computed as a weighted population covariance matrix. See the appendix for further computational issues. The remainder of the symmetric matrix is filled with covariances, where, e.g., $Cov(z_1, z_n) = Cov(z_n, z_1)$.

B-3. We end the census-related work by calculating the vector of partial regressions of fitness on each of the characteristics

$$\beta = \begin{bmatrix} \beta_{w,z_1} \\ \vdots \\ \beta_{w,z_n} \end{bmatrix}$$

We have an interesting case if, for example, the selection coefficient, $\beta_{w,z1}$, differs from β^{Total}_{w,z_1}.

These redefined steps in the procedure promote the analysis of multivariate selection. We can thus use the **P** matrix and the vector of selection gradients for the characteristics to describe the responses to selection pressures that act simultaneously on these characteristics. In condensed matrix format, the equation is

$$\Delta\bar{\mathbf{z}} = \mathbf{P}\beta \tag{5}$$

Let us, for example, expand the mean change in the first characteristic for the case in which there are only two characteristics, extending the assumption that $E(w\Delta z_1) = 0$ to $E(w\Delta z_j) = 0, j = (1, 2)$

$$\Delta \bar{z}_1 = \beta_{w,z_1} Var(z_1) + \beta_{w,z_2} Cov(z_1, z_2)$$

Here, the evolutionary response to selection on the first characteristic has two components. First, there is the direct response to selection $\beta_{w,z_1} Var(z_1) = \beta_{w,z_1} Cov(z_1, z_1)$, which consists of the change in the mean of characteristic z_1 due to selection acting directly on characteristic, z_1. Second, there is the indirect response to selection due to covariance. Thus, $\beta_{w,z_2} Cov(z_1, z_2)$ represents the indirect change in the mean of characteristic, z_1, due to its covariance with characteristic z_2.

It is, of course, possible that the change in the mean of characteristic z_1 is entirely or largely due to the direct selection on characteristic z_1. Another possibility is that the correlate response to selection on characteristic z_2 dominates the direct response. In the extreme case, direct selection tends to produce high levels of the first characteristic, while its mean becomes smaller due to negative covariance or to a low value of the other characteristic.

These and other possibilities are presented in Table 1. Here, we distinguish among five types of bivariate directional selection (cf. Connor and Hartl 2004, p. 223). If we ignore the case in which bivariate selection reduces to two univariate selections, we can classify the outcomes in terms of the signs of the selection coefficients and the covariance of characteristics. For example, negative covariance of the characteristics and selection with opposite signs leads to the negative augmentation of direct selection. However, when covariances remain negative

Table 1 Effects on evolutionary change of signs of selection coefficients and correlations of characteristics

Type of directional selection on two characteristics	Definition	Stylised example for $\Delta\bar{\mathrm{z}} = \mathbf{P}\beta$
Univariate selection	No covariance of characteristics	$\begin{bmatrix}\Delta\bar{z}_1\\ \Delta\bar{z}_2\end{bmatrix} = \begin{bmatrix}Var(z_1) & 0\\ 0 & Var(z_2)\end{bmatrix}\begin{bmatrix}>0\\ >0\end{bmatrix}$
Positive augmentation	Positive covariance of characteristics + gradients with same sign	$\begin{bmatrix}\Delta\bar{z}_1\\ \Delta\bar{z}_2\end{bmatrix} = \begin{bmatrix}Var(z_1) & >0\\ >0 & Var(z_2)\end{bmatrix}\begin{bmatrix}>0\\ >0\end{bmatrix}$
Negative augmentation	Negative covariance of characteristics + gradients with opposite sign	$\begin{bmatrix}\Delta\bar{z}_1\\ \Delta\bar{z}_2\end{bmatrix} = \begin{bmatrix}Var(z_1) & <0\\ <0 & Var(z_2)\end{bmatrix}\begin{bmatrix}>0\\ <0\end{bmatrix}$
Gradient constraint	Positive covariance of characteristics + gradients with opposite sign	$\begin{bmatrix}\Delta\bar{z}_1\\ \Delta\bar{z}_2\end{bmatrix} = \begin{bmatrix}Var(z_1) & >0\\ >0 & Var(z_2)\end{bmatrix}\begin{bmatrix}>0\\ <0\end{bmatrix}$
Correlation constraint	Negative covariance of characteristics + gradients with same sign	$\begin{bmatrix}\Delta\bar{z}_1\\ \Delta\bar{z}_2\end{bmatrix} = \begin{bmatrix}Var(z_1) & <0\\ <0 & Var(z_2)\end{bmatrix}\begin{bmatrix}>0\\ >0\end{bmatrix}$

while coefficients have the same sign, we are facing what might be called a correlation constraint on the evolution of the characteristics.

The taxonomy in Table 1 covers only characteristics that are subject to directional selection and only one confounding characteristic. It is this latter characteristic that augments or constrains the selection pressure that works on the focal characteristic. However, we can nevertheless use the taxonomic labels on the aggregate effects of several confounding characteristics. Even here, selection on the focal characteristic can still be augmented by selection on other characteristics. It can also be constrained. In the extreme case, a strong selection pressure on the focal characteristic can translate into zero evolutionary change due to selection on confounding characteristics. The taxonomy in Table 1 concerns directional selection, but it can be generalised to also include stabilising and diversifying selection. This would not require further categories, only more careful and less elegant definitions and examples in which the selection gradients are allowed to be zero. In the remainder of the paper, we focus on the taxonomy defined in Table 1 and avoid unnecessary complications following from further generalisation.

4 Modelling and Simulation Results

In this section, we will demonstrate how selection may be confounded. The modelling strategy has two steps: a data-generating algorithm and a deterministic selection process. The data-generating algorithm is a set of rules for defining the pre-selection population. It is at this step that we may introduce correlation among the traits of business units. The selection process determines how the pre-selection population evolves into the post-selection population. At this step, we may implement different selection functions based on different assumptions regarding the characteristics of firms. Finally, the evolution from the pre-selection to post-selection population is analysed using the method presented in the current paper: the identity in Eq. (5). This step is merely a measurement step, and we have no influence on the results at this step. The strategy is illustrated in Fig. 1.

When evaluating whether selection is confounded, we compare the selection gradients with the observed evolutionary change. Selection is argued to be confounded when these have opposite signs. That is, $\bar{z}_1 > 0$ while $\beta_{w,z_1} < 0$ entails that selection on z_1 is confounded in the sense that firms with relatively high values of z_1 have decreasing population shares, despite that the mean of z_1 is increasing in the population. Each simulation will be repeated 100 times for robustness and the results plotted in $\bar{z}_1$ by β_{w,z_1} space.

The pre-selection population will consist of 100 firms. Each firm is characterised by a vector of three characteristics: $z_i = (z_{1,i}, z_{2,i}, z_{3,i})$. In a more general model, firms might enter and exit, and the characteristics of a firm would change over time through adaptation and innovation, but these complications are not included here because they are inconsequential for the aim of the paper, as explained earlier.

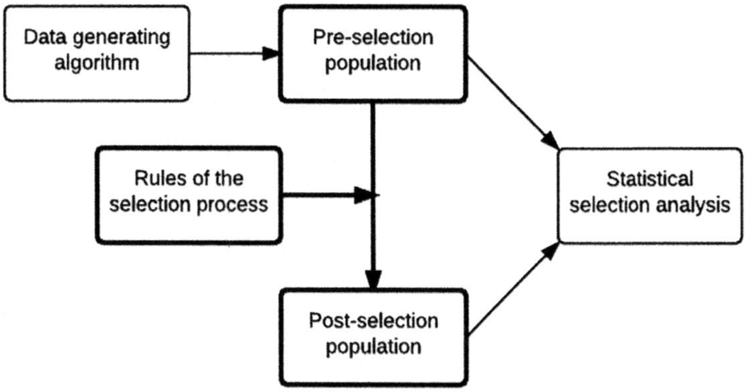

Fig. 1 The modelling strategy

Thus, the evolution of the characteristics in the population, $\Delta\overline{\mathbf{z}}$, is described fully by $\Delta\overline{\mathbf{z}} = \mathbf{P}\beta$. Any change in the means of the characteristics must come from the relative growth or decline of firms.

The data-generating algorithm proceeds as follows: the three characteristics are all drawn from standard normal distributions with correlation matrix ρ. All firms have equal population shares in the pre-selection population: $s_i = 0.01\forall i$.

For the rules of the selection process, we follow the general lines applied in Andersen and Holm (2014). This means that we specify a deterministic function for absolute fitness. We then transform the outcome into relative fitness and allow the population to evolve according to Eq. (6).

$$s_i' = s_i w_i \tag{6}$$

Relative fitness is defined as absolute fitness divided by population fitness, $w_i = W_i/\overline{W}$, and absolute fitness is determined by the following relationship

$$W_i = (1 + C)^{F(z_i)} \tag{7}$$

The general fitness function specified in Eq. (7) is an exponential function. The parameter C determines the pace of evolution in the sense that a firm will grow by $C * 100\%$ as many times as specified by the exponent. The specification of the exponent determines the type of selection. In the current paper, we have chosen a specification in which there is negative directional selection on z_1 and positive directional selection on z_2 and z_3. The exponent is determined as

$$F(z_i) = -\left(z_{1,i} - \overline{z}_i\right) + \left(z_{2,i} - \overline{z}_2\right) + \left(z_{3,i} - \overline{z}_3\right) \tag{8}$$

The rules of the selection process are uniform in all of the simulations presented in the current paper. C is fixed at 0.5. This sets a relatively high pace for evolution but allows us to disregard the possibility of multiple time periods between the pre and post-selection populations. The data-generation algorithm is also the same in all simulations except for the value of ρ_{12} and thus also ρ_{21}: the correlation between the standard normal distributions from which z_1 and z_2 are drawn.

$$\rho = \begin{bmatrix} 1 & \rho_{12} & 0 \\ \rho_{21} & 1 & 0 \\ 0 & 0 & 1 \end{bmatrix} \tag{9}$$

In all simulations, there will be positive directional selection on z_3, which is independent of the other characteristics. There will also be positive directional selection on z_2, but this characteristic will, to varying degrees, be correlated with the characteristic, z_1, upon which there is negative directional selection.

4.1 Baseline Simulation ($\rho_{12} = 0$)

In the first simulation, the three traits of the firms are uncorrelated; $\rho_{12} = 0$ in Eq. (9) above. The pre-selection population is described by the vector of mean characteristics, $\bar{\mathbf{z}}$. After having been subject to the deterministic selection process described in Eqs. (6) through (8), the post-selection population is created, and it is described by $\bar{\mathbf{z}}'$. The evolution of the population is described by the change in mean characteristics, $\Delta\bar{\mathbf{z}}$ (step B-1). This evolution is then decomposed into the variance-covariance matrix of the characteristics (step B-2) and the vector of selection gradients (step B-3). In a typical baseline simulation, the results look as presented in Fig. 2. The mean of the characteristic z_1 has decreased by 0.376, while the means of the remaining two characteristics have increased by approximately the same magnitude. This is in accordance with the assumed directional selection processes. The final product on the right is the decomposition of the selection differential, $\mathbf{P}\beta$. The selection gradients reflect the assumed selection processes and correspond to the observed evolution in means: z_2 and z_3 have positive selection coefficients (0.418 and 0.436, respectively), while z_1 has a coefficient of −0.406.

Figure 3 plots the results from Fig. 2 along with 99 additional simulations with the baseline specification. The values of the $\left(\beta_{w,z_1}, \Delta\bar{z}_1\right)$ pairs cluster in the bottom left while the values of $\left(\beta_{w,z_2}, \Delta\bar{z}_2\right)$ and $\left(\beta_{w,z_3}, \Delta\bar{z}_3\right)$ cluster at the top right corner.

Figure 3 also includes three regression lines, one for each characteristic. All three have a positive slope, indicating that there is a positive relationship between the gradient and the change in mean. The slope of the regression line and the clustering of the data points show that selection is not confounded: observing that a

$$\begin{bmatrix} \Delta\bar{z}_1 \\ \Delta\bar{z}_2 \\ \Delta\bar{z}_3 \end{bmatrix} = \begin{bmatrix} -0.376 \\ 0.469 \\ 0.350 \end{bmatrix} = \begin{bmatrix} -0.139 \\ 0.613 \\ 0.242 \end{bmatrix} - \begin{bmatrix} 0.239 \\ 0.145 \\ -0.108 \end{bmatrix} = \begin{bmatrix} 1.174 & 0.042 & 0.190 \\ 0.042 & 1.108 & 0.051 \\ 0.190 & 0.051 & 0.929 \end{bmatrix} \begin{bmatrix} -0.406 \\ 0.418 \\ 0.436 \end{bmatrix}$$

Fig. 2 Result from a baseline simulation

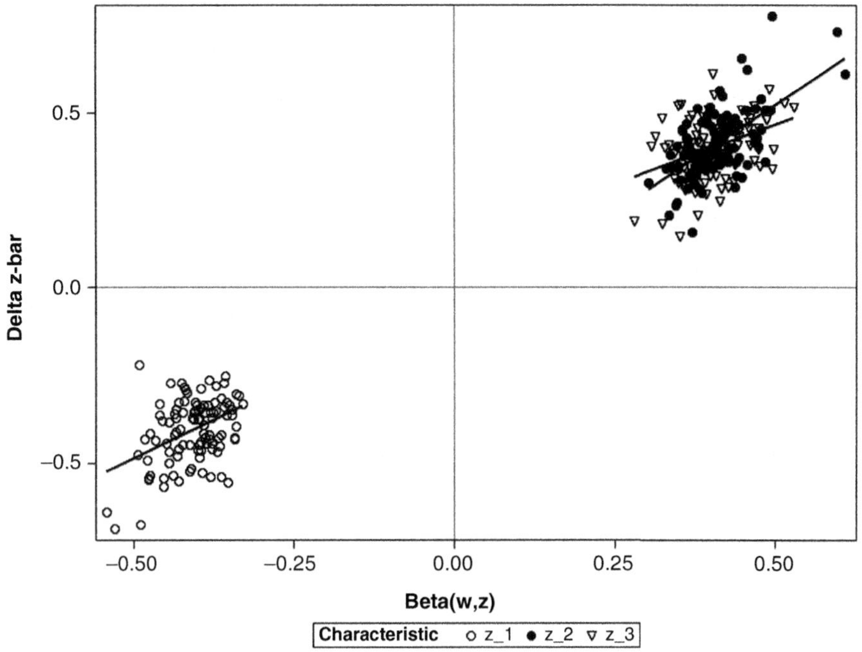

Fig. 3 1000 baseline simulations

characteristic is becoming more (less) frequent in the population allows us to assume that it is positively (negatively) related to firm growth. In a population where the change in the average characteristic is greater, we may even assume that the significance of the characteristic for firm growth is also greater.

4.2 *Simulations with Positive Correlation ($\rho_{12} > 0$)*

In this section, we will present the results from assuming that $\rho_{12} \neq 0$. Specifically, we will let the correlation approach unity in a stepwise manner that can be illustrated in a series of simulations. Adding correlation between z_1, upon which there is negative directional selection, and z_2, upon which there is positive directional selection, is expected to lead to confounded selection, as the selection mechanism will drive $\bar{z}_1$ down and $\bar{z}_2$ towards ever higher values, while they are positively correlated at the firm level. In the taxonomy introduced in Sect. 3, this is a case of gradient constraint selection. The correlation between z_1 and z_2 constrains $\bar{z}_1$ from decreasing, and it constrains the growth in $\bar{z}_2$ to be lower than would otherwise be the case.

The results from specifying $\rho_{12} = 0.05$ to $\rho_{12} = 0.95$ in increments of 0.3 are shown in Fig. 4. This yields a total of four different parameterisations. Compared to

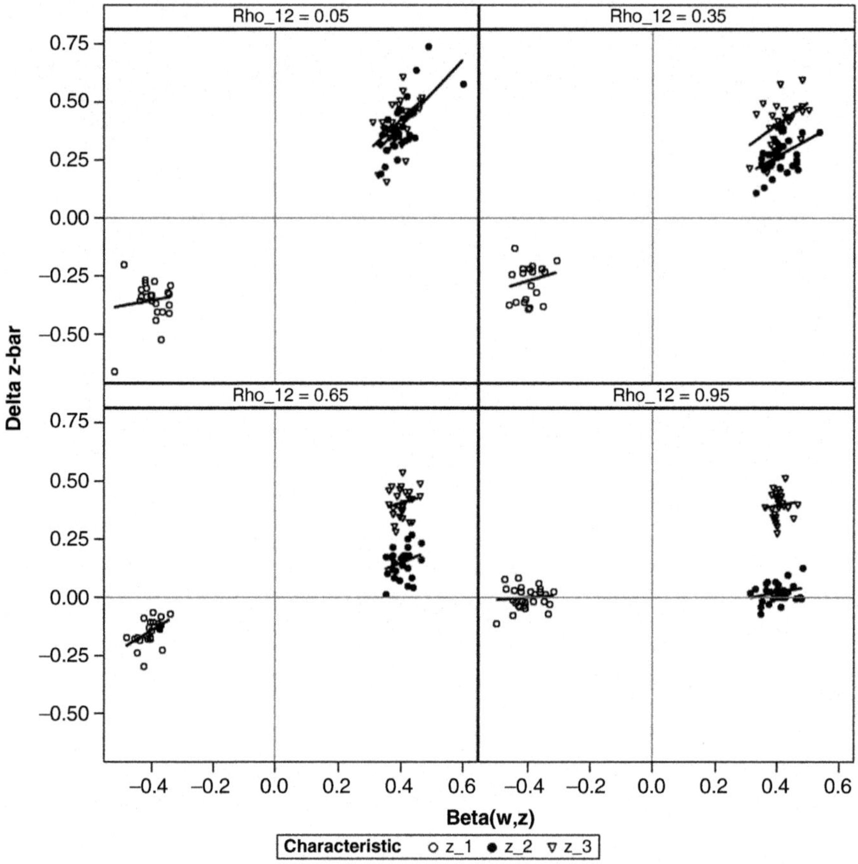

Fig. 4 Four different parameterisations for ρ_{12}

Fig. 3 (where $\rho_{12} = 0$), it does not make a substantial difference if instead $\rho_{12} = 0.05$. However, as the correlation increases, the data points describing the evolution of $\bar{z}_1$ and $\bar{z}_2$ cluster closer and closer to the horizontal axis. In this region, selection is confounded: $\Delta\bar{z}_1$ is positive, while $\beta_{w,z1}$ is negative, meaning that the average of z_1 is increasing in the population but firms with high values of z_1 have relatively low growth. The reason that this can happen is that z_1 is correlated with z_2, upon which there is positive directional selection, vice versa for the evolution of z_2.

Figure 5 shows one of the results from the bottom-right panel of Fig. 4 in greater detail. The selection gradients, the final element on the right, take approximately the same value as in Fig. 2. This is because evolution follows the exact same deterministic fitness function. Any variation is due to the stochastic data-generation algorithm. The observed evolution, however, differs from Fig. 2: $\bar{z}_2$ has only increased slightly (0.127) despite the strong selection on the characteristic, and $\bar{z}_1$ has even increased (0.079) despite strong negative selection.

$$\begin{bmatrix}\Delta\bar{z}_1\\ \Delta\bar{z}_2\\ \Delta\bar{z}_3\end{bmatrix} = \begin{bmatrix}0.079\\ 0.127\\ 0.583\end{bmatrix} = \begin{bmatrix}-0.042\\ 0.005\\ 0.656\end{bmatrix} - \begin{bmatrix}-0.121\\ -0.122\\ 0.073\end{bmatrix} = \begin{bmatrix}1.036 & 1.029 & 0.266\\ 1.029 & 1.122 & 0.264\\ 0.266 & 0.264 & 1.375\end{bmatrix}\begin{bmatrix}-0.513\\ 0.482\\ 0.431\end{bmatrix}$$

Fig. 5 A result from a simulation with $\rho_{12} = 0.95$

5 Conclusions

Economic evolution is the combined result of innovation in firms and selection within and between them. Selection is often modelled using replicator dynamics, and this entails assuming that selection is based on a single characteristic reflecting a single uniform selection environment in which all firms are treated equally. This assumption constrains the analysis of real selection processes in which the firm operates in several markets and has products with several characteristics. From a simplified perspective, this means that we are facing confounded selection that cannot be addressed by standard replicator dynamics. This paper develops a statistical approach that serves to analyse confounded selection explicitly and illustrates the proposed method by means of simulation.

The results show how observed evolutionary change may not convey the suspected information about selection gradients. As an example, consider a population in which there is selection on, inter alia, firms' wage costs and the adaptability of the work force. For the former, there is negative directional selection: lower costs mean higher growth; for the latter, there is positive directional selection: firms that can easily adapt their workforce grow more than others. However, the correlation between these two variables—labour turnover entails a loss of tacit knowledge and incurring retraining costs—means that we would not be able to infer the importance of either characteristic for firm growth from the observed change in the mean characteristic at the population level. In this example, it is plausible that neither characteristic's mean would change at all, despite that a micro-level regression analysis would show that both are important for firm growth. As in this example, the simulations show quantitatively how population dynamics constrain the evolution of aggregate variables towards values that would be deemed "optimal" in an atomistic study of firm behaviour. A regression analysis does not, on the contrary, necessarily allow for forecasting of evolutionary change. Even if the regression analysis shows that a characteristic has a large effect on firm growth, the characteristic will not become more frequent in the population if selection is confounded.

Despite this comparison it is important to keep in mind that methodologies for decomposing evolutionary change are very different from regression analysis. Regression analysis attempts to identify the effect of a characteristic on firm growth while decomposition analysis charts the role of differential growth on the change in average characteristic. Decomposition analyses rely on two or more full population censuses to quantify population dynamics, whereas regression provides estimates of effects at the level of population members from a sample of data.

Correlation is vital in evolution. It determines the direction of change in the characteristics of a population, but we may be mistaken if we interpret observed change as indicating correlation, as the correlation between a characteristic and fitness can be mediated by other characteristics, and hence the determinants of fitness fail to actually correlate with fitness.

The simulations and the above example were constructed around a process exhibiting gradient constrained selection, but we could easily have included the other types of confounded selection defined in Table 1. Positive or negative augmented selection would be created by setting $\rho_{23} > 0$ or $\rho_{12} < 0$, respectively. Correlation constrained selection could have been included by setting $\rho_{23} < 0$. It is even possible to go beyond directional selection processes and incorporate stabilising or diversifying selection in the simulations by adapting the $F(\cdot)$ function of Eq. (8). It is relatively simple to illustrate confounded selection as augmenting or constraining when selection is directional, but the phenomenon of confounded selection is not restricted to such cases.

In this paper we have developed an approach that serves to explicitly analyse confounded selection. The central elements are the selection gradients and the covariance matrix of the characteristics. Based on these, the method motivates a taxonomy of selection. The method is relatively formal but thinking in terms of confounded, augmented and constrained selection can be useful in a variety of different approaches to economic evolution. The discussions in this paper focus on the evolution of a characteristic in a population of firms, but the method is equally applicable to studies of populations of industries, regions, countries, etc. Future research applying the methodology will invariably also contribute to further generalisation of the method. Such research must necessarily consider that, for the methodology and its interpretation to be applicable, it is necessary to assume that the data are census data for the units of selection and that the measured characteristics are stable over time. Firms, or more generally business units, have characteristics that may be assumed to be stable. When instead studying a population of regions or industries, such an assumption becomes increasingly problematic, but it more likely that the data can be assumed to be a complete census. Further studies applying the methodology will have to discuss these assumptions and demonstrate the robustness of conclusions to the assumptions.

Acknowledgments We thank participants in the 2014 Conference of the International Schumpeter Society for very helpful comments on a draft version of this paper, as well as the editors of this journal and two anonymous reviewers. Remaining errors are our own.

Appendix: Guide for Empirical Application

The starting point for any decomposition of evolution is the absolute size of members and their characteristics, x_i and z_{ij}, where i denotes the members and j indexes the characteristics. The population share of a member is defined as

Table 2 Computations for empirical applications

Element	Dimensions	Definition
z_{ij}		Value of z_j for member i in the early census. $i = (1\ldots m), j = (1\ldots n)$
z	$m \times n$ matrix	Values of the n characteristics for the m members in the early census
s	$m \times 1$ vector	Population shares for the m members
$w = s'/s$	$m \times 1$ vector	Relative fitness (i.e. growth) for each member
$\bar{z} = E(z) = z^T s$	$n \times 1$ vector	Population mean values for the n characteristics
$\Delta\bar{z} = \bar{z}' - \bar{z}$	$n \times 1$ vector	Change in the n population level means from t to t'
$Var(z) = \left(z - z^T\right)^T \left(\left(z - \bar{z}^T\right) \bullet s\right) = P$	$n \times n$ matrix	Weighted population variance-covariance matrix of the n characteristics
$E(w\Delta z) = (w \bullet (z' - s))^T s$	$n \times 1$ vector	Intra member change (generally assumed to be zero in simulations; as in the main text)
β	$n \times 1$ vector	Slopes from the WLS regression $w = \beta_0 + \sum_j z\beta + error$ with s as weights

$s_i = x_i / \sum_i x_i$, and selection can then be discussed in terms of absolute fitness, $W_i = x_i'/x_i$, or relative fitness, $w_i = W_i / \left(\sum_i s_i W_i\right) = s_i'/s_i$. Recall that applying a decomposition requires the use of two censuses at each time t and t', with $t < t'$, and that the prime is also used to distinguish between values taken from each census. Relying on relative fitness rather than absolute fitness does not make the computations more arduous, but it facilitates interpretation, and at least in our case, it makes the decomposition equation more parsimonious.

Table 2 contains an overview of the computations necessary to conduct the decomposition of the evolution of a vector of characteristics. A superscript T indicates a transpose and • is the dot product. When performing the computations, one must note that $Var(z)$ is the population, not the sample, variance-covariance matrix and that the vector of selection gradients, β, is computed in a regression that also contains an intercept, although the intercept is not included in β, and that this is a WLS regression.

With the elements defined in Table 2, it holds as an identity for any size of the population m and any number of characteristics n that

$$\Delta\bar{z} = Var(z)\beta + E(w\Delta z) \tag{10}$$

As we assume in the expositions presented in the main text that there is no change within members, $\Delta z = 0$, the identity becomes $\Delta z = Var(z)\beta = P\beta$ as in Sect. 3 of the main text.

In any empirical application, the expectation term would have to be included, and in many cases so would entry and exit in some manner. The vector of selection gradients would be computed as

$$\beta^* = \begin{bmatrix} \beta_0 \\ \beta \end{bmatrix} = \begin{bmatrix} \beta_0 \\ \beta_1 \\ \vdots \\ \beta_n \end{bmatrix} = \left(\widehat{z*}^T \widehat{z*}\right)^{-1} \widehat{z*}\,\widehat{w} \tag{11}$$

where z^* is the $m \times (n+1)$ matrix

$$z^* = \begin{bmatrix} 1 & z_{11} & \cdots & z_{1n} \\ \vdots & \vdots & \ddots & \vdots \\ 1 & z_{m1} & \cdots & z_{mn} \end{bmatrix} \tag{12}$$

and hats denote weighted data, i.e.,

$$\widehat{z*} = \left(\sqrt{s} \bullet I_m\right) z^* \tag{13}$$

References

Agrawal AF, Stinchcombe JR (2009) How much do genetic covariances alter the rate of adaptation? Proc R Soc B 276(1659):1183–1191
Andersen ES (2004) Population thinking, Price's equation and the analysis of economic evolution. Evol Inst Econ Rev 1(1):127–148
Andersen ES, Holm JR (2014) The signs of change in economic evolution: an analysis of directional, stabilizing and diversifying selection based on Price's equation. J Evol Econ 24 (2):291–316
Baldwin JR, Gu W (2006a) Competition, firm turnover and productivity growth. Statistics Canada, Economic Analysis Research Papers 11F0027MIE No. 042
Baldwin JR, Gu W (2006b) Plant turnover and productivity growth in Canadian manufacturing. Ind Corp Chang 15(3):417–465
Baldwin JR, Rafiquzzaman M (1995) Selection versus evolutionary adaptation: learning and post-entry performance. Int J Ind Organ 13(4):501–522
Brodie ED, Moore AJ, Janzen FJ (1995) Visualizing and quantifying natural selection. Trends Ecol Evol 10(8):313–318
Cantner U (2014) Evolution in markets. Paper presented at the Economic Change and Evolution conference, Rome, Italy, 10–11 November
Connor JK, Hartl DL (2004) A primer of ecological genetics. Sinauer, Sunderland, MA
Endler JA (1986) Natural selection in the wild. Princeton University Press, Princeton
Fisher RA (1930) The genetical theory of natural selection. Oxford University Press, Oxford
Foster L, Haltiwanger J, Krizan CJ (1998) Aggregate productivity growth: lessons from microeconomic evidence. NBER Working Paper Series 6803
Hodgson GM, Huang K (2012) Evolutionary economics and evolutionary game theory: are they different species? J Evol Econ 22(2):345–366

Holm JR (2014) The significance of structural transformation to productivity growth: how to account for levels in economic selection. J Evol Econ 24(5):1009–1036
Hölzl W (2015) Sunk costs and the speed of market selection. J Evol Econ 25(2):323–344
Kingsolver JG, Hoekstra HE, Hoekstra JM, Berrigan D, Vignieri SN, Hill CE, Hoang A, Gibert P, Beerli P (2001) The strength of phenotypic selection in natural populations. Am Nat 157 (3):245–261
Kingsolver JG, Pfennig DW (2007) Patterns and power of phenotypic selection in nature. Bioscience 57(7):561–572
Lande R, Arnold SJ (1983) The measurement of selection on correlated characters. Evolution 37 (6):1212–1226
Metcalfe JS (1994) Competition, Fisher's principle and increasing returns in the selection process. J Evol Econ 4(4):327–346
Metcalfe JS (1997) Labour markets and competition as an evolutionary process. In: Arestis P, Palma G, Sawyer M (eds) Markets, unemployment and economic policy: essays in honour of Geoff Harcourt, vol 2. Routhledge, London, pp 328–344
Metcalfe JS (1998) Evolutionary economics and creative destruction. Routledge, London
Metcalfe JS (2008) Accounting for economic evolution: fitness and the population method. J Bioecon 10(1):23–49
Metcalfe JS, Ramlogan R (2006) Creative destruction and the measurement of productivity change. Revue de 'OFCE 97(5):373–397
Price GR (1970) Selection and covariance. Nature 227:520–521
Price GR (1995) The nature of selection. J Theor Biol 175(3):389–396
Rice SH (2004) Evolutionary theory: mathematical and conceptual foundations. Sinauer Associates, Sunderland, MA
Safarzynska K, van den Bergh JCJM (2010) Evolutionary models in economics: a survey of methods and building blocks. J Evol Econ 20(3):329–376
Safarzynska K, van den Bergh JCJM (2011) Beyond replicator dynamics: innovation-selection dynamics and optimal diversity. J Econ Behav Organ 78(3):229–245
van Veelen M (2011) The replicator dynamics with *n* players and population structure. J Theor Biol 276(1):78–85
Windrum P (2007) Neo-Schumpeterian simulation models. In: Hanusch H, Pyka A (eds) Elgar companion to neo-schumpeterian economics. Edward Elgar, Cheltenham, pp 405–439

The Roots of Growth: Entrepreneurship, Innovation and the Capitalist Firm

Michael Joffe

Abstract The spectacular growth record of capitalist economies in the past 200 years is frequently attributed to entrepreneurship and/or innovation. This cannot be the whole story, because entrepreneurship has a far more widespread historical and geographical distribution than these high-growth countries, and occurs particularly in rather stagnant societies; innovation contributes to economic growth, but it is unclear why it has become so much more prevalent in capitalist societies, or why it takes a form that is growth-promoting in that context. Thus, entrepreneurship and innovation only contribute to dynamism in a particular institutional context: a real economy that is dominated by capitalist firms, which are able to purchase all their inputs including labour, making it easy to change the technology, workforce, product, location, etc.

Because entrepreneurship and innovation have tended to be analysed in capitalist societies, this extra component has been taken for granted. But it is not a natural, ubiquitous feature—it has its specific history, notably the development of "entity shielding" that protects the firm from its shareholders as well as from outsiders, enabling it to accumulate assets, including premises and equipment, as well as less tangible items such as expertise, relationships and reputation.

These features of the capitalist firm shape entrepreneurship and innovation, and make them effective. The central imperative to make a profit provides direction for entrepreneurs and innovators, and the potential rewards of success provide an incentive both for their performance and for their choosing these roles. The capitalist firm's flexibility of inputs gives scope for the inventiveness of entrepreneurs and innovators, and its potentially large market magnifies the success of their efforts.

M. Joffe (✉)
Imperial College London, London, UK
e-mail: m.joffe@imperial.ac.uk

A. Pyka, U. Cantner (eds.), *Foundations of Economic Change*, Economic Complexity and Evolution, DOI 10.1007/978-3-319-62009-1_11

1 Modern Economic Growth

One of the outstanding features of economic change in the past two centuries has been the advent of the long-term dynamic economy. This started with the industrial revolution in Britain, and spread to other European countries and "European offshoots" during the nineteenth century—the "great divergence". Subsequently other parts of the world followed suit, starting with Japan and then other parts of East Asia. In the successful economies, positive economic growth became normal, albeit subject to cyclical fluctuations. Prior to this, there had been periods of economic growth in various parts of the world, e.g. imperial China around the tenth century AD (Kelly 1997), and more recently north-western Europe from the late sixteenth century and also Japan in a similar period—the "little divergences" (Broadberry 2013). However, the growth rates in these episodes of "Smithian growth" were low by modern standards, and the episodes proved transient. For example, China stagnated after its tenth-century acceleration, and the Netherlands experienced a severe decline even in absolute terms following its golden age (de Vries and van der Woude 1997). This raises the question, what is responsible for the dynamism of the successful economies? I argue that the key change has been the advent of the capitalist firm: competition between such firms has generated unprecedented abundance.

One influential explanation of this dynamism, following Schumpeter's vivid description of "creative destruction", is that it results from entrepreneurship and innovation, and a rich literature has explored their many important features. However, there are problems if either concept is taken in isolation as an explanation of modern economic growth.

In the case of entrepreneurship, its spatio-temporal distribution is quite different from that of long-term growth; in particular it is far more widely distributed. It is frequently observed that entrepreneurs are more prevalent in low-income societies than in rich ones, and also that entrepreneurship is less prized as a career path than "a proper job" in such conditions (Banerjee and Duflo 2011). It is not generally a path that leads either to individual or societal prosperity. These informal observations are confirmed by the annual Global Entrepreneurship Monitor (Singer et al. 2015), which finds that the most entrepreneurial countries in their sample are in sub-Saharan Africa, e.g. Cameroon and Uganda, followed by Latin America and low- or middle-income Asian countries. The cross-sectional analysis finds a strong negative relationship between per capita GDP and what they term the TEA (total early-stage entrepreneurial activity) rate, which reflects the adult population prevalence rates of nascent and new businesses.

In the case of innovation, the situation is somewhat different, as it is commonly defined in relation to success in commercialising a new idea, which could be seen as building a capitalist context into the definition, even if in an implicit and unacknowledged way. Schumpeter's concept of innovation was broad, encompassing organisational and structural measures as well as technical invention. This could include new products, new combinations, new trades, new sources of supply, and the creation or destruction of a monopoly. His account emphasised agency, which is important in the context of standard economic theory based on optimisation and therefore no independent role for individual action. However, in trying to account for the dynamism of capitalist economies since the industrial revolution, the concept of innovation would only succeed if it could be shown (a) that innovation increased in such societies, (b) that it was the type of innovation that led to economic growth. These may well be true, but in addition one needs to explain why they occurred—what changed. These questions tend not be addressed clearly in the literature on innovation. Furthermore, to the extent that the innovation literature focuses on the contribution of individuals, neglecting the institutional context, they are missing a large part of the story. In fact, as empirical research proceeds, the organisational context is increasingly being found to be central (Salge and Vera 2012).

To put it another way, although entrepreneurship and innovation may be necessary for the growth of firms and for wider economic dynamism, they are far from sufficient. An additional ingredient is necessary, an essential component that is missing from standard descriptions of economic change. The purpose of this paper is to explore the contribution to economic dynamism of an institution, in the sense of a particular type of organisation: the capitalist firm.

What then is a capitalist firm? One definition emphasises the employment relationship as the central feature (Hodgson 1999) (although that now needs to be extended to include e.g. subcontracting arrangements that are increasingly used by firms so as to avoid statutory duties to employees and/or tax). Crucially in the current context, the capitalist firm can buy in all its needs, which gives it a degree of flexibility unknown in other methods of organising production. This means that it can easily make changes in technology, workforce size and composition, product, location, etc. It provides the structure within which entrepreneurship and innovation have the consequence of producing continuing growth. Thus, entrepreneurship and innovation are behaviours that have been shown to be important in generating particular types of economic change, but they have this aggregate outcome only under specific conditions.

Similar remarks apply to another influential explanation of capitalist growth, especially as it occurred in trail-blazing societies such as nineteenth-century Britain (e.g. Mokyr 2002; Lipsey et al. 2003): exogenous technological change, otherwise known as "invention". This resembles entrepreneurship, in the sense that its spatio-temporal distribution is quite unlike that of capitalist growth. Inventiveness has characterised many societies, notably the great Islamic civilisations that flourished for centuries after the early expansion of Islam; Europe in medieval times; and imperial China throughout its long history. Yet for the most part these economies were stagnant, in contrast with the modern period. It is possible to explain their lack of dynamism by focusing on particular features of each society, but this is the wrong way round: the "deviant" pattern is the modern one that has generated exponential growth, and this raises the question of what the extra ingredient is. In addition, invention is a poor explanation of economic growth in, for example, Japan and other parts of East Asia, because this was mainly catch-up growth, i.e. the economic transformation was achieved by applying existing methods imported from elsewhere.

A further widespread idea is that capitalist growth is fundamentally about capital accumulation. Whilst it is undoubtedly true that capital accumulation regularly accompanies capitalist growth, its causal significance needs to be unpicked. Empirically, it has been established that growth leads to savings, but savings does not lead to growth (Carroll et al. 2000; Rodrik 2000). Another perspective on this issue is that a firm's success depends not only on accumulating capital, but crucially on how this is used—its future performance is related to the quality of an investment as well as its quantity. This is illustrated by the current situation: numerous large and successful corporations possess abundant capital, but lack promising investment opportunities.

2 The Institutional Context: Dominance of the Real Economy by Capitalist Firms

A large majority of the studies in the literature on entrepreneurship and innovation have been located in modern "advanced" economies. This means the institutional context tends to be taken for granted; it is invisible. It also means that the manner in which entrepreneurship and innovation are shaped by their institutional context is ignored—a real economy that is dominated by capitalist firms is more likely to generate entrepreneurship and innovation of the type that leads to economic growth, an insight that can be found in Schumpeter's works, but which was not highly developed by him (Joffe 2013). Furthermore, the outcome of the interaction of entrepreneurship and innovation with the intrinsic dynamic of the capitalist firm—arguably far more than the sum of the parts—is similarly neglected. These processes of shaping and of interaction are outlined below.

Capitalist firms should not be invisible: their existence is not some automatic or natural phenomenon, but has a particular history. Capitalist firms were rare before the industrial revolution, then in early nineteenth century England they emerged out of the factory system. Following pressure from the increasingly important industrialists, legal and institutional changes were adopted that enhanced their stability, thereby facilitating their further development. Foremost among these was entity status (Blair 2003), which gave firms the status of a singular legal person that could trade as an entity in its own right. The implication was that the law protected firms from their own shareholders, as well as from the state and those who might sue, a phenomenon known as *entity shielding* (Hansmann et al. 2006). This meant that they could have a continuing existence, relatively unthreatened as long as they continued to be solvent. It also meant that they could accumulate assets, including premises and equipment as well as less tangible items such as expertise, relationships and reputation.

This is the mirror image of limited liability, which has traditionally received more attention, but which only became a feature of industrial capitalism many decades later, by which time Britain had already become the dominant world economic power. This is owner shielding, which protects shareholders from the liabilities of the firm—in contrast to entity shielding which protects the firm from its shareholders (amongst others) (Hansmann et al. 2006).

Similar legal/institutional measures were subsequently adopted in other countries, and this allowed the spread of capitalism in the sense of a real economy dominated by such capitalist firms. The spatio-temporal distribution of capitalist firms corresponds with that of modern economic growth, except that there are in addition numerous examples of unsuccessful capitalist economies that have also been dominated by capitalist firms. This implies that there are additional conditions needed for continuing economic growth, beyond the institutional ones. These could be regarded as conditions for the successful thriving of capitalist firms, which came to be abundantly fulfilled in the dynamic East Asian economies, but were much less so in (for example) twentieth-century Latin America. The basic observation remains, that capitalist economies thrive when their constituent firms thrive.

The pervasiveness of capitalist firms in the modern world is a result of their success—they now dominate economic life, especially in the richer economies. This is not a question of their benefitting at the expense of the economy as a whole—on the contrary, the dynamism and prosperity of the capitalist real economy is largely traceable to the activities of its component firms. They generate the unique property of successful capitalism, long-term growth that is approximately exponential, albeit with cyclical fluctuations. Specifically, the extraordinary expansion in production and consumption in the modern world results from competition between capitalist firms, which can be analysed as an arms race (Joffe 2011). The institutional foundation gives rise to specific system properties, with reinforcing (positive) feedback, tending to result in exponential growth. How does this occur?

3 How Capitalist Firms Generate Growth

Like all types of firm, capitalist firms own and control the means of production, and rely on generating a surplus (a profit) for long-term survival and prospering. In addition, *capitalist* firms employ wage labour, and more generally are able to buy in whatever inputs are required. They consequently have flexibility in the combination of inputs they can bring together. This allows manipulation of the productive methods, of the scale of production, and therefore of costs. Flexibility is what enables capitalist firms to have effective control over what resources they use, how they use them, and what they are used for. A firm can alter its inputs, notably the number and type of workers, wage rates etc., and/or introduce a new production process, to try and maintain or enhance its market position by reducing unit costs, thereby raising productivity.

Alternatively a firm can introduce new products more easily than other organisational forms can, because of flexibility in opening and closing plants, radically altering the nature of their workforce, and so on. As a consequence, the scope of a capitalist firm is limited only by the abilities of the people who are taking the initiative: their imagination and competence—managerial capacity (Penrose 1959)—plus their access to resources. These resources include the availability of a workforce with particular types of skill and other types of tacit knowledge, as well as equipment and other more tangible assets. The ability to buy in the appropriate range of labour and equipment is central to capitalist firms' success in competing, and therefore for the dynamism and success of the capitalist real economy (Joffe 2011).

These options are not generally available in other ways of organising production. The only way that a petty producer, such as a handloom weaver in early nineteenth century England, could reduce costs was to pay himself lower "wages", and the same is true of present-day sole traders such as peasant farmers. Their flexibility in the number of workers is typically limited by their family circumstances, and they are similarly limited in their choice of production methods. Traders (merchants) whose costs are dominated by the merchandise itself are in a similar position of lacking flexibility; they can reduce the costs of their goods only if they are able to put pressure on existing suppliers or to source from a cheaper one, and they may also be able to reduce other costs, such as those of transport. In a world of petty production and trade, change is therefore mainly incremental, which is why Smithian growth is relatively weak. Traders largely take the stock of product as given, with only an indirect influence via suppliers' willingness to supply. Petty producers are similarly limited by the "stock" of their materials, labour time, skills and production methods.

Thus, capitalist firms have direct control over the volume of production, not being limited by fixed stocks of product, skills, etc. as petty producers and traders are—as long as they can purchase what is needed. This means that the volume of product, and hence the size of the market they can supply, is in principle unlimited—it is extendable without limit—as long as consumers are willing to buy it. The implication is that firms can conquer the market share of their competitors. The more successful ones grow at the expense of the less successful, leading to a highly skewed firm size distribution that typically follows a power law (Gabaix 2009).

The degree of flexibility varies from firm to firm, from sector to sector and in different historical times and places (e.g. for institutional reasons). But the unifying feature of capitalist production is that across all the dramatic changes that have occurred, for example in the presence/absence of limited liability, in market structure and in the role of science and technology, it is composed of firms that have this characteristic of potential flexibility both in inputs and in scale of output.

These key properties of the firm not only span the different organisational forms that have occurred in capitalist societies, but are also compatible with different types of ownership. Even the public sector, as with township-village enterprises in China (Qian 2003) and state-owned enterprises in China and in Vietnam (Ngu 2002), can function as capitalist firms if they are allowed to do so—this is the main difference from pre-reform organisations, and from the factories of the former USSR. Intermediate forms also exist, for example cooperatives, which have some similarities to capitalist firms but may be expected to have less flexibility and which have been observed to have lower growth rates in the long term (Gagliardi 2009). The state can also be important in innovation, by supporting basic research plus applied research and development, acting entrepreneurially, taking on risk, and creating and shaping markets (Mazzucato 2013).

The contributions of entrepreneurship and innovation need to be seen in this context. First, the central imperative of the capitalist firm to make a profit, while competing with other firms in the same sector, provides a clear *direction* for the talents of entrepreneurs and innovators to follow. The rewards of success in this endeavour are great, providing a powerful *incentive* for them to find ways to achieve it, and for those with relevant talents to *become* entrepreneurs and innovators. In these three ways the capitalist firm creates the conditions that develop, motivate and channel the types of entrepreneurship and innovation that power the system.

Secondly, the combination of the capitalist firm structure with these types of entrepreneurship and innovation has far-reaching consequences. The flexibility of *inputs* that is characteristic of capitalist firms gives scope for the inventiveness of entrepreneurs and innovators. The flexibility in the *size of the market* that can be supplied means that the introduction of a successful production technique or new product can lead to the expansion of production, limited only by the ability of the management team to purchase the required inputs and to coordinate the production at an increased scale. Success in entrepreneurship and/or innovation is thereby magnified, a synergy that generates the dynamism that we see in the real economy of the capitalist system.

4 Motivation and Consequences at Firm Level

The central role of profit in the success of the firm does not imply that profit *maximisation* is necessarily operating as an *aim*: it is possible that a firm aiming to maximise profit could be less successful than one that does not, if the latter firm has other attributes that give it an edge—the outcome of competition is a matter of consequences not of motivation.

The distinction between motivation and consequences is important more generally. Motivation, the combination of carrot and stick, is central for the individual firm. However, to understand the causes of growth we need to focus also on the consequences, both at the level of the firm and at the aggregate levels of the sector and the whole economy. A parallel distinction underlies the structure of Adam Smith's argument that differentiates the motivation of the trader from its consequence: "It is not from the benevolence of the butcher, the brewer, or the baker, that we expect our dinner, but from their regard to their own interest" (Smith 1776).

The unintended consequences at the level of the individual firm arise simply from its being in business, and are contributions that it makes to the wider economy. Among the most important are:

- provision of goods and/or services;
- generation of profit and therefore accumulation of capital;
- employment of workers and payment of wages, thereby providing buying power for other companies' products.

Simple aggregation applies here, that the economy-wide consequences are simply the sum of the firm-level effects—except that in the case of wages, a lower wage bill helps to keep costs down, benefiting the individual firm, whereas a higher wage bill contributes more buying power to other sectors of the economy, a form of externality; this is the "micro" (or meso) foundation of aggregate demand. But at the aggregate level, unintended consequences give the system its distinct properties.

5 How Cost Reduction Works: The Sector Level and the Wider Economy

Each firm pursues lower unit costs, attempting to maintain and improve its competitive position. Other firms in the same sector are similarly engaged, so that profit margins are constantly squeezed by the successes of one's competitors. An "arms race" takes place, aptly described by Lewis Carroll as running as fast as one can in order to stay in the same place [the "Red Queen" effect (Carroll 1872)].

A firm can use many different types of strategy to try and reduce its unit costs. Taking the example of a manufacturing firm (the question of generalisation outside manufacturing will be considered in the next section), these include:

- use of a technology with higher productivity to produce more units with the same resources;
- downward pressure on wages and/or employment levels;
- providing poor working conditions, and cutting corners on health and safety;
- sourcing of lower cost materials;
- superior organisation;
- mergers and acquisitions with elimination of overlaps;
- running at full capacity and thereby minimising fixed costs.

Such cost reduction can involve innovation in a technological sense, but this is by no means the only method. There are multiple ways, with cost reduction as the final common path.

For growth, the important consequences are at the level of the sector. Each firm's cost-cutting is a contribution to a continual reduction in costs in the sector as a whole—although the term "contribution" should not be seen as implying any more benevolence than in the case of the butcher, the brewer and the baker—it is an unintended consequence of how the system operates. In this way, a given output requires a constantly falling input of real resources over successive waves of cost reduction. Just as Smith's "invisible hand" operates as an unintended consequence at the level of the market, a sector composed of capitalist firms is here seen as embodying the emergent property that makes capitalism distinct and, specifically, more dynamic than other economic systems.

There are two ways in which this happens: (1) replacement of the less efficient firms and (2) survivors' behavioural response to lower their costs. Historically, the greater dynamism of capitalism in each geographical area starts when other forms of organisation begin to be replaced by capitalist firms that are able to undercut them, as when the English handloom weavers were driven into destitution by the more efficient factories in the early nineteenth century.

The process does not end with lower unit costs. A second effect of competition is to exert downward pressure on margins, so that the price also falls. With the same real wage, the consumer can now afford to buy more: thus a price fall increases the buying power of workers in other sectors, making them richer. In this way, cost-and-price reduction in each sector increases the prosperity of the rest of the economy. In other words, it releases buying power. Over time, as this process occurs in many sectors, society becomes more prosperous, the distribution of prosperity depending on the income distribution. After some decades, the economy is transformed into the mass-consumption type of capitalism.

The trajectory of each sector depends not only on this process of ever-greater efficiency, but also on the market. At the new lower price, the quantity demanded increases until the market becomes saturated; saturation is superseded when the next round of cost reduction occurs. In addition, a sector can be affected by exogenous developments in other sectors, for example, ones that render its product obsolete.

At the aggregate level of the whole economy, the most important unintended consequences are:

- increased buying power as a result of the previous level of consumption now costing less;
- capital accumulation;
- to the extent that cost-cutting results in higher labour productivity, less labour is required for the same output, and despite higher quantities being produced, eventually is likely to fall for the sector as a whole.

6 Generalisability Outside Manufacturing

The above description is based on manufacturing, but may well be more general, inviting the question, "what other sectors have similar properties?". The historical record shows that agriculture has followed a path similar to industry, at least in rich societies (Harley 2014, especially pp. 498–501). The development of retailing makes it clear that a similar dynamic must be operating in this sector too, as with

Wal-Mart in recent decades, and similar processes in earlier times leading to the rise of chain stores and supermarkets in America, Europe and elsewhere. Such developments are continuing, with the rise of internet-based sales companies such as Amazon.

The example of retail corporations such as Wal-Mart in using cost-cutting provides a clear illustration of a principle that is quite general: their increase in market power—to an extent that approaches monopoly in many locations—goes with lower not higher prices. This reverses the conventional logic found in mainstream economics, that given a monopoly position a firm will extract higher prices; whilst that is true, it does not allow for the way the monopoly position was arrived at. If it was achieved by cost-cutting, then the dominant company is likely to be the one charging lower not higher prices. This is readily observed in retailing, where displacement of small shops by supermarkets and chains is clearly evident, but present in manufacturing and probably other sectors as well. The same logic also makes clear that size itself is not necessarily an advantage; rather, size and influence are both consequences of being in a position of relative strength, whether through low costs or through new products—except in sectors where economies of scale impart a substantial reinforcing (positive) feedback impetus.

It is not immediately clear that the same description applies in non-financial services other than retailing. On one hand, the continuing dynamism of the US economy, in which services have largely replaced manufacturing, suggests that the processes are at least partly similar to those described for manufacturing. On the other hand, it is difficult to see how such services as personal (one-to-one) care can be analysed in this way—they are inherently more akin to petty production. Clearly the term "services" is highly heterogeneous in these terms. For example, in services such as a hotel or a language class, where fixed costs dominate, full occupancy/attendance (analogous to full capacity in industry) plays a central role. Consideration of this issue requires an analysis of the different sources of profit in different types of service industry, the strategies available and their aggregate-level effects, but this is beyond the scope of the present paper.

Similarly, sectors in primary production that have a limited stock of product, such as mining and oil/gas, with limited flexibility of supply, follow the market logic of a scarce resource. Capitalist cost-cutting logic only applies where there is scope for substantial reduction in input costs. And housing has its own characteristics: building methods are subject to cost reduction as well as to product innovation and quality improvement, but housing has a strong positional element in that land prices reflect the degree of desirability of different locations—a major zero-sum component.

7 Conclusion

Any account of economic change that sets out to explain the dynamism of capitalist economies since the industrial revolution needs to include the specific properties of the capitalist firm in its analysis. In particular, it must take account of the way that the capitalist firm uniquely enables entrepreneurship and innovation to generate enhanced productivity and/or new/better products.

References

Banerjee A, Duflo E (2011) Poor economics. PublicAffairs, New York

Blair MM (2003) Locking in capital: what corporate law achieved for business organizers in the nineteenth century. UCLA Law Rev 51:387–455

Broadberry S (2013) Accounting for the great divergence. LSE Economic History Working Papers No. 184/2013. http://www.lse.ac.uk/economicHistory/workingPapers/2013/WP184.pdf. Accessed 30 Mar 2016

Carroll L (2003 [1872]) Through the looking glass. Penguin Classics, London

Carroll CD, Overland J, Weil DN (2000) Saving and growth with habit formation. Am Econ Rev 90(3):341–355

de Vries J, van der Woude A (1997) The first modern economy: success, failure and perseverance of the Dutch economy, 1500–1815. Cambridge University Press, Cambridge

Gabaix X (2009) Power laws in economics and finance. Annu Rev Econ 1:255–293

Gagliardi F (2009) Financial development and the growth of cooperative firms. Small Bus Econ 32:439–464

Hansmann H, Kraakman R, Squire R (2006) Law and the rise of the firm. Harv Law Rev 119:1335–1403

Harley CK (2014) British and European industrialization. In: Neal L, Williamson JG (eds) The Cambridge history of capitalism, vol I: The rise of capitalism: from ancient origins to 1848. Cambridge University Press, Cambridge, pp 491–532

Hodgson GM (1999) Evolution and institutions: on evolutionary economics and the evolution of economics. Edward Elgar, Cheltenham

Joffe M (2011) The root cause of economic growth under capitalism. Camb J Econ 35:873–896

Joffe M (2013) What causes creative destruction? In: Pyka A, Andersen ES (eds) Long term economic development. Springer, Berlin, pp 431–438

Kelly M (1997) The dynamics of Smithian growth. Q J Econ 112:939–964

Lipsey RG, Carlaw KI, Bekar CT (2003) Economic transformations. Oxford University Press, Oxford

Mazzucato M (2013) The entrepreneurial state. Anthem Press, London

Mokyr J (2002) The gifts of Athena: historical origins of the knowledge economy. Princeton University Press, Princeton

Ngu VQ (2002) The state-owned enterprise reform in Vietnam: process and achievements. Institute of Southeast Asian Studies, Singapore, Visiting Researchers Series No. 4, available via https://bookshop.iseas.edu.sg/publication/1764#contents. Accessed 30 Mar 2016

Penrose ET (1959) The theory of the growth of the firm. Oxford University Press, Oxford

Qian Y (2003) How reform worked in China. In: Rodrik D (ed) In search of prosperity. Analytic narratives on economic growth. Princeton University Press, Princeton

Rodrik D (2000) Saving transitions. World Bank Econ Rev 14(3):481–507

Salge TO, Vera A (2012) Benefiting from public sector innovation: the moderating role of customer and learning orientation. Public Adm Rev 72:550–560

Singer S, Amorós JE, Moska D (2015) Global entrepreneurship monitor. 2014 Global Report. Available at: http://gemconsortium.org/report. Accessed 5 Sep 2017

Smith A (1970[1776]) The wealth of nations. Penguin Books, Harmondsworth

The Journey of Innovation

From Incremental to Radical Innovation and High-Tech Innovation Cascades: The Case of Biotechnology

Jorge Niosi

Abstract This paper argues that innovation has itself evolved, from the slow, path-dependent, and foreseeable world of technological trajectories, to the less predictable world of innovation cascades, after incorporating the analysis of radical innovation in the last three decades. Innovation cascades are long series of radical innovations in one or in related technological domains. Two types of innovation cascades are distinguished in the paper: those emerging before the Industrial Revolution and the modern high-tech ones. The previous innovation cascades usually petered out fairly soon by lack of institutional support, as inventors and innovators were individuals or companies trying out their luck in the market place in a less than friendly environment. Present day innovation cascades benefit from numerous innovating firms, research universities and government laboratories, science, technology and innovation policies, increasing numbers of countries investing in R&D and innovation, as well as reduced costs of access to information, communication and transportation. Today's innovation cascades tend to be more extended through time and space. Their systemic effects are also more widely diffused in global terms.

Innovation is the engine of economic growth. It is thus critical to understand how it proceeds. For several decades, evolutionary theories using the biological model were applied to innovation (Basalla 1988; Petroski 1994; McKelvey 1996): innovation was supposed to proceed in a leisurely way, over the centuries if not the millennia, one step at a time, in an incremental process. Similarly, organisations and institutions evolved clearly from one form to the next. The founding book of this current is that of Richard Nelson and Sid Winter (1982). Industries also evolve and several models have been advanced to explain this evolution (Malerba 2006). For most authors, including the author of this paper, this type of technological

A previous version of this paper was presented to the International Schumpeter Society conference, Jena, Germany, 25–30 September 2014. I gratefully acknowledge the many comments I received in that session.

J. Niosi (✉)
UQAM, Montréal, Canada
e-mail: niosi.jorge@uqam.ca

A. Pyka, U. Cantner (eds.), *Foundations of Economic Change*, Economic Complexity and Evolution, DOI 10.1007/978-3-319-62009-1_12

change is the most frequent. Arthur (2009) calls 'standard engineering' this evolutionary technical change. Bessant et al. (1994) underlined the fact that continuous innovation is sometimes difficult. Yet the vast majority of authors find evolutionary innovation is ubiquitous. Companies and governments alike abhor rapid technological change that may devalue their assets and sunk costs, and cannibalize their products (Christensen 1997).

Radical innovation (already identified by Schumpeter in his 1939 book *Business Cycles*) appeared and, again, it was deemed analogous to biological change, where saltation (Gould 1977) and short periods of rapid structural change interrupted long periods of stasis and incremental change. Both in biology and management, radical innovation and saltation were difficult to accept. In biology, the neo-Darwinian synthesis wiped out most ideas about saltation. They came back slowly since the 1950s and 1960s through the work of B. McClintock (Nobel Prize in physiology 1983). The idea was developed and popularized by S.J. Gould and N. Eldridge. How the markets accept these complex modifications of product and/or process? In the postwar period, radical innovation appeared in Britain in the works of Gibbons and Littler (1979), Rothwell (1980) and others. A few years later, several authors were discussing the multifarious dynamics between radical innovation, organizations and industry structure (Souder 1983; Achilladelis et al. 1990; Christensen and Bower 1996) as well as the importance of the necessary infrastructure for radical innovation to be adopted (McIntyre 1988).

Much more recently, innovation seems to be accelerating; new scientific disciplines appear. Thus, it cannot be properly depicted as a smooth path, punctuated by occasional changes in direction. It looks much more like a river where fast-moving water evolves from rapids to waterfalls, splits into several diverging flows that sometimes merge with other flows to form new estuaries. The concept of innovation cascades circumscribes evolutionary change (Antonelli 2008, 2009; Berkers and Geels 2011; Delapierre and Mytelka 2003; Lane 2012). Rothwell and Wissema (1986) had suggested that radical innovations arrive in clusters, much in line with the Schumpeterian view of business cycles. This paper suggests that **innovation cascades** are becoming much more frequent today for several reasons: because of the rise of science-based industries (Pavitt 1984), the increasing number of research universities in a growing number of emerging countries, more linkages between these loci of knowledge creation, and faster technology diffusion. Fastest imitation also increases the probability of new combinations between different strands of knowledge. Cascades have a definite Schumpeterian flavour.

The paper will bring some aggregate figures about the rise of science-based industries, and then it will illustrate one of the major (if not the major) present-day innovation cascade with the growth of biotechnology and the arrival in rapid succession of genetic engineering, monoclonal antibodies, genomics, epigenetics, proteomics, bioinformatics, gene therapy, pharmacogenomics, nanobiotechnology, metabolomics, stem cell technology, and other related disciplines. The growth of biotechnology publication and patenting by countries such as China, Japan, Singapore and South Korea is also presented (nbt. 2384). A table with the different disciplines, application and key companies will help.

1 Evolutionary Innovation: Natura Non Facit Saltum

Evolutionary or incremental innovation (small, continuous improvements in technology and organisation) is the most abundant type of innovation. Its predominance over other forms of innovation is easy to accept. Companies and individuals tinker on what they know best. Such behaviour reduces the risk associated with big jumps. Evolutionary product and process and organizational innovation is less expensive, because it requires minor adaption of marketing, and operations strategy and infrastructures. Markets recognize, and sometimes even trigger such slow changes. Many organizations almost continuously produce such small adaptations to environmental changes of their output and/or their structure. Large changes, both in biology and economics would produce monsters, which the environment often rejects as such, and do not survive. The organisation produces variety (at the level of technology, product, process, strategy and structure) in a bounded rational way, and the environment selects. Such slow process drives the organisation and its technologies to local optima. "Artifacts, like plant and animal life forms, can be arranged in continuous, chronological sequences./. . ./Butler, Pitt-Rivers, Gilfillan, Ogburn and Usher all stressed the accumulation over time of small variations that finally yielded novel artifacts." (Basalla 1988, p. 24) Yet, the author recognizes that short periods of rapid change may exist between long periods of slow change and stasis. However, the vast majority of authors on technology have adhered to an evolutionary perspective (Fig. 1).

In economics, Nelson and Winter (1982) have identified the sources of slow change: the firm's routines, which are the genes of organizations. Over time, organisations have developed ways of solving their search, production and marketing problems; such a learning process has been long and costly, and has been

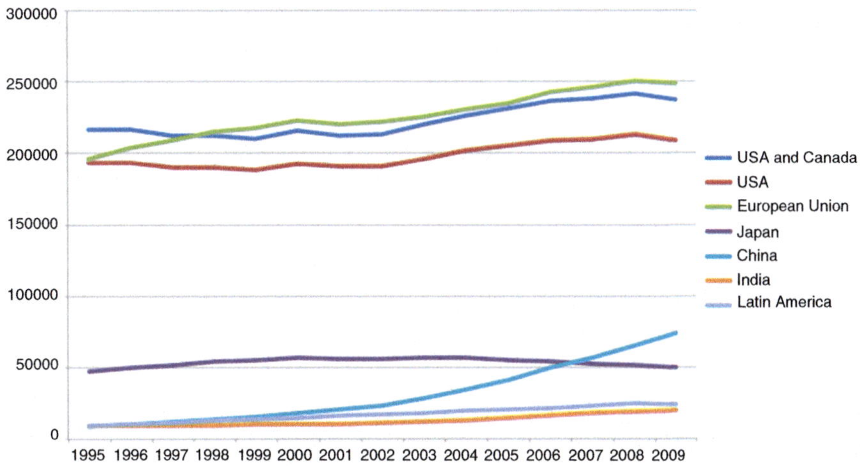

Fig. 1 The rise of scientific publication (1995–2009)

reinforced by the building of complementary infrastructures and practices. Maureen McKelvey (1996) has presented the basic principles of evolutionary innovation in biotechnology. They include variation (generation of novelty); selection; transmission and retention of certain traits over time; and non-optimization but adaptation to local environments. Like Basalla (1988), McKelvey argues that biological evolution cannot be deemed identical to economic evolution. Nelson (2006) has also adopted this perspective: biological evolution and human culture share a few major unifying themes, such as variation, selection and retention, but are split apart by major differences, including the speed of change and the goal-oriented action of humans in cultural evolution. Also, within cultural dynamics there are large differences between fields, such as linguistic and policy evolution.

A lively debate among evolutionary economists and management theorists is linked to the amount of inertia that organizations carry. At one extreme one finds the organisational ecology perspective, with such authors as Michael Hannan, John Freeman, and Glenn Carroll, for which organisational inertia is predominant, and firm level adaptation is limit. Populations of firms change by the birth and death of organizations; those that survive have usually from the start, the right genes. Organizational ecology is more Darwinian, while Nelson and Winter (1982) are more Lamarckian. The more the evolutionary approaches put the emphasis on the importance of strategy, including Nelson and Winter, the farther they are away from the organizational ecology perspective. Whatever the case, it is clear that most companies live and die with their original routines, technologies and strategies. These are the traditional small and medium-sized firms that Bhidé (2000) has shown to be the vast majority of firms. A few of them usually medium-sized and large ones, tend to change from time to time their range of technologies, strategies and structures. This paper adopts a mixed perspective: studies on firm mortality in all OECD countries show that the vast majority of firms disappear a few years after they were founded. A few of them manage to change and adapt to the environment. Even among those that adapt and change, many sometimes err in their choice of new routines, technologies and markets, and also disappear. The roads of industrial change of the latest years are littered with the remains of such companies as Blackberry and Nokia.

In this world of evolutionary innovation, technological trajectories abound, and technological discontinuities are amenable to modelling (Dosi 1982). New technological paradigms (discontinuities) are linked to the emergence of Schumpeterian companies and the process of innovation stabilises. The process is fairly structured:

> ...a technological paradigm (or research programme) embodies strong prescriptions on the directions of technical change to pursue and those to neglect. (Dosi 1982: 152).

Also, evolutionary innovation is the world of path dependency. Institutions, routines, technologies persist over time, even when they have outlived the social matrix in which they were born

2 Radical Innovation

Before turning to present day work about ***radical innovation***, let us recall that Schumpeter (1939: 90) had already made the distinction between major and minor innovations. By the way, his debate about new forms and innovation has a very deep organizational ecology flavour (ibid: 90–93). Very often new firms are founded to launch a major innovation, Schumpeter adds, and they cease to exist when the previous novelty is not new anymore.

The notion of radical innovation is also labelled **discontinuous** or ***disruptive innovation***. Radical innovation, when successful, has a much larger effect on firm's profitability, market share, and entire industries (Sainio et al. 2012). Key dimensions of radical innovation include technology novelty (clear advances in frontier technology, as in the I-Pad), and market novelty (products that address themselves to new markets, or to markets that were served by other products, such as MABs). Even if it often the special activity of entrepreneurial firms, it also occurs in large established companies (O'Connor and McDermott 2004).

Compared to the PC or even the portable computer, the I-Pad is a disruptive innovation, where large firms are bringing high technical novelty. The I-Pad is lighter (1.5 pounds), has a long life battery (up to 10 h), a powerful camera, a GPS, and fingers are used to tape and swipe the contents of the screen. The I-Pad corresponds to what Sainio et al. (2012) call radical innovation: launched in April 2010, it had sold over 100 million units by October 2012. In addition, other large manufacturers quickly entered the market; they include Google, Lenovo, Microsoft, Samsung and Sony. By the end of 2013, Apple remained the market leader in the tablet segment of the computer industry, and tablets contributed enormously to its profitability. Experts expect that in 2015, tablets sales will be larger than PC shipments (Table 1).

Biopharmaceuticals medicines represent radical innovations compared to traditional chemical-based drugs. Monoclonal antibodies (MABS) that bind to specific forms of cancer bring at the same time market novelty and technological novelty. Up to a few years ago, the only ways to treat cancer were early detection followed by surgery and/or chemotherapy. Ten years ago, in 2004, the first monoclonal antibody, i.e. bevacizumab, against breast cancer, made its appearance in the market. It was surrounded (and still is, like most radical innovations) by strong market uncertainty. The drug inhibits the growth of blood vessels that feed cancer tumours, but not on all patients; its high cost added to market uncertainty, as price inhibited the growth of demand. Many other MABS followed for treatment of different types of cancer.[1] All of them are still suffering from similar market uncertainty, due to high cost, and different effects on different patients.

Table 2 presents the most usual dimensions of radical innovation compared with incremental ones. Note the fact that all these characteristics of radical innovation

[1]See http://en.wikipedia.org/wiki/Category:Monoclonal_antibodies_for_tumors, the list of 71 antibodies approved or being developed against tumours.

Table 1 The biotechnology innovation cascade

Year	Discipline	Landmark event	Definition	Key organizations
1953	Biology	Drs. F. Crick and J. D. Watson (UK) discover the structure of DNA	NA	University of Cambridge, UK
1970	Bioinformatics	E. A. Kabat (USA) pioneer computer methods for biological sequence analysis	"The application of computer technology to the storage, management, and analysis of biological data."[a]	Genomodel, Integromics, Rosetta, SymBioSys
1972	Biotechnology: genetic engineering	Drs. H. Boyer and S. Cohen (USA) develop methods to combine and transplant genes	"Any technological application that uses biological systems, living organisms, or derivatives thereof, to make or modify products or processes for specific use." (UN)[b]	Amgen, Biogen, Genentech, Gilead, Serono, Vertex, UCSF and Stanford U.
1975	Monoclonal antibodies (MABS)	Drs. C. Milstein and G. Kohler (UK) develop hybridoma techniques to produce MABS	The development of monospecific antibodies made by identical immune cells, cloned from a unique parent cell. They bind to any organic substance, that they can detect, purify or destroy	Abbott, Amgen, Biogen, Eli Lilly, Genentech Genzyme, Glaxo, Novartis
1977	Genomics	Dr. F. Sanger (UK) publishes a key method to sequence DNA	Genomics is a discipline in genetics that applies recombinant DNA, DNA sequencing methods, and bioinfor matics to sequence, assemble, and analyze the function and structure of genomes (the *complete* set of DNA within a single cell of an organism)	Agilent, Illumina, Life Technologies, Myriad Genetics, Pacific Biosciences[c]
1994	Proteomics	Dr. R. Nelson (USA) develops the use of mass spectrometry in immunoassays	The large scale study of proteins, their structure and functions	Applied Biomics, Biacore, Proteome Sciences...[d]
1998	Stem cell therapy	Drs. Thompson and Gearhart (USA) develop stem cells	Introduction of adult stem cell in damaged tissue in order to treat disease or injury, I.e. bone marrow transplantation	Mostly experimental in hospitals and research universities

(continued)

Table 1 (continued)

Year	Discipline	Landmark event	Definition	Key organizations
2002	Gene therapy	Dr. Claudio Bordignon (Italy) publishes the first successful gene therapy treatment	Use of DNA as therapeutic agent to treat genetic diseases (replace mutated genes)	Ark Therapeutics Group, Ceregene (US) Glybera (Netherlands), Shenzen SiBiono GeneTech (China), Oxford BioMedica (UK)
2003	Pharmacogenomics	Completion of the Human Genome Project (international)	The application of genomics concepts and technologies to the study of drug activity and metabolism, including gene expression, or inactivation and SNP association studies	AnyGenes, DeCode Genetics, Gentris, Glaxo, Jackson Library[e]

[a]European Bioinformatics Institute (EBI)(2012): *In a Nutshell*, Cambridge, UK
[b]UN (1992): The Convention on biological diversity. (http://www.cbd.int/convention/articles/default.shtml?a=cbd-02)
[c]http://www.marketwatch.com/story/genomics-companies-ripe-for-flurry-of-mergers-2013-04-16
[d]http://www.proteinscience.com/companies.html
[e]http://www.jazdlifesciences.com/pharmatech/leaf/Drug-Discovery/Clinical-Research-Services/Pharmacogenomics.htm

Table 2 Incremental and radical innovation defined

Dimension of radicalness	Incremental	Radical
Impact on the industry	Low	High
Source of subsequent innovation	No	Yes
Older technology remains substitute for new	Yes	No
Cost reductions	Low	High
Competitive advantage to adopters	Low	High
Benefits brought if successful	Low	High
Adoption risks	Low	High
Technical uncertainty levels	Low	High
Market uncertainty levels	Low	High
Resource uncertainty levels	Low	High
Organizational uncertainty levels	Low	High

are difficult if not impossible to distinguish at the moment where the new product or service is launched. The impacts on the industry, future benefits and cost curves, risk and uncertainties are unknown at the beginnings of the market introduction, as are the subsequent innovations that may follow piggyback on the original radical one. Such phenomenon explains why the very innovators in all these science-based radical technologies are often confounded about the future adoption of the novelty. Radical innovation appears wrapped either under the look of incremental one, or as a monster that the market will reject. We know that an innovation was radical only when it is accepted by the market, and generates benefits, cost reductions, competitive advantages to adopters, and when major uncertainties and risks have been dealt with.

3 Innovation Cascades

Innovation cascades are streams of radical innovations usually concentrated in one industry or in contiguous industries. The idea of innovation cascades is already present in Schumpeter:

> First, that innovations do not remain isolated events, and are not evenly distributed in time, but that on the contrary they tend to cluster, to come about in bunches, simply because first some, and then most, firms follow in the wake of successful innovation; second, that innovations are not at any time distributed over the whole economic system at random, but tend to concentrate in certain sectors and their surroundings. (Schumpeter 1939, p. 98)

More recently, a few authors have explored the subject without arriving to a satisfactory explanation of the dynamics of the development of cascades. Delapierre and Mytelka (2003) link innovation cascades to the oligopolistic behaviour of large firms. Competition among large diversified corporations generates the exploration of new technological domains, and the creation of new technologies and new industrial sectors. They do not make any link between their work and Schumpeter's, in spite of the obvious similarities. Antonelli (2008, 2009) explains innovation cascades by the interplay of Marshall and Jacob externalities within clusters. Cascades would appear in regional innovation systems, not necessarily in concentrated industries, as in Delapierre and Mytelka (2003). Explains innovation cascades by a phenomenon called "exaptive bootstrapping". In biology, exaptation is the use of structure or feature for a function other than that for which it was developed originally through natural selection. "Exaption is a change in the function of a trait during evolution. "Bootstrapping," means to help oneself by one's own means and efforts. Thus, in the two previous explanations, the conscious efforts of economic agents launch a cascade; in Lane's approach, some agents would launch a cascade without even noticing it, just trying to solve a local specific problem. His example is Gutenberg's re-invention of the printing press by the introduction of the movable metal type around 1452–1854. Such innovation launched a cascade where new organizational forms (printing companies), new technical novelties (new ink, paper), new markets (for printed books), new types of printing characters (the *italics*) and new functionalities emerged, imitation from other economic agents increased both the market and the innovative activities, in a positive feedback dynamics that eventually extend over decades.

Once it is launched, the self-reinforcing dynamics is difficult to control or predict, even for those that actively involved in the process (Lane and Maxfield 1996). Under such conditions, optimization and strategy making become difficult, if not impossible. And predicting technological trajectories is highly improbable. Finally, Berkers and Geels (2011) use the same notion of innovation cascades to describe a positive feedback innovation mechanism that has taken place among traditional small and medium-sized enterprises using innovations generated elsewhere (mostly equipment suppliers, but also government laboratories and universities). The authors make a passing remark on the fact that these cascades are different from those studies in scale-intensive and science-based industries and/or government utilities (ibid, p. 243), but they do not cite any of the above mentioned papers on innovation cascades. They contribute to the theory of technological transitions.

Technological transitions are major long-term technological changes. These technological transitions come along through several mechanisms: niche-accumulation, technological add-on and hybridisation (Geels 2002). His idea of technological transitions is close to Schumpeter approach of innovation cascades. Technological transitions occur in all different types of industries, from science-based to scale intensive to government-supported sectors. However, "transitions are characterised by one major, radical innovation or discontinuity" (Berkers and Geels 2011, p. 230), while innovation cascades are more characterised by a stream of radical innovations.

In this paper I contend, following Mokyr (2002) that innovation cascades in Western economies before the Industrial Revolution, such as the printing press, failed to promote sustained economic growth. They are different from present day high-tech (information technology and biotechnology) cascades. The reasons why innovation cascades before 1800 where short lived are many. First, the institutional environment did not contribute to its adoption but blocked the diffusion of innovation and the emergence of new radical ones: indexes of prohibited books and censorship were widespread. Also, universities and private companies did not conduct R&D, and there were no public research laboratories to push the cascade further. Radical innovation depended on the individual efforts of remarkable luminaries like Galileo or Watt in physics, Dalton and Lavoisier en chemistry. Before 1800, the innovation centres of the world were just a few cities such as Amsterdam, London, Paris, and Venice, and within them there were few innovating organizations. Also, communications between those centres were slow and costly, and the scientific and technical knowledge of the times was scanty. Innovation came through serendipity, and was not the routine activity of thousands of organizations as it is today.

After the Industrial Revolution innovation cascades became more frequent. One can find several of them associated with the rapid improvements in steel-making technology, the railway, the internal combustion engine, and chemicals to name some of the most important in the nineteenth and early twentieth centuries.

Postwar innovation cascades are increasingly frequent in Western countries. The reasons are many. For one, the stock of knowledge grows by bounds and leaps. As a result, innovation, as measured by the number of patents and scientific publications increases continuously. So the scientific and engineering raw material for innovation is today much more abundant (Kortum and Lerner 1999; Larsen and von Ins 2010). Second, the rise of scientific collaboration (Grene 2007) and particularly of international scientific collaboration increases the number of new combinations that may be produced on the basis of this new knowledge. The growth of international scientific collaboration may be explained by the diffusion of scientific capacity both within industrial countries and among emerging countries (Wagner and Leydersdorff 2005). Also, rapid advances in communication and transportation technology increase today the chances that new combinations emerge from international and inter-regional collaboration. Third, the institutional landscape has enormously changed: in each advanced industrial and emerging country, thousands of innovative firms and hundreds of research universities, as well as public laboratories are now able to amplify and develop many technological trends in a way that was impossible to occur 200 years ago. Thus, all these elements launch positive and self-reinforcing feedback processes that are increasingly unstoppable. Other key innovation institutions contribute today that did not exist in the fifteenth or sixteenth centuries, namely policy incentives, such as those aiming to the commercialization of university research, policies increase the likelihood that scientific novelty is used in industry and launch an innovation cascade.

The previous world was one were technological trajectories and path dependencies were the name of the game. They still are numerous today, but innovation cascades, a world of self-reinforcing mechanisms, non-linear dynamics with many possible short-term equilibrium situations, make that technological trajectories are less evident than 50 years ago. Who could foresee the rise of Internet, or the advances in computational genomics 30 years ago? Technological path dependencies also seem to be often interrupted by these innovation cascades. The dictum "Natura non facit saltum" does not apply to these unpredictable cascades.

4 Biotechnology Innovation Cascade

Today two major innovation cascades are dominating the industrial landscape: information and communication technologies, and biotechnology. This paper will confine to biotechnology.

The discovery of the structure of DNA by Crick and Watson, in 1953 launched one of the most astounding innovation cascades in human history, only comparable with those that are taking place in information and communication technologies.

In a rapid succession, from the discovery of the structure of DNA by Crick and Watson in 1953, followed the development of methods to cut, transplant and recombine genes by Boyer and Cohen in the United states (1972), the development of bioinformatics in the 1970s, methods to produce monoclonal antibodies (UK, 1970s), and genomics and proteomics and pharmacogenomics, followed by stem cell and genomic therapies. While genetic engineering and MABS are already revolutionising the way biopharmaceutical companies operate and the drug market is organised, bioinformatics, genomics and proteomics are starting to produce new results that allow companies to identify the reasons why some drugs are effective on some people and not on others, and to improve them consequently. Between 2000 and 2009 US applicants filed 116,145 international biotechnology patent applications, against Japanese applicants with 37,754, Chinese applicants with 24,135 and Germans with 23,818.[2]

Any innovation cascade is punctuated by many intersections where the very people involved in the dynamics could not understand the nature of what was going on. In the late 1990s, gene or stem cell therapies were considered impossible. Today they are being experimented everywhere and the first successes take place in both bone marrow transplantation and cornea regeneration, among others.

It is important to underline the fact that today the biotechnology innovation cascade takes place essentially in North America and Western Europe. The United States are the cradle of some 80% of all biological drugs, with Britain, France, Germany and Switzerland following. Such a finding suggests that innovation cascades occur within innovation systems in advanced countries. Yet, several Asian countries, most prominently China, Japan and South Korea are entering this field at great speed, through massive public subsidies and through the hiring of hundreds of Chinese scientists trained in North America and Western Europe. The rise of stem cell research in China is just one of them (Dennis 2002). Similarly, Indian pharmaceutical companies are starting to innovate and patent in several advanced fields of biopharmaceuticals (Mueller 2006). And Brazil is now among the top countries in terms of biotechnology publication.

Also, the biotech innovation cascade, as the ICT one, is bringing forward a cornucopia of new business models, a big bang of new business organizations (Bourreau et al. 2012). The reason is that biotechnology firms operate in an environment of high uncertainty due to rapid technological change.

4.1 *The Genomics Revolution and Sequencing Technology*

A major part of the biotechnology revolution is linked to the fast improvement that took place in sequencing technology (Heather and Chain 2016). The following insert summarizes the main steps in the sequencing technical support of the revolution.

---

[2]http://www.uspto.gov/web/offices/ac/ido/oeip/taf/tecstc/classes_clstc_gd.htm (for US patents)

Date	Main inventor	Country	Contribution
First generation sequencing milestones			
1965	Robert Holley	USA	Describing the structure of tRNA
1977	Frederick Sanger	UK	Chain-termination sequencing technique
1983	Kary Mullis	USA	Polymerase chain reaction improved
	Kary Mullis	USA	Polymerase chain reaction improved
Second generation sequencing milestones			
1983	Kary Mullis	USA	Polymerase chain reaction (PCR) improved
2000	454 Life Sciences (in 2007, Roche acquired it)	USA	Mass parallelisation of sequencing reactions reducing cost and increasing ease of DNA sequencing through large scale pyrosequencing
Third generation sequencing milestones			
2003	Stephen Quake	USA	Single molecule sequencing
2004	Illumina	USA	Bridge PCR; ligation of fragmented DNA to a chip
2005	Complete Genomics	USA	DNA nanoballs and unchained sequencing by ligation

The performance of DNA sequencers has increased at a rate faster than Moore's law in computers, and allowed the biotechnology revolution to enter in a new era. Sequencer's applications include evolutionary biology (evolution of plants and animals), genetic tests, forensics, paternity tests, metagenomics (identification of organisms present in air or water), pharmacogenomics (identification of genes that may favour or block the efficacy of medicines in patients) and many others. The biotechnology innovation cascade would have never unfolded in so short period of time if not for the contribution of DNA sequencers.

5 Conclusion

For centuries, evolutionary innovation has taken place in Western countries at its own slow pace. Radical innovation, conversely, has taken place most often in advanced scientific and industrial nations, and occasionally in emergent nations. Innovation cascades of today exist in affluent (Europe, North America, and Japan) and emergent capitalist nations, China and South Korea.

We are not aware of innovation cascades taking place in developing countries, but occasionally such countries produce a radical innovation. Mokyr (1990) suggested that many Chinese innovations (silk, porcelain, gunpowder, clocks, printing, iron suspension bridges, advanced ships, etc.) were either suppressed or controlled by bureaucratic restraint of the Ming dynasty (1368–1644), and their diffusion was sometimes forbidden by the central government. In Europe, instead, political divisions favoured the diffusion of advanced scientific or technical ideas from one country to others. No autocratic European ruler or the Catholic Church could completely suppress technical and scientific advancement in Europe, thus leaving free course to innovation cascades.

Innovation cascades are taking place even more frequently within different sectors of the advanced economies. Up to now most of them, if not all, from those that occurred before the Industrial Revolution to modern times high-tech ones, have taken place in industrial advanced nations. To impact economic growth, such cascades require an ecosystem of institutions, one that is only provided by the national systems of innovation in those countries.

Innovation cascades seem not so much linked to regional knowledge spillovers, as argued by Antonelli, even if at the origins there may be a hub or several ones of knowledge creation. They are not either linked to large firm behaviour in oligopolistic markets, like Delapierre and Mytelka suggested. They are more often determined by a rapid increase in knowledge production in a rising number of countries and organisations. They are also linked to increasing international scientific and technical collaboration.

Innovation cascades are such that their technological trajectories are difficult to foresee. They have their own dynamics, and often confound their own main agents. By nature, radical innovation is difficult to foresee. Streams of radical innovation are even more so.

This paper suggest that innovation cascades have become more frequent in the past half century and will become more so in the years to come, as the frontiers of science advance very fast, the number of loci of knowledge creation increases, and international research collaboration soars multiplying the chances of radical recombination, and brand new novelty.

Also, innovation cascades force us to revise our evolutionary models including concepts such as path dependency, technological trajectories, and lock-in. Some room must be left to path creation, technological uncertainty and radical novelty.

References

Achilladelis B, Swarzkopf A, Cines M (1990) The dynamics of technological innovation: the case of the chemical industry. Res Policy 19(1):1–34

Antonelli C (2008) Pecuniary knowledge externalities: the convergence of technological change and the emergence of innovation systems. Ind Corp Chang 17(5):1049–1070

Antonelli C (2009) Localised appropriability: pecuniary externalities in knowledge exploitation. Tech Anal Strat Manag 21(6):727–742

Arthur WB (2009) The nature of technology: what it is and how it evolves. Free Press, New York

Basalla G (1988) The evolution of technology. Cambridge University Press, Cambridge

Berkers E, Geels FW (2011) System innovation through stepwise reconfiguration: the case of technological transitions in Dutch greenhouse horticulture (1930–1980). Tech Anal Strat Manag 23(3):227–247

Bessant J, Caffyn S, Gilbert J, Harding R, Webb S (1994) Rediscovering continuous improvement. Technovation 14(1):17–29

Bhidé A (2000) The origin and evolution of new businesses. Oxford University Press, New York

Bourreau M et al (2012) The impact of radical innovation on business models; incremental adjustments or big bang? Ind Innov 19(5):415–435

Christensen CM (1997) The innovators' dilemma. Harvard Business Review Press, Boston

Christensen CM, Bower JL (1996) Customer power, strategic investment and the failure of leading firms. Strateg Manag J 17(3):197–218
Delapierre M, Mytelka L (2003) Cascades d'innovations et nouvelles stratégies oligopolistiques. Rev Econ Ind 103:233–252
Dennis C (2002) China: stem cell rise in the East. Nature 419:334
Dosi G (1982) Technological paradigms and technological trajectories: a suggested interpretation of the determinants and directions of technological change. Res Policy 11:147–162
Geels FW (2002) Technological transitions as evolutionary reconfiguration processes: a multi-level perspective and a case study. Res Policy 31(8–9):1257–1274
Gibbons M, Littler D (1979) The development of an innovation: the case of Porvair. Res Policy 8 (1):2–25
Gould S (1977) Return of the hopeful monster. Nat Hist 86:24–30
Grene M (2007) The demise of the lone author. Nature 450(7173):1165
Heather JM, Chain B (2016) The sequence of sequencers: the history of sequencing DNA. Genomics 107:1–8
Kortum S, Lerner J (1999) What is behind the recent surge in patenting? Res Policy 28:1–22
Lane D (2012) The dynamics of innovation cascades: is the innovation society sustainable? In: A presentation to the ISS Conference, Brisbane, July
Lane D, Maxfield R (1996) Strategy under complexity: fostering generative relationships. Long Range Plan 29(2):215–231
Larsen PO, von Ins M (2010) The rate of growth in scientific publication and the decline of coverage provided by SCI. Scientometrics 84:575–603
Malerba F (2006) Innovation and the evolution of industries. J Evol Econ 16:3–23
McIntyre S (1988) Perspective: market adaptation as a process in the product life cycle of radical innovations and high technology products. J Prod Innov Manag 5(2):140–149
McKelvey M (1996) Evolutionary innovation: the business of biotechnology. Oxford University Press, Oxford
Mokyr J (1990) The lever of riches. Oxford University Press, Oxford
Mokyr J (2002) The gifts of Athena: historical origins of the knowledge economy. Princeton University Press, Princeton
Mueller JM (2006) The tiger awakens: the tumultuous transformation of India's patent system and the rise of Indian pharmaceutical innovation. Univ Pittsburgh Law Rev 68:491
Nelson RR (2006) Evolutionary social science and universal Darwinism. J Evol Econ 16:491–510
Nelson RR, Winter S (1982) An evolutionary theory of economic change. Belknap Press of Harvard University, Cambridge
O'Connor GC, McDermott CM (2004) The human side of radical innovation. J Eng Tech Manag 21:11–30
Pavitt K (1984) Sectoral patterns of technical change: towards a taxonomy and a theory. Res Policy 13:343–373
Petroski H (1994) The evolution of useful things. Random House, New York
Rothwell R (1980) The impact of regulation on innovation. Technol Forecast Soc Chang 17 (1):7–34
Rothwell R, Wissema H (1986) Technology, culture and public policy. Technovation 4(2):91–115
Sainio LM, Ritala P, Hurmelinna-Laukkanen P (2012) Constituents of radical innovation – exploring the role of strategic orientations and market uncertainty. Technovation 32:591–599
Schumpeter J (1939) Business cycles. McGraw-Hill, New York
Souder WE (1983) Organising for modern technology and innovation: a review and synthesis. Technovation 2(1):27–44
Wagner C, Leydersdorff L (2005) Network structure, self organization and the growth of international collaboration in science. Res Policy 34(10):1608–1618

Schumpeterian Incumbents and Industry Evolution

Guido Buenstorf

Abstract This essay explores the role of established firms in the evolution of innovative industries. Both direct and indirect contributions are discussed. Besides innovation in their own industries, established firms are often among the pioneering entrants into related markets. They enable spin-off entrepreneurship and provide exit options for startups through acquisition. Furthermore, established firms help shape and directly support public research activities. The multiple roles of established firms, their interaction with new entrants in the innovation process, and the dynamics on industry evolution in an increasingly globalized world are not sufficiently well understood.

1 Introduction[1]

"Schumpeterian entrepreneur" is a frequently used term in economics as well as in the broader populace. It generally characterizes the founders of innovative startups. Often, these startups are juxtaposed to rigid incumbent behemoths that are unwilling and/or unable to develop innovative products or processes. This essay will argue for a more nuanced view on established firms. There are indeed many instances of industry incumbents failing to react to innovative challenges or even proactively pursue innovations. At the same time, a sizeable theoretical and empirical literature shows that larger firms have stronger incentives to innovate, that incumbents often drive innovative changes in their own industries, and that established firms are

[1]This essay is based on a plenary talk given at the 2014 International Joseph A. Schumpeter Society Conference in Jena, Germany. I am grateful for a number of helpful comments and suggestions. The ideas expressed in this essay are strongly shaped by countless discussions with the late Steven Klepper, and also by his eminent contributions to entrepreneurship and industry evolution.

G. Buenstorf (✉)
Department of Economics and INCHER-Kassel, University of Kassel, Moenchebergstrasse 17, 34109 Kassel, Germany

Institute of Innovation and Entrepreneurship, University of Gothenburg, Göteborg, Sweden

Leibniz Institute of Economic Research (IWH), Halle, Germany
e-mail: buenstorf@uni-kassel.de

A. Pyka, U. Cantner (eds.), *Foundations of Economic Change*, Economic Complexity and Evolution, DOI 10.1007/978-3-319-62009-1_13

pioneering entrants into newly emerging markets. Incumbents moreover enable innovation by involuntarily training future entrepreneurs, by providing exit options for startup founders and investors, and by supporting public research. Thus, there are multiple ways in which established firms directly or indirectly contribute to innovation and drive industry evolution. These contributions justify the characterization of (some) established firms as "Schumpeterian incumbents". It is the purpose of this essay to draw attention to these contributions, and also to their implications for future research on industry evolution.

Arguing that both established and new firms can be innovative is of course anything but original. More than 100 years ago Schumpeter already allowed for both possibilities. Even though this *Theory of Economic Development* (Schumpeter 1911/1934) highlighted the role of individual innovators, it also recognized that some innovation was realized by large established firms. In Schumpeter's later work, incumbents took center stage in the innovation process (Schumpeter 1942). Inspired by these contributions, a sizable empirical literature has explored the relative merits of small versus large, as well as young versus old, firms in the innovation process. This research has led to numerous important insights and an improved understanding of both innovation and industrial dynamics. These achievements notwithstanding, we still do not fully understand the interaction of different types of firms in the dynamics of innovative change. It therefore seems about time to shift the conceptual focus from innovation "beauty contests" between startups and incumbents toward a more "systemic" view on how their activities interact and jointly drive the evolution of innovative industries.

The remainder of this essay is organized as follows. Section 2 discusses findings on innovation by industry incumbents. Sections 3 and 4 focus on diversification and the role of incumbents in the spin-off process. Section 5 proposes that acquisitions by incumbents are important to induce startup entry, and Sect 6 calls attention to the role of established firms in performing and inducing basic research. Implications for future research are presented in the concluding remarks of Sect 7.

2 Incumbents Are Important Innovators

How innovative are incumbents compared to new entrants, in particular startups? This is a key issue in the economics of innovation and industry evolution. Many have suggested that incumbents are structurally disadvantaged vis-à-vis entrants. A variety of reasons for incumbent failure in the face of "competence-destroying" (Tushman and Anderson 1986) innovations have been suggested. As established organizations, incumbent firms are constrained by the imprint they received at the time of founding (Stinchcombe 1965) and subject to structural inertia that limits their capacity to adapt to environmental change (Hannan and Freeman 1984). Internal division of innovative labor along product components may restrict incumbents in their ability to cope with "architectural" innovation altering the linkages between product components more than the individual components themselves (Henderson and Clark 1990). Subsequent work by Christensen famously emphasized incumbents' excessive focus on existing customers as a source of failure (Christensen 1993; Christensen and Rosenbloom 1995). His notion of "disruptive innovation" has attracted a great deal of attention among management scholars as well as practitioners, and "disruption" has become a buzzword (not only) in the Silicon Valley entrepreneurship community (Lepore 2014). But how general are these concerns? Are we really seeing that most innovations are introduced by new entrants, let alone startup or *de novo* entrants?[2] At least three bodies of literature suggest otherwise: first, empirical work on productivity changes in industries showing the importance of incumbents' increasing productivity, second, work inspired by the so-called "Schumpeter hypotheses" suggesting that larger firm size and market concentration are conducive to innovation, and third, the related work on industry evolution.

The development of productivity levels within firms and industries provides a first impression on how incumbents contribute to the development of industries.[3] While the discussion on measuring and explaining productivity is ongoing, existing work shows that growing productivity of existing firms substantially contributes to overall productivity increases (e.g., Cantner and Krueger 2008; Foster et al. 2008; Krueger 2014). In addition, more productive incumbents also tend to grow faster than less productive competitors. This evidence is relevant for the present discussion inasmuch as productivity changes are driven by innovation.

The literature on firm size and innovation is informative in the present context because firm size and age are not independent. While small firms need not be young, very few firms start big. The vast majority of large firms entered small and have taken years to grow to their present size (cf., e.g., Cabral and Mata 2003). Empirical results on the innovation performance of large firms can therefore tell us something about incumbents. A proportional relationship between firm size and R&D expenditure is generally observed, but the productivity of R&D efforts seems to decrease with firm size. In addition, smaller firms tend to engage in more radical innovation, whereas larger ones focus more on incremental and process-oriented innovation (cf. Cohen 2010, for a survey of the underlying literature).[4]

The cost spreading model (Cohen and Klepper 1996) can account for these findings. It is based on the insight that firms with large output volumes of a given product have stronger incentives to generate cost-reducing process innovations.[5]

[2]There is an important difference between new firm formation and entry into new industries. New entrants into an industry are not necessarily newly established firms. A conceptual distinction is therefore made between *de novo* entrants, i.e., new ventures, and *de alio* entrants, i.e., firms that have already been active in other industries. Hybrid forms also exist (cf. Helfat and Lieberman 2002).

[3]I am grateful to an anonymous reviewer for making this point.

[4]There is little systematic research into whether new entrants, notably startups, are particularly prone to generate radical innovation (Cohen 2010).

[5]A crucial assumption underlying the cost-spreading model is that there are no well-functioning markets for technology and firms engage in R&D activities for their own use (cf. Cohen 2010, for a discussion).

Costs of R&D do not increase if the ensuing process innovation is applied to a large production volume. This entails that costs of R&D *per unit output* decrease with increasing output scale, providing the larger firm with a stronger incentive to engage in R&D. With diminishing returns to R&D, the ability of larger firms to spread their R&D expenditures over a larger output base can also explain their poorer R&D productivity, as more marginal R&D projects may still be profitable for them, but not for smaller competitors. Importantly, then, it is differences in incentives, not capabilities, that underlie the lower R&D productivity of larger firms.

Innovation by entrants and incumbents has also been explored in the theoretical and empirical work on industry evolution (cf. Peltoniemi 2011, for a survey). In stark contrast to the conjectures about incumbent failure discussed above, this literature suggests and finds that incumbents may have systematic advantages over entrants in innovation. Klepper's (1996) seminal model of industry evolution incorporates the cost spreading model originally developed to understand the relationship between firm size and innovation. In this model profitable firms grow. The larger (and therefore older) they are, the stronger are their incentives to invest in cost-reducing process innovation and to grow further. Cost spreading thus generates dynamic increasing returns to process R&D, providing early entrants with a sustainable competitive advantage over later ones.

Given the disparate predictions derived from different theoretical perspectives, incumbents' (dis-) advantages in innovation are an empirical issue. In part drawing on data collected by other authors before (Abernathy et al. 1983, for automobiles; Warner 1966, for tires), Klepper and Simons (1997) have shown that in the U.S. automobile industry, the two market leaders, Ford and GM, accounted for 34% of the major product innovations before 1940, considerably below their joint market share. In contrast, both firms accounted for 21 of the 27 (or 78%) major process innovations listed for this time period, which exceeded their joint market share. An even more favorable (from the incumbent perspective) picture emerges for the historical U.S. tire industry, where incumbents dominated both process and product innovation (Klepper and Simons 1997). In particular, with cord and balloon tires they pioneered the most significant product design innovations introduced before World War 2. Numbers of tire-related patents confirms these results (Buenstorf and Klepper 2010). In the industry's first three decades, only a minority of firms had any patents, and those which did tended to be large. The Top 5 producers consistently accounted for more than 75% of all patents, which was considerably above their joint market share.[6]

[6]Other research has pointed out that U.S. tire producers eventually lost their dominance when they were challenged by the ascent of the radial tire in the 1970s (Sull 2001). It is noteworthy in this context that the radial tire was not introduced by innovative startups, but by established European producers (in particular, Michelin from France) diversifying into the U.S. market. A similar account can be given for the decline of the U.S. automobile industry after the entry of Japanese producers. Diversifying entry will be in the focus of the subsequent section.

The U.S. automobile and tire industries are well-known examples of industries that experienced severe shakeouts early in their evolution. A striking contrast is provided by the U.S. laser industry, where no shakeout was observable 35 years into the industry's history. Bhaskarabhatla and Klepper (2014) developed a theoretical model to explain the development of "submarket" industries such as lasers. In these industries a multitude of product types compete in separate submarkets, because substitutability across product types is severely limited and there are no pronounced economies of scope. As in Klepper (1996), the model is driven by dynamic increasing returns based on cost spreading for process innovations. However, initially all submarkets are too small to justify investments into process R&D. The dynamics of the Klepper (1996) model set in only when unexpected technological change gives rise to an escalation of R&D efforts causing one of the submarkets to grow. This growing "integrative" submarket successively gains in importance, while other submarkets become obsolete, which causes a shakeout at the aggregate industry level. Based on their stronger incentive to (process) innovate, the earliest entrants into the integrative submarket grow to dominate first this submarket and subsequently the entire industry.

Bhaskarabhatla and Klepper (2014) argue that diode-pumped solid state (DPSS) lasers constituted an integrative submarket and led to a severe shakeout of U.S. laser producers beginning in the mid-1990s. They show that the leading patenters in the core technology of this submarket (wavelength conversion) were Coherent and Spectra Physics, two early entrants into the laser industry and then the two largest U.S. laser producers. Both firms aggressively entered the new submarket, producing a larger variety of DPSS lasers than most of their competitors.

As these examples suggest, it is too simplistic to view incumbents as being large, bureaucratic behemoths that are blown away as soon as seriously innovative new entrants enter the stage. It is easy to find further evidence against a too pessimistic view on incumbents. For instance, established producers accounted for large shares of early entrants into new submarkets in the U.S. diagnostic imaging industry (Mitchell 1991). In the contemporary global automobile industry, incumbent producers are leading radical innovations such as hybrid and fuel cell vehicles (Toyota), electric automobiles (GM, Nissan/Renault and BMW—but of course also Tesla as an innovative new entrant), and even car-sharing platforms (BMW, Daimler).

In spite of this evidence, we still do not fully understand which incumbents are more successful and under what conditions they are able to outcompete entrants. As noted above, there is substantial evidence that incumbents tend to focus on the more incremental and process-oriented innovations. Possibly, however, it is not incumbency itself but rather a lack of competition in mature, oligopolistic industries that makes incumbents prone to complacency and thus vulnerable to innovative entry. In line with this conjecture, the DPSS laser was introduced in an industry that had not yet experienced a shakeout in the number of active producers, and competition in the global automobile market is intense.

3 Incumbents Diversify and Innovate in Related Industries

As the literature on industry evolution shows, the innovation performance of established firms can often not be assessed based on individual markets alone. Just because innovators come from outside an established industry they are not necessarily startups. As an illustrative case in point, consider Apple's iPhone, the radical innovation that disrupted the global market for mobile telephones. When the first-generation iPhone was launched in 2007, Apple Computers Inc. was 31 years old and, according to its 2006 Annual Report, had about 18,000 employees. Clearly, then, the iPhone was not developed by an entrepreneurial startup, but by a successful established firm that diversified into the market for mobile phones. In doing so Apple leveraged the capabilities it had previously built up in the computer and music player markets.[7]

Diversification of established firms into new markets is a "natural" phenomenon. It enables these firms to re-deploy resources that have been made redundant by organizational learning (Penrose 1959/1995). The crucial role of diversifying entrants in the emergence and evolution of industries has been demonstrated in a variety of industry contexts. Diversifying bicycle, carriage and engine producers figured prominently in the early history of the U.S. and German automobile industries (Klepper 2002; Cantner et al. 2006). In the German industry, the share of innovators was twice as large among experienced entrants as among non-experienced ones (Cantner et al. 2009). Similarly, the first U.S. pneumatic automobile tire was introduced in 1986 by B.F. Goodrich, a rubber goods producing firm established 25 years before (French 1991). The U.S. television receiver shows an even more extreme pattern (Klepper and Simons 2000). Not only were diversifiers from the radio industry numerous in this industry, but there was not a single significant TV producer that had *not* diversified from radios. Diversifying radio producers, in particular the larger ones, were also more innovative than other entrants. More recently, many of the pioneering entrants into the U.S. and German laser industries were diversifiers from electronics, optics, or mechanical engineering (Sleeper 1998; Buenstorf 2007).

These examples illustrate that the innovative record of incumbents is grossly underestimated when only their current industries are taken into account. Incumbents in one industry can be innovative diversifying entrants in other, often related, industries. Diversifiers account for a substantial share of entrants in many industries, and are often found among the pioneering innovators. This tendency of innovative diversification into related markets has important implications for the economic development of regions and entire economies. As Frenken and Boschma (2012) highlight in their "branching theory", it entails that new industries frequently

[7]Note also the similar origins of the conventional mobile phone that the iPhone successfully challenged. The mobile phone had first been commercialized in 1983/1984 by Motorola, then 55 years old, and Nokia, then 119 years old. Both firms were diversifiers with substantial experience in related markets.

emerge where related earlier industries are already found, thus giving rise to regional path dependence (Martin and Sunley 2006) and long-term regional imbalances. A similar argument can be made at the level of entire economies (Hidalgo et al. 2007).

4 Incumbents Are Seedbeds of Innovative Spin-Offs

The previous two sections focused on the innovative performance of established firms as incumbents in their own markets and as diversifying new entrants into related industries. This and the following sections will further broaden the perspective. They will argue that established firms make contributions to the evolution of innovative industries that go beyond their own innovation activities. To begin this discussion of indirect or enabling effects of incumbents, first their role in spin-off entrepreneurship will be scrutinized.

(Intra-industry) spin-offs are defined as entrepreneurial ventures started by former employees of incumbent firms active in the same industry that the spin-off enters. Spin-off entrepreneurship has received substantial scholarly attention in the past decades. Time and again, spin-offs have been found to outperform other types of *de novo* entrants and to be similar to diversifiers in their success (Klepper 2009). To date, there is no conclusive evidence showing that the performance of spin-offs is due to on-the-job learning of subsequent spin-off entrepreneurs. However, several empirical patterns are consistent with spin-offs benefitting from their founders' prior experiences. For instance, more successful incumbents tend to have more spin-offs, and their spin-offs are generally higher performers than those of humbler origins. The first-generation products of spin-offs moreover tend to be similar to those made by the parent firm (ibid., Golman and Klepper 2016). These patterns suggest that spin-off founders indeed acquired useful knowledge on their prior jobs, and that superior incumbents are superior training grounds for aspiring entrepreneurs.

A recurrent pattern in the spin-off process is that employees develop some innovative variant to the parent firm's product and/or some modification of the parent's strategy, and leave the parent firm after they fail to find support for their innovation from the firm's management (Garvin 1983; Klepper and Thompson 2010). Incumbents thus enable their employees (and future spin-off entrepreneurs) to generate new knowledge resulting in innovative products and processes, but are often unable or unwilling to employ this knowledge in the market. Empirical findings from the U.S. disk drive industry (Agarwal et al. 2004) nicely illustrate this tension. In this industry, both the technological capabilities of incumbent firms and their market-pioneering know how (proxied by early entry into new product submarkets) were associated with a higher propensity of (involuntarily) spawning spin-offs. However, the interaction effect of both types of capabilities was significantly negative. This indicates that spin-offs primarily formed in firms that produced more knowledge than they utilized themselves.

As others have pointed out before (e.g., Klepper and Sleeper 2005), incumbent firms may have good reasons not to pursue an innovative technology that they have developed. Product innovations may "cannibalize" their existing products and threaten their legitimacy or organizational identity (Hannan and Freeman 1984; Hannan et al. 2006). In other cases, failure to commercialize new technologies may reflect poor managerial decision making. Or highly innovative firms such as Intel may simply generate more employee inventions than they could possibly commercialize (Moore and Davis 2004). Either way, spin-off entrepreneurship is important to prevent the new technology from being "shelved". Incumbents then have an ambiguous role in the spin-off process. On the one hand, they are the ones that—for whatever reason—fail to innovate. But on the other hand, they provide the context in which the underlying invention is made. In this sense, incumbents enable innovative spin-off entrepreneurship. To the extent that the innovative technology could not, or not as quickly, have been developed in a different environment, they thus contribute to the evolution of the industry (and sometimes to their own eventual demise).

In this perspective, a "hotbed" of spin-offs such as Fairchild Semiconductors deserves credit for the innovations of its spin-offs (the proverbial "Fairchildren" including Intel and AMD), which contributed to the rapid development of information and communication technology as well as the ascent of Silicon Valley as the world's leading high-tech cluster. At the same time, spin-off entrepreneurship is one of the processes in which the interaction of incumbents and entrepreneurial entrants contributes to innovation and drives industry evolution. With the acquisition of startups by incumbents, a second form of interaction will be explored in the next section.

5 Incumbents Acquire Innovative Startups

Firm exit is a key element in the population dynamics of industry evolution. Even in industries that have not (yet) experienced a shakeout in the number of active firms, pronounced "churning" is generally observed within the firm population, with substantial numbers of firms entering and exiting the market. A large number of studies of industry evolution have analyzed firm performance using longevity as a performance measure, and exit as an indicator of poor performance. These studies often acknowledge that not all firm exit is equally indicative of failure. The precise nature of exit is rarely explored, however (for a notable exception, cf. Krueger and von Rhein 2009).

In many industries acquisition events contribute substantially to the observed rates of firm exit. When firms exit because they are acquired by another firm (often a larger competitor), it is particularly problematic to interpret their exit as indicating poor performance. Being acquired by a competitor may indeed constitute the last resort of a failing firm to prevent impending bankruptcy. However, in many cases acquisition reflects success rather than failure. In some contemporary industries, the acquisition of innovative startups by large incumbent firms with superior production and distribution capabilities to profit from innovations is a pervasive phenomenon. It is observable, for instance, in the laser industry, where large incumbents such as Coherent and Spectra Physics have acquired many of their smaller competitors. This has enabled them to broaden their product portfolios and to serve a wider spectrum of customer needs.

The importance of acquisition events has attracted attention in several lines of literature, including the research on university technology transfer. Studying the commercialization of inventions from the University of California system based on licensing to incumbents and inventor startups, Lowe and Ziedonis (2006: 183) observe: "Virtually all inventor-founded start-ups that commercialized an invention were acquired, and all but two of these firms were acquired prior to commercialization. Most unacquired firms remain in product development with no significant sales." Similarly, the division of labor between biotechnology inventors and pharmaceutical commercializers is a well-established pattern of innovation (cf., e.g., Powell et al. 2005).

Where acquisitions of innovative startups by incumbents are widespread, the respective incumbents play another indirect role in the innovation process. They provide an important channel of profitable exit for founders and investors. If prospective entrepreneurs and investors of innovative startups have reason to expect that in the event of success they may sell their venture to an established firm, this will *ceteris paribus* increase the attractiveness of the venture and its chances to be organized and funded in the first place. The importance of acquisition as an exit strategy for investors has further increased since the ascent of professional venture capital firms, particularly in countries where (and at times when) IPOs are rare events. As a consequence, the role of incumbents in facilitating entry through being potential acquirers has also been strengthened. And obviously, this role is even more important if incumbents become corporate venture capitalists themselves.

6 Incumbents Perform and Induce Basic Research

The corporate R&D laboratory was one of the key organizational innovations of the nineteenth century (Hounshell and Smith 1988). Its diffusion resulted in major shifts in the innovation process, which in turn helps explain the shifting locus of innovation suggested in Schumpeter's writings. Most research performed in corporate R&D laboratories is of an applied nature and directly feeds into the respective firm's innovation output. But this is not universally true: corporate R&D labs also engage in basic research activities. These activities warrant attention as another indirect contribution that incumbent firms make to the evolution of innovative industries.

By its very nature, basic research is fraught by uncertainty regarding its success as well as its range of potential applications. In his pioneering work on the economics of innovation, Nelson (1959) suggested that more diversified firms are more likely to engage in basic research because they are more likely to find a useful application of its uncertain results. This application may be within the scope of their existing activities, in which case basic research adds to their innovative performance in their industry of origin. In other cases, basic research activities may lead to results that motivate incumbents to diversify into new markets. Unexploited findings of incumbents' basic research activities may lead to spin-offs with or without parent firm involvement (a prominent case in point is Xerox PARC, cf. Chesbrough 2003).

A recent popular book (Gertner 2012) relates the history of the Bell Labs, AT&T's R&D laboratories that arguably constituted the most important corporate R&D establishment in history. The Bell Labs were the birthplace of numerous key discoveries and inventions. New knowledge from the Bell Labs provided the foundation of present-day high-technology industries, and also of a number of Nobel prizes. Scientists at the Bell Labs also invented or co-invented some of the technologies extensively studied in the empirical literature on industry evolution, including the transistor and the laser. This provides direct evidence that established firms can be crucial in the emergence of innovative new industries.

The Bell Labs were an extreme case of basic research activities by large firms. However, they were not unique. As an example from a different empirical context, consider the German Siemens firm and its entry into laser research in the early 1960s (Albrecht et al. 2011). Siemens' first laser was constructed in 1960/1961 by Dieter Röss, a young university graduate who had recently joined the firm's central research laboratory (Albrecht 1997). Röss (personal communication) enjoyed far-reaching autonomy to choose his objects of research. He had become interested in laser technology because he sensed it might become relevant for Siemens. However, much in line with the well-known quip that the laser initially was a solution in search of a suitable problem, Röss started his research into lasers without having a specific market or product in mind. He was able to initiate contacts to some of the leading U.S. research groups and quickly managed to catch up to the global frontier of laser research (Albrecht 1997). In 1961, Röss constructed an improved laser design, and subsequently Siemens became a pioneering producer in the German laser industry.

Other well-known examples notwithstanding, the role of incumbents' research activities in the, as it were, prehistoric phase on industry evolution has not been explored in much detail. It is conceivable that the direct involvement of incumbents in basic research has become less important in recent decades as competitive pressure and short-term profit orientations have tended to increase. Even if this were true, however, incumbents could still exert a relevant influence on basic research activities. Substantial evidence suggests that established firms help shape the research agendas of universities and government labs, thereby inducing basic research activities that promise to contribute to their own innovativeness. While possibly quite important for how innovative industries evolve, this indirect effect of incumbents on public research has largely been neglected in the empirical work on industry evolution. In contrast, reverse influences of universities and government labs on innovation and industry evolution have figured more prominently (cf., e.g., Stuart and Sorenson's (2003) work on U.S. biotechnology).

A detailed account how incumbent firms and related public research activities mutually condition and support each other is provided by Murmann's (2003, 2013) comparative historical study of the synthetic dye industry. Murmann adopts the conceptual framework of coevolution of industries and their environment (Nelson 1994) to highlight that the two are interdependent. While Murmann's historic case study presents substantial evidence of firms benefiting from public research, his findings on the "reverse" effects of dye producers on public research activities are most relevant from the perspective of this essay. Murmann (2013) stresses three conduits through which such effects were realized: exchange of personnel, commercial ties, and lobbying on behalf of research facilities that were of interest to the synthetic dye producers. He shows that industry demand for organic chemists influenced the structure of chemistry departments, that access to collaboration partners and industry grants affected the location choices of leading scientists, and that lobbying efforts contributed to the establishment of new government labs.

Using a conceptual framework similar to the one adopted by Murmann, Blankenberg and Buenstorf (2016) study the regional coevolution of firm population, private-sector R&D and public research in the more recent context of the German laser industry. Similar to the historical dye industry, qualitative evidence suggests that laser producers not only benefited from public research activities but also exerted a non-negligible influence on the scope and direction of these activities. Blankenberg and Buenstorf (2016) begin to quantitatively address these coevolutionary dynamics. For this purpose they utilize regional data on firm populations spanning over a 45-year period from the outset of the German laser industry. They combine these data with information about laser-related patent applications from the private sector, as well as with scientific publications and laser-related doctoral dissertations as proxies of public research activities. To probe into the idea of regional coevolution, they estimate a set of reduced-form vector autoregressions considering changes in firm population size, private-sector innovation and public research activities at the level of West German planning regions. For a variety of alternative lag lengths Granger causal relationships are obtained for the effect of public research on private sector activities, but also for the reverse effect of regional firm population size and private-sector patent output on laser-related public research activities. These results are consistent with the idea of coevolution. They indicate that, via their effect on public research, incumbents may perform another relevant indirect role in the evolution of innovative industries.

7 Concluding Remarks

What is the contribution of incumbent firms to innovation and industry evolution? In other words, how and in what sense can incumbents be "Schumpeterian"? To approach this issue, the present essay drew on diverse lines of scholarly work. It touched upon several processes through which established firms directly or indirectly influence innovation activities within and outside their own industry. These processes have all found some attention in the diverse literature on innovation. However, they are reflected to differing degrees in the theoretical and empirical work on industry evolution.

Starting point of the essay was the literature on firm size and R&D. I then broadened the focus and called attention to the importance of diversifying established firms as innovative entrants into new markets. I also emphasized the role of incumbents in (involuntarily) breeding innovative spin-off entrepreneurs. Diversification and spin-off entrepreneurship both figure prominently in the research on industry evolution. In contrast, little has been written in this literature about acquisition as an exit strategy for innovative startups. As has been argued above, acquiring competitors is another indirect role of incumbents in fostering innovation. By signaling the existence of profitable exit through acquisition, incumbents may induce the entry of innovative startups. This also allows them to "outsource" innovation activities for which startups may be better suited than they are themselves, and provides opportunities for mutually beneficial collaborative R&D projects (cf., e.g., Baum et al. 2000). We also know little about the extent to which industry incumbents are able to shape their environment, for instance by inducing public research to address issues that are relevant for their own innovation efforts.

The above discussion suggests at least four issues that future work on industry evolution could (and, in my view, should) address. First, the "division of innovative labor" between incumbents and startups is not fully understood. To improve our knowledge, it would seem fruitful to de-emphasize the relative merits of different types of firms as innovators and focus more on how these types of firms interact. Part of this interaction are the more indirect, enabling roles that incumbents may take in the innovation process. These indirect roles imply that innovative startups may require the presence of successful incumbents, and that successful incumbents may be the origin of self-reinforcing dynamics of industry evolution at various geographic scales. They also suggest that the evolution of innovative industries takes places in a broader systemic context including, among others, universities, policy makers, customers, suppliers, and horizontally related firms. This relevance of a broader context that exceeds the boundaries of a single industry, and is itself shaped by the evolution of the industry, is a core tenet of the work on innovation systems (e.g., Lundvall 1992; Nelson 1993; Malerba 2002)—a literature that still has the potential to enrich the research on industry evolution. At the same time, the population-based, dynamic approach taken in the empirical work on industry evolution has much to offer to inform empirical research on innovation systems and their evolution.

Second, we know little about how the various processes and interactions change over the life cycle of an industry. Existing evidence suggests that diversifying *de alio* entrants are most important in the early stage of a new industry, whereas spin-offs by their very nature can only emerge from incumbents that have entered before. But how does, for example, the importance of acquisitions change over time, and is the interaction with public research becoming more or less important as industries mature? More theoretical and empirical work seems to be required to provide answers to questions like these.

Third, and perhaps most importantly, the evolution of industry evolution is largely a black box. We know from the broader work on innovation that markets for technology are getting increasingly well established. As has been suggested before (Cohen 2010), increased tradability of technology may have profound effects on how industries evolve and on the extent to which first-mover and size advantages still matter. Other developments may also change the dynamics of industry evolution. These include the increasing societal interest in and policy support for entrepreneurship, which may affect the frequency but also the motivation and behavior of spin-off entrepreneurs. A similar case can be made for the increasing attention that policy makers (as well as university administrators) pay to industry-science interaction and technology transfer from public research. Last but not least, we are witnessing the rapid global expansion and integration of markets, which so far has not been sufficiently well addressed by the research on industry evolution. The widespread tendency to study national firm populations may be less and less appropriate in a world in which markets are increasingly global and the geography of industries may shift at a very rapid pace. Only a small number of internationally comparative studies on industry evolution have been produced (e.g., Chesbrough 1999). A more global outlook on industries will increasingly be required in future research.

In summary, there is still much to learned about industry evolution and how it is affected by Schumpeterian firms—both Schumpeterian startups and Schumpeterian incumbents.

References

Abernathy WJ, Clark KB, Kantrow AM (1983) Industrial renaissance: producing a competitive future for America. Basic Books, New York

Agarwal R, Echambadi R, Franco AM, Sarkar MB (2004) Knowledge transfer through inheritance: spin-out generation, development and survival. Acad Manag J 47:501–522

Albrecht H (1997) Laserforschung in Deutschland 1960–1970. Unpublished Habilitation Thesis, University of Stuttgart

Albrecht H, Buenstorf G, Fritsch M (2011) System? what system? the (Co-) evolution of laser research and laser innovation in Germany since 1960. Unpublished working paper, University of Kassel

Baum JAC, Calabrese T, Silverman BS (2000) Don't go it alone: alliance network composition and start up's performance in Canadian biotechnology. Strateg Manag J 21(3):267–294

Bhaskarabhatla A, Klepper S (2014) Latent submarket dynamics and industry evolution: lessons from the US laser industry. Ind Corp Chang 23(6):1381–1415

Blankenberg AK, Buenstorf G (2016) Regional co-evolution of firm population, innovation and public research? Evidence from the West German laser industry. Research Policy 45(4):857–868.

Buenstorf G (2007) Evolution on the shoulders of giants: entrepreneurship and firm survival in the German laser industry. Rev Ind Organ 20:179–202

Buenstorf G, Klepper S (2010) Submarket dynamics and innovation: the case of the US tire industry. Ind Corp Chang 19(5):1563–1587
Cabral LM, Mata J (2003) On the evolution of the firm size distribution: facts and theory. Am Econ Rev 93(4):1075–1090
Cantner U, Dressler K, Krueger JJ (2006) Firm survival in the German automobile industry. Empirica 33(1):49–60
Cantner U, Krueger JJ (2008) Micro-heterogeneity and aggregate productivity development in the German manufacturing sector. J Evol Econ 18(2):119–133
Cantner U, Krueger JJ, von Rhein K (2009) Knowledge and creative destruction over the industry life cycle: the case of the German automobile industry. Economica 76(301):132–148
Chesbrough H (1999) Arrested development: the experience of European hard disk drive firms in comparison with US and Japanese firms. J Evol Econ 9(3):287–329
Chesbrough H (2003) The governance and performance of Xerox's technology spin-off companies. Res Policy 32:403–421
Christensen CM (1993) The rigid disk drive industry: a history of commercial and technological turbulence. Bus Hist Rev 67(4):531–588
Christensen CM, Rosenbloom RS (1995) Explaining the attacker's advantage: technological paradigms, organizational dynamics, and the value network. Res Policy 24(2):233–257
Cohen WM (2010) Fifty years of empirical studies of innovative activity and performance. In: Hall B, Rosenberg N (eds) Handbook of the economics of innovation, vol 1. Elsevier, Amsterdam, pp 129–213
Cohen WM, Klepper S (1996) A reprise of size and R & D. Econ J 106:925–951
Foster L, Haltiwanger J, Syverson C (2008) Reallocation, firm turnover, and efficiency: selection on productivity or profitability? Am Econ Rev 98(1):394–425
French MJ (1991) The U.S. tire industry. Twayne Publishers, Boston
Frenken K, Boschma RA (2012) Economic development as a branching process. In: Buenstorf G (ed) Evolution, organization and economic behavior. Edward Elgar, Cheltenham, pp 185–196
Garvin DA (1983) Spin-offs and the new firm formation process. Calif Manag Rev 25:3–20
Gertner J (2012) The idea factory: bell labs and the great age of American innovation. Penguin, New York
Golman R, Klepper S (2016) Spinoffs and clustering. The RAND Journal of Economics, 47(2), 341-365.
Hannan MT, Baron JN, Hsu G, Kocak Ö (2006) Organizational identities and the hazard of change. Ind Corp Chang 15(5):755–784
Hannan MT, Freeman J (1984) Structural inertia and organizational change. Am Sociol Rev 49 (2):149–164
Helfat CE, Lieberman M (2002) The birth of capabilities: market entry and the importance of pre-history. Ind Corp Chang 11:725–760
Henderson RM, Clark KB (1990) Architectural innovation: the reconfiguration of existing product technologies and the failure of established firms. Adm Sci Q 35(1):9–30
Hidalgo CA, Klinger B, Barabási AL, Hausmann R (2007) The product space conditions the development of nations. Science 317(5837):482–487
Hounshell DA, Smith JK (1988) Science and corporate strategy: Du Pont R&D, 1902–1980. Cambridge University Press, Cambridge
Klepper S (1996) Entry, exit and growth, and innovation over the product life cycle. Am Econ Rev 86:562–583
Klepper S (2002) The capabilities of new firms and the evolution of the US automobile industry. Ind Corp Chang 11(4):645–666
Klepper S (2009) Spinoffs: a review and synthesis. Eur Manag Rev 6(3):159–171
Klepper S, Simons KL (1997) Technological extinctions of industrial firms: an inquiry into their nature and causes. Ind Corp Chang 6(2):379–460
Klepper S, Simons KL (2000) Dominance by birthright: entry of prior radio producers and competitive ramifications in the US television receiver industry. Strateg Manag J 21 (10–11):997–1016

Klepper S, Sleeper SD (2005) Entry by spinoffs. Manag Sci 51(8):1291–1306
Klepper S, Thompson P (2010) Disagreements and intra-industry spinoffs. Int J Ind Organ 28 (5):526–538
Krueger JJ (2014) Intrasectoral structural change and aggregate productivity development: robust stochastic nonparametric frontier function estimates. Empir Econ 46(4):1545–1572
Krueger JJ, von Rhein K (2009) Knowledge, profitability and exit of German car manufacturing firms. Econ Innov New Technol 18(2):107–122
Lepore J (2014) The disruption machine: what the gospel of innovation gets wrong. New Yorker Mag 23:30–36
Lowe RA, Ziedonis AA (2006) Overoptimism and the performance of entrepreneurial firms. Manag Sci 52(2):173–186
Lundvall B-A (1992) National systems of innovation and interactive learning. Pinter Publishers, London
Malerba F (2002) Sectoral systems of innovation and production. Res Policy 31(2):247–264
Martin R, Sunley P (2006) Path dependence and regional economic evolution. J Econ Geogr 6:395–437
Mitchell W (1991) Dual clocks: entry order influence on incumbent and newcomer market share and survival when specialized assets retain their value. Strateg Manag J 12:85–100
Moore G, Davis K (2004) Learning the silicon valley way. In: Bresnahan T, Gambardella A (eds) Building high-tech clusters: silicon valley and beyond. Cambridge University Press, Cambridge, pp 7–39
Murmann JP (2003) Knowledge and competitive advantage. Cambridge University Press, Cambridge
Murmann JP (2013) The coevolution of industries and important features of their environments. Organ Sci 24:58–78
Nelson RR (1959) The simple economics of basic scientific research. J Polit Econ 67:297–306
Nelson RR (1993) National innovation systems—a comparative analysis. Oxford University Press, New York
Nelson RR (1994) The co-evolution of technology, industrial structure, and supporting institutions. Ind Corp Chang 3:47–63
Peltoniemi M (2011) Reviewing industry life-cycle theory: avenues for future research. Int J Manag Rev 13:349–375
Penrose ET (1959/1995) The theory of the growth of the firm. Oxford University Press, Oxford
Powell WW, White DR, Koput KW, Owen-Smith J (2005) Network dynamics and field evolution: the growth of interorganizational collaboration in the life sciences. Am J Sociol 110 (4):1132–1205
Schumpeter JA (1911/1934) The theory of economic development. Transaction Publishers, New Brunswick
Schumpeter JA (1942) Capitalism, socialism and democracy. Harper and Brothers, New York
Sleeper SD (1998) The role of firm capabilities in the evolution of the laser industry: the making of a high-tech market. PhD Dissertation, Carnegie Mellon University, Pittsburgh
Stinchcombe AL (1965) Social structure and organizations. In: March JG (ed) Handbook of organizations. Rand McNally, Chicago, pp 142–193
Stuart T, Sorenson O (2003) The geography of opportunity: spatial heterogeneity in founding rates and the performance of biotechnology firms. Res Policy 32:229–253
Sull DN (2001) From community of innovation to community of inertia: the rise and fall of the U.S. tire industry. Acad Manag Proc 2001(1):L1–L6
Tushman ML, Anderson P (1986) Technological discontinuities and organizational environments. Adm Sci Q 31:439–465
Warner SL (1966) Innovation and research in the automobile tire and tire-supporting industries. PhD Dissertation, Harvard University

Incremental by Design? On the Role of Incumbents in Technology Niches

An Evolutionary Network Analysis

Daniel S. Hain and Roman Jurowetzki

Abstract In this paper, we study the evolution of governance structures in technological niches. At the case of public funded research projects and the resulting cooperation networks related to smart grid and systems in Denmark, we raise the questions which actors over time inherit a central position—associated with high influence on the development of research trajectories—in the network. We are particularly interested in what role incumbent actors, connected to the old regime of fossil based energy production, play in shaping future technological trajectories. The protected space theoretically created by such public research funding offers firms an environment to experiment in joint learning activities on emerging technologies, shielded from the selection pressure on open markets, thereby facilitating socio-technological transitions. Generally, the engagement of large incumbent actors in the development of emerging technologies, particularly in joint research projects with entrepreneurial ventures, is positively perceived, as their resource endowment enables them to stem large projects and bring them all the way to the market.

However, growing influence of incumbents might also alter niche dynamics, making technology outcomes more incremental and adapted to the current technological regime. Potential influence on rate and direction of the technological development can to a large extend be explained by actors' positioning in the network of the niche's research activities. We create such a directed network of project consortium leaders with their partners to analyze if network dynamics of joint research projects in technological niches favor incumbent actors in a way that they are able to occupy central and dominant positions over time. To do so, we deploy a stochastic actor-oriented model of network dynamics, where we indeed discover path-dependent and cumulative effects favoring incumbents. Our findings suggest a development of the network towards an incumbent-dominated structure.

D.S. Hain (✉) • R. Jurowetzki
Department of Business and Management, IKE, Aalborg University, Fibigerstræde 11, 9220 Aalborg, Denmark
e-mail: dsh@business.aau.dk

A. Pyka, U. Cantner (eds.), *Foundations of Economic Change*, Economic Complexity and Evolution, DOI 10.1007/978-3-319-62009-1_14

1 Introduction

In order to address the environmental sustainability challenge many of the established large infrastructure related systems have to be transformed. One central area is the energy system. The shift from fossil based to renewable energy production is increasingly embraced as the solution, but the intermittent characteristics of electricity generated by sun and wind lead to severe implications for the electricity grid in its current architecture that is designed to transport steady energy from large central power plants to consumers. The construction of a smart grid and working towards a smart energy system is seen as a possibility to address this challenge. One issue that emerges in relation to this upcoming transformation is the ambivalent role of established firms from the energy sector. Their resources, capabilities, and cooperation are needed for this new development, yet they are likely to be the players that have a strong interest in maintaining the established systems unchanged.

In this paper, we study the evolution of governance structures in technological niches. At the case of public funded research projects and the resulting cooperation networks related to smart grid and systems in Denmark, we raise the questions which actors over time inherit a central position—associated with high influence on the development of research trajectories—in the network. We are particularly what role incumbent actors connected to the old regime of fossil based energy production play in shaping future technological trajectories.

The multidisciplinary literature on system innovation, often empirically focused on sustainability transitions, outlines the significance of niches for the protection and development of path-breaking technologies in early stages (Geels 2002, 2004; Hoogma et al. 2004; Kemp et al. 1998). Public funded research, development and demonstration (R&DD) protects represent such a protected space, offering firms an environment to experiment in joint learning activities on emerging technologies. In the same vein, literature originating from the Technological Innovation Systems (TIS) approach also highlights the importance of creating protected spaces to foster market formation and diffusion (Hekkert et al. 2007; Bergek et al. 2008).

The engagement of large incumbent actors in the development of emerging technologies, and especially joint research projects together with young SME's, is generally positively perceived as they have the capabilities to fulfill necessary systemic functions in a better way than new start-up firms (Suurs and Hekkert 2005). Apart from the direct effect of the engagement, it is likely to have a positive signaling effect. Thus, it might contribute positively to the status of the niche, improving financial viability and triggering interest of other companies (Smith et al. 2005). Arguably, the involvement of incumbents might, however, alter niche dynamics, making technology outcomes more incremental and adapted to the current unsustainable socio-technical regime. This is particularly evident if the emerging technology is a potential substitution to the existing solutions (Tushman and Anderson 1986; Bower and Christensen 1996). Indeed, literature on sustainable transitions suggests that incumbent actors—who over time carried out fixed investments in infrastructure, developed technological competences and secured market shares—have a high incentive to protect and replicate the old regime's logic and reinforce existing technological trajectories rather than develop new ones (Geels 2011). This reflects a more critical and nuanced consideration of network structures in research collaborations, which may not necessarily be fully cooperative and consensus oriented, as mostly envisioned in innovation system and networks oriented approaches (Hain 2016).

The incumbents' ability to influence the trajectory of technological development can, to a large extent, be explained by their position in the niche network. Here, a large body of literature on networks of innovators has produced ample theoretical reasoning and empirical evidence on how a firm's strategic positioning in interorganizational networks affect it's innovative performance (e.g. Powell et al. 1996; Baum et al. 2000), and the structure of the overall network affects the innovation output on the aggregated (Fleming et al. 2007) and firm-level (Schilling and Phelps 2007; Kudic 2014) alike. Consequently, firm-level cooperation choices build the micro-foundation for the rate and direction of innovation and technological chance in innovation networks. It is further argued that networks of innovators by no means are static constructs in time and space, but rather constantly rearrange in an evolutionary process, which is to a large extend path dependent (Doreian and Stokman 2005; Powell et al. 2005; Kilduff and Tsai 2003). Existing ties often tend to become more persistent over time (Burt 2000), and preferential attachment makes the likelihood of creating new ties influenced by the actors stock (Barabási 2005)—leading to a process of structural reinforcement (Gulati 1999). This effects are also well known determinants influencing the allocation of public research grants (Viner et al. 2004). In the terminology of innovation and transition literature, that relates to the development of a niche into a "proto-regime" (Geels and Raven 2006) with increasingly established institutions and emerging stabilization mechanisms. While these stabilization mechanisms are well-known features of social networks (e.g. Barabási and Albert 1999), the question how characteristics and rationales of central actors affect the outcome of such networks is discussed seldom from a network perspective.

Yet, when envisioning public funded research networks as technological niches, this question becomes particularly important for two reasons. First, the organization of public funded R&DD projects distinguishing between a project consortium leader and further project consortium partners by design imposes a governance structure, where project leaders are able to determine main parts of the project's content. Consequently, actors in central positions of such networks are likely to have a high influence on the rate and direction of future research through their higher social influence and their role as "knowledge hubs". Second, a main argument put forward to protect the space within technological niches is that they offer the actors the opportunity for broad experimentation which is not influenced by the selection pressure of the current regime (Smith and Raven 2012).

Having that said, to allow path-breaking ideas to unfold in technological niches, it becomes crucial that they initially contain a broad set of actors with heterogeneous knowledge bases as well as "hidden preferences" regarding the future development of the niche's technological trajectory. While over time evolutionary processes will lead to a concentration and consolidation of the network, in early phases broad experimentation in different direction is needed. A requirement for this endogenous selection processes to unfold is the emergence of internal selection logics. However, the smart grid as a technological niche is heavily connected to the current energy system, in terms of infrastructure and other physical assets as well as applied knowledge. Furthermore, public authorities who allocate resources in this niche are likely to be in some way connected to the old regime.

To conclude, path-dependent and cumulative characteristics representing the old regime and favoring incumbent players are replicated in the technological niche of smart grid research, evolutionary processes will enable them to obtain central and dominant positions and thus shape the niche's further development by their will.

Following earlier argumentation, actor-strategy driven network dynamics in technological niches can be assumed to lead to more incremental outcomes which reinforce old technological paths if (i) the network evolution is driven by endogenous and cumulative effects, such as the actors size, age, reputation or network position; (ii) incumbent actors embodying such characteristics are involved; and (iii) there exist possible new niche trajectories which lead to an underutilization of their accumulated resources.

The empirical context is the evolution within the Danish electricity grid-infrastructure network of joint participation in public funded R&DD projects in the period 2009 until 2012. Companies and projects were identified by exploring the Danish research project database. The Danish case is of particular interest because of the explicit political aspiration to become a European technology hub for the development and testing of advanced energy grid technologies (KEMIN 2013). A national smart grid strategy from May 2013 emphasizes the importance of interaction between research institutes, utilities and technology producers, and the development of various technologies. A number of research programs were established to support R&DD projects from basic research to large-scale demonstration and commercialization.

The purpose of the present paper is to study structural dynamics and path dependencies of research networks in technological niches at the case of public funded research projects. In particular, deploying a stochastic-actor-based model (Snijders et al. 2010a), we analyze if network dynamics of public funded R&DD in technological niches favor incumbent actors in a way that they are able to occupy central and dominant positions. Against the empirical and theoretical background, we conceptualize the research network as consisting of directed ties between the actors, assuming the project-leader to project-partner link as a hierarchically ordered relationship. By doing so, we are able to analyze up to now unobserved cumulative and self-reinforcing effects of network dynamics.

As a result, we indeed find such path-dependent and cumulative effects in the development of the research network that favor incumbent actors, in the long run leading to a reinforcing process of structural stabilization with central and influential positions.

The remainder of this paper is composed as follows: The following Sect. 2 aims at linking different streams of literature that advocate for the creation and protection of technological niches with network theory. This connection is made to understand strategies of different niche actors and possible macro outcomes of their behavior. Section 3 provides an overview of the technological and policy context of the smart grid development in Denmark. In Sect. 4 we introduce the stochastic actor-based model deployed to identify the evolution in the niche-network, and describe the research networks data used for the analysis as well as our empirical strategy. Section 5 presents the results, and the final Sect. 6 concludes.

2 Theoretical Background

2.1 *Inertia at Micro and Meso Levels in Large Technical Systems*

The achievement of the environmental sustainability goals—such as the reduction of greenhouse gas emissions, exhaustion of natural resources, and destruction of ecosystems—in highly dependent on the determination and ability to transform a number of large technical systems (LTS's) worldwide. LTS's, such as the energy grid, the transportation or the agri-food sector build complex, extremely interwoven technical, economic, institutional and administrative structures (Hughes 1987). Such sectors heavily build and rely on existing tangible and institutional infrastructures (e.g. development and trial systems, supplier and distribution networks, energy transmission grids, and other complementary assets). This dependence leads to high entry barriers in aforementioned industries and explains why key players are likely to be large companies (e.g. electric utilities, car manufacturers, railway operators).

Incumbent firms with substantial shares of their resources bound in an established technological regime are said to struggle in maintaining a certain level of innovation activity—particularly when facing radical, discontinuous technological change (e.g. Wagner 2010; Bower and Christensen 1996).[1] In case of *competence-enhancing* technological innovation, established firms have incentives to actively engage in and support the development of the technology updating the existing (Gilbert and Newbery 1982) regime. *Competence-destroying* innovation in turn appears as more likely to be pioneered by newcomers (Anderson and Tushman 1990; Tushman and Anderson 1986).

[1]One can broadly distinguish between *competence-enhancing* innovation building upon existing technological and organizational structures, and *competence-destroying* innovation turning them obsolete (Tushman and Anderson 1986). This distinction to a certain extent reflects the notions of *incremental* and *radical* innovation.

Over time, incumbents might also develop adoptive capabilities, enabling them to absorb knowledge on more radical novelties and combine it with their stock of knowledge to develop superior products and processes (Bergek et al. 2013). This can be done i.e. by engaging in joint R&D projects with entrant firms or the acquisition of their technology (e.g. Wagner 2010). However, once internalized, the absorbed novelty is likely to be aligned with existing resources in a complementary way. Therefore, when engaging in joint R&D projects, we assume that established firms—given the power—will influence technological trajectories in a way that makes the outcomes more compatible with their established assets and therefore potentially less radical.

Once a LTS has gained momentum these strategies become part of the resistance mechanisms against change on the system level (e.g. Walker 2000; Van der Vleuten and Raven 2006). The resulting set-up creates a power and capability imbalance between usually small enterprises that are pioneering the development of sustainable solutions and incumbent actors (Hockerts and Wustenhagen 2010). As long as production and distribution processes within existing trajectories are economically favorable, incumbents will not see urgent reasons to make large investments and reorganize existing production structures. On the contrary, they are most likely to defend the system against change (Walker 2000). In the most extreme case this leads to inertia and lock-in (Arthur 1989), as one might observe in our current fossil fuel dependent energy system Unruh (2000, 2002).

2.2 System Innovation Thinking

Technological change embedded in large systemic context has been conceptualized and analyzed throughout the past three decades. The technological innovation system TIS sub-orientation (Carlsson and Stankiewicz 1991; Bergek et al. 2008; Hekkert and Negro 2009) within the innovation system (IS) literature is increasingly used for the analysis of emergent industries on the basis of radically innovative technologies and the institutional and organizational changes that accompany the technological development (Truffer et al. 2012). A number of system functions (Hekkert et al. 2007) focusing on the support and nurturing of emerging technologies are seen as intermediate variables between the structure of the system and its performance, emerging out of the interplay between actors and institutions (Jacobsson and Bergek 2011). While it is acknowledged that incumbent players may employ strategies to prevent disruptive innovation (Hekkert et al. 2007), their participation in the TIS is generally seen as fruitful—highlighting their resources, knowledge integration capabilities (e.g. Bulathsinhala and Knudsen 2013) and the positive signalling.

In the recent decade, a second stream of literature situated closer to the science, technology and society (STS) tradition gained considerable attention. The multi-level perspective (MLP) at the center of the transition literature explains socio-technical transitions by the interplay of three systemic concepts. The landscape on the macro-, the socio-technical regime on the meso-, and niches on the micro-level respectively (Geels 2002, 2005). The character and intensity of the interplay between the three levels define the paths, which a socio-technical transition might take. The key concept of the MLP is the regime, which represents a coherent, stable structure at the meso-level, combining established products, technologies, and institutions (routines, norms, practices). The regime is characterized by a high level of "structuration" (Coenen and Díaz López 2010), well articulated rules, and hence path-dependency and mechanisms for self-stabilization. It corresponds in many respects to the selection environment in terms of evolutionary economic theory and generates entry barriers for innovative technologies.

2.3 Niches and Protected Spaces

Niches are conceptualized as spaces that shield path-breaking innovations in early stages of development from selection pressure on mainstream markets (Kemp et al. 2001; Schot 1992; Hoogma et al. 2004). These spaces help overcome the lock-ins existing in the current unsustainable system due to economic scale and scope effects (Arthur 1989), and institutional regime stabilization mechanisms that are constantly reinforced by established actors (Unruh 2000). Given alternative selection criteria, population and interaction dynamics, niches can develop own technological trajectories substantially differing from the established regime.

The direct funding of R&DD in selected technologies of interest represents an integral component of modern innovation policy. Shielded from the selection pressure of open markets, these research projects present an ideal platform for a broad, experimental and long term oriented search for new technologies. Nurtured with public investments, new entrants and incumbents alike are able to stem projects which would, due to their high technological uncertainty and long payoff periods, not be carried out otherwise. Given the proper institutional set-up, public R&DD financing offers a powerful tool to directly influence rate and direction of research activities (Pavitt 1998) and to create technology niches.

A challenge for policy-makers is the selecting of the appropriate protection level as well as its continuous assessment. Failure to find the right balance between protection and exposure to the selection environment can result in overprotection of "poor innovations" (Hommels et al. 2007), incompatibility with the surrounding technological context, or a too low level of protection of promising emerging technologies (Smith and Raven 2012). The latter can happen when actors belonging to the established unsustainable technological regime achieve dominance in spaces that are actually meant for the development of solutions that are potentially meant to replace parts of the current regime. As Smink et al. (2013) conclude "innovations with significant sustainability gains tend to be non-incremental and are therefore likely to have adverse effects on the business interests of regime actors". Therefore, we assume that their presence as dominant actors—and especially positioning as project leaders—in such niches might undermine the efficiency of the sustainable innovations under development.

2.4 A Network Perspective on Technological Niches

Cooperation and interaction between various actors involved in processes of technology development such as universities, firms, intermediate, and end users, are said to be of high importance for the smooth functioning of innovation systems (e.g. Lundvall 1992; Hekkert et al. 2007; Malerba 2002). A major task for science and innovation policy is therefore to facilitate the development of favourable R&D network structures (Carlsson and Jacobsson 1997), triggering interaction between heterogeneous actors and the generation of technological variety. Organizations form collaborative alliances in order to get access to their partners' technological assets and capabilities. Yet, potentially fruitful interaction with other corporations also comes at the risk of opportunistic technology appropriation by the counterpart, making careful selection of partners crucial (Li et al. 2008).

One can broadly distinguish between two categories of information that actors can use in cooperation and partner selection decisions. First, reputation, mostly stemming from past performance in similar settings (Shapiro 1983), and their demonstrated capabilities. Second, information about an actor's position in relevant networks (Benjamin and Podolny 1999; Burt 1992; Granovetter 1973), where usually better connected actors appear also as more attractive partners for further cooperation. Both appear to be highly interdependent, since an actor's reputation can be influenced by the reputations of past and current exchange partners (Benjamin and Podolny 1999; Podolny 1993) and collective reputations can be transferred to the a groups individual actors (Schweizer and Wijnberg 1999).

From a network perspective, a certain level of progressive centralisation and increasing dominance of incumbent players is therefore expected. Against the backdrop of the argumentation found in the transition literature, a strong centralization would however mean that niche protection is only limited. Particularly if incumbent actors, increasingly assume project-leader roles, the development of sustainable innovation is virtually handed by the regime.

2.5 Summary

Overall, the above presented streams of literature draw a similar picture from their respective point of view: Innovation is particularly complex and costly in systemic set-ups. Path dependencies are especially pronounced in sectors with a high share of infrastructure. Frameworks that inform policy measures to spur change in these areas agree on the need to actively create technological and market niches in order to foster alternative technologies and in general solutions. Yet, the role of incumbent player within these niches needs more inquiry.

Innovation paths that are compatible with regime technologies are attractive for established firms. Resulting innovations can address some of the existing problems on the regime level—to use the MLP terminology—without compromising existing socio-technical structures. Established firms are therefore likely to initiate or engage in niche activities, such as R&DD projects, which investigate such applications.

Facing radical or architectural technological change, they will not directly support the early development of path-breaking innovations, but rather aim at gaining control, acquiring, and integrating novel and existing technologies (Pavitt 1986; Bergek et al. 2013). Strong ties to the existent structures and technologies on the one hand and technological uncertainty, on the other lead to a relatively late but determined entry of incumbents into the development of these technologies. We assume that this may alter the particular innovative technology towards a less radical solution. In the case of sustainable technologies that would mean that generally more desirable superior solutions are possibly devaluated as they become compatible with the existing unsustainable system. From a policy perspective, and in the particular context of public research funding, that also raises the question related to *outcome additionality*.

3 Sociotechnical Context of the Smart Grid Development in Denmark

In order to understand and assess the structural dynamics of Danish smart grid and systems R&DD projects, it is important to consider the technological and policy context of the smart grid development. This section will introduce the fundamental technological concepts, components, and challenges related to the ongoing paradigm shift in the Danish and many other energy systems. Furthermore, the second part of this section will provide a brief overview of the policy ambitions that inform and guide the setup of publicly funded research programs. We fully acknowledge that funding programs and specified calls are intended to direct the technological trajectories of research projects. To some extent selection procedures by public authorities also predetermine their composition in terms of which types of actors and consortia constellations are awarded with grants and which not. Yet, the duality of selection in content as well as actor characteristics might lead to politically unintended developments regarding the evolution in the resulting research network—such as the rapidly growing dominance of certain actors.

3.1 Paradigm Shift in Energy Production and the Response in the Grids

The traditional architecture of the electricity grid assumes a unidirectional energy flow from centralized energy plants via the transmission and distribution grids to consumers, where energy production levels are constantly adjusted to match the over time fluctuating energy demand (Farhangi 2010; Fox-Penner 2010). Embracing the renewable energy paradigm, centralized energy production is gradually replaced by decentralized energy farming. The harmonization between production and consumption has to move from the traditional generation side into the transmission and consumption areas. ICT technologies will play a central role in supporting this process (Mattern et al. 2010).

In the North European set-up, two options are possible and currently discussed. Firstly, the construction of a European transmission super-grid to allow, for instance, energy exports from Denmark to Germany in wind-peak times. Secondly, the development of a national *smart grid*, that is able to transmit energy and information in both ways, thus allowing for harmonization by the means of flexible consumption. This requires the upgrade of the existing grid by adding a *layer of intelligence*—advanced measurement, communication and control technology—thus making the grid able to handle a higher share of decentralized renewable energy generation and the recently evolving consumption patterns (Elzinga 2011). This process is not primarily related to the development of radically new technology but to the recombination and integration of existing technology in order to achieve new functionality that would optimize the efficiency of the established system. If flexible consumption can be activated by the introduction of smart functionality, costly investments in the reinforcement of the distribution system can be moved into the future or avoided (Forskningsnetværket, Smart Grid 2013). This may be a favorable outcome for the country as a whole but might undermine profits of established actors that would benefit from capacity increase of the system.

3.2 Danish Smart Grid Research and Aspirations

Denmark is already today counting the largest amount of R&DD projects within the smart energy area in Europe (Giordano et al. 2011, 2013). The extremely high ambition of the national energy agreement, passed by the government in 2012, targets a wind-power share of 50 percent by 2020, and the more recently announced Smart Grid Strategy sees the country as a European laboratory for innovative energy solutions (KEMIN 2013).

Following the target setting of the policy package, a "Smart Grid Research Network" with key organizations from the technical universities and practitioners from the Danish TSO energinet.dk, the Danish Energy Association, and the energy group within the Confederation of the Danish Industry were established. In 2013 the network published a report commissioned by the Ministry of Energy, Utilities and Climate, which draws up a roadmap for the development of the Danish smart grid. The report identifies fields which will require considerable research efforts but also areas with strong Danish competences and experience that can attract foreign investment or contribute to technology export. Overall, it concludes that the development of the smart grid should be put first but not seen in isolation. Rather the interactions with the other energy related systems, such as heating, cooling, gas, and transport should be considered at all times.

In their latest inventory report Giordano et al. (2013) outline, that compared with other European countries, Denmark manages to develop a large amount of smaller projects which spurs technological diversity (Borup et al. 2013). This is in line with the findings by Jurowetzki (2015). Exploring the scope of the national smart grid and systems research he found that, research projects span from topics that are closely related to the pure electricity smart grid, such as consumption flexibilization to the interaction areas of different systems (e.g. the role of electric vehicles, heat pumps, and the district heating system).

That can be interpreted as a sign of successful niche development and the gradual merge of the electricity, gas, cooling, and heating systems into one smart energy system (Copenhagen Cleantech Cluster 2014). This context also offers entry and influence opportunities for different types of established actors from technological areas that yet have not been associated with the electricity system.

At the core of this research is the question of whether public funded R&DD activities are well constructed to provide necessary shielding in order to develop and introduce the needed amount of technological variety in the changing energy grid sector. The here proposed evolutionary network analysis can not provide direct answers to this question. Yet, the evolving structure of the research network can shed light on the likely development of the technological field.

4 Modelling Network Evolution

4.1 Data

4.1.1 Network Data

As a source for public funded research projects, we utilize the database provided by *Energiforskning.dk*. Combining data from several energy technology research and development programs, this database represents the most comprehensive source for public funded energy research in Denmark, covering projects funded by the *Strategic Research Council, ForskEL, ForskNG, ForskVE, ELFORSK, Green Labs DK, Danish High Technology Foundation* and the *European Union*. For the current analysis records from the *smart grid and systems* category were exported containing information on projects from 2009 to 2012 on yearly basis—overall 75 projects with 277 participants, and 132 single firms. Among those actors we identify

27 incumbent firms and 21 research institutions with the rest being either established diversifier companies or new entrants.[2]

We include all private firms and other organizations that participated in at least one public funded R&DD project during the 2009–2012 period. Further Thereby we exclude actors which have unsuccessfully applied for public funding, actors who would have liked to join such a research project as partners but have not been selected, or have been selected in the initial project application but where for some reason excluded from the official consortium at the start of the project. When assuming such actors to be systematically different from successful project leaders and partners, this obviously introduces a selection bias and limits the concussions we are able to draw from this analysis. Consequently, we are able to analyze if public research grant allocation decisions *per se* favor actors with certain characteristics. Neither we can investigate the general mechanisms of partner selection in the "hypothetical" network of available research partners. Yet, working with the "revealed" network of realized cooperation still allows us—in line with our research objective—to analyze the emerging governance structure of public funded R&DD networks.

The directed edges in the network represent join affiliations with the same research project, which are active from the official -start until the end of the project, where they are set to be inactive again if no further joint project follows. Technically, we project the two-mode network of actors-to-project to a one-mode network of direct actor-to-actor affiliation. In line with our research objective to analyze governance structures in this network, we do not connect all participants of a project with each other, but only create one-directional edges between the assigned project consortium leader in direction of every other project partner.

In order to utilize models of network dynamics, the dataset under observation has to fulfill certain properties in line with the underlying assumptions of this model class. First, the network has to show some variation between its periods. However, too rapid changes indicate that the assumption of gradual change—compared to the observation frequency—is violated. To ensure the validity of the gradual change assumption, we consult the Jaccard index to be found in Table 1, a common measure of similarity between two networks.[3] Snijders (2002) suggest this index to be higher than 0.3 and never drop beyond 0.2, which is given in our data. Overall, after a first preliminary inspection, the network data appears to have suitable properties in line with the assumptions of stochastic actor oriented models. Some further descriptive statistics on structural network measures and their development over time are provided in Table 2.

[2]A detailed description of the applied classification methodology is described below

[3]The Jaccard index as a measure of similarity between two network waves is computed by $\frac{N_{11}}{N_{11}+N_{01}+N_{10}}$, where N_{11} represents the number of ties stable over both waves, N_{01} the newly created and N_{10} newly terminated ties in wave 2 (see Batagelj and Bren 1995).

Table 1 Network turnover frequency

Periods	0⇒1	1⇒0	1⇒1	Jaccard
1⇒2	22	3	42	0.627
2⇒3	30	2	62	0.660
3⇒4	53	39	53	0.366

Table 2 Network density indicators

Periods	1	2	3	4
Density	0.003	0.004	0.005	0.006
Average degree	0.341	0.485	0.697	0.803
Network rate	0.383	0.490	1.406	–
Number of ties	45	64	92	106
Mutual ties	0	2	4	3
Asymmetric ties	45	60	84	100

A graphical presentation of the network under observation and its change over time is provided in Fig. 1. On first glance, a formation of structural clusters around some incumbent actors can already be seen over time.

4.1.2 Actor Data

Data on firm characteristics, such as their age, size, legal form *et cetra* was extracted from the Danish firm database Navne & Numre Erherv (NNE). For additional information about firms' technological capabilities and their range of activity where gathered by studying annual reports, press articles, corporate websites *et cetra*.

4.2 Modeling Network Dynamics

Our attempt is to analyze the dynamics of interorganisational networks of joint participation in public funded research projects. In particular, we are interested in which firms over time move towards central positions in the network. The analysis of such dynamic networks represents an empirical challenge which calls for distinct statistical models and methods. The main problem stems from the very nature of social network formation processes. Many drivers of individual tie-formation decisions, such as transitivity, reciprocity, and popularity effects, by their very nature lead to endogeneity and dependencies of observations (Rivera et al. 2010), since multiple characteristics of the current network structure influence its future development. This usually violates the assumptions of most standard statistical model types at hand (Steglich et al. 2010).

The class of stochastic actor-oriented models (SAOM) originally developed by Snijders (1996) represents an attractive solution to address the inherent endogeneity

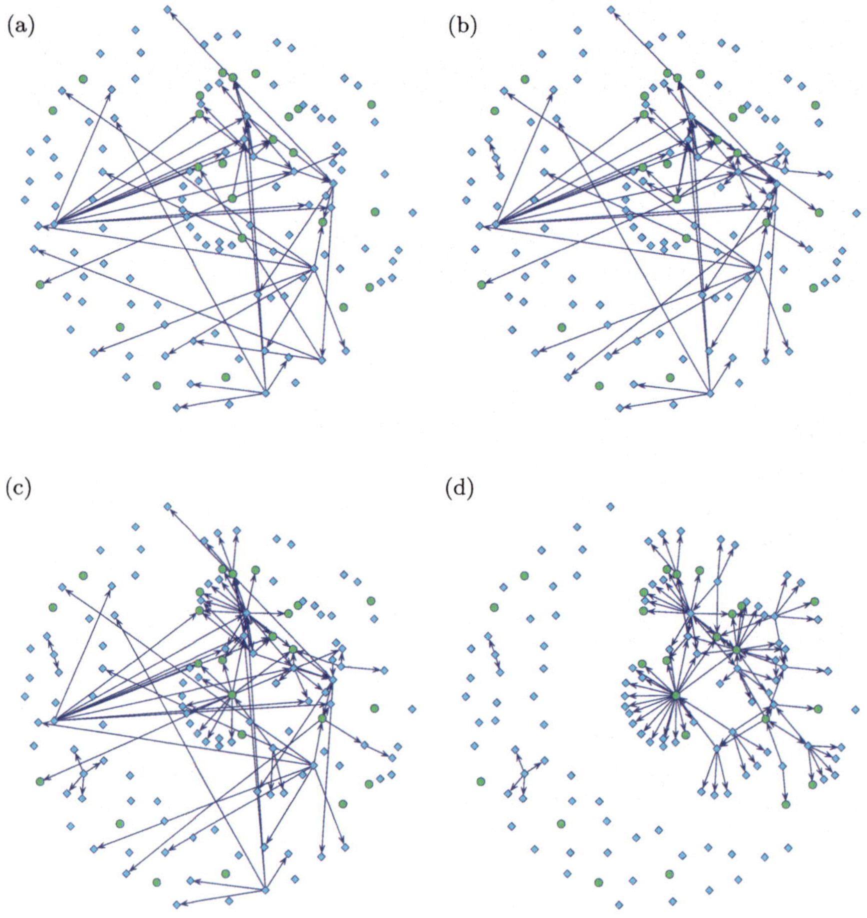

Fig. 1 Network Development in Public Funded R&D in Smart-Grid Research: (**a**) Network 2009, (**b**) Network 2010, (**c**) Network 2011 and (**d**) Network 2012. *Note:* Research network on basis of joint public funded research projects. Ties are directed from project-leader ⇒ project partner. *Circles* represent incumbents, *squares* all remaining types of organisations. The graphical presentation was done with the R package *Igraph*

problems of longitudinal network analysis, which scholars have lately started to deploy in the context of inter-organizational innovation networks (e.g. Balland 2012; Balland et al. 2012; Buchmann et al. 2014; Ter Wal 2013; Giuliani 2013). At its core, a SAOM combines a random utility model, continuous time Markov process estimation procedures, and Monte Carlo simulation. Originally, SAOM was developed in a sociological context and designed to model group dynamics in interpersonal networks (e.g. Van De Bunt et al. 1999). However, actor-oriented modeling has also proven to be suitable to depict the interaction between macro outcomes and firms' micro choices (Macy and Willer 2002; Whitbred et al. 2011) in inter-organizational alliance formation process. Here, structural change of the network is driven by individual firms' collaboration decision derived from a random utility model. Firms are assumed to observe the current network structure and characteristics of its population, and reorganize their ego-network in an utility-optimizing manner. Given the context of the study, we consider SAOM as the most suitable class of dynamic network models and deploy it for the empirical analysis to follow.

Snijders (1996) firstly proposed to address the problem of multiple endogeneity in the evolution of social network with transforming discrete datasets of panel waves into a continuous set of micro-changes (single reconfiguration decision) to be estimated by Markov-chain Monte Carlo simulation (MCMC).[4] Unobserved changes between the panel waves are simulated as continuous actor choices at stochastically determined points of time. Formally, following a Poisson function of rate λ_i, the actors (in our case, individual firms) are allowed to create, maintain, or dissolve ties until the network is transformed to the new structure χ. The decision of actor i to change the state of one tie to another actor j leads to a new overall state of the network χ, where the probability P_i for an actor choosing this structure is given by:

$$P_i(\chi^0, \chi, \beta_k) = \frac{\exp(f_i(\chi^0, \chi', \beta_k))}{\sum_{\chi' \in C(\chi^0)} \exp(f_i(\chi^0, \chi', \beta_k))} \qquad (1)$$

It technically resembles a multinomial logistic regression, modeling the probability that an actor chooses a specific (categorical) new network configuration P_i as proportional to the exponential transformation of the resulting networks objective function $f_i(.)$, with respect to all other possible configurations. The parameters' coefficients are stepwise adjusted by Monte Carlo simulation techniques in order to obtain convergence between the estimated and observed model, and finally, held fixed to allow their comparison and post-estimation analyses. The objective function contains actor i's perceived costs and benefits of a particular network reconfiguration leading to a network state χ, χ, which are represented by the random utility model:

$$f_i(\chi^0, \chi', \beta_k) = \sum_k \beta_k s_i(\chi^0, \chi, \nu_i, \nu_j, c_{i,j}, \varepsilon, r) \qquad (2)$$

It depends on the current state of the network χ^0, the potential new one χ, the ego i's and alter j's individual covariates ν_i and ν_j, their dyadic covariates c_{ij}, exogenous environmental effects ε, and a random component r capturing omitted effects. The underlying assumption is that the actors observe the current structure of the network χ^0 and the relevant characteristics of its actor set and make their collaboration decisions in order to optimize their perceived current utility (Jackson and Rogers 2007).

[4]Besides all its merits, the usage of estimations based on continuous-time Markov processes also has its drawbacks. It by definition does not allow for path dependencies. Yet, it is still possible to include variables aggregated over time to the current state.

4.3 Empirical Strategy

4.3.1 Theoretical Considerations

We model the tie creation process between ego *i* (project consortium leader) and alter *j* (project partner) as unidirectional from $i \Rightarrow j$. Thus, existing ties do not have to be reciprocal—a characteristic we find in many real-life networks such as friendships, mentorship, or producer-consumer relationships. Since we are interested in the ability to steer technological development of public funded research networks, we assume project consortium leader to have a significantly higher influence on the project's content than other participants. From this point of view, the directed network resembles the governance structure of there networks, and the actors outdegrees can be interpreted as a measure of influence. In our case, this appears as reasonable since the leaders of such projects are usually the ones applying for the corresponding grant, determining most of it's content, and selecting further partners. We chose a unilateral confirmation setup, where tie creating is only conditional to the ego's—but not the alter's—choice. By doing so, we assume potential partners to automatically join research projects when invited. This appears as a strong, but realistic assumption. Such a participation represents a safe source of income (and potentially knowledge), where the main upfront work, such as the grant application and determination of the content, is mostly carried out by the project leader. SAOM usually model tie creating as well as tie dissolution, where actors might choose to break up ongoing relationships which turn out to now offer negative utility. Since in our case the timeframe research projects is determined *ex-ante*, we only model the creation of new ties, where we exclude egos with already existing collaborations from the ego's choice set.

The nature of our network data calls for further consideration. In order to create a direct network among actors, we first have to project the two-mode network between actors and research projects to a one-mode network in actor space. Our resulting network is unweighed, meaning that the relationship between a project-leader and all project-members has the same quality, independent of the number of members. One might obviously assume that the size of project consortia systematically differs in a way that certain actors (probably larger and/or more experienced) actors show a tendency to include more members than others, thus establish more outdegrees per project than others. Further, it has been argued that the quality relationship between actors arising from a joint association with a second-mode differs with the number of actors this affiliation is shared. Newman (2001) for example argues that the quality relationship and interaction arising from scientific cooperation via co-authored publications substantially decreases with the amount of co-author. To account for this effect, one could weight the projected edges by the number of edges of the second mode (Opsahl 2013). While this is true for many types of relationships in different social settings, we do not believe it to be in our case. We explicitly aim to model governance structures emerging in public funded R&DD networks, given by the actors number of outdegrees. Consequently, the more alters a specific ego reaches increases their influence in determining research agendas, indecent of the fact that these outdegrees are established in one large or many small projects.

In addition, there undoubtedly exist some caveats when mapping networks based the common participation research consortia funded by public research grants. First, these networks only to some degree evolve naturally, since they are subject to a selection by the responsible public authorities. Selection criteria may be found, among others, in (i) the reputation and credibility based on past performance and other forms of accumulated advantage of consortia members, (ii) the characteristics of the project such as the applied technology, (iii) or the favoritism of certain consortia constellations. Second, since the actors are anticipating a selection according to these criteria, they have an incentive to consciously form consortia according to them. Thus, consortia formation are subject to selection biases *ex-ante* and *ex-post* to the project application (Hain and Mas Tur 2016). Consequently, the results have to be interpreted not as the outcomes of natural network evolution, but rather the channeled evolution in a socially constructed selection environment designed by public authorities, which might be subject to criteria (ii). With the choice of the study's empirical context, we attempt to minimize systematic biases caused by criteria (ii) and (iii). First, Danish research funding in renewable energy technology is designed to generate the broad technological variety necessary for the sustainable transition of the energy system (Lund and Mathiesen 2009), where favoritism of certain technology should explicitly be avoided. Second, by including several research funding programs of independent governmental and non-governmental agencies in Denmark and the EU, spanning different industries as well as preferred development stages of funded projects, we avoid systematic bias caused by preferences of particular programs or policy initiatives.

4.3.2 Dependent Variable

We model collaboration choices driving the evolution of the network as the outcome of the actors' mutual attempts to optimize their expected utility with respect to their own and their potential alters' covariates, and the current network structure. Thus, our model's dependent variable represents the probability P_i that the focal actor i chooses a reconfiguration of the own network that leads to a tie with a corresponding alter j. This tie is directed from the project-consortium leader (ego) to a participating project partner.

4.3.3 Independent Variables

In the following, we discuss our independent and control variables, where we integrate covariates referring to the characteristics of the actors, as well as effects

Table 3 Variable descriptions

Variable	Formal	Description
Outdegree	$s_{i1}^{net}(\chi) = \sum_j \chi_{i,j}$	Sum of outdegrees of ego i
Reciprocity	$s_{i2}^{net}(\chi) = \sum_j \chi_{i,j}\chi_{j,i}$	Sum of reciprocal ties between ego i and alter j
Transitivity	$s_{i3}^{net}(\chi) = \sum_{j<h} \chi_{i,j}\chi_{i,h}\chi_{j,h}$	Number of transitive patterns in ego i's relations (ordered pairs of alters (j, h) to both of whom ego i is tied, while also j is tied to h)
Size small		Dummy variable, taking the value of 1 if ego i is in size category small (<25 employees), 0 otherwise
Size large		Dummy variable, taking the value of 1 if ego i is in size category large (>100 employees), 0 otherwise
Role incumbent		Dummy variable, taking the value of 1 if ego i is categorized as incumbent, 0 otherwise
Age (ln)	$\ln(age^{year})$	Age of ego i in years, natural logarithm
Out-pop	$s_{i15}^{net}(\chi) = \sum_j \chi_{i,j} \sum_h \chi_{j,h}$	The sum of the out-degrees of alters j to whom ego i is tied
Out-act	$s_{i19}^{net}(\chi) = \left(\sum_j \chi_{i,j}\right)^2$	The squared out-degree of the ego i

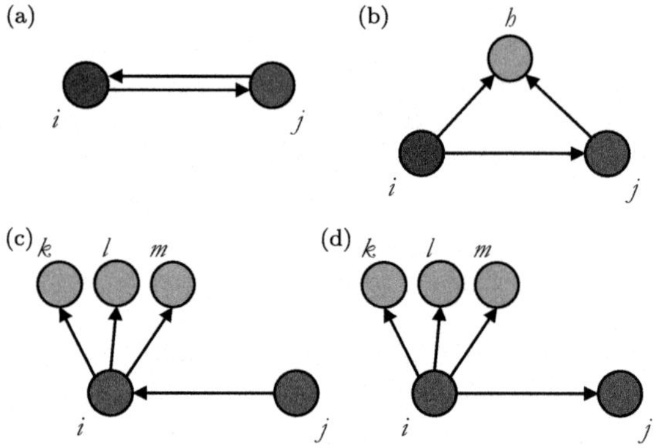

Fig. 2 Illustration of ego-network and degree-related effects: (**a**) Reciprocity, (**b**) transitive ties, (**c**) outdegree popularity and (**d**) outdegree activity. *Note:* The variables in the illustration are unrelated to the proposed model and analysis

referring to their position in the local and global network[5] Since we are primarily interested in what makes actors establish—rather than receive—new ties, all independent variables refer to the characteristics and network structure of the focal ego i. A detailed description of all independent variables—and their calculation—deployed is provided in Table 3, and all network related effects are illustrated visually in Fig. 2.

[5]Where local and global refer to the network position of the actor and not to a geographical context.

Actor Covariates This set of variables represents the effect of individual actor characteristics on their likelihood to establish new ties with other organizations.

In order to examine the role of actors in the combined network, we use a set of industry experts.[6] We differentiate between three roles, where we are particularly interested in the role of energy incumbents and the strategic deviations of these actors as compared to other actors involved in smart grid research projects. Role incumbent: This category aims at grouping actors with an origin in the energy sector that have an vested interest in protecting the established infrastructure from significant change. The experts were asked to identify "firms with a strong background/track-record and stakes in the traditional energy sector". This includes utilities, producers of transmission and distribution infrastructure, and producers of measuring devises. Apart from the utilities that went through a Europe wide policy induced organizational restructuring process, companies were founded before 2000. New Entrant: This group summarizes companies which were mostly founded after 2000 and have their main activity in the energy sector. The firms provide a broad range of products and services. Many of the firms develop ICT related solutions for the envisioned communication structure of the smart grid. Another large share are technology consultancies that are often responsible for analysis and system integration. It, however, also includes mature firms from other fields diversifying in the energy sector. Role Others: This class contains private and public actors that have shown interest in the development of a new grid infrastructure by participating in a research project. Actors are rather heterogeneous and have not had a background in the energy grid sector. This set of actors represents the reference group.

The size of a firm is also supposed to influence it's capabilities of successfully obtaining research grants, as well as to occupy central and dominant position in the resulting research networks. However, size is difficult to compare between different forms of organizations such as private companies, public organizations and research institutions. Therefore we only use a rough categorical classification of small (up to 25 employees, firm small), medium sized (up to 100 employees, reference groups), and large organizations (more than 100 employees, firm large). Generally, we expect large firms to establish more outdegrees for a set of reasons, where the most obvious is their higher internal capacity and resources to manage more projects at once than their smaller counterparts.

While maturing, firms are able to increase their competences in how to successfully formulate a research grant application, establish an intensify formal and informal relationships to industry partners and public authorities, and develop routines how to manage research partnerships. Since we expect these benefits to increase with decreasing marginal effects, and furthermore the distribution of firm age in our sample is highly skewed (start-ups as well as traditional firms established over a hundred years ago), we use the natural logarithm of the ego's age in years

[6]The experts are three energy related association managers from the Copenhagen Cleantech Cluster, Intelligent Energy alliance and the Lean Energy Cluster respectively.

Table 4 Descriptive statistics

Variable	Min.	Max.	Mean	Std. dev.
Size small	0	1	0.356	0.481
Size large	0	1	0.432	0.497
Role: incumbent	0	1	0.182	0.387
Role: Newcomer	0	1	0.106	0.309
Firm age	1	110	22.437	22.130

instead as control variable, which we generally expect to have a positive impact on the establishment of further outdegrees. Yet, the opposite might very well be true, if older firms loose their innovative edge and participate less in R&D projects.

Some further descriptive statistics of these actor-oriented measures are provided in Table 4.

Local (Ego) Network Effects This set of variables captures structural characteristics of the actor's ego-network, which include dyadic and triadic tie-configurations with other actors. Literature suggests these effects to be among the most important driving forces of network dynamics. Given the context of our study, however, they mostly represent control variables and are not emphasized in the following analysis. Reason therefore is the local nature of these variables, referring to effects only in and on the close neighbourhood in the network space.

The most basic effect is defined by the outdegree of actor i, representing the basic tendency to form an arbitrary tie to possible alters j, regardless of their individual characteristics. Since most social network structures observed in reality are rather sparse (meaning their density is way below 0.5), this effect tends to be negative, meaning the costs of establishing a tie *per se* in absence of a particular beneficial characteristic outweigh the benefits if no further characteristics make this tie particularly attractive (Snijders et al. 2010a).

Another basic feature of most social networks is reciprocity, the tendency of an ego i to respond to a former $j \Rightarrow i$ with the establishment of an $i \Rightarrow j$ tie (c.f. Wasserman 1979). In our context this effect captures a tendency of current project leaders to invite partners to join a project. In most social relationships such as friendship this effect has shown to be positive and of high explanatory power. Yet in our case of directed relationships, we expect this effect to be less pronounced, since project partners due to their characteristics might not necessarily qualify to be project leaders, thus might not have the chance for reciprocal action.

Transitivity is a measure for the tendency towards transitive closure, sometimes also called the clustering coefficient. Formally, it determines the likelihood a connection between $i \Rightarrow j$ and $i \Rightarrow h$ is closed by a connection between $j \Rightarrow h$ and/or $h \Rightarrow j$, or in other words that "partners of partners become partners" (e.g. Davis 1970). In our case we make use of the measure for transitive triads, which measures transitivity for actor i by the number of other actors h for which there is at least one intermediary j forming a transitive triplet of this kind. In line with a large body of earlier research, we expect this effect to be positive.

Global Network Effects Global network (or degree-related) effects express global hierarchies in a way that they reflect actors positions in the overall network. They capture the tendency of actors to send and receive ties according to their amount of out- and in-degrees, independent of their particular position in the network. Such effects can only be analyzed in a directed networks. They are of particular interest against the background of our study, since they are—in contrast to commonly applied triadic measures—suitable to analyze the tendency of certain actors to establish central and dominant positions in the overall network structure. Therefore, in our analysis we primarily focus on outdegree-related global effects.

Out-degree popularity captures the reputation and social recognition effect of the network on the activities of actor *i*. A positive parameter indicates that actors sending a higher amount of ties are also considered as more attractive to receive them in terms of higher indegrees. It in a way represents the global version of the local reciprocity effect, leading over time to a convergence of in- and outdegrees. This can in our case be interpreted in a way that actors leading many research projects also happen to often get invited to become partners in other projects. From a governance perspective, a positive Out-degree popularity effect leads to a more even distribution of power, since actors participate more equally in leading as well as following positions in research projects. Yet, in the same way as we argue in the case of reciprocity, we leave the direction of this effect to be an empirical question.

Of particular interest for this study is the Out-degree activity effect, which is the tendency of actors with high outdegrees to establish even more. A positive parameter indicates a self-reinforcing mechanism leading to an increasing dispersion of out-degrees in the network (Barabási and Albert 1999). It can be interpreted as the in network-structuralic impersonation of what is called the "Matthew Effect" (c.f. Merton 1968, 1988), cumulative advantage (Price 2007) or preferential attachment (Barabási and Albert 1999). Networks driven by this effect tend to stabilize towards a core-periphery structure around some very central, well connected, and influential actors. In the case of public funded research network, a positive Out-degree activity will lead to an ongoing and reinforcing concentration of governance structure and agenda-setting around particular actors. Technically, it resembles the squared version of an ego's outdegrees.[7]

Finally, we also include an interaction term between Out-degree activity and role incumbent, to test if the posited Matthew effect works particularly strong for incumbent actors.

[7]In the interpretation of this effect, one should take in the understanding that the outdegree effect itself is also included, and the parameters will be estimated such that the balance between creation and termination of ties agrees with the data. Taking a given function and then adding a positive coefficient multiplied by a quadratic function of the outdegree, (and note that the added quadratic function will because of the estimation be centered at the value where the balance occurs) imply that for current low oudegrees, the push to lower values will be relatively amplified, while for high outdegrees, the push to higher values will be relatively amplified.

4.3.4 Model Specification

To analyze the influence of actor characteristics and endogenous structural effects, we run a set of three models. All of them contain a set of standard structural dyadic and triadic ego-network control variables. Model I traditionally tests for ego (project leader) covariates, which are assumed to affect the capabilities of creating new outgoing ties. Model II instead tests for degree-related structural effects. In comparison to the set of dyadic and triadic structural effects, degree related effects are related to the overall number of in- and out-degrees of alter and ego, independent of their position in the others network. Thus, while the first set of controls refers to the local hierarchy of the actors ego network, degree related effects refer to a global hierarchy in the overall network. Finally, in model III we test for the joint effects of actor covariates and degree related effects simultaneously.

All parameters are estimated under full maximum likelihood according to the algorithm proposed by Snijders et al. (2010b), which has proven to be more efficient for small datasets. Technically, we make use of the SAOM application of SIENA (Ripley et al. 2013), a package for the statistical environment of R.

5 Results

5.1 Goodness-of-Fit Evaluation

As a first goodness-of-fit measure one can consider the t-convergence values of the parameters, indicating whether the simulated values deviate from the observed values. For a good model convergence, Snijders et al. (2010a) suggests to only include parameters with t-values of convergence between estimated and observed parameters below 0.1, what is given for all parameters in all corresponding models. The values in general show better convergence in later models, which confirms the effectiveness of our applied forward-selection strategy of model choice (cf. Lospinoso and Snijders 2011). Since the class of stochastic actor-oriented models is still under development, there exists no direct equivalent to the R^2 indicator of least squares regression models. Latest advances, however, offer a set of instruments to asses the model fit in stochastic settings. Score tests for each variable proposed by Schweinberger (2012), lead to overall satisfying results and gradually increased from model I to III. To account for changing dynamics over time, i.e. due to different policy focus and overall funding available, we carry out the test for time heterogeneity proposed by Lospinoso et al. (2011), which indeed shows a significant effect. As a result, an interaction term between year dummies and the actors outdegree is included in all models.

Also, we perform the Monte Carlo Mahalanobis Distance Test proposed by Lospinoso and Snijders (2011). Here we test the null hypothesis that auxiliary statistics such as indegrees, outdegrees and geodesic distance of observe data is distributed the results of Monte Carlo simulations on the estimated coefficients of our SAOM model, using the network in period one as point of departure. The purpose is to evaluate how well our stochastic model simulates transformation from the initial to the final network in terms of different degree distributions.

The underlying logic is to evaluate if a simulated process of network evolution based on our estimated coefficients leads to a network embodying the same structural characteristics as the observed one, the underlying mechanics of network change are appropriately modeled.[8] We here use the classical structural characteristics proposed by Lospinoso and Snijders (2011) indegree (how many nodes receive $1, 2, \ldots, n$ incoming ties), outdegree (how many nodes establish $1, 2, \ldots, n$ outgoing ties), geodesic distance (who many actor-dyads have a shortest path of $1, 2, \ldots, n$ that connects them in the network), and triad census (how many actor-triads show a certain connection pattern). We thereby also provide first validation of the ability of our model to predict future developments of research networks based on our estimated coefficients. The results are illustrated in Fig. 3.

The results suggest that our model is very well suited to predict the indegree and geodesic degree distribution, where the simulation results are very close to the observed values. Same holds for most forms of triad constellations. The only weakness of the model up to now appears to be the inconsistent identification of low outdegrees. While the model performs very well for high outdegrees, the simulated statistics for nodes with zero up to two outdegrees deviates highly from the observed values. However, since we are primarily interested in the distribution of the high degrees (the dominant nodes in the network), we consider the accuracy of prediction on the low end only as second priority.

Models of network dynamics generally have a tendency to suffer from collinearity problems, since a main share of variables originate from the same source, an actor's out- and indegrees. While building our models, we carefully checked for high correlations among the coefficients, where we in no case found a correlation of network related effects above 0.5. We also observed carefully the estimate stability when in- or excluding network-related variables, and found our models to be sufficiently stable.

5.2 SAOM Regression Models

Table 5 reports a set of SAOM on the probability of ego *i* to establish a new outgoing tie, depending on the egos characteristics, ego network, and global degree related effects. In our context that means that a project consortium leading firm *i* establishes a collaboration with some project partner firm *j*.

[8]Note: We here do not compare the characteristics of individual nodes, but the aggregated characteristics of the whole resulting network.

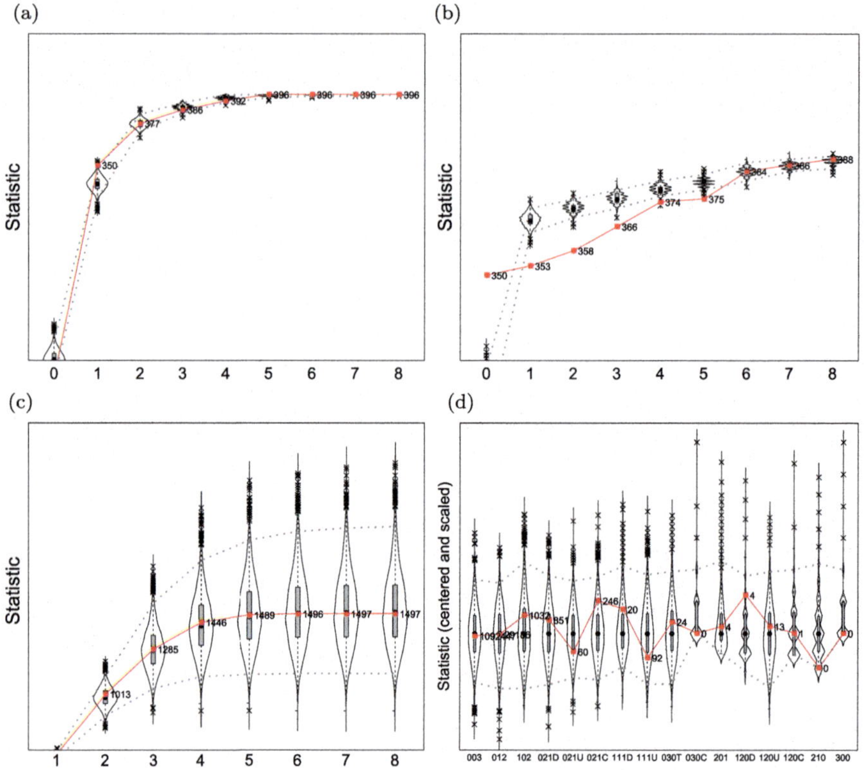

Fig. 3 Goodness-of-fit: Monte Carlo Mahalanobis distance test: (**a**) indegrees, (**b**) outdegrees, (**c**) geodesic and (**d**) triad census. *Note:* X-axis: P-value obtained by the Monte Carlo Mahalanobis Distance Test proposed by Lospinoso and Snijders (2011), testing null hypothesis that auxiliary statistics of observe data is distributed according to plot. Y-axis: Value of auxiliary statistic (indegree, outdegree, geodesic distance, triad census). *Solid red line* the observed values equal auxiliary statistic. "*Violin plots*" show simulated value of statistic as kernel density estimate and box plot of 95% interval

In the first model we jointly test for basic ego-network and ego-characteristic effects. The outdegree effect shows, as in most real-life sparse social networks, a negative coefficient. The positive and significant coefficient for transitive ties indicates local clustering over time, when partners of "partners become partners" on their on. Actors of size large as well as of size small establish significantly more outdegrees than their peers of the size medium reference group, where the coefficient is higher for large firms. This might reflect the preference of grant allocation decision makers for more stable large firms leading research consortia, or just the higher resource endowments of large players enabling them to manage the coordination of multiple research projects simultaneously. The age of the firm, however, *ceteris paribus* manifests in decreasing outdegrees. Allocation preferences towards stable project leaders again should lead to favoring older firms not subject to the liability of newness and the associated high failure rate (Freeman et al. 1983). An

Table 5 Stochastic actor-oriented model: probability of tie creation Ego → Alter

	Model I		Model II		Model III	
Variable	Coef.	Std. er.	Coef.	Std. er.	Coef.	Std. er.
Structural ego-network effects						
Outdegree	−4.314***	0.540	−5.913***	0.342	−6.264***	0.453
Reciprocity	1.143	0.622	1.411**	0.582	1.034	0.594
Transitivity	1.791***	0.345	0.319	0.228	0.229	0.191
Actor level effects						
Size small	0.990	0.873			1.601**	0.681
Size large	2.644***	0.832			1.629**	0.726
Role incumbent	3.424***	0.611			2.759***	0.476
Age (ln)	−0.793**	0.267			−0.448**	0.227
Degree related effects						
Out-pop			0.085**	0.029	0.077**	0.030
Out-act			0.372***	0.047	0.413***	0.073
Out-act * role incumbent					1.430***	0.347

Note: *, **, *** indicate significance at 10, 5, 1 percent level, two-tailed

explanation could instead be found on the demand side, when aging firms loose their innovative drive and stop engaging in early stage research. An interesting finding is the high positive and significant coefficient of role incumbent, providing first evidence that the smart grid research network indeed over time tends to be dominated by incumbent actors.[9] Since we are not able to disentangle supply and demand effects of public research funding, this finding again offers different explanations. First, it can be interpreted of revealed preferences of public authorities for consortia led by incumbents, possibly reflecting incumbents strategic advantage of infrastructure ownership or their exercised influence on policy making. On the other hand, it is also possible that incumbents actively strive for consortia leadership positions enabling them to influence early stage research on the future energy grid infrastructure—possibly to preserve the "old regime".

In model II, we test for ego-network and global network degree-related effects. An interesting finding is that, after introducing global degree related network effects, the coefficient of transitive ties drops in magnitude as well as significance. This finding demonstrates the usefulness and additional insights of including degree related effects when analyzing directed networks. Since actors increasing high outdegrees, they naturally will also have more potential to form reciprocal ties in their choice set. However, in this case global centralization outweighs local

[9]While we first categorized new entrants separately, we decided to in our final analysis only contrast incumbents with all other actors, who we assume to not share the same incentives to stabilize the existing system. Further, in an unreported analysis including also a dummy for new entrants, we find no significant effect for this variable.

clustering in the further evolution of the network, indicating the development towards a core-periphery rather than a small world like structure. Both outdegree popularity and outdegree activity show a high positive an significant coefficient, where outdegree activity dominates.[10] These findings indicate that the current selection environment in the technological niche of public funded smart grid R&DD indeed shows a tendency to develop towards a global hierarchy. This network-structural "Matthew Effect" over time leads to a development of the network towards a centralized network structure with a high dispersion of degrees. In such network structures, some actors continuously move in a reinforcing manner towards dominant positions. Such tendencies can be observed in many real-life networks.

Therefore, in model III we jointly test for the impact of ego-characteristic and global degree related network effects on an actor's establishment of further outdegrees. While ego-network effects remain roughly unchanged compared with the former model, the investigation of actor level effects reveal some interesting insights. Again, the effects of size large and role incumbent are significant and show positive coefficients, even though with decreased magnitude. However, the degree related effects outdegree popularity and outdegree activity both remain positive and significant, where the latter even increases in magnitude. Thus, outdegree-activity appears to be a major driving force in the evolution of public funded smart grid research networks, an effect that appears to be even stronger when controlling for firm characteristics.

Overall, the results of this final model suggests incumbents indeed to be in a favorable position to inherit dominant roles in the research network over time. While they are generally more likely to establish outgoing ties, preferential attachment and accumulated advantages reinforces this tendency over time. Finally we introduce an interaction term between outdegree-activity and role incumbent to test if degree-related effects work particularly in favor of incumbent firms, which appears to be the case. It shows a high positive coefficient, significant at one percent level, providing further evidence for the advantageous effects incumbents enjoy in the development of their network position. Here we are able to provide evidence not only of the benefits incumbents *per se* in leading research consortia, but also that powerful mechanisms of network evolution work in their favor. If these effects are driven by the demand or supply side of public research funding can only be speculated. So may it be that incumbents due to factors like their political influence and ownership of the energy grid infrastructure are generally more successful in grant applications, but the ones who decide to massively exercise their influence on energy grid technology development will enjoy structural forces of network evolution supporting them to do so.

This process can easily be forecasted in a simple Monte Carlo simulation of network evolution using the parameters estimated in our SAOM for calibration.

[10]Note that all parameters in SAOM are standardized (divided by their mean), thus making a direct comparison of their magnitude difficult within a model, but easier between models.

After 10 period, such a network already shows a very strong core-periphery structure, where the core is almost exclusively populated by incumbents.

5.3 Robustness Tests

Our main results are primarily dependent on a correct classification of the actors' roles, which in our case is determined by the categorization of industry experts. To cross-validate these sensible results, we ran all models with alternative classification strategies. First we apply a simple subjective classification strategy similar to the one used by Erlinghagen and Markard (2012), where we determine incumbents by certain combinations of NACE codes, size, and age of an actor. However, a classification exclusively based on these objective measures would often fail to identify actors. Second, we use a computational approach, where we collected approximately 550 Danish industrial publications related to energy system topics from the period 1995–2000 and used a fuzzy string matching process to identify actors that appear in the analyzed research projects within the description parts. We assume that actors that appear in a "energy context" can be considered established in the industry.

Furthermore, as already discussed, the number of an ego's outdegrees can in the projection of a two-mode network (project association $\rightarrow$ actor) to an one-mode network (actors $\rightarrow$ actors) be influenced by the number of projects lead by an actor as well as the number of participants in such projects. To test for bias arising from the tendency of certain actors to establish smaller or larger project-consortia, we rerun all models including a variable representing the average number of members in projects the ego-actor participated in, in the current and last year. In all cases, the results point in the same direction but are less pronounced, which speaks in favor of using industry experts for the identification of nuanced roles such as energy industry incumbents. All additional regressions mentioned are—for the sake of brevity—not reported, but available on request.

6 Conclusion

In this paper, we studied the influence of incumbent firms on the structural dynamics of research networks in technological niches at the case of public funded research projects. Drawing from innovation system, sociotechnical transitions, and network evolution literature, we identify a set of structural—as well as firm-characteristic—effects that might enable incumbents over time to move towards dominant positions in the research network. These effects generally originate from the supply side of public grant allocation, for instance the preferences of public authorities towards certain firms, technologies, project types. In addition, we identify demand side effects related to strategic motives of incumbents to participate in technological niches, and draw implications for the rate and direction of technological change as an outcome of research network dominated by incumbents. We thereby attempt to provide much needed insights (Christensen and Hain 2017) into the particular industry dynamics of the energy sector, but also to the evolution of interfirm networks more broadly.

To do so, we conduct a stochastic actor-oriented network analysis, where we model the hierarchy and power structure in the network with directed ties between research project leader and partners. We assume the leader of such projects as mainly influencing the context of conducted research as well as the selection of further participants, thus strongly influencing the development of technological trajectories in such niche networks. In contrast to mostly pronounced function of "knowledge diffusion" in research and innovation networks, we focus on governance structures as a result of project leadership. By doing so, we are able to analyse up to now unobserved cumulative and self-reinforcing effects of network dynamics and relate them to firm strategies and vested interests.

Our results indicate path-dependent and cumulative effects of firm characteristics such as size, and degree-related "Mathew effects" in the development of the research network, which over time lead to a centralization of the network structure. While we find incumbents *per se* to enjoy benefits in establishing new outgoing ties, we find path-dependent effects to work particularly in their favor. Overall, the observed dynamics suggest a development of the network towards a structure where incumbents occupy the most central positions.

By emphasizing governance and influence related aspects combined with firm characteristics and strategies, we provide an alternative—and perhaps more critical—perspective on research and innovation networks, and the role of the state in their coordination. The development of the electricity grid into a smart grid is not envisioned as a radical process that threatens the existence of the established regime. Rather it is a process of upgrading and adaptation to new types of energy generation. Yet, the strong centralization effects in the network and the high probability of incumbent players to lead research projects are surprising, particularly against the backdrop of the literature arguing for niche protection when developing sustainable technologies. Methodologically, we demonstrate the richness of stochastic actor-oriented models to answer such questions by modeling collaboration decisions on actor level, and relating them to macro outcomes of structural network evolution. We further contribute to a more nuanced discussion on the role and behavior of incumbents in sociotechnical transitions by identifying which firm-characteristics and structural forces of network evolution facilitate them to—for the better or the worse—increase their influence in the formulation of early stage research agendas. Our findings also provide implications for policy. Whether these increasingly incumbent-dominated networks are favorable or not is a rather normative discussion, which would go beyond the scope of this research.

However, the here unveiled interplay between firm characteristics, strategy and network dynamics have to be considered carefully, since they are to some extent policy orchestrated and not fully subject to natural evolution. The supply side selection environment is subject to *ex-ante* biases of grant allocation preferences of public authorities, as well as *ex-post* biases of firms observing these preferences and probably optimizing their project constellation patterns. Further, demand side effects related to firm strategies and vested interests affect the extent to which they participate in public funded research projects or choose other forms of collaboration, and which positions they prefer in such projects. While we derive some suggestions from theoretical reasoning and existing (mixed) evidence, we are not able to analytically disentangle supply and demand side effects. We yet do not provide a direct analytic link between the identified structural change of research networks and outcome characteristics in terms of more radical or incremental innovation.

Consequently, we consider future research separating supply and demand side effects of public funded research network formation as a promising avenue for further research. Here, the combination of rich supply side data, such as evaluations of project grant applications together with firm-level data on motives and strategies appears to be particularly promising to disentangle supply and demand side effects in public funding of R&D and the resulting network dynamics. The empirical link between the network structure and innovation outcomes can be—and has been—established using network data to explain innovation output measures such as patents.[11] However, the link between micro-level actor behavior and network dynamics with macro-level outcomes faces some empirical challenges. One obvious challenge is the endogeneity caused by interdependence of actor behavior and network position. Co-evolutionary models of networks and actor behavior as proposed by Snijders et al. (2007) and applied by Checkley et al. (2014); Veenstra and Steglich (2012); Steglich et al. (2010) could be an attractive solution. Lastly, additional empirical cross-country and cross-industry evidence is needed to clarify the role of incumbents in research networks and sustainable transitions in general. We hope our work stimulates further work on this issue, which we consider as a promising avenue for future research.

Acknowledgments We would like to thank all participants of the Jena ISS conference 2014, the Nice KID workshop 2014, the Copenhagen DRUID society conference 2014, the Stanford Network Forum ST2014, the IKE research seminar series 2014, the Oxford AIE conference 2013 and the Halle ENIC workshop 2013 for invaluable inspiration and feedback. All opinions, and errors, remain our own.

[11] Alternatively, dynamic approaches drawing from unstructured data, as demonstrated by Jurowetzki and Hain (2014), represent a promising new avenue to map an analyze the evolution of technology.

References

Anderson P, Tushman ML (1990) Technological discontinuities and dominant designs: a cyclical model of technological change. Adm Sci Q 35(4):604–633

Arthur WB (1989) Competing technologies, increasing returns, and lock-in by historical events. Econ J 99(394):116–131

Balland P (2012) Proximity and the evolution of collaboration networks: evidence from research and development projects within the global navigation satellite system (GNSS) industry. Reg Stud 46(6):741–756

Balland PA, De Vaan M, Boschma R (2012) The dynamics of interfirm networks along the industry life cycle: the case of the global video game industry, 1987–2007. J Econ Geogr 13 (5):741–765

Barabási AL (2005) Emergence of scaling in complex networks. Wiley-VCH, Weinheim, FRG, pp 69–84

Barabási A, Albert R (1999) Emergence of scaling in random networks. Science 286 (5439):509–512

Batagelj V, Bren M (1995) Comparing resemblance measures. J Classif 12(1):73–90

Baum J, Calabrese T, Silverman BS (2000) Don't go it alone: alliance network composition and startups' performance in Canadian biotechnology. Strateg Manag J 21(3):267–294

Benjamin B, Podolny J (1999) Status, quality, and social order in the California wine industry. Adm Sci Q 44(3):563–589

Bergek A, Jacobsson S, Carlsson B, Lindmark S, Rickne A (2008) Analyzing the functional dynamics of technological innovation systems: a scheme of analysis. Res Policy 37 (3):407–429

Bergek A, Berggren C, Magnusson T, Hobday M (2013) Technological discontinuities and the challenge for incumbent firms: destruction, disruption or creative accumulation? Res Policy 5, 8

Borup M, Klitkou A, Andersen MM, Hain DS, Christensen JL, Rennings K (2013) Indicators of energy innovation systems and their dynamics. a review of current practice and research in the field: Radar report. EIS Radar Report, EIS—Strategic Research Alliance for Energy Innovation Systems and their dynamics

Bower JL, Christensen CM (1996) Disruptive technologies: catching the wave. J Prod Innov Manag 1(13):75–76

Buchmann T, Hain DS, Kudic M, Müller M (2014) Exploring the evolution of innovation networks in science-driven and scale-intensive industries: new evidence from a stochastic actor-based approach, iWH Discussion Paper 1/2014, 42

Bulathsinhala NA, Knudsen MP (2013) The role of organizational knowledge integrators in large R&D projects, conference proceeding. In: 35th DRUID Celebration Conference, ESADE Business School, Barcelona, Spain

Burt RS (1992) Structural holes: the social structure of competition. In: Nohria N, Eccles R (eds) Networks and organizations. Harvard Business School Press, Boston, pp 57–91

Burt RS (2000) Decay functions. Soc Networks 22(1):1–28

Carlsson B, Jacobsson S (1997) Diversity creation and technological systems: a technology policy perspective. In: Edquist C (ed) Systems of innovation: technologies, institutions and organizations. Pinter, London, p 7

Carlsson B, Stankiewicz R (1991) In search of useful public policies: key lessons and issues for policy makers. J Evol Econ 1(2):93–118

Checkley M, Steglich C, Angwin D, Endersby R (2014) Firm performance and the evolution of cooperative interfirm networks: UK venture capital syndication. Strat Change 23(1–2):107–118

Christensen JL, Hain DS (2017) Knowing where to go: the knowledge foundation for investments in energy innovation. Energy Res Soc Sci 25:124–133

Coenen L, Díaz López FJ (2010) Comparing systems approaches to innovation and technological change for sustainable and competitive economies: an explorative study into conceptual commonalities, differences and complementarities. J Clean Prod 18(12):1149–1160
Copenhagen Cleantech Cluster (2014) The smart energy system. Technical report 10
Davis J (1970) Clustering and hierarchy in interpersonal relations: testing two graph theoretical models on 742 sociomatrices. Am Sociol Rev 35:843–851
Doreian P, Stokman FN (2005) The dynamics and evolution of social networks. In: Doreian P, Stokman FN (eds) Evolution of social networks, 2nd edn. Gordon & Breach, New York, pp 1–17
Elzinga D (2011) Smart grids roadmap. Technical report 9
Erlinghagen S, Markard J (2012) Smart grids and the transformation of the electricity sector: ICT firms as potential catalysts for sectoral change. Energ Policy 51(C):895–906
Farhangi H (2010) The path of the smart grid. IEEE Power Energy Mag 8(1):18–28
Fleming L, King C, Juda A (2007) Small worlds and regional innovation. Organ Sci 18 (6):938–954
Forskningsnetværket, Smart Grid (2013) Roadmap for forskning, udvikling og demonstration inden for Smart Grid frem mod 2020. Technical report 9
Fox-Penner P (2010) Smart power: climate change, the smart grid, and the future of electric utilities. Island Press, London
Freeman J, Carroll G, Hannan M (1983) The liability of newness: age dependence in organizational death rates. Am Sociol Rev 48(5):692–710
Geels F (2002) Technological transitions as evolutionary reconfiguration processes: a multi-level perspective and a case-study. Res Policy 31(8):1257–1274
Geels FW (2004) From sectoral systems of innovation to socio-technical systems. Res Policy 33 (6–7):897–920
Geels FW (2005) Technological transitions and system innovations: a co-evolutionary and socio-technical analysis. Edward Elgar, Cheltenham
Geels FW (2011) The multi-level perspective on sustainability transitions: responses to seven criticisms. Environ Innov Soc Trans 1(1):24–40
Geels FW, Raven R (2006) Non-linearity and expectations in niche-development trajectories. Tech Anal Strat Manag 18(3–4):375–392
Gilbert RJ, Newbery D (1982) Preemptive patenting and the persistence of monopoly. Am Econ Rev 72(3):514–526
Giordano V, Gangale F, Fulli G, Jiménez MS, Onyeji I, Colta A, Papaioannou I, Mengolini A, Alecu C, Ojala T (2011) Smart Grid projects in Europe: lessons learned and current developments. European Commission, Joint Research Centre, Institute for Energy, Luxembourg
Giordano V, Gangale F, Fulli G, Jiménez MS, Onyeji I, Colta A, Papaioannou I, Mengolini A, Alecu C, Ojala T (2013) Smart Grid projects in Europe: lessons learned and current developments. European Commission, Joint Research Centre, Institute for Energy, Luxembourg
Giuliani E (2013) Network dynamics in regional clusters: evidence from Chile. Res Policy 42 (8):1406–1419
Granovetter MS (1973) The strength of weak ties. Am J Sociol 78(6):1360–1380
Gulati R (1999) Network location and learning: the influence of network resources and firm capabilities on alliance formation. Strateg Manag J 20(5):397–4203
Hain D (2016) The network dynamics of financing technological (r-) evolution: the case of technological change in the renewable energy area. PhD thesis, Aalborg Univertsity, Department of Business and Management. doi: https://doi.org/10.5278/vbn.phd.socsci.00034
Hain DS, Mas Tur E (2016) Technological change and investments on a rugged landscape-an agent based simulation, iKE Working Paper Series, Aalborg University, Denmark
Hekkert MP, Negro SO (2009) Functions of innovation systems as a framework to understand sustainable technological change: emperical evidence for earlier claims. Technol Forecast Soc Chang 76(4):584–594

Hekkert MP, Suurs RA, Negro SO, Kuhlmann S, Smits RE (2007) Functions of innovation systems: a new approach for analysing technological change. Technol Forecast Soc Chang 74(4):413–432

Hockerts K, Wustenhagen R (2010) Greening goliaths versus emerging davids–theorizing about the role of incumbents and new entrants in sustainable entrepreneurship. J Bus Ventur 25 (5):481–492

Hommels A, Peters P, Bijker WE (2007) Techno therapy or nurtured niches? Technology studies and the evaluation of radical innovations. Res Policy 36(7):1088–1099

Hoogma R, Kemp R, Schot J, Truffer B (2004) Experimenting for sustainable transport: the approach of strategic niche management. Tech Anal Strat Manag 16(4):561–566

Hughes TP (1987) The evolution of large technological systems. In: Bijker WE, Hughes TP, Pinch T (eds) The social construction of technological systems: new directions in the sociology and history of technology. MIT Press, Cambridge, pp 51–82

Jackson MO, Rogers BW (2007) Meeting strangers and friends of friends: how random are social networks? Am Econ Rev 97(3):890–915

Jacobsson S, Bergek A (2011) Environ Innov Soc Trans 1(1):41–57

Jurowetzki R (2015) Unpacking big systems—natural language processing meets network analysis. A study of smart grid development in Denmark. SPRU Working Paper Series, 15, pp 1–36

Jurowetzki R, Hain DS (2014) Mapping the (r-) evolution of technological fields—a semantic network approach. In: Aiello LM, McFarland D (eds) Social informatics, lecture notes in computer science, vol 8851. Springer International, Heidelberg, pp 359–383

KEMIN (2013) Smart grid strategy. Technical report 4

Kemp R, Schot J, Hoogma R (1998) Regime shifts to sustainability through processes of niche formation: the approach of strategic niche management. Tech Anal Strat Manag 10(2):175–198

Kemp R, Rip A, Schot J (2001) Constructing transition paths through the management of niches. In: Garud R, Karnøe P (eds) Path dependence and creation. Lawrence Erlbaum, Mahwah, NJ, pp 269–299

Kilduff M, Tsai W (2003) Social networks and organizations. Sage, Thousand Oaks, CA

Kudic M (2014) Innovation networks in the German laser industry: evolutionary change, strategic positioning, and firm innovativeness. Springer, Heidelberg

Li D, Eden L, Hitt MA, Ireland RD (2008) Friends, acquaintances, or strangers? Partner selection in R&D alliances. Acad Manag J 51(2):315–334

Lospinoso J, Snijders T (2011) Goodness of fit for social network dynamics. Conference presentation, given at the Sunbelt XXXI, St. Pete's Beach, FL

Lospinoso JA, Schweinberger M, Snijders TA, Ripley RM (2011) Assessing and accounting for time heterogeneity in stochastic actor oriented models. ADAC 5(2):147–176

Lund H, Mathiesen B (2009) Energy system analysis of 100% renewable energy systems—the case of denmark in years 2030 and 2050. Energy 34(5):524–531

Lundvall BÅ (1992) National systems of innovation: toward a theory of innovation and interactive learning. Pinter Publishers, London

Macy MW, Willer R (2002) From factors to factors: computational sociology and agent-based modeling. Annu Rev Sociol 28:143–166

Malerba F (2002) Sectoral systems of innovation and production. Res Policy 31(2):247–2647

Mattern F, Staake T, Weiss M (2010) ICT for green. In: 1st International conference. ACM Press, New York, NY, pp 1–10

Merton R (1968) The matthew effect in science. Science 159(3810):56–63

Merton R (1988) The matthew effect in science, II: Cumulative advantage and the symbolism of intellectual property. Isis 79(4):606–623

Newman M (2001) Scientific collaboration networks. II. Shortest paths, weighted networks, and centrality. Phys Rev 64(1):016

Opsahl T (2013) Triadic closure in two-mode networks: redefining the global and local clustering coefficients. Soc Networks 35(2):159–167

Pavitt K (1986) 'Chips' and 'Trajectories': how does the semiconductor influence the sources and directions of technical change? In: Macleod R (ed) Technology and the human prospect. Frances Pinter, London, pp 31–55

Pavitt K (1998) The inevitable limits of EU R&D funding. Res Policy 27(6):559–568

Podolny J (1993) A status-based model of market competition. Am J Sociol 98(4):829–872

Powell W, Koput K, Smith-Doerr L (1996) Interorganizational collaboration and the locus of innovation: networks of learning in biotechnology. Adm Sci Q 41(1):116–145

Powell WW, White DR, Koput KW, Owen-Smith J (2005) Network dynamics and field evolution: the growth of interorganizational collaboration in the life sciences. Am J Sociol 110 (4):1132–1205

Price D (2007) A general theory of bibliometric and other cumulative advantage processes. J Am Soc Inf Sci 27(5):292–306

Ripley RM, Snijders TA, Preciado P (2013) Manual for siena version 4.0. Department of Statistics, Nuffield College, University of Oxford, Oxford

Rivera MT, Soderstrom SB, Uzzi B (2010) Dynamics of dyads in social networks: assortative, relational, and proximity mechanisms. Annu Rev Sociol 36:91–115

Schilling M, Phelps C (2007) Interfirm collaboration networks: the impact of large-scale network structure on firm innovation. Manag Sci 53(7):1113–1126

Schot J (1992) The policy relevance of the quasi-evolutionary model: the case of stimulating clean technologies. In: Coombs R, Saviotti P, Walsh V (eds) Technological change and company strategies: economic and sociological perspectives. Academic, London

Schweinberger M (2012) Statistical modelling of network panel data: goodness of fit. Br J Math Stat Psychol 65(2):263–281

Schweizer T, Wijnberg N (1999) Transferring reputation to the corporation in different cultures: individuals, collectives, systems and the strategic management of corporate reputation. Corp Reput Rev 2(3):249–266

Shapiro C (1983) Premiums for high quality products as returns to reputations. Q J Econ 98 (4):659–679

Smink MM, Hekkert MP, Negro SO (2013) Keeping sustainable innovation on a leash? Exploring incumbents' institutional strategies. Bus Strateg Environ 24(2):86–101

Smith A, Raven R (2012) What is protective space? Reconsidering niches in transitions to sustainability. Res Policy 41(6):1025–1036

Smith A, Stirling A, Berkhout F (2005) The governance of sustainable socio-technical transitions. Res Policy 34(10):1491–1510

Snijders TA (1996) Stochastic actor-oriented models for network change. J Math Sociol 21 (1–2):149–172

Snijders T (2002) The statistical evaluation of social network dynamics. Sociol Methodol 31 (1):361–395

Snijders T, Steglich C, Schweinberger M (2007) Modeling the co-evolution of networks and behavior. In: van Montfort K, Oud H, Satorra A (eds) Longitudinal models in the behavioral and related sciences. Lawrence Erlbaum, pp 41–71

Snijders T, Van de Bunt G, Steglich C (2010a) Introduction to stochastic actor-based models for network dynamics. Soc Networks 32(1):44–60

Snijders TA, Koskinen J, Schweinberger M (2010b) Maximum likelihood estimation for social network dynamics. Ann Appl Stat 4(2):567–588

Steglich C, Snijders TA, Pearson M (2010) Dynamic networks and behavior: separating selection from influence. Sociol Methodol 40(1):329–393

Suurs RA, Hekkert MP (2005) Naar een methode voor het evalueren van transitietrajecten. Functies van Innovatiesystemen toegepast op dBiobrandstoffen in Nederland. Utrecht University, Department of Innovation Studies, Utrecht

Ter Wal AL (2013) The dynamics of the inventor network in german biotechnology: geographical proximity versus triadic closure. J Econ Geogr 13(6):13

Truffer B, Markard J, Binz C, Jacobsson S (2012) A literature review on energy innovation systems. Technical report

Tushman ML, Anderson P (1986) Technological discontinuities and organizational environments. Adm Sci Q:439–465

Unruh G (2000) Understanding carbon lock-in. Energy Policy 28(12):817–830

Unruh G (2002) Escaping carbon lock-in. Energ Policy 30(4):317–325

Van De Bunt GG, Van Duijn MA, Snijders TA (1999) Friendship networks through time: An actor-oriented dynamic statistical network model. Comput Math Organ Theory 5(2):167–192

Van der Vleuten E, Raven R (2006) Lock-in and change: distributed generation in Denmark in a long-term perspective. Energ Policy 34(18):3739–3748

Veenstra R, Steglich C (2012) Actor-based model for network and behavior dynamics: a tool to examine selection and influence processes. In: Laursen B, Little TD, Card NA (eds) Handbook of developmental research methods. Guildford Press, New York, NY, pp 598–618

Viner N, Powell P, Green R (2004) Institutionalized biases in the award of research grants: a preliminary analysis revisiting the principle of accumulative advantage. Res Policy 33 (3):443–454

Wagner M (2010) Acquisitions as a means of innovation sourcing by incumbents and growth of technology-oriented ventures. Int J Technol Manag 52(1):118–134

Walker W (2000) Entrapment in large technology systems: institutional commitment and power relations. Res Policy 29(7):833–846

Wasserman S (1979) A stochastic model for directed graphs with transition rates determined by reciprocity. In: Schuessler K (ed) Sociological methodology. Jossey-Bass, San Francisco, pp 392–412

Whitbred R, Fonti F, Steglich C, Contractor N (2011) From microactions to macrostructure and back: a structurational approach to the evolution of organizational networks. Hum Commun Res 37:404–433. https://doi.org/10.1111/j.1468-2958.2011.01404.x 13

Entrepreneurs' Over-optimism During the Early Life Course of the Firm

Zornitza Kambourova and Erik Stam

Abstract Recent research on cognitive biases in decision making suggests that over-optimism critically influences entrepreneurs' decisions to establish and sustain new firms. This paper looks at entrepreneurs' over-optimism during the early life course of the firm, in order to uncover the dynamics and persistence of over-optimism. We use a representative sample of start-ups in the Netherlands, which we divide into solo self-employed and employer firms. We find that while there is a persistence of over-optimism for the solo self-employed, namely initial over-optimist are more likely to be overoptimistic in subsequent periods; this is not the case for the employer firms.

1 Introduction

While some new firms prosper, most of them stagnate and die shortly after start-up. Several authors attribute this high share of failing start-ups to the over-optimistic expectations of their founders (De Meza and Southey 1996; Storey 2011; Dawson and Henley 2013). This is quite in contrast to the dominant line of reasoning in economics, which emphasizes "rational expectations", i.e. that the predictions of economic actors about future values of economically relevant variables are not systematically wrong and that all errors are random. Much psychological evidence shows that subjects do not have rational expectations, but rather that they are unrealistically optimistic: 'According to popular belief, people tend to think that they are invulnerable. They expect others to be victims of misfortune, not themselves' (Weinstein 1980: 806). This hopeful outlook on life implies "a judgment error" which Weinstein called unrealistic optimism or optimistic bias. Interestingly, entrepreneurs are also regarded as economic actors specializing in judgmental decision making (Casson 1982). While overoptimism is positively associated with innovation, both at the micro and macro level (Dosi and Lovallo 1997), judgmental overconfidence is negatively linked to innovation (Herz et al. 2014).

Z. Kambourova (✉) • E. Stam
Utrecht University School of Economics, Utrecht, The Netherlands
e-mail: z.v.kambourova@uu.nl; e.stam@uu.nl

A. Pyka, U. Cantner (eds.), *Foundations of Economic Change*, Economic Complexity and Evolution, DOI 10.1007/978-3-319-62009-1_15

Overoptimism is a trend in the expectations, which are systematically estimated in a more optimistic manner with respect to the real potential of the projects (Pulford and Colman 1996). This personality trait of entrepreneurs has been highlighted in recent research due to the effect of their decision making on the performance of the company (Lowe and Ziedonis 2006; Hmieleski and Baron 2009; Landier and Thesmar 2009; Cassar 2010; Hogarth and Karelaia 2012; Hyytinen et al. 2014). On the one hand, it encourages the self-employed to follow their dreams and believe in their success, but, on the other hand, it also poses some problems for the sustainable growth and survival of new firms. The highly optimistic individuals tend to fail to recognize the true probabilities of future events. It enables them to discount with lower probabilities the lowest-profit probabilities, and to attribute unrealistically high probabilities to the high-profit events, luring them into risky situations with uncertain pay offs.

Does this trait of overoptimism change over time? Previous research shows that some entrepreneurs do learn to control their overoptimism and to account properly for the risk involved in their projects (Fraser and Greene 2006; Hmieleski and Baron 2009). According to Ucbasaran et al. (2010), having a failure serves to improve entrepreneurs' perception and attitude towards risk and is beneficial for their later performance as business-owners. However, this does not hold for all entrepreneurs. There are also examples of serial failures in the field, namely entrepreneurs who have consecutive failing businesses, who have a high level of over-optimism and do not learn from their experience (Ucbasaran et al. 2010).

So far the existing research is focused on the learning process after having had an entity, i.e. after entrepreneurial exit. It is interesting, however, if the entrepreneurs actually learn while they control their entity, namely if the learning actually happens when they see that their entity is underperforming (in comparison to their expectations) or are they overly optimistic and the learning process happens only after the (perhaps) more dramatic event of entrepreneurial exit? The aim of this paper is to analyze the relationship between initial optimism, as reported by the entrepreneurs, and the level of realism of their predictions of the future, measured as the discrepancy between their expectations for change in employment and realized employment growth. To do so, we will perform empirical tests on a large cohort of start-ups in the Netherlands. The insights from the analysis will contribute to a better understanding of optimism during the early life course of firms.

This paper contributes to the literature in two ways. The existing literature has taken a static view on over-optimism, by focusing on the differences in over-optimism between entrepreneurs and non-entrepreneurs, and as a determinant of exit. Our first contribution is to take a more dynamic view on over-optimism of entrepreneurs during the early life course of firms. Our second contribution is that we relate these over-optimism dynamics to other, non-varying characteristics of the firm and entrepreneur. In this paper, we consider whether entrepreneurial overoptimism is persistent over time (during the early life course of the firm) and whether this overoptimism over time can partly be explained by individual and firm level characteristics. To do so, we trace the overoptimism of entrepreneurs during the first 6 years of the new firm's life course, and relate this to individual and firm characteristics. Our analysis considers optimism in three moments in time: during start-up (are business plan expectations met?), in the first 3 years after start-up and the subsequent 3 years (are growth expectations met, 3 years after forecast?). Despite the prevalence of research on overoptimism in a wide variety of investment decision-making situations (including entrepreneurial decisions), there has been little research on the persistence of this characteristic and its determinants over time.

Before looking into the empirics, the next section will consider the existing literature on the topic. It will be used as a basis for developing the hypotheses about the factors influencing over-optimism. Afterwards, the data used in the empirical analysis will be described, as well as the methodology used to analyze it. The next section discusses the empirical results and the implications for the literature. The paper finishes with concluding remarks outlining the relevance of the research and proposing further steps.

2 Literature and Hypotheses

Good judgment is one of the most important factors for a successful business. Managers evaluate projects all the time and make investment decisions based on the expected pay offs. The main factors determining the quality of the judgment are: 1) the knowledge about the environment; and 2) the knowledge of the personal capabilities (or experience) (Hogarth and Karelaia 2012).

The evaluation of the environment is based mostly on previous experience in the sector. The longer a person has worked in a certain environment, the better is the quality of her decision making, since the experience accumulated reduces the 'noise' in the environment. The importance of the evaluation of the environment is noted by Hogarth and Karelaia (2012), who point out that even when individuals are realistic about their capabilities, if their evaluation of the working environment is 'noisy', they tend to make wrong decisions which can evolve into serious monetary losses.

The evaluation of the personal capabilities also comes from the past experience of the decision maker: relative optimism diminishes with experience, since entrepreneurs learn about their capabilities (Fraser and Greene 2006). The experience, however, may not be always pleasant. Ucbasaran et al. (2010) shows that failure has a positive effect on the quality of decision making: entrepreneurs report being less over-optimistic since they can picture themselves failing. This affects the probability-distribution they perceive: it increases the probability of a bad-event happening and corrects for their negligence of those events. Furthermore, such an outcome is seen as a 'clear signal' that something is wrong (Sitkin 1992). This encourages the entrepreneurs to re-evaluate their behavior and provides them with more knowledge about themselves, as well as about the environment.

However, not all authors agree that entrepreneurs can learn. According to Weiner (1986) entrepreneurs strive to keep their self-esteem and after a failure they tend to search for external facts that could have contributed to it instead of analyzing their own role in the situation. This serves as a barrier for acquiring knowledge on the (lack of) skills of the entrepreneur.

Over-optimism is seen as the tendency of individuals to see future outcomes in a more positive light than what could actually occur (Cassar 2010). This is related to the level of their over-confidence,[1] or their tendency to overestimate their ability to do well (Larwood and Whittaker 1977). According to Hmieleski and Baron (2009) high levels of over-optimism result in no learning effects for the entrepreneurs, since they focus on information that confirms their beliefs. Information that is contradictory is disregarded. This results in a biased analysis of the accumulated experience. So we hypothesize:

H1: Initial over-optimism of entrepreneurs is positively related to subsequent over-optimism in the early life course of the firm.

Furthermore, Storey (2011) argues that entrepreneurs do not learn. He pictures entrepreneurs as players in casino which derive satisfaction from "being at the table" and therefore do not try to analyze their capabilities in order to improve their future performance. However, most research in psychology on the relationship between risk propensity and optimistic biases shows that there is no clear evidence of the relation between the two within the overall human population, which seems to suggest that the two variables are not necessarily related (Hillman and Todesco 1999; Cohn et al. 1995). We hypothesize that:

H2: Risk propensity of entrepreneurs is positively related to over-optimism.

Bernardo and Welch (2001) describe the nature of the over-optimistic entrepreneurs as individuals more likely to diverge from the common behavior and use privately held information for decision making, rather than following the herd. They argue that this behavior decreases substantially in the cases when the "public information becomes sufficiently overwhelming" (Bernardo and Welch 2001: 13), otherwise it persists throughout the life time of individuals. From this it follows that without a major shock in the environment, the entrepreneurs will persist in their over-optimism and therefore we hypothesize that:

H3: Initial over-optimism and consequent over-optimism of entrepreneurs are positively related to subsequent measures of over-optimism in the early life course of the firm.

[1]Overconfidence relates to the ancient concept of hubris (going back to Greek tragedies), and the recent hubris theory of entrepreneurship (Hayward et al. 2006), which incorporate three separate psychological processes: overconfidence in knowledge, overconfidence in prediction, and overconfidence in personal abilities.

3 Data and Methodology

3.1 Sample

The data represents a random sample of all companies registered as start-ups at the Dutch Chamber of Commerce. The observations have been collected through a questionnaire designed by the research institute EIM Business and Policy Research. Initially 10,642 firms were contacted, out of which 1938 took part of the survey (see also Bosma et al. 2004; Stam and Wennberg 2009). These firms have been surveyed annually, which allows for a longitudinal analysis of their development. After 6 years, the number of observations declined to 612 due to unresponsiveness of the initial participants. The reasons for this could range from failure of the company, to change of location (which has been an obstacle for tracing them), to decline to participate further in the process. This substantial reduction of observations raises some concerns with respect to survivor bias.

3.2 Measuring Optimism

Since the pioneering articles by Scheier and Carver (1985) and Scheier et al. (1994), the optimism literature has developed quite extensively. Optimism is seen as generalized positive expectations about future events (Scheier and Carver 1985). Optimistic bias may vary from one setting to the next (Weinstein 1980), while dispositional optimism is a psychological trait that lies at the heart of an individual's outlook on life in general (Puri and Robinson 2007). In this paper we are focusing on optimistic bias in the setting of the early life course of the firm.

Measuring over-optimism entails comparison between predictions for the future and the realized performance at a later stage. The first opportunity for such a measurement is provided by the parameters of the business plan. Usually entrepreneurs develop a business plan when they start a new company. It reflects their vision of the company aims for the intermediate future. In our survey, the entrepreneurs are asked how the company is performing with respect to the initial business plan. The answers corresponding to the company performing worse and much worse represent the initial over-optimism of the entrepreneurs. In our data set this characterizes 66 people out of 612 (or approx. 11%). The others evaluate their company as performing the same as the plan or better, meaning that they were not overestimating the possible results of their entity.

An important question to ask here is whether the initial over-optimism is related to the subsequent firm performance, and in particular if it is associated with higher firm exit. In the first year of this cohort (including 1938 new ventures) 314 respondents had been found to be over-optimists, which corresponds to 16% of the total sample. This means that 248 initial over-optimists have exited the sample during the first 6 years. They constitute 19% of the $(1938 - 612 = 1326)$ non-survivors, meaning that over-optimism is positively related to subsequent firm exit (see also Dawson and Henley 2013). This implies that our analyses of subsequent over-optimism suffer from survivor bias (as expected), which could result in underestimation of the strength of the relation between initial and subsequent over-optimism, given that a relatively large share of the initial over-optimistic entrepreneurs did not manage to create a viable business.

Considering the survivors, at the same moment when they are asked to reflect on the development of their company with respect to their business plan, they are also asked to make predictions for the future, such as what is the expected change of profit in the next year (increase, decrease or no change), as well as what are the aims of their entity in the medium run. As such they could evaluate the importance of increase/decrease of personnel, improving their own skills, enjoying their work, extending their property, increasing the quality of their products etc. The discrepancy between these consequent predictions and the actual performance of the companies in 3 years' time indicates the level of optimism of the entrepreneurs in that point of time. A change of attitude, from being overly optimistic in their business plan predictions to being realistic in that second prediction, would be an indicator of a learning process. In that line of thought, we can compare the predictions about sales and employment. The other expectation categories are rather weak estimators of firm performance. However, the survey does not ask directly about the expected sales, but about the relative levels of profitability. The latter concept is not a good indicator of the development of most start-ups. They do not aim at high profit margins. Their focus is directed towards ensuring the viability of their business. In most cases, the new entity barely breaks even in the initial years of its existence. Thus, the expectations for profit are not an appropriate indicator for the future development of this type of companies. On the other hand, the amount of personnel is something highly correlated to the sales performance of the companies. The ones which perform better increase the number of employees in order to be able to cover their enlarged business needs. Therefore the aim of hiring new people is a good indicator of the expected future development of the company.[2] Comparing this prediction to the realized employment change in 3 years provides us with our second measure of optimism, from now onwards called Optimism2. It indicates over-optimism when the entrepreneur aims at increase of personnel, but this increase is not realized in 3 years' time. This measure is comparable to the measures used by other studies on over-optimism. For example, Landier and Thesmar (2009) compare a new venture's actual growth with its initial growth expectations.

The relation between the accuracy of the initial business plan prediction and the accuracy of the second prediction could indicate if there is a learning process happening while the entrepreneurs are working in their company.

[2]Other studies take these growth expectations as a key indicator of ambitious entrepreneurship (see Stam et al. 2012 for a review). In this study we take a more cautious view, by emphasizing the degree to which these expectations are realized.

Table 1 Distribution of initial optimism and consequent optimism

	Initial optimism business plan		
Optimism2	0	1	Total
0	405	41	446
	91%	9%	100%
	74%	62%	73%
1	141	25	166
	85%	15%	100%
	26%	38%	27%
Total	546	66	612
	89%	11%	100%
	100%	100%	100%

The column variable in Table 1 represents the initial optimism measured as a comparison between the business plan and the performance of the company: 1 indicates over-optimistic behavior and 0 otherwise. The variable Optimism2 is built analogically: 1 represents over-optimism with respect to the expected increase in employees, while 0 all other cases. Based on this, we can see that there are 405 realists that kept on being realists in their second evaluation.[3] Meanwhile, 141 (26%) of the realists became over-optimists while working in the company. The reasons could be initial luck, which increased their confidence and blurred their judgment. On the other hand from the initial over-optimists 25 are showing no learning behavior and kept their over-optimism. While 41 of the same group exhibit learning behavior, namely they improved their judgment. This means that in the population of initial over-optimists, 62% show learning behavior during the first years of their company. This could be attributed to the better insights from the work due to the accumulated experience, as we hypothesized. However, in order to be able to claim so, we should trace the persistence of this feature for at least two periods. While the second measure of over-optimism shows signs of divergence of behavior, this could as well be something different than learning (or non-learning). The noise could come from the abundance of factors that affect the initial years of development of the entity and therefore (may) affect the accuracy of judgment of the entrepreneur. However, those diminish in time and the perception of the entrepreneur becomes the main source of discrepancy between prediction and realization. Therefore, a consequent measure of judgment accuracy which provides with an overview of the trait on a longer time period could serve as an indicator of learning (or non-learning persistency). Such a measure could be retrieved from the data. The same process that enabled us to derive the second measure of optimism is available for developing a consequent measure: at the moment of judgment of accuracy of the second prediction (namely 3 years after the first questionnaire) the entrepreneurs are interviewed one more time and make predictions about the future.

[3]However, this could also be attributed to the fact that the individuals were lucky rather than having an accurate judgment (see Barney 1986).

At this moment they can see how accurate their judgment was and based on that knowledge, predict what will be the development of the entity in the next 3 years. Based on these expectations and the realized performance 3 years later, we were able to build Optimism3. The variable has the value of 1 when the entrepreneur expected to increase the number of employees and this did not happen, namely he was overoptimistic; and the value of 0 otherwise. It shows that there are 125 (or 20%) over-optimists at this third measurement point, versus 166 (27%) at the second measurement point and 66 (11%) at the initial point, namely the business plan. Would that mean that we have a learning curve?

To be able to claim so, we need to see how the accuracy of the predictions evolved in time. We can divide the sample into two groups: entrepreneurs who were over-optimistic in their business plan, and a group that does not possess this trait according to our measurement. Considering the initial over-optimists (outlined in Table 2), we can see that 62% of that group improved the accuracy of their judgment in the second measurement point. However, this improved performance was sustained only by 48% (or 32 people out of the 66 initial over-optimists) at the third measurement point. We call them 'learners' since the improvement of their judgment is persistent in time. The initial period may be prone to noise and the entrepreneurs may be claimed to be lucky in their accurate prediction. However, the persistence of this trait for more than one period cannot be classified as pure luck.

Considering the development of the other group, namely the entrepreneurs who were the non-over-optimists in their business plan (outlined in Table 3), we can see that there is a large group who were non-optimistic during the whole period, namely 57% (348 people out of the whole sample). This persistence of non-optimists results from the survivor bias present in the sample, according to which a large proportion of the over-optimists did not manage to establish a viable business. However, it is interesting to note that there is also a large group did suffer from a persistent deterioration of expectations, namely 9% (47) of the initial realists became persistently over-optimistic during the second and third measurement.

Besides the optimism levels of the entrepreneurs and their allocation of efforts, we also have information about their personal characteristics such as gender and age; their human capital (represented by their highest education level and if they

Table 2 Persistence of consequent optimism given being overoptimistic in the business plan

	Optimism2		
Optimism3	0	1	Total
0	32	13	45
	71%	29%	100%
	78%	52%	68%
1	9	12	21
	43%	57%	100%
	22%	48%	32%
Total	41	25	66
	62%	38%	100%
	100%	100%	100%

Table 3 Persistence of consequent optimism given being non-overoptimistic in the business plan

Optimism3	Optimism2		
	0	1	Total
0	348	94	442
	79%	21%	100%
	86%	67%	81%
1	57	47	104
	55%	45%	100%
	14%	33%	19%
Total	405	141	546
	74%	26%	100%
	100%	100%	100%

Table 4 Summary statistics

Variable	Obs	Mean	Std. dev.	Min	Max
OptimismBP (d)	612	0.108	0.310	0	1
Optimism2 (d)	612	0.271	0.445	0	1
Optimism3 (d)	612	0.204	0.403	0	1
Gender (d)	612	0.724	0.447	0	1
Age	612	1.792	0.768	1	3
Education (d)	612	0.286	0.452	0	1
Industry experience	612	1.982	0.914	1	5
Start-up capital	612	2.495	1.569	1	7
Unemployment (d)	612	0.114	0.319	0	1
Part time (d)	612	0.554	0.497	0	1
Self-employed (d)	612	0.838	0.369	0	1
Sector	612	69.516	18.922	20	99
Risk	612	3.755	0.773	1	5

(d) for discrete change of dummy variable from 0 to 1

have prior experience in the industry); the initial company characteristics (captured by the starting capital, the number of people in the first year and the sector of operations); and their risk propensity. The summary statistics for all variables is outlined in Table 4. Further information about the variables and a correlation table can be found in Appendix. The correlation exploration shows no high correlations between variables, making it possible to use all of them simultaneously in a regression model.

3.3 *Model and Methodology*

To determine the statistical significance of the initial level of judgment accuracy on the consequent one, we will use the following equation:

$$OptimismN_i = \beta_0 + \beta_1 Optimism(N-1)_i + \beta_2 OptimismBP_i + \gamma Control\ variables_i + \varepsilon_i \quad (1)$$

Where:

$OptimismN_i$ and $Optimism(N-1)_i$ capture the accuracy of the prediction of expected increase in employment in period N (and period N−1 respectively) of individual i. The value of the variable is equal to 1 if the entrepreneur is predicting increase in employment, but this has not been realized in the next 3 years. In that case there is a sign of being overly optimistic. In all other cases the variable has a value of 0.

$OptimismBP_i$ measures the initial level of over-optimism of individual i captured by the business plan. It is equal to 1 when the entrepreneur believes the company is performing worse than outlined in the plan. In all other cases the variable has a value of 0.

$Control\ variables_i$ capture the demographics (gender and age), human capital (education and experience in the same industry), initial company characteristics (starting capital and sector of operation), initial commitment (unemployment before start and part-time involvement in the entity), and risk propensity of individual *i*.

ε is the stochastic error term, which is assumed to have a normal distribution and to be independent from all other covariates.

We estimate Eq. (1) as a probit model, which enables us to capture properly the dual nature of the optimistic variable. Since we cannot read directly the magnitude of the coefficients from our estimation, we perform a post-estimation of marginal effects (or elasticities). Each marginal effect is calculated at the means of the other independent variables.

The equation has been estimated separately for the solo self-employed individuals and the entities with more than one person employed in them (i.e. employer firms). We evaluate the belonging to either of the two groups based on the start-up year. This separation is important due to the differences between the two forms of entrepreneurial activity.

4 Results and Discussion

4.1 Solo Self-Employed

The first four models look at the sample of solo self-employed individuals (see table 5). The initial model estimates the relationship between initial optimism measured by the business plan and the consequent level of optimism. It shows a statistically significant influence of the initial level on the consequent level, namely an initially overoptimistic person has 14.5% higher probability of being overly optimistic in the consequent measurement of this trend, if she is compared to a

Table 5 Regression models 1–4: self-employed

	Optimism2 (d)				Optimism3 (d)			
	Model 1		Model 2		Model 3		Model 4	
Variables	Raw	mfx	Raw	mfx	Raw	mfx	Raw	mfx
Optimism2 (d)					0.804***	0.234***	0.775***	0.219***
					(0.140)	(0.0448)	(0.145)	(0.0456)
OptimismBP (d)	0.411**	0.145**	0.413**	0.143**	0.397**	0.113*	0.407**	0.114*
	(0.184)	(0.069)	(0.191)	(0.0710)	(0.197)	(0.0630)	(0.203)	(0.0637)
Gender (d)			0.114	0.0353			0.00673	0.00162
			(0.144)	(0.0439)			(0.160)	(0.0385)
Age			−0.196**	−0.0619**			−0.0335	−0.00807
			(0.0843)	(0.0265)			(0.0930)	(0.0224)
Education (d)			0.0282	0.00894			0.120	0.0297
			(0.141)	(0.0447)			(0.156)	(0.0394)
Experience industry			−0.0168	−0.00532			−0.0683	−0.0164
			(0.0681)	(0.0215)			(0.0763)	(0.0184)
Start-up capital			0.0723	0.0228			0.0661	0.0159
			(0.0496)	(0.0156)			(0.0544)	(0.0131)
Unemployment (d)			−0.157	−0.0475			0.462**	0.130**
			(0.189)	(0.0546)			(0.190)	(0.0604)
Part time (d)			−0.268**	−0.0864*			−0.0939	−0.0229
			(0.135)	(0.0443)			(0.149)	(0.0367)
Sector			−0.00425	−0.00134			0.00139	0.000335
			(0.00335)	(0.00106)			(0.0038)	(0.00092)
Risk			0.120	0.0380			0.146	0.0350
			(0.0813)	(0.0256)			(0.0898)	(0.0216)

(continued)

Table 5 (continued)

	Optimism2 (d)				Optimism3 (d)			
	Model 1		Model 2		Model 3		Model 4	
Variables	Raw	mfx	Raw	mfx	Raw	mfx	Raw	mfx
Constant	−0.693***		−0.548		−1.225***		−1.879***	
	(0.0639)		(0.495)		(0.0870)		(0.561)	
Observations	513	513	513	513	513	513	513	513
Pseudo R^2	0.0083	0.0083	0.0521	0.0521	0.0807	0.0807	0.1096	0.1096

(d) for discrete change of dummy variable from 0 to 1
Standard errors in parentheses
***$p < 0.01$, **$p < 0.05$, *$p < 0.1$

person who has a better initial judgment. This confirms hypothesis 1 and shows that the initially over-optimistic person has a lower probability to learn from her misjudgment. To test hypothesis 3, namely if there is persistency in the over-optimism trait, model 3 extends model 1 by including all three measures of over-optimism in one model. It shows that the trait is persistent in time and the probability of an individual being overoptimistic in the third time period is twice more probable if the individual had shown that trait in the second measure versus if he had it in the first measure. This time-discrepancy shows the higher importance of the closest periods for the current judgment. Furthermore, these results show that individuals, who start as being over-optimistic, have a lower propensity to learn and are prone to carry this trait forward in time. Therefore, this provides evidence for hypothesis 3.

Model 2 and 4 extend the first two models by including controls for the demographics of the entrepreneur (gender and age), his human capital (education and previous experience in the industry), company effects (start-up capital and sector), commitment reasons (unemployment and part-time), and risk-taking propensity. Both models show a persistent impact of initial over-optimism on the consequent measurements of over-optimism. Furthermore, the trend revealed by model 3, namely the higher importance of the optimism trait in closer time periods, is also present in model 4: initial over-optimists have 11.4% higher probability of being over-optimistic at our third measure of the trait, while over-optimists in the second measure have a twice as big probability, 21.9%.

Model 2 also shows a statistically significant negative effect of working part time on the levels of over-optimism, while controlling for the previous levels of optimism. An entrepreneur working part time has 8.6% less probability of being over-optimistic during the initial period of the entity, than one working full time. However, model 4 shows that this impact is not present on the consequent level of optimism, which measures the trait in the time span after the first 3 years of the entity. However, model 4 reveals that if the individual was unemployed before the start of the entity, she is 13% more prone to be overly optimistic in our last measure of the trait.

Considering all the indicators, it is important not to forget the risk propensity of the entrepreneur. Her judgments, and the extent to which she is optimistic, are likely to be correlated to his risk preferences. Therefore both model 2 and model 4 consider this personality trait of the entrepreneur. The variable categorizes the risk propensity of the entrepreneur into five different levels, from low to high. The effect of this, however, is not statistically significant for the probability of the solo self-employed entrepreneur being overly optimistic in the second measure of the trait (Optimism2). There is also no indication of statistically significant impact of the risk propensity on our last measure of optimism (Optimism3). Therefore, overall there is no evidence for hypothesis 2.

4.2 Employer Firms

In the next four models, namely model 5 to model 8 (see table 6), we consider the optimism levels of the entrepreneurs who have a firm with more than one full-time

Table 6 Regression models 5–8: employer firms

	Optimism2 (d)				Optimism3 (d)			
	Model 5		Model 6		Model 7		Model 8	
Variables	Raw	mfx	Raw	mfx	Raw	mfx	Raw	mfx
Optimism2 (d)					0.0418	0.0151	−0.0179	−0.00638
					(0.277)	(0.100)	(0.321)	(0.114)
OptimismBP (d)	0	0	−0.214	−0.0719	0.0311	0.0112	0.0132	0.00470
	(0.399)	(0.145)	(0.459)	(0.146)	(0.400)	(0.145)	(0.414)	(0.148)
Gender (d)			−0.0917	−0.0326			−0.305	−0.113
			(0.394)	(0.142)			(0.391)	(0.149)
Age			0.420**	0.147**			0.162	0.0579
			(0.194)	(0.0683)			(0.199)	(0.0709)
Education (d)			0.281	0.102			0.00554	0.00198
			(0.341)	(0.126)			(0.333)	(0.119)
Experience industry			0.224	0.0785			0.169	0.0602
			(0.184)	(0.0647)			(0.167)	(0.0596)
Start-up capital			−0.298***	−0.105***			0.0668	0.0238
			(0.0907)	(0.0315)			(0.0909)	(0.0324)
Unemployment (d)			0.0358	0.0127			–	–
			(0.913)	(0.326)			–	–
Part time (d)			−0.380	−0.125			0.0416	0.0149
			(0.403)	(0.121)			(0.407)	(0.147)

Sector			0.00961	0.00337			0.0227**	0.00811**
			(0.0100)	(0.0035)			(0.0108)	(0.00381)
Risk			−0.174	−0.0610			0.265	0.0946
			(0.192)	(0.0675)			(0.189)	(0.0673)
Constant	−0.431***		−0.236		−0.476***		−3.577***	
	(0.139)		(1.120)		(0.168)		(1.277)	
Observations	99	99	99	99	99	99	96	96
Pseudo R^2	0	0	0.1653	0.1653	0.0002	0.0002	0.0842	0.0842

(d) for discrete change of dummy variable from 0 to 1
Standard errors in parentheses
***$p < 0.01$, **$p < 0.05$, *$p < 0.1$

working employee (including themselves). The models are estimated analogically to the one related to the solo self-employed entrepreneurs. While the first two consider the traits related to our second measure of optimism (Optimism2), the last two consider the factors associated with our third measure of optimism (Optimism3). None of the models show any impact of previous levels of over-optimism on consequent levels of the trait. Therefore, we can reject hypothesis 1 and 3 for the owners of multiperson companies. This is in contrast with the results for the solo self-employed entrepreneurs, where we found that the previous levels of over-optimism are related to later levels of the trait, as well as we found that the time span is of great importance for the intensity of the relationship. Furthermore, the models show no statistically significant relationship between risk propensity of the entrepreneur and his optimism levels, which results in rejection of hypothesis 2.

However, when we look at the second measure of optimism, two other covariates emerge as important: the start-up capital of the entity and the age of the entrepreneur (see model 6). Entrepreneurs with higher levels of start-up capital seem to be less over-optimistic. Older entrepreneurs strike as more over-optimistic. Never the less, those two characteristics do not persist as important for our last measure of optimism (Optimism3). Therefore, we can deduct that they are important during the initial years of the firm, but not later on. Lastly, the relationship that we found between unemployment before starting the entity and consequent levels of optimism; and between part-time work and later over-optimism for the solo self-employed entrepreneurs are not present for the entrepreneurs heading a firm with more than one full time working individual.

Over all, we can see that employers and solo self-employed entrepreneurs exhibit different traits. Table 7 reviews the empirical evidence for our hypotheses. We find strong persistence in over-optimism during the early life course of the firm, even after controlling for a large set of other variables, for the solo self-employed entrepreneur. However, this is not the case for the entrepreneurs involved in multiperson firms. Furthermore, we did not find any relation between risk preferences and the optimism levels of the two types of entrepreneurs.

Table 7 Hypotheses and empirical evidence

	Evidence	
Hypothesis	Self-employed	Employer firms
H1: Initial over-optimism of entrepreneurs is positively related to subsequent over-optimism in the early life course of the firm	+	0
H2: Risk preference of entrepreneurs is positively related to over-optimism	0	0
H3: Initial over-optimism and consequent over-optimism of entrepreneurs are positively related to latter measures of over-optimism in the early life course of the firm	+	0

5 Conclusion

The aim of this paper was to analyze the relationship between initial optimism and the level of realism of their predictions of the future, measured as the discrepancy between their expectations for change in employment and realized employment growth.

Over-optimism is said to be more prevalent amongst self-employed than amongst employees, and is likely to have a negative effect on the survival of newborn firms. But is this over-optimism homogeneous amongst the population of firm founders, and is it persistent during the early life course of the firm? Over-optimism is persistent once present, by diminishing the learning capabilities of the individual and providing her with an idea of more positive future outcomes than probable.

We have taken a more dynamic view on over-optimism of entrepreneurs then previous studies, by analyzing overoptimism during the early life course of firms. Our study reveals that initial over-optimism of entrepreneurs is positively related to subsequent over-optimism in the early life course of the firm, and that initial over-optimism and consequent over-optimism of entrepreneurs are positively related to latter measures of over-optimism in the early life course of the firm. However these findings only hold for solo self-employed, not for founders of employer firms. Over-optimism doesn't seem to be related to previous levels of overoptimism for founders of the employer firms. The over-optimism of founders of employer firms is reduced by those with relatively high start-up capital.

This study shows that overoptimism tends to be affected by the commitment of the entrepreneur to the new entity, with hybrid entrepreneurship showing a positive effect on improving the accuracy of decision making in the short term by keeping the individual more realistic with respect to the probable outcomes. However it does not affect the later accuracy. Previous research allocates the hybrid type of entry to individuals who feel the need to test the environment and their skills before they commit themselves fully (Folta et al. 2010). This seems to be a good technique for controlling the accuracy of expectations. However, this does not mean that more accurate decision making would lead to more profitable outcomes.

These findings can be related to a more outside view of hybrid entrepreneurs in contrast to full-time solo self-employed, lowering their biases in expectation (cf. Cassar 2010), both initially and over time. Founders of employer firms reveal to be more overoptimistic initially, but there seems to be no persistence of overoptimism for them, as it is for solo self-employed. Having high levels of start-up capital even seems to decrease over-optimism during the early life course, possibly also explained by a stronger outside view and enforced by external financiers.

Appendix

Description of variables

Variable name	Definition
OptimismBP	Captures the initial level of optimism measured by the fulfillment of the business plan. 1 indicates over-optimism; 0 otherwise
Optimism2	Represents the levels of optimism at the time of the first questionnaire. It is measured by the consequent fulfillment of the expected change of employees. 1 indicates over-optimism; 0 otherwise
Optimism3	Represents the levels of optimism at the time of the second questionnaire. It is measured by the consequent fulfillment of the expected change of employees. 1 indicates over-optimism; 0 otherwise
Gender	Dummy variable: 1 = male; 0 = female
Age	Categorical variable dividing the population into three groups, namely below 35, between 35 and 44, and older than 45
Education	Captures the higher level of education. Dummy variable: 1 = university degree; 0 = lower level of education
Industry experience	Captures if the entrepreneur has experience in the same industry as the one his/her company is currently operating in. The variable categorizes the experience into five levels, ranging from very little experience to high experience.
Start-up capital	Categorical variable separating the starting capital into seven different classes.
Self-employed	Captures if the individual is self-employed in the year 1994 or the firm has employees. 1 indicates self-employed, 0 otherwise.
Sector	Two digit industry classification
Unemployed	Dummy variable: has the value of 1 if the entrepreneur was unemployed right before engaging in his current position
Part time	Captures if the entrepreneur is working full time as such, or has another commitment. The variable has a dummy character, with 1 denoting working part time.
Risk propensity	Represented by a categorical variable, which captures the relative amount of risk taking of the entrepreneur. 1 indicates a very weak inclination to risk taking; and 5 very strong.

Correlation table for all variables

Variable	Obs	OptimismBP (d)	Optimism2 (d)	Optimism3 (d)	Gender (d)	Age	Education (d)	Industry experience	Start-up capital	Unemployment (d)	Part time (d)	Self-employed (d)	Sector
OptimismBP (d)	612	1											
Optimism2 (d)	612	0.0841	1										
Optimism3 (d)	612	0.0983	0.2288	1									
Gender (d)	612	0.0027	0.0562	0.0228	1								
Age	612	−0.0021	−0.0649	−0.0320	0.0663	1							
Education (d)	612	0.0947	0.0043	0.0382	0.0269	0.1475	1						
Industry experience	612	0.0587	−0.0121	−0.0344	−0.1202	0.0087	0.0797	1					
Start-up capital	612	0.0179	0.0464	0.1373	0.1740	0.0243	−0.0199	−0.1512	1				
Unemployment (d)	612	−0.0091	−0.0345	0.0599	−0.0077	0.0503	0.0339	0.0127	−0.0676	1			
Part time (d)	612	−0.0589	−0.1327	−0.1243	−0.2087	0.1000	0.0223	0.1694	−0.4441	−0.0080	1		
Self-employed (d)	612	−0.0189	−0.0614	−0.1297	−0.0927	0.0662	0.0423	0.0788	−0.4697	0.1160	0.3199	1	
Sector	612	0.0540	−0.0651	0.0095	−0.2207	−0.0101	0.1805	0.0471	−0.1677	−0.0261	0.1808	0.0923	1
Risk	612	−0.0056	0.0556	0.1083	0.0642	−0.0995	0.0042	−0.0850	0.0880	0.0077	−0.1230	−0.0302	−0.0515

(d) for a dummy variable with values 0 and 1

References

Barney JB (1986) Strategic factor markets: expectations, luck, and business strategy. Manag Sci 32(10):1231–1241
Bernardo AE, Welch I (2001) On the evolution of overconfidence and entrepreneurs. J Econ Manag Strateg 10(3):301–330
Bosma N, Van Praag M, Thurik R, De Wit G (2004) The value of human and social capital investments for the business performance of startups. Small Bus Econ 23(3):227–236
Cassar G (2010) Are individuals entering self-employment overly optimistic? An empirical test of plans and projections on nascent entrepreneur expectations. Strateg Manag J 31(8):822–840
Casson MC (1982) The entrepreneur: an economic theory. Martin Robertson, Oxford. 2nd ed. Edward Elgar, 1999
Cohn DL, Macfarlane S, Yanez C, Imai WK (1995) Risk perception: differences between adolescents and adults. Health Psychol 14(3):217–222
Dawson C, Henley A (2013) Over-optimism and entry and exit from self-employment. Int Small Bus J 31(8):938–954
De Meza D, Southey C (1996) The borrower's curse: optimism, finance and entrepreneurship. Econ J 106:375–386
Dosi G, Lovallo D (1997) Rational entrepreneurs or optimistic martyrs? Some considerations on technological regimes, corporate entries, and the evolutionary role of decision biases. In: Garud R, Nayyar PR, Shapira ZB (eds) Technological innovation: oversights and foresights. Cambridge University Press, Cambridge, pp 41–70
Folta TB, Delmar F, Wennberg K (2010) Hybrid entrepreneurship. Manag Sci 56(2):253–269
Fraser S, Greene FJ (2006) The effects of experience on entrepreneurial optimism and uncertainty. Economica 73(290):169–192
Hayward ML, Shepherd D, Griffin D (2006) A Hubris theory of entrepreneurship. Manag Sci 52 (2):160–172
Herz H, Schunk D, Zehnder C (2014) How do judgmental overconfidence and overoptimism shape innovative activity? Games Econ Behav 83:1–23
Hillman S, Todesco P (1999) Risk perception: unrealistic optimism or realistic expectancy. Psychol Rep 84:731–738
Hmieleski KM, Baron RA (2009) Entrepreneurs' optimism and new venture performance: a social cognitive perspective. Acad Manage J 52(3):473–488
Hogarth RM, Karelaia N (2012) Entrepreneurial success and failure: confidence and fallible judgment. Organ Sci 23(6):1733–1747
Hyytinen A, Lahtonen J, Pajarinen M (2014) Forecasting errors of new venture survival. Strateg Entrep J 8(4):283–302
Landier A, Thesmar D (2009) Financial contracting with optimistic entrepreneurs: theory and evidence. Rev Financ Stud 22(1):117–150
Larwood L, Whittaker W (1977) Managerial myopia: self-serving biases in organizational planning. J Appl Psychol 62(2):194–198
Lowe RA, Ziedonis AA (2006) Overoptimism and the performance of entrepreneurial firms. Manag Sci 52(2):173–186
Pulford BD, Colman AM (1996) Overconfidence, base rates and outcome positivity/negativity of predicted events. Br J Psychol 87(3):431–445
Puri M, Robinson DT (2007) Optimism and economic choice. J Financ Econ 86(1):71–99
Scheier MF, Carver CS (1985) Optimism, coping, and health: assessment and implications of generalized outcome expectancies. Health Psychol 4(3):219
Scheier MF, Carver CS, Bridges MW (1994) Distinguishing optimism from neuroticism (and trait anxiety, self-mastery, and self-esteem): a reevaluation of the Life Orientation Test. J Pers Soc Psychol 67(6):1063
Sitkin SB (1992) Learning through failure: the strategy of small losses. Res Organ Behav 14:231–231

Stam E, Wennberg K (2009) The roles of R&D in new firm growth. Small Bus Econ 33(1):77–89
Stam E, Bosma N, Van Witteloostuijn A, De Jong J, Bogaert S, Edwards N, Jaspers F (2012) Ambitious entrepreneurship. A review of the academic literature and new directions for public policy. Advisory Council for Science and Technology Policy (AWT), The Hague
Storey DJ (2011) Optimism and chance: the elephants in the entrepreneurship room. Int Small Bus J 29(4):303–321
Ucbasaran D, Westhead P, Wright M, Flores M (2010) The nature of entrepreneurial experience, business failure and comparative optimism. J Bus Ventur 25(6):541–555
Weiner B (1986) An attributional theory of motivation and emotion. Springer, New York
Weinstein ND (1980) Unrealistic optimism about future life events. J Pers Soc Psychol 39 (5):806–820

Part IV
Interaction

Knowledge Spillovers Through FDI and Trade: The Moderating Role of Quality-Adjusted Human Capital

Muhammad Ali, Uwe Cantner, and Ipsita Roy

Abstract The paper extends the findings of the Coe and Helpman (Eur Econ Rev 39(5):859–887, 1995) model of R&D spillovers by considering foreign direct investment (FDI) as a channel for knowledge spillovers in addition to imports. Deeper insights on the issue are provided by examining the inter-relationship between knowledge spillovers from imports and inward FDI. Furthermore, human capital is added to the discussion as one of the appropriability factors for knowledge spillovers, with special focus on its quality-content, using journal publications and patent applications. Applying cointegration estimation method on 20 European countries from 1995 to 2010, the direct effects of FDI-related as well as import-related spillovers on domestic productivity are confirmed. Furthermore, a strong complementary relationship is found between knowledge spillovers through the channels of imports and inward FDI. When considering quality-adjusted human capital, countries with better human capital are found to benefit not only from direct productivity effects, but also from absorption and transmission of international knowledge spillovers through imports and inward FDI. Finally, technological distance with the frontier does not appear to play a role in the absorption of import and FDI related knowledge spillovers.

1 Introduction

In the endogenous growth literature, the importance of international knowledge spillovers in explaining domestic productivity is widely acknowledged. Prior research on technological progress (Romer 1989; Aghion and Howitt 1992;

M. Ali (✉) • I. Roy
Faculty of Economics and Business Administration, Friedrich Schiller University Jena, Carl-Zeiss-Strasse 3, 07743 Jena, Germany
e-mail: m.alishuja@yahoo.com; ali.m@uni-jena.de

U. Cantner
Faculty of Economics and Business Administration, Friedrich Schiller University Jena, Carl-Zeiss-Strasse 3, 07743 Jena, Germany

Department of Marketing and Management, I2M Group, University of Southern Denmark, Campusveij 55, 5230 Odense, Denmark

A. Pyka, U. Cantner (eds.), *Foundations of Economic Change*, Economic Complexity and Evolution, DOI 10.1007/978-3-319-62009-1_16

Grossman and Helpman 1991; Coe and Helpman 1995; Engelbrecht 1997) proposes that a country's productivity depends not only on its own R&D efforts but also on foreign R&D, transmitted through channels of knowledge spillovers. In identifying the mechanism for knowledge spillovers, a considerable body of theoretical and empirical literature focuses on international trade as the most important channel through which knowledge and technology are transferred across boundaries. Other studies claim that international trade accounts for only 20% of productivity from foreign R&D and subsequently propose alternate spillover channels—such as outward and inward FDI (Wang and Blomström 1992; Borensztein et al. 1998; Glass and Saggi 1998; Xu and Wang 2000; Branstetter 2006), labor mobility and social networks (Bernard and Bradford Jensen 1999; Keller 2004), patent citations (Eaton and Kortum 1996, 1999; Xu and Chiang 2005) and cross-licensing (Lee 2006) to explain productivity growth.

While existing research addresses different channels through which external knowledge and foreign technologies are transferred across countries, this paper restricts its attention to knowledge spillovers via imports and inward FDI to ensure better identification of the spillover channels, as well as to provide for an easy comparability with standard literature on the topic (Grossman and Helpman 1991; Benhabib and Spiegel 1994; Coe et al. 1997; Coe and Helpman 1995). Trade in tangible intermediate inputs, manufactured goods and capital equipments result in efficient use of domestic resources and hence raises domestic productivity. Furthermore, it enables open communication among trade partners that leads to "cross-border" learning about foreign technologies and materials, production processes and organizational routines. Outward FDI enables greater returns on domestic investments by exploiting a foreign country's competitive advantage. Inward FDI, on the other hand, leads to greater access and diffusion of foreign technologies, productivity gains, forward and backward linkage effects and introduction of new skills and organizational practices in host countries. Furthermore, following from the literature on location choice and appropriability conditions relating to FDI (Feinberg and Majumdar 2001; Alcácer and Chung 2007), FDI enhances the ability of the country to absorb potential spillover-benefits related to investment.

Evidently, the literature on international trade and inward and outward FDI as spillover channels is extensive. However, what has been discussed so far are the respective effects of trade and of FDI on domestic productivity, assuming them to be two unrelated channels of spillovers. This constitutes an important drawback given the fact that trade and FDI are very much related (Brainard 1997) and therefore the complementarity or substitutability needs to be analyzed when examining their impact on productivity growth. Knowledge spillovers from trade can occur through the import of intermediate inputs and high-tech merchandise and services, while that from FDI can occur through channels of backward linkages (Javorcik 2004), vertical linkages in the form of spillovers to suppliers and customers (Lall 1980), worker mobility (Blomström and Kokko 1998) and demonstration effects in the form of imitation and reverse engineering (Saggi 2006). Yet, irrespective of the nature of spillovers through trade and FDI, empirical evidence remains inconclusive regarding their exact relationship (Fontagné 1999; De Mello and Fukasaku 2000).

The relationship between knowledge spillovers and productivity has also received much attention from labor economists in the last few decades. Education of the labor force and their accumulated stock of human capital significantly determine a country's ability to create new ideas and to adapt old ones (Lucas 1988; Nelson and Phelps 1966; Borensztein et al. 1998; Xu and Wang 2000). Apart from this direct effect on productivity growth, human capital also raises domestic productivity through greater absorption and diffusion of international technological spillovers and provision of suitable appropriability conditions for FDI. Existing literature in this regard suggests that an adequate level of human capital is necessary for technological spillovers to have a significant positive impact on domestic productivity. However, despite theoretical predictions, empirical findings on the exact relationship between channels of technological spillovers and the level of human capital in determining productivity growth remain inconclusive (Blomström et al. 2003). Various explanations for the inconsistent findings are provided in the literature, the most important being the way human capital stock is measured and compared across countries (Ramos et al. 2010).

Based on the above arguments, this study provides an integrated approach to better explain specific mechanisms by which spillover channels raise domestic productivity and the role of human capital therein. Specifically, it makes advances in the following directions: First, the Coe and Helpman (1995) model of R&D spillovers is extended by additionally analyzing FDI as an important channel for knowledge spillovers and the impact of trade and FDI-related knowledge spillovers on domestic productivity is investigated. However, unlike existing studies that explain trade and FDI as two independent channels of spillovers, the current study considers them as strongly overlapping and analyzes their relative and combined effect on productivity. Second, in this study human capital is considered not only as an ordinary input in the domestic production function, but also as a moderating variable that provides necessary conditions for absorption and transmission of trade and FDI-related knowledge spillovers and subsequent productivity growth. Accordingly, a quality-based index of human capital is proposed that allows for comprehensive and systematic comparison of human capital stocks across countries. Finally, this study builds on the catching-up hypothesis that countries farther away from the technological frontier benefit more from knowledge spillovers, and compares productivity effects of knowledge spillovers between countries with large distance to the technological frontier and countries with relatively smaller distance to the technological frontier.

The rest of the paper is organized as follows: Section 2 gives the conceptual background on knowledge spillovers through international trade and FDI and an overview of quality-based indicator of human capital. Section 3 introduces the econometric models and Sect. 4 discusses the data. Section 5 presents the econometric methodology considered to analyze the relevant research questions. Section 6 summarizes the main findings and Sect. 7 discusses the results.

2 Conceptual Background

2.1 *Knowledge Spillovers Through International Trade and Foreign Direct Investment*

Literature on the theory of endogenous technological progress presents mixed evidence on the importance and relative effectiveness of knowledge spillovers for the domestic economy. Earlier studies go back to Grossman and Helpman (1991), (henceforth GH) who formulate a theoretical model of product-variety where total factor productivity of a country increases with the number of varieties of intermediate products available in the market, and the share of labor employed in their production. Furthermore, the authors show that changes in the degree of openness of an economy, as measured by the level of trade promotion or trade protection, also affect the long-run growth rate, the transition to the steady state, the volume of bilateral trade and the level of social welfare. Extending GH, Coe and Helpman (1995) (henceforth CH) study the role of knowledge spillovers from foreign innovative activities through the channel of international trade. The authors argue that, in addition to domestic innovative efforts measured by profit maximizing R&D investments of entrepreneurs, foreign innovative activities also affect technological progress in the home country. Hence, total factor productivity is defined as a function of domestic R&D and foreign R&D. There can be direct and indirect benefits of foreign R&D to domestic economies. A direct impact arises from the direct transfer of technology while indirect benefits are realized through transmission channels such as trade and foreign direct investment. In the context of their paper, the extent to which these foreign R&D efforts can be transferred depends on how open the country is to international trade. Using the panel cointegration technique for long-run relationship on data for OECD countries for the period 1971–1990, the authors find that there is a close link between factor productivity and domestic as well as foreign R&D capital stocks. Moreover, trade is found to play an important role in transferring R&D related know-how from partners to home countries. Other empirical studies, such as Lichtenberg and Pottelsberghe de la Potterie (1998) and Kao et al. (1999) reach similar conclusions for different countries.

So far, most seminal papers analyzing the relationship between international knowledge spillovers and productivity have considered trade as the most important channel for knowledge spillover. Keller (1998), contrariwise, studies the robustness of CH results using Monte-Carlo-based test and challenges the findings that international R&D spillovers are trade related. In the Monte-Carlo experiment, international R&D spillovers are studied for randomly matched trade partners and comparison is then made between true values and ones generated by a simulation exercise. The findings suggest that the results of CH do not change even when the trade partners are randomly matched, which casts doubts on the claim that the pattern of international trade is important in knowledge spillovers. In response to Keller's critique, Coe and Hoffmaister (1999) show that a more sophisticated methodology for assigning random weights, as compared to Keller (1998), yields insignificant effects of spillovers on total factor productivity, a result that supports the earlier findings of Coe and Helpman (1995). Nevertheless, the results of Coe and Helpman (1995) appear to be sensitive to the choice of methodology and hints towards the need for the inclusion of trade unrelated channels of international technology diffusion. Consequently, a second strand of literature introduces FDI as an additional channel for international knowledge spillovers[1] and investigates the effect of FDI-related knowledge spillovers on domestic productivity. Hejazi and Safarian (1999) include FDI weighted R&D in the CH model in addition to import weighted R&D for G6 countries. Similar to the CH study, the authors find that both foreign and domestic R&D significantly affect domestic productivity. Additionally, the coefficient for FDI weighted foreign R&D is found to be higher than the trade weighted R&D variable, while the inclusion of FDI significantly reduces the significance of trade weighted foreign R&D. Moreover, they find that, when R&D variables are interacted with trade openness, they lose significance. The authors interpret this result suggesting that, irrespective of the extent to which the economy is open, technological spillovers do take place through FDI and trade. Branstetter (2006) studies the scope of technological spillovers through FDI by Japanese firms to US using patent citations from Japanese firms in the US patent office and argues that knowledge spillovers can go in either direction: firms investing in the host country bring knowledge from the home country and also learn from the domestic pool of knowledge in the home country. Results, robust to US-Japan technological alliances, suggest that FDI not only brings information into home country but also benefits the investing firm through the local stock of knowledge. Exploring further at the firm level, some studies examine the spillovers through backward and forward linkages. Javorcik (2004) uses panel data for Lithuanian firms and finds evidence only for backward linkages and not for forward linkages. Similarly, Kugler (2006) and Bwalya (2006) find evidence for backward linkages but not for forward linkages in Colombian and Zambian manufacturing sectors, respectively. Schoors and Tol (2002), however, in addition to evidence for spillovers through backward linkages, find negative spillovers effects through forward linkages.

In recent years, both international trade and FDI have been added as spillover channels in the productivity equation. Xu and Wang (2000), for example, examine the relationship between MNC activities (outward FDI) and trade in capital goods and technology diffusion for 21 OECD countries over the period 1971–1990 and find contrasting results. While a significant positive impact of foreign R&D spill-overs through the channels of international trade and outward FDI is found on domestic total factor productivity, no such effect is found with respect to inward FDI. The authors interpret the results in terms of methodological limitations and the unavailability of quality data, while acknowledging the need to give greater

[1]Our definition of knowledge spillovers in this paper includes both voluntary knowledge transfers and involuntary knowledge spillovers.

attention to econometric issues. Keller (2010) proposes a theoretical framework in identifying the contribution of international trade and FDI in the economic performance of a country and finds that geographical proximity is an important condition for knowledge diffusion. Furthermore, the author claims that the two channels are indeed correlated and therefore empirical studies should focus on understanding this relationship. Saggi (2002), in a detailed review of the literature, suggests that growth enhancing effects of FDI are larger in countries that follow export promotion rather than import substitution strategies. This is because countries that follow more open trade regimes usually target the bigger global market as against countries that undertake import substitution, and therefore attract more FDI. Thus the trade policy regime is found to be an important determinant of the effect of FDI on the domestic economy, necessitating the need to examine how they interact when included together in the productivity model.

While theoretical predictions on the inter-relationship between international trade and FDI are significant, empirical evidence remains scarce. Filippaios and Kottaridi (2008) compare the investment development path between the EU and CEEC and find a strong complementarity between inward FDI and imports in determining international investors' behavior. Fontagné (1999), in a review of literature, states that, while studies in the 1980s claimed international trade to have generated FDI, in recent years the causality has been reversed. Based on these claims, one can expect that the relationship between trade and FDI varies with several micro and macro characteristics such as firm attributes and market orientation, sectoral affiliation or the country under analysis. From the perspective of the investing (home) country, outward FDI can be considered a substitute for exports because of increased production and the sale of finished goods by the foreign multinational corporations (MNC) established in the host market. However, inward FDI can increase the host country's imports by acquiring raw materials and intermediate inputs necessary for production by foreign multinational corporations to be imported from the parent country. The unavailability of appropriate intermediate products, quality considerations or highly-specific production process of the foreign affiliates in the host country can trigger such a complementary relationship. The literature on gravity models (Brenton et al. 1999) also provides similar arguments. In summary, although the direction of correlation (complementarity or substitutability) between trade in imports and inward FDI is a matter of debate, these two channels seem to be interlinked in encouraging productivity growth. However, no evidence exists with respect to the dynamics of knowledge spillovers from inward FDI and imports and how they interact with one another in promoting domestic productivity growth. The first and foremost contribution of the study reflects this consideration. The a-priori assumption here is that inward FDI encourages imports of technologically intensive intermediate goods and services from the parent country and transfers the capabilities to use technologically advanced products to workers hired from the domestic labor market. Therefore, we expect a complementary relationship between the two spillover channels. Based on this expectation, we examine their individual as well as combined impact as a spillover mechanism on domestic productivity growth and propose the following hypotheses:

Hypothesis 1a: Knowledge spillovers through imports positively affect domestic productivity.

Hypothesis 1b: Knowledge spillovers through inward FDI positively affect domestic productivity.

Hypothesis 2: The productivity-enhancing effects of knowledge spillovers through imports are reinforced by high degrees of FDI.

2.2 *Moderating Knowledge Spillovers: Human Capital*

The relevance of trade and FDI as channels for knowledge transfer is crucial for productivity, to say the least. However, mere access to foreign R&D stock, technologies and know-how is not enough to drive a country on the path of long-term development. It is equally essential for the external knowledge to be sufficiently absorbed and diffused throughout the economy. Herein lies the role of human capital as a measure of absorptive capacity in moderating the relationship between productivity and knowledge spillovers, and forms the second most important contribution of the current study.

In their seminal paper on the two faces of R&D, Cohen and Levinthal (1989) argue that, while the existence of external knowledge linkages is beneficial, firms necessarily should have an adequate level of absorptive capacity in order to materialize beneficial spillovers from such external linkages. Accordingly, firms should invest in the development of such absorptive capacity by undertaking internal R&D activities. Discussing absorptive capacity within a human capital framework, Nelson and Phelps (1966) propose that, in a technologically progressive economy, the more educated the innovators, the quicker will be the speed of introduction of new techniques of production, and this will subsequently speed up the process of technological diffusion. Postulating two theoretical models of technological diffusion, the authors indicate that the payoff to increased educational attainment (that is, the rate of return to education) is greater the more technologically progressive the economy. Also, while the growth of technology frontier reflects the rate at which new discoveries are made, the growth of total factor productivity (TFP) depends on the implementation of these discoveries and varies positively with the distance between the technology frontier and the level of current productivity, which again depends on the level of human capital. Following similar arguments, Engelbrecht (1997) builds upon CH's model by including human capital as an additional variable accounting for non-R&D related innovation activities. Measuring human capital by interpolating Barro and Lee (1993) data on average years of education of the labor force above 25 years of age for 21 OECD countries, the author finds a direct effect of this variable on domestic productivity, technology catch-up and the absorption of foreign technology. Similar studies (Frantzen 2000; Griffith et al. 2002; Barrios et al. 2007; Kwark and Shyn 2006; Teixeira and Fortuna 2010) also confirm these findings.

Absorptive capacity measured in terms of human capital is also related to the literature on spillover channels where researchers have established the relationship between domestic human capital stock, international trade and FDI. Miller and Upadhyay (2000) suggest that the impact of human capital in a country is conditioned upon the degree to which the economy is open to international trade. Using data for a sample of developed as well as developing countries, the authors find that for low degrees of trade openness, the effect of human capital on total factor productivity is negative while for greater degrees of trade openness, the effect is positive and highly significant. While the relationship between trade and human capital is quite straightforward, the same cannot be said with respect to FDI. Borensztein et al. (1998) claim that the productivity effect of FDI will depend on the educational characteristics of the host or receiving countries. Examining the effect of FDI on economic growth in a cross-country analysis during 1970–1989 and measuring human capital as average years of schooling of male pupils (Barro and Lee 1993), the authors find direct as well indirect effects of FDI on productivity growth. Not only does greater FDI raise productivity, but the magnitude of the effect depends significantly on the domestic human capital stock of the country. Similarly, Blomström et al. (2003) suggest that, while FDI inflow leads to absorption and diffusion of foreign technology through the upgradation of local skills, a host country's level of human capital also determines the level of FDI it attracts. In other words, a greater level of human capital should attract more technologically intensive FDI and MNC operations as compared to weaker economies with lower level of human capital and absorptive capacity. Thus the extent and scope of knowledge spillovers from FDI depend on the readiness and absorptive capability of the domestic sector. This means that, while FDI reduces the cost of technology adoption, spillovers from FDI can also be negative because of the crowding out effect on domestic firms with insufficient absorptive capacity. Other studies that investigate the complex and non-linear relationship between channels of knowledge spillovers and human capital (Kokko et al. 1996; Kathuria 2002) suggest that FDI affects domestic productivity only in the presence of technological and market capabilities, a certain threshold level of human capital, and investment in learning and training.

It is evident from the studies mentioned above that the interrelationships between the channels of knowledge spillovers through FDI and trade and human capital have already been studied at various levels of aggregation. However, while theoretical predictions on the moderating role of human capital are substantial, empirical verification of the issue is mixed and rather inconclusive. The current study claims that the way human capital is measured in the existing literature might be one reason for the mixed evidence. So far, in previous studies, the human capital stock in a country is measured in terms of quantity-based indicators such as average years of schooling and graduation rates, and then related to knowledge spillovers and productivity growth. However, quantity-based indicators of human capital fail to account for quality differences in the education system and dimensions related to skills and competencies of human capital (OECD 2001). By this measure, an additional year of secondary education in a developed country, say the US, will be the same as in a less-developed country, say Bangladesh, even though US has a far superior education system in terms of quality. Furthermore, it neglects the differences in cognitive skills and problem-solving capabilities in students (Hanushek and Kimko 2000) and therefore renders the measure incomparable across countries. What is needed, therefore, is a systematic analysis of the role of human capital, taking into account the quality differences across countries that, in turn, affect the speed of absorption of knowledge spillovers through trade and FDI. To the best of our knowledge, no studies have so far provided a quality measure of human capital in analyzing the productivity effects of knowledge spillovers. Addressing this limitation, the paper uses secondary data for human capital based on average years of schooling and returns to education and adjusts it for quality using patents and publications. The following section explains the quantity-quality indicators and the choice of proxies for human capital measurement in more detail.

2.3 *Quantity vs. Quality of Human Capital*

Traditionally, three approaches to human capital measurement have been pursued in the literature: cost-based approach, income-based approach and indicator-based approach. The cost-based approach (Kendrick 1976; Eisner 1988) measures human capital in terms of past investments undertaken by individuals, households, employers or government, and more recently in terms of the value of time devoted to the education of students. The income-based approach (Weisbrod 1961; Graham and Webb 1979; Jorgenson and Fraumeni 1989) measures human capital as the expected future earnings generated from human capital investments over the lifetime of a person. Finally, the indicator-based approach uses various measures as proxy for the stock of human capitalfor example, school enrollment rates (Barro 1991; Mankiw et al. 1992; Levine and Renelt 1992), educational attainment of adults aged 25 years and above (Barro and Lee 1993), average years of schooling (Benhabib and Spiegel 1994; Barro and Sala-i-Martin 2004; O'Neill 1995; Barro 1997; Krueger and Lindahl 2001), student-teacher ratio (Wang and Wong 2011), graduation rates, dropout rates and adult literacy rates (Azariadis and Drazen 1990; Nehru et al. 1995; Barro and Lee 1996). However, these measures fail to account for differences in the education systems across countries and attach equal weights, irrespective of quality differences and mismatch in the cognitive skills of students. Because quality of human capital, and not mere quantity, is an important indicator of economic growth, the current study provides a new measure of the human capital stock adjusted by its quality and subsequently examines its effect in moderating the relationship between knowledge spillovers and productivity.

One approach that has gained much attention in recent years as a quality-based measure of human capital is international test scores that capture the cognitive performance of students globally (Hanushek and Kimko 2000). For example, the Trends in International Mathematics and Science Study (TIMSS) is a worldwide study program provided by the International Association for the Evaluation of

Educational Achievement (IEA) that assesses mathematics and science knowledge in fourth and eighth grade students. The study, first conducted in 1995 and thereafter conducted every four years globally, provides additional information on the learning conditions in countries and hence accounts also for the diversity in the education systems worldwide. A similar assessment program provided by the OECD is the Programme for International Student Assessment (PISA) that tests cognitive skills like reading, mathematics, science and problem solving of 15–16 year olds. This program, started in 2000 and repeated every three years, aims at measuring "education's application to real-life problems and lifelong learning" (OECD 2001). Another recent international study provided by the OECD is the Programme for the International Assessment of Adult Competencies (PIAAC) that tests skills and competencies of adults (aged 16–65) in terms of literacy, numeracy and problem-solving in technology-rich environments. PIAAC, first conducted in 2011–2012 in the US, therefore allows for systematic comparison across countries by focusing on the cognitive and workplace skills, educational background and occupational attainment of adults around the world. Other similar examples of standardized tests are the Graduate Record Examination (GRE), the Graduate Management Admission Test (GMAT) and the Scholastic Aptitude Test (SAT). Although most of these standardized tests provide time series across educational assessments for countries, the availability of annual data for a longer time frame and for all sample countries considered in the current analysis is a major issue. The International Mathematical Olympiad (IMO) serves as an alternative, by providing yearly scores in mathematics for pre-collegiate students worldwide. The IMO, first held in 1959 in Romania, is a 42-point mathematical Olympiad that ranks countries based on the cumulative test scores. It is not a proxy for basic skills in the population, rather a proxy for the beyond-the-classroom education a country provides to exceptionally high-skilled students in mathematics and science. IMO test scores are available for long time periods and for all our sample countries, with the only limitation arising from the structure of the test and sample-size.[2]

A second alternative in this regard is journal publications. An academic journal is a peer-reviewed periodical that constitutes publication of original research, review articles and book reviews in all fields of academia. It is frequently used as a proxy for the scientific environment, and the research activities undertaken in a country. Typically, the quality of an academic journal is measured by its 'impact factor', that is, the average number of citations received from later publications, and journals with higher impact factors are considered to be of higher quality than those with lower ones. Therefore, one can assume that higher the number of journal publications in a country, the richer is its knowledge base and human capital. Furthermore, data on publication is readily available for all countries in the sample for a long time frame.

[2]Please see Table 4 in the Appendix for an overview on pros and cons of using the different proxies for quality adjustment of human capital.

A third alternative is patents. Patents are generally used as a proxy for innovativeness in regional- and firm-level analysis. Although patents are a direct measure of innovative activity, they still suffer from some potential problems. Despite being very narrow in scope, patents can be used as a proxy for the quality of education. Countries with a better quality of education are more likely to innovate than countries with poorer quality. Therefore, the relatively higher number of patents in a given year can hint towards the better education system.

Subsequently, the current analysis uses data from the World Bank for journal publications in science and technology (S&T, having non-zero impact factors), and patent applications as weighting parameters for the Barro and Lee (2010) quantity-based measure of human capital. While the details of the construction can be found in the data section, Fig. 1 shows how the respective positions of the countries change when we adjust the conventional measure of human capital with quality. We rank 20 countries in our sample based on both adjusted and unadjusted human capital indices and subtract their respective ranks for 1995 and 2010. The figure shows the plots of differences in relative ranks of 20 European countries in the sample. The positive differences are the gains in ranks after adjustment for quality, which already points to the fact that the conventional human capital index underestimates the human capital of these countries and vice versa. Most significant differences are observed for Czech Republic for which the rank drops from 1st to 13th in 1995 and 1st to 15th in 2010. Similarly, Estonia goes down in the ranks from 8th to 18th in 1995 and 3rd to 19th in 2010. However, the rank for the United Kingdom increases from 18th to 4th in 1995 and 20th to 4th in 2010, which is similar to the rank of the United Kingdom according to TIMSS 2011.

Based on these differences, the second contribution of the study is the analysis of the moderating role of quality-adjusted human capital in the knowledge

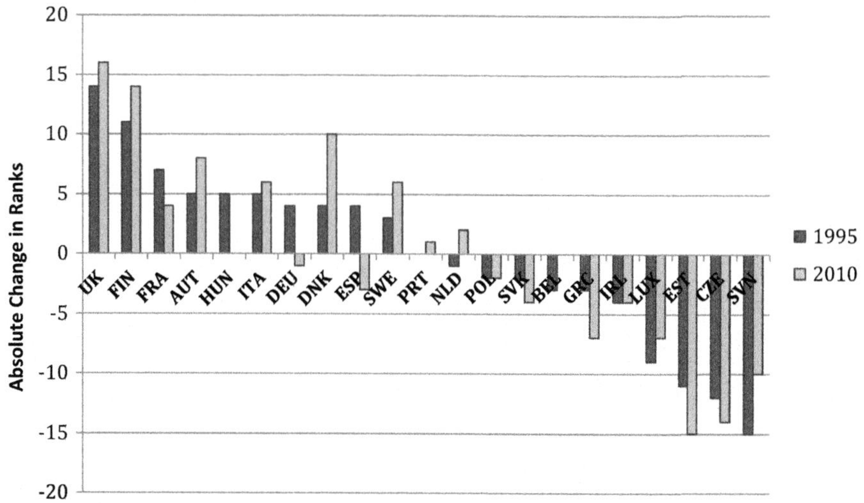

Fig. 1 Change in ranks after quality adjustment of human capital

spillover-productivity link. If imports, for example, are technology intensive and the importing country does not have adequate human capital to learn from the knowledge embedded in the imports, then spillovers will not adequately affect overall productivity of the economy. Proposing similar arguments with respect to FDI, it can therefore be argued that countries with better human capital benefit more from knowledge spillovers through channels of trade and FDI. We assess the moderation of human capital using interactions between knowledge spillovers and quality-adjusted human capital, while acknowledging the direct effect of human capital on domestic productivity. Accordingly, the following two hypotheses are proposed:

Hypothesis 3a: Human capital positively affects domestic productivity.

Hypothesis 3b: Human capital positively moderates the relationship between knowledge spillovers and domestic productivity.

Finally, in a cross-country analysis it is important to assess the heterogeneous country specific characteristics. Countries at different growth trajectories than others might benefit differently from the knowledge spillovers relative to their level of productivity. According to the catching-up hypothesis, countries with productivity levels significantly lower than the frontier are expected to gain more from international knowledge spillovers than countries closer to the frontier (Griffith et al. 2002; Castellani and Zanfei 2003). This is because technologically-backward countries benefit from imitation of technologies introduced in leader countries, and usually the cost of imitation is lower than that of innovation closer to the frontier (Barro and Sala-i-Martin 2004). Therefore, the wider the technology gap between the lagging country and the leader, the higher the scope of technology adoption and international knowledge spillovers and subsequently higher the gains in productivity. We capture this effect by introducing a technological gap variable in the main regressions and also interact with the spillovers variables to assess whether countries far away from the technological frontier gain more from knowledge spillovers.

Hypothesis 4: Countries significantly distant from the technological frontier gain more from international knowledge spillovers.

3 Models

3.1 Model 1: CH Specification

The main model to test our hypotheses 1a and 1b builds upon the CH specification (corresponding to Eq. (2) in the CH) and is formulated as follows:

$$logTFP_{i,t} = \beta_o + \beta_1 logR\&D_{i,t} + \beta_2 ImportSpill_{i,t} + \varepsilon_{i,t} \tag{1}$$

where *TFP* is total factor productivity of country *i*, R&D is per capita R&D stock in importing country (country *i*), $ImportSpill_{i,t} = \Omega \mathrm{logR\&D_{i,t}}$ represent per capita import-related spillovers where $R\&D_{i,t}$ is stock of R&D in the exporting country (country j) and Ω is the ratio of imports from country j to GDP in country i.

3.2 Model 2: Base Specification (Extension of Model 1)

We extend the CH model in Eq. (1) by including quality-adjusted human capital and FDI as an additional source of international knowledge spillovers in Eq. (2).

$$logTFP_{i,t} = \beta_o + \beta_1 logR\&D_{i,t} + \beta ImportSpill_{i,t} + \beta_3 logFDI_{i,t} + \beta_4 logHCQ_{i,t} + \varepsilon_{i,t} \tag{2}$$

where *HCQ* is the quality is adjusted human capital variable and *FDI* is per capita stock of inward FDI in country *i*. This, therefore, captures the direct impact of human capital on a country's productivity.

3.3 Model 3: Complementarity Between Import-Related Spillovers and FDI

Model 3 aims to capture the complementarity between import-related spillovers and FDI as outlined in hypothesis 2. The interaction between import-related spillovers and FDI is used to determine whether import-related spillovers and FDI are complements or substitutes.

$$logTFP_{i,t} = \beta_o + \beta_1 logR\&D_{i,t} + \beta_2 ImportSpill_{i,t} + \beta_3 logFDI_{i,t} + \beta_4 logHCQ_{i,t} + \beta_5 \left(ImportSpill_{i,t} * FDI_{i,t}\right) + \varepsilon_{i,t} \tag{3}$$

3.4 Model 4: Human Capital as a Moderator of Knowledge Spillovers

Interactions of import-related spillovers and FDI with quality-adjusted human capital are introduced in Model 4. Here we aim to test our hypothesis 3 where we expect human capital to moderate the relationship between knowledge spillovers and TFP.

$$logTFP_{i,t} = \beta_o + \beta_1 logR\&D_{i,t} + \beta_2 ImportSpill_{i,t} + \beta_3 FDI_{i,t} + \beta_4 HCQ_{i,t} + \beta_5 \left(ImportSpill_{i,t} * HCQ_{i,t}\right) + \beta_6 \left(FDI_{i,t} * HCQ_{i,t}\right) + \varepsilon_{i,t} \tag{4}$$

3.5 Model 5: Role of Technological Gap

Finally, in Model 5, to test our hypothesis 4, we include the technological gap between country *i* and the technological frontier in model 2 (Eq. 5a below).

$$logTFP_{i,t} = \beta_o + \beta_1 logR\&D_{i,t} + \beta_2 ImportSpill_{i,t} + \beta_3 logFDI_{i,t} + \beta_4 logHCQ_{i,t} + \beta_5 logGap_{i,t} + \varepsilon_{i,t} \quad (5a)$$

where *Gap* is the distance between country with highest TFP in the sample minus TFP of country *i*. In subsequent models, we include interactions of technological gap variable with import-related spillovers and FDI to test whether technologically distant countries benefit more from international knowledge spillovers (models 5b and 5c).

$$logTFP_{i,t} = \beta_o + \beta_1 logR\&D_{i,t} + \beta_2 ImportSpill_{i,t} + \beta_3 logFDI_{i,t} + \beta_4 logHCQ_{i,t} + \beta_5 logGap_{i,t} + \beta_6 (ImportSpill_{i,t} * Gap_{i,t}) + \varepsilon_{i,t} \quad (5b)$$

$$logTFP_{i,t} = \beta_o + \beta_1 logR\&D_{i,t} + \beta_2 ImportSpill_{i,t} + \beta_3 logFDI_{i,t} + \beta_4 logHCQ_{i,t} + \beta_5 logGap_{i,t} + \beta_6 (FDI_{i,t} * Gap_{i,t}) + \varepsilon_{i,t} \quad (5c)$$

4 Data

The data sample covers the period from 1995 to 2010 and includes 20 European countries: Austria, Belgium, Czech Republic, Denmark, Estonia, Finland, France, Germany, Greece, Hungary, Ireland, Italy, Netherlands, Poland, Portugal, Spain, Slovak Republic, Slovenia, Sweden and the United Kingdom. In what follows, we explain the construction and sources of the variables used in our empirical analysis.

4.1 Total Factor Productivity (TFP)

Total factor productivity is taken from Penn World Tables v8.0 and the following methodology has been used to calculate TFP:

$$TFP_{i,t} = \frac{Y_t}{Y_{t-1}} / Q_{t,t-1}$$

where

$$Q_{t,t-1} = \frac{1}{2}(\alpha_t + \alpha_{t-1})ln\frac{K_t}{K_{t-1}} + \left[1 - \frac{1}{2}(\alpha_t + \alpha_{t-1})\right]ln\frac{L_t}{L_{t-1}}$$

Y is real GDP, K is capital stock, L is labor force engaged and α is output elasticity of capital (share of gross fixed capital formation in real GDP). Details of the calculation can be found in Inklaar and Timmer (2013).

4.2 R&D Capital Stock

Since data for R&D capital stock are not available for long time series, we calculate R&D capital stock using the perpetual inventory method for each country. Data for R&D flows are taken from OECD Database: "Main Science and Technology Indicators" to estimate stock values, and subsequently R&D capital stock for the first year is calculated using following formula:

$$R\&D_{i,t=1} = \frac{R\&D^{flow}_{i,t=1}}{g + \delta} \tag{6}$$

where $R\&D^{flow}_{i,t=1}$ is R&D expenditure flow for the first year, g is the compound annual growth rate of R&D expenditure flows and δ is the depreciation rate of investment assumed at 15%.

Although our sample for estimations starts from 1995, for calculation of R&D capital stock, we use data from 1981 to minimize the potential bias in the construction of the first year's capital stock. For some countries such as the Czech Republic and Estonia, available data series start from 1991 and 1998, respectively. In such cases, initial capital stock is calculated for available years and linearly extrapolated wherever necessary. Similarly, linear interpolation is used to fill-in missing values of R&D expenditure flows. Capital stock for later years is calculated by adding the flow of R&D expenditure to the previous year's capital stock after adjusting it for depreciation. Formally:

$$R\&D_{i,t} = R\&D_{i,t-1}{}^{*}(1 - \delta) + R\&D^{flow}_{i,t}$$

4.3 Human Capital Variables

The unadjusted human capital index is taken from Penn World Tables v8.0. This index is based on averages years of schooling from Barro and Lee (2010) and assumed rate of return corresponding to Psacharopoulos (1994). The human capital variable based on the above mentioned criteria provides meaningful information about the quantity of human capital for the population above 15 years of age. However, it does not account for the quality of education. This caveat of the index limits its usefulness in cross country analysis, following which we weight human capital variable with proxies of quality of education. The variables used as proxies for the quality of education (as explained in Sect. 2.3) are (a) aggregated journal articles in science and technology (World Development Indicators (WDI) and (b) aggregated patents (WDI). The benefit of using aggregated patents and publications from WDI compared to the Web of Science Database is that OECD data are weighted for co-authorship. If there is more than one author for a publication or a patent, OECD distributes the share to all coauthors to avoid double counting. The quality adjusted human capital (HCQ) variable is calculated using Eq. (7).

$$HCQ_{i,t} = HC_{i,t}{}^{*}\left(\frac{Publications_{i,t}}{L_{i,t}} + \frac{Patents_{i,t}}{L_{i,t}}\right) \tag{7}$$

where HC is the human capital index based on average years of schooling and returns to education, Publications represents the journal publications in science and technology from the World Bank, Patents is number of patent applications per country in all fields and L is the engaged labor force.

4.4 Knowledge Spillovers

In the context of this study, knowledge from one country to another is transferred through the channel of imports and FDI. Countries spend on R&D to develop new knowledge. The pieces of new knowledge from R&D activities over the years jointly represent the knowledge stock of the country. Therefore, we use R&D capital stock as a proxy for the knowledge stock. Some component of the overall knowledge stock is embodied in every product a country produces. Therefore, by exporting its products to other countries, a country also shares some of its knowledge with the importing country. In order to simplify the presentation, the subscript for time is suppressed in Eq. (8). Formally:

$$ImportSpill_i = \sum_{j=1}^{n-1} \frac{Imports_{i,j}}{Y_i} logR\&D_j \tag{8}$$

where *Imports* represent imports of country i from country j. Y is the real GDP of country i and $logR\&D_j$ is R&D capital stock of country j.

We use bilateral imports data to calculate import-related spillovers for each country in each year. Spillovers are then aggregated across partners to calculate the overall spillover index for each country i. Assuming that knowledge embodied in technologically intensive products is larger than primary commodities, we expect spillovers to be greater for industries with a high level of technology and restrict our analysis to high-technology and medium-high-technology imports, according to the OECD intensity classifications.[3]

Calculation for knowledge spillovers through FDI ideally should also follow a similar strategy, as explained above. However, in the absence of quality data in bilateral FDI flows, such calculation is not possible. Therefore, we use the stock of inward FDI to approximate the knowledge flows through FDI.

4.5 Technological Gap

Growth theory suggests that countries that are technologically distant from the frontier tend to catch-up faster than the technologically proximate countries. In order to capture this effect, we use the technological gap (Gap) variable as shown in Eq. (9). The Gap variable for each country i in each year t is the difference between the TFP of the TFP leader and the TFP of country i for each time period t.

$$Gap_{i,t} = \frac{TFP_{leader,t} - TFP_{i,t}}{TFP_{leader,t}} \tag{9}$$

where $TFP_{leader,t}$ is the TFP of technological leader at time t and $TFP_{i,t}$ is the TFP of country i at time t ($2005 = 1$).

Table 1 provides an overview of descriptive statistics and Table 6 in the appendix provides the correlation matrix of variables used in the analysis. As shown by the number of observations, our dataset has a balanced panel structure. Apart from import spillovers, all variables are used in their natural logarithms. The *Gap* variable can take the value of 0 when the gap is calculated for the leading country. In such a case, the natural logarithm of a variable is undefined. Keeping this in view, we added 1 to Eq. (9) before applying natural logarithm. The correlation matrix in Table 6 shows that correlation coefficients are less than 0.5 for most of the variables. Two exceptions are correlation coefficients between *log(HCQ)* and

Table 1 Descriptive statistics

	log(TFP)	log(R&D)	ImportSpill	log(HCQ)	log(FDI)	log(Gap)
Mean	−0.031	−5.843	0.034	11.874	8.702	0.394
Median	−0.016	−5.882	0.018	11.886	8.746	0.438
Maximum	0.141	−1.712	0.274	14.677	11.397	0.650
Minimum	−0.406	−9.767	0.000	7.700	5.317	0
Std. Dev.	0.077	1.684	0.049	1.483	1.165	0.176
Observations	320	320	320	320	320	320

[3] ISIC Rev.2 Technology Intensity (See Table 5 in the Appendix).

ImportSpill and *log*(*HCQ*) and *log*(*Gap*). The presence of high correlation among explanatory variables could lead to a multicollinearity problem. Therefore, we relied on the mean variance inflation factor (VIF) for each estimated regression. Since all of the mean VIF scores are below 10, we conclude that multicollinearity is not present in our estimations.

5 Empirical Methodology

The data used in the current study are a panel of 20 European countries from 1995 to 2010. The natural candidates for estimation method in the case of panel data are fixed or random effects models, which are designed to account for country specific effects. However, there are at least two potential econometric problems that these methods do not take into account. First, the relationship between TFP and knowledge spillovers may not be unidirectional. Possible reverse causality in this case can result in endogeneity, where a crucial assumption of classical linear regression model $cov[X,c] = 0$ is violated and resulting estimates are biased. Second, variables used in our models have strong deterministic trend (Figs. 3, 4, 5, 6 and 7 in Appendix), the presence of which can result in spurious correlation. To avoid this problem, previous studies use variables in differences. However, by taking differences, important information embodied in the variables is lost (Coe and Helpman 1995).

In order to account for country specific effects and endogeneity in the absence of an ideal set of instruments at hand, generalized method of moments (GMM) provides a useful alternative. GMM uses lag structure of endogenous and predetermined variables to account for endogeneity and allows for dynamic modeling using lagged dependent variable. However, since GMM is designed for small T and large N, where N should be significantly larger than T, our $N = 20$ may not be large enough to satisfy this condition. Moreover, GMM is not designed to account for a long-run relationship in the presence of cointegration. Dynamic OLS provides a solution to the problems mentioned above, that is, it accounts for country specific effects, endogeneity, as well as the long run cointegrating relationship. Estimation using cointegration approach produces unbiased estimates without losing important information contained in data at levels. This procedure requires all variables to be $I1$ (integrated of order 1). Moreover, the variables are said to be cointegrated when the residual of the equations of interest are stationary. In other words, cointegration techniques for estimation can only be applied when all variables are stationary at first difference and their linear combination (residual) is stationary. In panel settings, a number of tests can be applied to test for unit-root as well as for cointegration. The most commonly used cointegration tests in panel data context are Pedroni (1999, 2004) and Kao (1999) tests. These tests use similar approaches but are based on slightly different assumptions. A brief overview of cointegration concept as well as tests for cointegration is presented in Appendix. There are two classes of panel unit root tests; one assumes a common unit root process for all cross sections (e.g. Levin et al. 2002; Breitung 2000) and the second one allows for individual unit-root processes (e.g. Im et al. (2003) (IPS), Fisher-type Dickey and Fuller (1979) (ADF) and Phillips and Perron (1988) (PP)). The assumption of a common unit root process across cross-sections can be too restrictive (Barreira and Rodrigues 2005). Therefore, we rely on IPS, ADF and PP tests for a unit root. Null hypothesis for these tests is the presence of a unit root.

6 Estimation Results

Estimation using panel cointegration methods, as explained in the previous section, requires all variables to be integrated of order 1 (non-stationary at levels but stationary at first difference) as well as their linear combination to be integrated of order zero (that is, the resulting residuals should be stationary at levels). The results of Pedroni and Kao tests for panel cointegration are presented under each model. Unlike the Kao test, the Pedroni test provides 11 test statistics under assumptions of joint unit root and individual unit root processes across cross sections. There is, however, no clear guideline on the decision rule to reach a conclusion on the existence of a cointegrating relationship. Moreover, the assumption of a common autoregressive process could be too restrictive (Barreira and Rodrigues 2005). Given these limitations, we rely, in addition to 11 test statistics of Pedroni, on the Kao test for cointegration. In most cases, 7 out of 12 tests show that the variables are cointegrated.[4]

The results of unitroot tests are provided in Table 2. The null hypothesis for the tests is the existence of a unit root. Test statistics show that all variables are non-stationary at levels and stationary at first difference (that is, they are $I(1)$) which is one of the necessary conditions for the use of the cointegration estimation method that we use further on.

Estimation results[5] for models (1)–(5c) are summarized in Table 3. Model 1, corresponding to Eq. (1) in the theory section, confirms the findings of CH. An increase in domestic R&D capital stock significantly increases TFP in the European countries considered. Additionally, and in line with hypothesis (1a), import related knowledge spillovers also have a positive relationship with TFP. The results show that, in addition to domestic R&D efforts (confirming the findings of CH), knowledge spillovers through imports in high and medium tech sectors are important for TFP in importing countries. This result shows support for hypothesis 1a. The result of the Kao cointegration test shows that the null hypothesis of no cointegration can be rejected at 1% level of significance. The Pedroni test for cointegration shows that

[4]Detailed results of cointegration tests are provided in Table 8 in the Appendix.

[5]Since our sample period includes the financial crisis in 2008–2009, an additional set of estimations was performed with a dummy for financial crisis (year 2008 and 2009). Even though the dummy was highly significant and negative, our findings were robust to its inclusion. Results are available from the authors on request.

Table 2 Unitroot tests[a]

Variables	IPS test (W-stat)	ADF test (Chi-square)	PP Test (Chi-square)
log(TFP)	0.96	37.25	30.82
Δlog(TFP)	−3.36***	76.68***	107.1***
log(R&D)	1.19	42.8	22.18
Δlog(R&D)	−3.76***	78.3***	153.25
ImportSpill	−1.44	18.94	17.09*
ΔImportSpill	−4.94***	95.04***	161.83***
log(HCQ)	3.67	24.15	44.57
Δlog(HCQ)	−3.23***	72.16***	180.59***
log(FDI)	3.24	17.68	16.34
Δlog(FDI)	−4.34***	88.63***	181.72***
log(Gap)	1.29	41.82	42.31
Δlog(Gap)	−2.41	68.68***	142.7***

Null Hypothesis: Variables contain unitroot
[a]*IPS* Im-Persaran-Shin, *ADF* Augmented-Dickey-Fuller, *PP* Philip-Perron

5 out of 11 cointegration tests reject the null hypothesis of no cointegration, at least at 5% level of significance. In summary, 6 out of 12 cointegration tests confirm the presence of cointegration.

In model 2, we extend the CH model by including FDI stock (hypothesis 1b) and quality adjusted human capital (already for hypothesis 4). For model 2, 7 out of 12 cointegration tests confirm the presence of cointegration in the model. An increase in the stock of human capital is expected to improve TFP, as labor with better human capital is expected to be more productive. Similarly, the FDI stock is expected to improve TFP if knowledge embodied in the multinationals is reflected in the TFP of domestic firms. Our results show support for hypotheses 1b and 3a, that is, an increase in the FDI stock and quality adjusted human capital increases TFP in host countries. Hence, the additional consideration of these two variables improves the findings of CH by showing that human capital and the FDI stock also significantly explain the variation in TFP and therefore should be included in the model.

Model 3 tests for the complementarity between import-related spillovers and FDI (hypothesis 2). Results of cointegration tests for model 3 show that 7 out of 12 tests confirm the presence of cointegration. Studies on the complementary relationship between imports and FDI provide mixed evidence on technologically intensive multinationals importing hi-tech merchandise and intermediate inputs from their home countries in the absence of suitable production facilities in the host country, on the one hand, and increased inward FDI substituting imports of finished goods and services, on the other hand. The current study contributes to an understanding of this specific relationship, with the a-priori expectation that, in the context of knowledge spillovers by importing hi-tech manufacturing goods, FDI not only brings potential sources of external knowledge but also diffuses the know-how to use hi-tech manufacturing goods. Following this line of argument, we expect import related spillovers and FDI to complement each other and we test for the complementarity using interaction between import-related spillovers and

Table 3 Estimation results

	Model(1)	Model(2)	Model(3)	Model(4)	Model(5a)	Model(5b)	Model(5c)
log(R&D)	0.267***	0.187***	0.262***	0.131***	0.206***	0.255***	0.218***
	(0.034)	(0.027)	(0.023)	(0.026)	(0.025)	(0.027)	(0.025)
ImportSpill	0.136***	0.738***	−0.422***	−0.909***	0.658***	0.759***	0.427
	(0.037)	(0.204)	(0.059)	(0.096)	(0.158)	(0.157)	(0.423)
log(HCQ)		0.380***	0.255***	1.090**	0.403***	0.381***	0.457***
		(0.042)	(0.033)	(0.043)	(0.042)	(0.046)	0.040
log(FDI)		0.056***	0.320***	−0.054	0.06***	0.054***	0.063***
		(0.004)	(0.004)	(0.041)	(0.005)	(0.005)	(0.004)
log(FDI) × log(HCQ)				0.009***			
				(0.003)			
ImportSpill × log(HCQ)				1.120***			
				(0.011)			
log(FDI) × ImportSpill			0.560***		0.033*	−0.001	0.037**
			(0.007)				
logGap					0.033*	−0.001	0.037**
					(0.014)	(0.086)	(0.013)
log(FDI) × logGap						0.007	
						(0.009)	
ImportSpill × logGap							0.181
							(0.616)
R^2	0.898	0.965	0.977	0.974	0.973	0.978	0.978
Adjusted R^2	0.874	0.978	0.971	0.969	0.967	0.973	0.974
No of observations	300	300	300	300	300	300	300
Mean VIF	1.12	1.82	5.04	1.73	1.94	2.87	1.97
Pedroni	5 out of 11	6 out of 11	6 out of 11	6 out of 11	6 out of 11	5 out of 11	5 out of 11
Kao cointegration test	−1.94**	−2.43**	−3.66***	−4.24***	−2.91***	−2.75***	−3.46***

Dependent variable is log(TFP)
Null hypothesis for cointegration test is "no cointegration"
Pedroni test results presented above are number of significant test results out of 11
$*p < 0.10$; $**p < 0.05$; $***p < 0.01$

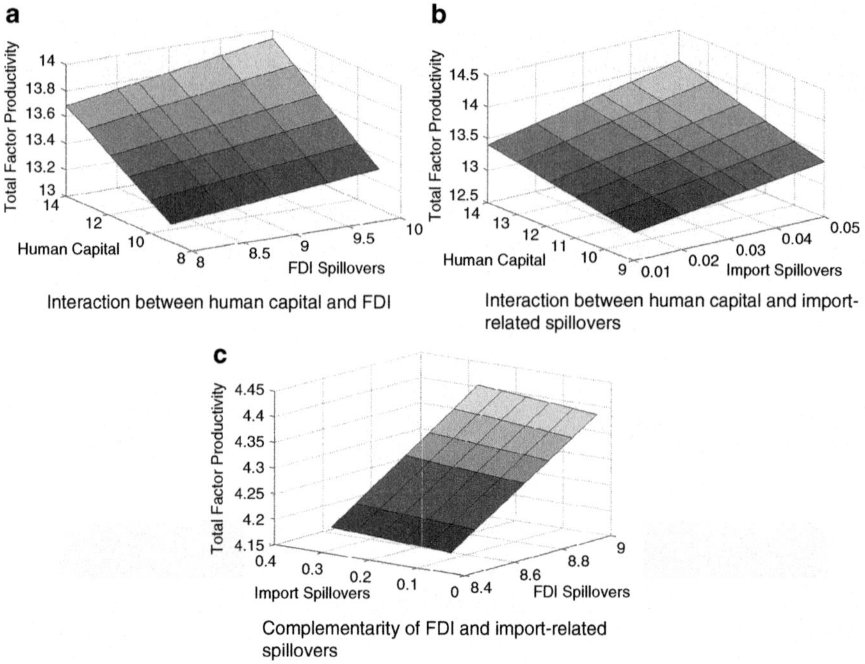

Fig. 2 Graphical representation of the interaction effects

FDI in the main model. The positive and significant coefficient of interactions shows support for the complementarity hypothesis. In other words, results show that not only do import related spillovers and FDI affect TFP but also their joint effect raise domestic productivity. These findings show support for hypothesis 2 and form the first major contribution of the study. Graphical representation of this effect is shown in Fig. 2c which shows that the effect of import-related spillovers is strengthened when FDI spillovers are high. The switch of sign from positive to negative for import-related spillovers deserves an explanation. Since interpretation of the main effects has to be done jointly with the interaction term, the joint effect should be positive. Since the resulting magnitude of the overall effect is positive (0.560–0.422) even at the minimum level of FDI (5.317), the minimal overall effect of import-related spillovers is always positive.

In model 4 we test our hypothesis 3b where we include interactions of human capital with the FDI stock and import related knowledge spillovers. Similar to models 2 and 3, 7 out of 12 cointegration tests for model 4 confirm the presence of cointegration. The purpose of this model is to test whether human capital moderates the relationship between knowledge spillovers and TFP. Countries with better human capital are expected to gain more from knowledge spillovers through external sources, as it is easier for them to absorb the inflow of knowledge. Positive and significant coefficients of interaction terms, both with import related knowledge spillovers and with FDI stock, show support for hypothesis 3b. In other words, results suggest that countries with better quality of human capital benefit not only from direct effects of productivity, but also from productivity effects from international knowledge spillovers. Graphical representations of the moderating effect of human capital for import-related and FDI-related spillovers are shown in Fig. 2b and a, respectively. The negative coefficient for the import-related spillover variable has to be interpreted the same way as in model (3) (with the minimal log(FDI) value of 7.7). To check the appropriateness of our quality-adjusted human capital variable, in Table 7 in the appendix we present the estimation results with a traditional human capital variable as a moderator. Insignificant interactions in model 2(a) of Table 7 show that the quality of education matters for the absorption of technological knowledge, and from an empirical point of view it reaffirms the necessity of using quality-adjusted human capital measures in cross-country analysis.

Finally, three models (5a, 5b and 5c) test our final hypothesis (hypothesis 4) concerning the technological distance from the frontier. For model 5a, 6 out of 12 tests, while for models 5b and 5c, 7 out of 12 tests, confirm the presence of cointegration. We hypothesize that the relationship between international knowledge spillovers and TFP is stronger for technologically-lagging countries. Technological distance (Gap) determines the potential to improve, implying that countries too distant from the frontier may not learn too much due to the lack of absorptive capacity while countries too close to the frontier may not have much to learn from the exporting (investing) partner. The existence of such a non-linear relationship can be tested using a quadratic version of the technological gap in the model. We, however, could not find support for the quadratic relationship. The linear version of the technological gap variable was introduced in model 5a. A positive and significant coefficient shows that technologically distant countries catch up faster than the ones closer to the frontier. In models 5b and 5c, we introduce interactions of the technological gap with FDI and import related spillovers. Using similar line of argument, we expect technologically distant countries to have a stronger relationship between international knowledge spillovers and TFP, as they have more to learn than countries technologically proximate to the frontier. The results do not show support for hypothesis 4. Both interactions, FDI with a gap variable and import related spillovers and gap, do not appear to have a significant relationship with TFP. In other words, the result shows that the relationship between international knowledge spillovers and TFP does not vary with the change in technological distance from the frontier.

7 Conclusion

The endogenous growth literature suggests that, while own R&D efforts as well as foreign R&D transmitted through channels of knowledge spillovers are necessary for explaining domestic productivity growth, it is not a sufficient condition. In order to understand the underlying mechanism through which international knowledge spillovers affect domestic productivity, it is essential to accommodate human capital in the analysis. However, the existing literature on the relationship between human capital and channels of knowledge spillovers provides mixed and inconclusive evidence, pointing towards methodological limitations associated with using quantity-based physical indicators of human capital to assess cross-country differences. The current study takes cue from this backdrop and proposes a quality-based indicator of human capital that incorporates quality-differences in the education systems. Furthermore, it incorporates inward foreign direct investment as an additional spillover channel and evaluates the findings of CH on domestic productivity. The extent to which knowledge spillovers from international trade and FDI overlap in shaping domestic productivity in the presence of human capital is examined. Finally, the gap towards the technology frontier and its effect on international knowledge spillovers is tested.

Employing cointegration estimation procedure on 20 European countries during 1995–2010, the productivity enhancing effects of FDI-related spillovers as well as import-related spillovers are confirmed. Looking closely at the inter-relationship between knowledge spillovers from trade and inward FDI, our results provide strong support for a complementary relationship between the two. This suggests that not only do these channels directly affect domestic productivity through greater knowledge spillovers, they also complement each other, resulting in a larger overall impact on productivity. The results are robust to model specifications, and to the best of our knowledge, constitute the first novel finding of this study. With respect to human capital, we construct a quality-adjusted indicator by weighing Barro and Lee (2010) quantity-based measure with S&T journal publications and patent applications, and find a direct as well as moderating effect of human capital on domestic productivity. Last but not least, we investigate the catching up hypothesis to test whether technologically lagging countries benefit more from international knowledge spillovers than countries closer to the technological frontier. However, contrary to our a-priori expectation, we do not find support for this argument, for FDI or for import-related spillovers.

While providing important implications relating to the literature on economic growth and human capital, our study is not free from limitations. First, the use of publications and patents as the proxy for quality of education has its limitations. Since publications largely represent only a small proportion of highly qualified academicians, it is difficult to generalize the results to the whole population, especially in the case of developing countries. However, since we do not have so-called developing countries in our sample, this problem might not be significant. Similarly, patents represent a very specific type of innovative activities that can be patented. The standardized tests such as TIMSS can be used as more generalizable quality proxies subject to data availability. Second, our analysis can be greatly improved by the use of bilateral industry level data. In the absence of a rich database at this moment, it is not possible to estimate the knowledge component of FDI using CH methodology. Third, since our sample covers 20 European countries, external validity is limited. Finally, future research can also point towards explaining the phenomenon on micro- and meso-levels of analysis.

Acknowledgments Authors gratefully acknowledge the financial support from DFG RTG 1411 "The Economics of Innovative Change". Authors are also thankful to the comments and suggestions from the participants of 15th International Joseph A. Schumpeter Society Conference in Jena and 7th Jena Summer Academy. Thanks is also due to Dr. Charles McCann for proofreading. The usual disclaimers apply.

Appendix

Table 4 Advantages and disadvantages of different proxies for quality of human capital

Proxies	Advantages	Disadvantages/limitations
TIMMS, PISA, PIAAC	Comprehensive test that includes many countries Many students examined at a time Homogenous test provides comparable results	Periodic tests, hence not available, for long time periods
International mathematical	Available for many countries	Only six students assessed per country
Olympiad (IMO)	Available for long time periods Homogenous test provides comparable results	Specific to mathematics
Journal publications	Provides good approximation for the final output of the education system Not specific to a particular field of study Available through various sources	Nationality of the authors is not available, therefore it is impossible to connect the publications based on author-origin Only provides output of the researchers
Patents	Patents cover a broad range of technologies Available from many different sources, both in aggregated and disaggregated forms Data are available for almost all countries for long period of time	Not all inventions are patented. Some technical fields are more likely to patent than others. Moreover, non-technical fields rarely patent Processes innovations are very important but are rarely patented Patents (as well as publications) may only be indicative of quality of education 20 years ago.

Patents—OECD Compendium of Patent Statistics 2008

Table 5 OECD Technology intensity classification

High-technology industries	Medium-high-technology industries
Aircraft and spacecraft	Electrical machinery and apparatus
Pharmaceuticals	Motor vehicles, trailers and semi-trailers
Office, accounting and computing machinery	Chemicals excluding pharmaceuticals
Radio, TV and communications equipment	Railroad equipment and transport equipment
Medical, precision and optical instruments	Machinery and equipment
Medium-low-technology industries	Low-technology industries
Building and repairing of ships and boats	Manufacturing; Recycling
Rubber and plastics products	Wood, pulp, paper, paper products, printing and publishing
Coke, refined petroleum products and nuclear fuel	Food products, beverages and tobacco
Other non-metallic mineral products	Textiles, textile products, leather and footwear
Basic metals and fabricated metal products	

Source: http://www.oecd.org/science/inno/48350231.pdf
Only medium-high and high-tech industries used in the analysis for international trade

Table 6 Correlation table

	(i)	(ii)	(iii)	(iv)	(v)	(vi)
(i) log(TFP)	1.000					
	–					
(ii) log(R&D)	0.129	1.000				
	(0.020)	–				
(iii) ImportSpill	−0.264	−0.323	1.000			
	(0.000)	(0.000)	–			
(iv) log(HCQ)	0.258	0.466	−0.721	1.000		
	(0.000)	(0.000)	(0.000)	–		
(v) log(FDI)	0.495	0.435	−0.084	0.221	1.000	
	(0.000)	(0.000)	(0.129)	(0.000)	–	
(vi) log(Gap)	0.034	−0.255	0.341	−0.584	−0.232	1.000
	(0.544)	(0.000)	(0.000)	(0.000)	(0.000)	–

p-Values in parenthesis

A.1 Country-Wise Time Plots of Variables

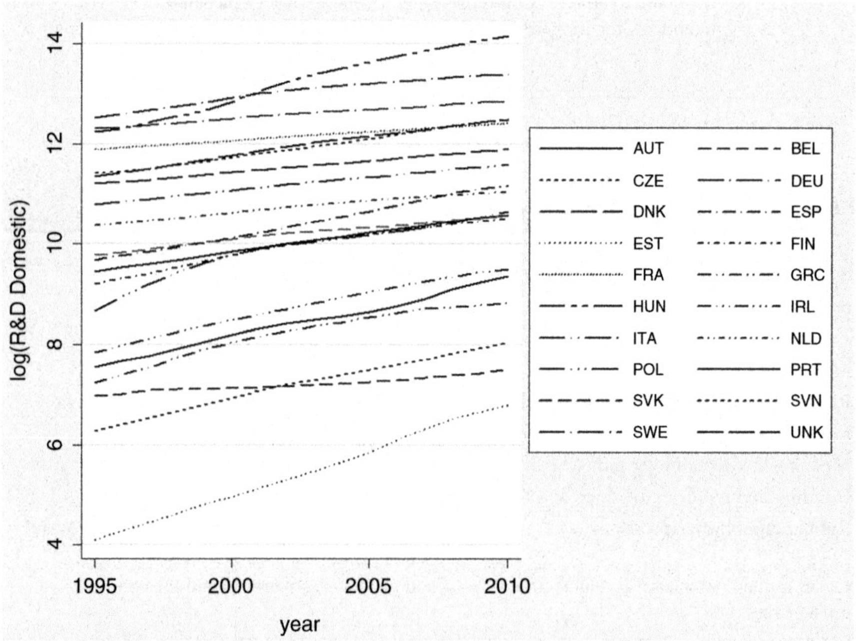

Fig. 3 log(R&D Domestic)

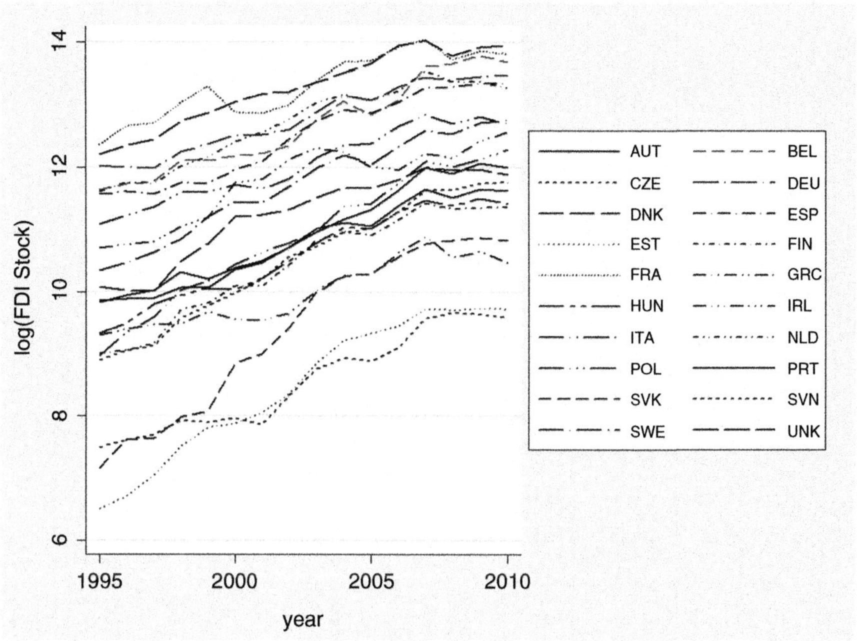

Fig. 4 log(FDI Stock)

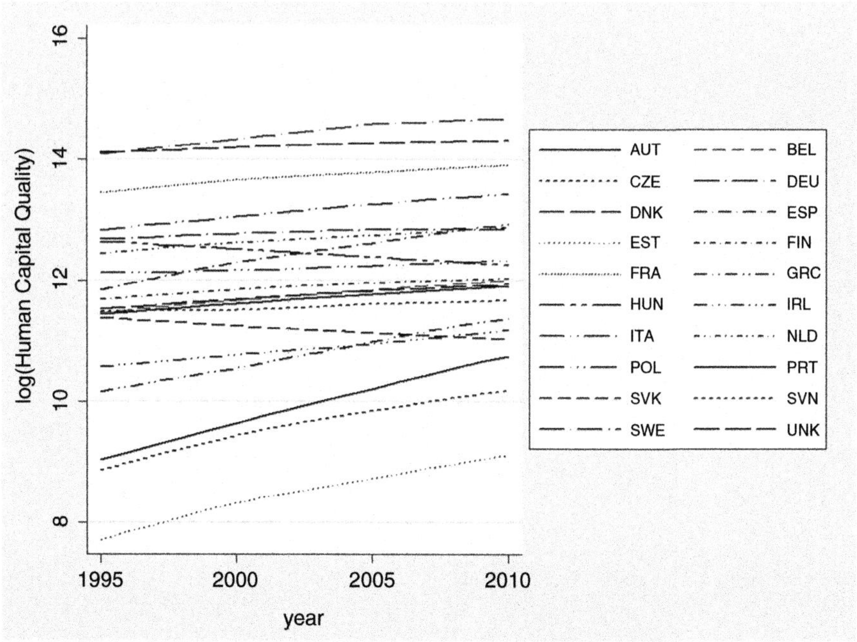

Fig. 5 log(Human Capital Quality)

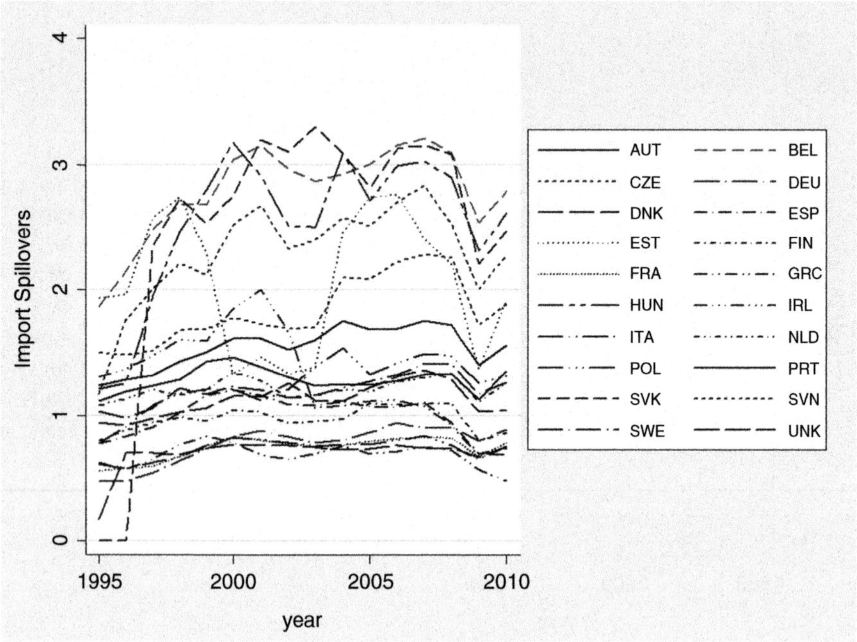

Fig. 6 Import related spillovers

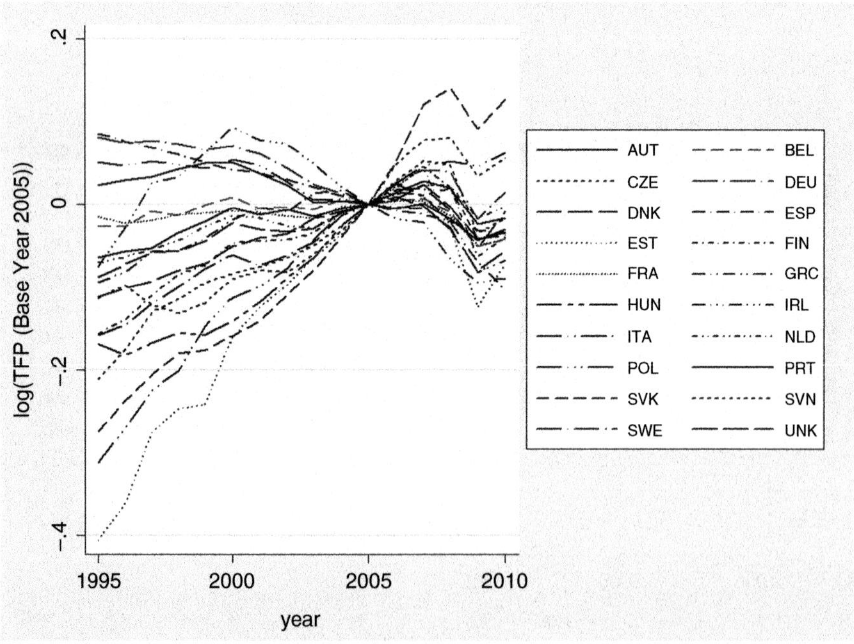

Fig. 7 log(Total Factor Productivity: Base Year = 2005)

Table 7 Estimation results: traditional human capital

	Model(1a)	Model(2a)	Model(3a)
log(R&D)	0.26***	0.30***	0.36***
	(0.03)	(0.03)	(0.03)
ImportSpill	1.44***	−0.35	−0.45***
	(0.24)	(0.56)	(0.07)
log(HC)	0.86***	1.09**	0.71***
	(0.11)	(0.51)	(0.09)
log(FDI)	0.07***	0.16**	0.39***
	(0.01)	(0.07)	(0.05)
log(FDI) × log(HC)		−0.09	
		(0.06)	
ImportSpill × log(HC)		0.38	
		(0.48)	
log(FDI) × ImportSpill			0.65***
			(0.07)
R^2	0.964	0.979	0.976
Adjusted R^2	0.957	0.974	
No. of observations	300	300	300
Pedroni	6 out of 11	6 out of 11	6 out of 11
Kao cointegration test	−3.21***	−2.58***	−2.59***

Dependent variable is log(TFP)
Null hypothesis for cointegration test is "no cointegration"
Pedroni test results presented above are number of significant test results out of 11
$*p < 0.10$; $**p < 0.05$; $***p < 0.01$

A.2 Additional Estimation Results with Traditional Barro-Lee Type Human Capital Variable

A.2.1 Brief Overview of Cointegration

Data in macroeconomics generally possess a strong deterministic trend, especially when there is a sufficiently long time series. The variables in such cases are generally non-stationary (that is, they do not have a constant mean and variance over time). In time series, when variables are non-stationary, conventional estimation techniques, such as ordinary least squares, are expected to be driven by spurious correlation (Phillips 1986). Engle and Granger (1987) show that linear combination of two or more $I(1)$ (non-stationary) variables could be $I(0)$ (stationary) in which case the series are said to be cointegrated. In other words, non-stationary variables are said to be cointegrated if the residuals from their relationship are stationary. By using cointegration, one can use full information embodied in the variables and also use the attractive properties of cointegration techniques such as super consistency when n goes to infinity (Stock 1987). Estimates generated by ordinary least squares, however, do not follow an asymptotic Gaussian distribution, therefore standard testing procedures are invalid unless they are significantly modified. Fully Modified OLS (FMOLS) and Dynamic OLS (DOLS) are generally considered as an alternative to simple OLS in the presence of cointegration. Since our data contain relatively large macroeconomic time series of 16 years, we test our variables for unit root, the presence of which motivates the test for cointegration.

In time series, the Engle and Granger (1987) cointegration test is used on *I* (1) variables to test for cointegration. If the residuals from the regression are *I* (0) then the variables are said to be cointegrated. On a similar principle, Pedroni (1999, 2004) and Kao (1999) propose cointegration tests for panel data. The Pedroni test consists of several tests under different assumptions on constants and trends across cross-sections. Consider the following regression:

$$y_{i,t} = \alpha_i + \delta_i t + \beta_1 x_{1(i,t)} + \beta_2 x_{2(i,t-1)} + \beta_M x_{M(i,t)} + \varepsilon_{i,t} \tag{10}$$

The variables x and y are assumed to be $I(1)$. The individual constant and trends are represented by α and δ, respectively. The null hypothesis of the test is 'no cointegration'. In the case of no cointegration, residuals c are integrated of order 1. If c is $I(0)$ then the variables are said to be cointegrated. Formally, the null hypothesis of no cointegration implies $\rho = 1$ in Eq. (11).

$$\varepsilon_{i,t} = \rho_i \varepsilon_{i,t-1} + u_{i,t} \tag{11}$$

Pedroni proposes two sets of hypotheses for between and within dimension. Under the test for between dimension, the test allows for different cointegrating relationships across cross-sections, while under the test for within dimension the cointegrating relationship is assumed to be homogenous across cross sections. Eleven statistics are calculated for the Pedroni test under the assumptions described above. For the decision rule, however, there is no concrete guideline for how many tests out of eleven should show a cointegrating relationship. In this study, we reject the null of no cointegration if six out of eleven statistics of Pedroni reject the null of cointegration. Kao (1999) uses the similar approach as that of Pedroni but allows for cross section specific constants and homogenous coefficients in the first stage regressions. The null hypothesis, similar to Pedroni test, is no cointegration. For robustness of the results, we have used both Kao and Pedroni tests for cointegration.

Table 8 Cointegration tests: detailed

	Model(1)	Model(2)	Model(3)	Model(4)	Model(5a)	Model(5b)	Model(5c)
Within dimension							
Panel v-statistic	−0.36	−2.4	−3.69	−4.47	−1.28	−2.04	−0.61
Panel rho-statistic	3.78	4.77	5.67	5.98	4.5	6.5	5.07
Panel PP-statistic	3.715	−1.57*	−3.33***	−8.38***	−0.03	−2.33***	−7.41***
Panel ADF-statistic	−2.69**	−4.59***	−5.69***	−4.63***	3.52***	−3.33***	−4.49***
Weighted-panel v-statistic	−1.72	−4.02	−3.17	−5.43	−2.88	−5.77	−5.15
Weighted-panel rho-statistic	1.74	3.81	4.86	6.01	3.48	5.43	4.98
Weighted-panel PP-statistic	−1.84**	−7.65***	−7.69***	−13.2***	−3.77***	−14.73***	−11.89***
Weighted-panel ADF-statistic	−4.62***	−7.47***	−7.21***	−5.92***	−2.14**	−4.06***	−4.38***
Between dimension							
Group rho-statistic	3.73	5.63	6.41	7.55	5.72	7.23	6.74
Group PP-statistic	−0.17	−10.82***	−14.68***	−20.17***	−2.88***	−20.35***	−17.38***
Group ADF-statistic	−3.33***	−5.96***	−7.39***	−7.12***	−1.61*	−5.79***	−5.88***
Kao residual cointegration test	−1.94**	−2.43***	−3.66***	−4.24***	−2.26**	−2.91***	−2.92***

References

Aghion P, Howitt P (1992) A model of growth through creative destruction. Econometrica 60 (2):323–351. Accessed 1 Feb 2016

Alcácer J, Chung W (2007) Location strategies and knowledge spillovers. Manag Sci 53 (5):760–776. Accessed 3 May 2015

Azariadis C, Drazen A (1990) Threshold externalities in economic development. Q J Econ 105 (2):501–526. Accessed 3 May 2015

Barreira AP, Rodrigues PMM (2005) Unit root tests for panel data: a survey and an application. Estudos II:665–685. Accessed 3 May 2015

Barrios S, Bertinelli L, Heinen A, Strobl E (2007) Exploring the link between local and global knowledge spillovers. http://mpra.ub.uni-muenchen.de/6301/. Accessed 3 May 2015

Barro RJ (1991) Economic growth in a cross section of countries. Q J Econ 106(2):407–443. Accessed 3 May 2015

Barro RJ (1997) Determinants of economic growth: a cross-country empirical study. MIT Press, Cambridge, MA

Barro RJ, Lee J-W (1993) International comparisons of educational attainment. J Monet Econ 32 (3):363–394

Barro RJ, Lee JW (1996) International measures of schooling years and schooling quality. Am Econ Rev 86(2):218–223. Accessed 3 May 2015

Barro RJ, Lee J-W (2010) A new data set of educational attainment in the world, 1950–2010. Working Paper 15902. National Bureau of Economic Research. Accessed 3 May 2015

Barro RJ, Sala-i-Martin X (2004) Economic growth. MIT Press, Cambridge, MA

Benhabib J, Spiegel MM (1994) The role of human capital in economic development evidence from aggregate cross-country data. J Monet Econ 34(2):143–173. Accessed 3 May 2015

Bernard AB, Bradford Jensen J (1999) Exceptional exporter performance: cause, effect, or both? J Int Econ 47(1):1–25. Accessed 3 May 2015

Blomström M, Kokko A (1998) Multinational corporations and spillovers. J Econ Surv 12 (3):247–277. Accessed 3 May 2015

Blomström M, Kokko A, Mucchielli J-L (2003) The economics of foreign direct investment incentives. In: Herrmann H, Lipsey R (eds) Foreign direct investment in the real and financial sector of industrial countries. Springer, Berlin, pp 37–60. Accessed 3 May 2015

Borensztein E, De Gregorio J, Lee J-W (1998) How does foreign direct investment affect economic growth? J Int Econ 45(1):115–135. Accessed 3 May 2015

Brainard SL (1997) An empirical assessment of the proximity-concentration trade-off between multinational sales and trade. Am Econ Rev 87(4):520–544. Accessed 3 May 2015

Branstetter L (2006) Is foreign direct investment a channel of knowledge spillovers? Evidence from Japan's FDI in the United States. J Int Econ 68(2):325–344. Accessed 3 May 2015

Breitung J (2000) The local power of some unit root tests for panel data. In: Advances in econometrics, Nonstationary panels, panel cointegration, and dynamic panels, vol 15. JAI Press, Amsterdam, pp 161–178

Brenton P, Di Mauro F, Lücke M (1999) Economic integration and FDI: an empirical analysis of foreign investment in the EU and in central and eastern Europe. Empirica 26(2):95–121. Accessed 3 May 2015

Bwalya SM (2006) Foreign direct investment and technology spillovers: evidence from panel data analysis of manufacturing firms in Zambia. J Dev Econ 81(2):514–526. Accessed 3 May 2015

Castellani D, Zanfei A (2003) Technology gaps, absorptive capacity and the impact of inward investments on productivity of European firms. Econ Innov New Technol 12(6):555–576. Accessed 3 May 2015

Coe DT, Helpman E (1995) International R&D spillovers. Eur Econ Rev 39(5):859–887. Accessed 3 May 2015

Coe, DT, Hoffmaister AW (1999) Are There International R&D spillovers among randomly matched trade partners? A response to keller. SSRN Scholarly Paper ID 880545. Rochester, Social Science Research Network. Accessed 7 Feb 2016

Coe DT, Helpman E, Hoffmaister AW (1997) North-South R & D spillovers. Econ J 107 (440):134–149

Cohen WM, Levinthal DA (1989) Innovation and learning: the two faces of R & D. Econ J 99 (397):569–596. Accessed 3 May 2015

De Mello LR, Fukasaku K (2000) Trade and foreign direct investment in Latin America and Southeast Asia: temporal causality analysis. J Int Dev 12(7):903–924. Accessed 3 May 2015

Dickey DA, Fuller WA (1979) Distribution of the estimators for autoregressive time series with a unit root. J Am Stat Assoc 74(366):427–431. Accessed 3 May 2015

Eaton J, Kortum S (1996) Trade in ideas patenting and productivity in the OECD. J Int Econ Symp Growth Int Trade: Empir Stud 40(3):251–278. Accessed 3 May 2015

Eaton J, Kortum S (1999) International technology diffusion: theory and measurement. Int Econ Rev 40(3):537–570. Accessed 3 May 2015

Eisner R (1988) Extended accounts for national income and product. J Econ Lit 26(4):1611–1684. Accessed 3 May 2015

Engelbrecht H-J (1997) International R&D spillovers, human capital and productivity in OECD economies: an empirical investigation. Eur Econ Rev 41(8):1479–1488. Accessed 3 May 2015

Engle RF, Granger CWJ (1987) Co-integration and error correction: representation, estimation, and testing. Econometrica 55(2):251–276. Accessed 3 May 2015

Feinberg SE, Majumdar SK (2001) Technology spillovers from foreign direct investment in the Indian pharmaceutical industry. J Int Bus Stud 32(3):421–437. Accessed 3 May 2015

Filippaios F, Kottaridi C (2008) Complements or substitutes? New theoretical considerations and empirical evidence on the imports and FDI relationship. SSRN Scholarly Paper ID 1121392. Rochester, Social Science Research Network. Accessed 3 May 2015

Fontagné L (1999) Foreign direct investment and international trade. In: OECD science, technology and industry working papers. Organisation for Economic Co-operation and Development, Paris. Accessed 3 May 2015

Frantzen D (2000) R&D, human capital and international technology spillovers: a cross-country analysis. Scand J Econ 102(1):57–75. Accessed 3 May 2015

Glass AJ, Saggi K (1998) International technology transfer and the technology gap. J Dev Econ 55 (2):369–398. Accessed 3 May 2015

Graham JW, Webb RH (1979) Stocks and depreciation of human capital: new evidence from a present-value perspective. Rev Income Wealth 25(2):209–224. Accessed 3 May 2015

Griffith R, Redding SJ, Simpson H (2002) Productivity convergence and foreign ownership at the establishment level. SSRN Scholarly Paper ID 388802. Rochester, Social Science Research Network. Accessed 3 May 2015

Grossman GM, Helpman E (1991) Trade, knowledge spillovers, and growth. Eur Econ Rev 35 (2):517–526. Accessed 3 May 2015

Hanushek EA, Kimko DD (2000) Schooling, labor-force quality, and the growth of nations. Am Econ Rev 90(5):1184–1208. Accessed 3 May 2015

Hejazi W, Safarian AE (1999) Trade, foreign direct investment, and R&D spillovers. J Int Bus Stud 30(3):491–511. Accessed 3 May 2015

Im KS, Hashem Pesaran M, Shin Y (2003) Testing for unit roots in heterogeneous panels. J Econ 115(1):53–74. Accessed 3 May 2015

Inklaar R, Timmer MP (2013) Capital and TFP in PWT8.0. University of Groningen. http://piketty.pse.ens.fr/files/InklaarTimmer13.pdf

Javorcik BS (2004) Does foreign direct investment increase the productivity of domestic firms? In search of spillovers through backward linkages. Am Econ Rev 94(3):605–627. Accessed 3 May 2015

Jorgenson DW, Fraumeni BM (1989) The accumulation of human and non-human capital 1948–1984. In: The measurement of savings, investment and wealth. The University of Chicago Press, Chicago, pp 227–282
Kao C (1999) Spurious regression and residual-based tests for cointegration in panel data. J Econ 90(1):1–44. Accessed 3 May 2015
Kao C, Chiang M-H, Chen B (1999) International R&D spillovers: an application of estimation and inference in panel cointegration. Oxf Bull Econ Stat 61(S1):691–709. Accessed 3 May 2015
Kathuria V (2002) Liberalisation, FDI, and productivity spillovers—an analysis of Indian manufacturing firms. Oxf Econ Pap 54(4):688–718. Accessed 3 May 2015
Keller W (1998) Are international R&D spillovers trade-related? Analyzing spillovers among randomly matched trade partners. Eur Econ Rev 42(8):1469–1481. Accessed 3 May 2015
Keller W (2004) International technology diffusion. J Econ Lit 42(3):752–782. Accessed 3 May 2015
Keller W (2010) Chapter 19—International trade, foreign direct investment, and technology spillovers. In: Hall BH, Rosenberg N (eds) Handbook of the economics of innovation, vol 2. North-Holland, pp 793–829. http://www.sciencedirect.com/science/article/pii/S0169721810020034
Kendrick JW (1976) The formation and stocks of total capital. NBER. Accessed 3 May 2015
Kokko A, Tansini R, Zejan MC (1996) Local technological capability and productivity spillovers from FDI in the Uruguayan manufacturing sector. J Dev Stud 32(4):602–611. Accessed 3 May 2015
Krueger AB, Lindahl M (2001) Education for growth: why and for whom? J Econ Lit 39(4). Accessed 3 May 2015
Kugler M (2006) Spillovers from foreign direct investment: within or between industries? J Dev Econ 80(2):444–477. Accessed 3 May 2015
Kwark N-S, Shyn Y-S (2006) International R&D spillovers re-visited: human capital as an absorptive capacity for foreign technology. Int Econ J 20(2):179–196. Accessed 3 May 2015
Lall S (1980) Vertical inter-firm linkages in LDCs. An empirical study. Oxf Bull Econ Stat 42 (3):203–226. Accessed 3 May 2015
Lee G (2006) The effectiveness of international knowledge spillover channels. Eur Econ Rev 50 (8):2075–2088. Accessed 3 May 2015
Levin A, Lin C-F, Chu C-SJ (2002) Unit root tests in panel data: asymptotic and finite-sample properties. J Econ 108(1):1–24. Accessed 3 May 2015
Levine R, Renelt D (1992) A sensitivity analysis of cross-country growth regressions. Am Econ Rev 82(4):942–963. Accessed 3 May 2015
Lichtenberg FR, van Pottelsberghe de la Potterie B (1998) International R&D spillovers: a comment. Eur Econ Rev 42(8):1483–1491. Accessed 3 May 2015
Lucas R (1988) On the mechanics of economic development. J Monet Econ 22(1):3–42
Mankiw NG, Romer D, Weil DN (1992) A contribution to the empirics of economic growth. Q J Econ 107(2):407–437. Accessed 3 May 2015
Miller SM, Upadhyay MP (2000) The effects of openness, trade orientation, and human capital on total factor productivity. J Dev Econ 63(2):399–423. Accessed 3 May 2015
Nehru V, Swanson E, Dubey A (1995) A new database on human capital stock in developing and industrial countries: sources, methodology, and results. J Dev Econ 46(2):379–401. Accessed 3 May 2015
Nelson RR, Phelps ES (1966) Investment in humans, technological diffusion, and economic growth. Am Econ Rev 56(1):69–75. Accessed 3 May 2015
O'Neill D (1995) Education and income growth: implications for cross-country inequality. J Polit Econ 103(6):1289–1301. Accessed 3 May 2015
OECD (2001) Education at a glance 2001. Organisation for Economic Co-operation/Development, Paris. Accessed 3 May 2015

Pedroni P (1999) Critical values for cointegration tests in heterogeneous panels with multiple regressors. Oxf Bull Econ Stat 61(S1):653–670. Accessed 3 May 2015
Pedroni P (2004) Panel cointegration: asymptotic and finite sample properties of pooled time series tests with an application to the PPP hypothesis. Econ Theory 3:597–625. Accessed 3 May 2015
Phillips PCB (1986) Understanding spurious regressions in econometrics. J Econ 33(3):311–340. Accessed 3 May 2015
Phillips PCB, Perron P (1988) Testing for a unit root in time series regression. Biometrika 75 (2):335–346. Accessed 3 May 2015
Psacharopoulos G (1994) Returns to investment in education: a global update. World Dev 22 (9):1325–1343. Accessed 3 May 2015
Ramos R, Surinãch J, Artís M (2010) Human capital spillovers, productivity and regional convergence in Spain. Pap Reg Sci 89(2):435–447. Accessed 3 May 2015
Romer P (1989) Endogenous technological change. Working Paper 3210. National Bureau of Economic Research. Accessed 3 May 2015
Saggi K (2002) Trade, foreign direct investment, and international technology transfer: a survey. World Bank Res Obs 17(2):191–235. Accessed 3 May 2015
Saggi K (2006) Foreign direct investment, linkages and technology spillovers. In: Global integration and technology transfer. Palgrave Macmillan/World Bank, Washington, DC, pp 51–65
Schoors K, Van Der Tol B (2002) Foreign direct investment spillovers within and between sectors: evidence from Hungarian data. Working Papers of Faculty of Economics and Business Administration, Ghent University, Belgium 02/157. Ghent University, Faculty of Economics and Business Administration. Accessed 3 May 2015
Stock JH (1987) Asymptotic properties of least squares estimators of cointegrating vectors. Econometrica 55(5):1035–1056. Accessed 3 May 2015
Teixeira AAC, Fortuna N (2010) Human capital, R&D, trade, and long-run productivity. Testing the technological absorption hypothesis for the Portuguese economy, 1960–2001. Res Policy 39(3):335–350. Accessed 3 May 2015
Wang J-Y, Blomström M (1992) Foreign investment and technology transfer: a simple model. Eur Econ Rev 36(1):137–155. Accessed 3 May 2015
Wang M, Wong MCS (2011) FDI, education, and economic growth: quality matters. Atl Econ J 39 (2):103–115. Accessed 3 May 2015
Weisbrod BA (1961) The valuation of human capital. J Polit Econ 69(5):425–436. Accessed 1 Feb 2016
Xu B, Chiang EP (2005) Trade, patents and international technology diffusion. J Int Trade Econ Dev 14(1):115–135. Accessed 3 May 2015
Xu B, Wang J (2000) Trade, FDI, and international technology diffusion. J Econ Integr 15 (4):585–601. Accessed 3 May 2015

Export, R&D and New Products: A Model and a Test on European Industries

Dario Guarascio, Mario Pianta, and Francesco Bogliacino

Abstract In this article we extend the model developed by Bogliacino and Pianta (Indus Corp Change 22:649, 2013) on the link between R&D, innovation and economic performance, considering the impact of innovation on export success. We develop a simultaneous three equation model in order to investigate the existence of a 'virtuous circle' between industries' R&D, share of product innovators and export market shares. We investigate empirically—at the industry level—three key relationships affecting the dynamics of innovation and export performance: first, the capacity of firms to translate their R&D efforts in new products; second, the role of innovation as a determinant of export market shares; third, the export success as a driver of new R&D efforts. The model is tested for 38 manufacturing and service sectors of six European countries over three time periods, from 1995 to 2010. The model effectively accounts for the dynamics of R&D efforts, innovation and international performance of European industries. Moreover, important differences across countries emerge when we split our sample into a Northern group—Germany, the Netherlands and the United Kingdom—and a Southern group—France, Italy and Spain. We find that the 'virtuous circle' between innovation and competitiveness holds for Northern economies only, while Southern industries fail to translate innovation efforts into export success.

1 Introduction

Technological efforts and international competitiveness are at the root of successful economic performance in advanced economies. Moreover, they are widely seen as key factors in the ability of European countries to return to growth after the 2008 crisis. The long-established debate on the relative importance of technological and

D. Guarascio (✉)
National Institute for the Analysis of Public Policies (INAPP), Rome, Italy
e-mail: d.guarascio@inapp.org

M. Pianta
University of Urbino, Centro Linceo Interdisciplinare "Beniamino Segre", Rome, Italy

F. Bogliacino
Universidad Nacional de Colombia, Bogota, Colombia

A. Pyka, U. Cantner (eds.), *Foundations of Economic Change*, Economic Complexity and Evolution, DOI 10.1007/978-3-319-62009-1_17

cost factors in determining international economic performances—opened up among others by Fagerberg (1988)—has recently seen a new set of contributions—including Cimoli et al. (2009), Laursen and Meliciani (2010), Evangelista et al. (2015) and Dosi et al. (2015)—that have empirically identified the key role played by technological factors at the micro, meso and macro level.

In order to investigate properly how technology contributes to export dynamics, we need to take into account the role of country and sectoral heterogeneity, the uneven distribution of technological capabilities, the uncertain, cumulative and irreversible nature of innovation as well as the structural interdependences involving technological advancements and economic performances. All these features can be identified and theoretically conceptualized adopting, in line with Dosi et al. (2015), a *partial disequilibrium* approach as well as an evolutionary view of trade and innovation.

In this article we develop a model for the structural relationships between R&D efforts, innovation success and export performance, and we carry out an empirical test for 38 manufacturing and service sectors of six major European countries, using a highly detailed database providing information on innovation, demand dynamics and international performances—the recently enhanced Sectoral Innovation Database. The theoretical framework moves from the model developed by Bogliacino and Pianta (2013a, b) and extends it to international competitiveness, captured by industries' export market shares. We use a model of simultaneous equations exploring feedbacks and structural linkages between our key variables. First, the ability of industries' R&D to lead to successful innovations is explored, combining supply push and demand pull drivers. Second, the determinants of export shares are identified, considering both the role of technological competitiveness and cost competitiveness factors (Soete 1981, 1987; Fagerberg 1988; Montobbio 2003; Dosi et al. 2015). Third, we investigate the feedbacks of export success and profits on further sectoral R&D efforts.

Our approach accounts for the role of innovation related heterogeneity—at the industry level—as well as feedback loops and structural interdependences between innovation inputs and outputs and international economic performance. A number of key elements of this complex nexus are explicitly assessed (Arthur 2013). First, we take into account the uncertainty of technological change, considering R&D efforts as distinct from the actual success in introducing new products. The contrast between technological and cost competitiveness strategies pursued by firms and industries is put at the center of the search for international competitiveness (Pianta 2001) and the broader links between technology and exports are fully addressed (Fagerberg 1988; Laursen and Meliciani 2010; Dosi et al. 1990, 2015; Evangelista et al. 2015). Second, similarly to what is done in Crespi and Pianta (2008b) and, more recently, in Lorentz et al. (2015), we jointly consider the role of demand and supply side factors. In particular, innovation is seen as the result of both demand pull and technology push factors (Schmookler 1966; Scherer 1982; Kleinknecht and Verspagen 1990; Lucchese 2011; Lorentz et al. 2015). Third, we analyze the relative importance of technology, on the one hand, and of cost factors on the other hand, in determining export performance. Among the latter, we explicitly consider the impact of international fragmentation of production, which is increasingly considered as a key factor—strongly interconnected with innovation—affecting firms and industries' ability to export and to gain advantage in international markets (Kleinert and Zorell 2012; Timmer et al. 2013).

In a recent set of contributions, there has been an effort to break down the innovation-performance nexus into different constituent phases in order to identify empirically its structural parameters. Usually, three equations are put forth: the decision to invest in R&D, the relationship between innovative inputs and outputs and the effect of R&D on economic performance (Crepon et al. 1998; Parisi et al. 2006). However, little attention has been devoted to the temporal structure and to feedbacks among such variables.

In addition to the large literature—both theoretical and empirical—on the relation between technology and competitiveness (see among others Dosi et al. 1990, 2015; Amendola et al. 1993; Carlin 2001; Landesmann and Pfaffermeyr 1997), international trade studies have recently moved towards a greater attention to intra-industry and intermediate input flows, and novel research has highlighted the role of technological content in shaping more complex trade patterns (Bas and Strauss-Kahn 2010; Colantone and Crinò 2014; Timmer et al. 2013). In our model we integrate such aspects of international trade—namely the role of offshoring and intermediate inputs flows—in the simultaneous and recursive explanation of innovation dynamics and export success. Our contribution bridges such different strands of literature, allowing us to frame in a clearer way the complexity involved in the investigated set of relationships.

To the best of our knowledge, Bogliacino and Pianta (2013a) is the first contribution to explore the feedback effect of the innovation-performance nexus, including the relevance of profits, leaving aside, however, the role of exports. This article fills in this conceptual gap and investigates empirically the regularities and differences across Europe in such relationships, using a simultaneous three equations model (3SLS). Data cover 21 manufacturing and 17 service sectors (two-digits NACE classification) and are drawn from STAN and WIOD databases for production and demand variables, and from the Community Innovation Surveys (CIS hereafter) for innovation variables. Our model and econometric strategy allows for greater efficiency by controlling for correlation among errors belonging to different equations, while identifying the impact of endogenous regressors through the instrumental variables technique. As a result, it is possible to estimate the role of feedbacks and loops in an efficient and statistically parsimonious way.

This article is organized as follows. The next section is dedicated to a theoretical overview of the issues, considering separately each equation of the system. In the third section, data are illustrated and some descriptive evidence is provided. In the fourth section, the econometric strategy is described. In the fifth section, the results are presented and we provide additional findings on the contrast between patterns in Northern and Southern countries. Section 6 offers some concluding remarks.

2 Theoretical Framework

At the root of our work is the circular loop of self-reinforcing relations between R&D, new products and profits (Bogliacino and Pianta 2013a, b). The extension proposed here has the following dynamics: R&D efforts lead to successful innovations; new products drive the acquisition of export market shares; strong exports (together with profits) enhance R&D efforts. In the following subsections, we first illustrate the theoretical foundations of our approach and the linkages with the existing literature; then we present the advantages of an analysis at the industry level; finally, we describe and conceptualize each equation of our model.

2.1 Innovation and Export Success: Concepts and Literature

The state of the literature addressing the three relationships we investigate—the determinants of R&D efforts, innovation and export success—shows different degrees of consensus.

(a) Building on evolutionary approaches, R&D is considered here as a path dependent process because the development of knowledge and technology is closely related to the relevant paradigm and trajectory of technological change, making the process of search eminently localized (Atkinson and Stiglitz 1969; Nelson and Winter 1982; Dosi 1982, 1988). The path-dependent nature of technological change has been pointed out by a recent set contributions focusing on innovation persistence (Malerba et al. 1997; Peters 2009; Antonelli et al. 2012; Triguero-Cano and Corcoles-Gonzales 2013). The latter is a key characteristic of innovation, affecting the relationships between input and output of innovation as well as the interaction of the two with economic performance. Theoretically, such persistence is explained in different ways. First, it is related to the cumulative and inexhaustible nature of innovation (Nelson 1959). Second, as argued by Arrow (1962) and Stiglitz (1987), persistency in innovation activities is associated with dynamic increasing returns that are connected, in turn, to the generation and accumulation of new knowledge. In the R&D equation of our model, we account for such persistence of commitments by including lagged R&D among the explanatory variables. The influence of technological factors on R&D operates on the one hand through the nature of the industrial structure, reflected in average firm size and, on the other hand, on the potential for new markets—two additional factors we consider in our model.

A second variables affecting R&D efforts is related to demand (Piva and Vivarelli 2007). Exports are the most dynamic component of demand in advanced countries and they lead to new demands for knowledge and competences required for international competition (Carlin 2001; Dosi et al. 1990, 2015). Moreover, export success, together with Schumpeterian profits, plays a key role in providing the resources required for R&D. The latter element has been recently highlighted by Harris and Moffat (2011), analyzing the behavior of a large panel of British firms.

A large literature has shown that R&D is financially constrained (Hall 2002; Cincera and Ravet 2010; Bogliacino and Gomez 2014) due the intangible nature of R&D, which is difficult to collateralize and also due to informational problems, namely the "radically uncertain" nature of research and the asymmetric distribution of information (Stiglitz and Weiss 1981). As a result, successful economic performance—expressed by both exports and profits—represents a vital source of resources for financing industries' R&D.

(b) The relationship between R&D and innovative performance is the least controversial one. A large literature on both firms and industries—using a variety of models and approaches—has found that greater research efforts are generally associated with better innovative outcomes (for instance, Griliches 1979, 1995; Crepon et al. 1998; Mairesse and Mohnen 2010; Loof and Heshmati 2006; Parisi et al. 2006 for firm level studies; Crespi and Pianta 2007, 2008a, b; Bogliacino and Pianta 2013b; Guarascio et al. 2015 for industry level approaches). Patterns of innovation are jointly affected by demand pull (Schmookler 1966; Scherer 1982) and technology push factors. Many authors have devoted efforts to identify the relative contribution of these mechanisms to technological progress. The available evidence is mixed; nevertheless, most of the contributions conclude that for innovation to occur, both push and pull must exist simultaneously (Mowery and Rosenberg 1979; Nemet 2009).

According to the demand-pull perspective, innovation is brought to the market when firms anticipate strong demand; in the latter view, innovation is supported by science related developments and is triggered by relative prices in a feasible production set. Such elements have been stressed earlier by Adner and Levinthal (2001) who identified demand—also accounting for its heterogeneity among consumers—as one of the main innovation drivers. More recently, Lorentz et al. (2015) emphasized the role of demand in shaping innovation and structural change.

Moreover, innovation is persistently characterized by the presence of specific technological and production capabilities (Pavitt 1984; Dosi 1988; Malerba 2002; Metcalfe 2010). We distinguished between the two mechanisms using the following strategy. On the technology side, in our analysis we build on the Schumpeterian distinction pointed out by Pianta (2001) between product and process innovation that helps identify heterogeneity in the determinants of innovative success. More precisely, we rely on the concepts of *technological* and *cost competitiveness* summarizing strategies, focusing either on new markets, new products and R&D, or on efforts directed at labor saving innovation, new machinery, efficiency gains and cost reductions.[1] On the demand side, our analysis is similar to the one proposed by Crespi and Pianta (2008b). The authors analyzed—at the industry level for 22 manufacturing sectors and 17 services sectors in Europe—the impact of

[1]In our equations, technological and cost competitiveness are proxied by specific CIS variables accounting for R&D efforts, on the one hand, and new machinery, on the other.

demand—distinguished between household consumption and exports—on innovation performance. In our specification, the demand pull effect on the development of new products is accounted for by a detailed consideration of the different components of demand, including internal demand for intermediate and final goods, and exports. In this way a comprehensive explanation of the drivers of innovative success is provided.[2]

(c) Today a broad agreement exists on the importance of innovation for international competitiveness of industries and countries. This has not always been the case. Traditional neoclassical trade theory disregarded differences in technology in explaining trade flows between countries, supposing that every country has access to the same technology set, while concentrating on factor endowments and hence on factor prices instead. For a long time, this led economists to concentrate on price as the only aspect of competitiveness (Dosi et al. 1990; Amable and Verspagen 1995). With the New Trade theory, the mainstream has started to stress the importance of non-price factors in determining international competitiveness. This approach has pointed out the importance of product differentiation and quality on the supply side and of preference for variety on the demand side (Krugman 1990). Innovation is crucial to both, leading to new products, while technology becomes a strategic variable to maintain market shares. R&D and innovation have also become important in growth theory where comparative advantages become endogenous and research policy and trade influence specialization and growth (Grossman and Helpman 1991; Aghion and Howitt 1992, 1998).

Similar arguments had been developed before in the Post Keynesian literature emphasizing non-price factors in country performance (Thirlwall 1979; Kaldor 1981); explanations of international competitiveness and specialization have later explicitly included R&D and technology (Fagerberg 1988; Archibugi and Pianta 1992; Fagerberg et al. 1997). In evolutionary approaches, technological differences among countries and industries have been considered as the basis for trade and for dynamic competition (Dosi et al. 1990; Amendola et al. 1993; Verspagen 1993).

The recent developments of international production and trade, however, have led to a greater international integration and to more complex trade patterns of intermediate inputs, shaped by global value chains (Feenstra and Hanson 1996; Hummels et al. 2001; Backer and Yamano 2012; Timmer et al. 2013). Imported intermediate inputs, on the one hand, may embody advanced technology and therefore increase the quality and variety of products and their technological competitiveness. On the other hand, they provide low cost inputs when production is outsourced to low wage countries, increasing in this way industries' cost

[2]In other contributions, Bogliacino and Pianta (2013a, b) and Guarascio et al. (2015) found a differentiation in the impact that demand components have on product innovation. Exports resulted as the most dynamic component having always a positive and strongly significant impact on product innovation (similar arguments are put forth by Crespi et al. 2008). Conversely, the growth of domestic demand—without distinction between consumption and demand for capital goods—has been found to have a non-significant and, in some cases, negative impact. The role of demand in fostering innovation diffusion has been discussed theoretically by Pasinetti (1981).

competitiveness (Daveri and Jona-Lasinio 2007; Bas and Strauss-Kahn 2010; Colantone and Crinò 2014). This complexity in the ways innovation affects international competitiveness has to be taken into account in modelling such relationships.

2.2 The Industry Level Approach

Studies on the topics addressed above have been carried out both at the firm and at the industry level. It is important to emphasize the differences between these two approaches and the specific value of industry level analysis.

Firm level studies have attracted increasing attention as a consequence of the emphasis on micro units of analysis that has emerged both in mainstream microeconometrics addressing causality issues, and in evolutionary approaches focusing on the heterogeneity of economic actors. While we share both concerns, we argue that firm level approaches cannot account for a number of explanatory factors in the analysis of innovation and performance that only emerge when the industry level is considered (Bogliacino and Pianta 2013a).

(a) In most cases, the small number of firms often included in panel based firm level studies is not representative of the universe. Moreover, these studies are usually focused on manufacturing alone, without taking into account service activities. Furthermore, when a panel is followed over a certain time span, it excludes firms exiting and entering the market—events where innovation, or the lack of it, is likely to play a major role. Therefore, the results of firm level studies are relevant only for the firms included in the analysis, and can rarely be generalized to other firms, or assumed to be relevant for the whole economy. On the contrary, an industry level approach identifies the changes in the structure of the economy and the links to macroeconomic patterns because sectoral data account for the totality of activities in a given sector, allowing leveling off gains and losses that may occur at the firm level (Pianta and Tancioni 2008; Bogliacino and Pianta 2013a).

(b) The specificity of technological trajectories and sectoral systems of innovation is at the heart of Neo-Schumpeterian and evolutionary approaches, which have widely documented the importance of industry level analysis. In this light, firms belonging to an industry are likely to share—to a large extent—the same technological opportunities, nature of knowledge, appropriability conditions and market structure (Dosi 1982, 1988; Pavitt 1984; Breschi et al. 2000; Malerba 2004). Technological heterogeneity of sectors is therefore effectively identifiable by an industry level approach, while in firm level studies such heterogeneity is generally expressed in a limited way by inadequate indicators of industries' technological characteristics, or is generally left uncharted and wrapped with all sorts of other factors in industry dummies.

(c) The consideration of the role of demand determines the emergence of another fundamental asymmetry between industry and firm-level approaches. At the micro level, a perfectly elastic demand can be assumed, since an individual firm can always grow and increase its market share at the expense of competitors. By contrast, an industry's demand has a downward slope and results from the part of aggregate demand directed to the products and services of that industry. Therefore, a fundamental difference emerges: at the firm level the relationship between innovation and improved economic performance can easily be found while, without a simultaneous expansion of demand, this relationship is much less identifiable at the industry level (Bogliacino and Pianta 2013a).

These fundamental differences between firm and industry level studies imply that the results obtained at one level cannot be automatically generalized at a more aggregate level; rather, a complementarity of analyses at the two level exists (OECD 2009). There are structural features—such as demand, technological trajectories and the macro and institutional context—that disappear when we focus on the micro level. Conversely, there are specific elements at the micro level which are lost in aggregation, such as the "turbulence underneath the big calm" (Dosi et al. 2012), rooted in the variety of firms' learning patterns and in the operation of selection processes in markets.

2.3 The Model: R&D Equation

The three equations we propose break down the innovation process into three steps: from drivers to innovation input, from the latter to innovation output, and finally to economic performance. We propose a non-linear model where performance feeds back into innovative effort, promoting both persistence and divergence. Each equation is grounded on basic evolutionary theorizing: innovative effort is path dependent and pulled by demand; innovative output is driven by technological and cost competitiveness, and finally, export performance is driven by innovative success, by demand and by labor cost competitiveness.

The first equation of the model explains the determinants of R&D efforts:

$$\begin{aligned} R\&D_{ijt} = \beta_0 + \beta_1{}^{*}R\&D_{ijt-1} + \beta_2{}^{*}DEMPULL_{ijt} + \beta_3{}^{*}SIZE_{ijt} \\ + \beta_4{}^{*}EXPSH_{ijt-1} + \beta_5{}^{*}PROF_{ijt-1} + \varepsilon_{ijt} \end{aligned} \quad (1)$$

where, i stands for sector at two digits level, j for country and t for time. The R&D variable is expenditure for research and development per employee (in thousands of euros); due to its path dependent nature, lagged efforts play a key role is shaping current R&D. DEMPULL stands for the potential for the introduction of new products, captured by the objective of opening up new markets reported by firms in innovation surveys (CIS). Following Schumpeterian insights, we expect that greater SIZE—average number of employees in firms—would go along with higher R&D efforts. EXPSH is the lagged export market share of industries, computed (following Carlin 2001) as the ratio between sector ij's real exports and the sum of real exports for that industry and period for all the countries included in the sample; we expect higher export shares to be associated with greater technological efforts. PROF is the lagged growth rate of gross operating surplus—average annual compound rate of change in profits in the previous period—and is considered as a key source for internal R&D financing. The last term is the standard error term.

In discussing the determinants of R&D, a short digression is needed on the so called 'Schumpeterian hypothesis'. According to this strand of literature it is possible to identify an effect of firm size on R&D (Cohen and Levine 1989; Cohen 2010). Since the introduction of the Schumpeter Mark II model, the concentration of R&D expenditures in larger firms has been identified as a stylized fact. However, this line of research has been criticized for being unclear as to whether it is innovation input or output that is affected by size and for the risk of endogeneity, given that both market structure and innovation are codetermined by the fundamental features of the sector (appropriability, cumulativeness and the knowledge base, as explained by Breschi et al. 2000). Relying on the contributions that have stressed the importance of past economic performance as a main driver of R&D investments (Schumpeter 1975; Brown et al. 2009), we emphasize the role of the incumbent position in export markets as a key element in determining R&D efforts in European countries. Industry level data make it possible to overcome the controversial evidence emerging from firm level studies (Greeve 2003) about the association of past economic performances and R&D efforts. From this point of view, considering lagged export market share as a performance variable allows us to take into account both the commitment of firms to exploit and reinvest the results of their past performances, and the perspectives of higher external demand as drivers of R&D. This allows including size as a control variable without incurring into the risk of endogeneity via omitted variable.

2.4 The Model: Product Innovation Equation

The specification of the product innovation equation, the second of the system, is the following:

$$\begin{aligned} NEWPROD_{ijt} = \beta_0 + \beta_1{}^{*}R\&D_{ijt-1} + \beta_2 MACH_{ijt} + \beta_3{}^{*}EXPGR_{ijt} \\ + \beta_3{}^{*}DEMGR_{ijt} + e_{ijt} \end{aligned} \quad (2)$$

where NEWPROD stands for the share of firms that are product innovators in the sector—an accurate indicator of the relative success in introducing new products in markets. Its first determinant is lagged R&D input (estimated in the first equation); the ability of new R&D expenditure to lead to successful innovations takes time and, for this reason, the R&D variable is inserted with a one period lag. In terms of innovation dynamics, we consider the complementary effect—or, possibly, the contrasting role—of innovation in processes, proxied by MACH—innovation related expenditure for machinery and equipment, in thousands of euros per employee. The success in the introduction of new products is also affected by demand factors; EXPGR is the compound annual growth of exports and DEMGR reflects the dynamics of internal demand, split into the growth rates of final demand and of demand for intermediate goods produced by the industry; ε the usual error term.[3]

The use of both expenditure for R&D and new machinery in this equation captures the potential complementarity stressed by Parisi et al. (2006) and Antonelli et al. (2012). The demand pull perspective and the literature on structural change (Pasinetti 1981) emphasize the positive effect that a strong demand dynamics has on the development and diffusion of new products. This is a complementary approach to the Schumpeterian analysis on the way major innovations change the economy (Saviotti and Pyka 2013). However, not all demand components may play the same role; when an economy—or an industry—operates in the Walrasian (or equilibrium) "circular flow", without major innovations, current demand for standard products may reduce the incentive to develop new products and delay their introduction. Therefore, we need to identify the more 'dynamic' components of demand—such as exports—that match current technological change and support the introduction of new products in a virtuous circle among capabilities, innovations and markets (as in the "learning by exporting" hypothesis assessed by Crespi et al. 2008). Conversely, demand that is related to the activity of industries where a "circular flow" prevails—such as demand for consumption and for intermediate goods—may lead to fewer incentives for the introduction of new products. In our estimations such an effect is captured by the growth of exports, while the aim of opening up new markets is already controlled for by the first equation, where demand pull is included among the regressors.

2.5 The Model: Export Market Share Equation

The specification of the market share equation, the third of the system, is the following:

$$\begin{aligned} EXPSH_{ijt} = \beta_0 + \beta_1 NEWPROD_{ijt-1} + \beta_2 MACH_{ijt} + \beta_3 ULC_{ijt} \\ + \beta_4 INTERM_{ijt} + \eta_{ijt} \end{aligned} \tag{3}$$

where success in international competitiveness is proxied by EXPSH—the export market share of sector i in country j with respect to the total of the exports of the same sector for the whole sample. For the method of calculation, we rely on the one used in Carlin (2001):

[3]In firm level literature, a recent contribution by Antonelli et al. (2012) highlights the persistence of product innovation through Transition Probability Matrices on annual data. Our data structure controls for that because it is based on long differences of 4 year windows (CIS waves).

$$EXPSH = \frac{EXP_{ijt}}{\sum_{j}^{j \in \{1,\ldots,6\}} EXP_{ijt}} \tag{4}$$
$$i \in \{NACE\}, j \in \{Ger, Sp, Fr, It, Nl, Uk\}$$

We considered the export market shares computed in (Eq. 4) as a reliable measure of relative competitiveness of our sample countries and industries since their position is highly stable; an extensive analysis of the reliability of this variable as a proxy for export performances is provided in the Appendix.

Competitive success is expected to result from both technological and cost competitiveness. The former is reflected in NEWPROD—the share of product innovators among the firms of sector i (in our system the variable estimated in the product innovation equation). Efforts in process innovation may strengthen competitiveness in various ways and is proxied by MACH—expenditure in thousands of euros per employee for innovation related machinery and equipment. The major source of cost competitiveness is related to labor costs, and is proxied by the compound average annual rate of change of unit labor cost (ULC), defined as follows (Carlin 2001):

$$UNITLC_{ijt} = \frac{\left(W_{ijt}/EMP_{ijt}\right)}{\left(VA_{ijt}/ENG_{ijt}\right)} \tag{5}$$

where the numerator is the wage per employee in real terms and the denominator is the ratio between the industry's value added and the number of total engaged—a measure of productivity. Finally, the complexity of current patterns of trade flows requires the consideration of the role different intermediate inputs (INTERM) may play in contributing to an industry's competitive success. In our equation we distinguish them on the basis of both their origin (domestic or imported) and their technological content (based on the revised Pavitt categories[4]: high when inputs are provided by Science Based and Specialized Supplier sectors, and low when they are provided by Scale Intensive and Supplier Dominated sectors, see the Appendix). The four variables accounting for the role of intermediate inputs therefore include the following: domestically sourced inputs of high technological content; domestically sourced inputs of low technological content; imported inputs of high technological content; imported inputs of low technological content. Indicators are computed as the sum of the expenditure devoted by each industry to the acquisition of different types of inputs, divided by the total production of each user sector (Yamano and Ahmad 2006). We expect that competitive success is driven by a greater use of inputs with higher technological content and of international origin.

Equation (3) is the crucial one in our model since it highlights the differences in terms of relevance of technological and cost competitiveness. Moreover, the estimated coefficients of this equation within our simultaneous system may allow the

[4]An extensive description of the revised Pavitt taxonomy is provided by Bogliacino and Pianta (2010).

identification of different types of relationships between innovation and international performance that will be examined later by splitting the sample between a group of 'Northern' and 'Southern' countries.

The full system is:

$$\begin{cases} R\&D_{ijt} = \beta_0 + \beta_1 {}^* R\&D_{ijt-1} + \beta_2 {}^* DEMBULL_{ijt} + \beta_3 {}^* SIZE + \beta_4 {}^* EXPSH_{tij-1} + \beta_5 {}^* PROF_{tij-1} + \varepsilon_{ijt} \\ NEWPROD_{ijt} = \beta_0 + \beta_1 {}^* R\&D_{ijt-1} + \beta_2 MACH_{ijt} + \beta_3 {}^* DEMGR_{ijt} + e_{ijt} \\ EXPSH_{ijt} = \beta_0 + \beta_1 NEWPROD_{ijt-1} + \beta_2 MACH_{ijt} + \beta_3 ULC_{ijt} + \beta_4 INTERM_{ijt} + \eta_{ijt} \end{cases} \quad (6)$$

3 Data and Descriptive Evidence

3.1 The Database

The database used in this paper is the Sectoral Innovation Database (SID) developed at the University of Urbino[5] that combines different sources of data at the two-digit NACE classification for 21 manufacturing and 17 service sectors; all data refer to the total activities of industries (Pianta and Lucchese 2011). For innovation variables data are from three European Community Innovation Surveys—CIS 3 (1998–2000), CIS 4 (2002–2004) and CIS 6 (2006–2008). Economic variables are obtained from the OECD-STAN database; demand, trade and intermediate inputs variables are drawn from the World Input Output Database (WIOD) (Timmer 2013). The country coverage of the database includes six major European countries—Germany, France, Italy, Netherlands, Spain, and United Kingdom—representing a large part of the European economy. The selection of countries and sectors has been made in order to avoid limitations in access to data, due to the low number of firms in a given sector of a given country, or to the policies on data released by national statistical institutes.

The time structure of the panel is the following. Economic and demand variables are calculated for the periods 1995–2000, 2000–2005 and 2005–2010. The export market shares variable is computed for each industry for the final year of each period—the years 2000, 2005 and 2010. Innovation variables refer to 1998–2000 (linked to the first period of economic variables); 2002–2004 (linked to the second period of economic variables) and 2006–2008 (linked to the third period of economic variables). The variables used and the main descriptive statistics are reported in Tables 1 and 2.

[5]Pianta et al. provide a comprehensive description of the database. CIS innovation data are representative of the total population of firms and are calculated by national statistical institutes and Eurostat through an appropriate weighting procedure. A detailed description of the procedure is provided in Bogliacino and Pianta (2013a).

Table 1 List of variables

Variable	Unit	Source
In-house R&D expenditure per employee	Thousands euros/empl.	CIS
New machinery expenditure per employee	Thousands euros/empl.	CIS
Share of product innovators	Percentages	CIS
Share of firms innovating with the aim of opening new markets	Percentages	CIS
Average firm size	Number empl. per firm	CIS
Rate of growth of exports	Annual rate of growth	WIOD I-O Tab.
Rate of growth of intermediate demand	Annual rate of growth	WIOD I-O Tab.
Rate of growth of final demand	Annual rate of growth	WIOD I-O Tab.
Rate of growth of imported interm. inputs (high and low-tech)	Annual rate of growth	WIOD I-O Tab.
Rate of growth of domestic interm. inputs (high and low tech)	Annual rate of growth	WIOD I-O Tab.
Rate of growth of wages	Annual rate of growth	STAN Isic Rev.3
Rate of growth of profits	Annual rate of growth	STAN Isic Rev.3

All economic variables are deflated using the sectoral Value Added deflator from OECD-STAN (base year 2000), corrected for PPP (using the index provided in Stapel et al. 2004). For the performance variable we compute the compound annual growth rate that approximates the difference in log. For innovation, we use the shares of firms in the sector or expenditure per employee; this can be justified considering innovative efforts as dynamic and capturing the change in the technological opportunities available to the industry.

The dataset is a panel dataset over three periods covering a time span from 1995 to 2010 across six major European countries. This kind of industry level dataset accounts for the complexity of innovation at the sectoral level, as well as for consideration of both supply and demand determinants of economic and innovative performance.

A summary of the strengths of this dataset is provided below:

- The industry level detail of the dataset allows us to identify the specificity of industries in terms of their innovation patterns and growth trajectories, considering both manufacturing and service sectors;
- The detailed nature of CIS data offers the possibility to take into account different innovation strategies (cost and technological competitiveness) as well as different aims of innovation;

Table 2 Descriptive statistics

Variables	Mean	SD overall (whole sample variability)	SD between (var. across industries)	SD within (var. across country and time)
In-house R&D expenditure per employee	2.65	4.86	4.36	2.07
New machinery expenditure per employee	1.70	2.69	2.51	1.44
Share of product innovators	35.03	43.15	61.83	13.28
Share of firms innovating with the aim to open new markets	25.58	15.88	13.36	9.33
Average firm size	0.364	1.90	1.51	1.38
Rate of growth of export	2.07	26.25	18.97	18.17
Rate of growth of intermediate demand	0.77	8.89	5.41	7.06
Rate of growth of $$	0.09	17.19	11.12	13.13
Export market shares	0.16	0.14	0.13	0.04
Rate of growth of operating surplus	3.72	17.25	16.2	8.01
Rate of growth of unit labor cost	−0.63	8.49	4.38	7.28

- Input–output data allow to distinguish the intermediate inputs used by a sector on the basis of their technological intensity (identified by the two digit NACE sector of origin of the inputs) and of their domestic or imported origin;
- The availability of consistent export data allows for the construction of reliable competitiveness indicators by industry.

The following table reports the main descriptive statistics:

In order to use these data in panel form, we need to test that the sample design or other statistical problems in the gathering of data are not affecting their reliability. Besides considering the time-effects capturing macroeconomic dynamics, we examined the stability of the database.

3.2 *Some Descriptive Evidence*

As we anticipated, one of the main objectives of this work is to analyze the connections and the feedbacks between innovation, labor cost and economic performances in terms of export market shares, with specific attention to the North–south divide in Europe. Table 3 contains data at the country level for the key economic and innovation variables used for the subsequent econometric analysis, providing information on national competitiveness. The figures also provide a first

Table 3 Economic and innovation variables, descriptive statistics by country (averages 1995–2010)

Country	R&D per empl. (%)	Mach. Exp per empl. (%)	New products (%)	New market Obj. (%)	Unit labour cost(%)	Export market share (%)
Germany	3.87	3.84	60.05	35.32	−3.05	0.29
Netherlands	3.08	1.19	36.79	26.50	1.90	0.12
UK	2.06	2.35	25.23	33.94	0.11	0.23
North	3.06	2.71	41.08	33.00	−0.34	0.64
Spain	0.99	0.68	25.23	16.79	−1.49	0.08
France	4.84	0.80	36.60	26.89	−2.15	0.14
Italy	1.37	1.42	29.04	16.00	0.88	0.14
South	2.38	0.99	30.24	19.85	−0.92	0.36

Notes: Labor Cost is the compound average annual rate of change of the indicator computation shown in Eq. (6), Export Market Shares is the average over the sample period, and totals for 'Northern' and 'Southern' groups are the sum of countries' shares. All the variables are in euros and in real terms. R&D expenditure and Process Innovation (Expenditure for Machineries and Equipments) are in thousands of euros for employee. New market objectives is a share variable computed dividing the respondents who declared that opening a new market is their main aim to innovate over the whole population of firms

snapshot of the North–south divide within the EU, highlighting the dynamics of technological and cost competitiveness across EU countries. Looking at R&D expenditure, Spain and Italy lag behind the rest of the countries in the sample. Regarding product innovation, the differences between Germany and the South are striking, and are paralleled by the distance in export market shares. Unit labour cost figures show an increasing trend in Italy, the Netherlands and the UK, with the opposite trend in the other countries.

The Italian case deserves a particular attention. Italy has maintained a significant market share despite weak performance in new products and processes and a rise in unit labor costs higher than in most countries. The complexity of the patterns involved—including the role of intermediate inputs, non price competitiveness and product quality—are relevant in the explanation of such outcome; a similar investigation has been carried out by Tiffin (2014) in a recent IMF paper exploring the "Italian productivity puzzle". In the Appendix, a more detailed descriptive analysis of the variables is provided.

4 Econometric Modelling Strategy

The estimation strategy adopted is the following. First, in order to verify the validity of the hypothesized relationships, we implement a WLS estimation equation-by-equation, carrying out all the needed diagnostic tests. Second, in order to identify the feedbacks and self-reinforcing loops among our variables, we use a model suitable for the estimation of systems of equations. We have chosen the Three

Stage Least Squares model (3SLS) since it allows estimating a simultaneous system of equations, addressing at the same time all the endogeneity issues. Third, we replicate the 3SLS estimation adopting the interaction terms technique in order to assess the extent of a divergent dynamics between Northern and Southern countries.

The 3SLS method generalizes the two-stage least squares (2SLS) method to take account of the correlations between equations in the same way that Seemingly Unrelated Regression (SUR) generalizes OLS. 3SLS requires three steps: first-stage regressions to get predicted values for the endogenous regressors; a two-stage least-squares step to get residuals to estimate the cross-equation correlation matrix; and the final 3SLS estimation step. The 3SLS method goes one step beyond the 2SLS by using the 2SLS estimated moment matrix of the structural disturbances to estimate all coefficients of the entire system simultaneously. The method has full information characteristics to the extent that, if the moment matrix of the structural disturbances is not diagonal (that is, if the structural disturbances have nonzero "contemporaneous" covariances), the estimation of the coefficients of any identifiable equation gains in efficiency as soon as there are other equations that are over-identified. Further, the method can take account of restrictions on parameters in different structural equations[6] (Zellner and Theil 1962).

Two further methodological points must be addressed: the choice of weights and the choice of instruments. As is well known, industry level data are grouped data of unequal size, and so we cannot expect all industries to provide the same contribution in terms of information. As a result, the consistency of the estimation is affected. Following Bogliacino and Pianta (2013a, b), we achieve consistency using the weighted least squares estimator (WLS) that allows taking the relevance of industries into account (Wooldridge 2002, Ch. 17). The use of a correct weight becomes crucial and the choice is usually limited to value added and number of employees. Statistical offices tend to use the latter since the former is more unstable and subject to price variations, and we follow them in the use of employees as weights.

In order to control for endogeneity, our baseline strategy is to use the lag structure; since our time lags are of 3–5 years, the autoregressive character of variables is considerably softened but not eliminated, which makes them suitable instruments (Kleinbaum et al. 1988). Moreover, 3SLS is a proper estimation technique to account for endogeneity when dealing with systems of equations. Anyway, there is always a trade-off between consistency and efficiency in choosing an estimator. Due to modest sample size (inevitable with industry level data), we solve the trade-off relying on consistency instead of efficiency. In fact, with 3SLS we only have to care about orthogonality inside each equation, without taking care of what is happening elsewhere in the system (ibid., 199). As a result, we can focus on the choice of instruments equation by equation in order to guarantee identification. We identified four endogenous variables: SIZE in the first equation, EXPGR in

[6]The simultaneous estimation performed in 3SLS further weakens the potential estimation biases associated with lagged dependent variables with respect to the 2SLS.

the second, MACH and INTERDEM in the third. The set of instruments we used include the rate of change of lagged value added, lags of the endogenous variables, country, Pavitt and time dummies. Additional endogeneity tests—carried out equation by equation—and the instruments validity tests are discussed in detail in the Appendix. Moreover, we controlled for the presence of multicollinearity and heteroscedasticity. All tests confirm the robustness of the approach we have followed.

5 Results

The results of our estimates are presented separately for each equation in the three tables below. We implement the model on all manufacturing and service industries (38 sectors, Nace Rev. 1), with two different specifications: a baseline estimation and a model with country and technology dummies; in the latter we control for country specificities and technological intensity—as well as for differences in technological trajectories among sectors—using dummies for the revised Pavitt taxonomy (Bogliacino and Pianta 2010). In principle, the use of rate of change is assumed to clear fixed effects at country and industry level, but dummies may capture differences in terms of trend across them.

5.1 The Weighted Least Squares Estimations

We first provide some comments over diagnostic tests. Multicollinearity is not an issue; we have conducted the VIF test over each of the three equations, obtaining respectively the following factors: 1.32 for the first equation, 1.26 for the second and 2.55 for the third. Since the critical value for the VIF statistic in order to detect multicollinearity among regressors is near to ten (Kleinbaum et al. 1988, p. 210), we can exclude the presence of multicollinearity in our regressions. Moreover, the results of the Breusch-Pagan test for heteroskedasticity reject for each equation the null hypothesis of constant variance. As a result, we carried out all the estimations with robust standard errors. The results of the R&D equation contained in Table 4 suggest that the theoretical framework developed in Sect. 2 is supported by the empirical results. Both the baseline and the model with country dummies show that R&D efforts are explained by the cumulative nature of R&D, identified by the coefficient of lagged R&D expenditure. The *demand pull* factor, proxied by the importance of firms innovating with the aim of entering new markets, is not significant; a possible explanation could be found in the major role played by lagged profit and export market share. The latter in particular can easily capture the motivation to invest in R&D related to the opening of new markets making the *New Markets Objective* variable less relevant.

Table 4 The R&D equation

	(1) Baseline model	(2) Baseline with dummies
Lagged R&D expenditure	0.58 [8.35]***	0.51 [6.90]***
Firm size	11.42 [6.66]***	12.05 [6.98]***
New markets obj.	0.03 [1.64]	0.02 [0.93]
Profits (first lag)	0.026 [2.25]**	0.03 [2.26]**
Export market share (first lag)	3.68 [1.68]*	4.04 [1.71]*
Country dummies		Yes
Pavitt dummies-industry groups		Yes
Constant	−1.01 [−0.94]	−1.88 [−3.06]***
N. observations	179	179
R^2 (Adj)	0.73	0.73

Dependent Variable: In-house R&D expenditure per employee
WLS with robust standard errors and weighted data (weights are the numbers of employee)
t-stat in brackets
*Significant at 10%, **Significant at 5%, ***Significant at 1%

Supporting the Schumpeterian assumption of R&D efforts driven by large firms able to earn monopolistic profits, the *Size* variable is significant and positively related to the dependent variable in both the baseline and the country dummy equation. Moreover, *lagged profits* have an important role in determining new R&D investment. Finally, the *lagged export market share* is significant and positive in both estimations.

Regarding the dummy variables inserted in the second equation, *country dummies* do not seems to play a clear role in the case of R&D efforts, while *Pavitt dummies* are both positive and significant for Science Based and Specialized Supplier sectors. The interpretation of the coefficients associated with *Pavitt dummies* is straightforward since we can expect that sectors characterized by an intensive use of technological inputs are also those where R&D efforts are relatively higher. Including country dummies in our baseline model does not harm the significance of the estimated coefficients, so we can proceed to analyze the New product equation.[7]

The results in Table 5 show that innovative performances are mainly driven by research efforts. The coefficient associated with past R&D efforts is positive and significant in both the baseline and the country/Pavitt dummy equation. On the contrary, the coefficient associated to process innovation—*Expenditure for new machinery and equipment*, a proxy for cost competitiveness strategies—is negative and is significant in the country dummy specification only. This result may suggest that at the industry level product and process innovation are more substitute than complement; industries tend to be characterized either by a prevalence of the search

[7]The full set of results, including the dummy variables' coefficients for all the three equations, are reported in the Appendix (Tables 12, 13 and 14).

Table 5 The new product equation

	(1) Baseline model	(2) Baseline with dummies
Lagged R&D expenditure	1.57 [6.23]***	1.60 [6.28]***
Expenditure for mach. and equipments	−0.45 [−0.69]	−1.16 [−1.73]*
Demand for final consumption (rate of growth)	−0.28 [−0.38]	−0.24 [−0.33]
Demand for interm. goods (rate of growth)	−0.55 [−2.88]***	−0.47 [−2.49]**
Exports (rate of growth)	0.01 [0.70]	0.009 [0.41]
Country dummies		Yes
Pavitt dummies-industry groups		Yes
Constant	37.79 [11.14]***	30.04 [6.75]***
N. observations	286	286
R^2 (Adj)	0.55	0.57

Dependent Variable: Share of firms carrying out product innovation
WLS with robust standard errors and weighted data (weights are the numbers of employee)
t-stat in brackets
*Significant at 10%, **Significant at 5%, ***Significant at 1%

for new products, or by efforts to introduce new processes. This further supports our distinction between technological and cost competitiveness.

Among demand variables the impact on innovation of the *rate of growth of exports* is always positive, although it is not statistically significant. The internal demand for final consumption and intermediate goods has negative and significant coefficients that could be explained by the lack of dynamism and innovative content of domestic demand with respect to exports. Such a result is in line with the previous findings of Bogliacino and Pianta (2013b) where, in an analogous specification, they found that only exports, out of the complete set of demand components, were able to explain innovative performances.

Dummy variables point out some divergent trends in this case. In the country dummy specification Germany and the Netherlands have a positive and strongly significant role in explaining innovative performances in our sample; these results begin to delineate the divergent dynamic between Northern and Southern countries. Looking at *technology dummies*, Science Based and Specialized Supplier sectors have—as expected—a positive and significant impact on innovative performances.

The results of Table 6 show that industries' export market shares are supported by both technological and cost competitiveness, confirming the view developed in the theoretical framework of Sect. 2. In the baseline equation, lagged new products, new processes and lower labor costs are all significant factors in strengthening exports shares. However, including country dummies in the second specification of the model leads to a loss in significance of product innovation and labor costs, as country specificities do play a key role in shaping national competitiveness.

The intermediate input mix is also relevant to explain performances of sectors. Industries' export performance is supported by the imports of inputs from hightechnology sectors that improve the quality and variety of goods produced,

Table 6 The export market share equation

	(1) Baseline model	(2) Baseline with dummies
Lagged product innovation	0.0015 [2.88]***	−0.0004 [−0.03]
Expenditure for mach. and equipments	0.014 [2.41]***	0.01 [1.83]*
Unit labor cost (rate of growth)	−0.005 [−3.39] ***	−0.004 [−3.07]
Domestic interm. inputs, low tech (rate of growth)	−0.012 [−3.51] ***	−0.12 [−3.80]***
Domestic interm. inputs, high tech (rate of growth)	−0.004 [−1.43]	−0.002 [−0.81]
Imported interm. inputs, low tech (rate of growth)	0.002 [1.02]	0.003 [1.77]*
Imported interm. inputs, high tech (rate of growth)	0.015 [5.31]***	0.011 [3.98]***
Country dummies		Yes
Pavitt dummies-industry groups		Yes
N. observations	287	287
R^2 (Adj)	0.79	0.81

Dependent Variable: Export Market Share
WLS with robust standard errors and weighted data (weights are the numbers of employee)
t-stat in brackets
*Significant at 10%, **Significant at 5%, ***Significant at 1%

improving technological competitiveness. Conversely, domestic low-tech inputs have a negative impact on export shares as industries more dependent from such factors are left out of innovation dynamics; this result is in line with the findings of authors who have already analyzed the relation between imported inputs and export performance (Bas and Strauss-Kahn 2010; Colantone and Crinò 2014).

The included dummies are all significant and, also in this case, the coefficient associated with Germany has the highest positive impact on the dependent variable In the next subparagraph, the results of the full system estimation and the test for the presence of the North–south divide are reported.

5.2 *The System of Equation for R&D, New Products and Export Market Shares*

This section provides the results of the structural 3SLS estimations. Table 7 contains the results for the whole sample estimation, while in Table 8, the results from the model with separate estimations for Northern and Southern countries are shown.

The estimated coefficients and goodness of fits are consistent with the previous regressions and—in the first two equations—with the version of the model developed in Bogliacino and Pianta (2013a, b). In the R&D equation (column 1), past R&D past profits and export market shares—with strongly significant

Table 7 The system of equations for R&D, new products and export market shares

	Equation 1 R&D per employee	Equation 2 Share of product innovators	Equation 3 Export market share
R&D per employee (first lag)	0.57 [0.61] ***	0.5 [0.28]***	
Rate of growth of profits (first lag)	0.03 [0.01] ***		
New market objective	0.05 [0.02]**		
Size	10.02 [1.65] ***		−0.14 [0.08]*
Export market share	4.64 [2.69] ***		
Rate of growth of export		0.93 [0.32]***	
Rate of growth of final consumption		−0.047 [0.06]	
Rate of growth of intermediate demand		−0.49 [0.20]**	
Share of product innovators			0.0034 [0.0006]***
New machinery per employee		2.26 [0.70]***	0.028 [0.006] ***
Rate of growth of unit labor cost			−0.006 [0.001]***
Rate of growth of domestic interm. input (low-tech)			−0.0081 [−0.004]*
Rate of growth of domestic interm. input (high-tech)			−0.005 [0.003]
Rate of growth of imported interm. input (low-tech)			0.004 [0.003]
Rate of growth of imported interm. input (high-tech)			0.009 [0.003] ***
Country dummies	Yes	Yes	Yes
Pavitt dummies-industry groups	Yes	Yes	Yes
Obs	172	172	172
RMSE	2.40	13.14	0.09
Chi^2 (*p*-value)	870.78 (0.00)	1741.75 (0.00)	1594.93 (0.00)

Three stage least squares. Standard errors in brackets
*Significant at 10%, **Significant at 5%, ***Significant at 1%

coefficients—support R&D efforts that are also 'pulled' by the presence of a potential market for new products and 'pushed' by the importance of firm *size*, confirming the "Schumpeter Mark II" perspective. R&D expenditures are driven by the presence of high technological opportunities, extensive profit-based financial resources and high export market power.

In the product innovation equation (column 2), the importance of new products is the result of past R&D—with a positive and significant impact—confirming the

Table 8 The system of equations for R&D, new products and export market shares for Northern and Southern countries

	Equation 1		Equation 2		Equation 3	
	R&D per employee (NORTH)	R&D per employee (SOUTH)	Share of Pr. innovators (NORTH)	Share of Pr. innovators (SOUTH)	Export market share (NORTH)	Export market share (SOUTH)
R&D per employee (first lag)	1.17 [0.13]***	0.58 [0.06]***	1.85 [0.86]***	1.45 [0.32]***		
Rate of growth of profits (first lag)	0.01 [0.01]	0.04 [0.01]***				
New market objectives	0.06 [0.01]**	0.07 [0.02]**				
Size	4.39 [2.23]*“	10.69 [4.91]			−0.07 [0.16]	−0.05 [0.09]
Export market share	6.53 [2.53]***	4.88 [2.64]***				
Rate of growth of exports			1.77 [0.46]***	−0.64 [0.48]		
Rate of growth of final consumption			−0.31 [0.21]	−0.04 [0.07]		
Rate of growth of intermediate demand			−0.89 [0.31]***	−0.30 [0.35]		
Share of product innovation					0.02 [0.00]***	−0.00 [0.00]
New machineries per employee			0.50 [0.21]	−1.90 [0.56]	0.01 [0.00]***	−0.03 [0.01]
Unit labor cost (rate of growth)					−0.01 [0.00]***	−0.00 [0.00]
Domestic intermediate inputs (low tech)					−0.00 [0.00]	−0.00 [0.00]
Domestic intermediate inputs (high tech)					−0.00 [0.00]	−0.00 [0.00]
Imported intermediate inputs (low tech)					0.00 [0.00]	0.00 [0.00]
Imported intermediate inputs (high tech)					0.08 [0.03]**	0.00 [0.00]

Country and Pavitt dummies	Yes	Yes	Yes	Yes	Yes	Yes
Obs	172	172	172	172	172	172
RMSE	2.04	2.04	13.14	13.14	0.09	0.09
Chi^2	870.78	870.78	1741.75	1741.75	1594.93	1594.93
(p-value)	(0.00)	(0.00)	(0.00)	(0.00)	(0.00)	(0.00)

Three stage least squares. Standard errors in brackets
Group of countries: NORTH (DE, NL, UK), SOUTH (ES, IT, FR)
*Significant at 10%, **Significant at 5%, ***Significant at 1%

close relationship between technological inputs a1nd outputs. The introduction of new processes appears here to play a complementary role to new products, with a positive and significant coefficient. Demand variables have—as expected—different effects on new products: export growth is associated with a higher presence of product innovators, in line with the "learning by exporting" hypothesis (Crespi et al. 2008); a large growth of final consumption and intermediate demand, conversely, is associated with lower product innovation (a result already detected in the simple OLS estimation); an increase in such components of demand may lower the need to introduce new products, a relationship that is typical of "traditional" industries and services with little R&D, more standard goods and less international openness.

Finally, export market shares (column 3) are positively explained by product and process innovation (again showing complementarity) and, negatively, by unit labor costs; competitive success is therefore driven by both technological and cost competitiveness. Firm size has a negative impact on export market shares, suggesting a greater dynamism of small firms, especially in sectors more open to trade and with higher technological intensity. The relevance of size in influencing high R&D efforts (found in Eq. 1) is then lost when such technological efforts have to be turned into success in international markets. Considering the intermediate input mix, we find that—as already detected in the WLS single equation estimation—a growth in imported high tech intermediate inputs has a positive and significant impact on export performance, as it may improve the technological competitiveness of an industry's output. Conversely, a negative and significant link is found with domestic low tech intermediate inputs; they may help reduce production cost, but are of no use in gaining foreign markets. The other two types of intermediate inputs do not have significant effects.

The variables in bold in Table 7 are the key drivers of our system of feedbacks and circular loops. Consistent with the 3SLS estimation technique, the dependent variables estimated and instrumented in the first steps are then used as regressors in the next steps. Such a technique allows us to increase estimation consistency and highlights the role of R&D, new products and export market shares as engines of the recursive relationships we investigate.

An additional test has been carried out in order to check the robustness of our estimations controlling for path dependent technology factors; in a separate estimation, we also included time dummies in the R&D equation, but the results are unchanged, and the dummies are not significant. Indeed, the use of long differences, industry level data, average rate of change, and autoregressive specification is a satisfactory strategy to account for a time varying production possibilities frontier. Once detected this system of feedbacks between R&D, innovation and export performance we can go a step further and investigate the existence and magnitude of two divergent loops affecting the Northern and Southern European countries (with the obvious constraint represented by the limited number of European countries that we consider in this analysis, due to the lack of data).

In order to achieve our objective, we use the interaction terms technique. We are able to estimate the different coefficients for the groupings of Northern and

Southern European countries. The interaction model allows different intercepts and slopes for all the variables considered in the model.

The North–south divide clearly emerges from the results of our 3SLS system estimation in Table 8. In the R&D equation (column 1), the *technology push* effect is important and significant in both areas, but in the North its value is more than twice the one in the South. Given the size of the standard error, it is clear that this difference is significant at the 5% significance level. The *demand pull* effect identified by the New Market Objective variable remains significant for both clusters. The common relevance of industry characteristics means that size has an equal significance in both areas, with a higher coefficient in the South where R&D is more likely to be concentrated in a few large firms. The internal financing of R&D through past profits is significant in the South alone, as external sources of R&D funds may be more accessible in Northern countries. Export market shares affect R&D efforts with positive and significant coefficients; their value, however, is greater in the North where the feedback loop between international market power and technological efforts appears to be stronger. Nevertheless, we cannot distinguish them at a statistically significant level.

In the new product equation (column 2), the path dependency of R&D appears to be strong both in Northern countries and in the South—both coefficients are positive and significant, the Northern is larger but not statistically different from the latter. The impact on new processes loses its significance in both areas—but in Southern countries, it shows a negative coefficient, stressing the substitution between new products and processes. Coming to demand variables, the 'pull effect' of export growth on new products is positive and significant for Northern countries only; a key link in the innovation-performance relationship appear to be missing in Southern countries. No other element of demand is significant in either area, with the exception of the domestic demand for intermediate production in the North, showing a negative sign and confirming the hypothesis discussed above on the lower innovative dynamism of such demand component.

The export market share equation (column 3) is the one where the patterns for Northern and Southern countries are most contrasting. The key determinants of competitiveness are found to operate in the former and appear to be missing in the latter. This applies to the impact of the share of product innovators on export market share; to the significance of the contribution of new machinery to competitiveness; and even to the support that lower unit labor costs provide for cost competitiveness. The coefficients of the variables capturing the average growth in the usage of imported high tech intermediate inputs again is significant for the North only, and maintains the same order of magnitude and sign as in the previous models. While the North confirms the characteristics of the 'virtuous circle' between innovation inputs and outputs and competitiveness, in the South such links appear to be largely missing. Competitiveness and export success for the industries of Southern countries are not supported by innovative performances and the other expected determinants, but rather by nontechnological sources that are not captured by the present model.

6 Conclusions

The results of our model—focusing on the industry level—account for important dimensions of the interconnected engines of economic change in a Schumpeterian perspective. The results derived from the system of three equations support empirically some of the main tenets of the evolutionary literature. The following figure depicts the circular and cumulative relationships we have identified.

First, R&D intensity in industries is the result of technological opportunities—summed up by the cumulative nature of research and knowledge, the demand pull effect of the potential for new products, and firm size—, of their market power, reflected in export shares, and of the resources available for financing R&D from lagged profits. Second, the determinants of product innovation show that, on the supply side, the cumulative nature of R&D is important, while new processes may reveal a complementary or a substitutive role; demand factors either stimulate the introduction of new products, in the case of strong export growth, or may delay it when consumption and intermediate demand characterize markets. Third, in the export market share equation we find that both technological and cost competitiveness matter. The direct effect of product innovation reflects a strategy of technological competitiveness in line with the literature that previously investigated the connection between technology and exports. The introduction of new machinery may improve technological capabilities and reduce costs at the same time. Lower unit labor costs contribute to higher cost competitiveness. Imported intermediate inputs originating from high technology industries also contribute to higher export market shares.

Four improvements on the existing literature emerge from our model and findings. First we strengthen the evidence on the innovation-performance links provided by Bogliacino and Pianta (2013a, b), through an enlargement of the time span (the previous analysis was limited to 2005) and using data from different sources. In this way we are able to show that the recursive set of relationships depicted in Fig. 1 persists over a longer time span.

Second, the role of exports is fully addressed, pointing out the fundamental role of competitive success in 'closing' the 'virtuous circle' between innovation and performance. Its determinants in technological factors—such as new products and processes—are, for the first time to our knowledge, combined with the importance of the intermediate input mix. Export success is shown to depend on high technology imported inputs, which are playing an increasing role in the current process of fragmentation of international production.

Third, we enrich the evolutionary literature that has traditionally focused on supply and technology factors, with a full consideration of demand, broken down into its major components. Our results lend support to the 'learning by exporting' thesis showing that exports represent the most dynamic component of demand capable to 'pull' the emergence of new products. Conversely, domestic demand, particularly for intermediate products, is much less dynamic and unable to stimulate innovation. These results echo the Schumpeterian distinction between novel

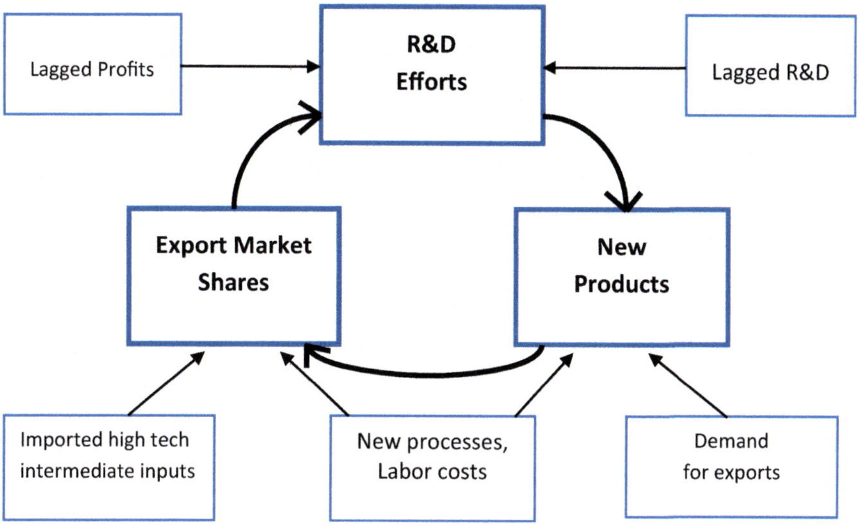

Fig. 1 The system of relations with feedbacks and loops

productions based on major innovations, on the one hand, and standard activities in the 'circular flow' of the economy (Schumpeter 1976).

Fourth, we show—on empirical grounds—that this set of relationships does not necessarily hold for all countries (and, possibly, for all times, as shown for the innovation-employment nexus by Lucchese and Pianta 2012). Northern European countries do provide evidence of a 'virtuous circle' between innovation and international competitiveness that, however, is largely missing in Southern ones. This result shows the relevance of national differences and may help explain the observed divergent dynamics in international competitiveness between different areas of the European Union. It also has important policy implications on the need for addressing the gaps in technological efforts and capabilities in Southern economies, and on the policy proposals that may support better and more converging performances in Europe.

Acknowledgments The authors wish to thank the editor Uwe Cantner, an anonymous referee and, for their comments, Jan Fagerberg and all the participants at the 15th ISS Conference held in Jena—Schiller University. We are particularly grateful to Luca Zamparelli for a previous discussion of this paper. Dario Guarascio is strongly indebted with Michael Landesmann, Robert Steherer, Mario Holzner, Sebastian Leitner, Roman Stöllinger and Julia Grübler for their comments and suggestions during his visiting period at the Vienna Institute for International Economic Studies. All the usual disclaimers apply.

Appendix

A.1 Descriptive Statistics

A.1.1 Export Market Shares

The six countries contained in our sample account for 95% of the EU-15 and for the 70% of the EU-28 exports (Table 9). The percentages are obtained dividing the sum of the exports of the considered countries by the total EU exports. Moreover, the export performance of the countries in our sample (measured by the export market shares) remain stable when different data sources are considered (calculations based on our SID database are compared with Eurostat data) and when exports are distinguished by destination. These elements bring us to consider the export market share variable used in the third equation of the system as a reliable proxy for industries performances in terms of international competitiveness.

A.1.2 Innovation vs. Performance Variables

The following scatter plots relate product innovation with export and value added as proxies for economic performance; they identify countries' heterogeneity and sectoral regularities, using Pavitt classes. Figure 2 shows a clear correlation between R&D efforts and innovation performance; Science Based and Supplier Specialized industries—those sectors for which innovation is most important—are located at the top right of the graph, as expected. Within technological intensive sectors, the best performers are from Northern countries and France. Figure 3

Table 9 Export market shares of the six major European countries DE, NL, UK, FR, ES, IT, EU15, EU28

Country	Export Mkt Sh. in the 6 major EU countries	Export Mkt Sh. in the EU 15	Export Mkt Sh. in the EU 28
Germany	0.29	0.26	0.22
Netherlands	0.12	0.10	0.08
UK	0.23	0.14	0.11
North	0.64	0.50	0.41
Spain	0.08	0.06	0.05
France	0.14	0.12	0.10
Italy	0.14	0.10	0.09
South	0.36	0.28	0.24

Averages over the sampled period 1995–2010
Sources: SID database (first column) and Eurostat
Notes: All values are in real terms deflated with OECD-STAN and Eurostat deflators (base year 2000) and corrected for PPP

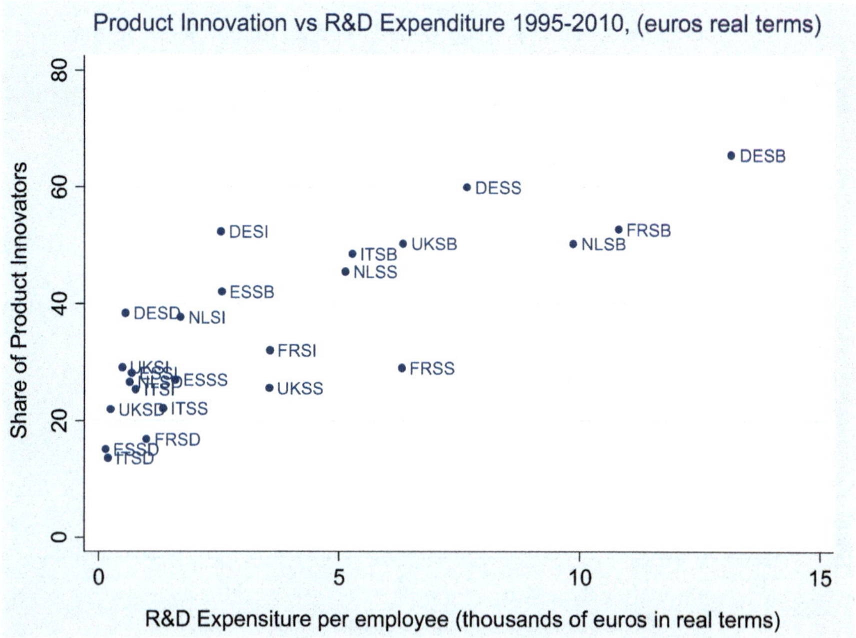

Fig. 2 Product innovation vs. R&D expenditure by country and Pavitt categories

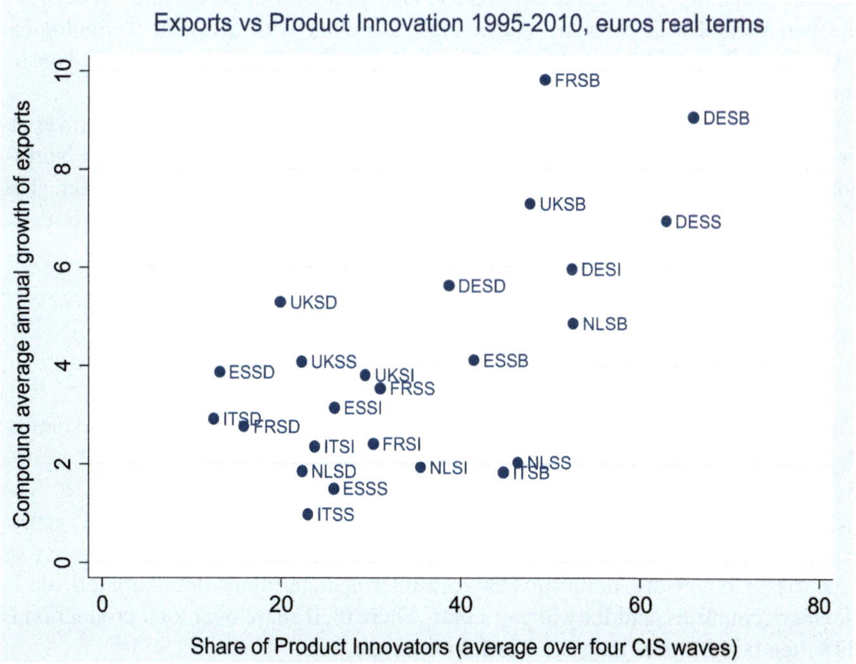

Fig. 3 Product innovation vs. exports by country and Pavitt categories

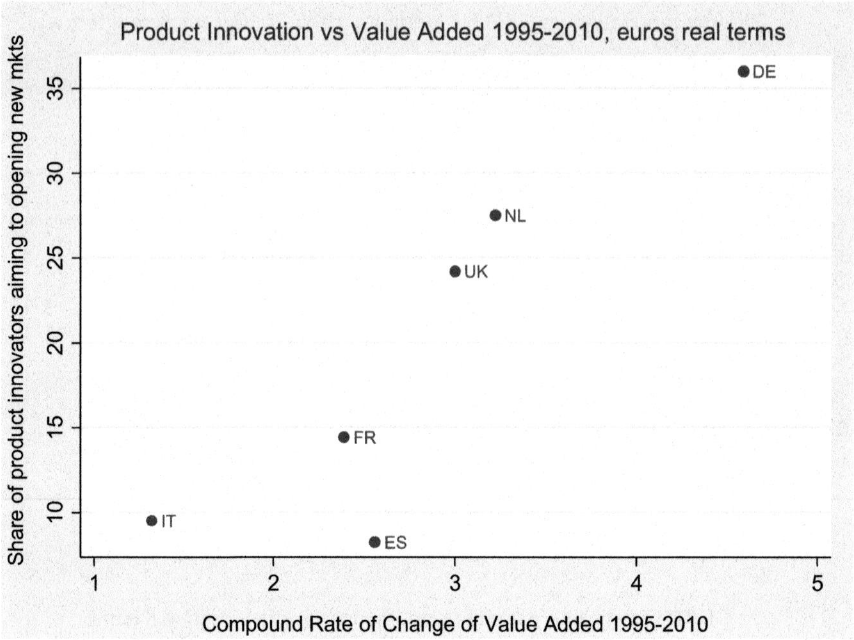

Fig. 4 Product innovation vs. value added by country

relates product innovation and exports and also, in this case, the correlation between the two variables is detected. As in Fig. 2, sectors with a higher technological intensity (SB and SS) are positioned in the top right of the graph and the North–south divide is again clear in the distribution.

Figure 4 provides a cross country comparison plotting product innovation versus the rate of change of value added over the sampled period. In this graph, the North–south divide is again clear, as well as the role of Germany as an outlier. The descriptive evidence provided is the background to the results of the econometric model developed in Sect. 5.

A.1.3 Intermediate Inputs

The final step of this data inspection regards the role played by intermediate inputs, distinguishing them in terms of technological content and source. Table 10 reports the share of each intermediate input over total industry production of countries. The numbers in Table 10 depict a situation where there is little variability across countries; even the high tech imported inputs have a highly stable relevance across countries. Conversely, domestic low tech intermediate inputs play a major role in Southern countries, and Italy in particular, where their share over total production is 32%, ten point higher than the Northern average.

Table 10 Intensity in the use of domestic and imported inputs by country (1995–2010)

Country	Domestic low tech	Domestic high tech	Foreign low tech	Foreign high tech
Germany	0.20	0.17	0.07	0.05
Netherlands	0.19	0.19	0.11	0.10
UK	0.23	0.14	0.06	0.05
North	0.21	0.17	0.08	0.05
Spain	0.26	0.15	0.06	0.05
France	0.24	0.18	0.06	0.05
Italy	0.32	0.17	0.06	0.04
South	0.27	0.17	0.06	0.05

Expenditures for the acquisition of input as a share of total production, average values
Notes: High Tech intermediate inputs are those originating sectors belonging to SB and SS Pavitt categories while Low Tech ones are those coming from SI and SD sectors

Table 11 Intensity in the use of domestic and imported inputs by revised Pavitt category (1995–2010)

Pavitt category	Domestic low tech	Domestic high tech	Foreign low tech	Foreign high tech
Science based	0.19	0.20	0.04	0.10
Supplier dom.	0.27	0.14	0.07	0.03
Scale intensive	0.26	0.17	0.11	0.05
Supplier spec.	0.18	0.19	0.03	0.08

Expenditures for the acquisition of input as a share of total production, average values
Notes: High Tech intermediate inputs are those originating from sectors belonging to SB and SS Pavitt categories while Low Tech ones are those coming from SI and SD sectors

Table 11 reports the intensity in the use of domestic and imported inputs by Pavitt Categories for the period 1995–2010. As expected, the variability across Pavitt Categories is higher than the one observed among countries. Sectors belonging to Science Based and Supplier Specialized categories rely mostly on high tech intermediate inputs, and their openness to the foreign market is also remarkable. Conversely, Scale Intensive and Supplier Dominated sectors are characterized by an intensive use of low tech inputs originating principally from the domestic market. A substantial divergence in terms of economic and innovative performances across our sample's countries emerges from this first data inspection. Moreover, technological factors turn out as a crucial element in the explanation of competitiveness for the EU countries we have considered.

A.2 Model Diagnostics

A.2.1 Dummy Variables Estimations

In this subsection, we report the estimations, equation by equation including the dummy variable coefficients (Tables 12, 13 and 14). The dummy variable coefficients have been discussed in Sect. 5.1.

The standard diagnostic tests are examined here, equation by equation. We try to detect the presence of heteroscedasticity and/or multicollinearity. To check we respectively use a Breusch-Pagan test and a Variance Inflation Factor (VIF, calculated on the baseline WLS regression). In order to address the endogeneity issue, we regress the explanatory variables over a set of instruments, compute the residuals and re-run a robust standard errors-WLS of the equation, with the residuals included as an explanatory variable. The *T*-test for the coefficient of the residuals included becomes a test of endogeneity; see Wooldridge (2002, p. 118) (Tables 15, 16, and 17).

The results are the following: we have to estimate robust standard errors since the Breusch-Pagan test rejected the null hypothesis of homoscedasticity, explanatory variables are orthogonal to the error term, and multicollinearity is not an issue;

Table 12 The R&D equation

	(1) Baseline model	(2) Baseline with country and Pavitt dummies
Lagged R&D expenditure	0.58 [8.35]***	0.51 [6.90]***
Firm size	11.42 [6.66]***	12.05 [6.98]***
New markets obj.	0.03 [1.64]	0.02 [0.93]
Profits (first lag)	0.026 [2.25]**	0.03 [2.26]**
Export market share (first lag)	3.68 [1.68]*	4.04 [1.71]*
Core dummy	−1.82 [−1.75]*	
Periphery dummy	−0.68 [−0.76]*	
Science based dummy	1.98 [2.48]**	2.66 [3.21]***
Supplier specialized dummy	1.17 [2.30]**	1.43 [2.79]***
Germany dummy		−0.58 [−0.61]
Spain dummy		−0.45 [−0.55]*
France dummy		1.45 [1.91]*
Italy dummy		−0.19 [0.78]
Netherlands dummy		−0.58 [−0.47]
UK dummy		−0.95 [−0.79]***
Constant	−1.01 [−0.94]	−1.88 [−3.06]***
N. observations	179	179
R^2 (Adj)	0.73	0.73

Dependent Variable: In-house R&D expenditure per employee
WLS with robust standard errors and weighted data (weights are the numbers of employee)
t-stat in brackets
*Significant at 10%, **Significant at 5%, ***Significant at 1%

Table 13 The innovation equation

	(1) Baseline model	(2) Baseline with country and Pavitt dummies
Lagged R&D expenditure	1.57 [6.23]***	1.60 [6.28]***
Expenditure for mach. and equipments	−0.45 [−0.69]	−1.16 [−1.73]*
Final demand (rate of growth)	−0.28 [−0.38]	−0.24 [−0.33]
Demand of int. goods (rate of growth)	−0.55 [−2.88] ***	−0.47 [−2.49]**
Exports (rate of growth)	0.01 [0.70]	0.009 [0.41]
Core dummy	3.99 [1.66]*	
Periphery dummy	−12.87 [−4.63] ***	
Science based dummy	14.73 [5.32]***	14.54 [5.38]***
Supplier specialized dummy	−7.49 [−4.34]**	−8.14 [−4.80]***
Germany dummy		15.52 [3.19]***
Spain dummy		−8.17 [−1.72]*
France dummy		−5.03 [−1.07]
Italy dummy		−1.03 [−0.29]
Netherlands dummy		7.56 [2.40]***
UK dummy		−0.27 [−0.06]
Constant	37.79 [11.14]***	30.04 [6.75]***
N. observations	286	286
R^2 (Adj)	0.55	0.57

Dependent Variable: Share of firms carrying out product innovation
WLS with robust standard errors and weighted data (weights are the numbers of employee)
t-stat in brackets
*Significant at 10%, **Significant at 5%, ***Significant at 1%

usually VIF is considered worrisome if it is higher than four (or higher than ten, according to different sources), and these thresholds are four to ten times higher than the value of our sample statistics. We cannot reject our formulation of WLS with robust standard errors. Regarding endogeneity (we developed standard endogenity tests on SIZE, EXPGR, MACH and INT_IMP_HT), our diagnostic rejects the hypothesis of endogeneity for the tested variables.

To go a step further in the endogeneity test, we report the results of the 2SLS estimation of each of our baseline equations (as already illustrated above, we instrumented our regressors suspected of being endogenous with their lag, the rate of change of value added, country dummies, time dummies and Pavitt dummies) (Table 18).

The basic formulation of the R&D (1) and New products (2) equations is not rejected by the results and the overidentification test supports the validity of the selected instruments. As a final step, we report the results of the 2SLS estimation for the third equation of the system (Tables 19 and 20).

Table 14 The export market share equation

	(1) Baseline model	(2) Baseline with country and Pavitt dummies
Lagged product innovation	0.0015 [2.88] ***	−0.0004 [−0.03]
Expenditure for mach. & equipments	0.014 [2.41] ***	0.01 [1.83]*
Unit labour cost (rate of growth)	−0.005 [−3.39]***	−0.004 [−3.07]
Domestic interm. inputs, low tech (rate of growth)	−0.012 [−3.51]***	−0.12, [−3.80]***
Domestic interm. inputs, high tech (rate of growth)	−0.004 [−1.43]	−0.002 [−0.81]
Imported interm. inputs, low tech (rate of growth)	0.002 [1.02]	0.003 [1.77]*
Imported interm. inputs, high tech (rate of growth)	0.015 [5.31] ***	0.011 [3.98]***
Science based dummy	−0.07 [−3.03] ***	−0.04 [−1.59]
Supplier specialized dummy	−0.011 [−0.11]	−0.022 [0.11]
Core dummy	0.22 [10.12] ***	
Periphery dummy	0.07 [6.38]***	
Germany dummy		0.31 [9.96]***
Spain dummy		0.08 [3.61]***
France dummy		0.12 [6.04]***
Italy dummy		0.13 [7.14]***
Netherlands dummy		0.19 [3.40]***
UK dummy		0.26 [9.17]***
N. observations	287	287
R^2 (Adj)	0.79	0.81

Dependent Variable: Export Market Share
WLS with robust standard errors and weighted data (weights are the numbers of employee)
t-stat in brackets
*Significant at 10%, **Significant at 5%, ***Significant at 1%

Table 15 R&D equation

Breusch-Pagan test	
Chi^2	107.30
p-value	0.0009
Multicollinearity	
Average variance inflation factor	1.32
Endogenity	
SIZE (p-value)	0.21
t-stat	−1.27
R&D (p-value)	0.35
t-stat	−0.93

Table 16 Innovation equation

Breusch-Pagan test	
Chi^2	46.76
p-value	0.0000
Multicollinearity	
Average variance inflation factor	1.26
Endogenity	
EXP (p-value)	0.12
t-stat	−1.54
EXMACHE (p-value)	0.19
t-stat	−1.31

Table 17 Innovation equation

Breusch-Pagan test	
Chi^2	35.92
p-value	0.0000
Multicollinearity	
Average variance inflation factor	2.55
Endogenity	
INT_IMP_HT (p-value)	0.13
t-stat	−1.52

Table 18 The R&D equation

	(1) Baseline model
Lagged R&D expenditure	0.70 [7.97]***
Firm size	1.73 [1.69]*
New markets obj.	0.03 [1.64]
Profits (first lag)	0.013 [2.16]**
Export market share (first lag)	3.27 [1.71]*
Constant	−1.01 [−0.94]
N. observations	256
Uncentered R^2	0.71
Overidentification test (Hansen J tests)	18.36
p-Value	0.04

Dependent Variable: *R&D expenditure per employee*
2SLS for panel data with robust standard errors and weighted data (weights are the numbers of employee) Included Endogenous: Size Excluded Instruments: rate of change of value added, country dummies, Pavitt dummies, time dummies
z-stat in brackets
*Significant at 10%, **Significant at 5%, ***Significant at 1%

Table 19 The innovation equation

	(1) Baseline model
Lagged R&D expenditure	2.32 [8.40]***
Expenditure for new machineries	1.67 [2.22]*
Final demand	−0.65 [−0.71]
Intermediate demand	−0.58 [−2.41]**
Compound rate of growth of exports	0.20 [1.95]**
Constant	−1.01 [−0.94]
N. observations	256
Uncentered R^2	0.73
Overidentification test (Hansen J tests)	7.31
p-Value	0.12

Dependent Variable: *Share of product innovators*
2SLS for panel data with robust standard errors and weighted data (weights are the numbers of employee) Included Endogenous: Compound rate of growth of exports. Instruments: lagged exports, rate of change of value added, country dummies, time dummies and Pavitt dummies) z-stat in brackets
*Significant at 10%, **Significant at 5%, ***Significant at 1%

Table 20 The export market share equation

	(1) Baseline model
Lagged product innovation	0.0015 [2.88]***
Expenditure for mach. and equipments	0.014 [2.41]***
Unit labour cost (rate of growth)	−0.005 [−3.39]***
Domestic interm. inputs, low tech (rate of growth)	−0.012 [−3.51]***
Domestic interm. inputs, high tech (rate of growth)	−0.004 [−1.43]
Imported interm. inputs, low tech (rate of growth)	0.002 [1.02]
Imported interm. inputs, high tech (rate of growth)	0.015 [5.31]***
N. observations	300
Uncentered R^2	0.56
Overidentification test (Hansen J tests)	16.78
p-Value	0.02

Dependent Variable: Export Market Share
2SLS with robust standard errors and weighted data (weights are the numbers of employee) Included Endogenous: Expenditure for new machineries for employee and Imported intermediate inputs—high tech. Instruments: lagged expenditure for new machineries, lagged imported intermediate inputs, rate of change of value added country dummies, time dummies and Pavitt dummies) z-stat in brackets
*Significant at 10%, **Significant at 5%, ***Significant at 1%

Also in this case, our formulation is consistent with the data and the instruments are properly selected.

References

Adner R, Levinthal D (2001) Demand heterogeneity and technological evolution: implications for product and process innovation. Manag Sci 47(5):611–628

Aghion P, Howitt P (1992) A model of growth through creative destruction. Econometrica 60 (2):323–351

Aghion P, Howitt P (1998) Endogenous growth theory. The MIT Press, Cambridge

Amable B, Verspagen B (1995) The role of technology in market shares dynamics. Appl Econ 27:197–204

Amendola G, Dosi G, Papagni E (1993) The dynamics of international competitiveness. Weltwirtschaftliches Arch 129(3):451–471

Antonelli C, Crespi F, Scellato G (2012) Inside innovation persistence: new evidence from Italian micro-data. Struct Chang Econ Dyn 23(4):341–353

Archibugi D, Pianta M (1992) The technological specialization of advanced countries. A report to the EC on international science and technology activities. Kluwer, Dordrecht

Arrow KJ (1962) The economic implications of learning by doing. Rev Econ Stud 29:155–173

Arthur B (2013) Complexity economics: a different framework for economic thought. Santa Fe Institute Working Papers Series 2013-4-012

Atkinson A, Stiglitz J (1969) A new view of technological change. Econ J 79(315):573–578

Backer K, Yamano D (2012) International comparative evidence on global value chains. STI Working Paper 3, OECD

Bas M, Strauss-Kahn V (2010) Does importing more inputs raise exports? Firm level evidence from France. MPRA Paper 27315. University Library of Munich, Germany

Bogliacino F, Gomez S (2014) Capabilities and investment in R&D: an analysis on European data. Struct Change Econ Dyn 31(C):101–111

Bogliacino F, Pianta M (2010) Innovation and employment: a reinvestigation using revised pavitt classes. Res Policy 39(6):799–809

Bogliacino F, Pianta M (2013a) Profits, R&D and innovation: a model and a test. Ind Corp Chang 22(3):649–678

Bogliacino F, Pianta M (2013b) Innovation and demand in industry dynamics. R&D, new products and profits. In: Pyka A, Andersen ES (eds) Long term economic development. Springer, Berlin

Breschi S, Malerba F, Orsenigo L (2000) Technological regimes and Schumpeterian patterns of innovation. Econ J 110:388–410

Brown JR, Fazzari SM, Petersen BC (2009) Financing innovation and growth: cash flow, external equity, and the 1990s R&D boom. J Financ 64:151–185

Carlin W (2001) Export market performance of OECD countries: an empirical examination of the role of cost competitiveness. Econ J 111:128–162

Cimoli M, Dosi G, Stiglitz JE (eds) (2009) Industrial policy and development: the industrial policy of capability accumulation. Oxford University Press, New York

Cincera M, Ravet J (2010) Financing constraints and R&D investments of large corporations in Europe and the USA. Sci Public Policy 37(6):455–466

Cohen W (2010) Chapter 4: Fifty years of empirical studies of innovative activity and performance. In: Rosenberg N, Hall B (eds) Handbook of the economics of innovation. Elsevier, Amsterdam

Cohen WM, Levine RC (1989) Empirical studies of innovation and market structure. In: Schmalensee R, Willig RD (eds) Handbook of industrial organization, vol 2. North-Holland, Amsterdam, pp 1059–1107

Colantone I, Crinò R (2014) New imported inputs, new domestic products. J Int Econ 92 (1):147–165

Crepon B, Duguet E, Mairesse J (1998) Research and development, innovation and productivity: an econometric analysis at the firm level. Econ Innov New Technol 7(2):115–158

Crespi F, Pianta M (2007) Innovation and demand in European industries. Econ Politic J Inst Anal Econ 24(1):79–112

Crespi F, Pianta M (2008a) Demand and innovation in productivity growth. Int Rev Appl Econ 22 (6):655–672
Crespi F, Pianta M (2008b) Diversity in innovation and productivity in Europe. J Evol Econ 18:529–545
Crespi G, Criscuolo C, Haskell J (2008) Productivity, exporting, and the learning-by-doing hypothesis: direct evidence from UK firms. Can J Econ 41(2):619–638
Daveri F, Jona-Lasinio C (2007) Off-shoring and productivity growth in the Italian manufacturing industries. Economics Department Working Papers 2007-EP08. Parma University
Dosi G (1982) Technological paradigms and technological trajectories: a suggested interpretations of the determinants and directions of technical change. Res Policy 11:147–162
Dosi G (1988) Sources, procedures and microeconomic effects of innovation. J Econ Lit 26:1120–1171
Dosi G, Pavitt K, Soete L (1990) The economics of technical change and International Trade. Harvester Wheatsheaf, Brighton
Dosi G, Grazzi M, Tomasi C, Zeli A (2012) Turbulence underneath the big calm? The micro-evidence behind Italian productivity dynamics. Small Bus Econ 39(4):1043–1067
Dosi G, Grazzi M, Moschella D (2015) Technology and costs in international competitiveness: from countries and sectors to firms. Res Policy. https://doi.org/10.1016/j.respol.2015.05.012
Evangelista R, Lucchese M, Meliciani V (2015) Business services and the export performances of manufacturing industries. J Evol Econ. https://doi.org/10.1007/s00191-015-0409-5
Fagerberg J (1988) International competitiveness. Econ J 98:355–374
Fagerberg J, Hansson P, Lundberg L, Melchior A (1997) Technology and international trade. Edward Elgar, Cheltenham
Feenstra R, Hanson GH (1996) Foreign investment, outsourcing and relative wages. In: Feenstra RC, Grossman GM, Irwin DA (eds) The political economy of trade policy: papers in honor of Jagdish Bhagwati. The MIT Press, Cambridge, pp 89–127
Greeve HR (2003) Organizational learning from performance feedback. Cambridge University Press, Cambridge
Griliches Z (1979) Issues in assessing the contribution of research and development to productivity growth. Bell J Econ 10:92–116
Griliches Z (1995) R&D and productivity: econometric results and measurement issues. In: Stoneman P (ed) Handbook of the economics of innovation and technological change. Blackwell, Oxford, p 5289
Grossman M, Helpman E (1991) Trade, innovation and growth. Am Econ Rev 80(2):86–91
Guarascio D, Pianta M, Lucchese M et al (2015) Business cycles, technology and exports. Econ Polit J Anal Inst Econ 32(2):167–200
Hall BH (2002) The financing of research and development. Oxf Rev Econ Policy 18(1):35–51
Harris R, Moffat J (2011) R&D, Innovation and exporting. SERC Discussion paper, Spatial Economic Research Center, LSE
Hummels D, Ishii J, Yi KM (2001) The nature and growth of vertical specialization in world trade. J Int Econ 54(1):959–972
Kaldor N (1981) The role of increasing returns, technical progress and cumulative causation in the theory of international trade and economic growth. Econ Appl 34(4):593–617
Kleinbaum DG, Kupper LL, Muller KE (1988) Applied regression analysis and other multivariate methods, 2nd edn. PWS Publishing, Boston
Kleinert J and Zorell N (2012) The export magnification effects of offshoring. European Central Bank – Working Papers Series, 1430
Kleinknecht A, Verspagen B (1990) Demand and innovation: Schmookler re-examined. Res Policy 19:387–394
Krugman P (1990) Increasing returns and economic geography. NBER Working Papers 3275. National Bureau of Economic Research

Landesmann M, Pfaffermeyr M (1997) Technological competition and trade performances. Appl Econ 29(2):179–196
Laursen K, Meliciani V (2010) The role of ICT knowledge flows for international market share dynamics. Res Policy 39(5):687–697
Loof H, Heshmati A (2006) On the relationship between innovation and performance: a sensitivity analysis. Econ Innov New Technol 15(4–5):317–344
Lorentz A, Ciarli T, Savona M, Valente M (2015) The effect of demand-driven structural transformations on growth and technological change. J Evol Econ. https://doi.org/10.1007/s00191-015-0409-5
Lucchese M (2011) Demand, innovation and openness as determinants of structural change. University of Urbino DEMQ WP
Lucchese M, Pianta M (2012) Innovation and employment in economic cycles. Comp Econ Stud 54:341–359
Mairesse J, Mohnen P (2010) Using innovations surveys for econometric analysis. NBER working paper, w15857
Malerba F (2002) Sectoral systems of innovation and production. Res Policy 31:247–264
Malerba F (ed) (2004) Sectoral systems of innovation. Cambridge University Press, Cambridge
Malerba F, Orsenigo L, Peretto P (1997) Persistence of innovative activities sectoral patterns of innovation and international technological specialization. Int J Ind Organ 15:801–826
Metcalfe J (2010) Technology and economic theory. Camb J Econ 34(1):153–171
Montobbio F (2003) Sectoral patterns of technological activity and export market share dynamics. Camb J Econ 27:523–545
Mowery D, Rosenberg N (1979) The influence of market demand upon innovation: a critical review ofsome recent empirical studies. Res Policy 8:102–153
Nelson RR (1959) The simple economics of basic scientific research. J Polit Econ 67:297–306
Nelson R, Winter S (1982) An evolutionary theory of economic change. The Belknap Press of Harvard University Press, Cambridge
Nemet GF (2009) Demand-pull, technology-push, and government-led incentives for non-incremental technical change. Res Policy 38:700–709
OECD (2009) Innovation in firms: a microeconomic perspective. OECD, Paris
Parisi ML, Schiantarelli F, Sembenelli A (2006) Productivity, innovation and R&D: micro evidence for Italy. Eur Econ Rev 50:2037–2061
Pasinetti L (1981) Structural change and economic growth. Cambridge University Press, Cambridge
Pavitt K (1984) Sectoral patterns of technical change: towards a taxonomy and a theory. Res Policy 13(6):343–373
Peters B (2009) Persistence of innovation: stylized facts and panel data evidence. J Technol Transfer 34:226–243
Pianta M (2001) Innovation, demand and employment. In: Petit P, Soete L (eds) Technology and the future of European employment. Elgar, Cheltenham, pp 142–165
Pianta M, Lucchese M (2011) The sectoral innovation database 2011. Methodological Notes, University of Urbino, DEMQ working paper
Pianta M, Tancioni M (2008) Innovations, profits and wages. J Post Keynesian Econ 31 (1):103–125
Piva M, Vivarelli M (2007) Is demand-pulled innovation equally important in different groups of firms? Camb J Econ 31:691–710
Saviotti P, Pyka A (2013) The co-evolution of innovation, demand and growth. Econ Innov New Technol 22(5):461–482
Scherer F (1982) Demand-pull and technological invention: Schmookler revisited. J Ind Econ 30 (3):225–237
Schmookler J (1966) Invention and economic growth. Harvard University Press, Cambridge, MA
Schumpeter JA (1975) Capitalism, socialism and democracy, 1st edn. Harper, New York
Schumpeter JA (1976) Capitalism, socialism and democracy. Harper, New York (1st edn 1942)

Soete LLG (1981) A general test of the technological gap trade theory. Weltwirtschaftliches Arch 117:638–666
Soete L (1987) The impact of technological innovation on international trade patterns: the evidence reconsidered. Res Policy 16(2–4):101–130
Stapel S, Pasanen J, Reinecke S et al (2004) Purchasing power parities and related economic indicators for EU, Candidate Countries and EFTA. Eurostat – Statistics in Focus
Stiglitz JE (1987) Learning to learn localized learning and technological progress. In: Stoneman P, Dasgupta P (eds) Economic policy and technological performance. Cambridge University Press, Cambridge
Stiglitz JE, Weiss A (1981) Credit rationing in markets with imperfect information. Am Econ Rev 71(3):393–410
Thirlwall A (1979) The balance of payment constraint as an explanation of growth rate differences. BNL Quarter Rev, Banca Nazionale del Lavoro 32(128):45–53
Tiffin A (2014) European productivity, innovation and competitiveness: the case of Italy. IMF Working Paper Strategy, Policy and Review Department
Timmer M (2013) The World Input Output Database (WIOD): contents, sources and methods. WIOD WP 10
Timmer M, Los B, Stehrer R, de Vries G (2013) Fragmentation, incomes and jobs: an analysis of European competitiveness. Econ Policy 28(76):613–661
Triguero-Cano A, Corcoles-Gonzales D (2013) Understanding the innovation: an analysis of persistence for Spanish manufacturing firms. Res Policy 42:340–352
Verspagen B (1993) Technological and social factors in long term fluctuations. Struct Chang Econ Dyn 4(1):210–213
Wooldridge JM (2002) Econometric analysis of cross section and panel data. The MIT Press, Cambridge
Yamano N, Ahmad N (2006) The OECD input-output database: 2006 Edition. OECD Science, Technology and Industry Working Papers 2006/8. OECD Publishing
Zellner A, Theil H (1962) Three-stage least squares: simultaneous estimation of simultaneous equations. Econometrica 30(1):54–78

Using Simulation Experiments to Test Historical Explanations: The Development of the German Dye Industry 1857–1913

Thomas Brenner and Johann Peter Murmann

Abstract In a simulation experiment, building on the abductive simulation approach of Brenner and Werker (Comput Econ 30(3):227–244, 2007), we test historical explanations for why German firms came to surpass British and France firms and to dominate the global synthetic dye industry for three decades before World War I while the U.S. never achieved large market share despite large home demand. Murmann and Homburg (J Evol Econ 11(2):177–205, 2001) and Murmann (Knowledge and competitive advantage: the coevolution of firms, technology, and national institutions. Cambridge University Press, 2003) argued that German firms came to dominate the global industry because of (1) the high initial number of chemists in Germany at the start of the industry in 1857, (2) the high responsiveness of the German university system and (3) the late (1877) introduction of a patent regime in Germany as well as the more narrow construction of this regime compared to Britain, France and the U.S. We test the validity of these three potential explanations with the help of simulation experiments. The experiments show that the second explanation—the high responsiveness of the German university system—is the most compelling one because unlike the other two it is true for virtually all plausible historical settings.

1 Introduction

The question of where and how new industries originate and develop is of great interest to policy makers. If one examines the industrial strength of countries and regions today, one usually finds that these strengths can be traced back to a dominating or, at least, strong role in the emergence or early developments of the industry. One example is the chemical industry in Germany. It is strongly connected

T. Brenner (✉)
Department of Geography, Philipps University Marburg, Deutschhausstr. 10, 35032 Marburg, Germany
e-mail: thomas.brenner@uni-marburg.de

J.P. Murmann
UNSW Australia Business School, Sydney, NSW 2052, Australia
e-mail: jee@professor-murmann.net

A. Pyka, U. Cantner (eds.), *Foundations of Economic Change*, Economic Complexity and Evolution, DOI 10.1007/978-3-319-62009-1_18

to the BASF and Hoechst companies, which were founded to sell synthetic dyes and related chemicals, and the firm Bayer, which, after being a trader of natural dyes, ventured into the early synthetic dye industry. There is wide agreement that the synthetic dye industry has been crucial for the development of the German chemical industry (Teltschik 1992). All three firms started not too far from each other along the Rhine river.

Understanding this spatial dimension of the development of industries—why firms producing similar products often cluster in particular regions—has become a very important area of research precisely because it is so important for economic policy making. Two strands can be observed. Some researchers study specific industries and their development in great detail, sometimes including spatial aspects (Klepper 2007; Buenstorf and Klepper 2009; Wenting and Frenken 2011; De Vaan et al. 2013). For other researchers the path-dependence of technology and industry development has become an important research topic in past three decades (David 1985; Arthur 1994; Krugman 1995; Sydow et al. 2009; Heimeriks and Boschma 2014).

While the development of the German chemical industry on the basis of the German synthetic dye industry can be explained on the basis of inter-technological path-dependence, these arguments do not apply to the exceptional developments of the German synthetic dye industry. When the first synthetic dyes were discovered (in France and UK), German firms were imitators and only much later became product innovators in their own right. Furthermore, the important raw materials and by far the largest market for synthetic dyes was in Great Britain, making it somewhat of a puzzle why Germany and not Britain dominated this industry in the period before World War I. Hence, understanding why Germany came to dominate this industry 15 years after the start of the industry requires a historical perspective (as done in Murmann 2003).

However, historical events are typically caused by a variety of factors. Because events do not recur in the exact same fashion multiple times, there are considerable challenges in developing causal accounts from the one run of history that we can observe. As a consequence, historical examinations are able to propose potential causes, but are not able to test the underlying mechanisms. In this sense, Murmann and Homburg (2001) and Murmann (2003) propose three potentially key explanations for the development of the German dye industry: (1) the high initial number of chemists in Germany at the start of the industry in 1857, (2) the high responsiveness of the German university system and (3) the late (1877) introduction of a patent regime in Germany as well as the more narrow construction of this regime compared to Britain, France, and the U.S. However, they are not able to make specific conclusions about the relative importance of these potential causes. Are all causal factors equally important? Could the dominating German market share in 1914 have been caused by a subset of these causal factors? Would the presence of these causal factors under all historically plausible conditions always have produced a dominance of German firms?

The present paper provides much more specific and robust answers to these questions on the basis of a simulation experiment. This is possible because in a simulation approach we are able to utilize at the same time general and case-specific knowledge and analyze counter-factual situations. Although the evolution of the dye industry shows many specific characteristics—some of which we will study in detail here—it is based on the development of firms, which follows some basic rules that hold for all industries. Firm characteristics and developments have been studied intensively in recent years and many facts that hold for all kinds of industries have been established (an overview is given in Brenner and Duschl 2014). We utilize this information and combine it with the specific knowledge about the development of the synthetic dye industry (provided in Murmann and Homburg 2001; Murmann 2003). This allows us to build realistic simulation models and to test the proposed set of causal reasons for the development with the help of counter-factual simulation experiments.

This is of interest for two reasons. First, we provide much more specific and robust conclusions about the relevance of the different factors for the unusual development of the German dye industry. Although, this development is quite specific (see Sect. 2), understanding the underlying causes provides information that is also relevant for other industry studies. Second, the combination of general and case-specific information for constructing an adequate simulation model goes beyond the existing approaches. Based on the abductive approach by Brenner and Werker (2007), we are able to produce validated and, hence, reliable results.

The remainder of the paper will proceed as follows. In Sect. 2 we will provide an overview of the historical development of the synthetic dye industry between 1857 and 1913. Based on the writings of Murmann and Homburg (2001) and Murmann (2003), we highlight three central historical explanations that they offered for why Germany came to dominate the dye industry in the period before 1913. We treat them as the three hypotheses that we test in this paper. Section 3 describes our simulation approach and how the simulation experiments carried out. Section 4 will present the results of the simulation experiments and provide conclusions on the causes of the developments in the German dye industry that are more robust than what a pure historical methodology can offer. Section 5 discusses the contributions of our paper.

2 The Synthetic Dye Industry, 1857–1913

2.1 A Brief History of the Industry

Human societies have dyed textiles for thousands of years, extracting coloring particles from plants and small animals. The first synthetic dye was produced in 1857 by Perkins and Sons. Wilhelm Henry Perkin—one of the two sons in Perkins's and Sons—was a student at the Royal College in 1856 when he made a serendipitous discovery. His professor had set the goal for him to synthesize quinine, a drug against malaria. He did not succeed with this task but 1 day he saw a purple coloring substance in his test tube. When textile dyers confirmed that the purple dye was able to dye silk in an appealing purple color, Perkins formed a company with his father and brother and pioneered the synthetic dye industry. The industry received substantial historical attention already in the late nineteenth century and early twentieth century (Caro 1892; Redlich 1914; Thissen 1922). For one, the industry was seen as the first example of a science based industry where a university based research discovery led to the development of a new technology and its commercialization within a very short period of time. Second, contemporaries found it surprising that Germany overtook the early leaders in Great Britain, which was endowed by a much larger home market and the source for raw materials in the first few decades of the industry. By 1913 natural dyes had been almost entirely replaced by synthetic dyes and synthetic dyes had become the largest export item of Germany (Murmann 2003). Furthermore, Germany had dominated the industry for three decades, making British, French, American firms into small players who could not compete effectively with the most successful German and Swiss firms. Thousands of dyes were synthesized in the period until 1914, rendering natural dyes uncompetitive in price and/or quality. After the initial development of aniline dyes in the wake of Perkins invention, the most important natural dyes were replaced by synthetic alizarine in the early 1870s and synthetic indigo in 1897.

Among scholars of science and technology, the striking case of the German dominance in one of the industries of the second industrial revolution had been widely known even in the English literature (see for example, Beer 1959; Landes 1969; Freeman 1982). What Murmann and Homburg (2001) added to this literature was that they created a demographic history of the entire global industry—all firms that left any historical trace, even if they were very short-lived, not just focusing on the most successful firms that previous historical writings had focused on. Adapted from Murmann (2013), we summarize some key demographic data on firm entries and exists, demand in individual countries, and country market shares in Table 8 (in the Appendix). What the data of Homburg and Murmann showed for the first time is that Germany before 1914 not only produced the largest number of firm start-ups (118) but also the largest number of firm failures (84). Great Britain, by contrast, had only 53 firm entries and only 43 firm failures (for other countries see Table 8). The failure rates in most of the countries were above 80%. The German global market share only amounted to 3% on 1862, but by 1873 the German global share had climbed to 50%, by 1893 Germany had 70% and by 1913 74%. This is not counting the German owned plants in foreign markets.

2.2 Central Explanations

Building on the existing historiography and the new data collected on the industry demography with Homburg (Homburg and Murmann 2001), Murmann (2003) offered co-evolutionary explanations for how and why German firms came to dominate the industry by 1873 and then cemented their dominance until World War I. In terms of explaining the higher numbers of start-ups compared to Great Britain, Murmann cited two key factors. Dye start-ups required some chemical knowledge and hence the larger number of chemists that existed in Germany before the start of the industry facilitated entry because start-ups could more readily find chemical knowledge. Second, Great Britain, France and U.S. issued product patents for synthetic dyes, providing a monopoly to a particular firm for the particular dye. So while patents in the UK inhibited firms from entering industry with the same dye, the absence of an effective patent regime before 1877 allowed German entrepreneurs to enter the industry imitating French and British innovations. The larger number of start-ups in Germany led to fiercer competition in Germany, only allowing the most efficient firms to survive. When British and French firms had their patent expired, they could not manufacture dyes at the same low cost as the strongest German competitors and hence the German firms acquired 50% world market share by 1873. By the early 1870s chemical theory had advanced to a point that it could guide more systematically the search for innovative dyes. When Germany became a unified country in 1871, the societal groups that wanted Germany also to adopt a patent system gained the upper hand. The representatives of the dye industry together with support from leading chemists, lobbied that in chemical, pharmaceutical and food products only process patents would be granted in order to maintain some competition in the dye industry that industry participants saw as the key reason why German firms outcompeted French and British firms in the previous two decades. After the passage of the all-German patent law in Germany in 1877, the leading German firms started to employ chemists who did nothing else but develop new dyes. This allowed them to develop innovative dyes that achieved higher profits in the market, in turn allowing them to invest more in R&D and increase their market shares compared to less innovative rivals. Through their trade organization, which was formed in 1877, they lobbied also for German states to increase the number of chemistry graduates who could then be hired to staff expanding corporate R&D laboratories. Between 1890 and 1914, three of the leading German firms (BASF, Bayer, and Hoechst) producing dyes increased the number of chemists recruited from universities from 350 to 930 (Murmann 2013). Germany universities (in part because federalist structure in Germany and a history of competition among states to possess leading universities) were more responsive to the needs of the dye industry than the British, French, and US universities, making it easier for German firms to staff their growing R&D laboratories. British firms overcame their own shortage of chemists created by the lower responsiveness of universities to train chemists by importing talent from Germany. But they could not get the same quality of talent at the same price as German firms could, giving Germany an advantage in hiring the best chemists.

2.3 Historical Questions

To examine parts of the causal claims in the co-evolutionary explanation for German dominance in the synthetic dye industry before World War I, we carry out a simulation experiment of the development of the industry in the five major producer countries: Britain, France, Germany, Switzerland, and the United States. In particular, we want to examine the influence of differences in scientific capabilities in the early years of the industry on the competitive position of national firms over the next five decades. As mentioned earlier, Murmann's (2003) empirical analysis suggests that one of the key reasons why German firms overtook their British and French competitors was that Germany had a larger number of chemists available during the early years of the industry who could become founders of dye firms.

H1: A larger (smaller) number of German chemists in the first year of the synthetic dye industry (1857) would have caused a larger (smaller) global market share of German firms in this industry in 1913.

When German firms had captured a dominant global market share by 1873 (50%), collective lobbying campaigns where more successful in Germany than in other countries because the dye industry in Germany due to its size had more political clout. Building on Rosenberg (1998), Murmann (2003) also argued that the German university system was more responsive to the need for additional chemists who could staff the R&D labs of the large dye firms.

H2: A higher (lower) responsiveness to the demand for chemists in the German university system would have caused a larger (smaller) global market share of German firms in this industry in 1913.

Furthermore, Murmann (2003) argued that the absence of product patents in Germany for the first 20 years and the lobbying efforts of German dye firms to only allow process patents subsequently also had a decisive influence on the market share in 1913.

H3: A larger ability to protect innovations in Germany would have caused a smaller global market share of German firms in this industry in 1913.

3 Methods

3.1 Basic Considerations

We are not the first ones to simulate historical processes. In a path-breaking work Allen (2003) studied the relative importance of key causal factors in determining economic growth in European countries from 1300 until 1800 by running simulations that were calibrated with historical data. While Allen (2003) focused on the key macro variables, we consider the macro and micro level in our approach. Therefore, we follow the abductive simulation approach proposed by Brenner and Werker (2007). To some extent the approach has commonalities with the history-friendly simulation approach developed by Malerba et al. (1999, 2008) but it is also different in important ways. The abductive simulation approach has three specific characteristics: First, two levels are explicitly distinguished: the level of the underlying mechanisms and the level of implications. Second, the simulation model should be kept as general as necessary, instead of aiming at developing exactly one simulation model. Third, available knowledge on both levels should be used as much as possible to narrow the set of potential simulation models.

In our case the level of underlying mechanisms contains the developments of the individual firms, the markets for dyes, the education and employment of chemists, the ability to obtain individual patents, as well as all processes and mechanisms important for these developments and their interaction. The level of implications is the global development of the synthetic dye industry, especially the distribution of market shares between the countries and the number of active firms.

We proceed in four steps: First, we develop a very general model (see Sect. 3.2). Then, historical knowledge on the implication level—such as the number of start-ups, the number of firms active and the distribution of market shares among the countries—is used to identify realistic parameter sets (see Sect. 3.3). In a third step, we conduct counter-factual simulation experiments in order to test our hypotheses (see Sect. 3.4). The results of the counter-factual simulations are studied statistically (see Sect. 3.5).

3.2 Simulation Model

The basic element of our simulation model is the development of each single firm. Brenner and Duschl (2014) proposed a general model of firm and market dynamics that is in line with all well-established stylized facts and offers the possibility to further specify and adapt the model to specific industries. Hence, this model provides an excellent starting point for modelling the development of the dye industry.

The model by Brenner and Duschl (2014) is based on the assumption that the considered market (in our case the market for synthetic dyes) consists of numerous separate submarkets (called market packages) and that firms compete in a monopolistic competition for these market packages, so that at each point in time each market package is satisfied by exactly one firm. Market packages appear and disappear and change in size randomly. There is a competition between firms (including a potential start-up) for existing and appearing market packages with the competition strengths crucially depending on the innovativeness of firms. Firms are characterized by the innovation strategy (ranging from an imitative to an innovative focus), their age and their competitive strength, which follows a random walk (see Brenner and Duschl 2014 for further details). Brenner and Duschl (2014) carefully tested whether their model is in line with the stylized knowledge about firm growth and firm characteristics. Therefore, we use this model but adapt a number of details to the historical situation in the synthetic dye industry, such as running a real time period from 1957 to 1913 (simulating each day as proposed by Brenner and Duschl (2014)) and using six independent regions: United Kingdom (UK), Germany (G), France (F), Switzerland (SW), United States (USA), and the rest of the world (*REST*). The first five regions represent the major dye producing countries before 1914, whose development and global market share is under investigation. We created the umbrella category "rest of the world" to represent the demand in all other countries. Each actor (firm, chemist, and patent) is assigned to one of the first five regions.

Furthermore, a number of aspects are of crucial relevance for testing our hypotheses. Therefore, we go into more details in the modelling of these aspects. In this sense, we make some smaller expansions of the model by Brenner and Duschl (2014) by allowing firms to change their strategies (see Appendix A.2.1), allowing firms to generate innovations dependent on firm characteristics such as the number of chemists employed (see Appendix A.2.2), and making the number of start-ups dependent on the availability of chemists in the countries (see Appendix A.2.2). Larger modifications are done in the definition of the market space and with respect to the two central aspects of our analysis: chemists and patents (both being not present in the model by Brenner and Duschl). These modifications are described in detail here.

3.2.1 Market Space

Historically dyes mainly compete with respect to two factors: Their type and their price-quality ratio. Therefore, we use a value, y_m, which defines the type of the product, and a value, a_m, which characterizes the technological advancement in price-quality ratio. The total market space is spanned by these two variables. We start the simulation always with two firms (one in UK and one in France) existing, supplying two market packages of a randomly drawn type and with a technological advancement of 0. All other market packages are not supplied by synthetic dye firms at the beginning (they are supplied by traditional dye firms). At the beginning of a simulation run these market packages are created with random values of y_m ranging between 0 and 1 and a_m ranging between 0 and $a_{init,natural}$. $a_{init,natural}$ reflects how much more attractive (price-quality ratio) the best natural dye is compared to the first synthetic dye. $a_{init,natural}$ is chosen randomly from a range between 20 and 100 for each simulation group. With time the synthetic dyes become more advanced due to innovations (see Appendix A.2.2) so that their values go beyond $a_{init,natural}$ and they finally replace (almost) all natural dyes on the market. The number of initial market packages is chosen such that it reflect the market for natural dyes in 1957, so that these market packages reflect the potential market that could have been overtaken by synthetic dyes. The strength of competition between market packages and the range of innovations within the market space are deduced from historical knowledge about the market (see Appendix A.2.3).

While the total market size develops randomly in the model by Brenner and Duschl (2014), the real market development is well known, at least in parts, in our case. We use the available historical information to determine at each point in time the total market size (see Appendix A.2.4). While we keep the occurrence of new market packages random (as in the original model), we make the total market size to fit the historical record by removing each day the required number market packages, instead of making their disappearance a random event as in the original model. The most unattractive market packages are removed first (see Appendix A.2.4 for details).

3.2.2 Chemists

According to the historical records on the synthetic dye industry, chemists play an important role in the development of this industry. Therefore, in contrast to the original model, chemists and their employment are explicitly modeled and each firm is assumed to employ at least one chemist. Furthermore, the number of chemists increases with the size of the firm and depends on the firm's innovation strategy (for details see Appendix A.2.5).

We assume that chemists first have to be trained in universities. Training is assumed to take 3 years. Hence, the number of chemistry students deciding to start university education at a particular time influences the number of available chemists 3 years later. Education is relevant within countries mainly because migration was historically a rare event, which we nevertheless consider in the simulation model according to the real data (see Appendix A.2.5).

The initial numbers of chemists in each country, denoted by $c_{init,reg}$, are set in accordance with the estimates given in Table 10 (in the Appendix). We assume that the study of chemistry can be started once a year and calculate every year the number of new students. This number depends on the national system of education and the conditions in the labor market. The actual demand for chemists is assumed to be represented well by the current number of employed chemists $c_{emp,reg}(t)$ in a country *reg* (*"reg" standing for our five explicitly modeled countries UK, Germany (G), France (F), Switzerland (S) and the US*). In 3 years time, when the now starting students enter the labor market the demand may have changed. We assume that national governments treat this issue differently. The largest increase in the number of chemists observed in the history of the dye industry before World War I is the jump from 380 to 900 chemists in Germany during the period from 1851 to 1865. On average, this implies that the number of chemists increased by 6.5% each year or by approximately 20% within 3 years. Education clearly responds to an increase of demand. The expected increase in the number of chemists is assumed here to be based on two factors: a basic preparation for increases, e_{reg}—which we call the responsiveness of the national university system—and additional education that is caused by lobbying. Lobbying is the more effective the higher the market share of the local firms is. For this reason each year the number of new chemistry students is chosen such that the number of chemists 3 year later is given by

$$c_{available,reg}(t + 3years) = c_{empl,reg}(t)^* \left(e_{reg} + \lambda_{reg} \cdot m_{reg}(t)\right)$$

where m_{reg} denotes the joint market share of all firms in country reg. λ_{reg} represents the influence of lobbying on the national education system. Our empirical analysis implies that λ_{reg} should not be greater than 0.2, because otherwise the lobbying might cause the number of chemists to increase by more than 20% (within 3 years) and an increase by 20% is the maximum that we observe in history. Therefore, its range is set to $0 < \lambda_{reg} < 0.2$. Given the historical information, we set $1 < e_{reg} < 1.2$.

3.2.3 Patents

Selling products is restricted by patent laws. Each time a firm discovers a new product (market package) the simulation program checks whether a patent exists for this product in the country in which the product should be sold. If such a patent exists and is held by another firm, the firm does not create and own this market package. If no such patent exists and has never existed (patents that have expired cannot be granted again) but the home country offers patent protection, the firm patents the product.

Different patent laws existed in the countries modeled. First, patent laws did not exist in all countries during the entire time span from 1857 to 1913. Second, patent laws differed between the countries. All countries in our simulation except Germany granted patents for product innovations. After 1877, Germany granted process patents. We model this by defining ranges within the product space that patents cover. This means that each patent has a range with respect to the technological type, y_m, and the technological advancement, a, of products.

Patent counts show that there were between 1000 and 4000 different types of dyes patented in the different countries. If we take this as an approximation of the number of different types of products in our simulation of patents, each patent covers a range of between 0.00025 and 0.001 in the type dimension. In addition, in Germany process innovations were patented. These cover only one innovation step, so that their range is assumed to be one in the dimension of the level of technological advancement.

Because successful litigation often cut short the life-span of a patent, all patents are assumed to hold for between 5 and 20 years (in accordance to the historical record). All characteristics of patents are summarized in Table 1.

In addition, in Great Britain numerous patent applications failed in the years 1856–1862. Therefore, the probability of obtaining a patent during that time in Great Britain is reduced to 50%. Once patents expire, it is assumed in the simulation that the same product cannot be patented again. The respective products can then be produced and sold by all firms forever.

Table 1 National patent characteristics

	Existence	Range in type dimension	Range in technological dimension	Minimum duration	Maximum duration
UK	1856–1913	0.001–0.0025	10–50	5–10 years	15–20 years
G	1877–1913	0.001–0.0025	1	5–10 years	15–20 years
F	1856–1913	0.001–0.0025	10–50	5–10 years	15–20 years
SW	1908–1913	0.001–0.0025	10–50	5–10 years	15–20 years
USA	1856–1913	0.001–0.0025	10–50	5–10 years	15–20 years

3.3 Calibration of Simulation Model

The model by Brenner and Duschl (2014), even in its restricted form, is designed to be flexible enough to capture all different kinds of industries. While we use the specific parameter settings in the Brenner and Duschl (2014) model that are able to generate all stylized facts about firm growth and market dynamics, we keep the additional parameters of our extension very general. Only those features, for which exact numbers are available from historical records, such as the initial number of chemists, the demand for dyes, the patent laws and so on are fixed in the simulation model.

Therefore, it is necessary to calibrate the model and find the parameter specifications that are in line with the real development of the synthetic dye industry. In line with the proposal of Brenner and Werker (2007) we do not aim to identify one specific parameter set that represents reality. The available knowledge on the real developments of the synthetic dye industry does not allow us to determine exactly one simulation model that represents reality for sure. For this reason, we have to identify a whole range of possibly realistic simulation models (parameter sets) and check for each of them whether our hypotheses are confirmed.

Historical records provide quite some information that can be used for checking whether each parameter set leads to realistic developments. We use information about macro patterns: In total there had been 289 start-ups in the dye industry in the five major producers countries between 1856 and 1913 (see Appendix 1). In Germany 118 start-ups are counted (Murmann 2013). We accept all simulation runs that lead to between half and twice these numbers (i.e., between 59 and 236 German start-up and between 144 and 578 start-ups in total). Furthermore, we know that the world market share by German firms had been approximately 75% in 1913, so that we accept only simulation runs that end in a German market share between 65 and 85%.

The time structure of the industry development is also an important aspect. Therefore, it is important that the simulation model also represents the time course adequately. We use the year 1871 as a point of time for checking whether the early developments are represented adequately. Historical records show that the world production of synthetic dye was 3500 t in 1871 (Murmann 2003, pp. 38). Simulation runs are accepted only if the total production in 1871 is between half and twice that value (between 1750 and 7000 t). The number of start-ups before 1871 was historically 25 in the UK, 38 in Germany, 36 in France, 15 in Switzerland and 3 in the US (Homburg and Murmann 2014). For this reason, we set the boundaries for accepting simulation runs again to half and twice the historical values: 12–50 for UK, 19–76 for Germany, 18–72 for France, 7–30 for Switzerland and 1–6 for the US.

3.4 Simulation Experiment

Given the simulation model and the validation criteria, the simulation experiment is conducted as follows. The simulation model contains many parameters for which quite large ranges are defined. We classify these parameters either into one group called "nuisance parameters" that contains all parameters that are not of core interest in our analysis or into a second group called "central parameters" that contains the parameters whose impacts we seek to study in detail. Central parameters are those parameters that are connected to our hypotheses, namely the number of initial chemists in Germany, the reactiveness of the German university system and the specific patent law in Germany.

For the simulation experiment we repeated the following procedure (see Fig. 1 in the Appendix) more than 7 million times. We draw a random set of parameters from their defined ranges, run the simulation and check whether this parameter set is able to reproduce history, meaning that it produces a simulation run that satisfies the calibration criteria defined above. If this is the case, we start the simulation experiment. This means that now the central parameters are varied systematically. For the initial number of chemists in Germany (the real value is 54) we use three different values: $c_{init,G} = 25, 54, 85$. For the responsiveness of the German university we also use three values: $e_G = 1, 1.1, 1.2$. For the patent laws we use two settings: One setting reflects the actual historical situation, while the other setting assigns Germany the same patent laws that existed in France. We run 100 simulations for each of these values of the central parameters in combination with the setting of the nuisance parameters that passed the calibration test. Each simulation run starts in 1857 and ends in 1913. We record for each simulation run the market share of German firms in 1913 since this is the key outcome variable that we want to study.

In total we conducted the simulation experiment for 4000 parameter sets. All simulation runs for one setting of the nuisance parameters is called a group of simulations.

Note that the method we use here represents a Monte-Carlo approach since we run simulations across the entire range of empirically possible parameter settings.

3.5 Statistical Methods

Each group of simulations reflects one model specification and, therefore, one potential representation of the real world. If a large number of such groups are randomly drawn from the parameter ranges, it is likely that some simulation groups contain nuisance parameter values that are very similar to the true historical values. If, furthermore, the overall structure of the model is adequately chosen, these simulation groups will approximate well the true description of reality.

The number of simulation runs has to be numerous enough so that within a group of simulations a sufficient number of data points are generated to make statistical analyses feasible. Remember that within a group of simulations all nuisance parameters are the same for all simulation runs. In a first step, we analyze each group of simulations separately, so that in this first analysis the nuisance parameter do not play a role. In order to obtain a detailed picture of the impact of our central variable we compare the results for seven pairs of settings. Namely, we compare the market share held by German firms in 1913 between the simulation runs with $c_{init,G} = 85$ and $c_{init,G} = 54$, between the simulation runs with $c_{init,G} = 85$ and $c_{init,G} = 25$, between the simulation runs with $c_{init,G} = 54$ and $c_{init,G} = 25$, between the simulation runs with $e_G = 1.2$ and $e_G = 1.1$, between the simulation runs with $e_G = 1.2$ and $e_G = 1$, between the simulation runs with $e_G = 1.1$ and $e_G = 1$, and between the simulation runs with the actual historical German patent laws and with counterfactual German patent laws that we set identical to those in France. The *U*-Test of Mann and Whitney is an adequate statistical tool for these (using a significance level of 5%). The comparison is done for each simulation group separately, making it possible to determine for each simulation group seven results. Each result can be reflected by "+" if the average market share of German firms $<m_G>$ is significantly higher for the first setting than for the second setting, by "−" if it is significantly smaller for the first setting, and by "0" if no significant difference is detected (see Table 2 for an example). Such a table is obtained for each simulation group.

Above we argued that a result only holds in general if it holds for each simulation group. One way, then, of analyzing the results across all simulation groups is to count up the number of simulation groups for which a positive difference is obtained in a certain comparison. Since we carry out 4000 simulation groups in total, we could present 4000 tables in the form of Table 2. It is more expedient, however, to present simply the share of "+"s in the analysis below, as will be done in Tables 3, 5 and 6. This means that each cell will represent the probability for a significant difference.

The set of results that we obtain for the different simulation groups represent all possible types of causal relations that might exist in the real world. Hence, the fact

Table 2 Comparison of the average value of the market share $<m_G>$ of German firms dependent on the setting of the central parameters

	$c_{init,G} = 85$ vs. $c_{init,G} = 54$	$c_{init,G} = 85$ vs. $c_{init,G} = 25$	$c_{init,G} = 54$ vs. $c_{init,G} = 25$	$e_G = 1.2$ vs. $e_G = 1.1$	$e_G = 1.2$ vs. $e_G = 1$	$e_G = 1.1$ vs. $e_G = 1$	Real patent law vs. French patent law
Comparison result	+	+	0	0	+	0	+

"+" represents cases in which the first setting causes a significantly higher value of $<mG>$ than the second setting, significance level: 0.05; "−" represents cases with the opposite finding; "0" represents cases with no significant difference that we are only able to restrict the (nuisance) parameters to certain ranges leads to the fact that we obtain also ranges of outcomes. To claim otherwise would be an exaggeration of what simulations can accomplish. If, however, the same causal relation is found for all groups of simulations and if the model is an adequate representation of reality, a very strong inference can be made that the causal process does indeed operate in the real world in the manner specified.

If non-uniform causal relations emerge, our approach provides the option to study how the various nuisance parameters influence the relationship between the central variables and the simulated outcome. For each group of simulation (meaning for each setting of the nuisance parameters) and each pair of settings of the central variables (e.g., $c_{init,G} = 85$ vs. $c_{init,G} = 54$) we obtain a statistical statement about whether one setting leads to a significant higher market share of German firms in 1913 than the other. We define this finding as the dependent variable with two possible values (significant higher share (= 1) or not (= 0)) and regress this variable with all nuisance parameters as independent variables, e.g.,:

$$P_g(m_G(c_{init,G} = 85) > m_G(c_{init,G} = 54)) = f(B \cdot X_g),$$

where *P()* stands for the probability of the statement in the bracket to be true, *f* represent a logistic function, *B* stands for the regression parameters, *X* represents all nuisance parameters of the model and the index *g* signifies the simulation groups. This regression approach allows us to identify for each comparison of central parameter settings the nuisance parameters that influence the result of the comparison.

4 Results

From the historical records we proposed above three different hypotheses about the causes for the high market share of German firms in 1913. The simulation experiment allows us to test whether the development would have been different if these three causes would not have been present. To this end, we examine the effects of each potential cause separately in the following.

4.1 Chemists (Hypothesis 1)

Let us start with the high number of chemists in Germany in 1857. While in the UK and France there have been around 21 and 34 chemists in 1857, the number was approximately 54 in Germany. Therefore, we test with our simulation experiment whether the developments would have been different if there would have been 25 (similar to UK and France) or 85 chemists in Germany in 1857. The results are given in Table 3.

Table 3 Percentage of simulation groups (settings of the nuisance parameters) for which the market share <m_G> of German firms increases significantly if the initial number of German chemists is increased

	$c_{init,G} = 25 \rightarrow c_{init,G} = 54$	$c_{init,G} = 25 \rightarrow c_{init,G} = 85$	$c_{init,G} = 54 \rightarrow c_{init,G} = 85$
Significance level: 0.05	48.6%	77.6%	25.4%
Significance level: 0.01	30.4%	63.2%	11.3%
Significance level: 0.001	15.2%	44.2%	2.8%

Table 3 shows that we do not obtain a clear result for the impact of the initial number of German chemists on the development of the German firms' market share. If this initial number would have been comparable to the numbers in UK and France ($c_{init,G} = 25$), the final market share of German firms would have been in nearly 50% of the cases significantly (significance level: 0.05) lower. However, this result is far from being general and it becomes less frequent if the significance level is decreased. Furthermore, it strongly depends on the setting of the nuisance parameters. All settings that are studied in our simulation experiments are potentially realistic, so that we are not able to conclude whether one of those settings leading to a significant influence of the initial number of German chemists or one of those settings leading to no significant change is most realistic. Hence, a final conclusion cannot be drawn.

However, we can study the nuisance parameters that influence whether initial German chemists have a significant impact on the development. To this end, we conduct a logistic regression with the question whether the initial German chemists have a significant influence as dependent and all nuisance parameters as independent variables (see Sect. 3.5). The results for all significant nuisance parameters are listed in Table 4.

It is no surprise that the relevance of the initial number of chemists for the dominance of the German synthetic dye industry in 1913 depends most crucially on $\Phi_{start\text{-}up,chem}$, denoting the dependence of the number of start-ups in a country on the number of unemployed chemists there. Further aspects that play a role are the stability of submarket (market package) sizes (σ_d), the ability of firms to adapt their production to demand changes ($\mu_{T,adapt}$), the responsiveness of the German, French and UK university system (e_G, e_F and e_{UK}), the influence of lobbying on the German university system (λ_G) and the duration of effect of innovation success on further innovations. Strongly changing market package sizes would mean that the whole synthetic dye demand fluctuated strongly in the required characteristics of the products, implying a lower relevance of the initial conditions (such as the initial number of chemists). Similarly, if innovation success leads to further long-lasting innovation capability, the initial conditions have a more permanent impact. It is less clear why the parameter $\mu_{T,adapt}$ has an influence. Maybe better adapting incumbents leave less room for start-ups and make the number of initial chemists less relevant. Finally, the impact of the initial number of chemists is stronger if the

Table 4 Nuisance parameters that significantly influence the relevance of the initial number of German chemists

Nuisance parameters	Estimate	p-value
Dependence of start-ups on chemists ($\Phi_{start\text{-}up,chem}$)	5.09***	0.000
Stability of submarket sizes (σ_d)	−75.2***	0.000
Adaptiveness of firms to demand changes ($\mu_{T,adapt}$)	−2.86***	0.000
Responsiveness of the German university system (e_G)	4.88***	0.000
Responsiveness of the French university system (e_F)	−2.63***	0.000
Responsiveness of the UK university system (e_{UK})	−1.83**	0.005
Influence of lobbying in Germany (λ_G)	3.38***	0.000
Duration of effects of past innovation success on further innovation performance	1.87***	0.000
Strength of market competition	−50.9**	0.001
Transportation costs between countries	−1.59*	0.012
Number of observations	4000	
AIC	4438.5	
Cox and Snell pseudo R^2	0.175	
Hosmer and Lemeshow's goodness-of-fit test	0.09814	

Significance levels: ***0.001, **0.01, *0.05

system keeps the number high due to lobbying and a strong response of the university system to the demand for chemists. A low responsiveness of the university system in the other important countries, France and UK, also helps.

To sum up, we find that the initial number of chemists plays an important role only under some specific historical conditions. Because we do not know whether all conditions were historically present, we are not able to draw a final conclusion about the contribution of the initial number of chemists to German firms becoming the dominant players in the synthetic dye industry (Hypothesis 1).

4.2 *University Responsiveness (Hypothesis 2)*

Our simulation model contains a parameter e_{reg} ("reg" standing for our five countries) that determines the number of chemists that are educated in relation to the number of chemists currently employed. We called this the responsiveness of the university system to the needs of firms. This parameter cannot be estimated from historical records, but historical records make values between 1 and 1.2 realistic and the historical literature makes it clear that the German university system is characterized by higher values than present in the other countries. This is confirmed by our simulation validation. Although the value of e_G is randomly drawn from the range [1,1.2], the average value is 1.14 for those settings that are validated as potentially realistic. Furthermore, in approximately 80% of the setting that are validated as potentially realistic the value for Germany is higher than those for the other countries. Hence, the value of e_G has to be quite high for the simulation model to be able to explain the high market share of German firms in 1913. Table 5,

Table 5 Percentage of simulation groups (settings of the nuisance parameters) for which the market share <m_G> of German firms increases significantly if the responsiveness e_G of the German university system is increased

	$e_G = 1 \rightarrow e_G = 1.1$	$e_G = 1.1 \rightarrow e_G = 1.2$	$e_G = 1 \rightarrow e_G = 1.2$
Significance level: 0.05	92.1%	93.1%	98.1%
Significance level: 0.01	88.3%	89.9%	96.8%
Significance level: 0.001	83.1%	84.8%	94.9%

presenting the share of simulation groups with a significant impact of e_G on the final German market share, confirms this.

The results in Table 5 provide a quite clear picture. In most simulation groups an increase in the responsiveness e_G of the German university system leads to a significantly higher market share of German firms in 1913. If we consider an increase from $e_G = 1$ to $e_G = 1.2$ this result is obtained in almost all simulation groups, even if we lower the significance level. Thus, although a very small probability for error remains, we can conclude that our simulation experiment confirms Hypothesis 2: In the development of the synthetic dye industry the high responsiveness of the German university system has played a strong role, contributing significantly to the development of the dominant German market position.

4.3 Patent Law (Hypothesis 3)

The German patent laws have been quite different from the patent laws in the other important countries in 1857 and this has been highlighted by Murmann (2003) as one of the reasons that Germany built up capabilities that allowed it to dominate the industry for decades. To examine this historical interpretation, it is useful to study whether the developments of the German synthetic dye industry would have been the same if the patent laws in Germany had been similar to those in the other countries. For this reason, we experiment in our simulations with patent laws in German similar to those in France. The results of this experiment are listed in Table 6.

Similar to the initial number of German chemists, the simulation experiment leads to mixed results on the question whether the specific patent law situation in Germany was important for the development of the German synthetic dye industry.

Again, we can study the nuisance parameters that influence whether the German patent law has a significant impact on the development. As in the case of the initial number of German chemists, we conduct a logistic regression with the question of whether the German patent law has a significant influence as dependent and all nuisance parameters as independent variables. The results for all significant nuisance parameters are listed in Table 7.

The results show that the relevance of patent laws depends crucially on a large number of characteristics. Six of these characteristics relate to market packages and their development. We find that the specific patent law in Germany contributes more

Table 6 Percentage of simulation groups (settings of the nuisance parameters) for which the market share<m_G>of German firms is significantly higher if the German patent laws are modeled as they have been in reality instead of as they have been in France

	German patent laws as in France → Real German patent laws
Significance level: 0.05	49.1%
Significance level: 0.01	31.8%
Significance level: 0.001	17.9%

Table 7 Nuisance parameters that significantly influence the relevance of the German patent law

Nuisance parameters	Estimate	p-value
Stability of submarket sizes (σ_d)	−99.2***	0.000
Maximal size of submarkets ($\mu_{d,max}$)	−.0054***	0.000
Responsiveness of the German university system (e_G)	7.07*	0.000
Responsiveness of the French university system (e_F)	−3.16***	0.000
Responsiveness of the UK university system (e_{UK})	−2.49***	0.000
Basic innovation rate ($\Phi_{inno,0}$)	−2.57***	0.000
Adaptiveness of firms to demand changes ($\mu_{T,adapt}$)	−2.04***	0.000
Dependence of start-ups on chemists ($\Phi_{start\text{-}up,chem}$)	1.86**	0.000
Strength of market competition	109.7***	0.000
Advantage of larger firms in competition	−22.7***	0.000
Influence of lobbying in Germany (λ_G)	3.28***	0.000
Initial technological advancement of natural dyes ($a_{init,natural}$)	−0.0067***	0.000
Range of innovation ($\Phi_{type,inno}$)	107.7***	0.000
Frequency of imitating entrants ($\mu_{T,new}$)	0.029*	0.040
Number of observations	4000	
AIC	4434.8	
Cox and Snell pseudo R^2	0.178	
Hosmer and Lemeshow's goodness-of-fit test	0.00473**[a]	

[a]A detailed look at the deviations from the logistic distribution does not provide evidence for any alternative distribution. The deviations seem to be rather random in their structure and the high number of observation seems to contribute to the detection of these deviations. Quadratic or interaction terms do not change the outcome of the goodness-of-fit test and do not lead to additional significant estimates
Significance levels: ***0.001, **0.01, *0.05

to the dominance of German firms in the synthetic dye industry if market packages (1) are small ($\mu_{d,max}$), (2) their size is very stable (σ_d), (3) they are replaced rarely due to innovations ($\Phi_{inno,0}$), (4) competition is strong, (5) larger firm have no advantage in competition, and (6) imitative entries are frequent ($\mu_{T,new}$). Remember that our model is based on monopolistic competition and that smaller and, thus, more market packages mean that the demand is more segmented offering more possibilities for entries and niche producers. Our results imply that patent laws have played an important role if demand was strongly segmented with strong competition and difficult conditions for large incumbents, while the market packages were characterized by a high stability and rare replacement by innovative new submarkets.

In addition, we find two nuisance parameters ($\mu_{T,adapt}$ and $a_{init,natural}$) to be relevant that make the initial development less dynamic (see Sect. 4.1). This seemingly implies that the non-existence of patent laws in Germany at the beginning is more important for the development of the German dye industry than the different structure of the later introduced German patent law. To examine this further, we conducted additional simulations. These simulations show that introducing a product patent law in Germany in 1877 instead of a process patent law would also have led to a similarly high German market share in 1913. However, introducing the Germany kind of process patent law already before 1856 would have led to an even higher German market share in 1913. Hence, the German timing and the German kind of patent law are both individually beneficial in at least 50% of the simulation settings. Interestingly, introducing the specific German process patent law earlier would have even been more beneficial than introducing it in 1877 (this is found in 63% of the realistic simulation settings).

Furthermore, we find an interaction between our potential explanations. If chemists are more relevant for the start-up activities ($\Phi_{start\text{-}up,chem}$), the responsiveness of the German university system is high (e_G) (especially in comparison to France and UK), and lobbying is influential in Germany (λ_G), patent laws in Germany have a higher influence, probably because there is more innovation activity in the synthetic dye industry in Germany. Hence, it is quite likely that although our results suggest that the responsiveness of the Germany university system was most crucial, the specific patent law development additionally increased the German market share even further.

5 Conclusions

In this paper, we use simulation experiments to examine whether specific circumstances are decisive for the observed historical developments. While historical analyses are able to provide detailed information about the development of industries, they are not able to examine with precision whether history would have been different if certain circumstances would have been different. Simulation experiments allow for such counter-factual analyses with multiple factors playing a role. The reliability of the results of such simulation experiments, however, crucially depend on the reliability of the basic simulation model. For this reason, we apply the abductive simulation approach of Brenner and Werker (2007), using as basic model the well-validated firm growth model by Brenner and Duschl (2014), and we further validate our simulation models with historical data. All models identified as potentially realistic are analyzed, providing stochastic statements about the relevance of the potential causes that are identified in the historical analyses.

We study the historical development of the synthetic dye industry between 1857 and 1913. The interesting development in this industry is that German firms managed to obtain a global market share of approximately 75% in 1913 even though British and French firms initially dominated the industry. Historical studies (Murmann and Homburg 2001; Murmann 2003) provide three potential explanations for this change in industrial leadership: (1) the high initial number of chemists in Germany at the start of the industry in 1857, (2) the high responsiveness of the German university system and (3) the late (1877) introduction of a patent regime in Germany as well as the more narrow construction of this regime compared to Britain, France and the U.S. With the help of counter-factual simulation experiments we test all three potential explanations.

Our main finding is that the high responsiveness of the German university system has almost surely contributed to the development of a dominant German position in the synthetic dye industry. The synthetic dye industry seems to be an industry in which the university system was crucial for its development. Interestingly, even though the inventor of the first synthetic dye was a student at the Royal College of Chemistry in London, many of the early dyes both in the UK and France were not developed in university laboratories. University professor as inventors of new dyes became more important later when they had learned how economically valuable these dyes would be. Still later, from the 1880s, the R&D laboratories of the big dye firms became the most important source of new dyes. These large R&D laboratories did not train chemists themselves but relied on universities for the training of their chemists. The education of chemists by universities has, according to our analysis, been the crucial factor giving a national industry a competitive advantage. Hence, our results contribute also to the discussion about the relevance of university education for the local economic development. On the national level our study shows rigorously that university education was crucial for the development of the synthetic dye industry. Whether this is also true in other industries has to be examined in further studies.

For the influence of the initial number of chemists and the patent laws we do not obtain conclusive results. The final answer depends on the question of which simulation setting is the realistic one. According to the arguments by Brenner and Werker (2007) it is not possible to identify one correct model. As a consequence, it may not be possible to draw a final conclusion from simulation experiments unless they show uniform results. We could not show uniform results for the influence of the initial number of chemists across all historically plausible conditions. However, from our analyses, we conclude that the number of chemists in Germany play a role if the number of start-ups depends crucially on the number of unemployed chemists. Furthermore, patent law are relevant if demand is strongly segmented and stable in its structure. Finally we find that the specific patent law made at least an additional contribution to the development of the Germany synthetic dye industry.

Additional studies of this kind on other industries will make it possible to assess whether our findings apply to all industries or only are specific to particular sectors in the economy.

Acknowledgements We would like to thank Peter Bearman, Sendil Ethiraj, Shayne Gary, Steve Klepper, Ray Levitt, Dan Levinthal, Richard Nelson, Charles Tilly, participants of a Seminar at the Max Plank Institute for Economics and participants at the Schumpeter conference for helpful comments on earlier, significantly different versions of this paper. We also like to thank two anonymous reviewers for making suggestions that helped us to improve the paper. We would like to thank in particular Ernst Homburg for helping us locate the historical information that was needed to specify important parameters of the simulation experiment that could not be specified from earlier work by Homburg and one of us (Murmann).

Appendix 1: Some Data on the Synthetic Dye Industry

Table 8 Indicators for the evolution of national synthetic dye industries and the rest of the world, 1857–1914

	Great Britain	Germany	France	Switzerland	U.S.	Rest of world
1. Total firm entries	53	118	68	32	28	
2. Entries until 1870	25	38	36	15	3	
3. Total firm exits	43	94	57	26	18	
4. Market size[a]	1857: 530–1610	1857: 390–1270	1857: 310–950	1857: 70–210	1857: 240–720	1857: 1400–4200
	1913: 2300	1913: 2000	1913: 900	1913:300	1913: 2600	1913: 8100
5. Share of global market[a,b]	1862: 50.0%	1862: 3.0%	1862: 40.0%	1862: 2.5%	1862: 0.0%	1862: 4.5%
	1873: 18.0%	1873: 50.0%	1873: 17.0%	1873: 13.0%	1873: 0.2%	1873: 1.8%
	1913: 6.5%	1913: 74.1%	1913: 5.4%	1913: 7.0%	1913: 3.3%	1913: 3.7%

The data comes from Homburg and Murmann (2014) except for market size and share data, whose sources are provided in notes a and b

[a]Exact figures for market demand in 1857 are not available. However, it is possible to specify lower and upper bounds. The number of consumers is assumed to increase linearly in each region. The number of consumers at the beginning of the simulation (1856) is estimated to be 59,000. This number is derived from the following considerations: In the UK 75,000 t of natural dyes were consumed in 1856. This amounts to around 14% of the world consumption. Hence, around 535,000 t of natural dyes were consumed worldwide. The literature reports that 1 t of synthetic dye replaced around 9 t of natural dye. Therefore, the consumption in 1856 would equal around 59,000 t of synthetic dyes. To distribute these consumers across the different countries two assumptions are made: First, there is a worldwide increase in the demand for dyes. Second, in each country the demand for dyes increases linearly with the growth of the population. Both increases are assumed to be linear, so that only data for the population in each country in 1856 and 1913 has to be used to calculate the number of consumers in each region in 1856. This leads to the following numbers for 1856: 10,700 in UK, 7800 in G, 6300 in F, 1400 in SW, 4800 in USA and 28,000 in the rest of the world. Since these numbers represent rough estimates of the real demand in 1856, we defined a range of values that could have represented the true historical demand. We determined the historical demand to range between 0.5 and 1.5 times the estimated demand and divided by a factor by 10 to make them more convenient for representation

Precise estimates are available for 1913 based on the following information: In the year 1913 almost only synthetic dyes were consumed. We use the number of tons of synthetic dyes consumed in each country as a proxy for the demand at this time. This data is provided in Reader (1970, p. 258)

[b]The 1862 figures are from Leprieur and Papon (1979, p. 207). The authors report that Germany and Switzerland together held 5% of the market. We estimate that Germany's share amounted to 3% and the Swiss share to 2%. The 1873 figures were put together by Ernst Homburg from Hofmann (1873, p. 108), Wurtz (1876, p. 235) and Kopp (1874, p. 153). The 1912 figures are from Thissen (1922). Except in the case of Germany, we did not have figures for the year 1893. We estimated the countries' market shares by assuming that market shares declined between 1873 and 1914 in a linear fashion

Appendix 2: Some Additional Description of the Simulation Model and Approach

A.2.1 Firm Strategy

In the model by Brenner and Duschl (2014) each firm is characterized by a strategy variable that ranges from 0 to 1 and determines whether a firm is more an imitator (0) or an innovator (1). In the original model (Brenner and Duschl 2014) this variable is randomly drawn when a firm is founded and remains constant during its existence. From historical records we know that in the dye industry many firms started as imitators and developed into innovators. Therefore, the strategy value is set to 0.01 for each firm at its foundation. Then, after each year it is tested whether the sales of a firm decreased by more than $\Phi_{strat,react}$ %. If this is the case, the strategy variable is increased by $\Phi_{strat,increase}$ as long as the value of 1 is not reached. The reaction level $\Phi_{strat,react}$ is randomly drawn for each firm at its foundation between 0 and 1. The strategy increase $\Phi_{strat,increase}$ is randomly drawn for each simulation between 0.05 and 0.25.

A.2.2 Innovation Processes and Start-Ups

The original model by Brenner and Duschl (2014) considers innovation as the appearance of new market packages that firms compete for, whereby those firms that follow an innovative strategy have a higher probability to win the new markets. We change two aspects of their original modeling: In our model market packages are characterized by two technological variables, namely technological advancement a_m and type y_m (see Sect. A.2.3) and firms are more active and determine the appearance of new market packages.

For the detection of a new market an basic innovation rate $\Phi_{inno,0}$ is defined. The probability of a firm to innovate (detect a new market) is given by this rate multiplied by the firms total market share and the free capacity of the firm as well as the R&D activities of the firm (as in Brenner and Duschl 2014). The R&D activities of a firm are defined to depend on the number of chemists employed (see above). If a firm is able to innovate, a new market package appears. The technology type y_m and technological advancement a_m are randomly drawn from an area that deviates maximally by 1 from the technological advancement and maximally by $\Phi_{type,inno}$ from the technology type of the existing products of the firm. A country is randomly assigned to the market package. Before the market package is finally created in the simulation it is checked whether an existing patent forbids the firm to produce this product. Only if this is not the case the market package is created and the innovative firm is the new owner.

We still assume that new firms might enter the industry with innovations (new market packages). To this end, the procedure above is repeated with a potential new firm innovating on the basis of an existing product (market package). The likelihood of such an event is given by

$$\phi_{inno,0} \cdot \phi_{inni,start-up} \cdot c_{reg,unempl}^{\phi_{start-up,chem}},$$

where $\Phi_{inno,start\text{-}up}$ is a parameter reflecting the probability of new firms entering with innovations in contrast to the innovation probability of incumbents, $\Phi_{start\text{-}up,chem}$ is a parameter defining the dependence of the start-up probability on the number of unemployed chemists in a country *reg* ("reg" standing for the countries UK, G, F, S and USA) (drawn randomly from a range between 0 and 1 for each simulation group), and $c_{reg,unempl}$ represents the number of unemployed chemists. This means that we make the number of start-ups dependent on the number of chemists that might found a firm. To determine the technological characteristics of the new market package, one existing market package is drawn randomly and the procedure described above is repeated including the check for patents. If the resulting technology is not covered by an existing patent, a new market package and firm is generated in the simulation model.

A.2.3 Market Space

Dyes differ with respect to many characteristics. The most obvious is their color. Further aspects are the underlying chemical technology, textiles for which it can be used or durability. In our simulation model we simplify the situation by using only one value, y_m, which ranges between 0 and 1 to reflect these characteristics. Each market package has a unique value (see above) reflecting the demand for one specific combination of characteristics.

Innovations lead to new values of y_m (see above). However, innovations usually do not change all characteristics at once. Hence, to estimate the technological distance, $\Phi_{type,inno}$, that can be bridged by an innovation, we use the following considerations. Historically there are around five product classes that differ in their underlying chemical technology (aniline, alizarin, azo dyes, sulfur dyes, and synthetic indigo). Furthermore, seven classes of color (red, orange, yellow, green, blue, violet, black) exist, which leads to 35 classes. Most innovations will appear within these classes. However, within these classes the synthetic dyes still differ in their durability, the textiles for which they can be used, and similar characteristics. In order to restrict our parameter not too much, we assume between 40 and 1000 different technologies leading to $0.001 < \Phi_{type,inno} < 0.025$.

A.2.4 Market Size

The initial (1857) potential market sizes can be estimated as between 530 and 1610 for UK, between 390 and 1270 for Germany, between 310 and 950 for France, between 70 and 210 for Switzerland, between 240 and 720 for the US and between 1400 and 4200 for the rest of the world. We draw random sizes from these ranges for each simulation run. The values reflect the whole demand for dyes. Of course, at the beginning most of this demand is not satisfied by synthetic dye producers (see above). If firms innovate (see above) and an existing market packages that is currently not owned by a synthetic dye firm (but by a natural dye firm, not explicitly modeled here) is technologically reachable, they will not generate a new market package but occupy such an existing market package. Such an innovation is by a factor $\Phi_{exist,inno}$ more likely than an innovation leading to a new market package. The total potential market size is assume to increase linearly over time to reach 2300 in UK, 2000 in Germany, 900 in France, 300 in Switzerland, 2600 in US and 8100 in the rest of the world by 1913. Since new market packages appear randomly due to innovation processes by the firms, we have to control the development of the market size. If the market size in the simulation model exceeds the presupposed market size development in a country, market packages are deleted until the values fit again. To this end, for each existing market package in a country the following value is calculated:

$$a_m + \phi_{dens} \cdot \sum_{n \neq m} | y_n - y_m | .$$

Each time the market package with the lowest value disappears. The first term implies that market packages with a lower technological advancement are more likely to disappear. The second term implies that market packages with more technologically similar other market packages are more likely to disappear. Φ_{dens} determines the relative importance of these two aspects. In contrast to the model by Brenner and Duschl (2014), market packages do not disappear randomly in our model but their disappearance is modeled such that the total market size follows the historically known path. This implies that a higher innovative activity (creating more new market packages) of firms increases the probability of the disappearance (in this sence replacement) of existing market packages.

A.2.5 Chemists

Historical records show that the number of chemists per tons of synthetic dyes sales ranges between 0.0006 and 0.01 (these are the minimum and maximum share of chemists that were employed by the firms Bayer, BASF, Jäger and Levinstein at the end of the period of time studied. For a detailed study of these firms, see Murmann 2003). Therefore, for each firm a random chemist rate $\Phi_{chem,rate}$ is drawn from this range when the firm is founded. In addition, the number of chemists also depends on a firm's innovation strategy s_f, because innovation processes require chemical expertise. Thus, the desired number of chemists of a firm f is given by

$$c_f(t) = 1 + T_f \cdot \phi_{chem,rate} \cdot S_f,$$

where T_f denotes the firm's sales.

If a firm cannot employ the desired number of chemists it employs as many chemists as it can get. The real strategy $s_{f,real}$ of a firm depends on the number of chemists that it is able to employ. If this number is lower than the one that matches the intended strategy, the strategy has to be adapted downwards and the firm acts less innovative than intended.

We assume that chemists prefer employment in a domestic dye company. Hence, if firms require additional chemists, they first employ unemployed chemists from the own country. If no unemployed chemists are available in the own country, firms search for chemists in other countries. Only a certain share of all chemists are willing to move to foreign countries. This share is fixed according to historical records as given in Table 9.

If the need of chemists decreases in a firm, chemists are fired and become unemployed.

Table 9 Migration probabilities for chemists

	Destination				
Origin	UK	G	F	SW	USA
UK	–	0.005	0.005	0	0.02
G	0.025	–	0.01	0.045	0.005
F	0.01	0.005	–	0.05	0
SW	0.003	0.1	0.006	–	0.001
USA	0	0	0	0	–

Table 10 Estimates of chemists and estimates for 1857 assuming exponentially increasing numbers

Year	F	G	UK	SW	USA
1850	25	35	15	8	5
1900	225	750	150	75	75
Estimate for 1857	34.0	53.8	20.7	10.9	7.3

Source: Ernst Homburg (E-mail, November, 2002)

A.2.6 Simulation Approach

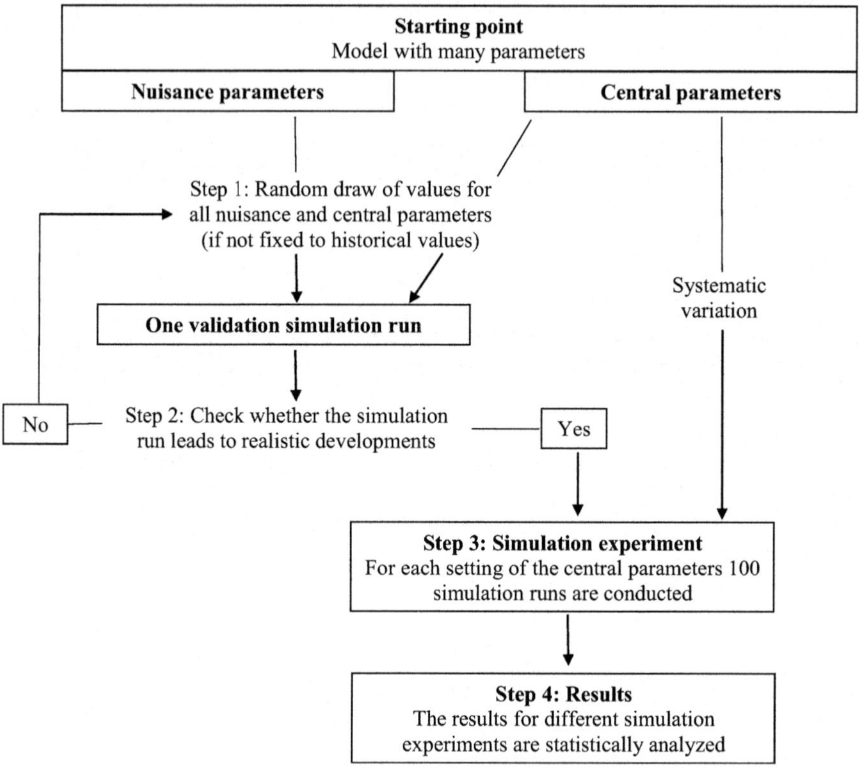

Fig. 1 Schematic graph of the successive steps in the simulation experiment method

References

Allen RC (2003) Progress and poverty in early modern Europe. Econ Hist Rev 56(3):403–443. https://doi.org/10.1111/j.1468-0289.2003.00257.x

Arthur WB (1994) Increasing returns and path dependence in the economy. University of Michigan Press, Ann Arbor

Beer JH (1959) The emergence of the German dye industry. University of Illinois Press, Urbana

Brenner T, Duschl M (2014) Modelling firm and market dynamics: a flexible model reproducing existing stylized facts. Working Papers on Innovation and Space, vol 07.14. Philipps-Universität Marburg

Brenner T, Werker C (2007) A taxonomy of inference in simulation models. Comput Econ 30 (3):227–244

Buenstorf G, Klepper S (2009) Heritage and agglomeration: the akron tyre cluster revisited. Econ J 119(537):705–733

Caro H (1892) Über die Entwicklung der Theerfarben-Industrie (About the develpment of the coal-tar industry). Ber Dtsch Chem Ges 25(3):955–1105

David PA (1985) Clio and the economics of QWERTY. Am Econ Rev 75(2):332–337
De Vaan M, Boschma R, Frenken K (2013) Clustering and firm performance in project-based industries: the case of the global video game industry, 1972–2007. J Econ Geogr 13 (6):965–991
Freeman C (1982) The economics of industrial innovation, 2nd edn. The MIT Press, Cambridge
Heimeriks G, Boschma R (2014) The path-and place-dependent nature of scientific knowledge production in biotech 1986–2008. J Econ Geogr 14(2):339–364
Hofmann AW (1873) Einleitung. In: Amtlicher Katalog der Ausstellung des Deutschen Reiches. Wiener Weltausstellung. Gruppe III: Chemische Industrie (Official Catalog of Exhibit by the German Empire. Vienna World Exhibition. Group III. Chemical Industry). Berlin, pp 95–139
Homburg E, Murmann JP (2014) Global database of synthetic dye firms and plants, 1857–1914. http://professor-murmann.net/dye-database.html. Accessed 28 Oct 2014
Klepper S (2007) Disagreements, spinoffs, and the evolution of Detroit as the capital of the US automobile industry. Manag Sci 53(4):616–631. https://doi.org/10.1287/mnsc.1060.0683
Kopp E (1874) Wiener Weltaustellung 1873 (Vienna World Exhibition 1873). In: Bericht über Gruppe III, Chemische Industrie (Report on Group III, Chemical Industrie), vol 8. C. Baader, Schaffhausen
Krugman P (1995) Development, geography, and economic theory. MIT Press, Cambridge
Landes DS (1969) The unbound prometheus: technological change and industrial development in Western Europe from 1750 to the present. Cambridge University Press, New York
Leprieur F, Papon P (1979) Synthetic dyestuffs: the relations between academic chemistry and the chemical industry in nineteenth-century France. Minerva 17(2):197–224
Malerba F, Nelson R, Orsenigo L, Winter S (1999) 'History-friendly' models of industry evolution: the computer industry. Ind Corp Chang 8(1):3–40
Malerba F, Nelson R, Orsenigo L, Winter S (2008) Vertical integration and disintegration of computer firms: a history-friendly model of the coevolution of the computer and semiconductor industries. Ind Corp Chang 17(2):197–231
Murmann JP (2003) Knowledge and competitive advantage: the coevolution of firms, technology, and national institutions. Cambridge University Press, New York
Murmann JP (2013) The coevolution of industries and important features of their environments. Organ Sci 24(1):58–78. https://doi.org/10.1287/orsc.1110.0718
Murmann JP, Homburg E (2001) Comparing evolutionary dynamics across different national settings: the case of the synthetic dye industry, 1857–1914. J Evol Econ 11(2):177–205
Reader WJ (1970) Imperial chemical industries: a history, vol I. Oxford University Press, London
Redlich F (1914) Die volkwirtschaftliche bedeutung der deutschen teerfarbenindustrie. Staats-und sozialwissenschaftliche forschungen 180. Duncker & Humblot, München-Leipzig
Rosenberg N (1998) Technological change in chemicals: the role of the university-industry interface. In: Arora A, Landau R, Rosenberg N (eds) Chemicals and long-term economic growth: insights from the chemical industry. John Wiley & Sons, Inc, New York, pp 193–230
Sydow J, Schreyögg G, Koch J (2009) Organizational path dependence: opening the black box. Acad Manag Rev 34(4):689–709
Teltschik W (1992) Geschichte der Deutschen grosschemie: entwicklung und einfluss in staat und gesellschaft (History of the large-scale German chemical industry: development and impact on state and society). VCH, Weinheim
Thissen F (1922) Die Stellung der deutschen Teerfarbenindustrie in der Weltwirtschaft (vor, in, und nach dem Kriege) [The Position of the German Tar Color Industry in the Global Economy before, during, and after the War]. Doctoral Dissertation, University of Giessen
Wenting R, Frenken K (2011) Firm entry and institutional lock-in: an organizational ecology analysis of the global fashion design industry. Ind Corp Chang 20(4):1031–1048
Wurtz A (1876) Progrès de L'industrie des Matières Colorantes Artificielles (The progress of the synthetic dye industry). G. Masson, Paris

The Marshallian and Schumpeterian Microfoundations of Evolutionary Complexity: An Agent Based Simulation Model

Cristiano Antonelli and Gianluigi Ferraris

Abstract The analysis of the Marshallian and Schumpeterian microfoundations of endogenous innovation enables to draw a line between the new emerging evolutionary complexity from biological evolutionary analysis and to overcome its limits. The paper integrates the Marshallian process of imitation and selection with the Schumpeterian creative response. In Marshall initial variety is given and exogenous, the dynamics of the process is driven by the selective diffusion of the best practice and long-term equilibrium stops the generation of externalities; firms are not expected to try and react to unexpected mismatches between planned and actual product and factor market conditions. In Schumpeter firms are allowed to try and react; the quality of knowledge externalities supports their creative response and may keep the system in a self-sustained process of growth. The Schumpeterian creative response can be regarded as a special case of the Marshallian dynamics that takes place when externalities—available to all firms including most performing ones—enable the introduction of innovations that account for the reproduction of superior performances and variety. The levels of reactivity of agents and of the quality of knowledge externalities, provided by the system, account for the growth of output and productivity. This hypothesis is tested by means of an agent based simulation model that shows how these microfoundations of endogenous innovation are able to generate aggregate dynamics based upon the interaction between individual decision making and system properties.

The authors thank the support of the Collegio Carlo Alberto with the project IPER and the University of Torino.

C. Antonelli (✉)
Dipartimento di Economia e Statistica "Cognetti de Martiis", Università di Torino, Torino, Italy

BRICK, Collegio Carlo Alberto, Moncalieri, Italy
e-mail: cristiano.antonelli@unito.it

G. Ferraris
BRICK, Collegio Carlo Alberto, Moncalieri, Italy

A. Pyka, U. Cantner (eds.), *Foundations of Economic Change*, Economic Complexity and Evolution, DOI 10.1007/978-3-319-62009-1_19

1 Introduction

The identification and appreciation of the Marshallian foundations of evolutionary thinking in economics is necessary to identify and overcome the limits of biological evolutionary framework of analysis and to contribute the new emerging evolutionary complexity with a consistent microeconomics of endogenous innovation that implements the reappraisal of the Schumpeterian notion of "creative response" (Arthur 2009; Kirman 2016).

The Schumpeterian notion of 'creative response' received very little attention so far and yet is indispensable to go beyond the shortcomings of biological evolutionary approaches (Antonelli 2015, 2017). Indeed, Schumpeter (1947: 150) provided a founding framework to grasping the endogenous microeconomic determinants of innovations. Innovation is the result of a creative response to unexpected events conditional to the availability of substantial externalities. Schumpeter defines the creative response as "something that is outside of existing practice", by highlighting three essential characteristics: "it cannot be predicted by applying the ordinary rules of inference from pre-existing facts"... "(it) shapes the whole course of subsequent events and their long-run outcome"... "its intensity and success or failure has.. to do.. with the socio-economic context". The notion of creative response—and its contrast with the adaptive one—enables to articulate an evolutionary complexity that puts the microeconomic determinants of the decision to innovate at the center of the analysis. In so doing, the reappraisal of the notion of creative response enables to articulate an endogenous model of the innovation process that can be enriched and implemented by the explicit identification and appreciation of the Marshallian legacy (Antonelli 2008, 2011, 2017; Antonelli and Ferraris 2011).

Specifically, the paper articulates the view that the analysis of the Marshallian and Schumpeterian microfoundations of endogenous innovation enables to elaborate a clear analytical separation between the evolutionary approaches based upon biological metaphors and the new emerging evolutionary complexity overcoming the limits of the former and contributing the latter. The integration of the Marshallian notions of imitation externalities and selection process with the Schumpeterian notion of creative as opposed to adaptive response, provides a rich and coherent microeconomic analysis of the determinants of the innovation process at the firm level that is able to take into account the effects of the system into which the individual decision making of heterogeneous agents takes place.

The rest of the paper is structured as it follows. Section 2 highlights the microeconomic limits of biological evolutionary approaches and calls attention on the lack of consistent microfoundations. Section 3 spells out the basic ingredients of the Marshallian-et-Schumpeterian frameworks of analysis and shows how their integration provides coherent microfoundations to the dynamics of evolutionary complexity. Section 4 presents an agent based simulation model (ABM) to test the coherence of the analysis. The conclusions summarize the main results of the paper and confirm the central role of the creative response in the introduction of innovation based upon the use of knowledge externalities as the basic mechanism of an effective and microfounded evolutionary dynamics able to move away from the ambiguities of biological evolutionary approaches.

2 The Limits of Biological Evolutionary Approaches

Different waves of evolutionary frameworks have been elaborated since the founding contribution of Thorstein Veblen (1898) focused on the role of heterogeneity of agents and institutions. After the decline of the second framework centered primarily by Armen Alchian (1950) on the role of uncertainty, evolutionary economics has been revived at the end of twentieth century by Richard Nelson and Sidney Winter with the grafting of biological metaphors. This (third) approach emphasizes the role of innovations and made crucial contributions to understanding industrial dynamics based upon the selective adoption and imitation of innovations. The biological evolutionary framework explores the effects of the exogenous introduction of a variety of innovations and their sequential and cumulative selection on the dynamics of market shares of firms and aggregate growth. The introduction of innovations, however, is assumed to be automatic and random. Biological evolutionary models pay very little attention to the endogenous determinants of innovation. The decision whether to innovate or not is poorly explored. The limits of this approach are becoming more and more evident. A new (fourth) generation of evolutionary economics is being implemented applying the tools of the economics of complexity that enable to focus the role of interactions among agents as the carriers of emerging system properties that include the introduction of innovations (Arthur 2007). The analysis of the Marshallian and Schumpeterian legacies enables to identify the discontinuity between biological evolutionary approaches and the new emerging evolutionary complexity stressing at the same time their common origins and their radical diversity.

2.1 The Incipit of the Biological Metaphor

The book by Nelson and Winter (1982) has been the basic reference for the evolutionary approach based upon biological metaphors. *An Evolutionary Theory of Economic Change* makes three important contributions: (i) it place innovation at the center of the analysis; (ii) it introduces the notion of routine to explain how firms change their conduct; (iii) it highlights the central role of the selective adoption of innovations and their diffusion. The introduction of routines is a major contribution to organization theory and helps understanding how—large—firms change their strategies. Routines are based upon satisficing rather than optimization. As a matter of fact the first chapters of the book pay much attention to explaining *how* do firms change their routines, but never explain *why* would firms change them. In the rest of the book the analysis of the determinants of the introduction of innovations is considered but is quite confusing. The volume swings between two opposite views: (A) the Lamarckian approach according to which firms innovate only when their performances fall below some thresholds[1]; (B) the Darwinian approach where innovation takes place as a random process.[2] Incumbents keep changing their routines and have occasionally the chance to introduce actual innovations i.e. new superior technologies. Nelson and Winter (1982) never try to reconcile their opposite views.[3]

The evolutionary approach framed by Nelson and Winter (1982), beyond the awareness of the authors and the related literature, is much closer to the Marshallian legacy and to its direct grafting by the early Schumpeter into *The Theory of Economic Development*, rather than to the Schumpeterian dynamics forged by the contributions of 1928 and 1942 that lead to the Schumpeterian synthesis of 1947 and to the Neo-Schumpeterian literature (Scherer 1986).

2.2 The Biological Evolutionary Literature

The evolutionary literature that impinges upon the pathbreaking contribution of Nelson and Winter fully retains their second assumption that the introduction of innovations is a spontaneous and automatic process that is not characterized by intentionality and has no microeconomic foundation. According to this literature all agents are potential innovators that have no risk aversion. The *homo oeconomicus* of this literature is automatically an innovator.

The history friendly models elaborated by Malerba et al. (2001) simply assume that some firms innovate: "At the beginning of our episode, the only available

[1]See Nelson and Winter (1982: 211): "...we assume that if firms are sufficiently profitable they do not 'searching' at all. They simply attempt to preserve their existing routines, and are driven to consider alternatives only under the pressure of adversity. Their R&D activity should thus be conceived as representing an *ad hoc* organizational response rather than a continuing policy commitment. This satisficing assumption is a simple and extreme representation of the incentives affecting technical change at the firm level". In the failure inducement hypothesis innovation is introduced only as a response to performances that fall below some satisficing levels. Firms with performances above the average, or simply in the average are not expected to innovate.

[2]Nelson and Winter are very clear: "In the orthodox formulation, the decision rules are assumed to be profit-maximizing over a sharply defined opportunity set that is taken as a datum, the firms in the industry and the industry as a whole are assumed to be at equilibrium size, and innovation (if treated at all) is absorbed into the traditional framework rather than mechanically. In evolutionary theory, decision rules are viewed as a legacy from firm's past and hence appropriate, at best, to the range of circumstances in which the firm customarily finds itself, and are viewed as unresponsive, or inappropriate to novel situations or situations encountered irregularly. Firms are regarded as expanding or contracting in response to disequilibria, with no presumption that the industry is "near" equilibrium. Innovation is treated as stochastic and as variable across firms." (Nelson and Winter 1982: 165–166).

[3]See Erixon (2016) for an articulated effort to reconcile the failure-induced hypothesis with an extended Darwinian approach.

technology for computer designs is transistors. *N* firms engage in efforts to design a computer, using funds provided by "venture capitalists" to finance their R&D expenditures. Some firms succeed in achieving a computer that meets a positive demand and begin to sell. This way they first break into the mainframe market. Some other firms exhaust their capital endowment and fail. Firms with positive sales use their profits to pay back their initial debt, to invest in R&D and in marketing. With R&D activity firms acquire technological competencies and become able to design better computers. Different firms gain different market shares, according to their profits and their decision rules concerning pricing, R&D and advertising expenditure. Over time firms come closer to the technological frontier defined by transistor technology, and technical advance becomes slower." (Malerba et al. 2001: 4–5). In history friendly models the microeconomic decision of whether to innovate or not is completely missing. Innovation is assumed as a given characteristic of the system.

The influential contributions of Iwai (1984, 2000) make this point very clear: the analysis moves from the assumption that an innovation has been introduced. The analysis does not explore who, why, when and where did try to innovate. His analysis of the characteristics of the selective diffusion of many competing technologies remains one of the key contributions of the biological evolutionary literature.

The inclusive review of the evolutionary literature of Safarzyńska and van den Bergh (2010: 347) concludes that: "Although innovations are intrinsically uncertain, and for this reason in most evolutionary-economic models treated as stochastic, it would be incorrect to consider the process of innovation as totally random. Innovations may be expected to occur in a systematic manner, namely preceded by the cumulativeness of relevant technical advances. The innovative process is often depicted as following relatively ordered technological path-ways, as is reflected by notions such as natural trajectories (Nelson and Winter 1977), technological guide points (Sahal 1985), technological paradigms (Dosi 1982), and socio-technological regimes (Geels 2002, 2005). Innovations are conceptualized in formal models in a number of ways: as a stochastic process (e.g., Poisson) that can result in structural discontinuity, variation and recombination of existing technological options, or random or myopic search on a fitness (technology) landscape. Innovations may be associated with a new vintage of capital (e.g., Iwai 1984; Silverberg and Lehnert 1993; Silverberg and Verspagen 1994a, b, 1995).

The models of industrial dynamics that impinge upon the basic contribution of Dosi et al. (1995) assume that innovations are determined by technological opportunities, but no analysis is provided about the specific characteristics of the decision process at the firm level: all firms are expected to innovate when, where and if technological opportunities are large. The determinants of technological opportunities are missing: as such they must be regarded as exogenous. The important contribution by Winter et al. (2000) explores an alternative route: innovation is the direct and automatic consequence of learning. Learning processes are deemed to engender the accumulation of technological knowledge and the eventual introduction of innovations. The introduction of innovations is simply the consequence of learning processes: as such they take place at all times, in all conditions, in all locations. There is no variety in these models with respect to the innovation process: all firms do equally learn and do equally innovate. The possibility that some firms learn and innovate (more) and (than) others do not is not taken into account.

Windrum and Birchenhall (2005) provide the basic reference for the analysis of the models of selective adoption and implementation. Windrum and Birchenhall (2005) highlight the role of network externalities in the selection of alternative—given—technological innovations. For a given set of potential technologies, network externalities play a critical role in sorting out those that have stronger chances of further development and implementation. Once more the analysis does not take into account the determinants of the process by means of which agents did try to introduce each of the many alternative innovations. The variety of possible technological innovations is assumed but not explained.

As Dawid (2006) shows in his comprehensive review of the biological evolutionary models of innovation and technological change that impinge upon the agent-based approach, the decision to innovate is little explored: the focus of the analytical exploration is concentrated on the characteristics of the selective diffusion process, rather than on the determinants of the innovation process.

2.3 Away from Biology, Back to Schumpeter: Towards Evolutionary Complexity

The microeconomic limits of the approach that impinges upon biological metaphors are becoming more and more evident. The empirical evidence documents, in fact, the large variance among firms in terms of rates of introduction of innovations as proxied by R&D expenditures, patents, total factor productivity levels, innovation counts, as well as rates of growth and strategies. This unexplained variance calls for an effort to build consistent microfoundations of endogenous innovations. To do so, it seems necessary to move away from biological metaphors.

Routines can be regarded as an attempt to elaborate an economic equivalent of the biological genotype, but the actual causes of the changes of phenotypes and their effects on the characteristics of the genotypes are never elaborated. The detailed exposition of the procedures by means of which firms change their routines, in fact, contributes understanding how do—large—firms implement their changing strategies, but does not provide a clear hint about the motivations that induce to change them. Their application to small firms, moreover, seems rather difficult. Routines apply to understanding how do corporations change their behavior, not why. Biological evolutionary theorizing seems to be trapped by its ambiguity between the Lamarckian metaphors where innovation is failure-induced—the changes in the phenotypes do affect the changes in genotype, but only when performances are not satisfactory—and Darwinian ones where, as a matter of fact, variation is fully random and exogenous: genotypes cannot be changed intentionally. This second view is fully consistent with the Darwinian legacy retained by the evolutionary literature of the last decades of the twentieth century: the changes in genotype take place by chance. The characteristics of the new species do not reflect the purposes of their relatives. Their selection, instead, is endogenous as it enables to identify, out of the many variations, those that fit better into the environment. The grafting of the biological metaphor into economics prevents the understanding of the determinants of the introduction of innovations at the firm level (Levit et al. 2011).

As Edith Penrose (1952, 1953) had already remarked more than 30 years before the publication of *An Evolutionary Theory of Economic Change*: "To abandon their (firm's) development to the laws of nature diverts attention from the importance of human decision and motives, and from problem of ethics and public policy, and surrounds the whole question of the growth of the firm with an aura of naturalness and inevitability" (Penrose 1952: 809).

The growing concern about the missing microfoundations of the biological evolutionary approach has been the main determinant of its progressive demise and of the attempts to implementing the new emerging framework provided by complexity economics. The identification of the central role of feedbacks engendered by interactions among heterogeneous learning agents credited with the capability to innovate and of the context into which such interactions take place lies at the hart of the new emerging complexity economics (Kirman 1997, 2011; Arthur 1989, 2007).

The innovative model of Yildizoglu (2002) based upon the application of genetic algorithms can be regarded as the starting point of the new approach because of its important merits: (i) it stresses the limits of the biological trap where decision making about innovation is automatic and is not sensitive to the changing conditions of the environment:" Firms invest a fraction rd_{jt} of their gross profits on R&D. A minimal investment is necessary to keep alive the R&D potential (research equipment and team)...... Learning of firms about their environment does not influence their R&D behaviour. This is the common approach retained in many evolutionary industry models" (Yildizoglu 2002: 55); and (ii) it articulates the basic argument of evolutionary complexity where interactions among agents play the central role. To overcome the limits of the "*common approach retained in many evolutionary industry models*"[4] Yildizoglu introduces an individual genetic algorithm in order to adjust the R&D strategy of firms to the changing conditions of the industry. In so doing he clearly overcomes the foundations of biological evolutionary models and paves the way to a reappraisal of the Schumpeterian approach based upon the notion of interactions and hence externalities. The analysis of firms strategies where the introduction of innovations is a strategic tool conditional to the characteristics of the environment (Bischi et al. 2003) adds innovative elements that enable to move away from biological evolutionary approach towards an evolutionary complexity.

[4]Italics added.

Recent evolutionary theorizing in a radical departure from the biological evolutionary approach abandons the hypothesis that innovation efforts are random and exogenous and explores the micro determinants of the innovation process stressing the role of consumers' preferences and exploring the microeconomic effects of the changes in the aggregate levels of demand implementing a microeconomic demand pull approach (Aoki and Yoshikawa 2002). Along these lines Napoletano et al. (2012) introduce the hypothesis that firms change their strategies according to the levels of profits that in turn are influenced by the dynamics of aggregate demand. Antonelli and Scellato (2011) test the hypothesis that firms try and innovate when they are found in out-of-equilibrium conditions: when they enjoy profits risk aversion and financial constraints are low and firms are more likely to try and innovate; when firms face losses, innovation is the single way to avoid exit. Lorentz et al. (2016) model the effects of changes of consumption preferences that are engendered by the changing distribution of income on the structural and technological change. According to Antonelli and Scellato (2013) social interaction is a specific form of interdependence whereby the changes in the behavior of other agents affect the structure of the utility functions for households and of the production functions for producers. They graft the methodology of social interactions to the knowledge externalities literature and the Schumpeterian notion of creative reaction to understanding innovation and technological change within the new evolutionary approach that builds on complex dynamics.

It seems more and more necessary to contribute the new evolutionary complexity with an explicit analysis, at the firm level, of the determinants of innovation and the role of externalities in the decision process that leads to their—possible—introduction (Arthur 2007; Pyka and Fagiolo 2007). In the new emerging evolutionary complexity the innovative strategies of firms are at the same time sensitive to the contextual conditions of product and factor markets and play a central role to understanding why do firms innovate: i.e. both a consequence and a cause of system dynamics. The changing characteristics of the context into which decision-making takes place are the complementary and indispensable variables. Agent based decision making that includes creativity and externalities are the two basic tools—provided respectively by Joseph Schumpeter and Alfred Marshall—that enable to articulate the shift away from the biological evolutionary approach and reintegrate in an evolutionary complexity major chapters of the economics of endogenous technological change ranging from the Hicksian induced technological change approach to the Kaldorian demand pull and the Schumpeterian oligopolistic rivalry, that biological evolutionary approaches had abandoned (Ruttan 1997; Dosi 1997).

The appreciation of the Marshallian roots enables to focus the attention on the role of imitation externalities not only in the selective adoption of new technologies but also and primarily in their introduction and the reappraisal of the Schumpeterian dynamics where innovation is not the outcome of a random process but the result of the creative response of firms and their intentional pursuit of new technologies made possible by the properties of the system into which the process takes place, provides key inputs to implementing the new evolutionary complexity. The analysis of the Marshallian origins of the Schumpeterian approaches enables to understand at the same time their complementarities and yet their diversities. This in turn makes it possible to draw a clear line between the evolutionary approaches that impinge upon biological metaphors and the emerging evolutionary complexity (Caldari 2015).

3 From the Marshallian Search for Equilibrium to the Schumpeterian Dynamics: The Basic Role of Externalities

In the essay in honor of Alfred Marshall Schumpeter (1941) acknowledges the many contributions of the Marshallian legacy to his own understanding of the role of the selective competition among heterogeneous firms. The Marshallian approach has been a fundamental and constant source of inspiration for Joseph Schumpeter from *The theory of economic development* to the *The creative response in economic history*.[5] The Marshallian approach, in fact, can be regarded as the basic foundation not only of the early contributions but also and primarily of the 1947 attempt to provide an endogenous understanding of the innovation process able to integrate the analysis at the firm level with the appreciation of the role of externalities embedded in the system.

The Marshallian model rests on three building blocks: (i) exogenous innovations; (ii) no appropriability, and (iii) imitation externalities. Let us consider them in turn. In the Marshallian framework innovations are the starting point. For unknown reasons they are introduced occasionally and randomly. Their exogenous introduction puts—and keeps—the system in motion. According to Marshall, knowledge cannot be appropriated by inventors and spills freely like information so that everybody is immediately aware of the details of the best practice. The perfect access to the best knowledge at each point in time is a key aspect of the notion of 'normal' cost: "But though everyone acts for himself, his knowledge of what others are doing is supposed to be generally sufficient to prevent him from taking a lower or paying a higher price than others are doing." (Marshall 1920, V, 3, p. 199). As a matter of fact Marshall introduced the notions of limited appropriability and spillover, well before Arrow (1962) and Griliches (1979). The imitation of exogenous innovations introduced randomly is the focus of the analysis and the engine of the dynamics both in Marshall and biological evolutionary models. Marshall considers two types of externalities: agglomeration externalities and imitation externalities. Agglomeration externalities have received much attention while imitation externalities did not. Yet imitation externalities are at the heart of the Marshallian dynamics that leads from variety to homogeneity by means of selection and from out-of-equilibrium to equilibrium. Marshall assumes that firm are heterogeneous: some firms perform better than others. Selective competition drives the system to generalize the competence of the most performing firm.

[5]See the contributions of Stan Metcalfe (2007a, b, 2009a, b) that have highlighted the Marshallian foundations of the early Schumpeterian framework.

In Marshall equilibrium is the result of a competitive process that reduces heterogeneity to homogeneity.[6] Exogenous and random innovations and consequently the variety of firms are the cause of the Marshallian imitation externalities. Externalities and variety decline together, along a competition process—intertwined with a selection process—that accounts for the growth of the system but reduces variety and consequently destroys the very origin of externalities. They display their effects along with the selection process and the reduction of heterogeneity to homogeneity. Marshallian imitation externalities are endogenous to the system and intrinsic to the Marshallian search for equilibrium. As such, however, they are bounded.

Marshall assumes that a variety of firms try and produce, enter and exit the market place with different levels of productivity and costs. At each point in time firms are confronted with partial equilibrium that unveils their heterogeneity in terms of production costs. Less efficient firms are sorted out while more efficient ones can enjoy the benefits of transient rents and increase their size. In the Marshallian process, new entrants and less performing incumbents, however, can imitate freely the most performing ones. The efficiency of most performing firms spills freely in the system and can be accessed and shared by any other agent.[7] The imitative entry of new competitors and the imitation of incumbents affect the shifting position of the supply curve that engenders a sequence of lower market prices and larger quantities. The variance of profitability levels shrinks. In the long term the process leads to the eventual identification of the equilibrium price according to which only most efficient firms can survive with normal profits. The identification of a stable equilibrium stops the endogenous generation of externalities. In equilibrium there is no growth. Growth lasts as long as the selection & imitation process that enables to push the allocation of inputs towards their most effective use is in place. Marshallian externalities are endogenous, but bounded.

The influence of Marshall on *The theory of economic development* is clear. The role of entrepreneurship is a first attempt to fill the Marshallian gap about the origin

[6]See Metcalfe (2007a: 10): "In a famous passage Marshall claims that the tendency to variation is the chief source of progress (Marshall 1920, V, 4, p. 355). This telling phrase captures in a single step the deep evolutionary content of Marshall's thought but "What is meant by this?" The rest of the Principles make clear that variation and progress are connected by a variation cum selection dynamic, Marshall's principle of substitution in which more profitable firms prosper at the expense of weaker brethren. Outcomes are tested in the market so that "society substitutes one undertaker for another who is less efficient in proportion to his charges" (Marshall 1920, V, 3, p. 341). Indeed, in introducing a discussion of profit in relation to business ability, Marshall is quite explicit that this principle of substitution is a "special and limited application of the law of "the survival of the fittest" (Marshall 1920, VI, 7, p. 597). Furthermore, innovation is inseparable from the competitive process. For the advantages of economic freedom "are never more strikingly manifest than when a business man endowed with genius is trying experiments, at his own risk, to see whether some new method or combination of old methods, will be more efficient than the old" (Marshall 1920, V, 8, p. 406). The relation runs two ways and mutually reinforces the links between free competition and business experimentation."

[7]See Ravix (2012: 53): "In Marshall, entry and exit appears in different contexts. For instance, economic change leads to the distinction between 'those who open out new and improved methods of business, and those who follow beaten tracks (Marshall 1920, VI, VII, 1, 496)".

of innovations. Schumpeter (1911–1934) however does not really provide an endogenous account of the origin and determinants of entrepreneurship. It remains unclear whether the flows of innovations introduced by entrepreneurs and their entry are steady through time and space, or do exhibit relevant and systematic changes. As a matter of fact the evolutionary models that impinge upon Nelson and Winter (1982) are intrinsically Marshallian and are consistent with the legacy of Schumpeter (1911–1934) where, following Marshall, innovations are exogenous as they are introduced by entrepreneurs that enter the economic system from outside without any economic causality, rather than the frame elaborated by Schumpeter with the 1928 and 1942 contributions and their greats synthesis of 1947.[8]

The Marshallian dynamics of imitation externalities provides the foundations for the path-breaking contribution of Schumpeter (1947). This frame can be regarded as a full-fledged evolutionary process based upon the notion of endogenous innovation as the outcome of a creative reaction able to reshape the existing map of

[8] Careful reading of the celebrated notion of "forest trees" introduced by Marshall (1920) is useful to support the hypothesis that young trees are the carriers of innovations that account for the growth of the system and the continual reproduction of out-of-equilibrium conditions: "We saw how these latter economies are liable to constant fluctuations so far as any particular house is concerned. An able man, assisted perhaps by some strokes of good fortune, gets a firm footing in the trade, he works hard and lives sparely, his own capital grows fast, and the credit that enables him to borrow more capital grows still faster; he collects around him subordinates of more than ordinary zeal and ability; as his business increases they rise with him, they trust him and he trusts them, each of them devotes himself with energy to just that work for which he is specially fitted, so that no high ability is wasted on easy work, and no difficult work is entrusted to unskillful hands. Corresponding to this steadily increasing economy of skill, the growth of his business brings with it similar economies of specialized machines and plant of all kinds; every improved process is quickly adopted and made the basis of further improvements; success brings credit and credit brings success; credit and success help to retain old customers and to bring new ones; the increase of his trade gives him great advantages in buying; his goods advertise one another, and thus diminish his difficulty in finding a vent for them. The increase in the scale of his business increases rapidly the advantages which he has over his competitors, and lowers the price at which he can afford to sell. This process may go on as long as his energy and enterprise, his inventive and organizing power retain their full strength and freshness, and so long as the risks which are inseparable from business do not cause him exceptional losses; and if it could endure for a hundred years, he and one or two others like him would divide between them the whole of that branch of industry in which he is engaged. The large scale of their production would put great economies within their reach; and provided they competed to their utmost with one another, the public would derive the chief benefit of these economies, and the price of the commodity would fall very low. (Book IV. XIII. 3). But here we may read a lesson from the young trees of the forest as they struggle upwards through the benumbing shade of their older rivals. Many succumb on the way, and a few only survive; those few become stronger with every year, they get a larger share of light and air with every increase of their height, and at last in their turn they tower above their neighbours, and seem as though they would grow on for ever, and for ever become stronger as they grow. But they do not. One tree will last longer in full vigour and attain a greater size than another; but sooner or later age tells on them all. Though the taller ones have a better access to light and air than their rivals, they gradually lose vitality; and one after another they give place to others, which, though of less material strength, have on their side the vigour of youth". (Book IV. XIII. 4). *The Theory of Economic Development* can now be read as the evident grafting of the Marshallian intuition about the role of entrepreneurs as the vehicles of innovation and growth.

isoquants that takes place in out-of-equilibrium conditions when firms' plans do not meet the actual product and factor market conditions, provided the system is able to support their reaction with the provision of knowledge externalities.[9] If knowledge externalities are not available the response of firms will be adaptive and consists only in the traditional movements on the existing map of isoquants.

The Schumpeterian dynamics elaborated in the 1947 essay differ from the Marshallian one for two key reasons: (i) in Schumpeter, externalities are knowledge externalities rather than imitation externalities. Knowledge externalities make it possible to every firm to introduce productivity enhancing innovations that keep the system in a cost-reducing process further reinforced by the increased levels of generation of new technological knowledge that is able to reinforce the further creation of endogenous knowledge externalities; (ii) in Schumpeter the creative reaction of firms supported by the self-sustained dynamics of knowledge externalities enables the introduction of innovations that are by definition the cause of unexpected changes in product and factor markets. Marshallian agents can imitate only from advanced firms. Advanced firms cannot take advantage of their transient competitive advantage to introduce new innovations. Schumpeterian agents, on the opposite, exhibit the distinctive characters of entrepreneurship that enable them to try and react both to bad and good performances. In both cases, in fact, they will try and introduce innovations either to contrast their decline and eventual exit or to take advantage of their competitive advantage and increase it with the introduction of new technologies. The levels of the actual reactivity of firms and of the quality of knowledge externalities provided by the system are the key variables of the Schumpeterian approach that enable to account for endogenous growth of output and productivity (Antonelli and Scellato 2011; Erixon 2016). Both are the results of implementation of the Marshallian framework. The identification of the Marshallian legacy enables to better appreciate the strength of the late contribution by Schumpeter.

4 The Simulation[10]

The typical bottom-up approach of interactions nested in a systemic context of ABM provides an excellent tool for theoretical investigations. This use of ABM, next to its traditional application to forecasting, seems to open an innovative field of investigation to validate the robustness and consistency of theoretical hypotheses (Pyka and Fagiolo 2007; Mueller and Pyka 2016). ABM seems most appropriate to

[9]As a matter of fact Schumpeter had already overcome, the limits of the exogenous role of entrepreneurship not only in the 1928 essay, but also and more consistently in *Business cycles* (1939) where the cause/effect relationship between the phases of the economic cycle and the flows of innovations is investigated in depth, at least at the aggregate level.

[10]See Antonelli and Ferraris (2011, 2017) for complementary specifications of the basic ABM presented in this paper.

show how the implementation of a microfounded evolutionary complexity that integrates the legacies of Marshall and the late Schumpeter (1947) is able to overcome the microeconomic limits of the biological evolutionary framework with an endogenous account of the innovation process. By setting appropriate values for the key simulation's parameters (imitation externalities, knowledge externalities, knowledge governance, and reactivity), the ABM, in fact, enables to compare the alternative bottom up system dynamics: the "Marshallian" and the full range of "Schumpeterian" ones determined by the varying levels of reactivity and knowledge governance.

The ABM used to compute the simulations reproduces a stylized economy where a variety of firms produce a unique output, useful both for investment and consumption. The simulated economy is closed—no import neither export activities are allowed—and systematically reach a state of local equilibrium—the whole production is sold, firms fully redistribute profits as well as shareholder immediately contribute to cover losses. No form of accumulation either in savings or equity is allowed. The levels of capitalization of firms are given and are maintained by the shareholders through immediate contributions to cover potential losses. Profits are always fully distributed, do not eat/add capital funds of any kind.

Wages (w) are constant and there is an unlimited supply of labor. The cost of labor per unit is set by a simulation parameter. Provided that new technological knowledge is produced by employing labor, all the costs the firms afford produced a monetary transfer to the workers. The utility and demand functions of consumers, employees, shareholders are not simulated explicitly: their behavior is summarized in the price equations of the goods. Output prices are set by a market maker that ensures that the whole—fixed—amount of money is totally allocated to consumption.

Because all of remuneration (dividends, wages, contribution to research activities) will be immediately used to buy all the goods produced and money circulates twice for each production cycle, the demand for goods, in value terms, is equal to the amount of money in the system. The velocity of circulation of money (per cycle) is equal to 2 (all the money is paid in the form of remuneration of workers, researchers and shareholders (either as positive amount in case of profits or negative one in case of losses). During the same cycle all the money is spent to buy goods.

At the aggregate level the model can be resumed as:

$$\mathrm{Gs} = \Sigma \mathrm{Y}_{\mathrm{i}}. \tag{1}$$

Where Gs represents the aggregate supply, and Y are the individual revenues.

$$\mathrm{Gd} = \mathrm{Gs}. \tag{2}$$

Where Gd represents the demand of goods, both for investment or consumption.

$$\mathrm{Gp} = \mathrm{M}/\mathrm{Gs}. \tag{3}$$

Where Gp represents the price of a single unit of production, and M the whole amount of money that circulates into the system. Note that the whole amount of M is always available for consumption: when enterprises are subject to losses, the aggregate expense for salaries is greater than the value of the production, so shareholder receive negative profits and vice versa: at the aggregate level the amount of money available for buying the productions sticks always to M.

The aggregate production function could be expressed as:

$$Y = (A)L. \tag{4}$$

Where A is the productivity and L the amount of labor the enterprises employ.

The productivity reflects both agglomeration effects and the purchase of knowledge as it may be influenced by the current amount of technological knowledge (T) that the firm is able to mobilize and by a small fraction (g) of the amount of technological knowledge mobilized in the past production cycles, as it follows:

$$A = \sum \left[L_i{}^* \left(a_i{}^* \left(1 + t_{i0} + g^* \sum t_{i-j}\right)\right]\right/ \sum L_i. \tag{5}$$

Equation (5) makes explicit the work of knowledge externalities: L_i represents the input the i-th enterprise employs, a_i represents its labour productivity, t_i represents the level of technological knowledge this enterprise has just bought and $\sum t_{i\text{-}j}$ the sum of the past technological knowledge acquisition, weighted by a decay parameter g (the small fraction the enterprises permanently acquire in their knowledge estate for each technological knowledge acquisition). New technological knowledge acquisition is a risky activity, so its effects on productivity levels take place with a risk coefficient (R): each new technological knowledge acquisition (t_{i0}) could fail and in that case the productivity of the single enterprise becomes:

$$A_i = \left(a_i{}^* \left(1 + g^* \sum t_{i-j}\right)\right. \tag{6}$$

Under the Marshallian restriction, the contribution of technological knowledge is zeroed. As a consequence the productivity is limited and it reaches a maximum that is given by the equilibrium level output in the system where all firms use the best technology. The productivity equation becomes:

$$A = \sum L_i{}^* a_i / \sum L_i. \tag{7}$$

Each period a_i can be upgraded by a fraction of the difference between its level and the productivity level of the best enterprise, due to imitation effects. This upgrade is subject to risk, too, in this way:

$$A_{i1} = a_{i0} + h(a_{max} - a_{i0}) \mid E >= R. \tag{8}$$

Where A_{max} is the productivity of the best in class enterprise, E is a random number tossed from a uniform distribution, and R measures the probability the imitation fails. When $E < R$ the productivity level of the enterprise remains at the latest reached level.

The cost equation includes both the labor cost (w) and the technological knowledge one (z):

$$TC = wL + zT. \tag{9}$$

where L is the single input labor and w are the unit wages, as well as z is the costs of a technological knowledge unit and T is the amount of employed technological knowledge.

Note that in Eq. (9) the effect of T on productivity is usually such that $\delta Y/\delta T = c > z$ where c is the cost of technological knowledge if it were a standard good while z is the actual market costs of technological knowledge. There is an equilibrium level c of knowledge costs that reflects the equilibrium conditions for its generation. If technological knowledge were a standard economic good its cost c would be equal to w, the cost of labor. The case for adaptive reaction takes place when the technological knowledge is acquired at its equilibrium cost c. The use of T will allow firms to introduce novelties without direct economic effects on output levels that are higher than the total cost of the technological knowledge acquired. There is no chance for firms to introduce innovations that enhance output beyond the levels of the costs incurred to purchase the technological knowledge. When $z = c$ the value of the technological knowledge T matches the equilibrium value of its marginal product.[11]

If positive pecuniary knowledge externalities are at work the reaction applies successfully and becomes creative. This amounts to assume that when the cost z of technological knowledge ($z < c$) falls below equilibrium levels, technological knowledge can be treated as a factor that enhances output beyond its costs. In this case, total factor productivity increases because of the discrepancy between the

[11]The recent advances of the economic of knowledge enable to substantiate the dynamics of knowledge costs. Technological knowledge as an economic good is characterized not only by limited appropriability, but also by non-exhaustibility and non-divisibility (Arrow 1962, 1969). Technological knowledge moreover has the unique characteristic to be at the same time the output of a dedicated process and a necessary, indispensable input into the generation of new knowledge as well as into the production of all other goods (David 1993). Finally, the generation of technological knowledge is a recombinant process characterized by the central role of the stock of existing knowledge, both internal and external to each learning agent (Weitzman 1996; Fleming 2001; Sorenson et al. 2006). The understanding of the unique characteristics of technological knowledge as an economic good and the features of its generation process enables to better grasp the dynamics of knowledge externalities. Each learning agent—not only least performing firms but also most advanced ones—can actually benefit from the spillovers of the knowledge generation processes at work in the system (Griliches 1979, 1984). The actual access conditions to knowledge generated at each point in time and hence the mechanisms governing its dissemination are crucial to make persistent the working of pecuniary knowledge externalities (Antonelli and Ferraris 2011, 2017).

equilibrium levels of technological knowledge costs c and its actual—lower—levels z. The economic effects of technological knowledge purchased at a cost z that is lower than the equilibrium cost c, consist in the positive outcome of the reaction: the creative reaction takes place exactly in these circumstances. Firms can enjoy an 'unpaid' increase of the productivity levels that is equal to the levels of pecuniary knowledge externalities i.e. the difference between the equilibrium levels of the technological knowledge costs and their actual levels as determined by the working of pecuniary knowledge externalities. When, instead, the actual costs of knowledge are in "equilibrium" the reaction of firms will be adaptive.

The stylized economy configuration depends on a wide set of parameters. The model allows different setups to compare the simulation outcomes of different theoretical frameworks. For each simulation some parameters have a key role and vary to configure different simulation scenarios, whereas the other ones are usually set at fixed values. The configuration of the economy used for the simulations was based on: (i) the presence of 1000 agents, (ii) the availability of 10,000 unit of money for the whole transactions, (iii) a fixed labor price—1 unit of money—and an infinite labor offer, (iv) out of business enterprises were replaced by new entrants with 20% probability, whereas enterprises went out of business when their demand for factor became less than one unit. In order to set up an initial variety of agents, the employed labor and the productivity at the start of the simulation have been tossed randomly; the labor was allowed to vary in the range]1,10[and the productivity in the range]0.001,0.2[. Some agents have been endowed with higher values, respectively labor was tossed in the range]10,20[and productivity in the range]0.2,1.0[, the number of such "smarter" agents was set to the 15% of the 1000 agents that populate the economy. Agents were endowed the capability to both adapt and react. Adaptation has been simulated by setting up the agents to increase or decrease the amount of the employed factor of 10%, respectively if the previous production cycle ended with a profit or a loss. In computing their results (either profits or losses) agents rounded the amount with a tolerance of 0.001 due to computation matters.

Externalities have been simulated as productivity enhancement subject to a failure risk of 10%; technological knowledge had set as suitable for one production cycle only, except for a small fraction (0.1% in the simulations) that is added to the knowledge estate of the firms to mimic the learning process that always takes places both at the workers level and organizational level during the innovation exploitation. In fact the contribution of new technological knowledge is immediately subject to a decay of 99.9% (the parameter is named "techDecay"). The Marshallian imitation externalities have been simulated simply by granting each cycle each agent a labor productivity increase of 1% (the value is set by the parameter "imitation") the difference between their own productivity and the one of the "smartest" agents, i.e. the firms that as the highest productivity in the whole simulated economy. As mentioned this upgrade may fail: the probability of success was set at 90%. The Schumpeterian scenario was based on the possibility for the agents to buy technological knowledge instead of receiving labor productivity upgrade—the parameter "imitation" was set to zero. The amount of technological knowledge each agent buys in each production cycle, depended on two key parameters: (i) "techRate" that measures the reactivity of firms as the percentage of the total output each agent would invest, and (ii) "governancePerformance" that measures the quality of the knowledge governance by means of the discount factor applied for the price of technological knowledge, as in Eq. (10):

$$z = \partial Y / \partial T^{*}(1 - \text{governancePerformance}). \tag{10}$$

Note that if governancePerformance is set to zero, the cost of technological knowledge becomes equal to its marginal contribution and no knowledge externalities are available in the system, in this way the behavior of the agents cannot be reactive, they can only adapt their factor allocation. The computation of $\partial Y/\partial T$ has been based upon the forecast of the production each agent is planned to obtain at the end of the production cycle, in order to forecast the level of price the produced good will be sold and set up a plausible base to compute the productivity of the technological knowledge in monetary terms to set up a plausible base to compute z. More details are available in Appendix 1.[11]

The amount each agent invests is subject to financial constraints: because, intentionally, no financial institution has been included into the model, the whole investment amount has to be covered either by profits or through savings obtained by reducing the input of factors. The amount an agent invests can be expressed as:

$$I = \min(Y_{-1}{}^{*}\text{techRate}, \text{profit}) \mid \text{profit} > 0; \quad \text{or as :} \tag{11}$$

$$I = \min(Y_{-1}{}^{*}\text{techRate}, \text{Labor}_{-1}{}^{*}0, 1^{*}w) \mid \text{profit} < 0. \tag{12}$$

Where I represents the investment the i-th firm is going to afford in the production cycle 0. Labor and Y stand, respectively, for the labor the i-th agent employed in the previous production cycle and the output of the i-th agent in the previous production cycle. Schumpeterian agents are credited with the capability to react to out-of-equilibrium conditions: they invest and purchase new knowledge both when they enjoy extraprofits (Eq. 11) or face losses (Eq. 12).[12]

Table 1 exhibits the six different simulations scenarios generated by alternative values of the three key parameters: (i) imitation, (ii) techRate, (iii) governancePerformance. The single scenario devoted to Marshallian externalities is the first one, named "Imitation", the second, named "Zero Gov" has been run to demonstrate the results achieved with no knowledge governance are close to them of the Marshallian scenario. The others explore the different combinations between high/low reactivity (techRate) and high/poor knowledge governance (GovernancePerformance). The parameter: (i) "techLife"—that indicates how many production cycles, after the current one, the benefits of a technological knowledge acquisition lasts—has always been set to 0, and (ii) "techDecay"—

[12]Agents that face losses reduce their input by a parametrical amount that was set to 0.1 in all the simulations.

Table 1 Simulation scenarios

Scenario	Parameter values		
	Imitation	TechRate	GovernancePerformance
Imitation	0.01	0.00	0.00
Zero Gov	0.00	0.05	0.00
Low Gov Low React	0.00	0.01	0.01
Low Gov High React	0.00	0.05	0.01
High Gov Low React	0.00	0.01	0.95
High Gov High React	0.00	0.05	0.95

that measures the fraction of the acquired technological knowledge that is lost after its usage—has always been se to 0.999; practically each knowledge acquisition gave productivity advantage only for one production cycle, with the exception of the 0.1% of the acquired technological knowledge that became a consolidated component of the knowledge of the enterprise.

The simulation process consists in repeating a sequence of actions, managed through a precise schedule to control the information level of the agents and compute some statistics and aggregate figures. Before starting the simulations the model is charged to:

- create the planned number of agents and assign each of them different size and productivity;
- create a random generator for each agent and assign one to each, in order to avoid indirect and uncontrolled influence among agents;
- create the market maker object, that will manage exchanges and set prices, either for goods, factor and knowledge;
- initializing a common variable, called theWatch used by agents and marketMaker to synchronize their actions.

Each simulation cycle mimics a whole production cycle as shown by the flow chart in Appendix 2,[13] that illustrate the sequence of orders the model gives the agents and other components each simulation cycle. To avoid single pseudo random distribution that could pollute the results, a large number of simulations have been run for each scenario and results have been resumed as average values, paying attention to their variance that was not significant. The evolution of the simulated economy has been studied by means of the trend of the global output and productivity and by computing concentration indexes: (i) sum of the relative contribution to the global output by the three larger firms (GB method), (ii) sum of the

[13]The set of Appendices is available on request.

contribution of the four larger firms (US method) and (iii) Hall and Tideman aggregation index.

Tables 2, 3 and 4 resume the results obtained during 100 simulations, 2000 production cycles long, by reporting the average values of the 100 results, for each scenario.

Table 2 Productivity and output obtained during the simulations of the different scenarios

	Productivity				Output	
Scenario	T_1	Var	T_{2000}	Var	T_1	T_{2000}
Imitation	0.254332	0.000100	0.994559	0.000022	1868	9946
Zero Gov	0.252382	0.000110	0.833257	0.000229	1858	9845
Low Gov Low React	0.253934	0.000136	0.798269	0.000065	1871	10,010
Low Gov High React	0.254936	0.000139	0.864955	0.000188	1877	10,229
High Gov Low React	0.252215	0.000143	1.261606	0.004393	1851	15,654
High Gov High React	0.254803	0.000150	7.177898	0.807940	1880	84,908

Table 3 Concentration

	Concentration					
Scenario	H & T—T1	H & T—T_{2000}	CR USA—T1	CR USA—T_{2000}	CR GB—T1	CR GB—T_{2000}
Imitation	0.003292	0.001845	0.038695	0.212997	0.029390	0.210496
Zero Gov	0.003279	0.044264	0.038486	0.941844	0.029220	0.938796
Low Gov Low React	0.003297	0.047324	0.038533	0.944353	0.029270	0.943503
Low Gov High React	0.003281	0.043585	0.038362	0.940119	0.029123	0.934742
High Gov Low React	0.003280	0.045686	0.038758	0.942979	0.029453	0.942099
High Gov High React	0.003281	0.036878	0.038203	0.926782	0.029004	0.890148

Table 4 Correlation between productivity and concentration and the three key parameters

	Correlation—Productivity			Correlation—Concentration		
Scenario	Imitation	TechRate	Governance Performance	Imitation	TechRate	Governance Performance
Imitation	0.223784	n.a.	n.a.	−0.707532	n.a.	n.a.
High Gov High React	n.a.	0.806627	0.277358	n.a.	−0.203093	−0.335518

All the simulations have been executed under the same parameter configuration but with different random distribution, the random seed has been set randomly for each run. The first evidence that come out of the figures is that the results are not depending on the random distributions, due to the fact the variance figures are negligible and confirm the results are robust and due to the endogenous dynamic the model is able to mimic.

Productivity and output values show that the Marshallian scenarios were systematically able to reach the highest productivity value the system was initially endowed with. In each of the 100 simulations, under Marshallian dynamic, the economy reached a stable equilibrium. The results of the Schumpeterian scenarios demonstrate the role played by the knowledge governance: with no governance at all or with poor governance, either with high or low reactivity, the economy had a slow growth achieving final figures close to those obtained under Marshallian simulation. No imitation was allowed in the Schumpeterian scenarios. Thus result confirms the importance of the quality of knowledge externalities. When knowledge governance is effective, externalities arise and both total output and productivity reach higher levels. The compound effect of good knowledge governance and high reactivity is able to push the system to overcome the initial limitation by achieving a productivity level that is seven times as large the highest level the best firm, as endowed at the start of the simulation. As Tables 3 and 4, and Fig. 1 confirm, strong knowledge externalities and high levels of reactivity lead not only to fast growth, but also to higher concentration, configuring product markets with a few large firms and many small competitors. The results of the High Gov High React scenario shows that more than 90% of the output is done by four firms (CR-USA value) and the three big ones cover the 89% of the production (GR-GB value), providing that they were able to spend a larger amount in investing to buy technological knowledge. Their higher productivity parallels a strong increase of total output.

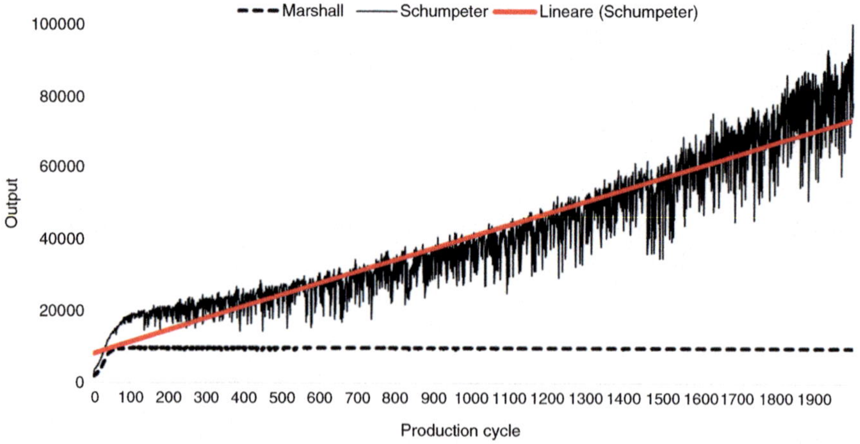

Fig. 1 Comparison of the trend of production between Marshallian and Schumpeterian scenarios

In the Schumpeterian scenario the system is always in evolution, with a growth that, in the presented case, is 10 times larger with respect to the results obtained by the Marshallian hypothesis, where the output reached a stable level when the system went to equilibrium. The Schumpeterian dynamic implies the impossibility to reach a stable equilibrium, with cycles of growth and decline, and a total output that oscillates with a trend to grow: the interpolation of the output level could be represented by the simple linear function (the straight line called "linear" in the graph) in Eq. (13), the interpolation is quite good, the r-square value is: $R^2 = 0.9005$

$$8146.400 + 32.881x. \tag{13}$$

The graph in Fig. 2 shows the output trend between the 500th and the 1000th cycles, in order to easier the catching of the cycles: there cycles where periods of decay and growth alternate are clearly visible.

In the Marshallian scenario the growth of output and productivity is larger, the larger the variance of the given distribution of firms: growth is exogenous and bound to the maximum given level of productivity at the onset of the process. The variance of the distribution of firms, at the onset, instead, has no impact on the Schumpeterian scenario: growth is endogenous.

The robustness of the exposed results has been investigated by computing correlation indexes between key parameters and results. In order to exclude that the tolerance value, used only for computational matter, would affect the results, a correlation has been computed between its values and the correspondent outputs. The named indexes have been computed using the results obtained by dedicated batches of simulations, where the parameters under investigation were randomly tossed each simulation and the other ones—including random distributions with the

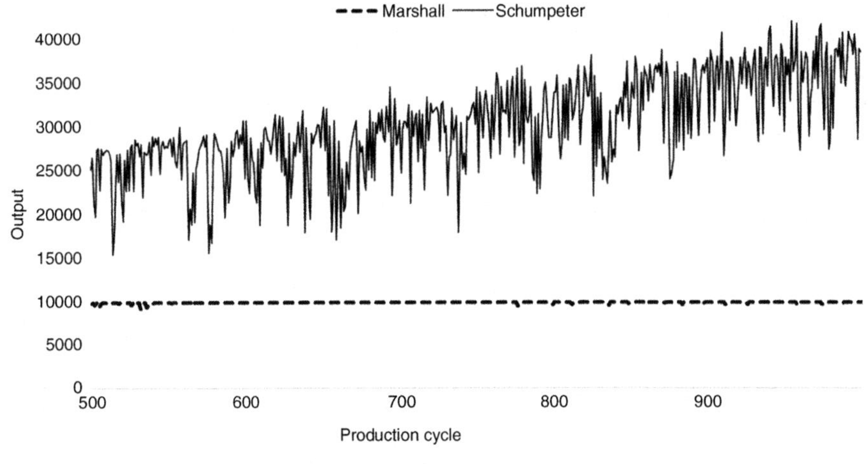

Fig. 2 Comparison of the trend of production between Marshallian and Schumpeterian scenarios: zooming cycles between 500 and 1000

Table 5 Correlation between values for the parameter "tolerance" and results of the simulations

			Correlation—Tolerance		
Scenario	Output	Productivity	H&T	CR USA	CR GB
High Gov High React	0.045423	0.015503	0.040802	0.072391	0.001194

exception of the distribution used to toss the parameter under investigation—were fixed in order to isolate the effect of each single investigated parameter. Table 4 reports the values of the correlation between the key parameters and output values.

Table 4 shows the weak correlation between imitation and the levels of productivity achieved at the end of the simulations (the weakness of the correlation is witnessed by the variance of the achieved output level that was 0.0038 to be compared with an average value of 9822.104, even if the values for the parameter imitation were tossed into the range]0,0.5[). Imitation level matters for concentration indexes, because determines the speed for reaching the equilibrium and the time better firms have to grow due to their adaptive reaction (highly productive enterprises make profits and each time upgrade their input by increasing it, so their production grows and the system becomes more and more concentrated). Under the Marshallian legacy enterprises are doomed to reach the best productivity due to the working of imitation, so the intensity of the phenomenon has influence only on the pattern the system follow to reach the results, not on the final result. As expected thecRate and GovernancePerformance exert a positive and significant impact on the Schumpeterian based simulations.

The results of Table 5 show that the "tolerance" parameters do not affect the results of the simulations: the correlation between its value and the results have been computed through 100 simulations with configuration High Gov High React and tolerance value randomly tossed between 0 and 0.0011. The correlation values are meaningless and confirm that even with smaller or even null values for tolerance the results of the simulations are the same.

No other correlations have been investigated as this paper aims to highlighting the differences of the results stemming from alternative theoretical configurations rather than forecasting values: the results of the simulation support the hypotheses outlined without any need of empirical evidence about the parameters configuration.

5 Economic Interpretation of the Results of the Simulation

The results obtained running the simulation model under various configurations (scenarios) and different random values for the key parameters demonstrated that the dynamic theorized by Marshall and Schumpeter is fully reproduced by the model. The results confirm the strong and effective role of the microeconomic foundations of the innovation process. The stronger is the reactivity of firms and the more effective the role of knowledge externalities the more dynamic is the system. The response of Schumpeterian innovative entrepreneurs to the unexpected mismatches in the product and factor markets supported by a rich environment able to secure the provision of high-quality knowledge externalities accounts for economic growth. Reactivity and knowledge governance are clearly the key parameters that enable the Schumpeterian scenario to outperform the Marshallian. These results of the ABM confirm the hypotheses and validate at the same time the proximity and yet discontinuity of the Marshallian and the Schumpeterian analytical framework. The introduction of reactivity conditional to the quality of the environment is the element that distinguishes and qualifies the Schumpeterian approach from the Marshallian one. The results have proven to be robust because the described effects emerged independently from different values of innovation risks and possibility that new firms can enter the market.

ABM enable to explore the working of the system of interactions, transactions and feedbacks between individual actions and the structure of the system, that qualify the simple but articulated Marshallian and Schumpeterian frames outlined in Sect. 3. ABM provide the opportunity to grasp the dynamics of competitive interactions among heterogeneous agents, that, because of the working of endogenous externalities are able to affect the structure of the system itself. This approach is actually able to model in a parsimonious and simple way the intrinsic complexity of the nested interactions among agents and the endogenous changes in the structure of the system that lay at the heart of both the Marshallian and the Schumpeterian frames (Mueller and Pyka 2016).

ABM operationalizes, through the interactions among a large number of agents of our systems, the comparison between the working of a typical complex process characterized by the key role of Marshallian externalities and the Schumpeterian notion of creative reaction conditional to the actual availability of knowledge externalities (Schumpeter 1947), enriched by the explicit assumption that the action of agents affects the structure of the environment including the actual amount of pecuniary knowledge externalities (Lane 2002; Lane et al. 2009). In so doing the ABM enables to identify and highlight both the complementarities and the sequential implementations and the theoretical differences between the Marshallian and the Schumpeterian frames. The Marshallian framework can be regarded as the case of zero reactivity and constrained externalities. The Schumpeterian frame starts as son as reactivity is larger than 0 and externalities affect the possibility to innovate.

The results of the Marshallian scenario show the high levels of elasticity of output to the distribution of productivity of firms. The larger is initial variance, the larger is output growth. The results of the replicator analysis are fully confirmed. The results of the Marshallian scenario also confirm that (i) growth is driven by exogenous assumptions about the distribution of the heterogeneity of firms; (ii) growth is bounded to the productivity of best performing firm. When all—surviving—firms reach it, growth stops. Growth can be resumed only by tossing new innovators with higher levels of productivity. Only the introduction of exogenous innovations enables the Marshallian scenario to generate further growth: this

Table 6 The ingredients of the different levels of Schumpeterian dynamics

	Low reactivity	High reactivity
Poor knowledge governance z = c	Quasi Marshallian convergence to equilibrium	Slow Schumpeterian regimes
Good knowledge governance z < c	Slow Schumpeterian regimes	High powered Schumpeterian dynamics

is exactly the basic engine of the biological evolutionary approach.[14] The automatic introduction of exogenous innovations can take place either by entrepreneurs as suggested by Marshall (1890/1920) and Schumpeter (1911/1934) or by the unexplained upgrading of the routines of corporations as in Nelson and Winter (1982). The hypothesis of exogenous innovation, as the single possibility to keep the dynamics of the system, retained by the evolutionary literature, is far away from the approach eventually sketched by Schumpeter in 1928, articulated in 1942 and fully elaborated in the 1947 contribution.

The results of the Schumpeterian scenario, in fact, confirm that the dynamics of the system is fully endogenous: the larger is the reactivity of firms and the better the quality of knowledge externalities, and the larger output growth. A growth that is endless, provided the system is able to regenerate high quality knowledge externalities. Table 6 provides a synthesis of the different Schumpeterian combinations of high and low levels of reactivity and poor and good knowledge governance that the ABM allows to explore.

The results of the simulation make it possible to compare the Schumpeterian simulations and to appreciate their substantial complementarity, highlighting the key innovations introduced by Schumpeter (1928, 1947) and their implementation (Antonelli 2008, 2011) upon the Marshallian frame.

The results of the simulation of the Marshallian model confirm five relevant issues: (i) in the Marshall innovation is exogenous. Marshall, as much as Schumpeter (1911–1934), assumes that some firms and agents are occasionally and randomly able to introduce better technologies and more effective organizations. (ii) Limited knowledge appropriability was well known by Marshall. All existing firms can imitate the superior technology. In Marshall, however, imitation can benefit only laggards. Marshallian externalities consist in imitation effects. Imitation externalities augment and accelerate the reduction of variety brought about by the parallel selection process. The increase of output stems from the selection and imitation processes with the exclusion of less performing firms and the progressive convergence of all production units to the best practice. When variety is erased and all the firms share the best practice, there is no longer room for growth and the positive effects of imitation level off. (iii) The Marshallian model is the first and most effective attempt to graft the Darwinian selection process in economics. Innovation is the exogenous source of variety. Variety is transient.

[14]See note 8.

Variety in fact exists at the onset of the process and is wiped out by the process itself. Growth is explained by the extent of variety and by the selection process itself. The larger is the variety at the onset of the process and the larger are the rates of growth. Growth stems from the sorting process of the firms that are less efficient and by the generalization of the best practice to all the surviving firms. The rate of growth declines together with the reduction of variety brought about by the selection process. Equilibrium, reduction of variety, exhaustion of endogenous externalities and the end of growth coincide. When the selection process is over, all firms are able to use the best practice and the allocation of resources cannot be improved any longer. There is no endogenous mechanism in the Marshallian process by means of which variety can be reproduced. (iv) The replicator dynamics introduced eventually both in biology and in economics is clearly at work in the Marshallian model (Foster and Metcalfe 2012). The evolutionary applications of the Marshallian model however make clear its intrinsic limitations: in the replicator dynamics variety is exogenous. (v) Biological evolutionary economics impinges upon the Marshallian legacy much more than currently assumed and, in any event, its exhibits stronger elements of continuity with the Marshallian framework than with the Schumpeterian approach.

In the scenarios that build upon Schumpeter (1947) innovation is the endogenous source of variety: it is path dependent as it may be continuously recreated by the endogenous dynamics of the system (Page 2011). Innovation and hence variety are generated by the reaction of firms to the changing conditions of product and factor markets. Innovation and variety are the product of internal feedback supported by the working of pecuniary knowledge externalities. Firms caught in out-of-equilibrium conditions by unexpected factor and product markets try and cope with either extra-profits or losses with the introduction of innovations. All firms, both advanced and laggard, try and innovate. In order to introduce innovations firms need knowledge externalities to generate technological knowledge and innovate. Their reaction will be adaptive when and where knowledge externalities are weak. The response of firms, instead, will be creative and successful so as to make the introduction of innovations possible when the cost of knowledge is below equilibrium levels. Endogenous variety is constantly reproduced by the dynamics of the creative response: firms in out-of-equilibrium conditions in fact dare to face the risks associated by means of the purchase, use and generation of technological knowledge to innovate. The creative reaction is persistent when and where knowledge externalities are reproduced and the best practice keeps moving ahead. The process rests upon the interaction between the entrepreneurial behavior of agents in out-of-equilibrium conditions and the systemic process that is at the origin of pecuniary knowledge externalities. Growth keeps increasing along the typical Schumpeterian cycles explained by the successful introduction of new technologies until knowledge governance mechanisms support the levels of pecuniary knowledge externalities.

6 Conclusions

Evolutionary models that impinge upon biological metaphors miss a consistent microeconomic analysis of the determinants of the introduction of innovations. The appreciation of the Marshallian framework clarifies the weaknesses of the evolutionary approaches that impinge upon biological metaphors: as a matter of fact they are more Marshallian than Schumpeterian. This enables to mark a clear distinction between the two evolutionary approaches: those that impinge upon biological metaphors and miss a consistent analysis of endogenous innovation and the new emerging evolutionary complexity. The integration of the Marshallian legacy and the late Schumpeterian frameworks, in fact, provides solid microfoundations to an evolutionary complexity that is able to account for the endogenous introduction of innovations. The integration in a single framework of the dynamic interaction of reactive decision making at the firm level and changing provision of externalities as determined by the evolving structure of the system are the cornerstones of the new evolutionary complexity.

Externalities play a central role both in the Marshallian and in the Schumpeterian analysis of the working of economic system. In the Marshallian legacy, however, imitation externalities are the cause and the consequence of the search for a stable equilibrium. In the Schumpeterian legacy, on the opposite, especially in the legacy of Schumpeter (1947), knowledge externalities are the cause and the consequence of the creative response of firms in out-of-equilibrium conditions that makes possible the introduction of innovations, persistent growth and evolution. The differences and yet the continuity and actual complementarity between the notions of externality implemented by Marshall and the Schumpeterian notion of creative response conditional to the availability of knowledge externalities seem clear. In both externalities are endogenous to the system. In Marshall they are bounded as they are intrinsically tied to the—transient—heterogeneity and variety of firms. In Schumpeter, instead, they may be continuously reproduced by the creative response of firms, the introduction of innovations and the consequent dynamics of the system.

Schumpeter builds his dynamics upon the Marshallian foundations. While Schumpeter (1911/1934) praises Leon Walras, Schumpeter (1928, 1941, 1947) relies on Alfred Marshall moving away from an ex-ante equilibrium that precede production to an ex-post quasi-equilibrium that follows production and market exchange, showing that equilibrium is impossible with innovation. Schumpeter (1911–1934) shares with Marshall the hypothesis that innovations are exogenous and random. Not surprisingly biological evolutionary models impinge upon this line of analysis. A line of analysis that had been overcome not only by Schumpeter (1942), but also by Schumpeter (1947) which draws from Marshall two key mechanisms: (i) the competition process as a selection process, and (ii) the endogenous dynamics of externalities, but implements radically the Marshallian frame with the notion of creative response conditional to the availability of endogenous knowledge externalities. The approach elaborated by Schumpeter (1928, 1947) is able not only to go beyond the limits of the unexplained origins of variety assumed by Marshall as the result of a Darwinistic grafting, but also to provide the foundations of an evolutionary complexity.

The understanding of the complementarities and linkages between the Marshallian and the Schumpeterian (1947) legacies enables to take advantage of the rich Marshallian framework and to use it to implement and strengthen the foundations of the new emerging approach to innovation as a creative response and an emerging system property where both agent based decision making and the properties of the system into which firms are embedded. The Schumpeterian frame elaborated in 1947 shares the basic microeconomic tools laid down by Marshall but departs from it—as well as from the earlier approach elaborated in *The theory of economic development*—as soon as firms in out-of-equilibrium conditions are credited with the capability to try and react to the unexpected conditions of both product and factor markets by means of the endogenous introduction of innovations.

In the Schumpeterian dynamics the reaction function of the firms plays a central role. The performances of each company are considered in equilibrium when the result for the year falls in a spherical neighborhood of zero, whose amplitude is parametrically determined by the researcher. Firms are in out-of-equilibrium conditions when their profits—either below or above 0—are far from equilibrium. Firms that experience performances below equilibrium try and reduce the use of the current input and to purchase knowledge. Firms that enjoy profits try and increase both the amount of labor and that of knowledge: output and productivity increase together.

In the Schumpeterian model, pecuniary knowledge externalities substitute and actually augment the transient Marshallian externalities associated to the imitation and selection processes. Because of the Arrovian characteristics of knowledge as an economic good such as limited appropriability and exhaustibility, non divisibility and hence cumulability, limited rivalry in use and the recombinant generation of new knowledge where existing knowledge is an indispensable input, the cost of knowledge may be actually lower than in equilibrium conditions. When the system properties are such that the costs of absorption and use of external knowledge are below equilibrium levels, the creative reaction can take place.[15] The Schumpeterian dynamics may be endless provided that knowledge governance mechanisms remain at work and hence the costs of knowledge keep falling below equilibrium levels.[16]

[15]In the simulation model we allow the actual costs of knowledge (z) to assume different values so as to show the effects of different types of knowledge governance mechanisms. In the first simulation run z is slightly smaller than the cost of knowledge-as-if-it-were a standard good (c) to mimic a system with weak knowledge governance mechanisms at work. In the second simulation run z is assumed to be much smaller than c so as to consider the case of high-powered knowledge governance mechanism.

[16]As noted, knowledge equilibrium levels would take place when the cost of external knowledge would equal the costs of a standard good or when absorption costs are so high that the total costs of effective use of external knowledge equals the costs of knowledge as a standard good.

The results of this paper provide a platform that can be enriched further to contribute complexity economics implementing the notion of innovation and knowledge as emergent properties of an economic system based upon the recursive interaction between individual action and the structure of the system.[17] The structure of the system makes available pecuniary knowledge externalities. The entrepreneurial attempts of agents—caught in out-of-equilibrium conditions—to introduce innovations have the multiple effects to: (a) bring new changes in product and factor markets altering the expected equilibrium conditions upon which agents elaborate their productive plans; (b) expand the generation of new additional technological knowledge modifying the structure of interactions and transaction and hence (c) change the actual amount of pecuniary knowledge externalities available in the system and (d) reproduce variety within the system and to push ahead the technological frontier so as to keep improving the best practice. In the frame that builds upon Schumpeter (1928, 1947) innovation, knowledge, variety and growth are endogenous and stochastic. This Schumpeterian frame enables to identify the forces that may limit its reproduction. At each point in time knowledge governance mechanism and hence the amount of pecuniary knowledge externalities may decline with the consequent decline of the reproduction of variety, the rates of introduction of innovation and the rates of growth. The continual implementation of effective knowledge governance mechanisms is crucial to keep the working of knowledge externalities. This dynamics is clearly path-dependent, as opposed to past dependent. When and if the system is no longer able to support the regeneration of pecuniary knowledge externalities, the innovation process stops and the system identifies a stable attractor. The recursive interaction between individual decision-making and the system properties enable to identify the introduction of innovations as an emergent and contingent system property (Antonelli 2008, 2011, 2013, 2015, 2017).

Evolutionary complexity empowered by the solid microfoundations of endogenous innovation derived from the Marshallian&Schumpeterian legacies seems far better equipped than evolutionary economics impinging upon the Darwinian legacy to grasp the endogenous drivers of innovation and economic dynamics. Growth, as a result of the endogenous and contingent reproduction of variety, made possible by the introduction of innovations, may be endless provided that appropriate knowledge governance mechanisms are implemented and supported. The recursive interaction between individual action and the evolution of the properties of the system paves the way to elaborate effective strategies at the firm levels to make it actually persistent. The implications for policy are most important as it becomes clear that all interventions aimed at increasing the quality of knowledge governance mechanisms that favor the persistence of pecuniary knowledge externalities and consequently the reproduction of innovative variety are likely to enhance economic growth.

[17] See Antonelli and Ferraris (2017).

ABM confirms to be a powerful theoretical tool as it enables to show how different theoretical frames are the result of the recombination of analytical bricks drawn from pre-existing models that alter the working of the system and yield new theories. In this case the shifting role of externalities plays a crucial role.

Appendix 1: Detailed Description of the Simulated Economy

The economy configuration depends upon the number of agents and their repartition between "smart" and "normal" agents. Smart agents are bigger and have a higher productivity than normal ones. Variable used to configure the economy are the following:

- "agents" it indicates the maximum number of firms the simulated economy is capable to host; at the start of the simulation the market hosts always the maximum allowed number of firms;
- "totMoney" is the fixed amount of money available into the simulated system;
- "labPrice" it quantifies the wage to be payed for a single unit of labour;
- "exitLabour" is the amount of work an enterprise has to employ in order to be considered alive; firms whose input falls under this threshold are automatically removed from the market;
- "smarterRatio" represents the probability a single enterprise can be initially set as smart;
- "normalLab" is the maximum amount of input (work) a normal firm could be given for the first production cycle, the minimum one coincides with the exitLabour, that is the quantity of input a firm needs to employ to survive;
- "smarterLab" is the maximum amount of input (work) a smart firm could be given for the first production cycle, the minimum one coincides with the maximum amount the normal firms could be given (i. e. normalLab);
- "normalPro" is the maximum amount of starting labor productivity (A) for normal firms, being the minimum one a non relevant amount bigger than zero for computational matters";
- "smarterPro" is the maximum amount of starting labor productivity (A) for smart firms, be the minimum the "normalPro";
- "turnover" is the probability a new firm enters the market when there is room for that.

The **behaviour of the agents** is influenced by the following parameters:

- "tolerance" measures the maximum distance from zero, agents consider as equilibrium. As computers are only able to deal with limited precision amounts, this confidence interval makes possible to reach equilibrium position.
- "labRate" represents the higher fraction of the actual input the firms use to compute the input adjustment. Each simulated cycle and for each agent the

upgrade for labor is randomly tossed between 0 and the parametrically set value. For each agent:

$$\Delta L_i = L_{i0}{}^{*}\mathrm{random}(]0, \mathrm{labRate}[). \tag{14}$$

Firms that enjoy profit will increase their demand of labour by this ΔL, provided that their profit will be enough to compensate the major expense, due to the fact that no financial institutions have been—intentionally—provided, in the simulated economy firms have to finance the hiring of additional labor with their profit. The affordable increase of labor depends upon the amount of profit(P) and the cost of the labor (w), as in the following equation:

$$L_{i1} = L_{i0} + \min\left(\Delta L_i, (P_{i0}/\text{labor price})\right) \mid P_{i0} > \text{tolerance}. \tag{15}$$

When a firm suffers a loss it simply reduce the labor input, with the lower limit of zero:

$$L_{i1} = \min\left(0, L_{i0} - \Delta L_i\right) \mid P_{i0} < -\text{tolerance}. \tag{16}$$

- "techRate" is the fraction of their proceeds the Schumpeterian firms invest to acquire knowledge. Investment has to be financed exactly like labor upgrade. Firms invest in both cases of profit or losses, whereas in the former case the amount of profit will be the maximum affordable investment, in the latter such amount is measured by the savings the enterprise realizes by reducing its input (labor) acquisition. The amount a firm invests can be computed as:

$$I_{i1} = \min\left((Y_{i0}{}^{*}Gp_0{}^{*}\text{techRate}), P_{i0}\right) \mid P_{i0} > \text{tolerance}; \quad \text{or as:} \tag{17}$$

$$I_{i1} = \min\left((Y_{i0}{}^{*}Gp_0{}^{*}\text{techRate}), (-\Delta L_{i1}{}^{*}\text{labor price})\right) \mid P_{i0} < -\text{tolerance}. \tag{18}$$

- "techDecay" measures the effects of time on the contribution of knowledge in increasing the productivity (A). The labor productivity (A) is subject either to Marshallian imitation externalities or Schumpeterian knowledge externalities, according to the scenario at work. The production function in the Schumpeterian approach has been operationalized into the simulation as:

$$Y_{i1} = L_{i1}{}^{*}A_{i1}{}^{*}(1 + T_{i1}). \tag{19}$$

Where T represents the technological knowledge the firm is able to exploit, the amount depends both by: (i) knowledge acquisition through investment, (ii) knowledge generation due to the competence rising from past technological knowledge acquisition. To simulate the two effects the level of T at a time is computed as sum of the acquired technological knowledge and the accumulation of a small fraction of the past acquisitions, accordingly with the parameter "techDecay" that measures the fraction of technological knowledge that cannot be cumulated. The level of knowledge is computed as:

$$T_{i1} = \sum t_{i-j}{}^{*}techDecay + I_{i1}/(Tp_1{}^{*}L_{i1}{}^{*}A_{i1}). \tag{20}$$

Where Tp represents the price the firm has to pay to apply a unit of technological knowledge to a unit of product, it is determined at the system level and depends on the effectiveness of the knowledge governance.

- "techLife" represents the number of production cycles a technological knowledge acquisition could be fully exploited.

Type and intensity of externalities are managed by four parameters:

- "risk" measures the risk of failure for imitation and knowledge acquisition, each time a firm acquires knowledge or tries to imitate better practices, a uniform random number E is tossed in the range]0,1[and compared with risk value: if the tossed number is less than risk value the result of the action is nullified.
- "imitation" is a variable used to enable the simulation of the imitation process; its value represents the fraction of the gap between the best performing firm labor productivity and the own one each firm can fulfill accordingly with the risk parameter. (See Eq. 25). If the parameter value is zeroed, no enhancement in productivity is allowed for existing firms nor for newcomers.
- "governancePerformance" is used to express the effectiveness of the knowledge management in the simulated environment; its value is set in the range [0,1] the higher the value the lower the cost of knowledge becomes, as follows:

$$z = \partial Y/\partial T^{*}(1 - governancePerformance), \tag{21}$$

where $\partial Y/\partial T$ measures the estimated monetary value of the effect of the new knowledge on the output of the enterprise.

Simulation control is performed by setting up three parameters:

- "randomSeed" is used to set a fixed random distribution based upon the indicated seed; by setting to zero the parameter value each run could be based upon a different random distribution.
- "stopAt" is used to set the number of production cycle to be observed by the simulation; when the number of cycles is reached the simulation is stopped and final results are collected.
- "prFlg" is a switch used to enable printing the values of the parameters directly into the results files.

A.1 The Computation of the Marginal Value of Technological Knowledge

Assuming c to be the marginal value of the technological knowledge, i.e.:

$$c = \partial Y / \partial T. \tag{22}$$

a creative reaction can be performed only if the price of technological knowledge (z) is less than c. In order to study and simulate such situations we need to know the value of c, but it depends upon the prices and the total output of the enterprises.

Starting from the assumption the value of c needs to be only a plausible starting point for figure out z, it has been decided to compute it through a simple two steps procedure:

(a) all the firms forecast the amount of output (F_{i1}) they will offer at the end of the current production cycle, without new knowledge acquisition as:

$$F_{i1} = L_{i1} {}^{*} A_{i1} {}^{*} (1 + T_{i1}). \tag{23}$$

(b) The market after summarizing all the forecasts computes a knowledge price per unit of knowledge and product as:

$$z = M / \sum F_{i1} {}^{*} (1 - \text{governancePerformance}). \tag{24}$$

Because z represents the cost for an amount of knowledge able to rise of one unit the total product, z has to be multiplied for the product unit the new knowledge is going to be applied: each firm computes the amount of knowledge its investment is worth by dividing the amount it invested by $z * A_{1i} * L_{1i}$; "governancePerformance" is a parameter to be set in the interval [0,1] that quantify how much z differs from c.

Even assuming a null performance of the knowledge governance mechanism, this process over-estimates the z if the production grows, due to the fact the price per unit will fall, as well as it under-estimates z if the whole production fall. Production amount depends not only upon the knowledge acquisition process, it may be influenced by the exit of some enterprises, as well as the decision to reduce or raise the amount of output, so the z value tends to equal c but it never estimate it exactly.[18]

With proper levels of knowledge governance that enable each learning agent to access and use the stock of knowledge available at each point in time in the system, including the knowledge being generated by all the other learning agents, knowledge externalities are being recreated as an endogenous process within the system

[18]This version of the model does not allow experimenting the specific case where c = z.

as soon as agents start relying on technological knowledge to feed their—creative—reactions. The lower the costs of accessing and using the stock of existing knowledge, and more specifically, the larger the gap between the actual costs of accessing external knowledge as an input into the internal recombinant generation of technological knowledge and its equilibrium costs, and the larger the opportunities for firms to react creatively to arising mismatches between actual and expected conditions of product and factor markets with the introduction of productivity enhancing innovations (Antonelli 2011).

The actual cost of access and use of knowledge in an economic system is influenced by the quality of the knowledge governance mechanism the system has been able to elaborate. Knowledge governance consists in an array of institutional settings that combine and integrate market transactions and personal interactions, ex-ante and ex-post coordination both among firms in the economic system and between them and the academic system created by the State. Knowledge governance is intrinsically dynamic. Its ingredients and mechanisms keep changing with the continual introduction of new modes. This dynamics exhibit the typical traits of an emergence process whereby the identification of limits and failures engenders a creative reaction that eventually leads to the articulation of a new mode. Knowledge governance can improve or deteriorate: the outcome is far from deterministic (Antonelli 2015).

A.2 Simulating Externalities: Marshall Versus Schumpeter

In the Marshallian scenario imitation is limited to less performing firms: the process allows the system to reach the productivity of the best firm at the level that has been tossed during the set up of the simulated economy. In the Marshallian scenario each time a firm takes advantage of imitation it enjoys a productivity upgrade that is a fraction of the gap between its productivity level and the one of the best enterprise in the economy. Imitation is a challenging process, may be an enterprise fails doing its upgrade. The effect of imitation is represented as:

$$A_{i1} = A_{i0} + (A_{max} - A_{i0})^{*} E_0 \mid E_1 > \text{risk}. \tag{25}$$

Where A_{i0} and A_{i1} are the productivity of the i-th enterprise respectively before and after the process, A_{max} is the productivity of the best firms, E_0 and E_1 are random uniformly tossed numbers: E_0 is tossed in the range]0,imitation], where imitation is a parametrical value used to manage the process, and E_1 is tossed in the range]0,1[. Risk represents the probability the imitation process fails.

Newcomers are able to exploit imitation externalities too, accordingly with the risk parameter new enterprises are given either: (i) the labour productivity of the old ones they replace or (ii) the average labour productivity of the system.

A small upgrade of its labor productivity granted to each agent mimics imitation externalities. The upgrade is computed on the basis of the difference between the productivity of the best agent in the system (A_{max}) and each other agent's own productivity (A_i). The granted amount is randomly tossed by multiplying the gap (A_{max}–A_i) by a random number in the interval]0,imitation[, where "imitation" is a parameter set between [0,1[(by setting it to zero the effects of imitation are automatically excluded); this upgrade is subject to failure with a probability that is specified by setting up the appropriate model parameter, called "risk". At the end of each production cycle, for each agent, the gap between its labor productivity (A_i) and the A_{max} is computed, then by comparing a random trial with the risk, the system decide if the agent would be granted an enhancement or not. If yes the agent is given a labor productivity enhancement that is a randomly tossed fraction of the gap as represented in the previous section. Note that 'imitation' does not work for knowledge that has to be bought as a kind of production factor.

A_{new} and L_{new} represent, respectively, the labor productivity and the input of a new firm, whereas A_{old} represents labor productivity of incumbents. The following relations describe how the "new" values are set:

$$A_{new} = \text{average A} \mid \text{imitation} > 0, \tag{26}$$

$$A_{new} = A_{old} \mid \text{imitation} = 0, \tag{27}$$

$$L_{new} = (\text{average L} - \text{exitLabour}^*2)^*\text{random}([0,1]) + \text{exitLaboour}^*2. \tag{28}$$

In the Schumpeterian scenario, instead, all firms can try and use external knowledge spilling in the system because of its limited capability to generate new technological knowledge and introduce productivity-enhancing innovations. Provided that knowledge externalities are available, each firm is capable to try and increase its productivity: also the best firm can evolve through knowledge acquisition and overcome its initial endowment. This process is subject to fail too: in the model it is subject to the same probability of failure of the imitation process. The innovation equation is split into two components: (i) the decision to try and innovate that depends on the performances and (ii) the knowledge generation function. In the Schumpeterian scenario firms decide to react each time they find themselves in out-of-equilibrium conditions, i.e. when their profit (P) differs from zero, provided a small tolerance range (d). Their reaction consists in the attempt to innovate by investing in knowledge acquisition a fraction of their output (F), but such acquisition has to be financed either by investing extra profits or through savings obtained by reducing the amount of employed labor.

Innovation is subject to failure risks as well as imitation, so results of each trial are subject to failure with a certain probability (risk). Once the new technological knowledge has been acquired it may be exploited during the next years, even obsolescence could reduce its effect on productivity. The decision to try and innovate can be resumed as the amount each enterprise invests each time to acquire new knowledge (Ii):

$$I_{i1} = \min\left[\left(Y_{i0}{}^{*}G_{p0}{}^{*}F\right), P_{i0}\right] \mid P_{i0} > d. \tag{29}$$

$$I_{i1} = \min\left[\left(Y_{i0}{}^{*}G_{p0}{}^{*}F\right), \left(-\Delta L_{i1}{}^{*}\text{labor price}\right)\right] \mid P_{i0} < -d. \tag{30}$$

Provided that innovation is subject to failure, as well as imitation, each investment decision is subject to fail accordingly with a probability parameter (risk). The levels of new knowledge—that may be exploited during the next period—takes into account the effects of obsolescence that limits its effect on productivity accordingly with a decay coefficient (decay).

$$T_{i1} = \left\{[I_{i1}/z_1/L_{i1}{}^{*}A_{i1})] \mid E > \text{risk}\right\} + \sum t_{i-j}{}^{*}\text{techDecay}. \tag{31}$$

Where z_1 represents the current price the firm has to pay to apply a unit of knowledge to a unit of product and E is a uniformly distributed pseudo-random number.

Schumpeterian externalities depend on the quality of the knowledge governance and the accumulation of knowledge. The quality of the knowledge governance mechanisms affects the access costs to the stock of knowledge. The second component of the Schumpeterian dynamic is the accumulation of knowledge that leads to a reduction of the cost of knowledge: by allowing firms to use the knowledge acquired in previous production cycles, paying for the first acquisition only, the model simulates this phenomenon. It is plausible that very old vintages of knowledge have little influence on production. Consequently, in order to account for the effects of obsolescence, at each production step, the amount of the stock of knowledge is reduced by dividing it per a decay parameter.

Both variables are controlled by a parameter: (i) techRate sets the fraction of the production the firms invest, whereas (ii) governanePerformance sets the effectiveness of the knowledge management. By specifying a zero value for techRate the firms remains simply adaptive, without performing any innovative reaction; by setting to zero the governancePerformance the cost of the knowledge becomes very close to c, i.e. to the value of its marginal productivity. Both techRate and governancePerformance manage the main component of the process.

Appendix 2

Table 7 Setup of the parameters for the different scenarios

Parameter name	Scenario					
	Imitation	Zero Governance	Low Gov Low React	Low Gov High React	High Gov Low React	High Gov High React
Random Seed	Random/ fixed	Random/ fixed	Random/ fixed	Random/ fixed	Random/ fixed	Random/ fixed
Tolerance	0.001	0.001	0.001	0.001	0.001	0.001
Imitation	0.01	n.a.	n.a.	n.a.	n.a.	n.a.
TechRate	n.a.	0.05	0.01	0.05	0.01	0.05
Governance Performance	n.a.	0.0	0.01	0.01	0.95	0.95
Risk	0.1	0.1	0.1	0.1	0.1	0.1
Turnover	0.2	0.2	0.2	0.2	0.2	0.2
Tech Decay	n.a.	0.999	0.999	0.999	0.999	0.999
TechLife	n.a.	0.0	0.0	0.0	0.0	0.0
Agents	1000	1000	1000	1000	1000	1000
TotMoney	10,000	10,000	10,000	10,000	10,000	10,000
SmarterRatio	0.15	0.15	0.15	0.15	0.15	0.15
SmarterLab	20.0	20.0	20.0	20.0	20.0	20.0
SmarterPro	1.0	1.0	1.0	1.0	1.0	1.0
NormalLab	10.0	10.0	10.0	10.0	10.0	10.0
NormalPro	0.2	0.2	0.2	0.2	0.2	0.2
LabRate	0.1	0.1	0.1	0.1	0.1	0.1
LabPrice	1.0	1.0	1.0	1.0	1.0	1.0
ExitLabour	1.0	1.0	1.0	1.0	1.0	1.0
StopAt	2000	2000	2000	2000	2000	2000
PrFlg	0/1	0/1	0/1	0/1	0/1	0/1

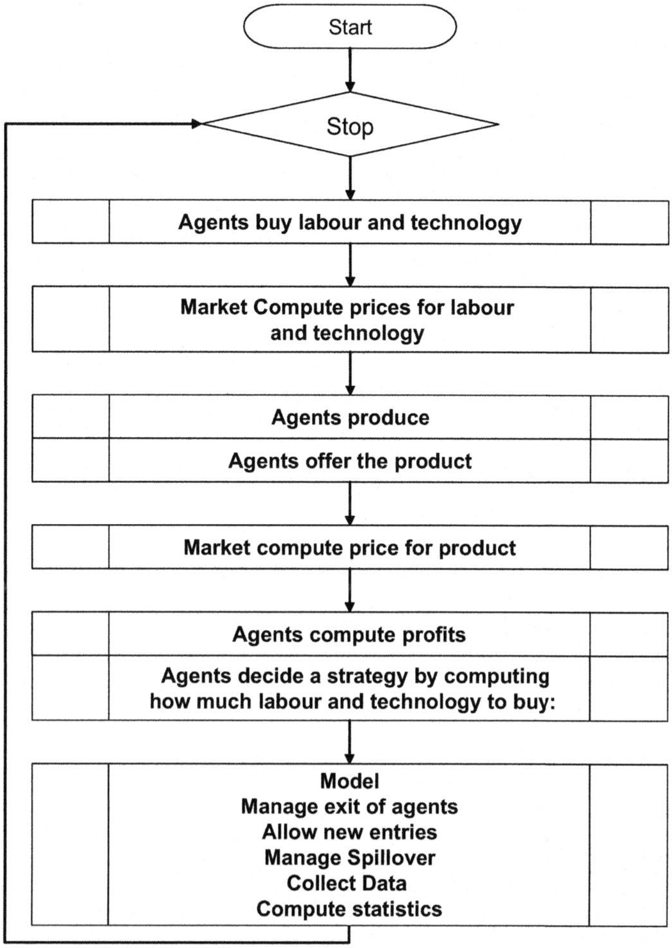

Fig. 3 The simulation process

References

Alchian A (1950) Uncertainty evolution and economic theory. J Polit Econ 58:211–221

Antonelli C (2008) Localized technological change. Towards the economics of complexity. Routledge, London

Antonelli C (ed) (2011) Handbook on the economic complexity of technological change. Edward Elgar, Cheltenham

Antonelli C (2013) Knowledge governance, pecuniary knowledge externalities and total factor productivity growth. Econ Dev Q 27:62–70

Antonelli C (2015) Innovation as a creative response. A reappraisal of the Schumpeterian legacy. Hist Econ Ideas 23:99–118

Antonelli C (2017) Endogenous innovation: the creative response. Econ Innov New Technol 26(8):689–718

Antonelli C, Ferraris G (2011) Innovation as an emerging system property: an agent based model. J Artif Soc Soc Simulat 14(2) no page

Antonelli C, Ferraris G (2017) The creative response and the endogenous dynamics of pecuniary knowledge externalities: an agent based simulation model. J Econ Interac Coord (forthcoming)

Antonelli C, Scellato G (2011) Out-of-equilibrium profit and innovation. Econ Innov New Technol 20(5):405–421

Antonelli C, Scellato G (2013) Complexity and innovation: social interactions and firm level productivity growth. J Evol Econ 23:77–96

Aoki M, Yoshikawa H (2002) Demand saturation–creation and economic growth. J Econ Behav Organ 48(2):127–154

Arrow KJ (1962) Economic welfare and the allocation of resources for invention. In: Nelson RR (ed) The rate and direction of inventive activity: economic and social factors. Princeton University Press for N.B.E.R, Princeton, pp 609–625

Arrow KJ (1969) Classificatory notes on the production and transmission of technical knowledge. American Economic Review 59:29–35.

Arthur B (1989) Positive feedbacks in the economy. Sci Am 262:92–99

Arthur B (2007) Complexity and the economy. In: Hanusch H, Pyka A (eds) Elgar companion to Neo-Schumpeterian economics. Edward Elgar, Cheltenham

Arthur WB (2009) The nature of technology. What it is and how it evolves. Free Press, New York

Bischi GI, Dawid H, Kopel M (2003) Gaining the competitive edge using internal and external spillovers: a dynamic analysis. J Econ Dyn Control 27:2171–2193

Caldari K (2015) Marshall and complexity: a necessary balance between process and order. Camb J Econ 39:1071–1085

David PA (1993) Knowledge, property and the system dynamics of technological change, in L.S. Summers and S. Shah (eds), Proceedings of the World Bank Annual Conference on Development Economics, Washington, DC: International Bank for Reconstruction and Development, pp. 215–48.

Dawid H (2006) Agent-based models of innovation and technical change. In: Tesfatsion L, Judd KL (eds) Handbook of computational economics, Agent-based computational economics, vol 2. North-Holland, Amsterdam, pp 1235–1272

Dosi G (1982) Technological paradigms and technological trajectories. A suggested interpretation of the determinants and directions of technical change. Res Policy 11:147–162

Dosi G (1997) Opportunities, incentives and the collective patterns of technological change. Econ J 107(444):1530–1547

Dosi G, Marsili O, Orsenigo L, Salvatore R (1995) Learning, market selection and the evolution of industrial structures. Small Bus Econ 7(6):411–436

Erixon L (2016) Is firm renewal stimulated by negative shocks? The status of negative driving forces in Schumpeterian and Darwinian economics. Camb J Econ 40:93–121

Fleming L (2001) Recombinant uncertainty in technological search. Manag Sci 47(1):117–132

Foster J, Metcalfe JS (2012) Economic emergence: an evolutionary economic perspective. J Econ Behav Organ 82:420–432

Geels FW (2002) Technological transitions as evolutionary reconfiguration processes: a multi-level perspective and a case-study. Res Policy 31(8–9):1257–1274

Geels FW (2005) Technological transitions and system innovations: a co-evolutionary and socio-technical analysis. Edward Elgar, Cheltenham

Griliches Z (1979) Issues in assessing the contribution of research and development to productivity growth. Bell J Econ 10(1):92–116

Griliches Z (ed) (1984) R&D patents and productivity. University of Chicago Press for NBER, Chicago

Iwai K (1984) Schumpeterian dynamics: an evolutionary model of innovation and imitation. J Econ Behav Organ 5(2):159–190

Iwai K (2000) A contribution to the evolutionary theory of innovation, imitation and growth. J Econ Behav Organ 43:167–198

Kirman A (1997) The economy as an evolving network. J Evol Econ 7:339–353

Kirman A (2011) Learning in agent-based models. East Econ J 37(1):20–27

Kirman A (2016) Complexity and economic policy: a paradigm shift or a change in perspective? A review essay on David Colander and Roland Kupers's complexity and the art of public policy. J Econ Lit 54(2):534–572

Lane DA (2002) Complexity and local interactions: towards a theory of industrial districts. In: Quadrio Curzio A, Fortis M (eds) Complexity and industrial clusters: dynamics and models in theory and practice. Physica-Verlag, Heidelberg, pp 65–82

Lane DA, Pumain D, Leeuw SE, West G (eds) (2009) Complexity perspectives in innovation and social change. Springer, Berlin

Levit G, Hossfeld U, Witt U (2011) Can Darwinism be "generalized" and of what use would this be? J Evol Econ 21:545–562

Lorentz A, Ciarli T, Savona M, Valente M (2016) The effect of demand driven structural transformation on growth and technological change. J Evol Econ 26:219–246

Malerba F, Nelson RR, Orsenigo L, Winter SG (2001) History-friendly models: an overview of the case of the computer industry. J Artif Soc Soc Simulat 4(3):195–226

Marshall A (1890–1920) Principles of economics, 8th edn. The Online Library of Liberty

Marshall A (1920 [1890]) Principles of economics, 8th edn. Macmillan, London

Metcalfe JS (2007a) The broken thread: Marshall, Schumpeter and Hayek on the evolution of capitalism. ESRC Centre for Research on Innovation and Competition, University of Manchester

Metcalfe JS (2007b) Alfred Marshall's Mecca: reconciling the theories of value and development. Econ Rec 83:S1–S22

Metcalfe JS (2009a) On Marshallian evolutionary dynamics, entry and exit. In: Vint J, Metcalfe JS, Kurz HD, Salvadori N, Samuelson PA (eds) Economic theory and economic thought: essays in Honour of Ian Steedman. Routledge, London, pp 350–373

Metcalfe JS (2009b) Marshall and Schumpeter: evolution and the institutions of capitalism. In: Pyka A, Cantner U, Greiner A, Kuhn T (eds) Recent advances in neo-Schumpeterian economics: essays in honor of Horst Hanush. Edward Elgar, Cheltenham, pp 53–77

Mueller M, Pyka A (2016) Economic behavior and agent-based modeling. In: Frantz R, Chen S, Dopfer K, Heukelom F, Mousavi S (eds) Routledge handbook of economics. Routledge, London, pp 405–415

Napoletano M, Dosi G, Fagiolo G, Roventini A (2012) Wage formation investment behavior and growth regimes: an agent based analysis. Revue de l'OFCE 124:235–261

Nelson RR, Winter SG (1977) In search of useful theory of innovation. Res Policy 6(1):36–76

Nelson RR, Winter SG (1982) An evolutionary theory of economic change. The Belknap Press of Harvard University Press, Cambridge

Page SE (2011) Diversity and complexity. Princeton University Press, Princeton

Penrose E (1952) Biological analogies in the theory of the firm. Am Econ Rev 42(5):804–819

Penrose E (1953) Biological analogies in the theory of the firm: rejoinder. Am Econ Rev 43 (4):603–609

Pyka A, Fagiolo G (2007) Agent-based modelling: a methodology for neo-Schumpeterian economics. In: Hanusch H, Pyka A (eds) Elgar companion to neo-Schumpeterian economics. Edward Elgar, Cheltenham, pp 467–502

Ravix JL (2012) Alfred Marshall and the Marshallian theory of the firm. In: Dietrich M, Krafft J (eds) Handbook on the economics and the theory of the firm. Elgar, Cheltenham, pp 49–54

Ruttan VW (1997) Induced innovation evolutionary theory and path dependence. Econ J 107 (444):1520–1529

Sahal D (1985) Technological guideposts and innovation avenues. Res Policy 14(2):61–82

Safarzyńska K, van den Bergh JCJM (2010) Evolutionary models in economics: a survey of methods and building blocks. J Evol Econ 20(3):329–373

Scherer FM (1986) Innovation and growth: Schumpeterian perspectives. MIT Press, Cambridge

Schumpeter JA (1911, 1934) The theory of economic development. Harvard University Press, Cambridge
Schumpeter JA (1928) The instability of capitalism. Econ J 38:361–386
Schumpeter JA (1939) Business cycles. A theoretical, historical and statistical analysis of the capitalist process. McGraw-Hill, New York
Schumpeter JA (1941) Alfred Marshall's Principles: a semi-centennial appraisal. Am Econ Rev XXXI:236–248
Schumpeter JA (1942) Capitalism socialism and democracy. Harper and Brothers, New York
Schumpeter JA (1947) The creative response in economic history. J Econ Hist 7:149–159
Silverberg G, Lehnert D (1993) Long waves and 'evolutionary chaos' in a simple Schumpeterian model of embodied technical change. Struct Change Econ Dyn 4:9–37
Silverberg G, Verspagen B (1994a) Learning innovation and economic growth: a long-run model of industrial dynamics. Indus Corp Change 3:199–223
Silverberg G, Verspagen B (1994b) Collective learning innovation and growth in a boundedly rational evolutionary world. J Evol Econ 4:207–226
Silverberg G, Verspagen B (1995) An evolutionary model of long term cyclical variations of catching up and falling behind. J Evol Econ 5:209–227
Sorenson O, Rivkin JW, Fleming L (2006) Complexity, networks and knowledge flow. Res Policy 35:994–1017
Veblen T (1898) Why is economics not an evolutionary science? Q J Econ 2(4):373–397
Weitzman ML (1996) Hybridizing growth theory. Am Econ Rev 86:207–212
Windrum P, Birchenhall C (2005) Structural change in the presence of network externalities: a co-evolutionary model of technological successions. J Evol Econ 15:123–148
Winter SG, Kaniovski YM, Dosi G (2000) Modeling industrial dynamics with innovative entrants. Struct Chang Econ Dyn 11(3):255–293
Yildizoglu M (2002) Competing R&D strategies in an evolutionary industry model. Comput Econ 19:51–65

Understanding the Complex Nature of Innovation Network Evolution

Muhamed Kudic and Jutta Guenther

Abstract In this article, we suggest a theoretical framework to explain how and why innovation networks emerge, change and eventually dissolve over time. We argue that network evolution is a multi-faceted phenomenon that needs to be studied at multiple levels. Our framework is based on the notion that network change is a result of exogenous and endogenous determinants. At the heart of our framework, we focus on four elementary network change processes at the micro level: the entry and exit of actors, and the formation and termination of the links between them. We integrate the actors' knowledge endowments and strategic orientations to emphasize the role of actor-specific decision making processes in explaining the emergence of characteristic network patterns over time. In doing so, we add still missing pieces of the puzzle to the contemporary network evolution literature.

1 Introduction

Previous empirical research shows that the structural configuration of innovation networks is characterized by typical properties. For instance, Barabasi and Albert (1999, p. 510) demonstrate that "[. . .] large networks self-organize into a scale-free state". Similarly, previous empirical studies confirm the emergence of small-world patterns (Kudic 2015; Tomasello et al. 2016). We also know that, over time, innovation networks tend to build up a densely connected core and a loosely connected periphery (Kudic et al. 2015a). This is usually referred to as a core-periphery structure (Borgatti and Everett 1999).

The configuration and positioning of actors within these structurally complex entities affects innovative outcomes in various ways. Powell et al. (1996) provide evidence that an actor's network positioning is closely related to its innovation performance. This insight was confirmed and extended by a number of subsequent studies (Stuart 2000; Baum et al. 2000). Several other studies have demonstrated that large-scale network characteristics, in particular small-world properties, are

M. Kudic (✉) • J. Guenther
Faculty of Business Studies and Economics, University of Bremen, Bremen, Germany
e-mail: kudic@uni-bremen.de; jutta.guenther@uni-bremen.de

A. Pyka, U. Cantner (eds.), *Foundations of Economic Change*, Economic Complexity and Evolution, DOI 10.1007/978-3-319-62009-1_20

likely to affect the exchange of information, ideas and knowledge and thus enhance the creativity and innovativeness of embedded actors (Uzzi and Spiro 2005; Fleming et al. 2007; Schilling and Phelps 2007). Others have studied the relationship between core-periphery structures at the overall network level and the creative performance of the actors involved (Cattani and Ferriani 2008). Their results show that individuals who occupy an intermediate position between the core and the periphery of their social system are in a favorable position to achieve creative results (ibid.). At the same time, it is important to note that innovation networks are anything but stable. Structural network properties, as well as the actors' network positions, continuously change over time.

The considerations mentioned above point to that fact that an in-depth understanding of how and why innovation networks emerge, change and eventually dissolve over time is crucial, especially when studying the relationship between network structure, the actors' network embeddedness, and their subsequent innovation performance. Over the past year, remarkable progress has been made in this research domain (Pittaway et al. 2004; Bergenholz and Waldstrom 2011). Nevertheless, evolutionary change of networks still constitutes a widely unexplored area of research (Brenner et al. 2011, p. 5). We still face more questions than answers, especially when it comes to holistic theoretical explanations of causes and consequences of structural network change processes.

Accordingly, the aim of this study is to contribute to an in-depth understanding of the multi-faceted nature of innovation network evolution.[1] We propose a framework that considers both exogenous and endogenous determinants of structural network change. It incorporates four network change processes at the micro level, i.e. the entry and exit of actors, and the formation and termination of the links between them. These processes explain the emergence and structural evolution of characteristic innovation network patterns at higher aggregation levels.[2] Our framework explicitly acknowledges the role of the actors' knowledge endowments and strategic orientations. In doing so, we add a highly relevant but still missing piece of the puzzle to the discussion on the structural evolution of innovation networks.

The remainder is structured as follows. Section 2 provides a literature review. In Sect. 3 we present the main building blocks of our conceptual framework and we introduce the theoretical arguments that allow us to substantiate the four micro-level networks change processes at the heart of our framework. In Sect. 4 we discuss the structural implications of these processes at the micro level against the backdrop of actors' knowledge endowments and strategic orientations. Section 5 concludes with some implications, critical reflections, and suggestions for future research.

[1]The general idea of this study is based on Kudic (2015).

[2]In a most basic sense, any kind of network consists of two basic elements: nodes and the ties between these nodes (Wasserman and Faust 1994). This justifies our focus on the four micro-level processes.

2 State of the Art

In this section we start with a brief discussion on the most influential empirical contributions to real-world network topologies. Next, we provide an overview of network change conceptualization, refer to recent empirical findings, and provide a critical discussion on the typically assumed network change mechanisms in these papers. Finally, we briefly look at the most recent directions research has taken in the broad and highly interdisciplinary field of network evolution research.

2.1 What Do We Know About Real-World Network Topologies?

One of the very first formal network conceptualizations is the random-graph model, originally proposed by Solomonoff and Rapoport (1951) and applied in the field of mathematical biophysics. Only a few years later a seminal paper on the evolution of random graphs was published by Erdős and Rényi (1960). These types of models assume that links are placed on a purely random basis which means that the resulting system is characterized by nodes that have approximately the same number of links (Barabasi and Bonabeau 2003, p. 52). Random-graph models have dominated the debate in network research since the mid-twentieth century, even though the large-scale network topologies produced by these models are far from network structures observable in real-world.

Empirical explorations show—for nearly all kinds of real-world networks, ranging from technical to socio-economic networks—that links are not homogenously distributed across nodes. More precisely, real-world networks are typically characterized by a strongly skewed degree distribution. This implies that some actors obviously attract ties at a higher rate than others. This recognition led to the development of a new generation of network models which were able to reproduce real-world network topologies in a more realistic way. In a seminal paper on large-scale network properties Barabasi and Albert (1999) suggest a "preferential attachment" based network model that self-organizes into a scale-free state. The underlying logic of the applied preferential attachment mechanism is straightforward: highly connected nodes are more likely to connect to new nodes than sparsely connected nodes (Albert and Barabasi 2002) which is mirrored in the emergence of a typical power law degree distribution at higher aggregation levels.

Only a few years after the development of the Erdős-Rényi random-graph model, psychologist Stanley Milgram conducted his famous "letter-passing experiment" in which he showed that people in the United States are separated by more or less six degrees of separation (Milgram 1967). Surprisingly, it took about 30 years to apply Milgram's initial idea in the field of socio-economic network research. Watts and Strogatz (1998) were the first to show that the small-world phenomenon can be explained and quantified by applying a graph-theoretical approach and using relatively simple network measures. The authors argued that a compression of real-world networks and randomly generated networks should reveal some systematic differences with regard to network clustering and actor reachability. They proposed using two simple graph theoretical indicators—"cluster coefficient" and "average distance"—and calculating two ratios—"clustering coefficient ratio" (CC ratio) and "path length ratio" (PL ratio)—in order to check for the existence of small-world properties in real-world networks. Since then a number of excellent empirical studies have been conducted analyzing the relationship between small-world properties and the creation of novelty and innovation (Uzzi and Spiro 2005; Fleming et al. 2007; Schilling and Phelps 2007) and the emergence and evolution of small-world structures in an innovation network context (Baum et al. 2003; Corrado and Zollo 2006; Mueller et al. 2014).

Finally, we refer to a so-called core-periphery (CP) structure in innovation networks. The CP concept is based on the notion of "[...] a dense, cohesive core and a sparse, loosely connected periphery" (Borgatti and Everett 1999, p. 375). The core of the network occupies a dominant position in contrast to the subordinated network periphery (Muniz et al. 2010, p. 113). Cattani and Ferriani (2008, p. 826) point to the fact that the core is typically composed of "[...] key members of the community, including many who act as network coordinators and have developed dense connections between themselves." The existence of such a CP structure in an innovation network is accompanied by important implications. Accordingly, Rank et al. (2006) argue that a firm embedded in the core of an industry's innovation network has better access to critical information and knowledge. Hence, the occupation of a prominent position by a firm, e.g. in terms of its network core embeddedness, is typically assumed to be positively related to above-average innovation outcomes. However, actors who bridge the gap between a network's core and its periphery also seem to fulfil an important role. Cattani and Ferriani (2008) looked at the relationship between core-periphery structures in social networks and the creative performance of the actors involved by analyzing data from the Hollywood motion picture industry between 1992 and 2003. Their results show that individuals who occupy an intermediate position between the core and the periphery of their social system are in a favorable position to achieve creative results.

2.2 *What Do We Know About the Emergence and Evolution of Real-World Networks?*

The literature on network dynamics is quite heterogeneous[3]. Several scholars have provided schemes to systematize the work that has been done in this field. In accordance with Parkhe et al. (2006), we draw upon a general systematization scheme, originally proposed by Van De Ven and Poole (1995). This enables us to

[3]For an in-depth discussion, see Kudic (2015).

categorize the most influential contributions to network dynamics into three groups: life-cycle model, teleological approaches and evolutionary approaches.

The use of life-cycle analogies is not new to economics and has been employed to capture product exploitation stages (Levitt 1965) as well as change patterns of industries (Klepper 1997) or clusters (Menzel and Fornahl 2009) over time. Life-cycle conceptualizations of network change are based on the notion of "[. . .] linear, irreversible and predictable progressions of events or states over time" (Parkhe et al. 2006, p. 562). The basic idea that underlies most of these models is that one can identify ideal development stages such as initialization, growth, maturity and decline. Thus, some authors often refer to these models as phase models (Schwerk 2000; Sydow 2003). Change is imminent in life-cycle models which indicates that the developing entity has an underlying logic within itself that regulates the process of change (Van De Ven and Poole 1995, p. 515). The change process itself is regarded as a linear sequence of events where all development stages are traversed only once without disruptions or feedback loops (ibid.). Literature often contains examples of life-cycle or phase models that address network change. For instance, Lorenzoni and Ornati (1988) introduce one of the first growth-oriented network formation models by arguing that expanding firms pass through three cooperation stages: unilateral relationships, reciprocal relationships and network constellations. However, these models have often been criticized. Sydow (2003, p. 332) puts forward the argument that the phase specification and the length of the stages in these models may vary arbitrarily. In addition, the notion of a linear change process that does not consider disruptions or feedback loops is—to formulate it in a cautious way—questionable in the least.

According to the teleological school of thought, change in organizational entities is explained by relying on a philosophical doctrine according to which the purpose or goal is the ultimate cause of change (Van De Ven and Poole 1995, p. 515). From this point of view, development is regarded as a "[. . .] repetitive sequence of goal formulation, implementation, evaluation and modification of goals [. . .]" whereas all of these sequences are affected by the experiences and intentions of an adaptive entity (Van De Ven and Poole 1995, p. 516). This means that organizational entities are able to learn at each stage of the repetitive sequence and reformulate their goals. In response to the limitations of the previously discussed lifecycle conceptualizations, scholars have applied this teleological perspective in order to gain more open-ended and iterative process models of alliance and network change in which the final goal guides the underlying change process (De Rond and Bouchiki 2004, p. 57).

Non-linear process models of network change are among the most prominent applications of teleological ideas in network research. This strand of research has been strongly influenced by the contributions of the IMP research group (Hakansson and Johanson 1988; Hakansson and Snehota 1995; Halinen et al. 1999). In these models, network change is driven by market access and internationalization goals. For instance, Halinen et al. (1999) have proposed a dynamic network model that includes radical and incremental change processes at the dyadic and network level. The framework integrates the ideas of mechanisms, nature and forces of change, and contains two interdependent circles of radical and incremental change which are affected by external drivers of change and stability. The strength of teleological conceptualizations lies in their rejection of simplistic, uniform and predictable sequences of change towards more realistic non-linear process models which recognize that unplanned events, unexpected results, as well as conflicting interpretations and interests can and do affect the change process over time (De Rond and Bouchiki 2004, p. 58).

Evolutionary conceptualizations of network change draw our attention to "[...] change and development in terms of recurrent, cumulative, and problematic sequences of variation, selection and retention" (Parkhe et al. 2006, p. 562). Evolutionary approaches seek to understand the forces that cause network change over time (Doreian and Stokman 2005, p. 5) which means that the focus is placed on the underlying determinants and mechanisms of network change processes. In other words, the understanding of "[...] the 'rules' governing the sequence of change through time [...]". Doreian and Stokman (2005, p. 5) provide an in-depth understanding of the network change process itself. These conceptualizations encompass the determinants that trigger the change processes at the micro-level, the mechanisms that generate change, and the structural consequences over multiple aggregation levels. Evolutionary conceptualizations of network change can be grouped into three partially overlapping categories: network emergence, network evolution and co-evolutionary approaches.

The first category—so-called network emergence or network growth approaches—focuses predominantly on determinants and mechanisms affecting alliance formations and associated network change patterns at the overall network level (Walker et al. 1997; Gulati 1995; Gulati and Gargiulo 1999; Hite and Hesterly 2001; Hagedoorn 2006; Kenis and Knoke 2002). These growth-oriented models consider both endogenous as well as exogenous factors of alliance and network change. They recognize the importance of previous network structures in current cooperation decisions (Gulati and Gargiulo 1999). However, these studies place little emphasis on tie termination processes and the associated structural consequences for the overall network configuration.

In response to these limitations, network evolution models explicitly account for both network formation processes as well as network fragmentation processes by simultaneously considering the determinants and mechanisms behind these processes (Venkatraman and Lee 2004; Powell et al. 2005; Amburgey et al. 2008; Doreian and Stokman 2005; Glueckler 2007). The main point of network evolution models is to understand how and why networks emerge, solidify and dissolve over time. For instance, Powell and his colleagues (2005) have analyzed the underlying mechanisms, such as "cumulative advantage", "homophily", "following the trend" and "multiconnectivity", in order to explain the structural evolution of complex networks in the US biotech industry. Others have analyzed the impact of tie formations and tie terminations on the component structure and connectivity of networks (Amburgey et al. 2008). Economic geographers have argued that evolutionary processes of retention and variation in network structure are affected by a spatial dimension (Glueckler 2007). The concept of co-evolution refers to the notion that two or more dimensions change simultaneously and affect each other while they evolve. Co-evolutionary network change models concentrate on simultaneous change processes between networks and other subjects of change, such as industries (Ter Wal and Boschma 2011), technologies (Rosenkopf and Tushman 1998), or even other types of networks between the same actors (Amburgey et al. 2008). The analytical focus lies on understanding the interdependencies between simultaneously evolving network change patterns. Theoretical contributions addressing the multi-faceted nature of innovation network evolution are still very rare (most notable exceptions: Glueckler 2007 and Hite 2008).

2.3 Recent Developments in Network Evolution Research

Two classes of network evolution models seem to have the potential to break new ground, i.e. stochastic and numerical agent-based simulation approaches.

The first class of models is typically referred to as SIENA models. SIENA stands for Simulation Investigation for Empirical Network Analysis (Huisman and Snijders 2003; Snijders 2004; Snijders et al. 2010). These types of simulation models allow us to analyze the mechanisms that fuel the structural change of networks between two or more discrete points in time. Stochastic actor-based models possess several distinctive features, including flexibility and accessibility of procedures to estimate and test the parameters which support the description of mechanisms or tendencies of network change (Snijders et al. 2010, p. 2).

Others have used agent-based simulation models to investigate the origins of variation in the structures of interorganizational networks across industries (Tatarynowicz et al. 2015). This study provides important insights into the relatedness between technological dynamics in six industries from 1983 to 1999 and the firms' collaborative behavior. Another example of agent-based models are simulation models based on the SKIN (Simulating Knowledge Dynamics in Innovation Networks) approach (Gilbert et al. 2001; Gilbert et al. 2007; Pyka et al. 2007). The general idea behind these models is to include firms' knowledge bases, market processes, individual and interorganizational learning processes, and the transfer of knowledge in the analysis of complex networks. These types of agent-based models were recently applied to analyze how the actors' strategies at the micro-level shape macro-level network patterns (Mueller et al. 2014).

3 Towards a Conceptual Framework for Explaining How Networks Change

We start by introducing the general principles of network evolution models. Next, we continue with a discussion on exogenous and endogenous determinants of network change which finally results in the derivation of the superordinate structure of our conceptual framework. Subsequently, we turn our attention to the very core of our model by taking a closer look at four micro-level network change processes. Finally, we incorporate the actors' knowledge-related cooperation strategies in our framework.

3.1 Some General Considerations on Evolutionary Network Change

We start in this section with some general principles of network evolution models proposed by Stockman and Doreian (2005). First, the instrumental character of networks provides the starting point for modeling network evolution. This means that the motives or goals of the actors involved have to be taken into consideration from the very beginning. Innovation research has identified a broad range of reasons for why firms participate in innovation networks (Pyka 2002). However, the exchange of knowledge and initialization of mutual learning processes can be regarded as the most salient for successfully generating novelty.

Secondly, in order to gain an in-depth understanding of the actors' actions and the structural consequences of those actions it is appropriate to assume that a network actor possesses only partial or limited local information. This means that network actors only possess global knowledge in the rarest of cases. Instead, Stockman and Doreian (2005, p. 245) argue that network actors should be seen and modeled as adaptive entities that learn through experience and imitation. This principle is consistent with the neo-Schumpeterian notion of bounded rational agents with incomplete knowledge bases and capabilities (Pyka 2002).

The third principle highlights the importance of the relational dimension of cooperation. This means that the parallel tracking of goals by network actors affects the emergence of ties in a sense that both entities have to agree upon common goals and parallelize decisions. From an innovation network perspective, this principle highlights the importance of integrating concepts that operate primarily on the dyadic level, such as mutual trust or tensions between partners (Lui 2009; Das and Teng 2000).

The fourth basic principle refers to the complexity of evolutionary processes in networks. Neo-Schumpeterian scholars have proposed a broad range of concepts about the complexity of agents, their decisions and their interaction patterns in complex adaptive systems.[4] Consequently, Stockman and Doreian (2005, p. 247) recommend designing network evolution models that are as simple as possible.

The fifth principle refers to the falsifiability of network evolution models. The authors suggest that network evolution models should have sufficient empirical reference and conclude that "statistical models are strongly preferred, as they enable the estimation of essential parameters and test the goodness of fit of the model" (Stokman and Doreian 2005, p. 249).

[4]For an overview of contemporary research in the field of complexity economics, see Antonelli (2011).

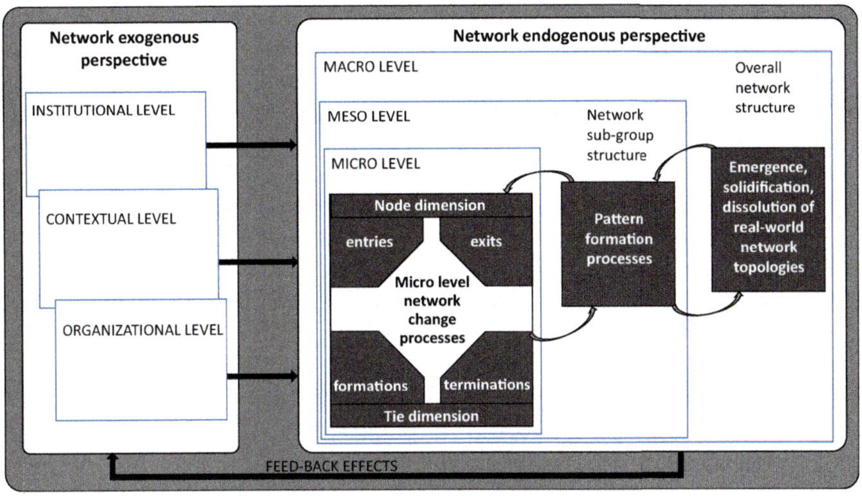

Fig. 1 Causes and consequences of evolutionary network change processes. Source: Authors' own illustration, based on Kudic (2015), modified

3.2 *Exogenous and Endogenous Determinants of Structural Network Change*

Based on the general considerations outlined above, we now introduce the overall structure of our conceptual framework (cf. Fig. 1), which will be specified in more detail in the course of this article. In the most general sense, the framework accounts for the following, closely related aspects of evolutionary network change processes (cf. Kudic 2015): (1) network exogenous determinants, (2) driving forces and mechanisms of network change at the micro level, (3) structural consequences along multiple levels of analysis, and (4) feedback effects, both within the network dimension and across network boundaries.

3.2.1 The Network Exogenous Perspective

Even though this article focuses on the network endogenous perspective (Fig. 1, right), we would like to take the opportunity to briefly outline and discuss the role of network exogenous factors. It is important to note that the institutional, contextual and organizational levels addressed here are not mutually exclusive.

To start with, we turn our attention to the role of institutions in explaining structural network change. It is common knowledge that institutions play a role in socio-economic processes.[5] Formal institutions (e.g. laws, rules, norms etc.) and

[5]For an in-depth discussion on the role of generic rules for economic evolution, see Dopfer and Potts (2008).

informal institutions (e.g. values or habits etc.) affect the extent and way in which organizations interact. In an innovation network context, institutions take on the role of enabling mechanisms that stabilize the environment in which knowledge transfer and interactive learning processes take place. On the other hand, institutions can also hinder or prevent organizations from cooperating with one another. Between these two extremes, there is a range of ways that cooperation among organizations can be orchestrated and can force cooperation into a desired direction through the setting of institutions. Funding initiatives, initialized by regional, national or supranational authorities aimed at promoting collective innovation though publicly funded cooperation, are only one example of how institutions affect the formation, structural configuration and stability as well as scientific productivity of R&D project consortia (Defazio et al. 2009). In summary, rules, norms, and institutions, are very likely to play an important role for explaining and understanding structuration processes in complex dynamic system. Yet they are barely considered in the network evolution literature. Over the past decades, institutional economists have developed a rich theoretical toolbox that has the potential to significantly contribute to an in-depth understanding of structural network change (Hodgson 2012; Elsner 2017).

Next, we move on to the contextual level. Innovation networks can be seen as an integral part of their surrounding innovation systems. According to Lundvall (1992), national innovation systems consist of elements and relationships between them which enable interaction in the production, diffusion and use of new, and economically useful, knowledge. The structural characteristics of innovation systems—such as the actors, types of relationships, system boundaries and the broader environments in which the system is embedded—affect the interactions of actors and subsequent innovation outcomes (Carlsson et al. 2002). Closely related to this strand of literature is the industry life-cycle perspective (Utterback and Abernathy 1975). Early studies show that some industries may be seen as evolving through this cycle several times. Studies in this tradition have significantly enhanced our understanding of how industries change over time (Jovanovic and McDonald 1994; Klepper 1997). Some researchers in this area (Buenstorf and Klepper 2010) have emphasized the importance of submarket dynamics in industries. Their findings suggest that the development of a new submarket can open up opportunities for new firm entries and stimulate innovation at the same time. They show that this situation can reinforce the advantages of the leading established firms, accentuating the shakeout of producers. Industry dynamics have some important implications for the entry and exit processes in innovation networks. An increasing number of firm entries due to new company founding, spin-offs etc. enhance the number of potentially new cooperation partners which are not yet part of the innovation network. Firm exits due to closures, failures, bankruptcies etc. can decrease the number of potential cooperation partners or disrupt an existing network structure.

Finally, we move on to the organizational determinants in our framework. In this context, organizations are considered to be the nodes (or potential nodes) of the network we look at. As we will establish in more detail later, firm characteristics such as size, age, origin, knowledge stock and cooperation capabilities etc. are likely to affect knowledge-related cooperation behavior in an innovation network context.

3.2.2 The Network Endogenous Perspective

The network endogenous perspective (Fig. 1, right) is conceptualized by differentiating between three analytical levels. The distinction between multiple analytical levels is not new in evolutionary economics (cf. Dopfer and Potts 2008). However, we apply this general idea in a network context.

Accordingly, we argue that the macro level refers to the overall network perspective. Empirical evidence on real-world innovation network topologies is now available for a range of technological fields and industries. The discussion in Sect. 2.1 shows that innovation networks are not randomly structured but rather characterized by typical patterns such as fat-tailed degree distributions, small-world properties, core-periphery patterns etc. It is important to note that these structural particularities of the innovation network do not exist from the very beginning but rather emerge and solidify throughout the network evolution process.

The meso level addresses sub-group structures which are an integral part of the overall network. These sub-groups are part of the surrounding innovation network; however, they follow a different logic than simple dyadic linkages. For instance, ego networks are centered around a focal actor.[6] The ego network constitutes a structural entity in itself which is, at the same time, an integral part of the overall network structure. These types of network sub-structures are strongly influenced by the strategy of a focal actor (Hite and Hesterly 2001) and each tie formation or tie terminations is evaluated against the backdrop of the existing portfolio structure. Complementarity and synergy considerations typically play a key role in this context (Hoffmann 2007). Other types of sub-structures within networks can be the result of, or at least strongly affected by, informal or formal institutions such as publicly funded R&D project consortia. Accordingly, the size, configuration, duration etc. of new components entering an industry's innovation network can be the result of formal rules set by the funding authority (Schwartz et al. 2012). The bottom line is that even though the formation or existence of each sub-structure in an innovation network can be traced back to basic micro-level network change processes (cf. next paragraph), the consideration of additional formation logics can be required to gain an in-depth understanding of structuration processes in these complex dynamic systems.

Now we turn our attention to the micro level in our framework. The evolution of networks is typically explained by referring to a number of frequently discussed network change mechanisms. These mechanisms are typically assumed to operate on the micro level. For instance, the preferential attachment concept provides one

[6]A firm's ego network consists of its set of direct, dyadic ties and the relationships between these ties (Hite and Hesterly 2001; Wasserman and Faust 1994).

of the most frequently discussed tie formation mechanisms in network studies. The underlying logic is quite simple: highly connected nodes are more likely to attract new nodes at a higher rate than sparsely connected nodes (Barabasi and Albert 1999; Albert and Barabasi 2002). The mechanism generates a relatively unique structural pattern at the overall network level which is characterized by a power law degree distribution. Several other mechanisms and the underlying logic of network formation processes have been discussed in the literature. These include "homophily" according to which actors with similarities are more likely to connect to one another (McPherson et al. 2001), "herding behavior" where actors follow the crowd (Kirman 1993; Powell et al. 2005) and "transitive closure" where two nodes, which are both connected to a third partner, attract one another (Snijders et al. 2010). Even though these mechanistic concepts provide us with some valuable insights, we argue that we need to take a closer look at node entries and exits as well as tie formations and terminations to gain an in-depth understanding of the structural evolution of innovation networks.

3.3 Micro-Level Network Change Processes at the Core of the Model: Node Entries and Exits as Well as Tie Formations and Terminations

Accordingly, we continue the debate by moving on to micro level network change processes at the core of the model (cf. Fig. 1, center). Only a few previous studies have analyzed the structural consequences of micro-level network change processes (Elfring and Hulsink 2007; Baum et al. 2003; Guimera et al. 2005; Amburgey et al. 2008). We follow Glueckler (2007, p. 623) who argues that "[. . .] a complete theory of network evolution [. . .] has to theorize both the emergence and disappearance of ties and nodes". Accordingly, both dimensions will be considered in this section. In accordance with Hite (2008), we explicitly acknowledge the particular importance of micro-level network change processes in the context of network evolution. In doing so, we draw upon evolutionary ideas and network change models proposed by Guimera et al. (2005) and Amburgey et al. (2008) to substantiate this part of the puzzle in our framework (cf. Fig. 2).

We start our argumentation by focusing on the node dimension and the concept provided by Guimera et al. (2005). In the most basic sense we can differentiate between system actors who participate (i.e. incumbents) and those who do not participate (i.e. newcomer) in a particular network (Fig. 2, top). The first group includes all actively cooperating network actors, whereas the second group provides a pool of potentially available network actors. The link to the contextual level in our framework (Fig. 1, left) is obvious. The innovation system approach entails all firms within well-specified system boundaries, irrespective of whether these firms are actively involved in the respective innovation network or not. We follow the suggestion made by Guimera et al. (2005) and differentiate between two groups

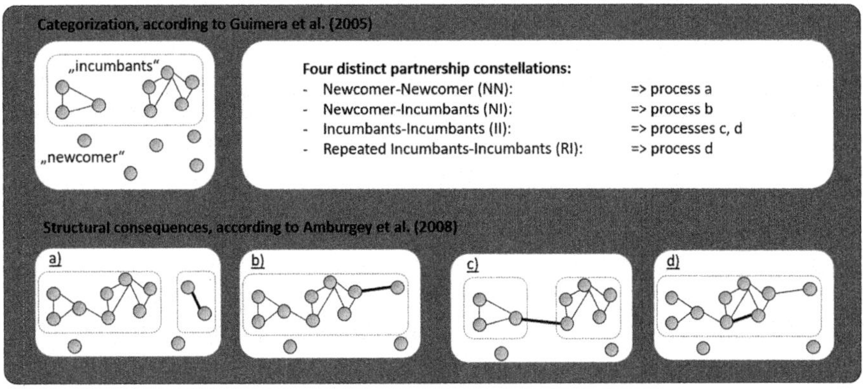

Fig. 2 Categorization and structural consequences of micro-level network change processes. Source: Authors' own illustration, based on Guimera et al. (2005) and Amburgey et al. (2008), modified

of potential network actors: "incumbents" and "newcomers" (Fig. 2, top). Both groups are subject to change due to dynamics at the industry level. Entries and exits affecting actors within the first group (i.e. active network actors) have direct consequences for the structural configuration of the network, whereas the same events affecting actors in the second group (i.e. potential network actors) have an indirect impact by enlarging or reducing the pool of cooperation partners that are potentially available. The distinction between "incumbents" and "newcomers" gives us four distinct partnership constellations: "newcomer-newcomer" (NN), "incumbent-newcomer" (IN), "incumbent-incumbent" (II) and "repeated incumbent-incumbent" (RI). Finally, it is important to note that the distinction between newcomers and incumbents—and all possible combinations, i.e. NN, NI, II and RI—implicitly acknowledges cooperation histories of the actors involved and the network paths traversed by these actors.

These four partnership constellations can be translated into structural consequences. To establish this link, we refer to the model proposed by Amburgey et al. (2008). The authors provide a conclusive theoretical explanation for structural consequences of tie formations and tie terminations by introducing four distinct structural processes (Amburgey et al. 2008, pp. 184–186): (a) the creation of a new component, (b) the creation of a pendant tie to an existing component, (c) the creation of a bridge between components, and (d) the creation of an additional intra-component tie (Fig. 2, bottom). Each of these processes shapes the size and/or the density of the network. Figure 2 also illustrates the relatedness of the two concepts. For instance, the constellation "newcomer-newcomer" (NN) is closely related to the creation of a new component in the network. Similarly, we can link the three remaining partnership constellations (IN, II, RI) to the structural processes (b, c, d).

Even though the consideration of this two concepts brings us closer to understanding the structural evolution of networks, a number of additional aspects needs to be account for. First, up to now the discussion on micro level network change processes has operated on a highly abstract level and the specific nature of innovation networks has yet to be considered adequately. Second, the knowledge endowment and the strategic orientation of the actors involved play no role in evolutionary network change processes. Finally, the structural implications that can be derived from the discussion so far are still too coarse-grained. For instance, the NN partnership constellation is very close to the notion of component-creating ties. However, no clear-cut differentiation can be made between the circumstances under which large or small components are established, enter the network and change their structural configuration (Fig. 2, process a). The NI partnership constellation and the formation of a pendent tie (Fig. 2, process b) contains no information about who the newcomer connects itself to—the most central network actor or a peripheral network actor. Similarly, the II partnership constellation, according to Guimera et al. (2005), can be related to both the establishment of a bridging tie (Fig. 2, process c) or to an intra-component tie (Fig. 2, process d) according to Amburgey et al. (2008).

All in all, it becomes obvious that a structural discussion is indispensable but reaches its limits sooner or later. We address this limitation by focusing on the actors' knowledge endowments and integrating a set of knowledge-related cooperation strategies into our framework. This shift from a purely structural discussion towards a content-driven elaboration allows us to gain a more differentiated picture and disentangle and refine our framework. In general, strategies and actions of network actors can result in the destruction of existing network paths (Glueckler 2007, p. 620) and determine, at the same time, the scope of future cooperation options and possibilities. Hence, we propose a classification of knowledge-related cooperation strategies along two dimensions (cf. Fig. 3) which allows us to integrate actors-specific R&D cooperation decisions in our framework. The first dimension is input-oriented and the second dimension is output-oriented.

To start with, we take a closer look at the input-oriented dimension. Organizations follow individual cooperation strategies that are guided by their individual goals and motives. Hagedoorn (1993, 2006) divides the broad variety of heterogonous and partially overlapping cooperation rationales into six groups: cost savings, risk reduction, time savings, access to national and international markets, status and reputation building, and knowledge-related motives. In R&D cooperation and innovation networks the latter category plays a particularly superordinate role. The reason for this is straightforward. Dosi (1988, p. 1126) argues that problem solving during the technological innovation processes involves the use of information drawn from previous experience, formal knowledge and various types of specific and uncodified capabilities. Knowledge and expertise which cannot be internally generated within the boundaries of a firm can be tapped via external channels (Malerba 1992).

When it comes to knowledge-related cooperation strategies, at least two qualitatively different types of exchange processes have to be distinguished (Grant and Baden-Fuller 2004; Buckley et al. 2009): the "knowledge accessing approach" and the "knowledge acquiring approach". At the very heart of the knowledge acquiring approach is the idea that firms cooperate to learn from one another and exchange non-codifiable (or "implicit") knowledge through multiple interactions. According

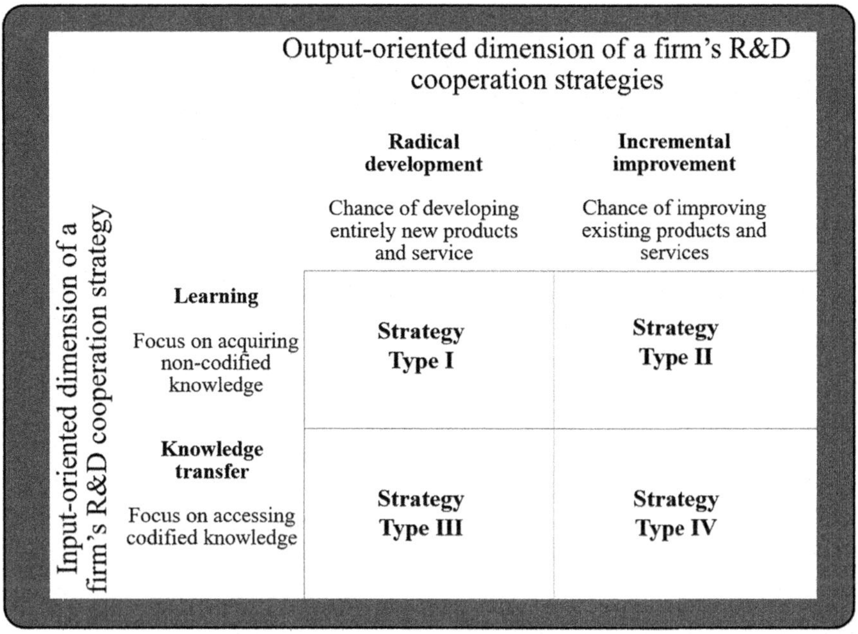

Fig. 3 Knowledge-oriented dimensions of R&D cooperation strategies. Source: Authors' own illustration

to Grant and Baden-Fuller (2004, p. 78) a knowledge acquiring strategy implies a limit to the number of cooperative partnerships a firm can pursue simultaneously due its constrained absorptive capacity. In addition, small teams of actors, interconnected by strong ties, provide the ideal basis for the generation of trust, a necessary prerequisite for the exchange of non-codifiable knowledge and the initialization of mutual learning processes. Prior research indicates that trust increases the amount of information that can be exchanged (Tsai and Ghoshal 1998) and decreases the cost of exchange (Zaheer et al. 1998). In contrast, proponents of the "knowledge accessing" perspective argue that R&D cooperation predominantly serves as a vehicle for accessing complementary stocks of codifiable (or "explicit") knowledge. The connectedness to as many partners as possible is important to get potential access to a broad variety on knowledge stocks. The knowledge accessing approach implies that a firm can engage in multiple alliances simultaneously without sharply declining marginal benefits (Grant and Baden-Fuller 2004, p. 78). Hence, large teams, interconnected by weak ties, provide the ideal basis for transferring tacit knowledge.

Our second dimension focuses on the output dimension of collective innovation processes. The main rational for firms to join forces, collaborate, exchange knowledge, and learn from each other is to generate novelty in terms of innovative products and services. We differentiate between incremental and radical innovations, even though this distinction is no always clear (Henderson and Clark 1990). On the one hand, technological change processes can be incremental in nature and innovation occurs rather gradually as a stepwise improvement process (cf. Levinthal 1998, p. 217). Thus, incremental innovations typically introduce minor changes to existing products and services, exploits existing potentials, and reinforces the dominance of established market actors (Henderson and Clark 1990, p. 9). On the other hand, innovations can also appear as spontaneous and rather discontinuous events (Levinthal 1998, p. 217). Radical innovation typically establishes a new dominant design and opens up entirely new market and new fields of application (Henderson and Clark 1990, pp. 9–11). We adopt and integrate this fundamental distinction between incremental and radical innovation in our framework by arguing that every kind of collective R&D process falls within one of these two output-oriented categories.

The combination of the input-oriented and output-oriented dimension leads to four distinct types of strategic R&D cooperation strategy. On the one extreme, we find actors who follow a Type I R&D cooperation strategy. In this case we assume that actors focus on acquiring new knowledge through the initialization of interorganizational learning processes (Hamel 1991; Lane and Lubatkin 1998; Kale et al. 2000) in order to have a realistic chance of developing entirely new products and services. On the other extreme, the Type IV R&D cooperation strategy constitutes cooperation efforts in which actors focus on knowledge transfer (Grant and Baden-Fuller 2004; Rothaermel 2001; Buckley et al. 2009) with the aim of achieving incremental improvements in existing goods and services. According to Grant and Baden-Fuller (2004) we assume that an organization acquires and accesses knowledge from a partner to extend its own knowledge base. However, the generation of novelty is a highly uncertain and risky endeavor (Henderson and Clark 1990) and interorganizational learning processes can be affected and hindered due to various reasons (Doz 1996). Hence, the Type II R&D cooperation strategy accounts for the fact that the desired outcome of the Type I R&D cooperation strategy cannot always be realized. As already outlined above, innovations can also occur as spontaneous events. The Type III R&D strategy reflects the case in which knowledge transfer processes lead to radical innovation. The important point in this context is that each of the four strategic options is accompanied by individual partner choices. As we will discuss later in more detail, not all strategic options are available to all actors over time. The respective consequences for the structural configuration of the industry's innovation network will be the subject of the discussion in Sect. 4.

4 Structural Consequences of Micro-Level Network Change Processes: An Exemplifying Discussion

In this section we bring together the preceding considerations by proposing a scheme that integrates partnership constellations, actors' strategic orientations, and structural network consequences. Based on our consideration in Sect. 3.3

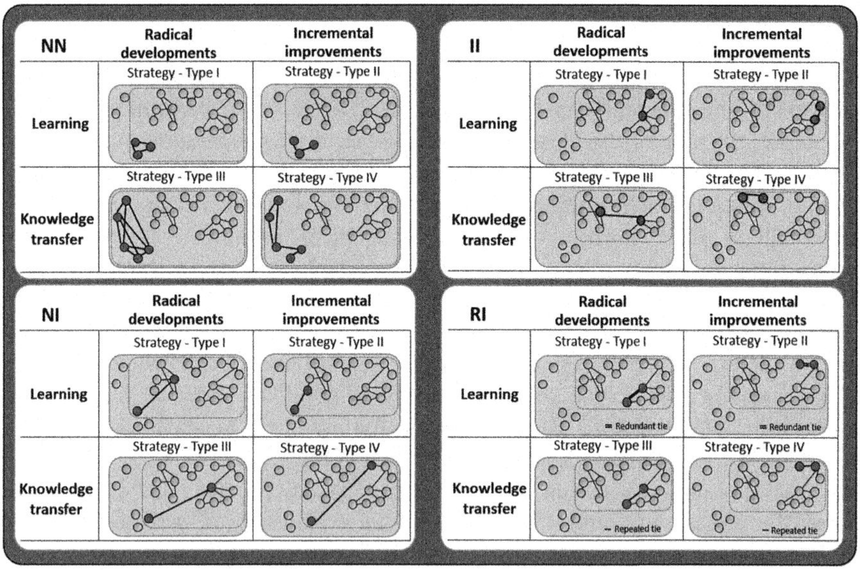

Fig. 4 Interrelatedness between partnership constellations, actors' strategic orientations and structural consequences. Source: Authors' own illustration

we have integrated the general distinction between newcomers (N) and incumbents (I) in the subsequent discussion. Figure 4 illustrates theoretically possible structural consequences resulting from actor-specific strategic orientations (i.e. Type I–Type IV) for each of the previously introduced partnership constellations (NN, NI, II, RI).

Figure 4 (top, left) points to the structural effects of cooperation events between newcomers (NN). These partnership constellations are typically reflected in the formation and entry of new network components into the system. Accordingly, the size of the network increases while changes to the network's density depend on the degree of connectedness within the new component. We argue that the formation of small components is closely related to an actors' strategic orientation towards learning. The rationale behind this assumption is straightforward. Small components can be interpreted as structural vehicles—or learning arenas—that provide the basis for intense interactions, initialization of trust building and interorganizational learning processes. In contrast, the formation of larger components is assumed to be accompanied by the knowledge exchange goals of the actors involved. Actors entering the network via the formation of large components rather aim at getting fast access to a broadly dispersed and easy absorbable knowledge stocks. A glance at the output-oriented dimension provides another important distinction. We argue that actors in densely connected components have a higher chance of realizing more radical innovations while the actors in sparsely connected components tend to generate relatively incremental innovations.

The partnership constellation reflecting cooperation activities between newcomers and incumbents (NI) is displayed in Fig. 4 (bottom, left). Each of the four actor-specific strategic orientations (i.e. Type I–Type IV) results in the attachment of a previously unconnected actor to the existing innovation network. As before, the size of the network increases due to NI cooperation events while the density of the system is not affected. The illustration shows that potential network entrants (newcomers) with a learning-oriented R&D cooperation strategy prefer to attach themselves to small components within the system. Actors oriented towards knowledge transfer aim to establish a link to larger components. The theoretical arguments behind these two attachment logics are the same as outlined above. Irrespective of a network component's size, we are able to identify more or less central actors. For instance, actors with an above average number of direct partners occupy a dominant role in their nearer cooperation environment. They are typically assumed to have qualitatively superior knowledge endowment compared to less integrated actors. Accordingly, we argue that the chances for developing entirely new products and services are higher for those newcomers who succeed in establishing a link to the most central actors in the respective component. In contrast, links between newcomers and peripheral incumbents are expected to be accompanied by rather incremental improvements.

Now we turn our attention to partner constellations displayed in Fig. 4 (top, right), a constellation in which incumbents establish links to other incumbents (II). First of all, it is important to note that an incumbent's cooperation environment strongly depends on its previous cooperation decisions. It also determines all future cooperation opportunities. In other words, an incumbent's network position is the result of previous cooperation events and reflects the path on which the respective actor has traversed through the network. As before, we distinguish between cooperation strategies that are oriented towards learning and those oriented towards knowledge transfer. In the first case, incumbents are expected to increase the density of their nearby cooperation environment through the establishment of intra-component ties. In the second case, incumbents seek to enlarge their nearby cooperation environment by acting as brokers and connecting otherwise unconnected (or loosely connected) components of the network.

Figure 4 (top, right) illustrates a learning-oriented R&D cooperation strategy between two incumbents which are located in the main component of the network. Again, the chances for realizing radical innovation are not equally distributed. We argue that learning-oriented incumbents who achieve an intra-component tie to the most central actor in the respective component have a higher chance of developing entirely new products or services. In contrast, incumbents following a learning-oriented strategy by establishing an intra-component tie to a peripheral incumbent in the same component are likely to generate incremental innovations. Now we turn attention to knowledge transfer oriented R&D cooperation strategy between two incumbents located in different network components. It is plausible to assume that two incumbents, which are not part of the same component, can maximize their potential information pool by acting as brokers. In this case, the chances of achieving a radical innovation are higher for those brokers who connect large components. In contrast, bridging the gap between two small components is accompanied by incremental improvements for the broker.

The last partnership constellation addresses repeated links between incumbents (RI). There are two qualitatively different types of repeated links which have to be differentiated. On the one hand, we can think of cooperation event sequences between two incumbents. In this case the termination of an existing link is directly followed by the establishment of a new, cooperative partnership between the same actors. Cooperation event sequences among the same partners ensure intertemporal structural stability of the system by simply reproducing existing network patterns. We argue that an incumbent's efforts to maintain its cooperation environment through sequential link formations is closely related to a knowledge-transfer oriented R&D cooperation strategy. On the other hand, there is the possibility that two incumbents establish more than one linkage. Technically speaking, in this case we have a redundant link structure. We argue that an incumbent's efforts to strengthen its nearer cooperation environment through redundant link formations is closely related to trust building and goes along with a learning-oriented R&D cooperation strategy. Similar like above, attachment processes among more or less central actors affect the chances of realizing radical innovations or rather increment improvements.

5 Conclusion, Limitations and Further Research

We intended to develop a theoretical framework that explains how micro-level activities of cooperation impact the overall structure of innovation networks. This is a subject with a clearly evolutionary nature. We refer to existing theoretical literature on network formation processes in order to differentiate between two types of actors (newcomers and incumbents) and derive a set of knowledge-related R&D cooperation strategies (differentiated by an input and output dimension) for these actors. At the very heart of this contribution we integrated elementary network change processes at the micro level and discussed the role of actors' knowledge endowments and strategic orientations for the emergence of characteristic network patterns. We ended up with a fine-grained systematization of structural network effects, each of which grounded in knowledge-related R&D cooperation decisions of actors at the micro level.

We do not claim that our theoretical concept is fully comprehensive or complete. Nonetheless, we strongly believe that a closer look at different types of knowledge-related R&D cooperation strategies significantly enhances our understanding of how and why structural large-scale networks patterns emerge and evolve over time. The distinction between newcomers and incumbents—and all possible combinations, i.e. NN, NI, II and RI—raises awareness for the importance of cooperation histories and network paths. We are convinced that the analysis of R&D cooperation cascades, against the backdrop of previous cooperation decisions and new cooperation options, is crucial for understanding structural network change. Our discussion revealed some highly interesting insights into the emergence of real-world network properties. First, our framework implies that the structuration processes at higher aggregation levels are not the result of individual actors' cooperation activities. Instead, the complex interplay of cooperation activities and structural consequences of multiple actors, operating at different stages of their individual cooperation paths, generate patterns that we typically refer to as real-world network properties. Second, we saw that structurally identical pattern formation processes at higher aggregation levels can be caused by completely different micro-level network change processes. Our framework raises awareness for this fact and provides a scheme that allows researchers to deepen and extend own knowledge on network evolution along these lines. Third, our theoretically motivated research raises awareness for the importance of policy interventions affecting the formation of sub-group structures at the meso level (cf. Fig. 1). Public support of collaborative innovation projects still ranks high in innovation policy agendas at different levels (local, regional, national and supranational). We should keep in mind that any public support means an intervention into otherwise "naturally" developing network structures. So far we know little about the interplay between different types of public support schemes and micro-level network change processes. This offers not only a great opportunity for further research but also for the intensification of the dialog between science and policy.

This study also has some limitations. For instance, we focus on economic actors, i.e. organizations as the smallest unit of analysis within the meaning of innovation system literature. R&D cooperation strategies, however, are always the result of decision processes at the individual or interpersonal level. Another issue is closely related to complex nature of networks. The exercise presented in Sects. 3 and 4 certainly provides some plausible explanations for pattern formation processes, but by far not all. We are well aware that the proposed and discussed interrelations between micro level network change processes, actors' knowledge endowments and strategic orientations, and structural network change processes provide at best one of several possible explanations.

In summary, the implications derived from our framework condense the complexity of possible structural consequences at the overall network level. They call for empirical tests and might be useful for conceptualizing data collection in further research projects. Some very initial steps in this direction have already been undertaken by using non-parametric (Kudic et al. 2015b) and parametric (Kudic et al. 2016) event history estimation techniques for analyzing network entry processes in the German laser industry. Beyond that, we believe there is high potential for applying agent-based simulation techniques in this context since these analytical tools allow the complex nature of network evolution and structuration processes to be dealt with—at least to some extent (cf. Mueller et al. 2014). Further refinements and empirical tests of the implications raised so far constitute the next steps in our research agenda.

References

Albert R, Barabasi A-L (2002) Statistical mechanics of complex networks. Rev Mod Phys 74 (1):47–97

Amburgey TL, Al-Laham A, Tzabbar D, Aharonson BS (2008) The structural evolution of multiplex organizational networks: research and commerce in biotechnology. In J. A. Baum, & T. J. Rowley, Advances in strategic management - network strategy, Vol 25. Emerald Publishing, Bingley, UK, pp 171–212

Antonelli C (2011) Handbook on the economic complexity of technological change. Edward Elgar, Cheltenham

Barabasi A-L, Albert R (1999) Emergence of scaling in random networks. Science 286 (15):509–512

Barabasi A-L, Bonabeau E (2003) Scale-free networks. Sci Am 288(5):50–59

Baum JAC, Calabrese T, Silverman BS (2000) Don't go it alone: alliance network composition and start ups's performance in Canadian biotechnology. Strateg Manage J 21(3):267–294

Baum JA, Shipilov AW, Rowley TJ (2003) Where do small worlds come from? Ind Corp Change 12(4):697–725

Bergenholtz C, Waldstrom C (2011) Inter-organizational network studies - a literature review. Ind Innov 18(6):539–562

Borgatti SP, Everett MG (1999) Models of core/periphery structures. Social Netw 21(4):375–395

Brenner T, Cantner U, Graf H (2011) Innovation networks: measurement, performance and regional dimensions. Ind Innov 18(1):1–5

Buckley PJ, Glaister KW, Klijn E, Tan H (2009) Knowledge accession and knowledge acquisition in strategic alliances: the impact of supplementary and complementary dimensions. Br J Manage 20(4):598–609

Buenstorf G, Klepper S (2010) Submarket dynamics and innovation: the case of the US tire industry. Ind Corp Change 19(5):1563–1587

Carlsson B, Jacobsson S, Holmen M, Rickne A (2002) Innovation systems: analytical and methodological issues. Res Policy 31(2):233–245

Cattani G, Ferriani S (2008) A core/periphery perspective on individual creative performance: social networks and cinematic achievements in the Hollywood film industry. Org Sci 19 (6):824–844

Corrado R, Zollo M (2006) Small worlds evolving: governance reforms, privatizations, and ownership networks in Italy. Ind Corp Change 15(2):319–352

Das TK, Teng B-S (2000) Instabilities of strategic alliances: an internal tensions perspective. Org Sci 11(1):77–101

Defazio D, Lockett A, Wright M (2009) Funding incentives, collaborative dynamics and scientific productivity: evidence from the EU framework program. Res Policy 38(2):293–305

De Rond M, Bouchiki H (2004) On the dialectics of strategic alliances. Org Sci 15(1):56–69

Dopfer K, Potts J (2008) The general theory of economic evolution. Routledge, London

Doreian P, Stokman FN (2005) The dynamics and evolution of social networks. In Doreian P, Stokman FN (eds) Evolution of social networks, 2nd edn. Gordon and Breach, New York, pp 1–17

Dosi G (1988) Sources, procedures, and microeconomic effects of innovation. J Econ Lit 26 (3):1120–1171

Doz YL (1996) The evolution of cooperation in strategic alliances: initial conditions or learning processes? Strateg Manage J 17(1):55–83

Elfring T, Hulsink W (2007) Networking by entrepreneurs: patterns of tie formation in emerging organizations. Org Stud 28(12):1849–1872

Elsner W (2017) Social economics and evolutionary institutionalism today. Theoretical components and heterodox convergence in a socio-economic perspective. Forum Soc Econ 46 (1):52–77

Erdős P, Rényi A (1960) On the evolution of random graphs. Publ Math Inst Hung Acad Sci 5:17–61
Fleming L, King C, Juda AI (2007) Small worlds and regional innovation. Org Sci 18(6):938–954
Gilbert N, Ahrweiler P, Pyka A (2007) Learning in innovation networks: some simulation experiments. Phys A Stat Mech Appl 378(1):100–109
Gilbert N, Pyka A, Ahrweiler P (2001) Innovation networks - a simulation approach. J Artif Soc Soc Simul 4(3):1–13
Glueckler J (2007) Economic geography and the evolution of networks. J Econ Geogr 7 (5):619–634
Grant RM, Baden-Fuller C (2004) A knowledge accessing theory of strategic alliances. J Manage Stud 41(1):61–84
Guimera R, Uzzi B, Spiro J, Armaral LA (2005) Team assembly mechanisms determine collaboration network structure and team performance. Science 308(29):697–702
Gulati R (1995) Social structure and alliance formation pattern: a longitudinal analysis. Admin Sci Q 40(4):619–652
Gulati R, Gargiulo M (1999) Where do interorganizational networks come from? Am J Sociol 104 (5):1439–1493
Hagedoorn J (1993) Understanding the rational of strategic technology partnering - organizational modes of cooperation and sectoral differences. Strateg Manage J 14(5):371–385
Hagedoorn J (2006) Understanding the cross-level embeddedness of interfirm partnership formation. Acad Manage Rev 31(3):670–680
Hakansson H, Johanson J (1988) Formal and informal cooperation - strategies in international industrial networks. In: Contractor FJ, Lorange P (eds) Cooperative strategies in international business. Lexington Books, Lexington MA, pp 369–379
Hakansson H, Snehota I (1995) Stability and change in business networks. In: Hakansson H, Snetota I (eds) Developing relationships in business networks. Thomson, London, pp 24–49
Halinen A, Salmi A, Havila V (1999) From dyadic change to changing business networks: an analytical framework. J Manage Stud 36(6):779–794
Hamel G (1991) Competition for competence and interpartner learning within international strategic alliance. Strateg Manage J 12:83–103
Henderson RM, Clark KB (1990) Architectural innovation: the reconfiguration of existing product technologies and the failure of established firms. Admin Sci Q 35:9–30
Hite JM (2008) The role of dyadic multi-dimensionality in the evolution of strategic network ties. In: Baum JA, Rowley TJ (eds) Advances in strategic management - network strategy, Vol 25. Emerald Publishing, Bingley, UK, pp 133–170
Hite JM, Hesterly WS (2001) The evolution of firm networks: from emergence to early growth of the firm. Strateg Manage J 22(3):275–286
Hodgson GM (2012) From pleasure machines to moral communities. an evolutionary economics without Homo economicus. University of Chicago Press, Chicago, IL
Hoffmann WH (2007) Strategies for managing alliance portfolios. Strateg Manage J 28:827–856
Huisman M, Snijders TA (2003) Statistical analysis of longitudinal network data with changing composition. Sociol Methods Res 32:253–287
Jovanovic B, McDonald G (1994) The life cycle of a competitive industry. J Polit Econ 102:322–347
Kale P, Singh H, Perlmutter H (2000) Learning and protection of proprietary assets in strategic alliances: building relational capital. Strateg Manage J 21(3):217–237
Kenis P, Knoke D (2002) How organizational field networks shape interorganizational tie-formation rates. Acad Manage Rev 27(2):275–293
Kirman A (1993) Ants, rationality, and recruitment. Q J Econ 108(1):137–156
Klepper S (1997) Industry life cycles. Ind Corp Change 6(1):145–181
Kudic M (2015) Innovation networks in the German laser industry – evolutionary change, strategic positioning and firm innovativeness. Springer, Berlin

Kudic M, Ehrenfeld W, Pusch T (2015a) On the trail of core-periphery patterns in innovation networks - measurement and new empirical findings from the German laser industry. Ann Reg Sci 55(1):187–220

Kudic M, Pyka A, Guenther J (2015b) Taking the first step - what determines German laser source manufacturers' entry into innovation networks? Int J Innov Manage (19)5. doi:https://doi.org/10.1142/S1363919615500504

Kudic M, Pyka A, Sunder M (2016) R&D cooperation in the German laser industry - an event history perspective. Ind Corp Change 25(4):649–670

Lane PJ, Lubatkin MH (1998) Relative absorptive capacity and interorganizational learning. Strateg Manage J 19(5):461–477

Levinthal DA (1998) The slow pace of rapit technological change: gradualism and punctuation in technological change. Ind Corp Change 7(2):217–247

Levitt T (1965) Exploit the product life cycle. Harvard Bus Rev 43(6):81–94

Lorenzoni G, Ornati OA (1988) Constellations of firms and new ventures. J Bus Ventur 3(1):41–57

Lundvall B-A (1992) National systems of innovation - towards a theory of innovation and interactive learning. Pinter, London

Lui SS (2009) Interorganizational learning the roles of competence trust, formal contract, and time horizon in interorganizational learning. Org Stud 30(4):333–353

Malerba F (1992) Learning by firms and incremental technical change. Econ J 102(413):845–859

McPherson M, Smith-Lovin L, Cook JM (2001) Birds of a feather: homophily in social networks. Annu Rev Sociol 27(1):415–444

Menzel M-P, Fornahl D (2009) Cluster life cycles - dimensions and rationales of cluster evolution. Ind Corp Change 19(1):205–238

Milgram S (1967) The small-world problem. Psychol Today 1(1):60–67

Mueller M, Buchmann T, Kudic M (2014) Micro strategies and macro patterns in the evolution of Innovation networks. In: Gilbert N, Pyka A, Ahrweiler P (eds) Simulating knowledge dynamics in innovation networks. Springer, Berlin, pp 79–95

Muniz AS, Raya AM, Carvajal CR (2010) Core periphery valued models in input-output field: a scope from network theory. Pap Reg Sci 90(1):111–121

Parkhe A, Wasserman S, Ralston DA (2006) New frontiers in network theory development. Acad Manage Rev 31(3):560–568

Pittaway L, Robertson M, Munir K, Denyer D, Neely A (2004) Networking and innovation: a systematic review of the evidence. Int J Manage Rev 5(6):137–168

Powell WW, Koput KW, Smith-Doerr L (1996) Interorganizational collaboration and the locus of innovation - networks of learning in biotechnology. Admin Sci Q 41(1):116–145

Powell WW, White DR, Koput KW, Owen-Smith J (2005) Network dynamics and field evolution: the growth of the interorganizational collaboration in the life sciences. Am J Sociol 110 (4):1132–1205

Pyka A (2002) Innovation networks in economics: from the incentive-based to the knowledge based approaches. Eur J Innov Manage 5(3):152–163

Pyka A, Gilbert N, Ahrweiler P (2007) Simulating knowledge-generation and distribution processes in innovation collaborations and networks. Cybernet Syst 38(7):667–693

Rank C, Rank O, Wald A (2006) Integrated versus core-periphery structures in regional biotechnology networks. Eur Manage J 24(1):73–85

Rothaermel FT (2001) Incumbent's advantage through exploiting complementary assets via interfirm cooperation. Strateg Manage J 22(6):687–699

Rosenkopf L, Tushman ML (1998) The coevolution of community networks and technology: lessons from the flight simulation industry. Ind Corp Change 7(2):311–346

Schilling MA, Phelps CC (2007) Interfirm collaboration networks: the impact of large-scale network structure on firm innovation. Manage Sci 53(7):1113–1126

Schwartz M, Peglow F, Fritsch M, Günther J (2012) What drives innovation output from subsidized R&D cooperation? Project-level evidence from Germany. Technovation 32(6): S.358–S.369

Schwerk A (2000) Dynamik von Unternehmenskooperationen. Duncker & Humbolt, Berlin
Snijders TA (2004) Explained variation in dynamic network models. Math Soc Sci 42(168):5–15
Snijders TA, Van De Bunt GG, Steglich CE (2010) Introduction to actor-based models for network dynamics. Soc Netw 32(1):44–60
Solomonoff R, Rapoport A (1951) Connectivity of random nets. Bull Math Biophys 13:107. https://doi.org/10.1007/BF02478357
Stokman FN, Doreian P (2005) Evolution of social networks: processes and principles. In: Doreian P, Stockman FN (eds) Evolution of social networks, 2nd edn. Gordan Breach, New York, pp 233–251
Stuart TE (2000) Interorganizational alliances and the performance of firms: a study of growth and innovational rates in a high-technology industry. Strateg Manage J 21(8):791–811
Sydow, J. (2003): Dynamik von Netzwerkorganisationen - Entwicklung, Evolution, Strukturation. In Hoffmann WH (ed) Die Gestaltung der Organisationsdynamik - Konfiguration und Evolution. Schäffer-Poeschel, Stuttgart, pp 327–357.
Tatarynowicz A, Sytch M, Gulati R (2015) Environmental demands and the emergence of social structure technological dynamism and interorganizational network forms. Admin Sci Q 61 (1):52–68
Ter Wal AL, Boschma R (2011) Co-evolution of firms, industries and networks in space. Reg Stud 45(7):919–933
Tomasello MV, Napoletano M, Garas A, Schweitzer F (2016) The rise and fall of R&D networks. Ind Corp Change 25(6). https://doi.org/10.1093/icc/dtw041
Tsai W, Ghoshal S (1998) Social capital and value creation: the role of intrafirm networks. Acad Manage J 41(4):464–476
Utterback JM, Abernathy WJ (1975) A dynamic model of process and product innovation. Omega 3(6):639–656
Uzzi B, Spiro J (2005) Collaboration and creativity: the small world problem. Am J Sociol 111 (2):447–504
Van De Ven AH, Poole MS (1995) Explaining development and change in organizations. Acad Manage Rev 20(3):510–540
Venkatraman S, Lee C-H (2004) Preferential linkage and network evolution: a conceptual model and empirical test in the U.S. video game sector. Acad Manage J 47(6):876–892
Walker G, Kogut B, Shan W (1997) Social capital, structural holes and the formation of an industry network. Org Sci 8(2):109–125
Wasserman S, Faust K (1994) Social network analysis: methods and applications. Cambridge University Press, Cambridge
Watts DJ, Strogatz SH (1998) Collective dynamics of 'small-world' networks. Nature 393 (6684):440–442
Zaheer A, McEvily B, Perrone V (1998) Does trust matter? Exploring the effects of interorganizational and interpersonal trust on performance. Org Sci 9(2):141–159

Why Does Sports Equipment Sometimes Become Too Sophisticated and Expensive? A Case Study of the Overshooting Hypothesis in Board Sports

Stuart Thomas and Jason Potts

Abstract This paper investigates innovation overshooting in equipment-based sports, using windsurfing as a case study. Sports, in particular equipment-based, "lifestyle" sports can experience a rapid rise in popularity but eventually technology-driven competition leads to equipment overshooting the capabilities and financial budgets of users. This 'innovation overshoot' leads to a decline in participation and the eventual collapse of the market for the sport's equipment. This progression can have significant adverse consequences for industry and allied sectors of the economy. Models of endogenous overshooting are established in the study of finance and business cycles, and more recently have been extended to the music and design industry. This paper extends this idea to the sports equipment sector where we find clear evidence of technological and market overshooting.

1 Introduction

The purpose of this paper is to better understand how the competitive introduction of new technologies affects the viability of a sport. The hypothesis explored is that overshooting will tend to occur, damaging not only the sport but sectors of the economy that rely on it. This paper uses the equipment-based sport of windsurfing as a case study for this phenomenon.

A sport such as windsurfing, kite-surfing, paddle-boarding or yachting can be economically analysed as an industry made of firms producing equipment, firms supplying the organization, training and competition, and consumers engaged in the sport. A sport has economic benefits, such as employment in manufacture, export, sales and service delivery, and also regional and complementary expenditure multipliers and spillovers associated with the sport's undertaking (clothing,

S. Thomas (✉) • J. Potts
School of Economics, Finance and Marketing, RMIT University, College of Business, 445 Swanston Street, Melbourne 3000, Australia
e-mail: stuart.thomas@rmit.edu.au

A. Pyka, U. Cantner (eds.), *Foundations of Economic Change*, Economic Complexity and Evolution, DOI 10.1007/978-3-319-62009-1_21

media, event tourism and regional branding, among others). Cultural and health benefits also accrue to the success of a sport.

Sports that are significantly dependant on equipment (i.e. most "lifestyle" sports, including board sports) can get caught in technological 'arms races' where oligopolistic competition at the elite high-performance end results in developments that significantly drive up the skill-level and cost of participation (Shah 2000). The unintended consequence of this competition is that it raises the cost of entry into the sport, thus harming, sometimes catastrophically, its long-run viability.

Earl and Potts (2013) , building on Christenson (1997) and Minsky (1982), call this the 'overshooting hypothesis' finding it to be a significant factor explaining the collapse of various genres in the cultural and creative industries where elite artists, competing with each other, overshoot the market tolerance and capabilities of music consumers. The same overshooting is observed in the car industry and in personal computing (Earl and Potts 2014).

The significance of this project is that we are concerned with the sustainability and long-run growth of the technology-driven sports economy, which, in Australia alone, is in the order of A$12 billion (Frontier Economics 2011). We identify technological overshooting as a source of instability and potential collapse in particular sports, and seek to understand that mechanism.

The key idea is that we identify this as an economic mechanism arriving from the unintended consequences of entrepreneurship and innovation-driven technological competition among (as we think of it) duopolists. We seek to understand how this competitive process plays out within and any consequences for the sport itself and associated industries, spillover effects into other sectors (media, tourism, clothing) and social welfare effects (health, community).

This study represents a new approach to sports economics as an application of the study of technology-driven Schumpeterian competition in industry dynamics (i.e. the overshooting model, Earl and Potts 2013). We also develop a new data source built on industry interviews, grey-literature and sports magazines that trace the technological changes, price points, governance concerns, and consumer issues through the trajectory of the industry. The paper is organized as follows: in Sect. 2 I present a review of the literature specific to sports innovation, in Sect. 3 I discuss the method of data capture, in Sect. 4 I present the history and innovation trajectory of the case study sport based on the primary interview and grey literature-based data. Section 5 summarises the case study findings, presents its conclusion and identifies further work required on the project.

2 Literature

Central to the technological innovation literature is the idea that firms, supported by strong intellectual property right regimes, drive product innovation (Schumpeter 1934; Demsetz 1967; Nelson and Winter 1977, 1982). This focus on firms has produced many important theoretical insights into the formative years of industry development, including the economics-influenced "product life cycle view" and the sociological literature on organizational fields and populations. In the product life cycle view, it is technological innovations, often in the form of spillovers, that give rise to new industries: firms enter the emerging industry under conditions of technological and market uncertainty and they experiment with various product designs and features to attract and satisfy customers. The combined effort of these firms leads to subsequent market development. (see, for example, Mueller and Tilton 1969; Abernathy and Utterback 1978; Utterback 1994; Klepper 1997; Agarwal and Bayus 2002). In this view, as in the organisational fields and populations view, the firm is the central actor (Shah 2000).

2.1 Innovation in Sports and the Formation of Sports Equipment Firms

In response to anecdotal evidence from certain sectors of the equipment-driven sports, Shah (2005) argues that existing models that rely solely on firms and research institutions to explain innovation fail to provide insight into the activities of "user-innovators" and the commercial consequences of their activities. Based on an examination of the boardsports industries (windsurfing, snowboarding, and skateboarding), Shah develops a model that illustrates how everyday innovations and social interactions among users can lead to the formation of firms and markets, beginning with "discovery through use." As users of products and services encounter new needs, wants, or use contexts, (e.g. the desire to sail faster, or move from flat water sailing to sailing on waves in surf) they modify existing equipment or a are motivated to seek out new design and/or construction. Some work alone, but many users seek out like-minded individuals with whom to collaborate, forming a *user innovation community,* typically characterized by voluntary participation, free exchange of ideas and innovations and a sense of mutual co-operation. At some point though some of these user-innovators will seek to capitalise on a potential mass market for their invention (or more particularly, the sport or activity that it facilitates) by creating firms to produce and market their goods. Shah finds that the majority of key equipment innovations made prior to the growth of the mass market are made by users and user-manufacturers. An increase in innovative activity by manufacturers occurs only after the mass market begins to grow rapidly and commercial enterprises (sometimes from other sectors) see the market potential of an emerging sport. This manufacturer activity is more often devoted to solving known problems for users or refining the performance characteristics of existing products (e.g. adding footstraps to a sailboard to allow a user to jump waves and remain in control of their board, or refining hull shapes or construction methods to make craft faster and lighter) rather than creating new product uses or truly novel new features.

In a similar vein, Hienerth (2006) documents the evolution of the fringe sport of "Rodeo Kayaking" from a user-innovation community to a "sport-industry". As in previous studies on user innovators (Shah 2000; Franke and Shah 2003), Hienerth chooses an extreme sporting industry to analyse the development and commercialization of innovations. The development of user innovations and commercialization in the rodeo kayak industry, similar to other sporting industries, came about from the matching of different stimuli (Lynn et al. 1996; Howells 1997). Some of these stimuli were more personal and technology oriented, others were created by a growing market. Lead users started innovating because of a technological gap—they had needs that could not be met by existing products or materials. The users themselves found new ways to shape and process materials, generating new, technically advanced products. As people bought new products, lead users had the chance to further develop new products and materials using external cash flow. The switch from personal demand and technological superiority to market demand leveraged the commercialization of user innovations. Similarly, Roberts (1988) has mentioned that market pull stimuli are responsible for the final success of innovations, although different kinds of stimuli can be sources for initiating innovations, and Gans and Stern (2003) have shown that a commercialised environment is important to the economic success of an invention.

Baldwin, Hienerth and Von Hippel extend this work to explore more thoroughly the examination to the formation of firms by user innovators and/or the adoption of their ideas by manufacturers. They find that in general, one or more communities of user-innovators will soon coalesce and begin to exchange innovation-related information. Sometime after user innovation begins, the first user-purchasers appear—these are users who want to buy the goods that embody the lead user innovations rather than building them for themselves, either as new users seeking a more convenient entry pathway to the sport or for existing participants to maintain a competitive position with the innovators. Manufacturers emerge in response to this demand. The first manufacturers to enter the market are likely to be user-innovators who have access to the flexible, high-variable-cost, low-capital production technologies they use to build their own prototypes. The relatively high variable costs of these user-manufacturers tends to limit the size of the market initially but as information about product designs is disseminated, and as market volumes grow, manufacturers, existing user-manufacturers and established manufacturers from other fields (who may bring their own innovations or refinements to generate manufacturing efficiencies) can justify investing in higher-volume production processes. These processes bring lower variable costs, their use may drive prices lower and expand the market. User-purchasers then have a choice between lower-cost standardized goods and higher-cost, more advanced models that user-innovators continue to develop. Finally, as a design space matures, the rate of user innovation within that space tends to decline because the expected returns from further design improvements decrease.

2.2 Overshooting

While the mechanism of innovation in equipment sports and the subsequent evolution of firms in the sector has been documented and is reasonably well understood, there has been little-to-no rigorous enquiry into what happens *later*... there is anecdotal evidence of equipment innovation in sports, driven by brands and manufacturers' desire to stay ahead of the pack by offering the faster, lighter, more specialised (and often more expensive) equipment, usually catering to the wants of elite, professional athletes (and promoted and endorsed by those athletes), to the extent that equipment design exceeds the technical capabilities and/or the budgets of the majority of participants. Recreational participants and even the most aspirational enthusiasts leave the sport, leading to eventual collapse of the market for the equipment, with spillover effects into other sectors of the economy (e.g. hospitality, event tourism).

This phenomenon has been identified and explored in other settings. Christenson (1997) argues, mainly in the context of computer equipment, that firms under competition tend to overshoot their markets by adding more features to products and making them more complex, to a point where they overshoot the appetites and/or capabilities of their target markets. Potts (2009) and Earl and Potts (2013) extend this thinking to other creative domains, including the performing arts and the automotive industry and observe that there had been no specific economic theory to explain it to that point. They observe that while under standard theories of production, conditions of diminishing returns will ensure that rational managers will not allow creative concepts to be pursued beyond what is optimal on a production frontier, but that rational choice about how far to pursue a creative product or concept is difficult because the work tends not to be consumable until it is developed to an advanced state. The desire to stay at the forefront, coupled with uncertainty about how far rival producers will take a concept, open the door to collective creative excess. Potts (2009) invokes a Schumpeterian aspect to this, with creative overshooting as a common (indeed expected) response to competition from other creative agents. The competition is for "attention" from consumers and creativity is a necessary input. In addition, the designers and manufacturers, as "creative producers", have more knowledge of their product and its technical nuances and will build more of that knowledge into the product, adding complexity.

In Earl and Potts (2013), the authors go on to propose a "Creative Instability Hypothesis" (CIH), modeled in part on Minsky's financial instability hypothesis. In part their hypothesis proposes that firms competing with each other by continual creation of novelty can systematically overshoot markets. They describe this as, among other things, a market process in which the complexity of creative products needs to match consumers' abilities to recognise, value and consume that complexity. With competitive escalation on the producer side, the consumer side is commonly overshot. This 'Schumpeterian economy' is, the authors argue, creatively unstable and with predictable Minsky-Christensen type outcomes leads to endemic market turbulence. As a market process they identify it as one in which the consumer is not always able to keep up with producer advances—consumers eventually fail to keep up and lose interest. At the margin, there are constraints on consumer attention and even consumer competence, that when violated lead to market collapse just as if they had violated a price point. To date this effect has not been canvassed at all in the domain of sports and sports equipment literature. As has been indicated earlier, it is the aim of this paper to establish whether there is compelling evidence that this overshooting has also occurred (or is occurring) in lifestyle/equipment sports.

3 Method and Data

Since the primary focus of the study was to understand the evolution of windsurfing as a case study sport, and there is no academic literature or empirical data as yet readily available I chose qualitative data collection procedures. Qualitative approaches are preferred in areas that require theory-building because they "make room for the discovery of the unanticipated" (Van Maanan 1998). Our approach is based upon primary data gathered through interviews with Australian pioneers of the case-study sport and through analysis of international and domestic industry publications and grey literature. Working within the meaning-based tradition of research I adopted an interpretative approach to interviews (Corbin and Strauss 2008). The primary data were derived from semi-structured, in-depth interviews with informants who are selected on the basis of their long standing and experience in various roles within the sector (see Table 1 for details). Long interviews allowed access to informants' first-hand personal experiences and meanings associated with their engagement in boardsports as participants and as long-established members of the associated industry, either as retailers or wholesale distributors.

Table 1 Informant profiles

Informants	Role in industry	Industry/sport tenure at 2014 (approx.)
1. WL	Retailer, instructor, former elite participant	28 years
2. AM	Retailer, former participant	24 years
3. DS	Retailer, current participant	12 years
4. LM	Distributor/manufacturer	32 years
5. GJ	Importer/distributor	38 years
6. HF	Importer/distributor/retailer	22 years
7. AQ	Importer/distributor, former elite participant	26 years
8. DJ	Former elite participant	35 years
9. MM	Importer/distributor/retailer (retired)	38 years
10. IF	Distributor/manufacturer	32 years

3.1 Procedure

Informants were asked a mix of grand tour questions and floating prompts (McCracken 1988). At the beginning of the interview, informants were asked to provide some background on their history in the sport and their current role in the industry. Since the informants would approach this question with personal stories or experiences, further prompts were used to understand the significance of their role in the sport/industry or user experiences. Following a general discussion interview questions then focused on: (1) interviewee background, experience and role in the industry (manufacturer/importer/distributor/retailer/athlete); (2) history and evolution/rise and fall of the sports as they saw it, such as how does it happen, how fast has it happened; (3) consequences of rise and decline for them and associated industries/business, (4) regional economic implications; (5) views how to avoid repeating the same 'mistakes' in the future.

Although the interviews were broad and only semi-structured, informants were asked to elaborate on various statements they made, provide more explanation for their experiences, comparisons of consumption or usage and brands they referred to, and elaborate on the personal relevance of the subject matter. Given this method, informants spoke for virtually the entire period, with the researchers only engaging in floating prompts (following the initial grand tour question), asking for clarification on certain terms and every so often, summarizing informant responses or views. Interviews lasted on average an hour (615 minutes total interview time). Interviews were audio recorded and transcribed *verbatim,* resulting in slightly more than 229 pages of text. Interviews were continued until saturation on the key themes of the trajectory of windsurfing as an industry and as a sport were exhausted (Creswell 2009).

Analysis began with the transcripts which were read in detail and meanings interpreted by the organisation, comparison and interpretation of various themes and meanings drawn from the transcripts (Malterud 2001). Throughout this procedure preliminary results were compared back and forward between the available trade, market and grey literature on the sport and includes both descriptive and interpretive explanations of the raw data (Kruegar 1988).

4 Case Study: The Rise and Fall of Windsurfing

4.1 Industry Inception and the Early Years 1970–1980

The "creation" of the windsurfer as a user-innovation has been documented in Shah (2000) and elsewhere (Pryde 2010; West 2012, among others). Briefly, several people have laid claim to inventing the windsurfer but Californians Hoyle Schweitzer and Jim Drake made the claim loudest. In 1968, Schweitzer and Drake filed the first patent on the craft, which was granted to them in 1970. U.S. Patent #3,487,800 was issued, and covered a "wind-propelled apparatus in which a mast is universally mounted on a craft and supports a boom and sail." The two inventors called their creation a sailboard.[1] The critical innovation in the patent was the incorporation of a molded rubber universal joint that secured the mast and sail rig to the board, allowing the rig to pivot freely and the user to steer the craft buy tipping the sail forward or aft.

Schweitzer and his wife Diana set up the company Windsurfing international to manufacture, promote and license windsurfing designs. The patent was jointly owned and wholly licensed by Drake and Schweitzer to their company Windsurfing International. In 1973 they registered the term "windsurfer" as a trademark and in that same year Drake sold his half of the patent to Windsurfing International for US $36,000 (Pryde 2010).

Schweitzer embarked on an ambitious licensing programme to encourage manufacturers to take up production using his patented universal joint. Early entrants into board manufacture were generally not from the surfboard industry (which was largely a cottage industry at the time) or otherwise associated with watercraft. Early windsurfer boards and their imitators were typically a roto-molded hollow structure or were constructed of a molded plastic skin bonded to an Expanded Polystyrene (EPS) foam core and seam-welded. The early manufacturers to adopt Schweitzer's design principles were in the main from the plastics industry—for example, in Europe, Mistral was a molder of plastic buckets, bins and brooms, BiC a manufacturer of ballpoint pens[2] and in Australia the "Bombora" and "Tyronsea" brands arose from an Adelaide-based molder of plastic lavatory seats and water tanks.

When Schweitzer first introduced the Windsurfer at boat shows in the early 1970s, some practical jokers outfitted the sailboard with a huge steering wheel and a portable toilet. But the joke was on the jokers. Windsurfing itself struggled initially to gain credibility in countries that had strong surfing and watersports traditions but in places like Germany, France and Holland that had no strong surfing culture it very quickly became a "cool" sport (Pryde 2010). Largely because the Schweitzers had been so dogged in promoting it, boardsailing had become the world's fastest growing sport. In Europe, where by the end of 1981 nearly 1 million boards had been sold, the sport was second only to skiing in the number of participants. According to Boardsailing U.S.A. figures of the day, 50,000 sailboards were sold

[1]The patent was ultimately challenged by several parties. British user-innovator Peter Chilvers claimed to have invented the concept in 1958 and American inventor Newman Derby published plans in 1965 in *Popular Science Monthly* magazine. Schweitzer strained his financial resources fighting big manufacturers over patent infringement through most of the 1970s. In *Windsurfing International vs Tabur Marine (Great Britain)*, Tabur, then a division of BiC, referenced the Chilvers and Derby designs to successfully argue that the design was not new. Schweitzer's patent was overturned in February 1980, reinstated on appeal in March 1981 and ultimately denied again on further appeal in June 1981 (Mamis 1982).

[2]After the withdrawal of Schweitzer's patent, BiC Sports entered the market in large scale in 1981 with the "DuFour Wing", a cheap sailboard package that "was to do for sport what the biro had done for office supplies" (Pryde 2010). The BiC package retailed in the USA for around $700 which at the time was 30–50% cheaper than other brands, some 12,000 were sold in the first year.

in the Unites States in 1981 with projections for 50–75% annual sales growth for the next five years. Outside the United States, there were over 100 sailboard makers, most of them doing business without a license from Windsurfing International (Mamis 1982). In 1982, a single sail manufacturer had sold 340,000 sails worldwide (Pryde 2010).

In Australia, the sport began in a modest way with the first Schweitzer windsurfers being imported in 1976 by a Sydney-based sailing enthusiast. A distribution agreement soon followed. By the early 1980s the sport in Australia was booming, with dozens of thriving retail outlets, particularly on the eastern seaboard.

> *"In its peak, through the early to mid '80s you had specialist retailers as well as camping stores that were selling windsurfers, as were ski shops and boating centres. In Victoria, (there were) upwards of 50 different outlets reselling windsurfers in some shape or form. On the eastern seaboard alone, there were in excess of 100 or 120 shops selling windsurfers. . .where I was working at [de-identified, retailer] it wouldn't be unusual to have 200 boards in stock wrapped up and on a busy weekend you might sell 80 windsurfers. . .we were like worker ants just running around unwrapping things and taking them out and tying them on people's cars"*
>
> *Retailer*

4.2 The Turning Point 1980–1985

After the initial drive for market footprint and the initial upsurge in worldwide board sales, there would be a fork in the road. BiC Sport among other European manufacturers would continue to follow the populist route, with an emphasis on simple, low-cost equipment and primarily flat-water, sailing-based participation. In parallel, new developments in Hawaii would kick-start the performance windsurfing movement (Pryde 2010). In Europe and North America, the sport was still very much recreational but in Hawaii, windsurfing was transformed into a much more technical, performance-based, athletic sport. Hawaii's consistent winds and big waves were encouraging a small group of designers and sailors to try new things. Elite users of the day, including Robbie Naish, Mike Walsh and Matt Schweitzer, among others, stretched the capabilities of the bulky, long boards of the day to perform fantastic acrobatic stunts (Pryde 2010).

"The Hawaiians", as they became known, started to make significant changes to their equipment to exploit their local conditions. Boards became shorter to make them more maneuverable, were made lighter and with less flotation to make them faster, but with this, the boards (and sailing rigs) required a higher level of skill to use them. Requests from enthusiasts interested in purchasing the equipment began to come in as people saw or heard about the Hawaiians' innovative equipment. Eventually, their brand, Sailboards Maui, became one of the most popular in windsurfing industry (Shah 2000).

"The marketing no doubt was probably 75 or 80 per cent skewed towards the advanced sailor. People aspired to be Robby Naish. They didn't want to be Joe Blogs on a heavy windsurfer at a resort with a chewed up sail. They wanted to be either shredding the waves at Diamond Head or winning a race in Europe"

Retailer

Meanwhile, In Europe and North America, the emphasis was still on more sailing-oriented participation, but the design elements that were emerging out of Maui to make boards faster soon found their way over. In 1982, French rider Pascal Maka bought a sailboard from Sailboards Maui but shaper Jimmy Lewis made a mistake with his planer and decided to turn the accidental gouge in the bottom into a double-concave shape. Maka paired that board with an innovative sail from sail-maker Neil Pryde and the very first hip harness from Maui sails (a device used to suspend the rider from the rig to free up hands and allow the rider to use body weight to control the sail in in stronger winds and at higher speeds). Maka took his setup to Weymouth, England in October 1982 and set a new speed record of 27.82 knots, a better than ten percent increase on the previous record. Briton Fred Haywood took another Lewis/Pryde setup to Weymouth in 1983 and broke the 30-knot barrier, then the holy grail of speed sailing. At a Paris trade show in December of that year a film of Haywood's record run ran more than 1000 times and so many people came to watch it, the aisles in the screening venue were regularly blocked. This attracted many of the then-biggest names in the sport to speed sailing. Sailmaker Neil Pryde, whose sails were used in setting these records said:

we went after the biggest name riders we could find. . .because we absolutely wanted our brand to be associated with fantastic athletes. . .speed and performance.

With this new emphasis on high-performance, manufacturing technology, in particular board manufacture, shifted from relatively inexpensive but heavy, high-volume plastics to lighter, stiffer (and more expensive) "sandwich" construction, consisting of an expanded polystyrene foam core, often hand-shaped and wrapped in a fiberglass and epoxy resin skin. This method of manufacture relied less on complex and expensive tooling that required a long product life and high volume to recover the investment in tooling. The product was, therefore able to be adapted, prototyped and brought to production much more quickly to satisfy the competitive drive of the manufacturers' elite "team" riders and the consequent appetites of aspirational consumers.

"I guess there were manufacturers that were learning new processes. So to buy a good lightweight epoxy race board. . .even back then a handmade race board was in the vicinity of two and a half to three grand just for the board. . .then brands having world cup team with 10 people on their payroll, paying them big bucks, so they had to provide them with the top end equipment. Of course the trickledown effect, the consumer thought they wanted or needed that as well. I think that's when consumers started to invest big dollars just to stay up with the Joneses."

Retailer

"Very quickly, within a couple of years. . .the emphasis really became about the top end performance of the equipment so it was really about high wind performance, high skill level . . . driven by the professionals. It was a positive. The equipment became a lot more high

performance which was great for the more advanced **but** *(emphasis added) all the companies there at that time put most of their efforts into technology changes that would benefit only the elite end of the sport"*

Manufacturer/Distributor

"Gear. . .well you'd be spending upwards of 10 to 12 grand a year just to stay at the pointy end. That's before you even think about time on water which maybe means time away from work or family. The keen guys wanted to turn theirs [gear] over every year. The gear was driven hard by the manufacturers to make you think it was that much better than the years before so you had to have it. Also the gear then wasn't well made. You'd break boards, break booms. I'm not heavy but I'd typically break three booms a year, so even a moderately priced boom, $400 or $500 bucks each, a broken board was 2 to 3 grand to replace. . .just for starters. I think in the boom time I had a van, personally I had this van, I probably had four or five boards, anything ranging from a speed board through to two wave boards, a mid-range board, maybe even a race board so maybe five boards. The amount of rigging, sails, booms. masts I think a couple of years I insured my gear it was about $13,000 bucks worth back then, in the early 80's."

Retailer, former elite competitor

4.3 Decline and Fall 1985–2000

In the early days of the sport, the equipment was rudimentary, despite a high degree of enthusiasm there was still a relatively steep learning curve for most newcomers:

The equipment was heavy, hard to use, had a fairly broad wind range of use but comfortable in none of them. I think the way to describe it at that was the early part of it was just positive energy, sponsors were involved, media were involved, anyone you spoke to wanted to have a go, most of your mates were doing it. It was the thing you dropped everything for and went as soon as there was a sign of wind or a nice day you—everyone in my social group was sort of dropping that] they were doing to go for a sail or a windsurf. That unified feeling of being part of a movement was pretty powerful.

Importer/Distributor

Windsurfing schools were established wherever there was a suitable body of water and for many new users the pathway into the sport was via lessons from a qualified instructor. As their clients wanted equipment of their own, many of the windsurfing schools evolved into board resellers to capitalise on the business opportunity this presented. As the equipment became more sophisticated and expensive, there was more money to be made (with less effort) by selling equipment than teaching people how to use it. The retailers began to neglect their school operations and many schools closed down. The (unexpected) consequence of this was to close off the "pipeline" of new entrants into the sport (*GJ, importer/distributor, in interview*).

". . . the companies had forgotten about the grassroots level of the sport, forgotten about the entry level part of the sport. The participation at that grassroots level. . .was lost."

Manufacturer/Distributor

> *"No one was thinking about the longevity or the health of the sport because it was bomb proof, it was going through the roof. So I probably—in '85 roughly when I entered or it might have been a little bit earlier, '83 or '84 the sport was probably nearing the apex. But no one was really talking about managing post the apex of the sport. So at that stage of the sport as a brand to survive you had to be new and innovative."*
>
> *Importer/Distributor*

Along with the decline in take-up by new entrants, as the sport and the equipment became more technically demanding, early acolytes and even aspirational enthusiasts began to lose interest and leave the sport:

> *"... when the focus of the sport takes the sport in a certain direction ... .it sometimes leads it away from what its core was. Windsurfing... .to most people was getting together with your mates, blasting around having a good time. Then the marketing came that unless you're in the waves, surfing big waves on highly refined wave gear, you weren't cool. Then two things happened, people either felt they're not cool so they won't do it. Or they went and bought the highly refined gear and sunk to the bottom, hated the sport and left."*
>
> *Importer/Distributor*

In 1985, as the performance market boomed, the recreational side of windsurfing crashed and several of the biggest mass producers went bankrupt in that year (Pryde 2010). The decline in entry-level participation also had its effect on the distribution and retail sectors.

> *"... you'd have those families coming in, buying a package on a Saturday morning and going out, just wasn't occurring. The sustainability of the stores wasn't there. A rep from [a surviving manufacturer] recently said that in windsurfing's heyday they were manufacturing and selling 700,000 boards worldwide per annum. They're currently doing 70,000. It's a huge decline in the sport."*
>
> *Retailer*

By way of example, on east coast of Australia the number of retail outlets for sailboards in Victoria declined from approximately 120 to approximately fewer than 12 by 2000.

5 Conclusions and Further Work

The sport of windsurfing began in the 1970s as a casual and fun leisure pursuit that was reasonably accessible to consumers. Equipment in the early period was relatively inexpensive and somewhat easy to use but relatively unsophisticated, with many new brands and manufacturers entering the market and bringing cross-over manufacturing skills. As seems almost inevitable with physical pursuits, the pastime eventually developed into a highly competitive sport with a range of specialised disciplines (e.g.: speed, surf, racing), necessitating more specialised, sophisticated (and expensive) equipment. In the initial stages of development, at least some of the development was by communities of users frustrated with the performance limitations of stock equipment, experimenting with modifications to what was available and in some instances the more entrepreneurial of these enthusiasts established firms to bring their developments into production. Driven partly by the demands of elite competitors and partly by relentless competition for market share, manufacturers refined their equipment and materials to the point where using it became beyond the skills and budget of the "average" or recreational user. Indeed, we find that rapid developments in materials and manufacturing process also left many of the early manufacturers behind.

The sport (and its associated industries) then went into rapid decline, with some severe economic consequences for those directly connected with the industry such as manufacturers, distributers and retailers. A view emerged that further decline could be avoided by regulating or standardising equipment, at least for competition, but attempts to do this came too-little-too-late to arrest the decline.

There is clear support for the overshooting hypothesis in this case, with adverse consequences for the sport's manufacturing, distribution and retail sectors. With this evidence, the next phase of this research will be to develop and calibrate a model of sports overshooting, focused on the competitive mechanism, the institutional rules, and the spillover consequences. The intent is to calibrate this against the case study of windsurfing discussed in this paper, extended using back-catalogue studies of trade publications and other archival material including manufacturer and distributor catalogues and price lists where available to estimate real prices of equipment and costs of access. The purpose of the extended work will be to study how this overshooting happens in sports—by what mechanisms and with what cost, with a view to developing economic models of this market and technology process and to arrive at recommendations to both sports governance bodies (in relation to rules and institutions) and to public policy (in relation to funding support) that might mitigate this endogenous instability and the economic harm and social welfare costs that this overshooting causes.

Acknowledgements The author wishes to acknowledge the support of the RMIT College of Business Seed Grants programme for financial support. I would also like to thank the representatives of the board sports industry who have given generously of their time and knowledge in support of this research and Jason Potts for invaluable support and guidance in establishing this research.

References

Abernathy WJ, Utterback JM (1978) Patterns of industrial innovation. Technol Rev 80:40–47

Agarwal R, Bayus B (2002) The market evolution and sales takeoff of product innovations. Manag Sci 48:1024–1041

Christenson C (1997) The innovators dilemma. Harvard University Press, Cambridge, MA

Corbin J, Strauss A (2008) Basics of qualitative research, 3rd edn. Sage, Los Angeles

Creswell J (2009) Research design: qualitative, quantitative, and mixed methods approaches, 3rd edn. Sage, Los Angeles

Demsetz H (1967) Towards a theory of property rights. Am Econ Rev 57:347–359

Earl P, Potts J (2013) The creative instability hypothesis. J Cult Econ 37:153–173

Earl P, Potts J (2014) The management of creative vision and the economics of creative cycles. Working paper (RMIT & UQ)
Franke N, Shah S (2003) How communities support innovative activities: an exploration of assistance and sharing among end-users. Res Policy 32(1):157–178
Frontier Economics (2011) The economic contribution of sport to Australia. https://secure.ausport.gov.au/__data/assets/pdf_file/0008/449171/4Frontier_Economics_Final_Report_2009.pdf
Gans JS, Stern S (2003) The product market and the market for "ideas": commercialization strategies for technology entrepreneurs. Res Policy 32(3):333–350
Hienerth C (2006) The commercialization of user innovations: the development of the rodeo kayak industry. R&D Manag 36(3):273–294
Howells J (1997) Rethinking the market-technology relationship for innovation. Res Policy 25 (8):1209–1219
Klepper S (1997) Industry life cycles. Ind Corp Chang 6:145–181
Kruegar RA (1988) Focus groups: a practical guide for applied research. Sage, Newbury Park, CT
Lynn LH, Reddy NM, Aram JD (1996) Linking technology and institutions: the innovation community framework. Res Policy 25(2):91–106
Malterud K (2001) Qualitative research: standards, challenges and guidelines. Lancet 358 (9280):438–488
Mamis RA (1982) INC magazine. http://www.inc.com/magazine/19820201/2262.html. Accessed 17 June 2014
McCracken GD (1988) The long interview. Sage, Newbury Park, CT
Minsky H (1982) Stabilizing an unstable economy. McGraw Hill, New York
Mueller DC, Tilton JE (1969) R&D cost as a barrier to entry. Can J Econ 2(4):570–579
Nelson RR, Winter SG (1977) In search of useful theory of innovation. Res Policy 6:36–76
Nelson RR, Winter SG (1982) An evolutionary theory of economic change. Harvard University Press, Cambridge, MA
Potts J (2009) Creativity under competition and the overshooting problem. In: Potts J (ed) Creative industries and economics evolution. Edward Elgar, Cheltenham
Pryde N (2010) The will to win: the remarkable story of Neil Pryde Limited. Neil Pryde Limited, Hong Kong
Roberts EB (1988) Managing invention and innovation. Res Technol Manag 31(1):12–29
Schumpeter J (1934) The theory of economic development, 7th edn. Harvard University Press, Cambridge, MA
Shah S (2000) From innovation to firm formation in the windsurfing, skateboarding and snowboarding industries. Working Paper #05–0107. University of Illinois
Shah S (2005) From innovation to firm formation in the windsurfing, skateboarding and snowboarding industries. Working paper, University of Illinois
Utterback JM (1994) Mastering the dynamics of innovation. Harvard University Press, Boston, MA
Van Maanan J (1998) Different strokes: qualitative research in the administrative science quarterly from 1956 to 1996. In: Van Maanan J (ed) Qualitative studies of organizations. Sage, Thousand Oaks, CA, pp ix–xxxii
West S (2012) Stand up paddle—a paddlers guide. Kanu Culture/Batini Books, Gold Coast

Printed by Printforce, the Netherlands